Reading Culture

CONTEXTS FOR CRITICAL READING AND WRITING

Sixth Edition

Diana George
Virginia Tech University

John Trimbur
Worcester Polytechnic Institute

PEARSON
Longman

New York   San Francisco   Boston
London   Toronto   Sydney   Tokyo   Singapore   Madrid
Mexico City   Munich   Paris   Cape Town   Hong Kong   Montreal

Senior Acquisitions Editor: Lynn M. Huddon
Director of Development: Mary Ellen Curley
Development Editor: Katharine Glynn
Senior Marketing Manager: Sandra McGuire
Senior Supplements Editor: Donna Campion
Media Supplements Editor: Jenna Egan
Production Manager: Ellen MacElree
Project Coordination, Text Design, and Electronic Page Makeup: Electronic Publishing Services Inc., NYC
Cover Designer/Manager: Nancy Danahy
Cover Photo: Amadeo Sandoval's Living Room, Rio Lucio, New Mexico, June 1985. Photograph by Alex Harris.
Photo Researcher: Photosearch, Inc.
Manufacturing Manager: Mary Fischer
Printer and Binder: Quebecor World
Cover Printer: Phoenix Color Corps.

For permission to use copyrighted material, grateful acknowledgment is made to the copyright holders on pp. 585–588, which are hereby made part of this copyright page.

Library of Congress Cataloging-in-Publication Data
Reading culture: contexts for critical reading and writing/[edited by] Diana George,
    John Trimbur.— 6th ed.
        p.   cm.
    Includes bibliographical references and index.
    ISBN 0-321-39169-1 (pbk.)
    1. College readers.   2. English language—Rhetoric—Problems, exercises, etc.
    3. Critical thinking—Problems, exercises, etc.   4. Academic writing—Problems,
    exercises, etc. I. George, Diana, 1948–   II. Trimbur, John.
PE1417.R38 2007
808'.0427—dc22   2005025817

Please visit our website at www.ablongman.com/george

ISBN 0-321-39169-1

2 3 4 5 6 7 8 9 10—QWT—09 08 07 06

Contents

CHAPTER 1

Reading the News   13

CHAPTER 4   IMAGES   198

CHAPTER 7　Storytelling　344

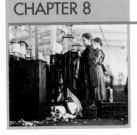

CHAPTER 10

Living in a Postcolonial World   521

Visual Resources

Alternate Contents

Preface

Every edition of *Reading Culture* has opened with these words from Raymond Williams: "Culture is ordinary; that is where we must start." We start, then, with the world that surrounds us and the experience of everyday life. In *Reading Culture*, we ask students to look at culture as a way of life that organizes social experience and shapes the identities of individuals and groups. We will be using the term *culture* in this textbook to talk about how people make sense of their worlds and about the values, beliefs, and practices in which they invest their energies and allegiances. We want to provide students with reading and writing assignments so they can understand how their familiar ways of life fit into the diverse, mass-mediated, multicultural realities of contemporary America.

Reading Culture assumes that students are already immersed in a wealth of cultural information and that their experiences of everyday life can usefully be brought to attention as material for reflection and deliberation. The reading and writing assignments in *Reading Culture* are designed to promote a critical distancing so that students can begin to observe and evaluate as well as participate in contemporary America. To this end, *Reading Culture* asks students to read in two ways. First we ask students to read carefully and critically the range of writing about culture we have assembled here. We ask them to identify the purposes and assumptions writers bring to the study of culture and the rhetorical patterns they use to enact their aims. Second, we ask students to read the social world around them, to identify the patterns of meaning in the commonplace, and to put into words the familiar experiences of everyday life that often go without saying.

Reading Culture is organized into ten chapters. The first chapter, "Reading the News," introduces students to the study of culture by looking at the American news media. The chapter includes critical strategies for reading the news on television, in print, and over the Internet, as well as a sequence of reading and writing activities about reporting war.

The chapters that form the main part of *Reading Culture*, as in past editions, are arranged under several broad topics. "Generations" and "Schooling" explore the personal experience of growing up and going to school. "Images," "Style," and "Public Space" emphasize the visual dimension of culture—in the popular media, in design and packaging, and in the way public space is planned, legislated, and used. The next three chapters, "Storytelling," "Work," and "History," investigate narratives Americans tell themselves, the experience of the workplace, and the meaning of the past in the contemporary United States. The final chapter, "Living in a Postcolonial World," examines the movement of people, cultures, and languages in an era of globalization.

In the third edition of *Reading Culture*, we included two new features—Visual Culture and Fieldwork—that are now standard in the textbook. In each chapter, a Visual Culture section presents strategies for analyzing and interpreting films, photographs, television shows, ads, public health messages, page design, signs in public places, and other forms of visual communication. In addition, most chapters include a Fieldwork section that provides ways of studying culture through interviews, participant observation, questionnaires, oral histories, and other forms of on-site research.

The fourth edition introduced Mining the Archives, Perspectives, and instructions on Reading the Web; with the fifth edition, we began to include a Classic Reading in the study of culture. These selections offer students a perspective on how the issues raised in each chapter have been written about in the past by men and women whose thinking we still return to—writers and thinkers such as James Agee, Roland Barthes, Margaret Mead, and W. E. B. Du Bois. All of these features have been carried over into the sixth edition. Many have been revised to accommodate new readings and assignments.

Reading Culture is designed to be used flexibly and creatively. Instructors may wish to ask students to work on the chapters in *Reading Culture* as they are arranged, but this is only one possible order.

The *Reading Culture* Companion Website, located at **www.ablongman.com/ george**, and the Instructor's Manual (available to qualified adopters of the book) also provide a wealth of resources for instructors wishing to extend their students' investigations on any of the chapter topics or individual readings.

New to the Sixth Edition

This sixth edition includes new and expanded features to help students investigate contemporary and past cultures. These additions come in large part from discussions we've had with writing teachers who have used previous editions of *Reading Culture*.

- *Wired Culture.* Wired Culture focuses on digital media and how such new means of communication as blogs, instant messaging, cell phones, iPods, and video games are changing the way people work and play. Each chapter now includes a reading about digital culture to investigate the immediacy, interactivity, and connectivity of new media, the increasingly blurry distinction between the virtual and the real, and the use of electronic communication in outsourcing jobs and forming antiglobalization networks.

- *Film Clips.* To enable teachers and students to examine films in some detail, chapters include a Film Clips feature that provides concepts and tools of analysis—from discussion of such film genres as documentaries, westerns, and Bollywood movies to storyboarding, set design, costumes, and screenplays to the Hollywood star system.

- *Guide to Visual Analysis.* The Guide to Visual Analysis (pages 7–12) provides a brief introduction to the kinds of questions students and teachers can ask of all sorts of visual communication. It also offers a comprehensive list of the concepts and tools of analysis *Reading Culture* includes for the study of visual culture.

- *New Readings.* The readings in *Reading Culture* draw on a variety of resources, including popular press features, academic scholarship, and news reports. In this Sixth Edition, we've included over 50 new readings from a wide array of voices such as Edward Tufte, Andrew Sullivan, Katha Pollitt, Martin Espada, Peggy Noonan, Studs Terkel, Frederick Jackson Turner, and Jamaica Kincaid. Also new to this edition are a graphic novel, Marjane Satrapi's "The Veil" from *Persepolis,* and Joe Sacco's graphic report "Complacency Kills."

The sixth edition of *Reading Culture* offers opportunities extending across chapters to work with visual communication, literacy events, and microethnography. The work you do with this text will, however, depend on your needs and your students' interests. We think that with this edition, *Reading Culture* has become a more flexible resource for teaching writing and critical reading and for asking students to write about, and in the culture of, contemporary America.

Acknowledgments

We want to thank a number of people for their insight and advice. Lynn Huddon and Katharine Glynn provided the editorial support for this edition. We appreciate as well the careful readings we received by reviewers of this book: Karen Auvinen, *Front Range Community College*; Jennifer Brezina, *College of the Canyons*; Shahara Drew, *Tufts University*; Kristin Girard, *Georgia Institute of Technology*; Ruth Hoberman, *Eastern Illinois University*; Shari Horner, *Shippensburg University*; Megan Knight, *University of Iowa*; Beverly J. Reed, *Stephen F. Austin State University*; John Schilb, *Indiana University*; Robert C. Spirko, *University of Tennessee*.

We want to thank the teachers who have used the first five editions of *Reading Culture*. The feedback, suggestions, and insights they have offered us over the years have enabled us to see the book in new ways and to plan the sixth edition with their ideas in mind. We thank our students at Michigan Technological University and Worcester Polytechnic Institute, and Clare Trimbur, Lucia Trimbur, and Catherine Trimbur for the best confirmation of our intentions we could possibly receive: they recognized themselves and their peers in this project and let us know that the cultural resources we are seeking to tap are vitally important to students in contemporary America.

We dedicate this book to the late Jim Berlin, whose work challenged a generation of teachers and students to turn their attention to the small things of everyday life—those ways of living and communicating that constitute a culture.

Diana George

John Trimbur

Introduction: Reading Culture

> **culture:** education, enrichment, erudition, learning, wisdom, breeding, gentility, civilization, colony, community, crowd, folks, group, settlement, society, staff, tribe, background, development, environment, experience, past, schooling, training, upbringing, customs, habits, mores, traditions.

Culture is Ordinary; that is where we must start.

—Raymond Williams

The British cultural historian Raymond Williams has written that culture "is one of the two or three most complicated words in the English language." This is so, Williams explains, because the term *culture* has acquired new meanings over time without losing the older meanings along the way. Therefore, writers sometimes use the term *culture* in quite different and incompatible ways. Even a simple list of synonyms, such as the one that opens this chapter, can illustrate the truth of Williams's observation.

For some, culture refers to great art in the European tradition—Beethoven's symphonies, Shakespeare's plays, Picasso's paintings, or Jane Austen's novels. *Culture* in that tradition refers to something that you read; something that you see in a museum, an art gallery, or a theater; or something that you hear in a concert hall. It is often called "high culture" and is closely linked to the idea of *becoming* cultured—of cultivating good taste and discriminating judgment. A cultured person, according to this sense of the term, is someone who has achieved a certain level of refinement and class.

We encounter this use of the term frequently. For example, advertisers who want their products to seem "high class" will draw on this idea of culture, as in the Absolut Vodka campaign that pays homage to such artists as Vermeer, Rubens, and Modigliani.

Those who equate culture with high art would most likely think, for example, that rock musicians like Jimi Hendrix and Nirvana or pop stars like Marilyn Monroe or Madonna do not belong in the domain of culture. They would not include popular entertainment like *The Daily Show, Sin City, American Idol*, the latest graphic novel, or NASCAR stock car racing in that category either. In making a distinction between high and low art, this view of culture is largely interested in the classics and in keeping serious art separate from popular culture.

Others, however, take an alternative approach to the study of culture. Instead of separating high from low art, they think of culture in more inclusive terms. For them, culture refers not only to the literary and artistic works which critics have called masterpieces but also to the way of life that characterizes a particular group of people at a particular time. Developed since the turn of the twentieth century by anthropologists, though it has now spread into common use, *culture* offers a way to think about how individuals and groups organize and make sense of their social experience—at home, in school, at work, and at play.

ABSOLUT HOFMEKLER.
HOMAGE TO JAN VERMEER

Ori Hofmekler is an artist on the staff of *Penthouse* magazine. For this ad campaign, he was asked to reproduce works of old masters, inserting an Absolut bottle in the ad as though it belonged in the original. Richard Lewis, *The Absolut Story.*

Culture includes all the social institutions, patterns of behavior, systems of belief, and kinds of popular entertainment that create the social world we live in. Taken this way, *culture* means not simply masterpieces of art, music, and literature, but lived experience—what goes on in the everyday lives of individuals and groups.

Reading Culture explores the interpretation of contemporary culture and how cultural ideas and ideals are communicated. When we use the term *culture* in this book, we are using a definition that is much closer to the second definition than to the first. The distinction between high and low art is indeed an important one but not because high art is necessarily better or more "cultured" than popular entertainment. What interests us, instead, is how the two terms are used in an ongoing debate about the meaning of contemporary culture in the United States—about, say, what languages should be taught in the schools, about the way media interpret daily events, or about the quality of popular tastes. We will ask you to explore these issues in the following chapters to see how arguments over media or schooling or national identity tell stories of contemporary U.S. culture.

In short, the purpose of this book is not to bring you culture or to make you cultured but to invite you to become more aware of the culture you are already living. According to the way we will be using the term, culture is not something you can go out and get. Rather, culture means all the familiar pursuits and pleasures that shape people's identities and that enable and constrain what they do and what they might become. Our idea is to treat contemporary American culture as a research project—to understand its ways of life from the inside as we live and observe them.

Reading Culture—Getting Started

The following chapters offer opportunities to read, research, and write about contemporary culture. The reading selections present writers who have explored central facets of culture and who offer information and ideas for you to draw on as you do your own work of reading and writing about culture. Each chapter raises a series of questions about how culture organizes social experience and how individuals understand the meaning and purpose of their daily lives.

In these chapters, we will be asking you to think about how the writers find patterns in culture and how they position themselves in relation to contemporary cultural realities. We will be asking you to read not only to understand what the writers are saying but also to identify what assumptions they are making about cultural issues such as schooling, the media, or national identity. We also will be asking you to do another kind of reading, where the text is not the printed word but the experience of everyday life. We will be asking you to read culture—to read the social world around you, at home and in classrooms, at work and at play, in visual images and public places.

Reading a culture means finding patterns in the familiar. In many respects, of course, you are already a skilled reader of culture. Think of all the reading that you do in the course of a day. You read not only the textbooks assigned in your courses or the books and magazines you turn to for pleasure. You probably read a variety of other "texts" without thinking about what you are actually reading. You read the logos on clothes people wear, the cars they drive, and the houses they live in. As you read these texts, you might make guesses about people's social status or about how you will relate to them. You read the way social experience is organized on your campus to determine who your friends will be, who the jocks are, where the geeks hang out.

You read all kinds of visual images in the media not only for the products advertised or the entertainment offered but for the lifestyles that are proposed as attractive and desirable. Most of your reading takes place as you move through the day, and it often takes place below the threshold of consciousness. Often, people just take this kind of reading for granted.

To read culture means *not* taking that reading for granted. Reading culture means bringing forward for analysis and reflection those commonplace aspects of everyday life that people normally think of as simply being there, a part of the natural order of things. Most likely you do some of that kind of reading when you stop to think through an ad or a history lesson or anything that makes you connect what you are seeing or reading with other ideas coming your way every day. Very likely, you do not accept without question all that you see and read. You probably turn a skeptical eye to much of it. Still, to read culture you will have to be more consistent as you learn to bring the familiar back into view so that you can begin to understand how people organize and make sense of their lives. To read the world in this way is to see that culture is not simply passed down from generation to generation in a fixed form but rather is a way of life through which individuals and groups are constantly making their own meanings in the contemporary world.

We are all influenced by what cultural critics call mainstream culture, whether we feel part of it or not. Everyone in the United States, to one extent or another (and whether they embrace or reject America's tenets), is shaped by what is sometimes called the "American way of life" and the value that it claims to place on hard work, fair play, individual success, romantic love, family ties, and patriotism. This is, undoubtedly, the most mass-mediated culture in human history, and it is virtually impossible to avoid the dominant images of America past and present—whether of the Pilgrims gathered at that mythic scene of the first Thanksgiving or of retired pro football players in a Miller Lite commercial.

Yet for all the power of the "American way of life" as it is presented by schools, the mass media, and the culture industry, U.S. culture is hardly monolithic or homogeneous. The culture in which Americans live is a diverse one, divided along the lines of race, class, gender, language, ethnicity, age, occupation, region, politics, economics, religion, and more. Ours is a multicultural society, and in part because of that diversity, contemporary culture is constantly changing, constantly in flux. To read culture, therefore, is to see not only how its dominant cultural expressions shape people but also how individuals and groups shape culture—how their responses to and interpretations of contemporary life rewrite its meanings according to their own purposes, interests, and aspirations.

In 1958 Raymond Williams wrote the essay "Culture Is Ordinary" explaining why, in his thinking, culture is not limited to high art or a university degree. It is also embodied in our ordinary, everyday ways of understanding how to make a life in the world.

Read the following excerpt from Williams's essay "Culture Is Ordinary" and use the Suggested Assignment that follows it to begin your own investigation of culture today.

CULTURE IS ORDINARY

— Raymond Williams

Raymond Williams (1921–1988) has been called Britain's foremost culture theorist and public intellectual. In the excerpt we have chosen, Williams tells the story of traveling from Cambridge, where he was attending college on a scholarship, back to his home in a working-class village in Wales. Cambridge was then and continues today to be a bedrock of high culture, the place where students from all over the world come to study. Perhaps that is why Williams, who grew up in a world of farmers, servants, and railway workers, repeats several times here that "culture is ordinary." In other words, culture is not only high art; culture is everything around us.

SUGGESTION FOR READING   As you read, notice those places where Williams explains different meanings of the word *culture* and how he describes his own encounters with the different ways people identify what it means *to be cultured*.

1 The bus stop was outside the cathedral. I had been looking at the Mappa Mundi, with its rivers out of Paradise, and at the chained library, where a party of clergymen had got in easily, but where I had waited an hour and cajoled a verger before I even saw the chains. Now, across the street, a cinema advertised the *Six-Five Special* and a cartoon version of *Gulliver's Travels*. The bus arrived, with a driver and a conductress deeply absorbed in each other. We went out of the city, over the old bridge, and on through the orchards and the green meadows and the fields red under the plough. Ahead were the Black Mountains, and we climbed among them, watching the steep fields end at the grey walls, beyond which the bracken and heather and whin had not yet been driven back. To the east, along the ridge, stood the line of grey Norman castles; to the west, the fortress wall of the mountains. Then, as we still climbed, the rock changed under us. Here, now, was limestone, and the line of the early iron workings along the scarp. The farming valleys, with their scattered white houses, fell away behind. Ahead of us were the narrower valleys: the steel-rolling mill, the gasworks, the grey terraces, the pitheads. The bus stopped, and the driver and conductress got out, still absorbed. They had done this journey so often, and seen all its stages. It is a journey, in fact, that in one form or another we have all made.

I was born and grew up halfway along that bus journey. Where I lived is still a farming valley, though the road through it is being widened and straightened, to carry the heavy lorries to the north. Not far away, my grandfather, and so back through the generations, worked as a farm labourer until he was turned out of his cottage and, in his fifties, became a roadman. His sons went at thirteen or fourteen on to the farms, his daughters into service. My father, his third son, left the farm at fifteen to be a boy porter on the railway, and later became a signalman, working in a box in this valley until he died. I went up the road to the village school, where a curtain divided the two classes—Second to eight or nine, First to fourteen. At eleven I went to the local grammar school, and later to Cambridge.

Culture is ordinary: that is where we must start. To grow up in that country was to see the shape of a culture, and its modes of change. I could stand on the mountains and look north to the farms and the cathedral or south to the smoke and the flare of the blast furnace making a second sunset. To grow up in that family was to see the shaping of minds: the learning of new skills, the shifting of relationships, the emergence of different language and ideas. My grandfather, a big hard labourer, wept while he spoke, finely and excitedly, at the parish meeting, of being turned out of his cottage. My father, not long before he died, spoke quietly and happily of when he had started a trade-union branch and a Labour Party group in the village, and, without bitterness, of the 'kept men' of the new politics. I speak a different idiom, but I think of these same things.

Culture is ordinary: that is the first fact. Every human society has its own shape, its own purposes, its own meanings. Every human society expresses these, in institutions, and in arts and learning. The making of a society is the finding of common meanings and directions, and its growth is an active debate and amendment under the pressures of experience, contact, and discovery, writing themselves into the land. The growing society is there, yet it is also made and remade in every individual mind. The making of a mind is, first, the slow learning of shapes, purposes, and meanings, so that work, observation, and communication are possible. Then, second, but equal in importance, is the testing of these in experience, the making of new observations, comparisons, and meanings. A culture has two aspects: the known meanings and directions, which its members are trained to; the new observations and meanings, which are offered and tested. These are the ordinary processes of human societies and human minds, and we see through them the nature of a culture: that it is always both traditional and creative; that it is both the most ordinary common meanings and the finest individual meanings. We use the word culture in these two senses: to mean a whole way of life—the common meanings; to mean the arts and learning—the special processes of discovery and creative effort. Some writers reserve the word for one or other of these senses; I insist on both, and on the significance of their conjunction. The questions I ask about our culture are questions about our general and common purposes, yet also questions about deep personal meanings. Culture is ordinary, in every society and in every mind.

SUGGESTIONS FOR DISCUSSION

1. In the opening paragraph of this selection, Williams explains how he had tried and failed to get into the library but watched a group of clergymen get in easily. He stands there between the locked library and the cinema that is showing a cartoon version of *Gulliver's Travels*. How does that opening scene establish for Williams's readers his character and his reason for insisting that culture is ordinary?

2. Williams says that the nature of a culture is "both traditional and creative; that it is both the most ordinary common meanings and the finest individual meanings" and that it is "a whole way of life." With a group of your classmates, discuss what he must mean by that. List examples of each aspect of culture (common meanings vs. arts and learning). Compare your lists with those of your classmates. Discuss the principles of selection for the lists (what each group member decided to list and how each choice was made).

3. At the end of the description of his bus trip from Cambridge to the Black Mountains in Wales, Williams writes that this is a "journey . . . that in one form or another we have all made." What does he mean? What does this journey tell us about culture?

SUGGESTED ASSIGNMENT

Work together with a group of classmates. Think of as many instances as you can where the term *culture* or *cultured* appears. For example, when do you hear other people that you know (family, friends, coworkers, neighbors, teachers, and so on) use the terms? When do you use them yourself? Where have you seen the terms in written texts or heard them used on radio and television or in the movies? Make a list of occasions when you have encountered or used the terms. Categorize the various uses of the terms. Are they used in the same way in each instance or do their meanings differ? Explain your answer. How do you account for the similarities and differences in the use of the terms? Compare the results of your group discussion with the results of other groups.

Analyzing Visuals

Throughout *Reading Culture* you will be asked to analyze visual texts of all sorts. The following brief guide is designed to introduce some of the questions you can begin with. It will also help you locate various tools of visual analysis that appear in *Reading Culture*.

A Guide to Visual Analysis

Reading Images

Most of the images you will be asked to examine are still images—photographs, advertisements, logos, graphic novels, comics, and so on. As with the 1936 Dorothea Lange documentary photograph of Florence Thompson (often called *Migrant Madonna*) reprinted here, the way you analyze a still image depends very much on the questions you ask.

Dorothea Lange, "Florence Thompson 1936."

✔ What do you see in the photo? What details do you notice first? Who are these people?

✔ What does the photograph seem to be about?

✔ How do you respond to the image? Does it remind you of anything you have seen before?

✔ What is the medium (photography, painting, digital image, painting, drawing, etc.)?

✔ What kind (*genre*) of image is it (documentary photo, publicity photo, family snapshot, news photo, etc.)?

✔ Who took the photo and for what purpose? Where can you find out about the photographer and her career?

✔ When was it made? What do you know about the historical background?

✔ Who is the intended audience for the image?

✔ How are the people in the image arranged and what relationships are indicated by the arrangement?

✔ What is the relationship between the people in the photograph and the viewer? How would that relationship change if the woman were looking at the camera instead of away from it?

✔ How would the meaning change if you saw this photograph in a family album?
In a history book?
On a poster about hunger in America?
In a news story?
In an advertisement for antidepressants?

Resources for Reading Images

Visual analysis is the process of explaining how an image works, so it is important to keep in mind the tools useful for performing that analysis. While Chapter 4, Images, offers a good introduction to visual analysis—especially to reading print advertisements—you will find resources for analyzing the visual throughout *Reading Culture*.

■ Composition

Visual composition usually refers to how elements of an image are arranged within the space or frame and how that visual design conveys meaning and sets up a relationship with the viewer or reader.

page layout—arrangement of elements on the page; this includes attention to the text-to-graphics ratio, use of color, choice of font size and style (in Chapter 1, see the section "The Look of the Front Page: Analyzing Visual Design," p. 32).

vectors—arrangement of subjects or elements that set up or complete a story or action and establish relationships among elements in the image (in Chapter 3, see the section "Picturing Schooldays," p. 186).

perspective—angle of vision; also, a technique for representing three-dimensional objects and depth relationships in a two-dimensional space to give the appearance of depth; how camera angle establishes a point of view (in Chapter 3, see the section "Picturing Schooldays," p. 188).

the gaze—the direction in which a subject looks at or away from the viewer, creating either an *offer* (offering the subject to the viewer to be looked at) or a *demand* (engaging the viewer in a direct way); common term in visual analysis of gender (in Chapter 4, see "Reading the Gaze—Gender in Advertising," p. 219).

■ Genre Analysis

Genres are familiar acts of communication that take place across a broad range of media. Genre analysis examines a visual in terms of how it conforms to or breaks with various genres of visual representation. Documentary photography, news photos, and landscape paintings, for example, are different visual types or genres that carry with them the expectations and forms of their type. Genres featured in *Reading Culture* for visual analysis include:

packaging—see "Sweet-Talking Spaghetti Sauce: How to Read a Label," p. 290 (Chapter 5).

logos—see "Graphic Design in Rock Culture," p. 256; Chief Wahoo in "Race and Branding" p. 295 (Chapter 5).

product design—see "American Car Culture," p. 266; "Wired Culture: iPods," p. 268 (Chapter 5).

documentary photography—see "A Way of Seeing: An Introduction to the Photographs of Helen Levitt," p. 238 (Chapter 4); "Camera of Dirt," p. 430 (Chapter 8); "Photographing History," p. 506 (Chapter 9).

landscape photography—see "The Troubled Landscape," p. 333 (Chapter 6).

glamour photography/publicity shots—see "Hollywood Stars: Brando, Dean, and Monroe," p. 120 (Chapter 2); "The Face of Garbo," p. 292 (Chapter 5).

news photos—see "The Iraq Invasion and Occupation," p. 510 (Chapter 9).

graphic narrative/comics—see "Complacency Kills," a graphic news report, p. 45 (Chapter 1); "This Modern World," a comic strip, p. 27 (Chapter 1);

"The Veil," an autobiographical graphic novel, p. 382 (Chapter 7); "Dil-bert," a comic strip, p. 404 (Chapter 8).

print advertising—see Chapter 4, Images, especially "Suggestions for Reading Advertising," p. 210.

publicity campaign—see "Public Health Messages," p. 227 (Chapter 4).

performance art—see Coco Fusco and Guillermo Gomez Peña, "Postcolonial Representation," p. 581 (Chapter 10).

■ Analyzing Visual Representations

In visual theory, *representation* is a term that refers to how cultural ideas, ideals, and attitudes are popularized and presented visually. See "Visual Culture: Representations of Youth Culture in Movies," p. 114 (Chapter 2) for a good brief overview of cultural representation in visual media.

images of gender—an examination of how women and men are treated visually. See "The Iron Maiden: How Advertising Portrays Women," p. 211 (Chapter 4); "Reading the Gaze: Gender in Advertising," p. 219 (Chapter 4); "When You Meet Estella Smart, You Been Met!" p. 231 (Chapter 4); "Advertising Through the Ages," p. 249 (Chapter 4); "The Veil," p. 382 (Chapter 7).

images of difference—an examination of how difference—racial, ethnic, economic, etc.—is treated visually; sometimes called the process of "othering." See "Race and Branding," p. 295 (Chapter 5); "Self-Portraits," p. 530 (Chapter 10); "Passport Photos," p. 533 (Chapter 10); Coco Fusco and Guillermo Gómez-Peña, "Postcolonial Representation," p. 581 (Chapter 10); Jean Gerome's "The Slave Market" and "The Snake Charmer," p. 584 (Chapter 10).

■ Historical Analysis

Though historical analysis can refer to the history of the image itself or to the history of the technology that is used to create an image (glass plate, film, and digital technology are all a part of the history of photography), in *Reading Culture*, historical analysis refers to an examination of the relation of an image to historical events (what the image can tell viewers about those events as well as the role it might have played in events) and to public memory of the past (how images are selected to represent the past and what this selection can tell us about the present).

"Lewis Hine and the Social Uses of Photography," p. 444 (Chapter 8), a discussion of documentary photography and its relationship to social movements.

"Contra Curtis: Early American Cover-Ups," p. 473 (Chapter 9), rereading history by using original photographs and photographic technology as the basis for telling a different story; "reinventing" history.

"Photographing History," p. 506, and "The Iraq Invasion and Occupation," p. 510 (Chapter 9), an examination of the role of photography in establishing a collective memory of history; making meaning from the "uncoded message" that is the photographic image; how readers create historical accounts from the photographic image.

■ Visual Parody/Satire

Visual parody and satire is the process of overturning or overwriting the original image as a commentary on the original message or the politics of the image. Parody begins with analysis—to understand what the original is saying and how it conveys that message in order to rewrite or satirize the original message.

"Rewriting the Image," p. 223 (Chapter 4)—rewriting advertising; visual parody.

"Contra-Curtis: Early American Cover-Ups," p. 473 (Chapter 9)—rewriting/re-inventing history using original technology—platinum prints—to bring to mind the original images and reveal the politics unspoken in those original prints.

Coco Fusco and Guillermo Gómez-Peña, "Postcolonial Representation," p. 581 (Chapter 10)—performance art that uses references to stereotypes and mainstream history as political commentary.

■ Reading Visual Displays of Information

We provide examples of information design for discussion and analysis of the visual display of data and information.

> ***bar graphs***—see "It's Time to Grow Up . . . Later," p. 84 (Chapter 2).
>
> ***PowerPoint***™—see "PowerPoint Is Evil," p. 170 (Chapter 3).
>
> ***quantitative information***—charts, graphs, tables—see "Reading Visual Displays of Information," p. 18 (Chapter 1).
>
> ***charts and tables***—see "The Cocktail Waitress," p. 438 (Chapter 8); "Reconstructing the Network of the Workplace," p. 437 (Chapter 8).

Reading Film

Dominic Monaghan, Elijah Wood, Billy Boyd, and Sean Astin, 2001, in a scene from *The Lord of the Rings: The Fellowship of the Ring.*

Film adds elements of movement, camera work, lighting, design, storyline, and sound to visual. Notice, however, that many of the questions you will begin with are similar to those you would ask about still images. Imagine you are watching *The Lord of the Rings: The Fellowship of the Ring.* You begin to ask questions as the film unfolds.

✔ What is your first impression of the film?

✔ What is it about? (What is the storyline? Who are the characters?)

✔ Who are the actors? Do they influence your response? Did they influence whether you wanted to see the film or not?

✔ Is it a Hollywood movie or an independent production? Is it a network or cable production?

✔ Who directed the film? Do you know of other films by this director? Is this one similar to those others?

✔ When was the film made? If it is an older film, what do you know about that period?

✔ What kind (genre) of film or program is it (documentary, drama, comedy, action/adventure, fantasy, feature-length animation, etc.)? How do you know?

✔ How does lighting contribute to the way you read this film? Is it brightly lit? Dark and grainy? Idealistic? Brooding?

✔ What do you notice about camera work? Does the camera move like a handheld camera might, to give the impression of walking or running with a character? Does the camera stay at a distance? When do you see close-ups? What characters or objects are at the center or in the foreground of the camera frame?

✔ How does costuming and make-up contribute to the way you read this film or respond to the characters?

✔ Describe the set design. Does it look like a town, city, or landscape you recognize, or is it a fantasy setting?

✔ Is the film a remake of a novel, play, short story, graphic novel, or video game that you know well? How does your knowledge of the original influence your reading of the film?

You will find a good introduction to writing about film (reviews, history, and criticism) in "Film Clip: Reading and Writing About Film," p. 190 (Chapter 3). For a list of terms useful for writing about film, see "Camera Work and Editing: Some Useful Terms," p. 247 (Chapter 4). Additional resources on film (as well as television) analysis are listed below:

Resources for Film and Television Analysis

■ Camera Work and Editing

A focus on camera work and editing means examining how a film is shot, how the camera is used, and the way those shots are then assembled and sequenced to create a storyline.

"Reading Television News," p. 22 (Chapter 1).

"Visual Codes," p. 28 (Chapter 1), set and screen design, camera space, special arrangement, sequencing.

"Storyboarding: Editing and Camera Work," p. 244 (Chapter 4), a sketch of a scene, shot-by-shot to examine how the scene works.

■ Genres

As with still images, films can be grouped into genres that have characteristic features and recognizable conventions.

"Reading Television News," p. 22 (Chapter 1), an examination of the visual and verbal codes typical to television news programming.

"The Gangster as Tragic Hero," p. 378 (Chapter 7), an analysis of the gangster film genre as a story of outlaw heroes.

"Film Documentary and the Narrator," p. 436 (Chapter 8), a discussion of point of view and the convention of the voice-over narrative in film documentary.

"Film Genres: The Western," p. 514 (Chapter 9), an examination of the formula western as an expression of the mythology of westward expansion and the cowboy hero.

"Film Genres: Bollywood," p. 583 (Chapter 10), a discussion of the film industry in India and the extravaganza productions of Bollywood.

■ Film Representations

Film representation analysis is an examination of the way film representations are filtered through cultural codes and ideals.

"Representations of Youth Culture in Movies," p. 114 (Chapter 2), an examination of the ways youth, especially juvenile delinquency, has been represented in film.

"Hollywood Stars: Brando, Dean, and Monroe," p. 120 (Chapter 2), an exploration of the iconic power of Hollywood stars.

■ Design

Design analysis is an examination of elements that give a film or television program a specific look.

"Visual Codes," p. 28 (Chapter 1), a discussion of how set design establishes the character and authority of news programming.

"Make-up and Costumes: Monsters and the Middle Ages," p. 288 (Chapter 5), an examination of how make-up and costuming account for the look of a film, with a focus on monster movies and period films.

"Analyzing Set Design: Cities in Decay," p. 339 (Chapter 6), an examination of the film set design as a crucial component in conveying meaning, tone, and symbol, with a focus on dystopia.

■ The Script

The script is the text used for making a film. An analysis of script can lead to content and audience analysis or to an examination of how the script translates or interprets an original text.

"Analyzing Content and Audience in Television News," p. 22 (Chapter 1), detailed outline example of stories on one evening news program as the basis for analyzing content and audience.

"Book to Film: The Adaptation," p. 392 (Chapter 7), a discussion of the film adaptation as an interpretations of literature.

CHAPTER ONE

Reading the News

Self-Portrait with Newsboy, by Lewis W. Hine. The J. Paul Getty Museum, Los Angeles. © The J. Paul Getty Museum

A newspaper should have no friends.

—Joseph Pulitzer

One of the basic troubles with radio and television news is that both instruments have grown up as an incompatible combination of show business, advertising and news. Each of the three is a rather bizarre and demanding profession. And when you get all three under one roof, the dust never settles.

—Edward R. Murrow

News is what powerful people want to keep hidden; everything else is publicity.

—Bill Moyers

Any time major dramatic events break—the 2005 funeral of Pope John Paul II, the 2004 Southeast Asia tsunami, the 2001 attack on New York's World Trade Center, the 1991 Persian Gulf War, the 1986 *Challenger* space shuttle disaster, the 1963 assassination of President John F. Kennedy—the media scramble to maintain round-the-clock coverage of the action as it unfolds. That means reporters must both sort out and be faithful to the facts of the story at the same time that they are

13

pressured to keep the audience reading their newspaper or watching their cable or network news program. Edward R. Murrow in the 1950s saw the real struggle for the television and radio journalist as one between entertainment and news reporting. That tension has not relaxed in the half-century since Murrow's groundbreaking news show. If anything, it has gotten stronger as cable and network television, newspapers, news magazines, bloggers, and even Comedy Central have all become involved in the business of reading the news.

The job of the news media is to report, as honestly and completely as possible, what is happening in the world. That is a task that requires more than organizing a series of events in the order they occurred. Reporting the news involves selection and interpretation. Whether it is in hourly updated Internet news sites, nightly television news programs, daily newspapers, or weekly news magazines, the news media select which events to report and which aspects of those stories to emphasize. News media tell us what is news and what is not. They sell the news.

Of course, "reading the news" means reading all kinds of news—everything from sports to celebrity to business to local news. This chapter looks at how the news media shape news for viewers, readers, and Internet users.

Where Do People Get Their News?

In March 2004, the following Associated Press report appeared on the CNN.com website. Before you read, take time to write your own account of where you get your news. Do you watch television news, read one or more newspapers or news magazines, catch the news on the Internet, or some combination of those? How informed would you say you are about current events in the news?

YOUNG AMERICA'S NEWS SOURCE: JON STEWART
But *Daily Show* Staffers Hope Viewers Turn to Others, Too

— *Associated Press*

1 Tom Brokaw, Peter Jennings, Dan Rather . . . and Jon Stewart?

Readers over 30 might scoff at Stewart's inclusion—assuming they know who he is. For many under 30, the host of Comedy Central's "The Daily Show" is, improbably, an important news source.

A poll released earlier this year by the Pew Research Center for the People and the Press found that 21 percent of people aged 18 to 29 cited "The Daily Show" and "Saturday Night Live" as a place where they regularly learned presidential campaign news.

By contrast, 23 percent of the young people mentioned ABC, CBS or NBC's nightly news broadcasts as a source.

5   Even more startling is the change from just four years ago. When the same question was asked in 2000, Pew found only 9 percent of young people pointing to the comedy shows and 39 percent to the network news shows.

The people at "The Daily Show" ridicule the idea of people looking to their show as a primary news source.

"A lot of them are probably high," Stewart cracked. "I'm not sure, coming off of robots fighting and into our show, what we're dealing with out there."

Think again, Jon.

Random conversations with nine people, aged 19 to 26, waiting to see a taping of "The Daily Show" last week revealed two who admitted they learned much about the news from the program.

10   None said they regularly watched the network evening news shows.

"I'm not really interested," said Michelle Cohen, a 20-year-old New Yorker. "A lot of those shows focus on topics that have absolutely nothing to do with me, like old people's health care."

AHEAD OF RUSSERT, KOPPEL, HANNITY

As if to drive the Pew survey's point home, "The Daily Show" reached a ratings milestone during the two weeks of the Iowa caucus, New Hampshire primary and State of the Union address. For the first time, Stewart's show had more male viewers aged 18 to 34 than any of the network evening news shows.

One newspaper, Newsday, has Stewart listed atop a list of the 20 media players who will most influence the upcoming campaign. Tim Russert, Ted Koppel, Sean Hannity, among others, trailed.

Stewart's success at skewering news people, and not just newsmakers, has particularly scored with his audience.

15   "They poke fun at how cheesy the regular news shows are, and somebody needs to do

that," said Joe Van Vleet, a 25-year-old Californian attending college in New York City. He mimicked a news anchor's voice and marveled at how they all sound the same.

Nicole Vernon, a 24-year-old bartender from New York City, said she finds much of television news "silly."

Stewart, she said, "keeps it very truthful and straightforward."

Hold on there, said Ben Karlin, the show's executive producer. A "Daily Show" viewer who doesn't supplement it with real news isn't very well-informed, he said. Pew confirmed that; its survey showed that people who regularly learned news from the comedy shows were less likely to know basic facts of the campaign.

Jim Murphy, "CBS Evening News" executive producer, read the Pew study closely. "I've passed being depressed about that," he sighed.

20   Evening news producers have long recognized their audience is older; the common theory is that when people get jobs, mortgages and children, they'll take a greater interest in their programs.

The worry is that with so many other sources of news available now, young people will become accustomed to them and not make the evening news a priority.

Steve Capus, "NBC Nightly News" executive producer, said he had a sense that more young viewers were watching right after the 2001 terrorist attacks. Now, he's not so sure.

The challenge is to get young viewers more consistently, not simply when there are monumental stories, he said.

Murphy said he's constantly trying to keep up with new technology and trends in how people get news. Ultimately, he said, you simply have to make the best newscast you can.

25   Vernon's companion at "The Daily Show" taping, 25-year-old graduate student Yvgeni Sverdlov, may be a typical young news consumer. He said he absorbed news from various sources—a little bit of CNN, a newspaper, even reading news tickers while walking in Manhattan. . . .

Both Stewart and the evening news anchors essentially have the same goal: to take the daily flood of news and distill it for a viewer. Brokaw does it seriously, Stewart looks for laughs.

Which one is a 21-year-old most likely to watch?

In Capus' Rockefeller Center office, the "Nightly News" staff often gathers after its morning news meeting to watch the 10 a.m. rerun of the previous night's "The Daily Show."

Stewart, in turn, knows their world intimately. In conversation, he drops the name of "The Note," ABC News' Web site for political junkies.

30   NBC invited Stewart to give commentary after President Bush's State of the Union address in January. CBS' evening news ran a weekly segment during the 2000 campaign on what comedians were saying, and it's returning this year.

The danger, one Capus and Murphy readily recognize, lies in network news programs that overreact to the comedy shows' growing influence by obviously groping for ways to connect with young people.

Stewart knows when he sees a newsmagazine correspondent in a leather jacket standing on a dark street to introduce a story about washing machines that he has a joke that needs no punch line.

"I shudder to think of Dan Rather up there trying to riff like Jon Stewart," said Rob Vincent, 26, an Oklahoma City native attending law school in New York. "That seems a little scary to me."

His friend, 25-year-old law student Jason Rogers of Phoenix, agreed.

35   "It would alienate their core audience—which is my parents and grandparents," he said.

SUGGESTIONS FOR DISCUSSION

1. This AP wire story reports that one study found that 21 percent of people age 18 to 29 got their news for the last U.S. presidential campaign from *The Daily Show*. How close is this report to your own experience of watching the news? Share the writing you did before you read this report with a group of your classmates. In what ways are your experiences with news sources similar? Where do they differ?

2. Where do you think your parents' generation gets most of their news? How would you compare their knowledge of news events to yours? To your friends'?

3. Why might it concern the news media that young people trust Jon Stewart for their news? What do you know about the other news personalities listed in this story—Tim Russert, Ted Koppel, and Sean Hannity, for example? How would you compare their news commentaries to Jon Stewart's?

Exercise 1.1   Audience Survey

1. Form a group with three or four classmates. Each group member can use the following questions to interview five to ten friends, classmates from other courses, coworkers, teachers, and/or family members about the news. Use written questions so people can answer on paper or via e-mail, or ask the questions in person and record the answers in a notebook. If possible, interview people from different age groups and walks of life.

   You might wish to preview this exercise by first interviewing each other in class; then make plans to interview people who are not your classmates.

■ Do you read a daily newspaper? What is it? How often? Why?

■ Do you listen to news on the radio? What stations? How long is the news program that you listen to?

■ Do you read a weekly news magazine such as *Time* or *Newsweek*? Do you subscribe or read it only when you are in a waiting room and it is available?

■ If you watch news on television, would you consider yourself:

__ A regular viewer?

__ An occasional viewer?

__ Someone who watches only when a major story breaks?

__ Someone who watches during your workout in a local gym or who catches television news when you see it being broadcast in a public space like an airport or hotel lobby?

■ Do you read news on the Internet? Which sites? How often?

■ If you get your news from the Internet, do you read only the headlines, or do you look for specific stories on specific topics? How often do you follow the headline link to read an entire story? Describe the story you read most recently.

■ Do you watch Comedy Central's *Daily Show* or *Saturday Night Live*'s news satire? How close would you say these shows are to real news?

■ Are there other sources you rely on for news? What are they?

■ Which news sources do you trust to give you accurate reports?

■ Which news sources do you consider biased, incomplete, or trivial?

Look at this list of journalistic principles. How closely do you think news media today follow them? Are some but not other principles practiced?

■ Journalism's first obligation is to the truth.

■ Its first loyalty is to citizens.

■ Its essence is a discipline of verification.

■ Its practitioners must maintain an independence from those they cover.

■ It must serve as an independent monitor of power.

■ It must provide a forum for public criticism and compromise.

■ It must strive to make the significant interesting and relevant.

■ It must keep the news comprehensive and proportional.

■ Its practitioners must be allowed to exercise their personal conscience.

Age:

__ 16–23   __ 35–45   __ 45–60   __ over 60

Gender:

__ male   __ female

Profession: _____

2. With your group, summarize the findings of your interviews. Tally how many people were interviewed and note their age, gender, and profession. Where do the people you interviewed get their news—television, radio, newspapers, news magazines, the Internet? Do these news sources vary depending on age, gender, or profession? How do people seem to assess the accuracy of the news? How did they respond to the list of journalistic principles? What patterns do you see in how people assess the accuracy and bias in the news and whether they think the news media stick to journalistic principles?

3. Report your findings in class. Compare them with the findings of other groups. What do you see as the significance of these findings?

Reading Visual Displays of Information

Tables, charts, lists, maps, timelines, and diagrams are some of the kinds of visual displays of information you are likely to encounter in books, journal articles, magazines, newspapers, Internet sites, and even on television and in film documentaries. That is because visual displays can give readers a quick overview of the material in a form that is meant to be clear and easy to understand.

In the charts reprinted here, notice how different kinds of charts are useful for displaying different types of information. A **line chart** can display patterns of data over time. Notice, for example, that Chart 1.1 indicates that newspaper readership between the years 1996 and 2004 has been consistently highest in the 65 + age group and lowest among readers age 18 to 29. The chart also indicates that readership in all of these age groups has dropped somewhat in those years, though most dramatically in readers age 30 to 49, rising a bit in that group after the bombing of Afghanistan in 2002 and the beginning of the war in Iraq in 2003. During that same period, the 18- to 29-year-old readership continued to drop, suggesting perhaps that young people were turning to other sources for their news.

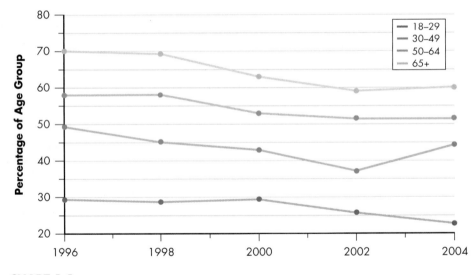

CHART 1.1

Newspaper Audience, by Age Group 1996–2004
Source: Pew Research Center for the People and the Press, "Pew Research Biennial News Consumption Survey," June 8, 2004.

By contrast, a **column chart**, like Chart 1.2 indicating the audience's perception of the reliability of Internet news sites, can be used to compare data in a single time period or compare a few items in a single time period.

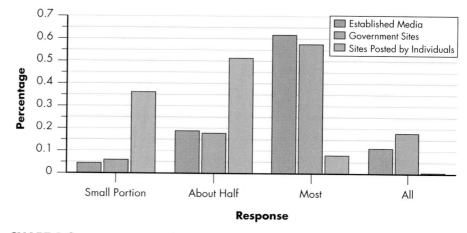

CHART 1.2

Perceptions of Internet's Reliability, Overall

Survey question: "How much of the information on the Internet do you think is reliable and accurate?"
Source: The Digital Future Report, USC Annenberg School Center for the Digital Future, September 2004.

A **pie chart** is most useful when your data total 100 percent and you are look-ing at data from a single source. For example, in order to use a pie chart to display the same information that is displayed in the column chart on attitudes toward Internet credibility (Chart 1.2), you would need three different pie charts, one for each type of site (Charts 1.3–1.5).

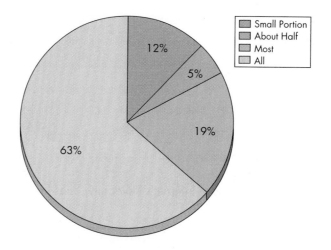

CHART 1.3

Perceptions of Internet's Reliability: Sites of Established Media

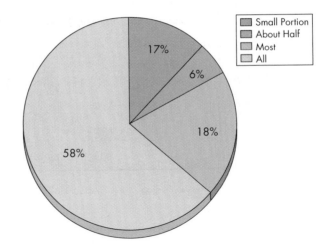

CHART 1.4
Perceptions of Internet's Reliability: Government Sites

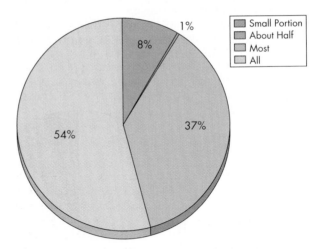

CHART 1.5
Perceptions of Internet's Reliability: Sites Posted by Individuals

All of these figures can also be expressed in **tables** which organize and display information so that readers can compare data easily. The table reprinted here, Table 1.1, contains the original data from the Internet reliability question.

TABLE 1.1 How Much of the Internet Is Reliable and Accurate?

User perception by type of Web site.

	Sites of Established Media	Government Sites	Sites Posted by Individuals
Small Portion	5%	6%	36%
About Half	19%	18%	52%
Most	62%	57%	8%
All	12%	17%	1%

Survey question: "How much of the information on specific types of Internet sites do you think is reliable and accurate?"

Responses are from people who use the Internet for news at least once in a typical week. Responses do not add up to 100 due to rounding.

Source: The Digital Future Report, USC Annenberg School Center for the Digital Future, September 2004.

SUGGESTIONS FOR DISCUSSION

1. Look at the information contained in each chart. To what extent does this information compare to the information you gathered in your survey of where people get their news?

2. What do the charts tell you that you could not get in the smaller survey you conducted?

3. With a group of your classmates, study the Internet reliability column chart (Chart 1.2) with the same information presented as a series of pie charts (Charts 1.3–1.5) and the same information presented again in Table 1.1. Which visual display of information do you find most useful? Clearest? Does any one type of visual indicate relationships or percentages any better than the others? What are the advantages and disadvantages in each type of visual display of information?

SUGGESTED ASSIGNMENT

Visit **http://www.stateofthemedia.org/2005/index.asp**. There you will find these and many other charts and tables displaying information from a larger report on the State of the Media in 2005. Choose a chart that interests you, and use the "Design Your Own Chart" feature to change it from its original to a different kind of chart—a column chart to a stacked bar chart, for example. How does the new chart change what is emphasized in the survey? What charts could not be used for the information you selected?

Reading Television News

This section offers strategies for reading and analyzing television news. That means you will be asked to pay attention to the content of evening network news, who watches these programs, and how the shows—using visual and verbal codes—convey information, provide entertainment, and aim for a loyal viewer base.

The task of television news programming is to inform citizens, entertain viewers, and advertise to consumers, all at the same time. There is little question that television news is a commercial enterprise and that the ratings (or the percentage of viewers who watch a news program) matter. Therefore, news programmers seek the widest audience by combining hard news about the important national and international events of the day with soft news about lifestyle, celebrities, and entertainment.

The exact combination of hard and soft news will vary, depending in large part on the type of news show. The traditional mainstays of television news—national network news and local news—differ in important respects. National network news, with well-known anchors, claim the greatest authority and have extensive resources to send reporters anywhere in the world to cover breaking stories or to develop special investigative feature stories. Local news typically features a limited number of national and international stories, along with local news, weather, sports, and lifestyle features.

The advent of cable television has made possible for the first time continuous news programming; networks such as CNN, MSNBC, and Fox News have round-the-clock coverage of national and international news as well as separate segments on financial, health, legal, sports, and entertainment news. With its on-the-spot coverage, CNN gained public recognition initially during the Persian Gulf War of 1991. Since then, cable news has become a fixture in American life, and the networks are likely to be playing nonstop in such places as airports, hotel lobbies, and health clubs.

Other types of news programs include news magazines such as *60 Minutes, 20/20,* and *Nightline,* which show investigative reporting and interviews; news commentary such as Chris Matthews's *Hardball;* and interview shows such as *Larry King Live.* Information and entertainment tend to blur together in these types of news shows—to create what is often called "infotainment."

Analyzing Content and Audience in Television News

A perennial question in television news programming is whether a story is newsworthy. What counts as news on television depends on the station or network, the type of news show, its audience, and whether the primary focus is to entertain or to inform. In Exercise 1.2, you analyze evening news programming on the major networks ABC, CBS, NBC, PBS, and Fox to obtain insight into three areas.

First, by noticing how news shows select and interpret the major events of the day, you will see how some events, such as the war in Iraq and the 2004 U.S. presidential election, influence news programming not only in headline stories but also in related features.

Second, by examining the content of the evening network news, including the commercials, you can draw inferences about who the intended audience is and how the news show addresses viewers' age, interests, and social position.

Third, by investigating what appears on the evening news, you can begin to formulate your own conclusions about the meaning of news programming—and respond to the critics who claim that by reducing the coverage of hard news, television news programming has become increasingly frivolous and has defaulted on its journalistic responsibilities.

TERMS TO KEEP IN MIND AS YOU READ TELEVISION NEWS

Hard News. Hard news consists of the important events of the day in international, national, and local affairs. Hard news tends to focus on serious issues with real consequences. Reports on the U.S. presidential election, an earthquake and tsunami in Southeast Asia, prisoner abuse scandals in Iraq and Afghanistan, a nationwide strike in South Africa, and stories of genocide in Congo are all hard news. Hard news may also include reporting on the law, business, science, and education when the story has wide interest, such as the Supreme Court decision on school vouchers, the corporate scandals at Haliburton, or new studies on global warming and environmental exposure and breast cancer. Sometimes the hard news overlaps with celebrity news, as in the imprisonment of Martha Stewart or the Michael Jackson child abuse trial.

Soft News. Soft news is meant to entertain as well as to inform viewers by focusing on celebrities, the entertainment world, and lifestyle. Soft news tends to emphasize the human interest side of things—sometimes with an eye for scandal and the sensational: another Hollywood star checking into rehabilitation, the latest super-couple break-up, the flap over *American Idol* voting mix-ups, or the latest drugs to hit the rave scene. Soft news can also emphasize heartwarming aspects of the news: third graders raising money to send to an Afghani elementary school, a teenager rescuing two people trapped in a burning car, or neighbors helping a black family repaint its house after vandals spray-painted racist slogans on it.

Feature Stories. Feature stories can be based on either hard or soft news. Features are different from news stories in the way they can go beyond reporting the events of the day to presenting more in-depth background, interviews, and analysis. Some feature stories try to get behind the news to reveal trends and underlying patterns. Feature stories might focus on the debate about mammography in medical circles, the controversy over the hunting rights of Native Americans in Alaska, or the European movement against genetically modified food. Major investigative feature stories sometimes run in two- or three-part series.

Breaking News. Breaking (sometimes called "developing") news refers to events that are just unfolding. Television news teams will sometimes interrupt regularly scheduled programming to announce an important piece of news such as election results, a national leader rushed to the hospital, or the rising death toll from Hurricane Katrina in 2005.

Continuing News. Continuing news refers to ongoing stories that unfold over a period of time and spin off related stories. For example, stories continue to grow out of the war in Iraq—reports on injured military men and women, on inadequate armor for Humvees, on corporate scandal relating to companies doing business in the Middle East, on prisoner abuse scandals, and on the failure of the intelligence community in the weeks before the war to report accurately on weapons of mass destruction.

Recording Content

1. Choose for this project the evening news on one of the major networks—ABC, CBS, NBC, PBS, or Fox. It will help if you can tape the program in its entirety. Construct an outline of the news show by doing the following:
   - Identify the exact title of the news program. Note date and time of the broadcast.
   - Record the headlines that appear at the beginning of the news.
   - Organize your outline by segments, using commercial breaks as the boundaries for the segments. Note that these segments are often titled. Record the titles that appear on the screen or that the anchor uses.
   - Time each story.
   - Note the program sponsors that appear during commercial breaks.

Sample Outline of a News Program
NBC Nightly News with Brian Williams
April 11, 2005—6:30–7:00 p.m. EDT
Opening Titles
Montage of the faces of former NBC News anchors come together toward the center of the screen and then move apart. Voices of Cameron Swazey, Chet Huntley, David Brinkley, John Chancellor, and Tom Brokaw introducing themselves in voice-over as pictures of each appear onscreen.

Headlines (00:56)
Rough Ride—story on presidential nomination for UN ambassador
Give and Take—story on meeting between President George W. Bush and Israeli Prime Minister Ariel Sharon
Tax Gap—income tax collecting story
Silicone Breast Implants—story on whether to put silicone implants back in the market
Stupid Pet Trick—Internet scam story

Segment 1 (11:35)
(02:21) Bolton nominated for UN ambassador story
(03:32) Sharon report with interview
(02:15) American taken hostage in Iraq; report from Baghdad
(02:28) Story on training Iraqi forces to take over from U.S. forces
(00:30) Story on controversy in Vatican
(00:15) Promos for upcoming segment

Commercial Break *(02:21)*: St. Joseph Aspirin for heart attacks; Transitions lenses; Prilosec heartburn medication; Beneful, natural dog food; promo for upcoming NBC shows

Segment 2 (3:35)
(03:25) Report on income tax investigations
(00:10) Promo for upcoming segment

Commercial Break *(02:39)*: Vesicare bladder control medication; Edward R. Jones investment agency ad; Bayer aspirin for arthritis and heart attack; Gas-X stomach medication; Round-up weed killer for lawns

Segment 3 (4:09)
(00:25) Report on man arrested at White House and dragged away by security guards. No weapons were discovered.

(03:03) Lifeline feature on silicone breast implants
(00:39) Story on what the president has on his iPod playlist
(00:05) Promo for upcoming story

Commercial Break (2:57): Just for Men hair color; Aqua Velva aftershave; Minwax wood stain product; Quiznos subs; Waterhouse brokerage firm; Levitra erectile dysfunction medication; Tylenol for arthritis; promo for local news programming

Segment 4 (2:43)
(02:30) Internet threat to kill Toby the rabbit unless $50,000 is sent to website
(00:10) Report that another website claims the "Toby the rabbit" threat is an Internet hoax
(00:03) Sign-off

2. Use your outline to write a brief summary of the program's content. Use the following questions to help you focus your summary.
   ■ What were the top stories introduced at the beginning of the broadcast?
   ■ How many hard news stories appeared in the broadcast compared with soft news stories such as human interest, lifestyle, celebrity, or entertainment? How much time was given to hard news and how much time to soft news?
   ■ Which stories are given the most time and which are brief notes?
   ■ How much international news is broadcast in relation to national news and how much time is allotted to each?
   ■ What kinds of stories dominate national news? What kinds of stories dominate international news?
   ■ How much time do commercials take?

Sample Summary

On April 11, 2005, *NBC Nightly News with Brian Williams* featured three kinds of stories: stories related to international tensions, stories featuring financial news, and stories featuring medical reports on approving silicone implants for use again in this country. This night, the programming had very few short reports. Most were longer (over two minutes) and focused on one of the three issues—international security, taxes, or women's medical news.

Of the thirty minutes set aside for this program, almost two minutes were devoted either to headlines at the beginning of the show or to promotions throughout announcing what stories would be coming up after the commercial breaks.

Commercials took up nearly eight minutes.

Of the remaining eighteen-plus minutes, approximately twelve minutes were spent on hard news and about one minute on two soft news headlines, including one story about what is on the president's iPod playlist. In all, about ten minutes were spent on headline stories primarily covering international security and finance, though both the Sharon and the finance stories went from hard news announcements to feature stories that included an interview with Sharon on a number of topics and a more general story about tax auditing, in general. I am assuming the tax story only came up because the deadline for filing taxes (April 15) was coming up. The international stories were solely about Iraq and the Israel/Palestine dispute over the Gaza strip. No stories about other international issues or nations were mentioned.

About three minutes were taken up with the Lifeline feature story, and 2:40 were taken up with the Internet rabbit threat story that, it was briefly reported after, was likely a hoax.

3. Now consider the target audience for the news program. Take into account the stories in the broadcast and the commercials that aired during the time you watched. Use this information to write a one-page analysis of the target audience for this program.

Sample Audience Analysis

The target audience for *NBC Nightly News* on April 11, 2005, is middle-aged adults, probably professionals, and many near retirement. That conclusion is based on the fact that, by far, the largest number of products advertised are aimed at the fifty-five and over age group. These include ads for retirement investments as well as several pharmaceutical products that treat gastric problems, arthritis, and heart trouble. Those commercials account for more than eight minutes of the thirty-minute broadcast.

In addition, six minutes or more of the broadcast are devoted to stories about threats to finances and to health issues, including the comment that uncollected taxes could fund an entire year's worth of Medicare. In other words, at least half of the time of this broadcast goes to some message—either news or commercial—directed at this older audience.

Analyzing Visual and Verbal Codes

Understanding how television news works requires paying attention to visual and verbal codes. A *code* is a system of signs that conveys meaning. Words, numbers, images, even body language can act as a code. Visual codes such as corporate logos identify companies, trademarks identify consumer brands, and male and female icons identify restrooms. Codes are also used to organize information, such as the periodic table in chemistry or maps of continents and countries. And codes can be used for persuasive purposes. Consider, for example, the way the "V for Victory" sign of World War II (holding up the forefinger and middle finger to form a V) became a peace sign in the 1960s.

The codes of television news are the ways television sends messages to viewers so that they recognize what they see on the news as real events that have taken place in the world. In the case of television news, viewing involves putting together sight and sound—or the visual, verbal, and aural codes that identify this type of program.

Notice, for example, the music that introduces and closes the evening news. It is brief but dramatic—like an announcement that says, "Pay attention. Something serious and important is about to happen." The music works in conjunction with the news anchor's voice—usually serious and low (even if the anchor is a woman)—and with the headlines and video footage that appear on the screen. It all happens together and so quickly that you may notice only that the evening news just came on. These are common television news codes that work together to take viewers into the special domain of the nightly news show.

In the comic strip *This Modern World*, shown here, the cartoonist Tom Tomorrow draws on readers' familiarity with the codes of television news programming to make a satiric point.

© Tom Tomorrow

The comic strip has reproduced such codes of television news as the "talking heads" of anchor Biff and special correspondent Wanda in close-up behind the news desk, looking straight into the camera and talking authoritatively to the audience. That is the look Tom Tomorrow expects his readers to recognize, even if they don't realize it, in his parody of news commentary.

A GUIDE TO VISUAL AND VERBAL CODES

Visual Codes

Set and screen design. The set and screen design refers to both the physical setting of the news show and the graphics that appear on the screen. The set of *NBC Nightly News*, for example, is designed to focus viewers' attention on anchor Brian Williams sitting behind a desk. The camera rarely pulls back far enough to include even the top of the desk. The background is a stylized screen in colors that make the anchor stand out. When the camera pulls back at the end of the broadcast, it shows Williams at his desk, a bank of television monitors in the background, and the NBC logo appearing at the right of the screen over them. The design of the set is simple, as though to emphasize the seriousness of working journalists but with the main visual emphasis on Williams as the anchor and star of the show.

By contrast, *CNN Live* and *CNN Headline News* both feature busy screens with weather, stock quotes, sports scores, and headlines or news promos running continuously across the bottom of the screen while the anchor is delivering the news. *CNN Headline News*, in fact, made a point of redesigning its screen to mimic a web page, suggesting, perhaps, that it identifies its viewing audience as being Internet savvy.

Spatial arrangement. Spatial arrangement refers to how people are placed within the camera frame—or the area you can see on your television screen. A news anchor is normally at the center of the screen, sitting behind a news desk, a talking head who speaks directly to the camera—and the viewer. This spatial arrangement emphasizes the stability and authority of the anchor as a trusted source of the news.

Sometimes, news reports use a *split screen*, which shows the anchor asking questions on one side of the screen and a reporter on location or an interview subject on the other side. The use of a split screen adds visual variety and makes news reporting more dynamic by creating a conversational exchange.

Camera space. Camera space refers to how close the camera is to what appears on the screen. Camera space indicates the social intimacy or distance between the viewer and what is represented on the screen—whether a close-up (head and shoulders), a medium close-up (chest, head, shoulders), a medium shot (waist on up), a full shot (head to toes), or a wide shot (the entire set or stage). In general, the closer the camera is to the subject, the more intimate the feeling, whereas the more distant the camera is from a subject, the less intimate. (See Figure 1.1.)

News anchors are typically shot in medium close-up. When, for example, you see Brian Williams behind his news desk, you usually see his chest, head, and shoulders, which is a respectful, formal, and not too intimate social distance.

The movement of the camera can alter the social distance established on the screen.

Medium shot

Close-up

FIGURE 1.1

Two examples of camera space.

When, for example, the camera moves in for a close-up of a news anchor, viewers sense they are being brought closer to the source of the news because something important is being said. By the same token, when the camera pans to a wide shot of the news room at the end of the program, it distances the viewer and signifies visually the close of the show.

Sequence of visuals. The sequence of visuals refers to the order in which images appear on the screen. The sequence of visuals in a news report can suggest meanings and relationships that may not be stated explicitly but take place nonetheless through a process of visual association.

Take, for example, the relationships implied in the following four visual elements that appeared sequentially in a news story on a school shooting—first, the headline, "Another School Shooting," and a picture of a handgun; second, video footage of the high school student accused of the shooting walking into a courtroom handcuffed and in prison uniform; third, an on-site interview with a tearful student at the high school where the shooting occurred; and fourth, a medium close-up of a psychiatrist seated behind a desk, explaining possible motives in school shootings.

As the camera moves from the headline and picture of a gun to a shot of the teenage boy in court, the implied logic is to associate the gun with the boy. In turn, the movement from the boy in court to the crying high school student associates the boy in prison uniform and handcuffs with the cause of the tears, and the psychiatrist in the final part of the sequence appears as an expert capable of bringing some order and explanation to an otherwise chaotic situation.

On-location reporting. Reporting on location brings the credibility of the eyewitness to news stories. A news reporter on the streets of Jerusalem, London, or Johannesburg or a weather reporter standing in wind and rain gives viewers the experience of being where the news is breaking. The language an on-location reporter uses can be less formal and more speculative than the language used in the studio, taking on a sense of urgency or uncertainty in the face of unfolding events.

Verbal Codes

Headlines. Headlines identify the key stories selected as the news of the day. Television news programs typically use brief headlines at the top or bottom of the screen to interpret the news. For example, in our sample news outline, the headline "American Kidnapped" appears behind Williams as he begins the story of the hostage taking. Similarly, the headline "Tax Gap" at the top of the story on income tax investigations gives viewers a slant on the story to follow.

Voice-over. Voice-over is a narrator speaking off-camera while scenes from a news report are shown onscreen. Viewers typically ascribe a high degree of authority to voice-over narration, just as readers do to the omniscient narrator in novels and short stories. The disembodied speech of voice-over suggests that the viewer is listening to someone able to see and explain everything that is going on.

Subtitles. Subtitles are written translations of what the onscreen speaker is saying when the speaker is using a language other than English or is speaking English with an accent that news producers think their audience will find difficult to understand. In both cases, the use of subtitles identifies the speaker as someone outside the U.S. mainstream, which can affect his or her credibility.

Outlining Visual and Verbal Codes

1. Choose a cable or network news broadcast and analyze the visual and verbal codes. Tape the show so you can watch it several times. (You can use the same news program you taped for Exercise 1.2 on page 24.) Choose at least one story or segment, and make a detailed outline of the story's visual and verbal codes. Then write a summary description of the show, focusing on visual and verbal codes. Refer to the next page for a sample of the kinds of notes you might take while watching for visual and verbal codes. These codes have been detailed from the headlines segment and from one top story in the broadcast.

Sample Outline of Visual and Verbal Codes

Verbal Codes	Visual Codes
Titles: NBC Nightly News **Voice-over:** I'm Cameron Swazy, David Brinkley, Chet Huntley, John Chancellor, Tom Brokaw	As names of former anchors are spoken, their faces framed in tv monitors emerge from center screen with older NBC news logos; these scatter to leave a stylized globe with the Nightly News logo then fade into headlines.
Headline: Rough Ride **Voice-over:** The President's choice for UN Ambassador faces tough questions about past statements slamming the UN	Footage of Bolton framed by blue screen and news logo testifying before the Senate confirmation committee. Senators questioning Bolton.
Headline: Give and Take **Voice-over:** President Bush and Israeli leader Sharon on the agreements and disagreements between the two men and tonight our exclusive with the Israeli leader.	Israeli flag flies across headline. Fade to footage of Bush at microphone; Sharon at microphone; then wide shot showing both at separate microphones in same press conference; fade to Sharon walking and talking in what looks like a casual and friendly way with the reporter who will later interview him.
Headline: Tax Gap **Voice-over:** $350 billion of uncollected taxes, enough to pay for a year's worth of Medicare. What's being done to collect what's owed?	Shots of NBC peacock logo fading to shots of tax forms, business office, people filling in tax forms, camera moves to close-up of sign identifying the IRS building.
Headline: Silicone Breast Implants **Voice-over:** Stories today of success and heartbreak. Should they be allowed back on the market?	NBC peacock logo fades to shots of medical symbols; footage of women speaking in microphone; doctors in surgery; silicone implants being prepared by a gloved hand. FDA logo appears in left corner of screen. Back frame shows form of a woman.
Headline: Stupid Pet Trick **Voice-over:** A website says send money or the rabbit dies. Is it a bad joke or just bad?	NBC peacock logo fades to image of laptop computer; dissolve to Internet site with picture of Toby the rabbit; close-up on words from the site "Toby will die"; more pictures of Toby from site ends in close-up of rabbit looking at camera.

Headline: NBC Nightly News Logo **Voice-over:** From NBC world headquarters in New York, this is NBC Nightly News with Brian Williams	Logo of news show appears over shot of New York, camera pans up Rockefeller Center. Fade to news studio, long shot of Williams standing on stage, news room behind him; April 11, 2005, in upper left of studio, Williams standing stage right near desk. Camera shifts to medium shot and gradually moves to medium close-up.
Top Story: **Headline:** Give and Take	Williams medium close-up, Israeli and US flags flying together over his left shoulder as he introduces the story. Shift to split screen with reporter David Gregory; cut to David Gregory on location in Crawford, Texas (a falling down barn behind him); cut to Bush and Sharon walking toward microphones; Bush talking to reporters in medium close-up.
Headline: One-on-One **Voice-over:** Gregory reads report of conflict with Israelis and Palestinians in Gaza Strip removal; stories of Israeli's fighting their neighbors and Israeli children and families who live peacefully in the area.	cut to Gregory on location in a field near the Bush ranch where he introduces the Gaza strip conflict with footage of people rioting, praying, and fighting; cut to Sharon sitting in interview and when talking about Israeli settlers, cut to children on swings.

2. Once you have completed a visual/verbal code outline of one story, write a brief (one- to two-page) description of the visual and verbal codes of the broadcast you watched. Share with several classmates the visual/verbal outline and description summary you wrote. As you read each other's outlines and descriptions, what differences do you notice? How do the shows resemble one another? How do they differ?

3. When you have completed your investigations and discussions with classmates, write an essay examining the ways that verbal and visual codes work together in any segment of the news program you watched. What story do they combine to tell? Is the visual just the backdrop of the story or does it represent an unfolding event? How does the anchor or the on-location reporter frame the story? How would the story read if the sound were turned off and you only had the visual and the words onscreen?

Reading Newspapers

Washington Post editors Leonard Downie Jr. and Robert G. Kaiser have argued that, although September 11, 2001, was a day of television, September 12 belonged to newspapers. The *Washington Post* sold a million copies on September 12, 2001, over 150,000 more than it usually sells. Other major papers experienced a similar increase in sales, some printing and selling 50 percent more papers than usual. If viewers were glued to their television screens round-the-clock on September 11, on September 12 they wanted to read the kind of coverage that newspapers provide.

This incident raises interesting questions about the differences between television and print news. One difference has to do with the sheer amount of news presented daily in the two media. Network evening news shows, for example, typically broadcast less than fifteen minutes of hard news in their daily thirty-minute time slots. Moreover, a typical *NBC Nightly News* program contains about 3,600 words, whereas an issue of *The New York Times* or the *Washington Post* contains roughly 100,000 words a day.

There are also important differences in the scope of news coverage. Although the cable news networks such as CNN and MSNBC offer continuous coverage, they do not cover the range of national and international stories that are covered in major newspapers such as *The New York Times*, *Washington Post*, *St. Louis Post-Dispatch*, *Chicago Tribune*, *Miami Herald*, and *Los Angeles Times*.

These differences in the amount and scope of news coverage point to key differences in the expectations of newspaper readers compared with those of television viewers. People turn to television for updates, daily headlines, sports, and weather. In times of crisis, they expect television news to provide ongoing coverage of events such as the attack on the World Trade Center. But for in-depth coverage with background information, analysis, and commentary, people rely on newspapers. This does not mean that all newspapers are the same. In fact, there are different types of newspapers, with different readerships. The three most popular types of newspaper are **local** newspapers, **nationally distributed** newspapers, and **tabloids**.

Local newspapers have a readership based in a town, city, or region. These newspapers typically feature news of local interest, such as stories on the school budget, the zoning board, and the mayoral race, along with international and national news taken from the Associated Press, *The New York Times*, or *Washington Post* wire services.

Newspapers with national circulation, such as *The New York Times*, *Washington Post*, *Wall Street Journal*, and *USA Today*, are read throughout the United States. The *Wall Street Journal* presents the news from a pro-business perspective, whereas *USA Today*, at least in the opinion of its critics, offers a lite version of the news. *The New York Times* and *Washington Post* are considered by many to be the pillars of respectable, influential, and responsible journalism, with a national audience of educated, well-informed readers in business, government, and the professions.

The third type of newspaper is the tabloid. Though often scorned for emphasizing gossip, crime, and scandal—and in the case of the *National Enquirer* and *Weekly World*, for being outright crackpot—daily news tabloids such as the *New York Daily News* and *Boston Herald* offer their working-class readership a popular alternative that presents a sensationalistic and sometimes anti-authoritarian slant on the news.

Reading newspapers means reading both the "look" of the paper—the visual composition or layout of the front page—and examining how a paper writes about and keeps up with particular stories. In the following two sections, you will have an opportunity to examine page design ("The Look of the Front Page") and then to pay attention to how a paper actually covers a story ("Continuing News: Covering a Story).

The Look of the Front Page: Analyzing Visual Design

Readers recognize different types of newspapers—and decide which to read—in part by their visual design. The visual design of a newspaper's front page is meant to send a message about its identity and intended readership. Based on visual cues, readers make assumptions about the authority, credibility, seriousness, and respectability of the newspaper. Tabloids, for example, are easily identified by their front-page graphics and sensationalistic screamer headlines, whereas newspapers with national circulation, such as *The New York Times, Washington Post*, and *Wall Street Journal*, project a more conservative and respectable image, with less graphics, more restrained headlines, and visual emphasis on the columns of newsprint.

By the end of the twentieth century, *The New York Times* had reduced the number of columns on its front page from eight to six and had added color to front-page photos. Although traditionalists objected to such changes, *The New York Times* was in many respects following the lead of *USA Today*, the national daily that broke with the conventional look of newspapers by featuring less print, shorter news stories, more white space, more and larger pictures, and lots of color to attract a younger, media-savvy readership. In recent years, many local and national newspapers have been redesigned to heighten their visual appeal and compete with television and the Internet.

GUIDELINES FOR ANALYZING THE VISUAL DESIGN OF FRONT PAGES

Page layout. Draw a sketch of one of the front pages reprinted on page 34 that identifies each separate visual element. Label these elements. Are they headlines, photos or other graphics, news stories, weather reports, sports scores, previews of stories inside the paper, short features (such as "On this day 50 years ago" or "Fact of the day"), or something else? This sketch should help you see how much space is devoted to hard news (whether local, national, or international) and how much to other features. Notice too how many news stories there are, how they are positioned on the page, and how their layout gives them greater or less emphasis.

Gray space. Gray space is the amount of unbroken text that appears on the page. The greater the gray space, the denser a page will seem. Gray space often indicates longer, more in-depth news reporting. Notice how much gray space appears on the front page and how it affects the apparent seriousness and credibility of the newspaper.

Graphics-to-text ratio. Pages with more graphics have less gray space and hence a more open, less dense feeling. Use your sketch of the front page layout to get a rough estimate of the graphic-to-text ratio. Consider what readership would prefer a less dense page with more graphics, such as a tabloid or *USA Today*, and what readership would prefer front pages with fewer graphics and more gray space, such as the *Wall Street Journal*.

Use of color. The use of color gives front pages a contemporary look, whereas black and white signifies more traditional news formats. Notice how, or whether, color is used, not just in news photos but also in headings and borders that highlight features.

Print fonts. The size and type of fonts used in headlines, stories, and captions contribute to the overall visual design of the front page. For example, big, bold headlines that extend across the front of a newspaper signal something important, catastrophic, or surprising. Notice how or whether the print fonts vary on the front page. If they do vary, how does this direct readers' attention?

Reprinted with permission from the NEW YORK POST, 2005, Copyright, NYP Holdings, Inc.

Exercise 1.4 **Analyzing the Visual Design of Newspapers**

1. Work with a group of your classmates. Use the guidelines to analyze the visual design of the front pages reprinted here, or bring in front pages of your own. Consider how each of the front pages selects the news of the day and what inferences you can draw about the intended readership. Compare the front pages. Based on the visual design of these pages, how do they differ in terms of credibility and respectability? How would you describe the image they project? What are the most important visual cues that establish this image?

2. Take an issue of the *Wall Street Journal* and redesign its front page to look like a tabloid. It won't be possible to include all the stories on the *Wall Street Journal*'s front page, so you'll have to select those that will appeal most to tabloid readers. Consider how to rewrite the headlines and include more graphics to give the stories a sensationalistic tabloid look.

Copyright © 2005 The New York Times Company. Reprinted by permission.

Reprinted by permission of The Wall Street Journal, Copyright © 2005 Dow Jones & Company, Inc. All Rights Reserved Worldwide.

Continuing News: Covering a Story

Newspapers report events as they take place—the attack on the World Trade Center, the war in Iraq, and reports of prisoner abuse in Abu Ghraib and the American base at Guantanamo Bay, Cuba. But national and local newspapers also provide other types of coverage, such as analysis of policymaking, feature stories based on investigative reporting or the human interest side of the latest news, editorials that state the official position of a newspaper, op-ed commentary in which regular columnists and others express their views, and letters to the editor.

Newspapers are typically divided into sections—news, arts and lifestyle, business, and sports. These sections may cover major news stories from their specific angles—for example, the business section reports on the war on terrorism's link to rising oil prices or the arts section might include stories on architectural proposals for redesigning the space where the World Trade Center once stood.

Exercise 1.5 asks you to follow a major news story and see how different types of newspapers have covered it, not only in news reporting but also in the other parts of a newspaper.

Tracking Coverage

For this project, pick a major news story. Follow its coverage in three to five different newspapers over the course of about a week. Use a local newspaper, your school newspaper, and a national newspaper.

1. Write down the headlines each newspaper uses to announce the story.

2. Note the section in which the story appears in each newspaper.

3. Which papers offer analysis of the event or feature stories covering different angles on the event? What aspects of the event do these analyses or features highlight?

4. Are there editorials or op-ed pieces that provide commentary on the news event? What perspectives on the news story do these provide?

5. Are there letters to the editor that offer readers' opinions? How do they compare with the newspaper's official editorial position and op-ed perspectives?

6. Taking all of this coverage into account, write a report on how the news story is covered in the newspapers you followed.

Reading About the News: Reporting War

Now that you have looked at how the news is reported on television and in newspapers, you are ready to investigate and enter into the debates over how the media handle the news, especially major news stories like the war in Iraq. Like any major and ongoing news story, this one has been addressed continuously throughout the media in a number of different forms. As direct news reporting, the media gives us stories of what is happening. But even direct reporting is not without controversy. As you will see in what follows, some of the controversy has come because of the administration's decision to "embed" journalists with combat troops. That is, reporters have not been locked out of the news, as they complained they had been during the 1991 Persian Gulf War, but in being assigned a particular unit under the command of the military, reporters are also not entirely independent.

As with any major story, the story of the Iraq war has been spun in a number of different directions. Besides straight reporting, you will find op-ed pieces in which a commentator argues a position, like Amy Goodman and David Goodman's *Baltimore Sun* commentary "Un-Embed the Media" or Aaron Barnhart's *Kansas City Star* column on the same topic. Other stories or commentaries might not seem, initially, to be related to the war at all. Frank Rich's "Nascar Nightly News," for example, appears initially to be a review of Brian Williams as Tom Brokaw's replacement for NBC news anchor. After all, it appeared in the Arts and Leisure section, not on the op-ed page, and yet, Rich centers his review on the issue of what television news ought to be covering, especially in a time of war. Bloggers comment on media coverage, offer chat space, and even track media accuracy. Iraq war coverage has even appeared as a comic strip in the hands of reporter and comics artist Joe Sacco.

Reading Strategies

Although you may be familiar with many of the reading strategies described below because you have used them throughout your education, it is useful to review them. They all involve writing, and all can help you to read more carefully and to write your way into the texts you are reading as you develop your own analysis and your position on the issues.

Underlining or highlighting. Most students underline or highlight what they are assigned to read—whether it's a textbook, a journal article, or a novel. The purpose is to catch the key points or memorable passages so that you can return to them easily when you need to study for a test or write a paper. This strategy works best if you keep in mind that you are looking for key points or noteworthy moments in the writing. If you underline or highlight too much of a reading selection, the strategy isn't likely to work well.

Annotating. Sometimes as students underline, they also write comments in the margins. This practice, annotation, is a more active kind of reading than underlining because it provides readers with a written record of their experience of the text. It offers readers a technique to write their way into the text. Annotations might include one- or two-word paraphrases of the content, notes on how the writer has structured the piece of writing ("key supporting evidence" or "refutes opposing views"), reactions ("I've never seen that"), or questions about difficult passages.

Summarizing. Not many students who underline or annotate take the next step to summarize. This is unfortunate because summarizing allows you to spend time thinking through what you have read. Summarizing builds on underlining and annotating by providing you with a brief account, in your own words, of what you have been reading. This strategy can be enormously useful for difficult material.

Exploratory writing. Exploratory writing offers a way to think out loud—on paper—about what you have been reading. It allows you to go beyond summary and annotation and begin to make decisions about what you have read, what it connects to, how it helps you understand issues, or how it seems to confuse an issue. With exploratory writing, you can experiment with ways of explaining and justifying your own reactions so that others will take them seriously, even if they don't agree. Exploratory writing can be personal in tone, but it isn't private. It is a level between the reactions you recorded in those annotations ("this is truly idiotic" or "I couldn't agree more") and the public voice you eventually will need to assume in a more formal, deliberative essay.

Synthesis. When you do research, you must do more than explore your own responses to what different writers have said about a topic and how they have said it. You also need to compare how these writers have written on the same topic, how they have positioned themselves in different ways in relation to what other writers have argued, or how they have identified a different set of issues to address within the topic. Comparing writers' positions and perspectives to see how they work in relation to one another is synthesis. Synthesis literally means to combine several separate elements or substances to create something new. To synthesize the arguments from two or more writers, look for places where the writers share common ground, where they depart from one another, and how one writer's position might help you understand the other writer's position.

KNOWING WHAT YOU READ

Just as in television news, print news offers straight reporting, opinion, commentary, entertainment, reviews, and feature stories. As you read, remember to keep these distinctions in mind.

(continued)

News Reports. Whether hard or soft news, a report is just that; it is what is often called a *straight news* story that reports on what happened and offers answers to the famous *who, what, where, when, why,* and *how* questions you might have been taught in a beginning journalism class. In fact, news reports often address who, what, where, when, and how, leaving the why for analysis, feature stories, commentary, or op-ed pieces.

Op-Ed or Commentary. The word *op-ed* appeared in the 1940s as an abbreviation for "opposite the editorial page." Commentary appearing on the op-ed page is written with a particular point of view, does not represent itself as news but rather as opinion, and is not necessarily the opinion of the newspaper editors. Official statements from the editors appear as *editorials* on the editorial page.

Feature Story. A feature is a longer story that might appear in any section of the paper—news, arts and entertainment, business, sports, style—and usually offers a more thorough analysis and background than you would get in an op-ed piece or in most news stories.

In all of these types of print journalism, it is only the straight news report that attempts to be free of bias and report on only "the facts."

Reading and Writing Exercises

The following reading and writing exercises, Exercises 1.6 through 1.10, have been developed as a sequence, but they do not have to be completed in this order. These are flexible strategies that can be combined in several ways.

Exercise 1.6

Highlight, Annotate, and Summarize

Read "The Times and Iraq" and the two op-ed articles that follow it, Amy Goodman and David Goodman's "Un-Embed the Media" from the *Baltimore Sun* and Aaron Barnhart's "Embedded Journalists Offer Riveting Reporting" from the *Kansas City Star*. Note that we have highlighted, annotated, and summarized the *Times* editorial. Highlight (or underline), annotate, and summarize the op-ed pieces that follow it.

THE TIMES AND IRAQ

From the Editors of The New York Times

By the spring of 2004, reports began appearing that U.S. intelligence assessments leading to the war in Iraq had been faulty. Like many of their counterparts, *The New York Times* had covered the period leading up to the war, but with little serious probing of the Bush administration's claims of WMDs (weapons of mass destruction) inside Iraq. In May of that year, after several press scandals, including the firing of one *Times* reporter for falsifying stories, *Times* editors published the following analysis and apology.

FROM THE EDITORS

MAY 26, 2004

1 Over the last year this newspaper has shone the bright light of hind-
sight on decisions that led the United States into Iraq. We have examined the failings of American and allied intelligence, especially on
the issue of Iraq's weapons and possible Iraqi connections to international terrorists. We have studied the allegations of official gulli-
bility and hype. It is past time we turned the same light on ourselves.

The point of the article.

In doing so—reviewing hundreds of articles written during the
prelude to war and into the early stages of the occupation—we found
an enormous amount of journalism that we are proud of. In most
cases, what we reported was an accurate reflection of the state of our
knowledge at the time, much of it painstakingly extracted from intelligence agencies that were themselves dependent on sketchy information. And where those articles included incomplete information
or pointed in a wrong direction, they were later overtaken by more
and stronger information. That is how news coverage normally
unfolds.

Establishing their authority
here.

But we have found a number of instances of coverage that was
not as rigorous as it should have been. In some cases, information
that was controversial then, and seems questionable now, was insuf-
ficiently qualified or allowed to stand unchallenged. Looking back,
we wish we had been more aggressive in re-examining the claims as
new evidence emerged—or failed to emerge.

An understatement?

The problematic articles varied in authorship and subject matter,
but many shared a common feature. They depended at least in part
on information from a circle of Iraqi informants, defectors and exiles
bent on "regime change" in Iraq, people whose credibility has come
under increasing public debate in recent weeks. (The most prominent
of the anti-Saddam campaigners, Ahmad Chalabi, has been named
as an occasional source in Times articles since at least 1991, and has
introduced reporters to other exiles. He became a favorite of hard-
liners within the Bush administration and a paid broker of information from Iraqi exiles, until his payments were cut off last week.)
Complicating matters for journalists, the accounts of these exiles were
often eagerly confirmed by United States officials convinced of the
need to intervene in Iraq. Administration officials now acknowledge
that they sometimes fell for misinformation from these exile sources.
So did many news organizations—in particular, this one.

Setting up the problem.

All of this seems like a weak
excuse.

5 Some critics of our coverage during that time have focused
blame on individual reporters. Our examination, however, indicates
that the problem was more complicated. Editors at several levels who
should have been challenging reporters and pressing for more skepticism were perhaps too intent on rushing scoops into the paper.
Accounts of Iraqi defectors were not always weighed against their

Not just blaming individuals.

This is interesting.

strong desire to have Saddam Hussein ousted. Articles based on dire claims about Iraq tended to get prominent display, while follow-up articles that called the original ones into question were sometimes buried. In some cases, there was no follow-up at all.

> *A nice example of how editors can bias news in selection and placement.*

On Oct. 26 and Nov. 8, 2001, for example, Page 1 articles cited Iraqi defectors who described a secret Iraqi camp where Islamic terrorists were trained and biological weapons produced. These accounts have never been independently verified.

> *That's a lot to admit.*

On Dec. 20, 2001, another front-page article began, "An Iraqi defector who described himself as a civil engineer said he personally worked on renovations of secret facilities for biological, chemical and nuclear weapons in underground wells, private villas and under the Saddam Hussein Hospital in Baghdad as recently as a year ago." Knight Ridder Newspapers reported last week that American officials took that defector—his name is Adnan Ihsan Saeed al-Haideri—to Iraq earlier this year to point out the sites where he claimed to have worked, and that the officials failed to find evidence of their use for weapons programs. It is still possible that chemical or biological weapons will be unearthed in Iraq, but in this case it looks as if we, along with the administration, were taken in. And until now we have not reported that to our readers.

> *Not good.*

On Sept. 8, 2002, the lead article of the paper was headlined "U.S. Says Hussein Intensified Quest for A-Bomb Parts." That report concerned the aluminum tubes that the administration advertised insistently as components for the manufacture of nuclear weapons fuel. The claim came not from defectors but from the best American intelligence sources available at the time. Still, it should have been presented more cautiously. There were hints that the usefulness of the tubes in making nuclear fuel was not a sure thing, but the hints were buried deep, 1,700 words into a 3,600-word article. Administration officials were allowed to hold forth at length on why this evidence of Iraq's nuclear intentions demanded that Saddam Hussein be dislodged from power: "The first sign of a 'smoking gun,' they argue, may be a mushroom cloud."

> *A really good example of editorial mishandling.*

Five days later, The Times reporters learned that the tubes were in fact a subject of debate among intelligence agencies. The misgivings appeared deep in an article on Page A13, under a headline that gave no inkling that we were revising our earlier view ("White House Lists Iraq Steps to Build Banned Weapons"). The Times gave voice to skeptics of the tubes on Jan. 9, when the key piece of evidence was challenged by the International Atomic Energy Agency. That challenge was reported on Page A10; it might well have belonged on Page A1.

> *I wonder how many readers notice things like this?*

10   On April 21, 2003, as American weapons-hunters followed American troops into Iraq, another front-page article declared, "Illicit Arms Kept Till Eve of War, an Iraqi Scientist Is Said to Assert." It

> *Interesting to see how they examine individual articles.*

began this way: "A scientist who claims to have worked in Iraq's chemical weapons program for more than a decade has told an American military team that Iraq destroyed chemical weapons and biological warfare equipment only days before the war began, members of the team said."

The informant also claimed that Iraq had sent unconventional weapons to Syria and had been cooperating with Al Qaeda—two claims that were then, and remain, highly controversial. But the tone of the article suggested that this Iraqi "scientist"—who in a later article described himself as an official of military intelligence—had provided the justification the Americans had been seeking for the invasion.

Good example of how language can bias a piece.

The Times never followed up on the veracity of this source or the attempts to verify his claims.

The bottom line.

A sample of the coverage, including the articles mentioned here, is online at nytimes.com/critique. Readers will also find there a detailed discussion written for The New York Review of Books last month by Michael Gordon, military affairs correspondent of The Times, about the aluminum tubes report. Responding to the review's critique of Iraq coverage, his statement could serve as a primer on the complexities of such intelligence reporting.

Check site. I wonder if it's still up.

We consider the story of Iraq's weapons, and of the pattern of misinformation, to be unfinished business. And we fully intend to continue aggressive reporting aimed at setting the record straight.

The promise.

Sample Summary of "The Times and Iraq"

The New York Times editorial staff lays out a simple and direct apology for what they describe as their failure to "turn the same light" on themselves that they have turned on other news organizations, especially in the period leading up to the decision to go to war with Iraq. In their apology, they make it clear that the *Times* is a solid news organization that publishes "an enormous amount of journalism that [they] are proud of." Still, the stories relying on unreliable informants dealing with weapons inside Iraq were obviously wrong and badly handled.

The editorial details coverage that was not entirely wrong but certainly biased, and they take the blame, as the editors, for that bias. They point both to where stories were placed that gave credence to their informants and where information that questioned those informants was "buried," to use their language.

The editorial ends both with a confession: "The *Times* never followed up on the veracity of this source or the attempts to verify his claims"; and with a promise. They promise to keep the story of Iraq's weapons an open one and "to continue aggressive reporting aimed at setting the record straight."

In the sample, our highlights and annotations help us summarize this editorial. We did not include our reactions to the article because reactions are more appropriate for an exploratory writing that records a response to what is written. We also incorporated brief quotes into our summary. By quoting a few short passages, you are reminding yourself of those parts of a reading that you find the most important.

As you compose comparable summaries of the two op-ed articles that follow, be sure to incorporate brief quotes into your writing. In your underlinings and annotations, pay particular attention to the places where these writers are making their arguments and what support they use for those arguments.

UN-EMBED THE MEDIA

— *Amy Goodman and David Goodman*

Amy Goodman is the host of the radio show *Democracy Now!* With her brother David Goodman, she is the author of *The Exception to the Rulers: Exposing Oily Politicians, War Profiteers, and the Media That Love Them,* a scathing assessment of mainstream news media. The op-ed piece that follows originally appeared on April 7, 2005, in the *Baltimore Sun.*

1   Recent revelations that the Bush administration has been fabricating news stories, secretly hiring journalists to write puff pieces and credentialing fake reporters at White House news conferences has infuriated the news media.

Editorials profess to being shocked—shocked!—by the government's covert propaganda campaign in which, as *The New York Times* revealed March 13, at least 20 federal agencies have spent $250 million creating and sending fake news segments to local TV stations.

But the media have only themselves to blame for most people—including TV news managers—not being able to distinguish journalism from propaganda. The line between news and propaganda was trampled not only by the public relations agencies hired by the government but also by reporters in the deserts of Iraq.

The Pentagon deployed a weapon more powerful than any bomb: the U.S. media. Embedded journalists were transformed into efficient conduits of Pentagon spin. Before and during the invasion of Iraq, the networks conveniently provided the flag-draped backdrop for fawning reports from the field.

5   As if literally adopting the Pentagon's propagandistic slogan—"Operation Iraqi Freedom"—for their coverage weren't enough, the networks bombarded viewers with an unending parade of generals and colonels paid to offer on-air analysis. It gave new meaning to the term "general news."

If we had state-run media in the United States, how would it be any different?

The media have a responsibility to show the true face of war. But many corporate journalists, so accustomed by now to trading truth for access (the "access of evil"), can no longer grasp what's missing from their coverage. As CBS' Jim Axelrod, who was embedded with—we would say in bed with—the 3rd Infantry Division, gushed: "This will sound like I've drunk the Kool-Aid, but I found embedding to be an extremely positive experience. . . . We got great stories and they got very positive coverage."

It should come as no surprise that the Bush administration, having found the media so helpful and compliant with their coverage of the Iraq war, would seek to orchestrate similarly uncritical coverage of other issues that they hold dear.

TV viewers nationwide have watched and heard about how the "top-notch work force" of the often-criticized Transportation Security Administration has led "one of the most remarkable campaigns in aviation history," how President Bush's controversial Medicare plan will offer "new benefits, more choices, more opportunities," how the United States is "putting needy women back in business" in Afghanistan, and how Army prison guards, accused of torturing and murdering inmates in Iraq and Afghanistan, "treat prisoners strictly, but fairly."

10   Such crude government-supplied propaganda would be laughable were it not being passed off as news on America's TV stations. Even sadder, nothing about the sycophantic reports seems out of the ordinary.

The first casualty of this taxpayer-financed misinformation campaign is the truth.

Mr. Bush must have been delighted to learn from a March 16 *Washington Post*-ABC News poll that 56 percent of Americans still thought Iraq had weapons of mass destruction before the start of the war, while six in 10 said they believed Iraq provided direct support to al Qaeda.

Americans believe these lies not because they are stupid but because they are good media consumers. The explosive effect of this propaganda is amplified as a few pro-war, pro-government media moguls consolidate their grip over the majority of news outlets. Media monopoly and militarism go hand in hand.

It's time for the American media to unembed themselves from the U.S. government. We need media that are fiercely independent, that ask the hard questions and hold those in power accountable. Only then will government propaganda be seen for what it is and citizens be able to make choices informed by reality, not self-serving misinformation. Anything less is a disservice to the servicemen and women of this country and a disservice to a democratic society.

EMBEDDED JOURNALISTS OFFER RIVETING REPORTING

— Aaron Barnhart

Aaron Barnhart is television critic for the *Kansas City Star*. This column appeared in the *Star* in April 2003, not long after a Columbia University Project for Excellence in Journalism report appeared analyzing stories filed by journalists embedded with the U.S. military in Iraq.

1 It is unusual to hear news junkies complain about the quality of their fix.

But these days you can't click on a media Weblog or open a magazine without reading about some poor soul left dazed and confused by the media's coverage of the war in Iraq. The sight of journalists in fatigues, it seems, now brings on viewer fatigue.

That's too bad, because journalists who are "embedded" with combat units shouldn't get the blame. They're the show. Without their straight-ahead accounts and otherworldly video, the networks would be making do right now with overhead maps of Baghdad and Donald Rumsfeld behind his enormous lectern.

This may or may not be the most picked-over war in history, as Rumsfeld seems to think. But it is certainly the most picked-over war coverage since Thucydides gave his side of the Athens-Sparta conflict.

5   So it's no surprise that a study is already out regarding the media and Iraq. The quickie analysis, being released today by the Project for Excellence in Journalism, looked at dispatches from embedded TV reporters during the first six days of war. The nonpartisan group works under the auspices of Columbia University.

Of the 108 news reports studied, an overwhelming number—94 percent—consisted entirely of factual reporting in a no-spin zone. As the war progressed, fewer live reports were used and embeds got to write scripts and edit their video. These prepared stories, the study's authors said without irony, often compared to the best radio reporting.

"On balance," they concluded, "Americans seem far better served by having the embedding system than they were from more limited press pools during the gulf war of 1991 or only halting access to events in Afghanistan."

What's more, as the study notes and further viewing confirms, the work of the embeds seems to be getting better by the day. An example: CBS reporter Mark Strassman filed a riveting, fact-filled report for the Tuesday "Evening News." He was in the holy city of Najaf, where a unit of the 101st Airborne was attempting to root out fedayeen.

For those who wondered when televised pictures would start measuring up to those from still photographers covering this war, Strassman's report opened with a stunning montage of battle video and close-ups of Iraqi civilians. (It helps if you can pause the picture.)

10   The embeds can rightfully claim their place in war journalism history even as they are writing it. They've proved adept at conveying both the boredom of war (you're eating *how* many times a day?) and the danger (Ted Koppel calmly describing his 3rd Infantry unit as it charges through a perilous gap west of Karbala).

As for the networks, it's tempting to blame them for leaving viewers in the fog of war. But that simply hasn't been the case, at least since the wall-to-wall coverage stopped. "Nightline," Dan Rather and CNN's Aaron Brown all set aside time each night for a segment each calls, intuitively enough, "The Big Picture."

As citizens of a robust democracy, we have the right to whine about our news. But with rights come responsibilities. In the chaos of battle, the media have quickly adapted to new technology and the military's new openness. The very least we can do is adapt too. Whether you get it from Brit Hume or Jim Lehrer, the BBC or print media, the big picture is out there, hiding in plain sight.

SUGGESTIONS FOR DISCUSSION

1. Compare with other members of your class the summaries you have written. To what extent are the summaries your classmates have written similar? To what extent do they differ? If they differ, how do you account for those differences? Don't assume that one person's summaries are necessarily better or more accurate than anyone else's. Instead, try to identify the principles of selection each writer used. Discuss how others' summaries change or add to your own understanding of what the writers are saying in these articles.

2. With a group of your classmates, look back at the highlighting/underlining and annotations you made. What details, language choices, or incidents seem to each of you particularly striking or crucial for following the two arguments?

3. Explain what each of these articles identifies as the real issue with "embedded journalists." How does your own position on the issues surrounding the Iraq war and media coverage influence the way you read the Goodmans or Barnhart? To what extent do these writers complicate your position or convince you to think differently about the issue of war coverage and the relationship between the military and journalists?

COMPLACENCY KILLS

— *Joe Sacco*

"Complacency Kills," a report on Joe Sacco's time spent as a journalist traveling with U.S. military troops in Iraq, first appeared on February 21, 2005, in the British newspaper the *Guardian*. Sacco is a cartoonist and journalist. He is the creator of the series *Palestine* (1993–1996), an account of Sacco's two months living in the Occupied Territories. The series won a 1996 American Book Award and has been released as a single volume.

SUGGESTION FOR READING   Before you read, write a brief account of what kind of story you normally expect when you see comics in a newspaper.

First published in *The Guardian Weekend* and reprinted by permission of **Joe Sacco** and Aragi Inc.

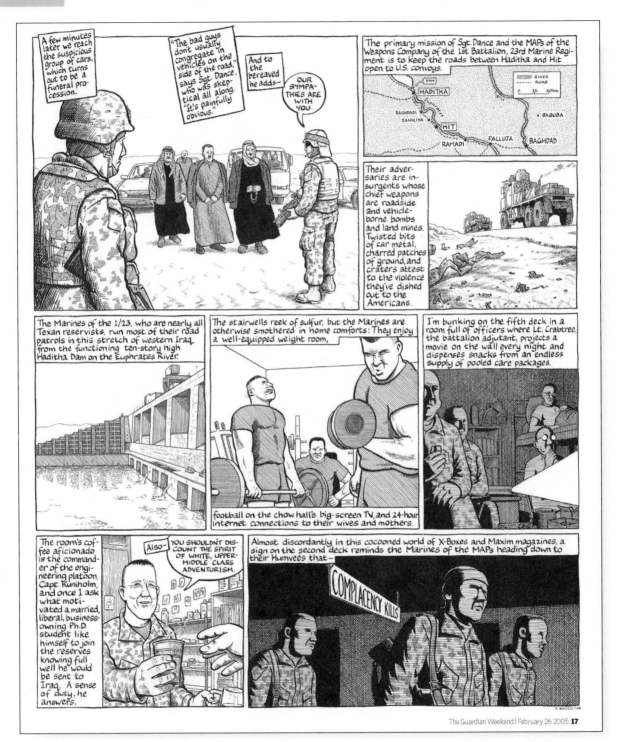

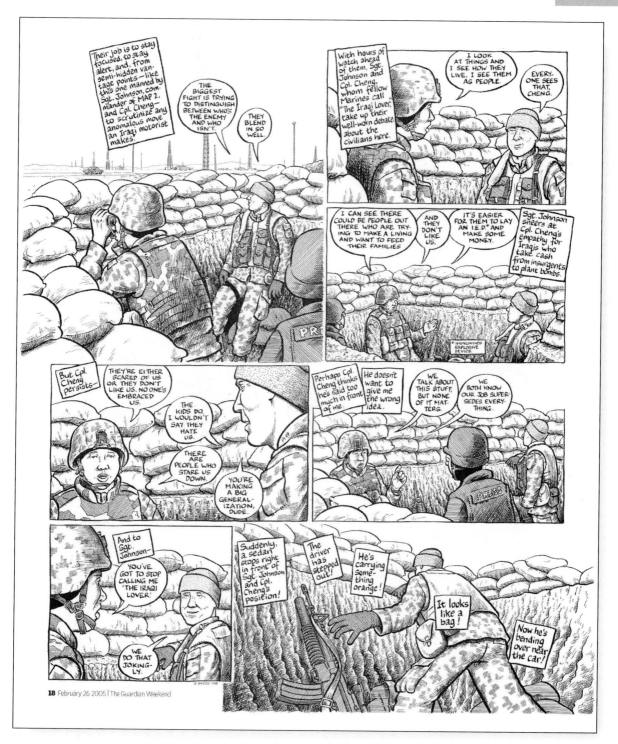

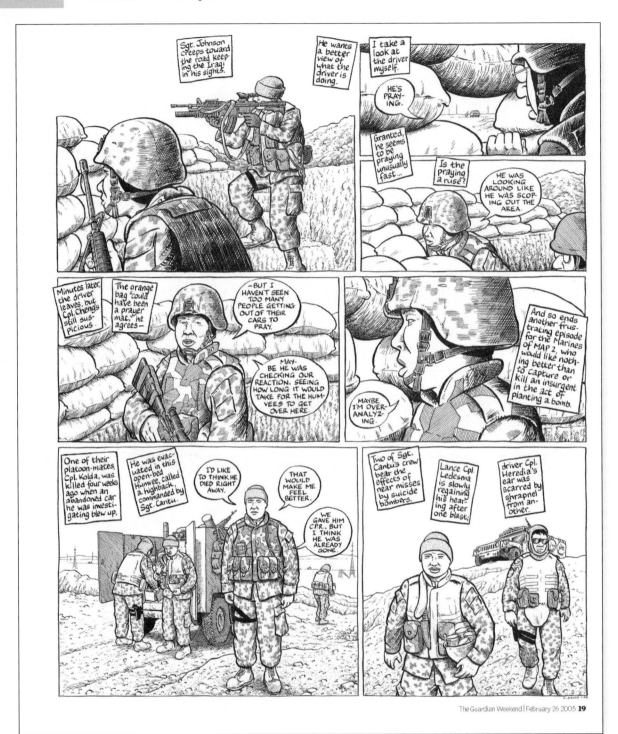

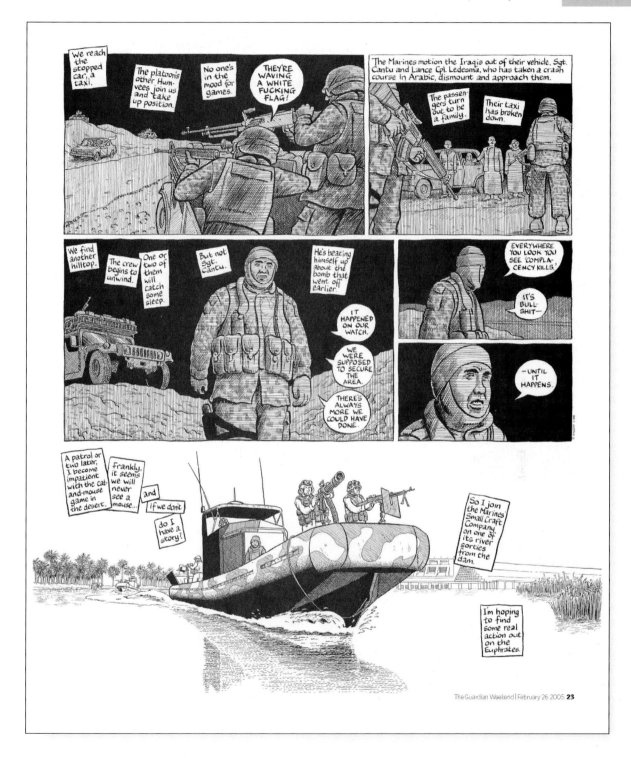

Exercise 1.7

Reading Comics as News

Although "Complacency Kills" is in the form of a comic strip, Joe Sacco has written that he does not make comics; he writes news reports. After you have read "Complacency Kills," copy all of the words of the report and write them so that they look like the sort of newspaper report most people are familiar with. Don't add anything; copy the words as they are written and simply eliminate the drawings.

Next, eliminate the words from this report, leaving only the pictures. You can do that either by photocopying the comics and blacking out the words, scanning the comics into a photo program and erasing the words, or simply taking small sticky notes and temporarily placing them over the words in your textbook.

After you have completed that task, write an analysis of this news report focusing on the use of words and pictures to tell the story. How is the story different without one or the other? Does the tone or the meaning change when you take away the relationship between the two? At what points are the words in this story necessary? At what points do the pictures tell the story or convey tone?

WIRED CULTURE   Reporting War in the Blogosphere

WWW

To learn more about news and blogs, visit
www.ablongman.com/george/101

In January 2005, CyberJournal.Net, a project of the Media Center at the American Press Institute, reporting on two surveys from the Pew Internet and American Life Project, wrote that blog readership was up by 58 percent in 2004. Yet, in the same study, 62 percent of Internet users said they didn't really know what a blog is.

Blog usage certainly went up during the 2004 U.S. presidential election, but the war in Iraq and the possibilities for first-person reports, alternative news, and outright political flaming may seem limitless in what has come to be known as the blogosphere.

The term *blog* is short for web log, a site on the Internet where an individual or a group logs entries, sometimes daily. The individual blog is a kind of public journal or diary, and when associated with war reporting, the blog can seem to convey the kind of credibility mainstream media is apparently losing with some people. War journalists, self-appointed war journalists, media pundits, organizations supporting or opposing the war, media watchdog groups, and the mainstream media them-selves—all of these have blogs and have become a part of the larger landscape of reporting the war.

'WEBLOGGERS' SIGNING ON AS WAR CORRESPONDENTS

Howard Kurtz

Howard Kurtz is a staff writer for the *Washington Post*. This column appeared in the *Post* on March 23, 2003.

SUGGESTION FOR READING Before you read, visit a blog devoted to the war in Iraq. To find one, simply use your search engine and type in Iraq war blog. You will find many. Choose one. Read what you can, and write your impressions of it.

1 L.T. Smash provided a terse after-action report on one close encounter with the Iraqis:

"Saddam fired a couple of those Scuds that he doesn't have at me this afternoon.

"He missed."

No need for embedded reporters when you've got a keyboard and a modem. "Smash" is the pseudonym of a military officer who is chronicling his exploits amid the desert sandstorms—and getting 6,000 hits a day on his Web site.

5 For all the saturation coverage of the invasion of Iraq, this has become the first true Internet war, with journalists, analysts, soldiers, a British lawmaker, an Iraqi exile and a Baghdad resident using the medium's lightning speed to cut through the fog of war. The result is idiosyncratic, passionate and often profane, with the sort of intimacy and attitude that are all but impossible in newspapers and on television.

Many of these so-called Weblogs eliminate the middleman—the news outlets whose reach was once needed for a broad audience—and allow participants to have their say, typos and all, without being run through the media's Cuisinart.

"The most interesting thing about the blog coverage is how far ahead it is of the mainstream media," says University of Tennessee law professor Glenn Reynolds, whose InstaPundit.com site has seen a surge in traffic as the Iraq crisis has heated up, doubling to 200,000 hits a day. "The first-hand stuff is great. It's unfiltered and unspun. That doesn't mean it's unbiased. But people feel like they know where the bias is coming from. You don't have to spend a lot of time trying to find a hidden agenda."

The New Republic is running an online diary by Kanan Makiya, a leading Iraqi dissident based in Cambridge, Mass., who, among other things, recently met with Vice President Cheney.

"Today there are hundreds—if not more—of Iraqis in America, Britain and the rest of the diaspora who are quitting their jobs and boarding planes to help rebuild their ravaged country," Makiya writes. "With the tyrant's destruction finally at hand, I am elated and worried."

10 Says Chris Orr, the magazine's executive editor: "This is history taking place, and he has a unique and extraordinary perspective on that history. If Iraq becomes a democracy, Kanan will be one of the founding fathers."

Tom Watson, a British member of Parliament, is blogging on such matters as the resignation of the former foreign minister to protest Tony Blair's war policy:

"Another sleepless night. . . . Yesterday I ended up three down from Robin Cook when he made his resignation speech. What I would have done to have moved to the end of the row, but once you're in, you're in. His speech was typed (so he must have been writing it for some time) and his hands were quivering (it must have been very difficult)."

The strength of this new form of communication is the sheer variety of voices. Despite some Internet chatter that he might be a disinformation agent, a self-described Baghdad resident posting under the name of Salam Pax at Dear_raed.blogspot.com, is being taken seriously by several Web columnists.

"The all clear siren just went on," he wrote Thursday. "The bombing would come and go in waves, nothing too heavy and not yet comparable to what was going on in 91. All radio and TV stations are still on and while the air raid began the Iraqi TV was showing patriotic songs and didn't even bother to inform viewers that we are under attack. At the moment they are re-airing yesterday's interview with the minister of interior affairs. The sounds of the anti-aircraft artillery is still louder than the booms and bangs which means that they are still far from where we live, but the images we saw on Al Arabia news channel showed a building burning near one of my aunt's house."

15 Some of the online commentators have a mordant sense of humor. L.T. Smash, who often rails about the stupidity of his superiors, posted the following memo to Saddam Hussein:

"You may have noted some blasting noises and disconcerting rumbling of the ground in your general vicinity over the past several hours. Do not be alarmed, these shock waves are the result of a long-planned demolition and urban renewal project for the greater Baghdad area."

Smash even provides his own self-interview:

"Q. Can't you get in trouble for this sort of thing? Isn't this a violation of Military Regulations?

"A: I'm in the military—I can get in trouble for just about anything. But generally speaking, this form of communication is bound by the same rules as e-mail. . . . I am voluntarily observing my own, stricter guidelines in regards to operational security."

20 On another Web site, a 29-year-old Army Reserve officer named Will provides regular updates on his mission:

"My Official Army job is Nuclear, Chemical and Biological Weapons Specialist (impressive, isn't it). What that really means is that I go in after a Nuclear, Chemical or Biological attack, and wash cars and help people clean up their gear (in Omaha, my home, that's called Merry Maids). It's very detail oriented, and requires a lot of practice because if I, or any of my soldiers, make a mistake, it could cost lives."

There are "warblogs" of every conceivable stripe and, inevitably, a No WarBlog, which declared during Friday's bombing of Baghdad:

"W is a war criminal.

"I weep for what W has now done to this nation.

25 "This looks like an attack with nuclear weapons."

Even some journalists are moonlighting as bloggers. Kevin Sites, a CNN correspondent, is posting pictures, audio and commentary on his personal Web site from the Kurdish section of Iraq.

"What I'm looking at right now is long line of trucks packed with all kinds of belongings of Kurdish people moving north," he writes. CNN told Sites to suspend the blog Friday, with spokeswoman Edna Johnson saying that covering war "is a full-time job and we've asked Kevin to concentrate only on that for the time being."

One benefit of the global electronic village is that Americans who don't fully trust their own media can check reports from overseas. In January, according to Wired News, half the 1.3 million visitors to the Web site for Britain's Guardian and Observer newspapers were from the Americas.

"Given how timid most U.S. news organizations have been in challenging the White House position on Iraq, I'm not surprised if Americans are turning to foreign news services for a perspective on the conflict that goes beyond freedom fries," Wired News quotes former Newsweek contributing editor Deborah Branscum as saying.

30 InstaPundit Reynolds sees bloggers acting as a fact-checking force. "The value we add is in unpacking the spin in the media coverage," he says.

SUGGESTIONS FOR DISCUSSION

1. With a group of your classmates, compare what each of you knows about or has heard about bloggers and blogs. What were your impressions of the blog you visited?

2. Kurtz writes that Iraq is "the first true Internet war." What does he mean by that?

3. What would you say is Kurtz's attitude toward blogging and war reporting? What in the article gives you an indication of his position?

Exercise 1.8 **Reviewing Web Sites**

Visit several different kinds of war reporting blogs—first-person blogs by military people or peace activists in Iraq, blogs created by mainstream reporters like Kevin Sites from CNN, and blogs that gather reports from several different sites and archive them with comments. Write a review of one of these sites as a source of news about the war. Who created it? What was the blogger trying to accomplish? Does it seem like a very personal site—like a diary—or is it more like a news log—like an Internet version of a newspaper? How thorough is it? How does it compare to mainstream media news reports? To what extent does it do what Kurtz suggests—"eliminate the middleman"—in getting the news to the public? How trustworthy is it?

READING WEB SITES

One of the attractions of the Web is that anyone with an Internet connection and some technical knowledge can put up a site. There is little question that, despite the growing commercialization of the Web, it still provides broad access to the means of communication and a new forum for discussion and debate. At the same time, it is also important to understand that the information and perspectives that show up on the Web are largely unregulated—they can range from the thoroughly reliable to the utterly crackpot. That's part of the creative and chaotic anarchy of the Web that makes it so interesting and so much fun. But it also means that web users need to learn to read in a new way, so they can assess the various sites they visit—to identify who put up a site, what its purposes are, and what can be expected from it in terms of the reliability of the information and ideas it contains.

What to Look For

Though there is great variation among web site designs, several standard features have emerged that users come to expect when they get to a site.

URL

The header at the top of your screen gives you the web page address, or URL (Uniform Resource Locator). You can find out a good deal about a website from the URL alone. Take, for example, the URL for Journalism.org, from the Columbia School of Journalism Graduate School's Project for Excellence in Journalism and the Pew Charitable Trust: http://www.journalism.org

The URL of the main page offers the host name www.journalism.org, which identifies where the page is located (Web), the name of the organization that owns the site (Journalism.org), and the domain (org).

Domain names identify the kinds of organizations that sponsor websites: ".edu" refers to educational institutions, ".org" to nonprofit organizations, ".gov" to government agencies, ".mil" to the military, and ".com" and ".net" to commercial enterprises.

If you click on a story link at the Journalism.org site, you will get an address that looks like this:

http://www.journalism.org/resources/briefing/default.asp

The second half of that address (resources/briefing/default.asp) identifies the file path—the path that takes you to the page you want to read. In this case, the path leads first to the Resources page and from there to the Daily Briefing page.

Organizational Logo and Title

Web pages often feature an organization's logo or a common header at the top of each page. This feature helps to unify a website visually and to identify the sponsoring organization from page to page. It is often more difficult to locate where you are on a site that does not repeat the logo or header on each page.

Links

Links appear as text or graphics to help you navigate from place to place, both within a particular website and to web pages at other sites. They may appear at the top or bottom of the page or both places. But wherever they appear, links offer clues about the purpose of the site because they indicate the range and type of information and opinion the website considers relevant.

Signature and Credits

Signatures give the name and often the e-mail address of the person who maintains the web page, information on when the web page was established, when it was last updated, those who have contributed to it, and sometimes a postal address and phone number for the person or organization responsible for the site. Often this information is on the home page.

Advertising

As the Web becomes increasingly commercialized, more and more advertising appears. The type of products and services advertised can help give you a sense of the kind of website you're visiting, much as you can draw some inferences about how magazines see themselves and their readers from their ads. The absence of advertising can also offer you information on how the organization or institution wants to relate to its readers.

What Can You Do at the Site?

The possibilities that web sites offer readers can give you further information to assess the site. Some, such as journalism.org, offer a number of reports, links to other sites covering media issues, and information about the organizations responsible for the site. Some sites invite you to sign a guest book, send e-mail, fill out surveys, enter contests, watch animation and videos, listen to music, or take part in message-board discussions. Commercial sites, of course, want you to buy something. Consider whether the website you're visiting provides you with choices about where you can go and whether it invites you to participate interactively. What purpose do these possibilities serve? What kind of relationship does the site seem to want to establish with people who visit it?

Exploring Ideas from Your Reading

Read Frank Rich's "The Nascar Nightly News: Anchorman Get Your Gun," highlighting/underlining and annotating as you read. Respond to the article in an exploratory writing.

Here is a sample of exploratory writing, written in response to *The New York Times* piece, "The Times and Iraq," reprinted earlier in this chapter. Notice how exploratory writing is a much more immediate and personal response to the ideas represented in the article than a summary is. A summary is an attempt to record a shortened version of what is said in the writing. In exploratory writing, you are following your response and seeing if it will lead to connections or ideas for future writing or research.

Sample Exploratory Writing

I was surprised by *The New York Times* piece. I've read "corrections" in newspapers and news magazines before, but this was an outright admission that the *Times* just didn't do its job the way it was supposed to do.

Very likely, the apology had the effect, on me anyway, that it was meant to. I had more respect for the paper after I read the article than before. In other words, once they pointed out what they did wrong and gave examples of that, I think their credibility was just higher for me. It is interesting, though, that if I read carefully, I notice they don't exactly take full responsibility. They take pains to point out that most of their coverage was solid and that the errors they made were errors everyone seemed to be making. And, they blamed the Administration for giving credibility to sources, when it seems to me that the whole point of journalism is that you do your own investigating. It would be interesting to follow up and see if they actually made good on their promise not to let the story drop or get buried. That would take research.

As you can see from this sample, exploratory writing does just that—it explores the reader's attitudes about a reading selection, it opens possible directions for further research and examination, and it allows the reader to begin moving toward a position on the subject at hand.

When you do exploratory writing, feel free to take some of the ideas the writer has raised and run with them, even if it seems that this will take you far afield from the reading. You may choose to dwell at length on a particular detail or incident in the reading that strikes you, even if it isn't the main point you'd identify in a summary. You may find that a particular reading selection reminds you of something you know or something you've read in a different context. It can be valuable to record this kind of connection.

THE NASCAR NIGHTLY NEWS: ANCHORMAN GET YOUR GUN

— *Frank Rich*

Frank Rich is an op-ed columnist for the *New York Times*. From 2003 to 2005, he served as the front-page columnist for the Sunday Arts and Leisure section of the *Times*. This article is a critique of television news at a time of war and especially of NBC's choice of Brian Williams as the new anchor for *NBC Nightly News*. It appeared in the Arts and Leisure section on December 5, 2004.

SUGGESTION FOR READING   As you read, pay attention to how Rich sets up his argument and how the language he has chosen might shape reader opinion.

1   If Democrats want to run around like fools trying to persuade voters in red America that they are kissing cousins to Billy Graham, Minnie Pearl and Li'l Abner, that's their problem. Pandering, after all, is what politicians do, especially politicians as desperate as the Democrats. But when TV news organizations start repositioning themselves to pander to Nascar dads and "moral values" voters, it's a problem for everyone.

There's a war on. TV remains by far the most prevalent source of news for Americans. We need honest information to help us navigate, not bunkum skewed to flatter one segment of the country, whatever that segment might be. Yet here's how Jeff Zucker, the NBC president, summed up the attributes of Brian Williams, Tom Brokaw's successor, to Peter Johnson of USA Today: "No one understands this Nascar nation more than Brian." Mr. Zucker was in sync with his boss, Bob Wright, the NBC Universal chairman, who described America as a "red state world" on the eve of Mr. Brokaw's retirement. Though it may come as news to those running NBC, we actually live in a red-and-blue-state country, in a world that increasingly hates all our states without regard to our provincial obsession with their hues. Nonetheless, Mr. Williams, who officially took over as anchor on Dec. 2, is seeking a very specific mandate. "The New York-Washington axis can be a journalist's worst enemy," he told Mr. Johnson, promising to spend his nights in the field in "Dayton and Toledo and Cincinnati and Denver and the middle of Kansas." (So much for San Francisco—or Baghdad.)

I don't mean to single out Mr. Williams, who is prone to making such statements while wearing suits that reek of "New York-Washington axis" money and affectation. But when he talks in a promotional interview of how he found the pulse of the nation in Cabela's, a popular hunting-and-fishing outfitter in Dundee, Mich., and boasts of owning both an air rifle and part interest in a dirt-track stock-car team, he is declaring himself the poster boy for a larger shift in our news culture. He is eager to hunt down an audience, not a story.

He's not an isolated case. You know red is de rigueur when ABC undertakes the lunatic task of trying to repackage the last surviving evening news anchor, the heretofore aggressively urbane Peter Jennings, as a sentimental populist. In a new spot for "World News Tonight," Mr. Jennings tells us that "this is a really hopeful nation, and I think there's a great beauty in that." This homily is not only factually inaccurate—most Americans continue to tell pollsters that the nation is on the wrong track—but is also accompanied by a tinkling music-box piano and a montage leaning on such Kodak tableaus as a fishing cove, a small-town front porch and a weather-beaten man driving a car with a flag decal. Mr. Jennings is a smart newsman, but his just-folks incarnation is about as persuasive as Teresa Heinz Kerry's chow-down photo op at Wendy's.

5   If the Nascarization of news were only about merchandising, it would be a source of laughter more than concern. But the insidious leak of the branding into the product itself has already begun. Last Sunday morning both NBC's "Meet the Press" and ABC's "This Week" had round-table discussions about—what else?—the "moral values" fallout of the election. Each show assembled a bevy of religious and quasi-religious leaders and each included a liberal or two. But though much of the "values" debate centered on abortion and gay marriage, neither panel contained a woman, let alone an openly gay cleric. Allowing such ostentatiously blue interlopers into the "values" club might frighten the horses—or at least the hunting dogs.

A creepier example of the shift toward red news could also be found last weekend when ABC's prime-time magazine show "20/20" aired an hourlong "investigation" into the brutal 1998 murder of Matthew Shepard in the red state of Wyoming. "20/20" added little except hyperventilation to previous revisionist accounts of the story, most notably JoAnn Wypijewski's 1999 Harper's article filling in the role crystal meth might have played in driving the crime. But ABC had obtained the first TV interviews with the killers and seemed determined to rehabilitate their images along the way. The reporter, Elizabeth Vargas, told us that while the pair had been "variously portrayed in press reports as 'rednecks' and 'trailer trash,' " they were actually just all-American everymen with "steady jobs, steady girlfriends and classically troubled backgrounds." Aaron McKinney, the killer who beat Shepard into an unrecognizable pulp, wasn't even challenged on camera when he said he had "gay friends" (none of whom were produced or persuasively vouched for by ABC) and that he had only invoked a homophobic "gay panic" defense in his trial because that's what the lawyers told him to do. What's not to like about the guy?

As chance would have it, this episode of "20/20" ran opposite the special "Dateline NBC" farewell to Mr. Brokaw. There could hardly be a more dramatic illustration of the changing of the tone, as well as of the guard, in network news.

Though the retrospective paid tribute, as Mr. Brokaw often has, to his roots in deeply red South Dakota, the career highlights that unfurled were not tied to any agenda but the stories the anchor reported. The newsmakers who made freshly shot guest appearances in the program to augment Mr. Brokaw's own accounts included not just George H.W. Bush and Norman Schwarzkopf but also Betty Friedan (who talked of how women of the 1950's "were supposed to have orgasms waxing the kitchen floor"), the AIDS activist Larry Kramer (whom Mr. Brokaw identified as his friend), Tom Hayden and, for the Watergate recap, a "former impeachment committee staffer" who happened to be Hillary Clinton. If Mr. Brokaw were arriving as anchor instead of leaving, this genuinely fair-and-balanced account of his career would have been vilified by the right-wing press and blogosphere 24/7—assuming the red-state-besotted suits at NBC would have allowed him anywhere near the anchor chair in the first place.

That both Mr. Brokaw and Dan Rather are going into retirement in the aftermath of the election is a coincidence of timing but widely seen as a fateful one. It's been a cue to roll out once more the funeral rites for network news. We know the litany. The evening newscasts' ratings have been sinking for years, their budgets slashed, their audience forever slipping into the pharmaceutical demographic. The investigation into Mr. Rather's apparent reliance on forged documents in a "60 Minutes" exposé of President Bush's National Guard record is an added embarrassment, perhaps rivaling Rupert Murdoch's publication of the "authenticated" Hitler diaries two decades ago. But the perennial demise of network news has been the slowest final curtain in the history of show business, and is likely to continue indefinitely. All three network newscasts, not to mention the morning-news franchises led by "Today," draw exponentially more viewers than even Fox News's top-rated hits and make tons of money. Though more and more Americans use the Web as a news source, even there they often turn to the sites run by TV news. In the real world of 2004, it's still a TV culture—just look at the flat-screen set breaking some relative's bank this Christmas.

10 And so network news still counts. The idea, largely but not exclusively fomented by the right, that TV news might somehow soon be supplanted by blogging as a mass medium may remain a populist fantasy until Americans are able to receive blogs by iPod. (At which point they become talk radio.) The dense text in the best blogs often requires as much of a reader's time and concentration as high-end print journalism, itself facing declining circulation. Since blogging doesn't generate big (if any) profits, there's no budget for its "citizen reporters" to reliably blanket catastrophic and far-flung breaking news. (There are no bloggers among the 36 journalists thus far killed in the Iraq war.) Bloggers can fact-check documents (as in the Rather case), opine, organize, talk back, leak early exit polls and publish multimedia outings of the seemingly endless supply of closeted gay Republican officials. But if

bloggers are actually doing front-line reporting rather than commenting upon the news in a danger zone like Falluja, chances are that they are underwritten by a day job on the payroll of a major news organization.

Kevin Sites, the freelance TV cameraman who caught a marine shooting an apparently unarmed Iraqi prisoner in a mosque, is one such blogger. Mr. Sites is an embedded journalist currently in the employ of NBC News. To NBC's credit, it ran Mr. Sites's mid-November report, on a newscast in which Mr. Williams was then subbing for Mr. Brokaw, and handled it in exemplary fashion. Mr. Sites avoided any snap judgment pending the Marines' own investigation of the shooting, cautioning that a war zone is "rife with uncertainty and confusion." But loud voices in red America, especially on blogs, wanted him silenced anyway. On right-wing sites like freerepublic.com Mr. Sites was branded an "anti-war activist" (which he is not), a traitor and an "enemy combatant." Mr. Sites's own blog, touted by Mr. Williams on the air, was full of messages from the relatives of marines profusely thanking the cameraman for bringing them news of their sons in Iraq. That communal message board has since been shut down because of the death threats by other Americans against Mr. Sites.

The attempt to demonize and censor Mr. Sites simply for doing his job is not an anomaly. Last spring The New York Post smeared Associated Press television cameramen as having "a mutually beneficial relationship with the insurgents in Falluja" simply because their cameras captured the horrific images of the four American contract workers slaughtered there. Well before the National Guard fiasco at CBS, red-state newshounds tried to discredit Mr. Rather's scoop on the photos of Abu Ghraib as overblown if not treasonous. This hysterical rage at the networks is a testament to their continued power—specifically the power of pictures in each of these cases.

Such examples notwithstanding, the networks were often cautious about challenging government propaganda even before the election. (Follow-ups to the original Abu Ghraib story quickly fell off TV's radar screen.) As far back as last spring Ted Koppel's roll-call of the American dead on "Nightline," in which the only images were beatific headshots, was condemned as a shocking breach of decorum by the mostly red-state ABC affiliates that refused to broadcast it. If full-scale Nascarization is what's coming next, there will soon be no pictures but those promising a mission accomplished, no news but good news. And that's good news only if you believe America has something to gain by fighting a war in the dark.

SUGGESTIONS FOR DISCUSSION

1. Rich is critical of the choice of Brian Williams as anchor for the NBC news because, Rich says, "when the TV news organizations start repositioning themselves to pander to Nascar dads and 'moral values' voters, it's a problem for everyone." Explain what he means by that. Why is this choice more than a liberal/conservative debate or a party politics split?

2. With a group of your classmates, compare the exploratory piece you have each written in response to Rich's article. How do your responses differ? In what ways are they similar? What about Rich's article might account for the ways you and members of your group have responded?

3. In the course of his article, Rich returns several times to the issue of war reporting. Mark those passages in this article where that happens. How does Rich connect the issue of war reporting with what he calls the "full-scale Nascarization" of the news?

Writing a Synthesis

Reread Rich, summarize his article, and then write a synthesis that includes the articles by the *Times* editorial staff, Amy Goodman and David Goodman, Aaron Barnhart, and Frank Rich. In your synthesis, pay attention to the way each of these arguments touches on the discussions of the others. How would, for example, some of Rich's comments place him in alliance with the Goodmans and the *Times* editors as well as with Barnhart? Where does he depart from them? What questions or concerns do all of these writers raise in common?

In preparation for this assignment, reread the articles, but also go back and look at those portions of the articles you have highlighted or underlined as well as at the annotations you have written in margins. If you have summarized articles, those summaries will help you see what each writer is doing in these separate discussions. Think of a synthesis as a place where you report on a conversation: Who said what? Where does each writer stand on the issues? What seems interesting or different? How do their arguments compare with and contrast with one another?

In a synthesis, you are trying to get a handle on how a topic or issue has been discussed by others. Don't offer your opinion on the issues or the way these writers have handled the issues. In a synthesis, you simply want to focus on analyzing how different writers have presented a position or an argument. Set forth the terms and shape of the public conversation so that, eventually, you will be able to position yourself or other writers within that conversation.

Writing About the News

Your ideas about how the news is reported have likely begun to form as you watched news programming, read newspapers, and read what the critics have said. Now it is time for you to formulate a position on your own. Below are suggestions for writing assignments, but the paper you write will be determined primarily by your own interests and the turn your thinking has taken as you have done the work throughout this chapter.

SUGGESTIONS FOR WRITING

1. Much of the discussion about television news—and especially about the coverage of the Iraq war—is about whether or not television is actually covering the news or simply competing for a viewing audience, thereby putting too much emphasis on soft news that features celebrities, scandal, entertainment, and lifestyles. Review the viewing notes you took, the chart you and your classmates made, and the readings in this section, and write your own analysis of the state of television news. Consider in your analysis what television news does best as well as what seems lacking in television coverage of the news.

2. If you are interested in doing Internet research on issues surrounding the media coverage of Iraq, you will discover hundreds of active websites. Remember that Internet sites are notoriously fleeting things. Those sites sponsored by news organizations, national museums, and libraries, however, tend to be much more stable. What are the issues connected to the war and the continuing occupation of Iraq as they are currently represented on the Internet, in archives, and in memorials? If you have some knowledge of putting together a site, you can even devise a website of your own to address these issues. Make sure your site has a central

purpose or argument and that the material you choose for it adds to the information already available or offers a different way of understanding all of that information.

3. Media scholar William Uricchio writes that there is an impulse in a news report to make it into a "story," that is, to find a compelling narrative, heroes, villains, and ultimately, a resolution to the conflict. Uricchio is also suggesting that reporters may be trying to find a neat way of tying up the ends and of keeping their audiences satisfied. Review the current major news stories. Choose one to follow in several media—television, radio, newspaper, news magazine, Internet—and examine that story for the narrative that seems to be emerging from it. What is lost when the press sticks to one particular narrative? What other narratives might be written from this story?

Looking Ahead

To learn more about the topics covered in this chapter, visit
www.ablongman.com/george/102

What you have been doing in the assignments throughout this chapter amounts to a cultural analysis of the news. The assignments have asked you to rely on your own observations, learn firsthand what others think, read what critics and analysts have written, and write your position on or analysis of those issues. As you have read, taken notes, summarized, and synthesized others' writing, you have been analyzing how writers seek to shape public opinion and how the news media represent what is happening in American culture. This amounts to a cultural analysis of the role of the news media at a moment of crisis in American life and thought.

Throughout the chapters that follow, we will be presenting further opportunities to do this kind of cultural analysis—to read and write your way into some of the meanings of contemporary U.S. culture. The work you do will be informed by what others have written, but it will also rely on your own knowledge of the culture you live in and on the observations you will be able to make from your own fieldwork. At times, you will be asked to go beyond analysis to produce your own texts. You are, after all, not only a reader of culture but a user and producer of that culture.

Generations

TV *happiness shared by all the family!*

Model 17F6—in mahogany and limed oak. 17 inch TV... FM and AM radio

This is not your father's Oldsmobile. This is the new generation—of Olds.
—1990 television commercial for Oldsmobile

Children are always episodes in someone else's narratives.
—Carolyn Steedman

The United States is a nation of immigrants, and it is common to distinguish between first and second generations—between those who first came to the United States, voluntarily and involuntarily, from Europe, Asia, Africa, and Latin America and their children who were born here. The two generations are biologically related to each other as well as to older generations as far back as people can trace their ancestry. Yet first-generation and second-generation Americans often differ in the way they live their lives, in the hopes they have for themselves and their children, and in the ties they feel to the traditions and customs of their places of ancestry.

People are also members of a historical generation that is formed by a common history and common experiences shared by others their age. To be a member of a generation in cultural terms, then, is to belong both to a family you are related to biologically and to a group of people you are related to historically.

In this chapter, you will be asked to read, think, and write about what it means to be a member of and a participant in your historical generation. Whether you are straight out of high school or returning to college, it can be valuable for you to consider how your own personal experience has been shaped by growing up at a particular moment in a particular historical generation.

The term *generation* denotes change. It suggests new life and new growth—new styles, new values, and new ways of living. Americans hear generational voices all the time in everyday conversation, when young people tell their parents not to be "so old-fashioned" and their parents reply, "It wasn't like that when we were growing up." Advertisers too, as the Oldsmobile commercial at the beginning of this chapter indicates, like to make consumers believe that the new generation of goods—cars, stereos, computers, household appliances—is smarter, better designed, and more high-tech than its predecessors.

Each generation produces its own way of speaking and its own forms of cultural expression. Cultural historian Raymond Williams says that "no generation speaks quite the same language as its predecessor." Young people, for example, use their own slang to recognize friends, to distinguish between insiders and outsiders, to position themselves in relation to the older generation. Whether you say "whatever," "sweet," or "far out"; the kind of music you listen to; the way you dance; your style of dress; where you go to hang out—all of these reveal something about you and your relation to the constantly changing styles of youth culture in the contemporary United States.

How a generation looks at itself is inevitably entangled in the decisive historical events, geopolitical changes, and popular entertainment of its day. Events such as the Great Depression, World War II, the Vietnam War, the Reagan years, the dot.com boom and bust of the 1990s, and now 9/11 and the invasion and occupation of Iraq have influenced a generation profoundly. To understand what it means to belong to your generation, you will need to locate your experience growing up as a member of your generation in its historical times—to see how your generation has made sense of its place in American history and its relation to past generations.

From the invention of the American teenager and juvenile delinquency in movies such as *Rebel Without a Cause* and *The Wild One* in the 1950s, American media have been fascinated by each new generation of young people. Each generation seems to have its own characteristic mood or identity that the media try to capture in a label—the "lost" generation of the Jazz Age in the 1920s, the "silent" generation of the Eisenhower years in the 1950s, the "baby boomers" of the 1960s, the "yuppies" of the 1980s, the Generation X "slackers" of the 1990s, and the "millennials" of the 2000s. When people use these labels, they are not only referring to particular groups of people but are also calling up a set of values, styles, and images, a collective feeling in the air. When thinking about your generation, look at how the media have represented it and how these media representations have entered into your generation's conception of itself.

This is not to say that everyone in the same generation has the same experience and the same feelings. A generation is not a monolithic thing. In fact, every generation is divided along the same lines of race, class, gender, and ethnicity that divide the wider society. But a generation is not simply a composite of individuals either. To think about the mood of your generation—the sensibility that suffuses its lived experience—you will need to consider how the character of your generation distinguishes it from generations of the past, even if that character is contradictory or inconsistent.

KISWANA BROWNE

— Gloria Naylor

Gloria Naylor's highly acclaimed novel *The Women of Brewster Place* (1980) tells the stories of several African American women who live in a housing project in an unnamed city. "Kiswana Browne" presents a powerful account of the encounter between a mother and daughter that explores both their generational differences and the aspirations that they hold in common. Naylor's story reveals how the much publicized generation gap of the 1960s is never simply a matter of differences in politics and lifestyle but rather is complicated by the intersecting forces of race, class, and gender. The cultural shift signified by Kiswana's change of name represents both a break with the past and, as Kiswana discovers, a continuation of her family's resistance to racial oppression.

SUGGESTION FOR READING As you read, highlight/underline and annotate the passages where the story establishes conflict between the two characters and where (or whether) it resolves the conflict.

1   From the window of her sixth-floor studio apartment, Kiswana could see over the wall at the end of the street to the busy avenue that lay just north of Brewster Place. The late-afternoon shoppers looked like brightly clad marionettes as they moved between the congested traffic, clutching their packages against their bodies to guard them from sudden bursts of the cold autumn wind. A portly mailman had abandoned his cart and was bumping into indignant window-shoppers as he puffed behind the cap that the wind had snatched from his head. Kiswana leaned over to see if he was going to be successful, but the edge of the building cut him off from her view.

A pigeon swept across her window, and she marveled at its liquid movements in the air waves. She placed her dreams on the back of the bird and fantasized that it would glide forever in transparent silver circles until it ascended to the center of the universe and was swallowed up. But the wind died down, and she watched with a sigh as the bird beat its wings in awkward, frantic movements to land on the corroded top of a fire escape on the opposite building. This brought her back to earth.

Humph, it's probably sitting over there crapping on those folks' fire escape, she thought. Now, that's a safety hazard. . . . And her mind was busy again, creating flames and smoke and frustrated tenants whose escape was being hindered because they were slipping and sliding in pigeon shit. She watched their cussing, haphazard descent on the fire escapes until they had all reached the bottom. They were milling around, oblivious to their burning apartments, angrily planning to march on the mayor's office about the pigeons. She materialized placards and banners for them, and they had just reached the corner, boldly sidestepping fire hoses and broken glass, when they all vanished. A tall copper-skinned woman had met this phantom parade at the corner, and they had dissolved in front of her long, confident strides. She plowed through the remains of their faded mists, unconscious of the lingering wisps of their presence on her leather bag and black fur-trimmed coat. It took a few seconds for this transfer from one realm to another to reach Kiswana, but then suddenly she recognized the woman.

"Oh, God, it's Mama!" She looked down guiltily at the forgotten newspaper in her lap and hurriedly circled random job advertisements. By this time Mrs. Browne had reached the front of Kiswana's building and was checking the house number against a piece of paper in her hand. Before she went into the building she stood at the bottom of the stoop and carefully inspected the condition of the street and the adjoining property. Kiswana watched this meticulous inventory with growing annoyance but she involuntarily followed her mother's slowly rotating head, forcing herself to see her new neighborhood through the older woman's eyes. The brightness of the unclouded sky seemed to join forces with her mother as it high-lighted every broken stoop railing and missing brick. The afternoon sun glittered and cascaded across even the tiniest fragments of broken bottle, and at that very moment the wind chose to rise up again, sending unswept grime flying into the air, as a stray tin can left by careless garbage collectors went rolling noisily down the center of the street.

5   Kiswana noticed with relief that at least Ben wasn't sitting in his usual place on the old garbage can pushed against the far wall. He was just a harmless old wino, but Kiswana knew her mother only needed one wino or one teenager with a reefer within a twenty-block radius to decide that her daughter was living in a building seething with dope factories and hang-outs for derelicts. If she had seen Ben, nothing would have made her believe that practically every apartment contained a family, a Bible, and a dream that one day enough could be scraped from those meager Friday night paychecks to make Brewster Place a distant memory.

As she watched her mother's head disappear into the building, Kiswana gave silent thanks that the elevator was broken. That would give her at least five minutes' grace to straighten up the apartment. She rushed to the sofa bed and hastily closed it without smoothing the rumpled sheets and blanket or removing her nightgown. She felt that somehow the tangled bedcovers would give away the fact that she had not slept alone last night. She silently apologized to Abshu's memory as she heartlessly crushed his spirit between the steel springs of the couch. Lord, that man was sweet. Her toes curled involuntarily at the passing thought of his full lips moving slowly over her instep. Abshu was a foot man, and he always started his lovemaking from the bottom up. For that reason Kiswana changed the color of the polish on her toenails every week. During the course of their relationship she had gone from shades of red to brown and was now into the purples. I'm gonna have to start mixing them soon, she thought aloud as she turned from the couch and raced into the bathroom to remove any traces of Abshu from there. She took up his shaving cream and razor and threw them into the bottom drawer of her dresser beside her diaphragm. Mama wouldn't dare pry into my drawers right in front of me, she thought as she slammed the drawer shut. Well, at least not the bottom drawer. She may come up with some sham excuse for opening the top drawer, but never the bottom one.

When she heard the first two short raps on the door, her eyes took a final flight over the small apartment, desperately seeking out any slight misdemeanor that might have to be defended. Well, there was nothing she could do about the crack in the wall over that table. She had been after the landlord to fix it for two months now. And there had been no time to sweep the rug, and everyone knew that off-gray always looked dirtier than it really was. And it was just too damn bad about the kitchen. How was she expected to be out job-hunting every day and still have time to keep a kitchen that looked like her mother's, who didn't even work and still had someone come in twice a month for general cleaning. And besides . . .

Her imaginary argument was abruptly interrupted by a second series of knocks, accompanied by a penetrating, "Melanie, Melanie, are you there?" Kiswana strode toward the door. She's starting before she even gets in here. She knows that's not my name anymore.

She swung the door open to face her slightly flushed mother. "Oh, hi, Mama. You know, I thought I heard a knock, but I figured it was for the people next door, since no one hardly ever calls me Melanie." Score one for me, she thought.

10 "Well, it's awfully strange you can forget a name you answered to for twenty-three years," Mrs. Browne said, as she moved past Kiswana into the apartment. "My, that was a long climb. How long has your elevator been out? Honey, how do you manage with your laundry and groceries up all those steps? But I guess you're young, and it wouldn't bother you as much as it does me." This long string of questions told Kiswana that her mother had no intentions of beginning her visit with another argument about her new African name.

"You know I would have called before I came, but you don't have a phone yet. I didn't want you to feel that I was snooping. As a matter of fact, I didn't expect to find you home at all. I thought you'd be out looking for a job." Mrs. Browne had mentally covered the entire apartment while she was talking and taking off her coat.

"Well, I got up late this morning. I thought I'd buy the afternoon paper and start early tomorrow."

"That sounds like a good idea." Her mother moved toward the window and picked up the discarded paper and glanced over the hurriedly circled ads. "Since when do you have experience as a fork-lift operator?"

Kiswana caught her breath and silently cursed herself for her stupidity. "Oh, my hand slipped—I meant to circle file clerk." She quickly took the paper before her mother could see that she had also marked cutlery salesman and chauffeur.

15 "You're sure you weren't sitting here moping and day-dreaming again?" Amber specks of laughter flashed in the corner of Mrs. Browne's eyes.

Kiswana threw her shoulders back and unsuccessfully tried to disguise her embarrassment with indignation.

"Oh, God, Mama! I haven't done that in years—it's for kids. When are you going to realize that I'm a woman now?" She sought desperately for some womanly thing to do and settled for throwing herself on the couch and crossing her legs in what she hoped looked like a nonchalant arc.

"Please, have a seat," she said, attempting the same tones and gestures she'd seen Bette Davis use on the late movies.

Mrs. Browne, lowering her eyes to hide her amusement, accepted the invitation and sat at the window, also crossing her legs. Kiswana saw immediately how it should have been done. Her celluloid poise clashed loudly against her mother's quiet dignity, and she quickly uncrossed her legs. Mrs. Browne turned her head toward the window and pretended not to notice.

20 "At least you have a halfway decent view from here. I was wondering what lay beyond that dreadful wall—it's the boulevard. Honey, did you know that you can see the trees in Linden Hills from here?"

Kiswana knew that very well, because there were many lonely days that she would sit in her gray apartment and stare at those trees and think of home, but she would rather have choked than admit that to her mother.

"Oh, really, I never noticed. So how is Daddy and things at home?"

"Just fine. We're thinking of redoing one of the extra bedrooms since you children have moved out, but Wilson insists that he can manage all that work alone. I told him that he doesn't really have the proper time or energy for all that. As it is, when he gets home from the office, he's so tired he can hardly move. But you know you can't tell your father anything. Whenever he starts complaining about how stubborn you are, I tell him the child came by it honestly. Oh, and your brother was by yesterday," she added, as if it had just occurred to her.

So that's it, thought Kiswana. That's why she's here.

25 Kiswana's brother, Wilson, had been to visit her two days ago, and she had borrowed twenty dollars from him to get her winter coat out of layaway. That son-of-a-bitch probably ran straight to Mama—and after he swore he wouldn't say anything. I should have known, he was always a snotty-nosed sneak, she thought.

"Was he?" she said aloud. "He came by to see me, too, earlier this week. And I borrowed some money from him because my unemployment checks hadn't cleared in the bank, but now they have and everything's just fine." There, I'll beat you to that one.

"Oh, I didn't know that," Mrs. Browne lied. "He never mentioned you. He had just heard that Beverly was expecting again, and he rushed over to tell us."

Damn. Kiswana could have strangled herself.

"So she's knocked up again, huh?" she said irritably.

30 Her mother started. "Why do you always have to be so crude?"

"Personally, I don't see how she can sleep with Willie. He's such a dishrag."

Kiswana still resented the stance her brother had taken in college. When everyone at school was discovering their blackness and protesting on campus, Wilson never took part; he had even refused to wear an Afro. This had outraged Kiswana because, unlike her, he was dark-skinned and had the type of hair that was thick and kinky enough for a good "Fro." Kiswana had still insisted on cutting her own hair, but it was so thin and fine-textured, it refused to thicken even after she washed it. So she had to brush it up and spray it with lacquer to keep it from lying flat. She never forgave Wilson for telling her that she didn't look African, she looked like an electrocuted chicken.

"Now that's some way to talk. I don't know why you have an attitude against your brother.

He never gave me a restless night's sleep, and now he's settled with a family and a good job."

"He's an assistant to an assistant junior partner in a law firm. What's the big deal about that?"

35 "The job has a future, Melanie. And at least he finished school and went on for his law degree."

"In other words, not like me, huh?"

"Don't put words into my mouth, young lady. I'm perfectly capable of saying what I mean."

Amen, thought Kiswana.

"And I don't know why you've been trying to start up with me from the moment I walked in. I didn't come here to fight with you. This is your first place away from home, and I just wanted to see how you were living and if you're doing all right. And I must say, you've fixed this apartment up very nicely."

40 "Really, Mama?" She found herself softening in the light of her mother's approval.

"Well, considering what you had to work with." This time she scanned the apartment openly.

"Look, I know it's not Linden Hills, but a lot can be done with it. As soon as they come and paint, I'm going to hang my Ashanti print over the couch. And I thought a big Boston Fern would go well in that corner, what do you think?"

"That would be fine, baby. You always had a good eye for balance."

Kiswana was beginning to relax. There was little she did that attracted her mother's approval. It was like a rare bird, and she had to tread carefully around it lest it fly away.

45 "Are you going to leave that statue out like that?"

"Why, what's wrong with it? Would it look better somewhere else?"

There was a small wooden reproduction of a Yoruba goddess with large protruding breasts on the coffee table.

"Well," Mrs. Browne was beginning to blush, "it's just that it's a bit suggestive, don't you think? Since you live alone now, and I know you'll be having male friends stop by, you wouldn't want to be giving them any ideas. I mean, uh, you know, there's no point in putting yourself in any unpleasant situations because they may get the wrong impressions and uh, you know, I mean, well . . ." Mrs. Browne stammered on miserably.

Kiswana loved it when her mother tried to talk about sex. It was the only time she was at a loss for words.

50 "Don't worry, Mama." Kiswana smiled. "That wouldn't bother the type of men I date. Now maybe if it had big feet . . ." And she got hysterical, thinking of Abshu.

Her mother looked at her sharply. "What sort of gibberish is that about feet? I'm being serious, Melanie."

"I'm sorry, Mama." She sobered up. "I'll put it away in the closet," she said, knowing that she wouldn't.

"Good," Mrs. Browne said, knowing that she wouldn't either. "I guess you think I'm too picky, but we worry about you over here. And you refuse to put in a phone so we can call and see about you."

"I haven't refused, Mama. They want seventy-five dollars for a deposit, and I can't swing that right now."

55 "Melanie, I can give you the money."

"I don't want you to be giving me money— I've told you that before. Please, let me make it by myself."

"Well, let me lend it to you, then."

"No!"

"Oh, so you can borrow money from your brother, but not from me."

60 Kiswana turned her head from the hurt in her mother's eyes. "Mama, when I borrow from Willie, he makes me pay him back. You never let me pay you back," she said into her hands.

"I don't care. I still think it's downright selfish of you to be sitting over here with no phone, and sometimes we don't hear from you in two weeks—anything could happen—especially living among these people."

Kiswana snapped her head up. "What do you mean, these people. They're my people and yours, too, Mama—we're all black. But maybe you've forgotten that over in Linden Hills."

"That's not what I'm talking about, and you know it. These streets—this building—it's so shabby and rundown. Honey, you don't have to live like this."

"Well, this is how poor people live."

65 "Melanie, you're not poor."

"No, Mama, *you're* not poor. And what you have and I have are two totally different things. I don't have a husband in real estate with a five-figure income and a home in Linden Hills—*you* do. What I have is a weekly unemployment check and an overdrawn checking account at United Federal. So this studio on Brewster is all I can afford."

"Well, you could afford a lot better," Mrs. Browne snapped, "if you hadn't dropped out of college and had to resort to these dead-end clerical jobs."

"Uh-huh, I knew you'd get around to that before long." Kiswana could feel the rings of anger begin to tighten around her lower backbone, and they sent her forward onto the couch. "You'll never understand, will you? Those bourgie schools were counterrevolutionary. My place was in the streets with my people, fighting for equality and a better community."

"Counterrevolutionary!" Mrs. Browne was raising her voice. "Where's your revolution now, Melanie? Where are all those black revolutionaries who were shouting and demonstrating and kicking up a lot of dust with you on that campus? Huh? They're sitting in wood-paneled offices with their degrees in mahogany frames, and they won't even drive their cars past this street because the city doesn't fix potholes in this part of town."

70 "Mama," she said, shaking her head slowly in disbelief, "how can you—a black woman—sit there and tell me that what we fought for during the Movement wasn't important just because some people sold out?"

"Melanie, I'm not saying it wasn't important. It was damned important to stand up and say that you were proud of what you were and to get the vote and other social opportunities for every person in this country who had it due. But you kids thought you were going to turn the world upside down, and it just wasn't so. When all the smoke had cleared, you found yourself with a fistful of new federal laws and a country still full of obstacles for black people to fight their way over—just because they're black. There was no revolution, Melanie, and there will be no revolution."

"So what am I supposed to do, huh? Just throw up my hands and not care about what happens to my people? I'm not supposed to keep fighting to make things better?"

"Of course, you can. But you're going to have to fight within the system, because it and these so-called 'bourgie' schools are going to be here for a long time. And that means that you get smart like a lot of your old friends and get an important job where you can have some influence. You don't have to sell out, as you say, and work for some corporation, but you could become an assemblywoman or a civil liberties lawyer or open a freedom school in this very neighborhood. That way you could really help the community. But what help are you going to be to these people on Brewster while you're living hand-to-mouth on file-clerk jobs waiting for a revolution? You're wasting your talents, child."

"Well, I don't think they're being wasted. At least I'm here in day-to-day contact with the problems of my people. What good would I be after four or five years of a lot of white brainwashing in some phony, prestige institution, huh? I'd be like you and Daddy and those other educated blacks sitting over there in Linden Hills with a terminal case of middle-class amnesia."

75   "You don't have to live in a slum to be concerned about social conditions, Melanie. Your father and I have been charter members of the NAACP for the last twenty-five years."

"Oh, God!" Kiswana threw her head back in exaggerated disgust. "That's being concerned? That middle-of-the-road, Uncle Tom dumping ground for black Republicans!"

"You can sneer all you want, young lady, but that organization has been working for black people since the turn of the century, and it's still working for them. Where are all those radical groups of yours that were going to put a Cadillac in every garage and Dick Gregory in the White House? I'll tell you where."

I knew you would, Kiswana thought angrily.

"They burned themselves out because they wanted too much too fast. Their goals weren't grounded in reality. And that's always been your problem."

80   "What do you mean, my problem? I know exactly what I'm about."

"No, you don't. You constantly live in a fantasy world—always going to extremes—turning butterflies into eagles, and life isn't about that. It's accepting what is and working from that. Lord, I remember how worried you had me, putting all that lacquered hair spray on your head. I thought you were going to get lung cancer—trying to be what you're not."

Kiswana jumped up from the couch. "Oh, God, I can't take this anymore. Trying to be something I'm not—trying to be something I'm not, Mama! Trying to be proud of my heritage and the fact that I was of African descent. If that's being what I'm not, then I say fine. But I'd rather be dead than be like you—a white man's nigger who's ashamed of being black!"

Kiswana saw streaks of gold and ebony light follow her mother's flying body out of the chair. She was swung around by the shoulders and made to face the deadly stillness in the angry woman's eyes. She was too stunned to cry out from the pain of the long fingernails that dug into her shoulders, and she was brought so close to her mother's face that she saw her reflection, distorted and wavering, in the tears that stood in the older woman's eyes. And she listened in that stillness to a story she had heard from a child.

"My grandmother," Mrs. Browne began slowly in a whisper, "was a full-blooded Iroquois, and my grandfather a free black from a long line of journeymen who had lived in Connecticut since the establishment of the colonies. And my father was a Bajan who came to this country as a cabin boy on a merchant mariner."

85 "I know all that," Kiswana said, trying to keep her lips from trembling.

"Then, know this." And the nails dug deeper into her flesh. "I am alive because of the blood of proud people who never scraped or begged or apologized for what they were. They lived asking only one thing of this world—to be allowed to be. And I learned through the blood of these people that black isn't beautiful and it isn't ugly—black is! It's not kinky hair and it's not straight hair—it just is.

"It broke my heart when you changed your name. I gave you my grandmother's name, a woman who bore nine children and educated them all, who held off six white men with a shotgun when they tried to drag one of her sons to jail for 'not knowing his place.' Yet you needed to reach into an African dictionary to find a name to make you proud.

"When I brought my babies home from the hospital, my ebony son and my golden daughter, I swore before whatever gods would listen—those of my mother's people or those of my father's people—that I would use everything I had and could ever get to see that my children were prepared to meet this world on its own terms, so that no one could sell them short and make them ashamed of what they were or how they looked—whatever they were or however they looked. And Melanie, that's not being white or red or black—that's being a mother."

Kiswana followed her reflection in the two single tears that moved down her mother's cheeks until it blended with them into the woman's copper skin. There was nothing and then so much that she wanted to say, but her throat kept closing up every time she tried to speak. She kept her head down and her eyes closed, and thought, Oh, God, just let me die. How can I face her now?

90 Mrs. Browne lifted Kiswana's chin gently. "And the one lesson I wanted you to learn is not to be afraid to face anyone, not even a crafty old lady like me who can outtalk you." And she smiled and winked.

"Oh, Mama, I . . ." and she hugged the woman tightly.

"Yeah, baby." Mrs. Browne patted her back. "I know."

She kissed Kiswana on the forehead and cleared her throat. "Well, now, I better be moving on. It's getting late, there's dinner to be made, and I have to get off my feet—these new shoes are killing me."

Kiswana looked down at the beige leather pumps. "Those are really classy. They're English, aren't they?"

95 "Yes, but, Lord, do they cut me right across the instep." She removed the shoe and sat on the couch to massage her foot.

Bright red nail polish glared at Kiswana through the stockings. "Since when do you polish your toenails?" she gasped. "You never did that before."

"Well . . ." Mrs. Browne shrugged her shoulders, "your father sort of talked me into it, and, uh, you know, he likes it and all, so I thought, uh, you know, why not so . . ." And she gave Kiswana an embarrassed smile.

I'll be damned, the young woman thought, feeling her whole face tingle. Daddy into feet! And she looked at the blushing woman on her couch and suddenly realized that her mother had trod through the same universe that she herself was now traveling. Kiswana was breaking no new trails and would eventually end up just two feet away on that couch. She stared at the woman she had been and was to become.

"But I'll never be a Republican," she caught herself saying aloud.

100 "What are you mumbling about, Melanie?" Mrs. Browne slipped on her shoe and got up from the couch.

She went to get her mother's coat. "Nothing, Mama. It's really nice of you to come by. You should do it more often."

"Well, since it's not Sunday, I guess you're allowed at least one lie."

They both laughed.

After Kiswana had closed the door and turned around, she spotted an envelop sticking between the cushions of her couch. She went over and opened it up; there was seventy-five dollars in it.

105 "Oh, Mama, darn it!" She rushed to the window and started to call to the woman, who had just emerged from the building, but she suddenly changed her mind and sat down in the chair with a long sigh that caught in the upward draft of the autumn wind and disappeared over the top of the building.

SUGGESTIONS FOR DISCUSSION

1. Gloria Naylor tells this story from Kiswana Browne's point of view. How would the story be different if Naylor had chosen to tell it from Kiswana's mother's point of view? What would be gained? What lost?

2. Consider how Naylor has organized this story—how she establishes a central conflict, leads up to the story's climax, and finally resolves the conflict. Does this type of plot seem familiar? Does the story achieve closure or does it seem open ended? What kinds of satisfaction do readers derive from plots such as this one? What, if anything, do such plots leave out or ignore?

3. Is Naylor making a judgment, whether implicit or explicit, about her characters? Explain your answer.

SUGGESTIONS FOR WRITING

1. Take the perspective of either Kiswana Browne or her mother and write an essay that explains how the character you have chosen sees the other. If you wish, write the essay in the voice of the character. Or you may choose to comment on the character's perceptions of the other and their generational differences in your own voice. In either case, be specific in your use of detail to define generational differences between the two women.

2. On one level, the chapter "Kiswana Browne" seems to be concerned with a generation gap between Kiswana and her mother. At the same time, other factors—race, class, and gender—affect the way generational differences are played out between the two characters. Write an essay that explains to what extent the chapter presents a version of the generation gap and to what extent other factors determine what happens between Kiswana and her mother. Do Kiswana and her mother have things in common, as well as generational differences? How do these factors influence the outcome of the story?

3. "Kiswana Browne" tells of the encounter between a young woman and her family and explores generational differences that have to do with issues such as lifestyle, names, and politics. Can you think of an encounter that you have had with your parents, or that someone you know has had with his or her parents, that involves such telling generational conflicts? (The conflict should be something that highlights differences in generational attitudes, values, or styles—not just "normal" disagreements about using the car or what time curfew should be.) Write an essay that explores such a conflict and explains what generational differences are at stake.

GEN (FILL IN THE BLANK): COMING OF AGE, SEEKING AN IDENTITY

Arlie Russell Hochschild

Arlie Russell Hochschild is a professor of sociology at the University of California, Berkeley, where she codirects the Center for Working Families; she is also the author of such sociological studies as *The Time Bind: When Work Becomes Home and Home Becomes Work* (2001) and *The Managed Heart: Commercialization of Human Feelings* (1985). This article appeared in a special section of the *New York Times* on "Generations" on March 8, 2000.

SUGGESTION FOR READING   Arlie Russell Hochschild, unlike the other writers in this chapter, provides a definition of the idea of a generation based on sociologist Karl Mannheim's 1927 essay "The Problem of Generations." As Hochschild notes, according to Mannheim, "a generation is a cohort of people who feel the impact of a powerful historical event and develop a shared consciousness about it." As you read, pay attention to how Hochschild uses this definition to analyze the generation of twenty- and thirty-year-olds and how she finds, in the absence of a large historical crisis in the life of this generation before 9/11, an underlying trend.

1   "I'm not part of the 1960's generation," said Sandy de Lissovoy. "I don't feel part of Gen X or Gen Y. I'm sure not part of the 'Me Generation.' Who made up that term? I hate it. What's really in front of me is my computer, but even with it, I'm between the generation that barely tolerates computers and the one that treats them like a member of the family."

Mr. de Lissovoy, a 29-year-old graphic designer in San Francisco, was expressing as well as anyone the feelings that, as a sociology professor, I frequently hear during office hours. At this moment he was having a hard time defining his generation. He raised his eyebrows quizzically, smiled and said, "Call me the @ Generation One and a Half."

Can we make up our generation, as Mr. de Lissovoy playfully did, or is it imposed upon us, like it or not?

These are questions that the German sociologist Karl Mannheim took up in his classic 1927 essay, "The Problem of Generations." Is a generation a collection of people born in the same span of years? No, he thought, that is a cohort, and many cohorts are born, come of age and die without becoming generations. For Mannheim, a generation is a cohort of people who feel the impact of a powerful historical event and develop a shared consciousness about it. Not all members of a generation may see the event the same way, and some may articulate its defining features better than others. But what makes a generation is its connection to history.

5   Americans who came of age in the 1930's, 40's and 60's have been branded by large events—the Great Depression, World War II, Vietnam—and the collective moods they aroused. But from the 70's through the 90's, history's signal events happened elsewhere. Communism collapsed, but not in the United States. Wars raged in Rwanda, the Balkans and elsewhere, but they had little effect here. The forces in the United States have been social and economic, and they have shifted the focus to personal issues—matters of lifestyle that are shaped by consumerism, the mass media and an increasing sense of impermanence in family and work.

"There is no overarching crisis or cause for our generation," Mr. de Lissovoy said. "It's more a confusing, ambiguous flow of events. There's a slow, individual sorting out to do."

But underneath this confusing, ambiguous flow of events is a trend toward a more loosely jointed, limited-liability society, the privatizing influence of that trend and the crash-boom-bang of the market, which, in the absence of other voices, is defining generations left and right.

People in their 20's and early 30's are often called Gen X'ers, a term derived from a novel by Douglas Coupland. The book, *Generation X*, was followed by a film, *Slacker*, directed by Richard Linklater, about a group of overeducated, under-employed oddballs who drop to the margins of society. But for Jim Kreines, a 32-year-old grad-uate student of philosophy at the University of Chicago, the label fit loosely, if at all.

When I asked him what generation he belonged to, Mr. Kreines replied, "I'm not sure I care enough to argue about this." He had read the Coupland book and seen the film. But did the Gen X'er label apply to him? He was not sure it mattered.

10   Many Gen X'ers may be trying to sort out a certain cultural sleight of hand. They feel luck-ier than previous generations because they enjoy many more options. In the 50's, said Charles Sellers, a 28-year-old urban planner in Portland, Ore., there was only one choice. "If you were a woman you were a housewife," he said. "If you were a man you married and supported your family. Today, except for the Mormons, Ameri-cans have a long cultural menu to choose from. If you're a woman, you can be a single woman, a career woman, a lesbian, a single mom by choice, a live-in lover, a married-for-now wife, a married-forever wife. And the same for work: I'm on my third career."

But the wider menu of identities comes with a decreasing assurance that any particular iden-tity will last. This is because a culture of dereg-ulation has slipped from our economic life into our cultural life. Gen X'ers, at least in the middle class, can be more picky in finding "just the right mate" and "just the right career." But once you've found them, you begin to wonder if you can keep them.

In his book *The New Insecurity*, Jerald Wal-lulis, a philosopher at the University of South Carolina, observed that in the last 30 years, peo-ple have shifted the way they base their identity: from marriage and employment to marriageabil-ity and employability. Old anchors no longer hold, and a sense of history is lost. For the gen-erations of the 80's and 90's, this rootlessness is their World War II, their Vietnam. And it pre-sents a more difficult challenge than the one faced by the 60's generation.

Mr. de Lissovoy's parents divorced when he was a baby and now live on opposite coasts. Consider, too, the shifting family ties of a 27-year-old computer programmer in Silicon Valley, who asked that her name be withheld. "My mother divorced four times and is living on uncertain terms with her fifth," she said, "so I'm not sure if she'll stay with him either. I haven't gotten attached to any of my stepdads. My dad remarried four times, too, only now he's married to a woman I like."

When her parents divorced, she spent every other weekend with her father. "My dad was glad to see me, but I'd have to remind him of the name of my best friends," she said. "He didn't know what mattered to me. After a while it just got to be dinner and a video, and after that, I didn't feel much like going to his apartment."

15   Talking about her love life, she said: "If I meet someone I really like, I become shy and tied up in knots. I can't talk about anything per-sonal." It was as if she did not dare to begin a relationship for fear of ending it.

After the parents of another young woman divorced, her father married a woman as young as his daughter, and is very involved with his new, young children who are the same age as his grandchildren. Now, when his daughter tries to arrange a visit between her father and his grand-children, he is often too pinched for time to see them. His daughter feels hurt and angry—first to miss out on a father, then a grandfather.

Reflecting on these generational jumbles, Mr. de Lissovoy commented: "Today's hype is that 'You can get it if you really want it'—a mate, career and love still sells a lot of tickets. We're the Generation of Individual Choice. Which? Which? Which? But the bottom can fall out from some of those choices. And in the end, we're orphans. We're supposed to take care of ourselves. That's our only choice."

phiveberbat Not every young person I have talked with has felt so adrift. The 20-somethings of the 90's have more material resources than their predecessors—ample job opportunities, for example.

Still, Mr. de Lissovoy's feelings reflect something true about America these days. Despite the recent economic miracle, we are experiencing a care deficit. Social services have been cut; hospitals release patients 24 hours after surgery to recover at home. But who is home to do the caring? Two-thirds of mothers are working. One-quarter of households are headed by single mothers; they need help, too. Paradoxically, American individualism and pride in self-sufficiency lead us to absorb rather than resist this deficit: "Care? Who needs care? I can handle it," thus adding one problem to another.

20   If in previous decades large historic events drew people together and oriented *dia histong* them to action, the recent double trend toward more choice but less security leads the young to see their lives in more individual terms. Big events collectivize, little events atomize. So with people facing important but private problems, and thinking in individual, not collective, terms, the coast became clear in the 80's and 90's for the marketplace to stalk into this cultural void and introduce generation-defining clothes, music and videos.

Generations X and Y function as market gimmicks nowadays. The market dominates not just economic life, as the economist Robert Kuttner argues in "Everything for Sale," but our cultural life as well. It tells us what a generation is—a Pepsi generation, a Mac generation, an Internet generation. And a magazine about shoot-'em-up computer games calls itself *NextGen*.

Advertisers are appealing to children over the heads of their parents. Juliet B. Schor, an economics lecturer at Harvard, suggests that the younger generation is the cutting edge of a full-blown market culture. More than $2 billion is spent on advertising directed at them, 20 times

the amount spent a decade ago. Most of the advertising is transmitted through television; it is estimated that youngsters increased their viewing time one hour a day between 1970 and 1990. Three out of five children ages 12 to 17 now have a TV in their bedroom. Advertisers are trying to enlist children against their parents' better judgment, Dr. Schor said recently, and overworked parents sometimes give in and go along. If Dr. Schor is correct, Generation Y might be defined even more than Generation X by what its members buy than by what they do or who they are.

Marketing strategists, meanwhile, are turning over all the generations faster, slicing and dicing the life cycle into thinner strips. In the computer industry, an advertising generation is nine months; in the clothing industry, a season. In department stores, between the displays for girls in their preteens and teens, is a new age, "tweens." The identity promised by a style or a brand name for one generation is marked off from an increasing number of others. And the styles continually replace old with new.

This creates a certain consumer logic. Older consumers buy what makes them feel young, while young consumers, up to a point, buy what makes them feel older. So the preteenager will buy the tween thing while the teenager will buy the 20-something jacket, and the 40-year-old will browse in the racks for 30-year-olds.

25   To be sure, every American decade has fashion marketeers define generational looks and sounds, but probably never before have they so totally hijacked a generation's cultural expression. Allison Pugh, a 33-year-old married mother of two and a graduate student in sociology at the University of California at Berkeley, said: "I definitely feel like people just two or three years younger than me are the beginning of another generation. But I can only say why by pointing to superficial things, like how many pierces they have, how high their shoes are and what kind of music they listen to. I roomed with a girl just two years younger and she listened to Smashing Pumpkins, Nirvana and Hole. I was 'old'—as in

out of it—even just a few years out of college. I started to sound like my mother: 'That's not music; what is that noise?' "

Like Ms. Pugh, Mr. de Lissovoy is considered old to the generation at his heels. He is wired, but feels ambivalent about it. "What I don't like is disposability, hyperspeed, consumption," he said. "I'd like to reduce these. What I want more of is face-to-face interaction, a value on repair, families living nearby each other. I'd love to live in a multigenerational, multiracial cohousing project. And a more leisurely pace of life. I want some pretty old-fashioned things."

The 60's generation is hitting 60, and with some computer nerds striking it rich, 60's-era protests are not defining the new generation. But that era's flame is not dead. In front of a large gathering at the Pauley ballroom on the Berkeley campus a few months ago, the Mario Savio Young Activist Award for 1999—named after the leader of the 1964 Free Speech Movement—was given to Nikki Bas, a 31-year-old American of Filipino descent who coordinates Sweatshop Watch, a campaign against the poor pay and working conditions of third-world workers who make football uniforms and other clothing sold on American college campuses. Mr. de Lissovoy remembers hearing about Mr. Savio from his 60's activist mother, but he does not know Nikki Bas, is no longer a student and is under time pressure at work. So he is not signing up.

Still, from a distance he watched the protests in Seattle against the World Trade Organization late last year, and they kindled a sense of the importance of history that he feels the market is driving out. "I hated the mindless anarchists who broke shop windows," he said. "But the other protesters who went there to speak up against mega-corporations running the show, and for the family farm, local communities, monarch butterflies and sea turtles—they are taking the long view of the planet. We usually think it's the older generation that wants to preserve the past, and it's the young who don't mind tearing things up. In Seattle, the young environmentalists had their eye on history, and it was the old who had an eye on their pocketbooks."

Ultimately, market generations are generations of things, and they can make us forget generations of people. "My generation doesn't know how globalization will turn out," Mr. de Lissovoy said. "But we won't see how globalization is messing us up if we've forgotten how the world used to be. Whichever way, we don't see that what we are doing is forgetting the past. And we're nobodies without a sense of history."

30   He recalled how baseball caps with X's became popular with teenagers, especially in Detroit, after Spike Lee's film on Malcolm X came out. "When a TV interviewer asked a kid about the X on his cap, he didn't know who Malcolm X was," Mr. de Lissovoy said. "He didn't even know he was a person. We need to appreciate the work it takes to get us where we are. Otherwise we aren't anywhere."

SUGGESTIONS FOR DISCUSSION

1. Looking for a defining feature of the generation of young people at the beginning of the twenty-first century, Arlie Russell Hochschild suggests that there "is a trend toward a more loosely jointed, limited-liability society, the privatizing influence of that trend and the crash-boom-bang of the market." What exactly does she mean by this trend? In what sense does it help explain the collective mood of a generation?

2. Hochschild cites the sociologist Karl Mannheim's idea that a "generation is a cohort of people who feel the impact of powerful historical events and develop a shared consciousness about it." "Gen (Fill in the Blank)" was written before 9/11, the "war on terrorism," and the invasion and occupation of Iraq. Do these events define a generation in the way that the Great Depression, World War II, and Vietnam defined the generations

coming of age in the 1930s, 1940s, and 1960s? If Hochschild were writing the article today, to what extent would she have to revise her findings?

3. Neither Hochschild nor her informants offer a term to "fill in the blank" and characterize the current generation of young people. Consider the terms used to characterize earlier generations—the greatest generation of World War II, the Beat generation, baby boomers, the Me generation, Generation X, slackers, and so on. What do such terms highlight about the generations they are meant to define? What purposes does the naming of generations serve? What might the terms leave out?

SUGGESTIONS FOR WRITING

1. Consider Hochschild's claim that the "market dominates not just economic life . . . but our cultural life as well." Write an essay that applies the statement to your generation. You'll want to take into account, of course, how individual identities are shaped by what people buy and consume—whether styles of clothes or music or digital technology. But consider also how the market permeates people's thinking, their relationships with others, and their capacity to experience the world.

2. Assume that Hochschild has hired you to help her update her article. Write a memo to her that first explains to what extent her findings remain valid and why. Then provide an explanation of what she would need to add or revise in order to update the article.

3. Gloria Naylor in "Kiswana Browne" and Arlie Russell Hochschild in "Gen (Fill in the Blank)" have written of the issue of generational identity, though in quite different ways, using different genres of writing. Naylor has written a fictional account, which is a chapter from her novel *The Women of Brewster Place*; Hochschild's "Gen (Fill in the Blank)" is an article based on academic research. Because each of these writers uses such a different genre and writing strategy, he or she is likely to have different effects on his or her readers. Write an essay that compares the writing strategies. What do you see as the advantages and disadvantages of each writer's attempt to address the issue of generational identity? What effects are the various genres likely to have on readers?

GOTHS IN TOMORROWLAND

— *Thomas Hine*

Thomas Hine is well known for his writing about architecture and design. He is the author of *Populuxe* (1987), a book on American design in the 1950s and 1960s, and *The Total Package* (1995), a study of brand names and packaging. The following selection comes from his most recent book, *The Rise and Fall of the American Teenager* (1999). Hine explores the diversity of teen culture and its relation to adult society.

SUGGESTION FOR READING   Hine begins with an anecdote about the goth "invasion" of Disneyland in 1997 and the "zero tolerance" policy adopted by Disney's security forces. Notice that Hine wants to do more than just tell his story. He sees in it a larger issue about how the "mere presence of teenagers threatens us." As you read, keep in mind this general theme of the alienation of teenagers from adult society, how adults enforce it, and how teenagers maintain it.

I feel stupid and contagious.

Kurt Cobain, "Smells Like Teen Spirit" (1991)

1   In the summer of 1997, the security forces at Disneyland and the police in surrounding Anaheim, California, announced a "zero tolerance" policy to fend off a new threat.

Hordes of pale, mascaraed goths—one of the many tribes of teendom—were invading. It was an odd onslaught. Unlike their barbarian namesakes, they weren't storming the gates of the walled Magic Kingdom. They had yearly passes, purchased for $99 apiece. Many of them had not even been goths when their parents dropped them off at the edge of the parking lot. Rather, they changed into their black sometimes gender-bending garments, applied their white makeup accented with black eyeliner and gray blush-on. The punkier among them accessorized with safety pins and other aggressively ugly, uncomfortable-looking pierceables. And most important of all, they reminded themselves to look really glum. Once inside, they headed for Tomorrowland, Disneyland's most unsettled neighborhood, and hogged all the benches.

It was a sacrilege. Disneyland, said those who wrote letters to the editor, is supposed to be "the happiest place on earth," and these young people with their long faces clearly didn't belong. The presence of sullen clusters of costumed teens showed, some argued, that Disney had given up its commitment to family values. It was no longer possible to feel safe in Disneyland, came the complaints, and that was about the last safe place left.

Actually, the safety of Disneyland was part of the attraction for the goth teens. They told reporters that their parents bought them season passes because the theme park's tight security would assure nothing bad would happen to them. In the vast sprawl of Orange County, California, there are very few safe places where teens are welcome, and Disneyland has always been one of them.

5   Those who complained spoke of the goths as if they were some sort of an alien force, not just white suburban California teenagers. Only a few years earlier, they had been kids who were delighted to go with their parents to meet Mickey. And only a few years from now, they will be young adults—teaching our children, cleaning our teeth, installing our cable television. But now they insist on gloom. And the adult world could not find a place for them—even in Tomorrowland.

Unlike Minnesota's Mall of America—which became a battleground for gang warfare transplanted from Minneapolis and which eventually barred unescorted teenagers from visiting at night—the perceived threat to Disneyland was handled in a low-key way. Teenagers were arrested for even the tiniest infractions outside the park and forced by security guards to follow Disneyland's quite restrictive rules of decorum within the park. After all, the theme park's administrators had an option not available to government; they could revoke the yearly passes. While Disneyland doesn't enforce a dress code for its visitors, it can keep a tight rein on their behavior.

Yet, despite its lack of drama, I think the situation is significant because it vividly raises many of the issues that haunt teenagers' lives at the end of the twentieth century. It is about the alienation of teenagers from adult society, and equally about the alienation of that society from its teenagers. The mere presence of teenagers threatens us.

It is also a story about space. How, in an environment devoid of civic spaces, do we expect people to learn how to behave as members of a community? And it is about the future. Is a meaningful tomorrow so far away that young people can find nothing better to do than engage in faux-morbid posturing? (Even Disney's theme parks are losing track of the future; they are converting their Tomorrowlands into nostalgic explorations of how people used to think about the future a century and more ago.)

And even its resolution—a stance of uneasy tolerance backed by coercion and force—seems symptomatic of the way Americans deal with young people now.

10   Inevitably, a lack of perspective bedevils efforts to recount the recent past, but the problem is more than that. The last quarter of the twentieth century has, in a sense, been about fragmentation. Identity politics has led to a sharpening of distinctions among the groups in the society, and a suspicion of apparent majorities. Postmodern literary theory warns us to mistrust narratives. Even advertising and television, which once united the country in a common belief in consumption, now sell to a welter of micromarkets. Thus we are left without either a common myth, or even the virtual common ground of *The Ed Sullivan Show.*

It seems crude now to speak of teenagers and think of the white middle-class, heterosexual young people that the word "teenager" was originally coined to describe. The "echo" generation of teenagers, whose first members are now entering high school, is about 67 percent non-Hispanic white, 15 percent black, 14 percent Hispanic, and 5 percent Asian or American Indian. The proportion of Hispanic teens will grow each year, and the Census Bureau also reports significantly greater numbers of mixed-race teens and adoptees who are racially different from their parents.

Even the word "Hispanic" is a catch-all that conceals an enormous range of cultural difference between Mexicans, Cubans, Puerto Ricans, Dominicans, and other groups whose immigration to the United States has increased tremendously during the last quarter century. Urban school systems routinely enroll student populations that speak dozens of different languages at home.

Differences among youth do not simply involve differences of culture, race, income, and class—potent as these are. We now acknowledge differences in sexual orientation among young people. Today's students are also tagged with bureaucratic or medical assessments of their abilities and disabilities that also become part of their identities.

There are so many differences among the students at a high school in Brooklyn, Los Angeles, or suburban Montgomery County, Maryland, that one wonders whether the word "teenager" is sufficient to encompass them all. Indeed, the terms "adolescent" and "teenager" have always had a middle-class bias. In the past, though, working-class youths in their teens were already working and part of a separate culture. Now that the work of the working class has disappeared, their children have little choice but to be teenagers. But they are inevitably different from those of the postwar and baby boomer eras because they are growing up in a more heterogeneous and contentious society.

15   What follows, then, is not a single unified narrative but, rather, a sort of jigsaw puzzle. Many pieces fit together nicely. Others seem to be missing. It's easier to solve such a puzzle if you know what picture is going to emerge, but if I were confident of that, I wouldn't be putting you, or myself, to such trouble.

These discussions do have an underlying theme: the difficulty of forging the sort of meaningful identity that Erik Erikson described at midcentury. But if we look for a picture of the late-twentieth-century teenager in these fragments, we won't find it. That's because we're expecting to find something that isn't there.

The goths who invaded Tomorrowland are examples of another kind of diversity—or perhaps pseudo-diversity—that has emerged gaudily during the last two decades. These are the tribes of youth. The typical suburban high school is occupied by groups of teens who express themselves through music, dress, tattoos and piercing, obsessive hobbies, consumption patterns, extracurricular activities, drug habits, and sex practices. These tribes hang out in different parts of the school, go to different parts of town. Once it was possible to speak of a youth culture, but now there is a range of youth subcultures, and clans, coteries, and cliques within those.

In 1996 a high school student asked fellow *tóng chí,* *Thong Car* readers of an Internet bulletin board what groups were found in their high schools. Nearly every school reported the presence of "skaters," "geeks," "jocks," "sluts," "freaks," "druggies," "nerds," and those with "other-colored hair," presumably third-generation punks. There were also, some students reported, "paper people," "snobs," "band geeks," "drama club types" (or "drama queens"), "soccer players" (who aren't counted as jocks, the informant noted), "Satanists," "Jesus freaks," "industrial preps," "techno-goths," and "computer dweebs." Several took note of racial and class segregation, listing "blacks," "Latinos," "white trash," and "wannabe blacks." There were "preppies," who, as one writer, possibly a preppie herself, noted, "dress like the snobs but aren't as snobbish." "Don't forget about the druggie preps," another writer fired back.

This clearly wasn't an exhaustive list. Terms vary from school to school and fashions vary from moment to moment. New technologies emerge, in-line skates or electronic pagers for instance, and they immediately generate their own dress, style, language, and culture.

20 The connotations of the technologies can change very quickly. Only a few years ago, pagers were associated mostly with drug dealers, but now they've entered the mainstream. Pagers became respectable once busy mothers realized that they could use them to get messages to their peripatetic offspring. Young pager users have developed elaborate codes for flirtation, endearment, assignation, and insults. They know that if 90210 comes up on their pager, someone's calling them a snob, and if it's 1776, they're revolting, while if it's 07734, they should turn the pager upside down and read "hELLO."

Most of the youth tribes have roots that go back twenty years or more, though most are more visible and elaborate than they once were. Many of these tribes are defined by the music they like, and young people devote a lot of energy to distinguishing the true exemplars of heavy metal, techno, alternative, or hip-hop from the mere poseurs. Hybrid and evolutionary versions of these cultures, such as speed metal, thrash, or gangsta rap make things far more confusing.

One thing that many of these subcultures have in common is what has come to be known as modern primitivism. This includes tattooing, the piercing of body parts, and physically expressive and dangerous rituals, such as the mosh pits that are part of many rock concerts. Young people use piercing and tattoos to assert their maturity and sovereignty over their bodies.

"Can this be child abuse?" Sally Dietrich, a suburban Washington mother, asked the police when her thirteen-year-old son appeared with a bulldog tattooed on his chest. "I said, 'What about destruction of property?' He's my kid." Her son was, very likely, trying to signal otherwise. Nevertheless, Dietrich mounted a successful campaign to bar tattooing without permission in the state of Maryland, one of many such restrictions passed during the 1990s.

It may be a mistake to confuse visible assertions of sexual power with the fact of it. For example, heavy-metal concerts and mosh pits are notoriously male-dominated affairs. And the joke of MTV's *Beavis and Butt-head* is that these two purported metalheads don't have a clue about how to relate to the opposite sex. Those whose costumes indicate that they have less to prove are just as likely to be sexually active.

25 In fact, visitors to Disneyland probably don't need to be too worried about the goths, a tribe which, like many of the youth culture groups, has its roots in English aestheticism. As some goths freely admit, they're pretentious, and their morbid attitudes are as much a part of the dress-up games as the black clothes themselves.

The goth pose provides a convenient cover. For some males, it gives an opportunity to try out an androgynous look. The costumes, which emphasize the face and make the body disappear, may also provide an escape for young women and men who fear that they're overweight or not fit. Black clothes are slimming, and darkness even more so. "Until I got in with goths, I hadn't met other people who are depressed like I am and that I could really talk to," said one young woman on an Internet bulletin board. Another said being a goth allowed her relaxation from life as a straight-A student and a perfect daughter.

Although young people recognize an immense number of distinctions among the tribes and clans of youth culture and are contemptuous of those they regard as bogus, most adults cannot tell them apart. They confuse thrashers with metalheads and goths because they all wear black. Then they assume that they're all taking drugs and worshipping Satan.

The adult gaze is powerful. It classes them all as teenagers, whether they like it or not. The body alterations that young people use to assert that they are no longer children successfully frighten grown-ups, but they also convince them these weird creatures are well short of being adults. The ring through the lip or the nipple merely seems to demonstrate that they are not ready for adult responsibility. What they provoke is not respect but restrictions.

Tribes are about a yearning to belong to a group—or perhaps to escape into a disguise. They combine a certain gregariousness with what seems to be its opposite: a feeling of estrangement. The imagery of being alone in the world is not quite so gaudy as that of modern primitivism, yet it pervades contemporary youth culture.

30   While youthful exploration of the 1920s, 1940s, 1950s, or 1960s often took the form of wild dancing, more recently it has been about solitary posing. This phenomenon is reflected, and perhaps encouraged, by MTV, which went on the air in 1981. In contrast with the rudimentary format of *American Bandstand*, in which the viewer seemed simply to be looking in on young people having fun dancing with one another, MTV videos tend to be more about brooding than participation. They are highly subjective, like dreams or psychodramas. They connect the viewer with a feeling, rather than with other people.

And while the writhing, leaping, and ecstatic movement of the mosh pit seems to be an extreme form of *American Bandstand*-style participation, it embodies a rather scary kind of community. One's own motions have little relationship to those of others. And there's substantial risk of injury. The society implied by the dance is not harmonious and made up of couples. Rather, it is violent and composed of isolated individuals who are, nevertheless, both seeking and repulsing contact with others. If this sounds like a vision of American society as a whole, that's not surprising. Figuring out what things are really like is one of the tasks of youth. Then they frighten their elders by acting it out.

When a multinational company that sells to the young asked marketing psychologist Stan Gross to study teenagers around the country, he concluded after hundreds of interviews and exercises that the majority of young people embraced an extreme if inchoate individualism. Most believe that just about every institution they come in contact with is stupid. When asked to choose an ideal image for themselves, the majority selected a picture that depicted what might be described as confident alienation. The figure sits, comfortably apart from everything, his eyes gazing out of the image at something unknown and distant.

Such studies are done, of course, not to reform the young but to sell to them. And the collective impact of such knowledge of the young has been the proliferation of advertising that encourages young people not to believe anything—even advertising—and to express their superiority by purchasing the product that's willing to admit its own spuriousness.

The distance between spontaneous expression and large-scale commercial exploitation has never been shorter. Creators of youth fashion, such as Nike, go so far as to send scouts to the ghetto to take pictures of what young people are wearing on the streets and writing on the walls. Nike seeks to reflect the latest sensibilities, both in its products and its advertising. The company feeds the imagery right back to those who created it, offering them something they cannot afford as a way of affirming themselves.

35   One result of this quick feedback is that visual symbols become detached from their traditional associations and become attached to something else. Rappers, having made droopy pants stylish in the suburbs, began to wear preppie sportswear, and brand names like Tommy Hilfiger and Nautica became badges of both WASP and hip-hop sensibilities. Thus, even when the fashions don't change, their meaning does. Such unexpected shifts in the meaning of material goods cannot be entirely manipulated by adults. But marketers have learned that they must be vigilant in order to profit from the changes when they come.

More overtly than in the past, many of today's young are looking for extreme forms of expression. This quest is just as apparent in sports, for example, as in rock culture. The 1996 Atlanta Olympics began with an exhibition of extreme cycling and extreme skating. These and other extreme sports, categorized collectively as "X-Games," have become a cable television fixture because they draw teenage males, an otherwise elusive audience. "Extreme" was one of the catchwords of the 1990s, and it became, by 1996, the most common word in newly registered trade names, attached either to products aimed at youth or which sought to embody youthfulness.

Young people are caught in a paradox. They drive themselves to extremes to create space in which to be themselves. Yet the commercial machine they think they're escaping is always on their back, ready to sell them something new.

Thomas Hine points to a social dynamic in which "extreme" forms of cultural expression such as tattooing and body piercing are meant to affirm group identities but, from an adult perspective, only reinforce the view that young people "are not ready for adult responsibility." What is the lure, for young people, of such extreme expressions? What cultural meanings do tattoos and body piercing carry?

SUGGESTIONS FOR DISCUSSION

1. Thomas Hine uses the opening anecdote about goth teens and Disneyland to announce the theme of this piece. As Hine presents it, what is this story meant to represent about the relations between teenagers and adults? What further examples and evidence does Hine offer in the rest of the selection to support his point?

2. Consider your high school or college. What "tribes" are represented? Develop a classification of the various groups. What do you see as the leading ways in which groups of young people define themselves? What are the meanings of the identities they take on?

What are the relationships among the various groups? What are the various groups' relationship to adult society?

3. Notice how Hine's perspective differs from Arlie Russell Hochschild's in the previous reading selection. Hochschild is interested in characterizing the collective mood of a generation, while Hine sees instead diverse "tribes of youth" defined by different styles of dress, music, body ornamentation, extracurricular activity, drug use, and sexual practices, as well as racial and ethnic markers. Compare the two perspectives. What does each bring into view about young people? What does each neglect?

SUGGESTIONS FOR WRITING

1. Write an essay that classifies the various groups (or "tribes") of youth culture at the high school you attended or your college. Describe the leading groups, their styles, behaviors, values, and attitudes. After providing an overview of the groups, explain their relationship to each other and to the adult society that surrounds them.

2. Hine suggests that some of the groupings of youth culture are seen as a threat by adult society. Consider what Hine thinks is the source of this fear. Why would adults be so worried about young people? What exactly is at stake in the fears and anxieties of the older generation?

3. At the end of this selection, Hine says that young people are "caught in a paradox": No matter how much they rebel against adult society to create a space for themselves, the "commercial machine" they're trying to escape from reincorporates their cultural styles in the form of new products and merchandise. Do you think this is a reasonable assessment? Why or why not? Write an essay that explains your answer—and whether you think young people can establish their own way of doing things, independent of the market and the workings of adult society.

IT'S TIME TO GROW UP—LATER

— *Sharon Jayson*

This reading selection provides a good example of a newspaper feature article. "It's Time to Grow Up—Later" appeared in *USA Today* on September 30, 2004. Notice that Sharon Jayson is not so much reporting a news event as identifying a trend in contemporary American culture, in this case to prolong adolescence. Jayson draws on interviews with young people and with experts who have studied the transition between adolescence and adulthood.

SUGGESTION FOR READING   As you read, consider the various types of evidence Sharon Jayson presents to establish a "new phase of life"—the gap between adolescence and adulthood—as a significant trend in contemporary culture. There are interviews with young people, interviews with sociologists and psychologists, and quantitative information displayed in the two boxes "What's 'grown up'?" and "Times have changed." Consider how these various sources of evidence add credibility and authority to Jayson's feature article.

1 Today's twentysomethings won't have the lives their parents had. And that's OK by them.

They're going to school longer, delaying marriage and children, job-hopping and apartment-swapping. They're also moving back home after college to save money, traveling to faraway places to work and generally taking "me" time to decide what they want their futures to be.

While their baby boomer parents lament that they've somehow gone wrong, experts studying why these kids aren't more like their parents' generation say there's a clear explanation: It takes longer to grow up these days.

What's "grown up"?

Many measure it in milestones: finishing school, leaving home, getting married, having a child, reaching financial independence. Those who had reached these goals by age 30:

Source: American Sociological Association

Researchers, sociologists and psychologists say there's a new phase of life—only recently acknowledged—that covers this gap between adolescence and adulthood. What was once the purview of academia has crossed into the popular culture. A plethora of how-to-cope books are declaring a world-wide shift in what it means to be an adult.

5   "It's the harbinger of a basic transformation of adulthood," says James Côté, a sociologist at the University of Western Ontario who has coined the term "youthhood." "The traditional adulthood of duty and self-sacrifice is becoming more and more a thing of the past."

Recent findings published by the American Sociological Association and based on U.S. Census data show a sharp decline in the percentage of young adults who have finished school, left home, gotten married, had a child and reached financial independence, considered typical standards of adulthood. In 2000, 46% of women and 31% of men had reached those markers by age 30, vs. 77% of women and 65% of men at the same age in 1960.

"What I'm talking about is very widespread and across countries and not peculiar to the United States," says Frank Furstenberg Jr., a University of Pennsylvania sociologist who headed the research team. "It isn't just an aberration. It's become normal behavior."

Shana Finkelstein, a May graduate from the University of Massachusetts–Amherst with a degree in communications and legal studies, says her family has been supportive—even though she's changing her mind "daily" about going to law school. She is also toying with becoming an event planner. Until she decides, Finkelstein is waiting tables at The Cheesecake Factory in Cambridge.

"I'm not in a rush to get to a job that I may or may not like," she says. "I'm 22. What's the rush? At this point, I don't really know what I want to do."

IT'S A TOUGHER CLIMB TO THE TOP

10   In the 1970s, a bachelor's degree could launch a career and support a family. Not anymore. Now, graduate school is almost a necessity and that means greater expenses, often when students are still saddled with college loans. More years of schooling also mean a delay entering the workforce. In this down economy, there's also stiffer competition for jobs. Financial independence is but a dream for many.

The need to save money brought 23-year-old Lindsey Engelman home to Austin after earning a bachelor's degree in legal studies in June from the University of California–Santa Cruz. She initially moved to New York, but when jobs and living arrangements got too tangled, she came

Times Have Changed

Median age of first marriage

Men

Year	Age
1970	23.2
2003	27.1

Women

Year	Age
1970	20.8
2003	25.3

Median age of women for first childbirth

Year	Age
1970	22.1
2003	24.8

Heads of household ages 25–34

Year	Percent
1970	20.7%
2003	18.6%

Young adults living with their parents (ages 18–24)

Year	Percent
1970	47.3%
2003	50.3%

Unmarried cohabitation

Year	Number
1970	523,000
2003	5.1 million

College completed by people 25 and older

4 or more years (in millions)

Year	Value
1970	12.0
2003	50.4

1–3 years (in millions)

Year	Value
1970	11.2
2003	46.9

Source: U.S. Census; Bureau of Labor Statistics; National Center for Health Statistics

home, got a job at a law office and is saving for a move next year to South America to work for a non-profit. Graduate school in public policy is part of her plan.

"I am tremendously proud of the idealism that Lindsey has and the dedication to making a difference in the world," says her mother, Merle Dover, a 54-year-old attorney. "But then the parent in me comes out and says, 'That's fine, but you're going to have to support yourself.' "

Engelman is among those some call "boomerang kids" because they return home after college. According to Twentysomething Inc., a market researcher that tracks youth trends, 65% of this year's grads expect to live with their parents after earning degrees.

Katie Foster, 22, did more than live at home after graduating in December with a psychology degree from Austin College in Sherman, Texas. In the future, she plans to head to graduate school. In the interim, Foster, who graduated a semester early, returned to the elementary, middle and high schools she attended, this time working as a substitute teacher.

15 "Since it was my 'freebie' semester, I didn't feel the need to have a 'real job,' " she said of her life as a sub from Nabari, Japan. She's now teaching high school English for the Japanese government.

Debate over what's driving these changing attitudes is fodder for academic conferences, research grants and books for this first generation of parents living through an odd dichotomy. Their highly educated, seemingly sophisticated, media-savvy and worldly kids just don't seem very mature compared with where they were at the same point in their lives.

"We were in a hurry to graduate, get out, get a job, get married. I didn't know there was anything else you could do," says Finkelstein's mother, Abby, of Houston. She is 48 and was married at 23. "These kids are not in a hurry to do those big things."

GETTING IT "RIGHT" NOW

Society is also an enabler. The advent of birth control pills led to changes in sexual mores, with less pressure for marriage, Twenty-somethings have seen their parents' early marriages end in divorce and the jobs their parents thought they'd have for 30 years end with corporate downsizing. As boomers resist aging and watch TV programs like *Nip/Tuck* that glorify youth, their offspring are paying attention.

"Twentysomethings are proving they want to get it 'right' now," says Alexandra Robbins, co-author of the 2001 book *Quarterlife* Crisis. "Our generation does not want to make our parents' generation's mistakes."

20   Terri Apter, a social psychologist at the University of Cambridge in England, says the young people she has dubbed "thresholders" are not the product of overly indulgent boomers spoiling their kids.

"What worries me is that a lot of parents think they need tough love and they should not be helping them. That ain't so," she says. "These young people need a lot of practical and emotional support from their parents."

Matt Twyman, 23, says he got a bit of initial financial help from his family after he graduated in December with a bachelor's degree in physics from the University of Texas–Austin. Right now, he's working two jobs and facing about $16,000 in college loans. Still, he and his girlfriend of almost three years returned just six weeks ago from a three-month trip to New Zealand.

"I know I'll end up doing something strongly related to physics," he said. "I wanted a cool down period to decide."

He's studying for the GRE in November, in case he decides on graduate school. Meanwhile, he's working at a climbing gym and UT library storage facility to pay the bills.

25   Jeffrey Jensen Arnett, a developmental psychologist who has studied this age group since 1992, explores the mind-set of young people in a new book, *Emerging Adulthood: The Winding Road from the Late Teens Through the Twenties.*

"They're not as mature because they're not required to be," he says. "It's really the society and culture as a whole."

Sociologists expect this prolonged adolescence to be solidified by the economic decline and jobs displaced by technology, which may mean job preparation will take longer. Also, with longer life spans, people will be on the job into their golden years.

Arnett notes that some emerging adults forged a clear path and knew early what they wanted to do. They are the exception, he says, estimating that only 10% to 20% of those interviewed for his book had settled lives by their mid-20s.

"This is a generation that has grown up in an accelerated culture and forced them to be older before they're ready," says David Morrison, president of Twentysomething Inc. "Now that they have their independence, they are going to squeeze every ounce of that sponge before they settle down."

SUGGESTIONS FOR DISCUSSION

1. The task that Sharon Jayson sets for herself in this feature article is to establish the gap between adolescence and adulthood as a social reality—a trend that can be verified with supporting evidence. Identify the various sources of evidence Jayson draws on. How does each help to establish the credibility of the article? Do some sources carry more authority than others? If so, why is this? What gives some sources more authority than others?

2. What explanations does Jayson offer to explain the growing gap between adolescence and adulthood? Identify the source of the various explanations. Do these explanations have approximately equal authority? Do some seem more persuasive than others? What gives an explanation persuasiveness?

3. How does the article represent the relationship between today's twentysomethings and their baby-boomer parents? What role does the article suggest this relationship between generations plays in the prolonged gap between adolescence and adulthood? Are there other ways to make sense of the relationship?

SUGGESTIONS FOR WRITING

1. Imagine you are writing an e-mail or a letter about "It's Time to Grow Up—Later" to a friend at another college. Assume your friend hasn't read the article. In your correspondence, explain the major findings that the article presents. Add your own observations about twentysomethings and the passage between adolescence and adulthood that are pertinent. Then explain what you see as the significance of the article to young people in general and to you, your friend, and others you know in particular.

2. Use the information contained in "It's Time to Grow Up—Later" to write a commentary about the dilemmas of twentysomethings and the transition to adulthood that would appear on an op-ed page in a local or national newspaper that's read by a broad audience of various ages and backgrounds. Your task here is to go beyond simply presenting the information to explaining its significance. What are the larger implications for contemporary American culture of the prolonged gap between adolescence and adulthood? Keep in mind the nature of your readership—and how your commentary can intersect their interests and concerns.

3. Conduct an informal survey by interviewing ten to fifteen seniors at your college about their plans following graduation. You can do this project individually or in a group, depending on your instructor's directions. Write a report that presents the results of your research. Set up the report by explaining the findings in "It's Time to Grow Up—Later" as background. Present what you've found about the plans of graduating seniors and explain how and why these plans conform to or depart from the national trends established in Sharon Jayson's article. Close your report by noting the significance of your research and the larger issues involved in the transition from college to adulthood.

TRAPPED IN DECLINE CULTURE

— Margaret Morganroth Gullette

Margaret Morganroth Gullette is a resident scholar at the Women's Studies Research Center at Brandeis University and the author of *Declining to Decline: Cultural Combat and the Politics of Midlife* (1997), which won the Emily Toth award as the best feminist book on popular culture, and *Aged by Culture* (2004), from which "Trapped in Decline Culture" was adapted for publication in the October 25, 2004, issue of *In These Times.* Gullette is a pioneer in the field of Age Studies, a new field of inquiry that seeks to understand how age shapes people's identities and how ageism or the fear of decline influences American culture.

SUGGESTION FOR READING   Margaret Morganroth Gullette opens with an anecdote that describes children's experience at the "Face Aging" exhibit at the Boston Museum of Science. In many ways, the rest of the article amounts to unpacking the meanings of the anecdote. As you read, consider how Gullette draws out these meanings. Notice, in particular, how she uses two questions—"What exactly is wrong here?" and "What does increased longevity and improved health accomplish, if so many people are afraid of being old?"—to mark the two main sections of the article.

1 The "Face Aging" booth at the Boston Museum of Science attracted the longest lines of children. Access was forbidden to those over 15, so I watched from outside. The youngsters had their photographs taken and soon their digitized image appeared on a TV monitor. Then, tapping

a button like a VCR remote, each child could call up simulations of what she or he would supposedly look like at one-year intervals up to their 60s. In seconds the computer added pouches, rouged skin and blotches; faces became elongated and then wider and then saggy; lines became heavier. Boys lost hair. Hair turned gray. The heads of both boys and girls grew and then shrank.

The children came out distracted, most edging away fast, not knowing what had happened to them. One 8-year-old girl moaned, "I don't want to get old!" A boy said about another child, "He's disgusting at 42."

Everything promised scientific truth—its location in the Museum of Science; the title of the show, *Secrets of Aging*; the prestigious technologies involved. But next to nothing was scientific. The increasing facial redness as the children aged was an accident of the Kodak film they used. The blotches were unintentional, developing from freckles, moles and pimples the kids already had on their faces. The software, by C.O.R.E. Digital, which specializes in TV animation, added the wrinkles, swags and grayness.

The programmer wouldn't say how the designers conceptualized "aging." But they started with a photo of an 8-year-old girl and asked the staff if the image of her at 60-something was believable. The responses made them add more effects. These were arbitrary decisions. As Digital's project manager observed: "It was only entertainment. We streamed together six or seven different ideas; we're a special-effects studio."

5   What exactly is wrong here?

First of all, the software engineers didn't ask, "What's the algorithm for making people look more beautiful, expressive or individual as they grow up?" because they worked from our culture's preexisting notions of decline. Gerontologists on the Science Museum Exhibit Collaborative didn't ask, as age critics should, "What future does this project for children? What story of aging does it tell?" They may not believe decline should be the acceptable life-course

narrative for the young, but had they been warier about American age culture, the taunting title, "*Face* Aging," would have raised an alarm.

People don't realize that aging is a narrative. Where age is concerned, we are made to focus endlessly on the body, as if we had no minds, concepts or attitudes about age that influence how we look to ourselves. Before anything called aging happens in the body, it is a set of stories children hear about their future. These stories create expectations, lay the ground rules of life, shape what it means to be human.

Prospective age narrative in a normal American childhood is about progress, not decline. In a narrative of progress, the implicit meanings of aging run from development to survival, resilience, recovery and then on to collective resistance to decline forces.

Adults—middle-class people, mostly women—read books that tell them how to "get over" getting older, how to be successful at retirement. But such positive aging isn't on display at the booth. Its monitor provides a startling example of decline forecasting: a wreck foretold about each and every tender body. "Face Aging" suggests that adults can't believe in aging-as-progress anymore; aging-as-decline is the default story.

10   Something historic has changed, some new era has begun.

What does increased longevity and improved health accomplish, if so many people are afraid of being old?

The real truth is that we are aged by culture. In our American case, the dominant culture reflects the needs and viewpoints of international capitalism in an era of globalization and inequality. The economy downsizes people at midlife; "anti-aging" ads and surgeries address people in their 40s and 30s; businesses outsource not just manufacturing, but white-collar jobs held by educated middle-class people. All of these cultural phenomena superannuate us prematurely, long before old age or retirement. Seniority systems—which provide the economic basis for respecting midlife workers—are eroding as labor unions weaken. Patriarchy used to protect midlife men in the middle and upper classes, but now—if we follow male midlife economic stagnation over the last 30 years—patriarchy seems weak in the face of capitalism's race to the bottom.

Age is politicized to explain history: growing inequality, rising displacement, high unemployment, job scarcity. Baby Boomers allegedly war against Generation X because they are jealous of their youth, while younger people are told that aging Boomers hold the good jobs and only as they retire will they be available to the young. People aging into their middle years are told they are under-skilled, overpaid, narcissistic and over-entitled. Age is doing the same kinds of dirty work as gender, race and sexuality.

Despite the American Dream, decades of feminist anti-ageism and the much touted power of the Boomers, American age culture uglifies time and passes off its squint as truth. Now we are telling our underlying national narrative of decline to people under 15. Economically and psychologically, we are losing the progress narrative of aging to which our national wealth, improved health and longevity should entitle us. Children are being prepared for decline as their future.

15   Thoughtful people wonder why we are so obsessed by age in America, why it seems so hard to hold on to respect for aging, to the values that make the life course feel valuable.

Children feel helpless looking into the crystal ball of aging because they don't know it's a fake. But how much better off are the grownups? Adults too are being made to stumble along the life course. The pain of decline, unless we are very privileged, will hit us long before the body begins to fail. Sexism, racism and homophobia are devastating. So is decline. Worse than ageism, worse than middle ageism, it is backing down the life course to ever-younger ages. We won't need anti-aging products if we can identify the forces that endanger us. We need political resistance and will.

My hope is that thoughtful people learn to fight collectively against the forces producing decline. Perhaps it is utopian to imagine our children and ourselves feeling at home in the life course at every age. But no lesser goal can drive us to maintain the systems like seniority that work in favor of American age culture and progress narrative, and to overthrow the forces that can still be fought.

SUGGESTIONS FOR DISCUSSION

1. Consider the two main questions Margaret Morganroth Gullette asks about the "Face Aging" exhibit—"What exactly is wrong here?" and "What does increased longevity and improved health accomplish, if so many people are afraid of being old?" How does the answer she gives to the first question lead her to the second question? How does the answer to the second question set up her concluding remarks?

2. Gullette suggests that before "anything called aging happens in the body, it is an endless set of stories children hear about their future." Gullette mentions two general types of story—"aging-as-progress" and "aging-as-decline"—but she does not give any specific examples. What does she mean by "aging-as-progress" and "aging-as-decline"? What examples can you think of to illustrate each type of story? How do such stories shape children's attitudes toward aging?

3. How does Gullette explain the fact that so many Americans are afraid of being old? How does she relate this fear of aging to "the needs and viewpoints of international capital in the era of globalization and inequality"? What does she mean by saying that age is "politicized to explain history"?

SUGGESTIONS FOR WRITING

1. Write an essay that explains the cultural sources of your own feelings about aging. You'll need first of all, of course, to identify how you feel about aging. Don't assume these

feelings are simple and straightforward. They may well be complicated, conflicted, contradictory, ambivalent. Next consider how these feelings have been shaped by various sources in American culture: stories you heard as a child, the media, advertising, religion, visual images, and so on. Your task is to explain how these stories and images of aging influenced your perspective on the life cycle.

2. It is hard to deny that Americans are obsessed by age. The question over which people are likely to differ is why is this so—why are Americans so obsessed? Write an essay that presents your own point of view on the question. Incorporate Gullette's explanation of Americans' obsession into the essay and point out what it helps us see and what it might overlook. Use it to find points of agreement and disagreement and to clarify your own thinking.

3. Take seriously Gullette's analysis of America as the "decline culture." First explain what she means by the term and what the consequences are. Next, explain what could be done to change things—to undermine, resist, or redirect the decline culture and present alternative views of aging.

4. In September, 2004, Dove, the global beauty products brand, launched the Campaign for Real Beauty to raise questions about standards of beauty and to serve as the starting point for widening the definition and discussion of beauty. According to Dove, only 2% of women described themselves as beautiful in recent global survey. Consider the two images of women shown above. How does the Campaign for Real Beauty ask viewers to reconsider their assumptions about beauty and age? How would current notions of beauty have to be revised to see "real beauty" in these women's faces? Would a more expansive sense of beauty really do much to change attitudes toward aging?

WIRED CULTURE   Instant Messaging

To learn more about this technology
and communication, visit
www.ablongman.com/george/103

New digital technologies—cell phones, e-mail, wireless laptops, blackberries, instant messaging (IM) systems, teleconferencing, and so on—have changed the way people communicate with each other in contemporary culture. It is easy enough, of course, to identify the technical advances in these new means of communication and what they enable at work and in everyday life. But there is more involved than just what you can do in the new wired culture. There are also questions to ask about what wired culture does to the nature of communication itself. IM offers an interesting example of some of the key ways that digital culture is changing how people communicate with each other—and, in this sense, offers an opportunity to think about how we as humans are wired into the very technologies we use. Three terms are especially useful in thinking about the dynamics of communication in wired culture: immediacy, connectivity, and interactivity.

- *Immediacy* refers to the sheer speed of communication—the difference, say, between e-mail and snail mail. The time lapse between sending and receiving messages is reduced to nearly zero.
- *Connectivity* is the felt sense that digital communication links individuals to larger networks of people and information. The world seems immediately available and present through the workings of wired culture.
- *Interactivity* means that the capacity to respond is built into the technology. It's the difference, for example, between watching television and surfing the Web: people feel more like participants than spectators.

These terms can be used to think about a range of new media. The following reading selection begins to look at the processes of digital communication by focusing on instant messaging. Part of the work here is to push on to further questions about wired culture.

CONFESSIONS OF AN INSTANT MESSENGER

— *Conor Boyland*

Conor Boyland was a sophomore at Northeastern University when "Confessions of an Instant Messenger" was published on the op-ed page of the *Boston Globe* in 2005. As you will see, Boyland uses the genre of the confession to call attention to his own experience in order to make a wider point about instant messaging.

SUGGESTION FOR READING   As you read, notice how Conor Boyland uses the metaphor of addiction to characterize his behavior online. Consider how this helps him organize his confession and bring out his main point.

1   I was sitting at my computer, and I realized something: I spend way too much time sitting at my computer. Granted, I'm a college student, and my options on where to sit in my room are limited, but that just makes it easier to justify the time I waste every day online, mostly instant messaging. Admit it, you do it too. We all do, to different degrees. It's just one of the most commonly accepted things to do when you have a computer; "I think, therefore IM."

It seems fairly harmless, but it snowballs, and before you know it, you can't stop or you'll go into withdrawal. When you get to the point where you can't take a shower without putting up that witty away message that says, "I'm all hot and steamy," you're officially addicted—welcome to the club. You're also really sick.

One of the lamest aspects of addiction to AIM, America Online's instant messaging system, is that even if you have people on your buddy list you haven't talked to in years, you can still keep up on their day-to-day activities by checking their away messages when you're bored. Or when you're doing homework. Or when you're supposed to be in class. The funny thing is, some of them are probably doing it to you too, but it doesn't matter. Next thing you know, you're fiending for recent pictures of them, who they're dating, where they're living, and what their favorite movies are.

Enter: The facebook. If AIM is a gateway drug, the facebook is Internet crack. If you're in college, you know the deal: upload your picture, add in some interests, list every single band you've ever listened to, girls write down your favorite "I love shopping and my best friends" quote from "Sex and the City," and guys write down that you like "Scarface" and "The Da Vinci Code." Then you browse through different profiles and compile a list of friends, some of which you know and some of which you've (maybe) met once but never talked to after that. You can even hunt down people from your hometown that now go to other colleges. That way you can ignore over the Internet the same people you used to ignore in high school!

5   If you're one of those people who like to stay up on the latest trends, like striped shirts and quoting Napoleon Dynamite, you're probably thinking, "Idiot! Facebook is so last semester, gosh!" Well, there's a new friend-making site for you folks called Catch27, which is basically the facebook with attitude. You actually trade friends here based on how hot they are, and if you can't get hot friends on your own you can even pay money for them. "99Â¢for a Wax Pack of 3: just like real life, only cheaper," writes the site's creator, E. Jean Carroll, who is either really desperate for friends or is laughing all the way to the bank. Now, don't get me wrong here, if you want to spend money to create an online list of "friends" you've never actually met, that's your own business. Just remember (and I quote my roommate on this one), "FBI agents make the sexiest cyber babes."

I don't have a problem with gimmicky websites, but I do take issue with the rapidly growing trend of communicating online rather than in person. I hate it, but I find the temptation increasingly hard to resist. When it comes down to it, reading someone's profile is so much easier than actually talking to them, and it carries no risk of them not liking you. Therein lies the problem: Online directories like the facebook make it possible to find out quite a lot about a person without ever speaking to them, which not only appeals to stalkers but ruins your social skills as well. Actually, I shouldn't speak for anybody else, but I admit that mine have certainly suffered.

On top of that, browsing the facebook can quickly go from being fun to becoming a compulsion, just like with AIM. It's not that we don't know this compulsive behavior is unhealthy; it's just another one of those guilty pleasures you know is bad for you but that you don't care enough about to stop doing. The Internet is so addicting that in many ways it has now become the most popular way to contact new people. A friend of mine met a cute girl at a party recently, and as he was leaving he told her to look him up on the facebook, no joke. I waited until he left and then got her *phone number.*

If drug addiction damages your mental capacities, then Internet addiction damages your social ones (Do you really think my friend has any chance with that girl?), and as with any addiction, admitting that you have a problem is only the first step. I'm just as guilty as the next guy, so I'm not going to say something preachy like "seize the day," or "get out and live life to the fullest," but I will say this: We need to sign off AIM and facebook and get up off our asses a little more often. Go run around outside, read a book, or—God forbid—talk to a stranger. Practice the dying art of conversation.

Communicating online is convenient, but no amount of smileys or pokes can substitute for real human connection, which is far more worthy of our time than anonymous facebook connections (of which I have 2,137 by the way). As for the compulsive behavior, I'm quitting cold turkey. I just have to put one more witty away message up, one last fix, and then I'm done. TTYL.

SUGGESTIONS FOR DISCUSSION

1. Consider Conor Boyland's use of the addiction metaphor. This is certainly in keeping with the genre of the confession. Like any metaphor, however, the notion of addiction will bring some things to light while ignoring or suppressing others. What does the addiction metaphor enable Boyland to show? What does it leave out? What other metaphors would you propose to characterize instant messaging?

2. Notice that Boyland does not say much about instant messaging as a form of literacy. How would you describe instant messaging in its relations to writing, speaking, and reading? How is it similar to and different from earlier forms of communication, such as the letter or the telephone? What do you see as the significance of these differences and similarities?

3. Evaluate the conclusions that Boyland draws about instant messaging being a "substitute for real human communication." Notice he does not define exactly what he means by "real" communication or why instant messaging is not "real" but seems to expect his readers will understand his meaning. What are the shared but unstated assumptions Boyland is counting on here? Do they seem reasonable? What other assumptions might you or other readers hold?

SUGGESTIONS FOR WRITING

1. Write an essay that analyzes instant messaging (or another form of new digital communication). Your task here is to explain what the new technology is, what it does, and how people use it. Hold off on making the kind of judgments Boyland makes about whether the technology is good or bad. Concentrate instead on understanding why and how it changes the way people communicate and what it reveals about the new wired culture.

2. Write a second essay on the same topic you chose in Writing Suggestion #1. This time, however, use the confession genre in the way Boyland does to draw on your own experience and make a judgment. (You might also read Andrew Sullivan's "Society Is Dead: We Have Retreated into the iWorld," in Chapter 5, for another example of the technology confession.)

3. Write an essay that examines the addiction metaphor Boyland uses. How does the metaphor relate to the immediacy of online communication and the connectivity of wired culture? Is the term adequate, in your view, to characterize the use of instant messaging? What other metaphor or metaphors would you propose?

PERSPECTIVES

The New Momism: Interviews with Susan J. Douglas and Judith Warner

Figuring out the best way to raise children has long been a central topic in American culture, generating books of advice such as Dr. Benjamin Spock's classic, articles in women's magazines, reports from panels of experts, new trends such as "attachment parenting," and lots of anxiety. Childrearing, for the most part, has traditionally been seen as the domain of mothers, though the role of fathers has also been the subject of intense discussion. The very notion of motherhood, of course, has a deep cultural resonance and a nearly sacred character. Still, feminism, changes in the American family, and pressures on women to hold jobs and raise children have called into question conventional understandings of what it means to be a mother.

The two readings that follow take a look at motherhood in contemporary American culture. Both are interviews with noted authors, Susan J. Douglas and Judith Warner, that took place when their new books on motherhood appeared in 2004 and 2005. As you will see, both Douglas and Warner offer critical views, from a feminist perspective, of the recent idealization of motherhood and its effect on women. At the same time, Douglas and Warner differ in their analyses of the cultural sources of this idealization.

THE MOMMY MYSTIQUE

— An Interview with Susan J. Douglas by Amy Reiter

Susan J. Douglas is Catherine Neafie Kellogg Professor of Communication Studies at the University of Michigan and the author of *Listening In: Radio and the American Imagination* (2004) and *Where the Girls Are: Growing Up Female with the Mass Media* (1994). The following interview by Amy Reiter about Douglas's most recent book, *The Mommy Myth: The Idealization of Motherhood and How It Has Undermined Women* (2004), coauthored by Meredith W. Michaels, professor of philosophy at Smith College, appeared on salon.com in February 2004.

SUGGESTION FOR READING As you read, notice how Susan J. Douglas defines the "new momism," what causes it, and what effects it has on women. Consider the evidence Douglas offers as support for her analysis.

1   When Jennifer Lopez holds forth, as she often has, on how she won't really feel complete until she births a few babies, or when new mother Sarah Jessica Parker proclaims, as she recently has, that her infant son is a "wonderful burden," whatever that means, are the mothers of America getting hosed?

Susan J. Douglas, who with Meredith W. Michaels has co-authored the buzz-gathering book "The Mommy Myth: The Idealization of Motherhood and How It Has Undermined Women," thinks so. And it pisses her off.

"If you're like us—mothers with an attitude problem—you may be getting increasingly irritable about this chasm between the ridiculous, honey-hued ideals of perfect motherhood in the mass media and the reality of mothers' everyday lives," Douglas and Michaels write. "And you may also be worn down by media images that suggest that however much you do for and love your kids, it is never enough."

Using dual tools—fantasy and fear—the media has created a standard for mothers that is wholly impossible to live up to—and spawned a generation of guilt-plagued, anxious mamas who are far worse off than their mothers before them.

5   "The Martha Stewartization of America, in which we are meant to sculpt the carrots we put into our kids' lunches into the shape of peonies and build funhouses for them in the backyard" has set the women's movement back decades, say the authors, both of whom balance careers in academia and motherhood.

Douglas and Michaels dream of a day when the mothers of the world rise up, raise their fists at their televisions and at Catherine Zeta-Jones looking fit and well-rested as she snuggles her latest nanny-nurtured bundle of joy on the cover of People magazine and yell, "Give me a %$#$% break."

A modest dream, to be sure. In fact, some might call it a bit pat or naive. After all, it's hard to see how talking back to your TV and shouting from the rooftops will change much. But Douglas, a feminist, insists that "naming and denouncing the enemy" is a "crucial" first step, noting the galvanizing power of Betty Friedan's 1963 book, "The Feminine Mystique," and the consciousness-raising movement it helped spawn.

During a recent visit to New York, Douglas sat down with Salon to discuss the corrosive effect of the media on mothers' self-esteem and her contention that the small acts of rebellion she prescribes will lead the way to a mothers' movement of epic proportions.

In "The Mommy Myth," you talk a lot about a trend you call the "new momism." What exactly is it and why is it so pernicious?

10   The "new momism" is an extremely romantic and demanding myth of the perfect mother in which the standards for success are so high that no woman can achieve them. People then say, "Well, what about June Cleaver? What about the '50s, isn't this the same?" And if it was the same, that would be bad enough. Who wants to go back to 1956? But it's actually worse. I mean, June Cleaver was not expected to drill the Beaver with algebra flashcards when he was 6 months old. June Cleaver was not expected to drive 10 hours round trip to a soccer match. June Cleaver wasn't expected to home-school and, by the way, look sexy the whole time doing it. So even June Cleaver couldn't meet these standards today, which are absolutely through the roof. So it's actually different from the '50s: It's more intense.

How did we get here?

First of all, the media discovered that the family was changing in the late '70s, early '80s, and children became a big story. But *endangered* children became an even bigger story, and so you got these media panics. You got sensationalized stories about children in danger: razor blades in Halloween candy, pajamas that caught on fire by themselves almost, day-care centers staffed by Satanists and pedophiles. That was all out of proportion to the risks that real children were facing, but it made mothers terrified to let their kids out of their sight. So fear was important.

The other thing was fantasy. Again, the media responded to women when we were looking for role models. Who's a better role model, in some ways, than a celebrity mom because celebrity mothers were working outside the home, but they were having children. So we got the explosion in the '80s of the celebrity mom profile, something you just didn't see in '70s women's magazines.

What's so bad about the celebrity mom profile?

15   They create this impossible ideal of motherhood. You know, I had a kid that didn't sleep. She got up at 4:30 and was up for the day, so I'd be at the supermarket at 7:30 in the morning, exhausted—I'd already been up for hours—in my husband's sweat pants, the only thing that fit, sweat shirt covered with spit-up, hair that hadn't seen a comb in two days, a kid screaming. I'm at the checkout line and there's some celebrity mom saying, "Motherhood is sexy." There she is, her perfect hair, her perfect makeup, no spit-up—her kid's even made up, you know? The inside of her house is decorated in *white furniture*. She's got a perfect, doting husband. And you're there, like, "What is wrong with this picture?"

But it laid out a fantasy that a lot of us wanted to enter. A fantasy of a world where you could work and enjoy your children and it would be easy and stress free. Who doesn't want to go there? This fantasy of course helps sell magazines. But the norms and the standards for motherhood that are in these celebrity mom profiles are also completely impossible. Occasionally you get the reference to the SWAT team of nannies and personal assistants who are making this woman's life possible. But for mothers who don't have the SWAT team, it's a different story.

What about the role of race in all this? While the book primarily focuses on white middle- and upper-middle-class mothers, you mention that the "new momism" is something

of an exclusive white club and that women of color have been portrayed as the anti-new-mom.

At the same time that the celebrity mom was going through the roof in the media, so was the welfare mother. There were awful attacks on welfare mothers from the right. Welfare mothers were supposedly responsible for everything wrong in America: [drugs, crime, loss of productivity]. And of course most of the welfare mothers that we saw in the media were African-American women.

The stories were sensational, they were newsworthy, so they got focused on. And everybody thought, Oh my god, welfare is comprised entirely of African-American women who come from three generations of welfare families and who refuse to work and are neglectful of their children. The number of welfare mothers who came from several generations of welfare mothers, in real life? That's a tiny fraction of welfare mothers.

20 It's such an awful stereotype. I think one of the worst things that emerged from the '80s was the stereotype of the African-American mother as a bad mother. Because of course we didn't see middle-class African-American women, of which there are some, by the way, who love their children and are fabulous mothers. Look, we're all in this together. If there are poor women whose children aren't getting enough to eat, they're going to crappy schools, they're learning a way of violence very young, that's not just a heartbreak for them, it's bad for us as a society, and it's morally wrong.

To highlight the contrast, you give a great example in the book of how Christie Brinkley is never described as having "three children by three different men," but if she were a black woman on welfare, she would be.

Right.

Can we really blame the media for our sense of maternal inadequacy and anxiety?

We can blame the media and marketing. Mothers and kids really got discovered in the '80s and '90s, when niche marketing took over.

Kids started getting divided into ever and ever smaller niches and there's a load of products that you're supposed to buy for each developmental stage. And if you don't by them, your kid's left in the dust. If you fail to buy a Leap Pad or Einstein Junior or the correct teething ring, 20 years from now, your kid will be working at the Dunkin' Donuts and the other kids will be CEOs.

25 Politics have also played a big role. In the '80s and beyond, the far right really slammed working mothers and single mothers, really sought to guilt-trip them under the frame of "family values," which by the way had nothing to do with supporting everyday families. And of course they were central to blocking anything resembling federal support for decent day care; paid maternity leave, which sounds scandalous in this country, but you know every other civilized country has paid maternity leave, some for up to a year; decent public schools; after-school programs; healthcare for everybody, including for little kids so parents don't have to worry about that. So mothers, rightly, looked around and they saw institutions collapsing all around them. And of course, what's a mother going to say? "I've got to pick up the slack." Mothers have been revered in rhetoric, but reviled in public policy.

You mention the vilification of the working mother by the far right. Do you see politicians on the left addressing the plight of these mothers at all?

I don't hear any of the Democratic candidates [for president] talking about women's issues. We had the so-called soccer mom in '96, whose vote people wanted to get. But they are not talking to us—and they should be. I really think mothers are realizing that politically we have not been seen as citizens. We've only been seen as consumers, not as a constituency. And that's got to change.

Have you ever been to Denmark?

No.

30 Oh, god. It'd break your heart. They have made a choice as a culture that's very different than the choices we've made as a society. Their

choice has been work is work and family is family—and family matters. So everybody leaves work between 4 and 5 o'clock. *Everybody.* Dads, moms. They go home and spend time with their families. You have a child, a baby nurse comes to your house once a week for, like, six weeks. So if you're not sure what you're doing, she helps you. Is their tax rate about 50 percent? Yeah. Would Americans put up with that? Probably not. But we can do a lot better than we're doing now. And once you see a culture in which there's really a commitment to family that makes it possible for fathers and mothers to work, it's a revelation.

It sounds great.

Well, you know, Japan, France, Norway, Sweden, they all have day-care centers for little kids, and they regard it not as a special interest for working mothers: They regard it as an investment in the future of the country because it's an investment in kids. If a kid goes into day care or nursery school when he or she is 2 or 3, by the time they get to kindergarten, they know their colors, they often know the alphabet, they've learned how to share with other kids, they've painted—all these cool things that are so enriching developmentally. Why don't we think that that's important? We should.

How did mothers get so disenfranchised?

I think they've been too busy dealing with their lives to notice or to take action. But there's an incipient mothers movement going on in this country. You can feel it. You can hear it. Women are joining organizations like the Motherhood Project, the Motherhood Movement and MOTHERS (Mothers Ought to Have Equal Rights). There are Web sites going up: the Welfare Warriors, the Children's Defense Fund, Ann Crittenden's Web site. Mothers are saying, "I've had it." And this is true of stay-at-home mothers as well as working mothers.

35 **In the book you talk about the "Mommy Wars" the media has created between "stay-at-home *moms*," which you point out is a friendly term, and "working mothers," more formal and distant.**

Right. I think it's a big red herring. Of course there are tensions and differences between stay-at-home mothers and working mothers. But the media has suggested that they have become mutually exclusive categories. You know, stay-at-home mothers have often been working mothers in the past. Working mothers have sometimes been stay-at-home mothers. We move back and forth between these categories. And in my limited experience, stay-at-home mothers and working mothers bail each other out all the time. We carpool together, we watch each other's kids. There's been a real divide and conquer in the media. We're supposed to be involved in this big catfight instead of saying, "What happened here?"

Are we mothers at all culpable here? Is it really Sarah Jessica Parker's and Catherine Zeta-Jones' fault that we're feeling so stressed out?

Look, images in the media don't come from Mars. It's not like somebody manufactures them out of some alien material. They come from what's in our culture. And people who work in the media are not all evil. Mass media is filled with all kinds of people, many of whom mean well—a lot of women work in the media too.

But there have been a series of very heavy-duty commercial pressures on television shows, on magazines, that have to do with selling products, that have to do with making women feel inadequate. After all, if you don't feel inadequate, why are you going to buy the next product. It's very important for selling things.

40 And if you talk to women who work in magazines, for example, or women who produce TV shows, they'll tell you how they feel besieged by this stuff, too, but they have to put out certain kinds of stories, certain kinds of idealized images. Then these scare stories come out and they gain traction. And so what happens to the regular mother is that she sees in the media a construction of what seems like the norm. "Oh, if it's in the media, everybody must believe it. If Kathy Lee Gifford can have this very high-powered job and still read the

Bible to Cody and look beautiful all the time, then those are expectations that I guess everybody has of me."

Should we really be basing our self-images on TV talk-show hosts and sitcom characters?

Well, it's not what we should do, but it's what does happen. The mass media is a kind of giant Home Depot of identities that colonizes our most basic hopes and dreams and fears about who we are as people, and as mothers.

But I think that we need to look to each other more to validate who we are. We need to use our common sense and just say, "This feels right to me. End of story. No, I'm not baking you 40 blueberry muffins at 10 o'clock at night so you can bring them in for snacks tomorrow. We'll go to the store tomorrow to buy something."

Are we presented with any realistic examples of motherhood in the media?

45   When "Roseanne" came on, the mothers of America said, "Thank you!" That show flew to the top of the ratings because it took the schmaltz out of motherhood. And I think "The Osbournes" took the schmaltz out of family values. And "Married With Children" was another one. A lot of people hated that show, but it was a huge hit. Why? Peg Bundy was the absolute anti-mom. She wouldn't do anything. It was funny, because it was a relief.

The book is funny, but it's also angry. Are you angry? Should we be?

Yeah, we should be angry. We're not supposed to be angry. We're supposed to be all sweetness and light and understanding. Well, where did that come from? You know, if mothers had never gotten angry in this country, there would never have been social change, including, I might note, widows' benefits in the 1930s. We wouldn't have child labor laws if mothers hadn't gotten mad. Birth control would be illegal if mothers hadn't gotten mad. So yeah, it's time for mothers to get mad. I don't know why mothers are not all opening their windows and saying, "I'm not gonna take it anymore."

We have been completely let down by our government, and many of us have been really let down by our places of employment. There are still so many companies with no day care, no flextime, incredibly punishing hours. It's *so* hard to work 60 hours a week and be a mother. I mean, it's hard enough to work 40 hours a week and have a child. So I think mothers have every, every right to be angry. There are plenty of other interest groups much smaller than mothers who, because they got angry, got what they wanted.

So what's the solution?

50   The most important first step is to rip the veneer off the Mommy Myth. It's important for mothers to get together and talk back to and make fun of these ridiculous ideals in the media, and the book tries to lay out some examples of how to do this.

What happened with the women's movement in the 1970s is that, once women began to see through the "Feminine Mystique," which was a crucial first step, they then got political. They did start agitating for child-care centers and equal pay and we made a lot of progress as a result of that.

I think it's time for mothers to get more political, and that is not as time-consuming as you might think. If every mother who has access to a computer spent five minutes, sat down and wrote an e-mail to her presidential candidate of choice, her congressional and senatorial candidates of choice, and said, "Excuse me, what are you going to start doing for mothers and children?" And if millions of mothers did that and kept doing that, I think the political agenda might change. Mothers' voices have to be heard. But what the women's movement taught us is that first you have to see things differently. First you have to see what's keeping you down, and once you do that, then you can move ahead politically. I think that's already starting to happen for mothers. Why shouldn't we have the same things that European women have? We deserve it!

MOMMY MADNESS

An Interview with Judith Warner by Katy Read

Judith Warner has written two biographies, *Hillary Clinton: The Inside Story* (1999) and *Newt Gingrich: Speaker to America* (1995), as well as her book *Perfect Madness: Motherhood in an Age of Anxiety* (2005). The following interview by Katy Read appeared on salon.com in February 2005 when the latter book appeared.

SUGGESTION FOR READING   Notice that Katy Read gives a brief summary of *Perfect Madness* in her introduction to the interview. Keep in mind this summary of Judith Warner's view of the "new momism" as you read. Look for what Warner considers the causes and the effects.

1   Playing Mozart to fetuses. Waving flashcards at infants. Indulging preschoolers with back-straining, eye-glazing "floor time." Hauling school kids around to a dizzying whirl of extracurricular lessons and activities. Tossing everything else aside in order to shower children with nonstop attention and encouragement and enrichment and self-esteem enhancement and, and . . .

Have today's mothers gone crazy?

Yes, in a way, according to Judith Warner's buzz-generating new book, "Perfect Madness: Motherhood in the Age of Anxiety." Warner warns, on the basis of media reports, sociological studies, historical analysis and her own interviews with 150 women, that middle- and upper-middle-class mothers have gone off the deep end trying to do everything right. Whether they're working in paid jobs or staying home with their children or some combination of the two, the overwhelming pressure of trying to orchestrate an ideal upbringing exhausts women, messes up marriages, and spoils children, she says. It leaves women feeling "a widespread, choking cocktail of guilt and anxiety and resentment and regret."

Warner says she recognized the problem after returning to this country after a few years in France, where attitudes toward motherhood were very different. In France, Warner found, mothers are expected to take time for themselves. Their lives are made easier by social supports such as high-quality childcare and generous parental-leave policies. French mothers, in Warner's view, enjoy a lifestyle that Americans might find almost incredible. "Guilt just wasn't in the air," she writes.

5   "Perfect Madness" landed last week with a burst of publicity—a Newsweek cover story, an excerpt in Elle, a Valentine's Day Op-Ed in the New York Times by Warner, and the lead review in the New York Times Book Review—and it is sparking debate from kitchen tables to the blogosphere. But Warner, who has written biographies of Hillary Clinton and Newt Gingrich, is hardly the first to decry the trend toward hyper-intensive mothering and the stress it places on women. Like some of her predecessors, she blames such factors as the popularity of the "attachment parenting" philosophy (which holds that even brief separations from a mother can scar young children), a therapy culture that traces adults' insecurities to their parents' mistakes, and a shortage of social supports like decent childcare and family-friendly workplace policies.

In contrast to previous observers, however—notably Susan J. Douglas and Meredith W. Michaels, authors of "The Mommy Myth: The Idealization of Motherhood and How It Has Undermined Women," *last* year's high-profile book on the topic—Warner downplays the impact of parenting magazines, child-rearing gurus and other media influences, contending that women enter motherhood already receptive to zealous messages. She points to some unexpected culprits: a diet consciousness that trains women to address external problems through intense self-control, and conservative government policies that, by shifting wealth to the rich, have left middle-class families frantic to improve their children's long-term economic prospects any way they can, even if it means signing them up for swimming lessons when they're 4 months old.

Salon spoke to Warner by phone from her home in Washington.

You spent your first few years as a mother in France, where attitudes toward motherhood are more relaxed. Then you moved back to States and you were immediately sucked in to the mommy madness in America. Why?

It takes a lot of inner strength to fend off the pressures that are all around you. It's very, very easy to get sucked in.

10   Washington is the most competitive place I've ever been in my life, in terms of the kinds of ambitions parents have and the kinds of ambitions they have for their children. I find it even more competitive and ambition driven than New York City, where I'm from. It's a real pressure cooker. And I think it was easy for me to get sucked in to that because I am from Manhattan. I'm from that kind of environment. It's what comes naturally to me. I found myself, as a mother, kind of flipping back into the person I was in high school, of just wanting to do everything perfectly and always having that worry of falling behind and not getting the best possible grade on a test.

How did you become aware of it and manage to extricate yourself?

The awareness was immediate, because the culture shock hit me right away. And because of that, I had the gift of having something of a more anthropological perspective than I would have had if I'd never left the country, where this would have just been normal life and I would have been sucked in to it without thinking.

And I would say that working on the book, in a way, helped me from being completely sucked under. Once I was thinking about these issues and making them a conscious thing rather than something I should just live through, then life became material. And when life becomes material, it's a lot more controllable and the

pressures become less toxic, because you have this distance toward everything at the same time that you're going through it.

But I'm still not outside of these pressures. I listen to the stories women tell and I totally identify with them. There are new pressures that come up all the time, and it is incredibly difficult to stay centered as a parent.

15   **What kinds of pressures?**

As my kids get older, there are social pressures that kick in. How many sleepovers are the right number of sleepovers? How many activities should my daughter be doing in a given week? I live in a well-off community, so people can afford to do lots of stuff, and they invite my daughter to do them. Fortunately, in a sense, I can say, "No, sorry, we can't afford to have you do ice skating, horseback riding, swimming lessons, violin and whatever else simultaneously. So you've got to make choices."

The higher up you go on the socioeconomic spectrum, the more ridiculous it gets, because there's more money and time to be spent on things.

Other women who have written about these issues—for example, Naomi Wolf in her book "Misconceptions: Truth, Lies and the Unexpected on the Journey to Motherhood"— have been criticized for focusing on problems experienced primarily by middle- and upper-middle-class women. But you decided very deliberately to do so: You interviewed women in that demographic, and your analysis focuses on issues affecting that demographic. Why?

I think of myself as a middle-class person. I live in a middle- to upper-middle-class area. My book sprang from personal observation of the world around me. I also became very interested in comparing the lives of women today with those described in [Betty Friedan's 1963 classic] "The Feminine Mystique." I became interested in looking back in time, not just of the conditions women were living in but also at their inner world. It became clear to me that it was consistent to keep that focus on the middle class, because that was where the focus has been always, in the mainstream women's magazines and women's writing, and in the question of motherhood from the 1960s onward.

20   I also realize that one book can't do everything. I would have liked in the book to write more about working-class women and poor women, but there was only so much I could do in this particular book.

The image of the hyper-intensive mother still contradicts a widespread stereotype of contemporary motherhood. People assume that since so many mothers are working at paid jobs, they're doing far less for their children than they used to.

There are a couple of studies that show that mothers today actually spend about the same amount of one-on-one-time with their kids as mothers did in the past, because they've upped the intensity of their mothering so much. One generation back, our mothers didn't put the same pressures on themselves to be sitting on the floor, building with Legos. They were ironing or gardening or cooking dinner or talking on the phone, and not feeling guilty about doing that.

Yet, we don't have a sense of being abused by mothers who didn't do enough "floor time."

No. Absolutely not. The bad memories that women seem to have, interestingly enough, is of overinvolved mothers who were frustrated and unhappy with their lives and who were overinvested in their children as a result.

25   There were also a certain number of women I talked to who grew up under more modest circumstances, whose mothers worked at a time when a minority of mothers worked. It became a real ambition for them to be stay-at-home moms because they remembered coming home in the afternoon after school to an empty house, and they remembered a mother—often a single mother—who was scrambling, never having enough money, getting fired from jobs when she tried to be with her kids or go to doctor's appointments and things like that. And they

reacted to that and said they did not want that kind of life for their kids.

The predicament of modern mothers is sometimes referred to [as] "the unfinished business of feminism." Did feminists drop the ball on this?

It isn't fair to say that they dropped the ball entirely. I think there has always been a kind of tension on this issue, because at the outset there was this desire to get away from seeing women in their traditional roles and certainly not to have them defined—legally and professionally—by their biology. This was the thing to accomplish. So in pursuit of that goal, you didn't want to have too much emphasis on women's roles as mothers, because those roles were limiting them, in the popular imagination, in what they could do with their lives.

Over the years, there were always calls for better childcare, for a greater valorization of the roles of mothers, that kind of thing. But I think what happened is that the abortion issue became so big, it became the major battlefield, and I think that everything else got kind of crammed to the side.

But it's unfair to the people who were working in women's movement throughout the '70s and '80s and '90s to say that they dropped the ball on motherhood.

30   **Many people point to parenting experts, to magazines and manuals, that have encouraged this intensive mothering style. But you argue that their advice wouldn't have much effect if mothers weren't already primed to accept it.**

I'm resistant to arguments that there's this sort of top-down pressure from the media. That doesn't make sense. These things exist in our marketplace. If they didn't resonate with people, people wouldn't buy the books and the magazines. They wouldn't take in these messages and run with them the way they do. Frequently what we do with the stuff we read is we push it even further in the way we apply it. The media isn't shoving some conspiracy down our throats. We're not passive consumers.

What do you mean?

Let me give you an example. My older daughter was born in 1997, just at the moment when brain research in children was getting a lot [of] coverage. There was all this talk about what you could do to optimally stimulate your child and help your child's development. And wherever you looked, the message was that you needed to talk to your child as much as possible, read to your child as much as possible, sing, play games. So I did this during my child's every waking moment. Until years went by and I was really, really depleted. I felt like I was losing an inner life. I also realized that my child was dependent on me for stimulation, kind of like the way kids can get dependent on television, and that I needed to wean her off it. And that's been a difficult process, frankly, with both my kids ever since.

Both my kids were born at about that same time, and there was this sense that if you stopped the stimulation for even a few minutes, then the synapses would start withering away.

35   The funny thing is that when, in the course of writing this book, I went back to the same articles that I had read then, I realized that they weren't so very over the top. There were little sentences embedded along with all the rest: "Don't overdo it." "You don't have to do this 24 hours a day." But that's not what most of us, I think, took away. We took away the same message that people always take away [in the United States] when it's a question of diet or anything else: that if a little bit is good, a lot has got to be better.

There is, obviously, a certain amount of sacrifice that parents do have to make on behalf of their children, financially and in terms of time and labor. Yet it seems like mothers are taking on most of the burden, as opposed to sharing it with fathers. A lot of women wonder, how can they get fathers to do their share?

I don't know. I think at this point it's largely a lost cause for our generation. It's too late.

Wow.

It just plain hasn't happened. The statistics overall will tell you that there's a grotesque inequality of who does what. When you have families where the mother is at home full time, she does almost everything.

40   **So men figure, as long as she's home, why can't she just toss in a load of laundry?**

This isn't necessarily a Stepford wives situation where the men are fantasizing about turning their wives into these perfect housewives so they can rule over them. You see a lot of wives caught up in this desire to be this perfect mother and this perfectly functioning creature, and the husbands are kind of shunted off to the side and often made to feel like impediments to the smoothly functioning household. I don't think they're necessarily getting a whole lot out of this, easy though it is to get enraged with them.

In terms of what's going to happen long term and what can we do, I don't know. An earlier generation would have said go on strike, get divorced—right? But we're a generation that was deeply scarred by divorce. It's a little bit hard to imagine someone cavalierly deciding that she's going to get divorced because her husband doesn't help out enough around the house.

But resentment and conflicts over this issue put huge pressure on marriages.

The pressure is huge. The divorce rate is down, but the percentage of couples saying that they're living in less-than-happy marriages is up. I think that there's a lot of long-simmering resentment and a lot of unhappiness in marriages. And I think it's quite toxic and very sad and I wonder what will happen 10 years from now, in terms of the divorce rate, if things go on like this. What's going to happen when the kids are older?

45   **You suggest that getting too much parental attention harms children, leaving them "stressed and anxious and, at the very least,**

often badly behaved." That sounds a lot like what experts very recently were saying would happen to children who didn't get *enough* attention, who were put in daycare or whatever. It seems that no matter how faithfully mothers try to follow experts' advice, they get blamed for wrecking their children. Is there any real evidence that kids' problems are the result of mistakes by well-intentioned mothers?

I think that parents have to take some responsibility for their children's behavior. In the past, I know, mothers were blamed for absolutely *everything*, and this was ridiculous and hateful. I am very clear to say in the book that I don't want to play into that same history of mother blaming.

However, I think that we have gone too far now in the direction of *avoiding* parent blaming—and this is an issue of parental behavior, not just of mothers'. It is now politically incorrect to even talk about the family environment as playing a role in children's "issues"—behavioral or emotional. Everything now is brain chemistry and genetics, and, frankly, while that is up to a point true, it also lets parents *and* society, which is the larger point of the book, entirely off the hook.

While I in no way want to add to mothers' guilt, I think it does our children a great disservice to not even open our minds and hearts to the possibility that some of the things we do— and by "we" I mean mothers *and* fathers *and* educators *and* society; I can't make this point strongly enough—have deleterious effects.

Specifically, what do you think parents do wrong, and what effect does it have on kids?

50   I think we can make our children self-centered by giving them too much attention and making them feel like they're the center of the universe. I think there are a lot of discipline problems in schools now, a lack of respect for adults, an inability to listen and make eye contact when somebody's speaking to you. A general lack of empathy. Children are lacking empathy for others because they're being raised in a way that makes them too self-centered.

I also have heard psychologists make the link between the pressures we put on children and the rise of anxiety and depression among children and people in their 20s.

You ultimately hold our conservative government responsible for a lot of what's ailing mothers because they're the ones who have created policies that force middle-class families to work ever harder just to keep up.

I think there's much greater harm done to women and families by the fiscal-conservative part of right-wing ideology . . . let me rephrase that—"fiscal conservative" is too mild—that's been done by the stripping away of social supports, the redirecting of the nation's wealth from the middle class to the wealthy, the tax policies, the benefit cuts, etc. All of that has contributed to the enormous wealth gap between the rich and poor in America and has made the middle class feel the squeeze and become worried about having their families fall off the map, fall onto the side of the losers. Because to be a loser in our society is such a terrible thing—or rather, not to be a *winner* in our society is, at this point, such a bad thing.

Things that, in the past, could be counted on to be staples of the middle-class existence— access to good public schools, access to decent healthcare, the ability to buy a house in a nice neighborhood—these are now luxuries. So you've really got to be in there, making money, and making sure that your kids have the ability to make money, just to have a middle-class existence. All of that is, at least in large part, a direct result of social policies that stem from right-wing political beliefs. And that, I think, is much more toxic than whatever kinds of so-called traditionalist, family-values rhetoric might come from the right wing.

55   **But if these pressures are mainly affecting middle-class people, how do you explain the frenzy getting more intense as you go up the socioeconomic ladder?**

In my mind all this exists on a continuum. It seems to get more absurd the higher up you go because there's more time and money to spend.

It's always been a bit of a mystery to me why it is that wealthy people can't sit back and relax a bit, but they don't seem capable of it.

What advice do you have for women who read your book and see themselves reflected in it? How do mothers get to a place where they are more relaxed? What are your public prescriptions for change?

In terms of what society can do, we need to think creatively to find more support for families. We need to lessen the financial burden on middle-class families, change our tax policies so that the middle-class isn't underwriting the wealthy as it is now. We need to have public education that people can believe in. We need better support for parents such as part-time daycare for part-time working and at-home mothers. We need universal government standards for daycare and preschool.

On a personal level, stressed-out mothers should talk to other women. Discover that you're not alone. Think about if there's anything you can do in your own life to make things less crazy.

SUGGESTIONS FOR DISCUSSION

1. What is the "new momism" according to Susan J. Douglas? Compare this idea to Judith Warner's notion of "mommy madness." To what extent are they pointing to the same thing? Do you see any differences in how they define the situation of contemporary mothers? How do their views compare with your own understanding of what it means to be a mother at the present time? Both Douglas and Warner seem to concentrate on middle-class and upper-middle-class mothers. What happens if you consider poor and working-class mothers as well?

2. How do Douglas and Warner explain the underlying causes of the "new momism"? What do their main differences seem to be? What assumptions do they seem to be making in their analyses? How would you evaluate the explanatory power of their respective analyses? Does one seem more persuasive than the other? Are there ways they could be synthesized? Are there other causes they do not mention?

3. Both Douglas and Warner write about the "new momism" to show that it poses a very real problem for women. What do they see as the effects on women? What do they think should be done to deal with the problem? Evaluate the arguments they are making. Do you accept their perspective that the "new momism" is a problem that needs attention?

SUGGESTIONS FOR WRITING

1. Write a paper that considers the two perspectives on the "new momism" Douglas and Warner offer. First, define what the term means to them. Then consider what you see as the main differences and similarities in explaining the causes of the "new momism." Identify the underlying assumptions each makes in her analysis. Your task here is not necessarily to agree or disagree with either perspective but to understand how they go about analyzing the current situation of mothers.

2. Write an advice column that might appear in a newspaper or women's magazine. Explain to your readers what the "new momism" is and what its causes and effects are. Imagine that your readers are middle-class and upper-middle-class mothers who will recognize the phenomenon. What advice, then, would you offer these mothers about how to deal with the pressures of the "new momism"?

3. Douglas and Warner focus on the "new momism" as a problem for women. Write an essay that considers its effects on fathers.

xei

WE ARE ALL THIRD GENERATION

— *Margaret Mead*

Margaret Mead (1901–1978) was an anthropologist interested in the way culture influences the development of individual personality. Curator of ethnology at the American Museum of Natural History in New York City from 1926 to 1969, Mead produced a series of books, including *Coming of Age in Samoa* (1928), *Growing Up in New Guinea* (1930), *Sex and Temperament in Three Primitive Societies* (1935), and *Culture and Commitment* (1970). This selection comes from *And Keep Your Powder Dry: An Anthropologist Looks at America* (1942). As you will see, Mead believed the "American character" could be described and analyzed as "shared habits and view of the world." Of particular pertinence to the discussion of generations in this chapter is her view—now commonly held—that by the third generation, immigrants become fully "American."

SUGGESTION FOR READING   As you read, keep in mind the title of this selection, "We Are All Third Generation." Notice how Margaret Mead traces the changes from one generation to the next. Consider how she sets up her line of analysis to explain how the "American character" reaches "its most complete expression in the third-generation American."

1 What then is this American character, this expression of American institutions and of American attitudes which is embodied in every American, in everyone born in this country and sometimes even in those who have come later to these shores? What is it that makes it possible to say of a group of people glimpsed from a hotel step in Soerabaja or strolling down the streets of Marseilles, 'There go some Americans,' whether they have come from Arkansas or Maine or Pennsylvania, whether they bear German or Swedish or Italian surnames? Not clothes alone, but the way they wear them, the way they walk along the street without awareness that anyone of higher status may be walking there also, the way their eyes rove as if by right over the façade of palaces and the rose windows of cathedrals, interested and unimpressed, referring what they see back to the Empire State building, the Chrysler tower, or a good-sized mountain in Montana. Not the towns they come from—Sioux City, Poughkeepsie, San Diego, Scotsdale—but the tone of voice in which they say, 'Why, I came from right near there. My home town was

Evansville. Know anybody in Evansville?' And the apparently meaningless way in which the inhabitant of Uniontown warms to the inhabitant of Evansville as they name over a few names of people whom neither of them know well, about whom neither of them have thought for years, and about whom neither of them care in the least. And yet, the onlooker, taking note of the increased warmth in their voices, of the narrowing of the distance which had separated them when they first spoke, knows that something has happened, that a tie has been established[1] between two people who were lonely before, a tie which every American hopes he may be able to establish as he hopefully asks every stranger: 'What's your home town?'

Americans establish these ties by finding common points on the road that all are expected to have traveled, after their forebears came from Europe one or two or three generations ago, or from one place to another in America, resting for long enough to establish for each generation a 'home town' in which they grew up and which they leave to move on to a new town which will become the home town of their children. Whether they meet on the deck of an Atlantic steamer, in a hotel in Singapore, in New York or in San Francisco, the same expectation underlies their first contact—that both of them have moved on and are moving on and that potential intimacy lies in paths that have crossed. Europeans, even Old Americans whose pride lies not in the circumstance that their ancestors have moved often but rather in the fact that they have not moved for some time, find themselves eternally puzzled by this 'home town business.' Many Europeans fail to find out that in nine cases out of ten the 'home town' is not where one lives but where one did live; they mistake the sentimental tone in which an American invokes Evansville and Centerville and Unionville for a desire to live there again; they miss entirely the symbolic significance of the question and answer which say diagrammatically, 'Are you the same kind of person I am? Good, how about a coke?'

Back of that query lies the remembrance and the purposeful forgetting of European ancestry. For a generation, they cluster together in the Little Italies, in the Czech section or around the Polish Church, new immigrants clinging together so as to be able to chatter in their own tongue and buy their own kind of red peppers, but later there is a scattering to the suburbs and the small towns, to an 'American' way of life, and this is dramatized by an over acceptance of what looks, to any European, as the most meaningless sort of residence—on a numbered street in Chicago or the Bronx. No garden, no fruit trees, no ties to the earth, often no ties to the neighbors, just a number on a street, just a number of a house for which the rent is $10 more than the rent in the old foreign district from which they moved—how can it mean anything? But it does. . . .

If this then, this third-generation American, always moving on, always, in his hopes, moving up, leaving behind him all that was his past and greeting with enthusiasm any echo of that past when he meets it in the life of another, represents one typical theme of the American character structure, how is this theme reflected in the form of the family, in the upbringing of the American child? For to the family we must turn for an understanding of the American character structure. We may describe the adult American, and for descriptive purposes we may refer his behavior to the American scene, to the European past, to the state of American industry, to any other set of events which we wish; but to understand the regularity of this behavior we must investigate the family within which the child is reared. Only so can we learn how the newborn child, at birth potentially a Chinaman or an American, a Pole or an Irishman, becomes an American. By referring his character to the family we do not say that the family is the cause of his character and that the pace of American industry or the distribution of population in America are secondary effects, but merely that all the great configuration of American culture is mediated to the child by his parents, his siblings, his near relatives, and his nurses. He meets American law first in the warning note of his mother's voice: 'Stop digging, here comes a cop.' He meets American economics when he finds his mother unimpressed by his offer to buy another copy of the wedding gift he has just smashed: 'At the 5 and 10 cent store, can't we?' His first encounter with puritan standards may come through his mother's 'If you don't eat your vegetables you can't have any dessert.' He learns the paramount importance of distinguishing between vice and virtue; that it is only a matter of which comes first, the pleasure or the pain. All his great lessons come through his mother's voice, through his father's laughter, or the tilt of his father's cigar when a business deal goes right. Just as one way of understanding a machine is to understand how it is made, so one way of understanding the typical character structure of a culture is to follow step by step the way in which it is built into the growing child. Our assumption when we look at the American family will be that each experience of early childhood is contributing to make the growing individual 'all of a piece,' is guiding him towards consistent and specifically American inconsistency in his habits and view of the world.

5   What kind of parents are these 'third generation' Americans? These people who are always moving, always readjusting, always hoping to buy a better car and a better radio, and even in the years of Depression orienting their behavior to their 'failure' to buy a better car or a better radio. Present or absent, the better car, the better house, the better radio are key points in family life. In the first place, the American parent expects his child to leave him, leave him physically, go to another town, another state; leave him in terms of occupation, embrace a different calling, learn a different skill; leave him socially, travel if possible with a different crowd. Even where a family has reached the top and actually stayed there for two or three generations, there are, for all but the very, very few, still larger cities or foreign courts to be stormed. Those American families which settle back to maintain a position of having reached the top in most cases moulder there for lack of occupation, ladder-climbers gone stale from sitting too long on the top step, giving a poor imitation of the aristocracy of other lands. At the bottom, too, there are some without hope, but very few. Studies of modern youth dwell with anxiety upon the disproportion between the daydreams of the under-privileged young people and the actuality which confronts them in terms of job opportunities. In that very daydream the break is expressed. The daughter who says to her hard-working mother: 'You don't know. I may be going to be a great writer,' is playing upon a note in her mother's mind which accepts the possibility that even if her daughter does not become famous, she will at least go places that she, the mother, has never gone . . . .

With this orientation towards a different future for the child comes also the expectation that the child will pass beyond his parents and leave their standards behind him. Educators exclaim impatiently over the paradox that Americans believe in change, believe in progress and yet do their best—or so it seems—to retard their children, to bind them to parental ways, to inoculate them against the new ways to which they give lip service. But here is a point where the proof of the pudding lies in the eating. If the parents were really behaving as the impatient educators claim they are, really strangling and hobbling their children's attempts to embrace the changing fashions in manners or morals, we would not have the rapid social change which is so characteristic of our modern life. We would not go in twenty years from fig leaves on Greek statues to models of unborn babies in our public museums. It is necessary to distinguish between ritual and ceremonial resistances and real resistances. Among primitive peoples, we find those in which generation after generation there is a mock battle between the young men and the old men: generation after generation the old men lose. An observer from our society, with an unresolved conflict with his father on his mind, might watch that battle in terror, feeling the outcome was in doubt. But the members of the tribe who are fighting the mock battle consciously or unconsciously know the outcome and fight with no less display of zeal for the knowing of it. The mock battle is no less important because the issue is certain.

Similarly, on the island of Bali, it is unthinkable that a father or a brother should plan to give a daughter of the house to some outsider. Only when a marriage is arranged between cousins, both of whose fathers are members of the same paternal line, can consent be appropriately given. Yet there flourishes, and has flourished probably for hundreds of years, a notion among Balinese young people that it is more fun to marry someone who is not a cousin. So, generation after generation, young men carry off the daughters of other men, and these daughters, their consent given in advance, nevertheless shriek and protest noisily if there are witnesses by. It is a staged abduction, in which no one believes, neither the boy nor the girl nor their relatives. Once in a while, some neurotic youth misunderstands and tries to abduct a girl who has not given her consent, and as a result the whole society is plunged into endless confusion, recrimination, and litigation.

So it is in American society. American parents, to the extent that they are Americans, expect their children to live in a different world, to clothe their moral ideas in different trappings, to court in automobiles although their forebears courted, with an equal sense of excitement and moral trepidation, on horsehair sofas. As the parents' course was uncharted when they were young—for they too had gone a step beyond their parents and transgressed every day some boundary which their parents had temporarily accepted as absolute—so also the parents know that their children are sailing uncharted seas. And so it comes about that American parents lack the sure hand on the rudder which parents in other societies display, and that they go in for a great deal of conventional and superficial grumbling. To the traditional attitudes characteristic of all oldsters who find the young a deteriorated version of themselves, Americans add the mixture of hope and envy and anxiety which comes from knowing that their children are not deteriorated versions of themselves, but actually—very actually—manage a car better than father ever did. This is trying; sometimes very trying. The neurotic father, like the neurotic lover in Bali, will misunderstand the license to grumble, and will make such a fuss over his son or daughter when they behave as all of their age are behaving, that the son or daughter has to be very unneurotic indeed not to take the fuss as something serious, not to believe that he or she is breaking father's heart. Similarly, a neurotic son or daughter will mistake the ceremonial grumbling for the real thing, and break their spirits in a futile attempt to live up to the voiced parental standards. To the average child the parents' resistance is a stimulus. . . .

By and large, the American father has an attitude towards his children which may be loosely classified as autumnal. They are his for a brief and passing season, and in a very short while they will be operating gadgets which he does not understand and cockily talking a language to which he has no clue. He does his best to keep ahead of his son, takes a superior tone as long as he can, and knows that in nine cases out of ten he will lose. If the boy goes into his father's profession, of course, it will take him a time to catch up. He finds out that the old man knows a trick or two; that experience counts as over against this new-fangled nonsense. But the American boy solves that one very neatly: he typically does not go into his father's profession, nor take up land next to his father where his father can come over and criticize his plowing. He goes somewhere else, either in space or in occupation. And his father, who did the same thing and expects that his son will, is at heart terrifically disappointed if the son accedes to his ritual request that he docilely follow in his father's footsteps and secretly suspects the imitative son of being a milksop. He knows he is a milksop—so he thinks—because he himself would have been a milksop if he had wanted to do just what his father did.

10   This is an attitude which reaches its most complete expression in the third-generation American. His grandfather left home, rebelled against a parent who did not expect final rebellion, left a land where everyone expected him to stay. Come to this country, his rebellious adventuring cooled off by success, he begins to relent a little, to think perhaps the strength of his ardor to leave home was overdone. When his sons grow up, he is torn between his desire to have them succeed in this new country—which means that they must be more American than he, must lose entirely their foreign names and every trace of allegiance to a foreign way of life—and his own guilt towards the parents and the fatherland which he has denied. So he puts on the heat, alternately punishing the child whose low marks in school suggest that he is not going to be a successful American and berating him for his American ways and his disrespect for his father and his father's friends from the old country. When that son leaves home, he throws himself with an intensity which his children will not know into the American way of life; he eats American, talks American, dresses American, he will be American or nothing. In making his way

of life consistent, he inevitably makes it thin; the overtones of the family meal on which strange, delicious, rejected European dishes were set, and about which low words in a foreign tongue wove the atmosphere of home, must all be dropped out. His speech has a certain emptiness; he rejects the roots of words—roots lead back, and he is going forward—and comes to handle language in terms of surfaces and clichés. He rejects half of his life in order to make the other half self-consistent and complete. And by and large he succeeds. Almost miraculously, the sons of the Polish day laborer and the Italian fruit grower, the Finnish miner and the Russian garment worker become Americans.

Second generation—American-born of foreign-born parents—they set part of the tone of the American eagerness for their children to go onward. They have left their parents; left them in a way which requires more moral compensation than was necessary even for the parent generation who left Europe. The immigrant left his land, his parents, his fruit trees, and the little village street behind him. He cut the ties of military service; he flouted the king or the emperor; he built himself a new life in a new country. The father whom he left behind was strong, a part of something terribly strong, something to be feared and respected and fled from. Something so strong that the bravest man might boast of a successful flight. He left his parents, entrenched representatives of an order which he rejected. But not so his son. He leaves his father not a part of a strong other-way of life, but bewildered on the shores of the new world, having climbed only halfway up the beach. His father's ties to the old world, his mannerisms, his broken accent, his little foreign gestures are not part parcel of something strong and different; they are signs of his failure to embrace this new way of life. Does his mother wear a kerchief over her head? He cannot see the generations of women who have worn such kerchiefs. He sees only the American women who wear hats, and he pities and rejects his mother who has failed to become—an American. And so there enters into

the attitude of the second-generation American—an attitude which again is woven through our folkways, our attitude towards other languages, towards anything foreign, towards anything European—a combination of contempt and avoidance, a fear of yielding, and a sense that to yield would be weakness. His father left a father who was the representative of a way of life which had endured for a thousand years. When he leaves his father, he leaves a partial failure; a hybrid, one who represents a step towards freedom, not freedom itself. His first-generation father chose between freedom and what he saw as slavery; but when the second-generation American looks at his European father, and through him, at Europe, he sees a choice between success and failure, between potency and ignominy. He passionately rejects the halting English, the half-measures of the immigrant. He rejects with what seems to him equally good reasons 'European ties and entanglements.' This second-generation attitude which has found enormous expression in our culture especially during the last fifty years, has sometimes come to dominate it—in those parts of the country which we speak of as 'isolationist.' Intolerant of foreign language, foreign ways, vigorously determined on being themselves, they are, in attitude if not in fact, second-generation Americans.

When the third-generation boy grows up, he comes up against a father who found the task of leaving his father a comparatively simple one. The second-generation parent lacks the intensity of the first, and his son in turn fails to reflect the struggles, the first against feared strength and the second against guiltily rejected failure, which have provided the plot for his father and grandfather's maturation. He is expected to succeed; he is expected to go further than his father went; and all this is taken for granted. He is furthermore expected to feel very little respect for the past. Somewhere in his grandfather's day there was an epic struggle for liberty and freedom. His picture of that epic grandfather is a little obscured, however, by the patent fact that his father does not really respect him; he may have been a noble character, but he had a foreign accent. The grandchild is told in school, in the press, over the radio, about the founding fathers, but they were not after all *his* founding fathers; they are, in ninety-nine cases out of a hundred, somebody else's ancestors. Any time one's own father, who in his own youth had pushed his father aside and made his own way, tries to get in one's way, one can invoke the founding fathers—those ancestors of the real Americans; the Americans who got here earlier—those Americans which father worked so very hard, so slavishly, in fact, to imitate. This is a point which the European observer misses. He hears an endless invocation of Washington and Lincoln, of Jefferson and Franklin. Obviously, Americans go in for ancestor worship, says the European. Obviously, Americans are longing for a strong father, say the psycho-analysts.[4] These observers miss the point that Washington is not the ancestor of the man who is doing the talking; Washington does not represent the past to which one belongs by birth, but the past to which one tries to belong by effort. Washington represents the thing for which grandfather left Europe at the risk of his life, and for which father rejected grandfather at the risk of his integrity. Washington is not that to which Americans passionately cling but that to which they want to belong, and fear, in the bottom of their hearts, that they cannot and do not.

This odd blending of the future and the past, in which another man's great-grandfather becomes the symbol of one's grandson's future, is an essential part of American culture. 'Americans are so conservative.' say Europeans. They lack the revolutionary spirit. Why don't they rebel? Why did President Roosevelt's suggestion of altering the structure of the Supreme Court and the Third-Term argument raise such a storm of protest? Because, in education, in attitudes, most Americans are third generation, they have just really arrived. Their attitude towards this country is that of one who has just established membership, just been elected to an exclusive club, just been initiated into the rites of an exacting religion. Almost any one of them who inspects

his own ancestry, even though it goes back many more generations than three, will find a gaping hole somewhere in the family tree. Campfire girls give an honor to the girl who can name all eight great-grandparents, including the maiden names of the four great-grandmothers. Most Americans cannot get this honor. And who was that missing great-grandmother? Probably, oh, most probably, not a grandniece of Martha Washington.

We have, of course, our compensatory mythology. People who live in a land torn by earthquakes have myths of a time when the land was steady, and those whose harvest are uncertain dream of a golden age when there was no drought. Likewise, people whose lives are humdrum and placid dream of an age of famine and rapine. We have our rituals of belonging, our DAR's and our Descendants of King Philip's Wars, our little blue book of the blue-blooded Hawaiian aristocracy descended from the first missionaries, and our *Mayflower*, which is only equaled in mythological importance by the twelve named canoes which brought the Maoris to New Zealand. The mythology keeps alive the doubt. The impressive president of a patriotic society knows that she is a member by virtue of only one of the some eight routes through which membership is possible. Only one. The other seven? Well, three are lost altogether. Two ancestors were Tories. In some parts of the country she can boast of that; after all, Tories were people of substance, real 'old families.' But it doesn't quite fit. Of two of those possible lines, she has resolutely decided not to think. Tinkers and tailors and candlestick makers blend indistinctly with heaven knows what immigrants! She goes to a meeting and is very insistent about the way in which the Revolutionary War which only one-eighth of her ancestors helped to fight should be represented to the children of those whose eight ancestors were undoubtedly all somewhere else in 1776.

15   On top of this Old American mythology, another layer has been added, a kind of placatory offering, a gesture towards the Old World which Americans had left behind. As the fifth- and sixth- and seventh-generation Americans lost the zest

which came with climbing got to the top of the pecking order[5] in their own town or city and sat, still uncertain, still knowing their credentials were shaky, on the top of the pile, the habit of wanting to belong—to really belong, to be accepted absolutely as something which one's ancestors had NOT been—became inverted. They turned towards Europe, especially towards England, towards presentation at Court, towards European feudal attitudes. And so we have had in America two reinforcements of the European class attitudes—those hold-overs of feudal caste attitudes, in the newly-come immigrant who carries class consciousness in every turn and bend of his neck, and the new feudalism, the 'old family' who has finally toppled over backwards into the lap of all that their remote ancestors left behind them.

When I say that we are most of us—whatever our origins—third-generation in character structure, I mean that we have been reared in an atmosphere which is most like that which I have described for the third generation. Father is to be outdistanced and outmoded, but not because he is a strong representative of another culture, well entrenched, not because he is a weak and ineffectual attempt to imitate the new culture; he did very well in his way, but he is out of date. He, like us, was moving forwards, moving away from something symbolized by his own ancestors, moving towards something symbolized by other people's ancestors. Father stands for the way things were done, for a direction which on the whole was a pretty good one, in its day. He was all right because he was on the right road. Therefore, we, his children, lack the mainsprings of rebellion. He was out of date; he drove an old model car which

couldn't make it on the hills. Therefore it is not necessary to fight him, to knock him out of the race. It is much easier and quicker to pass him. And to pass him it is only necessary to keep on going and to see that one buys a new model every year. Only if one slackens, loses one's interest in the race towards success, does one slip back. Otherwise, it is onward and upward, *towards* the world of Washington and Lincoln; a world in which we don't fully belong, but which we feel, if we work at it, we some time may achieve.

NOTES

1. I owe my understanding of the significance of these chronological ties to discussions with Kurt Lewin and John G. Pilley.
2. Sibling is a coined word used by scientists for both brothers and sisters. The English language lacks such a word.
3. Cf. Samuel Butler's definition: That vice is when the pain follows the pleasure and virtue when the pleasure follows the pain.
4. I owe my classification of the American attitude towards the 'founding fathers' to a conversation with Dr. Ernst Kris, in which he was commenting on the way in which Americans, apparently, wanted a strong father, although, in actual fact, they always push their fathers aside.
5. Pecking order is a very convenient piece of jargon which social psychologists use to describe a group in which it is very clear to everybody in it just which bird can peck which, or which cow can butt which other cow away from the water trough. Among many living creatures these 'pecking orders' are fixed and when a newcomer enters the group he has to fight and scramble about until everybody is clear just where he belongs—below No. 8 chick, for instance, and above old No. 9.

SUGGESTIONS FOR DISCUSSION

1. What does Margaret Mead mean when she says that we are all "third generation"? Why do you think she has chosen to locate the formation of the American "character structure" in the dynamics of the American family? Consider her analysis of the immigrant family from first to second to third generation.

2. How does Margaret Mead answer the question she begins with—what is "this American character"? Do you accept Mead's assumption that there is an "American character" that can be described and analyzed? What evidence does she provide to support this assumption? What evidence might contradict the idea?

They knew they had to learn English to survive.

How come today's immigrants are being misled?

They learned without bilingual education. And without government documents in a multitude of languages. They knew they had to learn English before anything else.

But today, a whole new generation of Americans are being fed a lie by bureaucrats, educators and self-appointed leaders for immigrant groups. The lie says "you don't have to learn English because you can make it here without assimilating." The truth is this: without learning our shared language, an immigrant's dream of a better life will fade.

With nearly 700,000 members, we're the largest organization fighting to make English the official language of government at all levels. *Join us. Support us. Fight with us.* Because now more than ever, immigrants need to be told the truth.

Speak up for America. Call 1-800-U.S.ENGLISH

U.S.ENGLISH

1747 Pennsylvania Avenue, NW, Suite 1100
Washington, DC 20006

3. Consider the ad from U.S. English, "They knew they had to learn English to survive," reproduced above. To what extent does the ad draw on a representation of American immigrant generations that is similar to Mead's? What is the ad's purpose in comparing older waves of immigration to more recent immigration?

SUGGESTIONS FOR WRITING

1. Use Mead's idea that "We Are All Third Generation" to analyze your own family. She offers a predictable sequence from first to second to third generation. Begin by describing this sequence and then show how it fits or fails to fit the experience of your family. What modifications, if any, would you want to make?

2. Mead wrote this chapter in 1942. Is it possible to update it—to identify a common "American character" today as confidently as Mead did sixty years ago? Is the notion of an "American character" useful at all? Explain your answers to these questions by either proposing an updated version or explaining why the notion doesn't work in contemporary America. (Consider also whether it ever worked.)

3. Consider Mary Gordon's sense of what it means to be an American in "More Than Just a Shrine: Paying Homage to the Ghosts of Ellis Island," in Chapter 9, and compare that with Mead's sense in "We Are All Third Generation." Pay particular attention to how each writer uses the notion of generation.

VISUAL CULTURE   Representations of Youth Culture in Movies

To learn more about youth culture and advertising, visit www.ablongman.com/george/104

The identity of a generation takes shape in part through the movies. Since the 1950s, movies about teenagers and youth culture have explored generational identities and intergenerational conflicts. In *The Wild One, Blackboard Jungle,* and *Rebel Without a Cause* (the 1950s); *The Graduate* and *Easy Rider* (the 1960s); *Saturday Night Fever* and *American Graffiti* (the 1970s); *River's Edge, The Breakfast Club,* and *Fast Times at Ridgemont High* (the 1980s); *Do the Right Thing, Boyz 'n the Hood, Slackers,* and *Clerks* (the 1990s); and *Elephant* and *Dogtown and Z-Boys* (2000s), to name some of the best-known movies, Hollywood and independent filmmakers have fashioned influential representations of young people.

This section considers how movies represent various youth cultures and their relations to adult culture. Think about what the term *representation* means. A key term in cultural analysis, it is more complex than it appears. At first glance, it seems to mean simply showing what is there, reflecting life as it occurs. But the complexity comes in because the medium of representation—whether language or moving images—has its own codes and conventions that shape the way people see and understand what is being shown. By the same token, representation is not just the result of a writer's or filmmaker's intentions. Readers and viewers make sense of the codes and conventions of representation in different ways, depending on their interests and social position. So to think about the representation of youth cultures in films in a meaningful way, consider how the images of youth culture in film have been filtered through such conventions as the feature film, the Hollywood star system, and the available stock of characters and plots viewers will recognize and respond to.

JUVENILE DELINQUENCY FILMS

James Gilbert

James Gilbert is an American historian at the University of Maryland. The following selection is taken from Gilbert's book *A Cycle of Outrage: America's Reaction to Juvenile Delinquency in the 1950s* (1988). Here, Gilbert traces the emergence in the 1950s of juvenile delinquency films and popular responses to them. This selection consists of the opening paragraph of Gilbert's chapter "Juvenile Delinquency Movies" and his analysis of *The Wild One, Blackboard Jungle,* and *Rebel Without a Cause.*

SUGGESTION   Notice how Gilbert sets up his dominant theme in the opening paragraph, when he explains
FOR READING   that widespread public concern with juvenile delinquency presents Hollywood with "dangerous but lucrative possibilities." Take note of how Gilbert defines these "possibilities" in the
opening paragraph and then follow how he traces this theme through his discussion of the
three films.

Whereas, shortly after the screening of this movie the local police had several cases in which the use of knives by young people were involved and at our own Indiana Joint High School two girls, while attending a high school dance, were cut by a knife wielded by a teen-age youth who by his own admission got the idea from watching *Rebel Without a Cause.*

Now Therefore Be It Resolved by the Board of Directors of Indiana Joint High School that said Board condemns and deplores the exhibition of pictures such as *Rebel Without a Cause* and any other pictures which depict abnormal or subnormal behavior by the youth of our country and which tend to deprave the morals of young people.

*Indiana, Pennsylvania, Board of Education
to the MPAA, January 9, 1956*

1   The enormous outpouring of concern over juvenile delinquency in the mid-1950s presented the movie industry with dangerous but lucrative possibilities. An aroused public of parents, service club members, youth-serving agencies, teachers, adolescents, and law enforcers constituted a huge potential audience for delinquency films at a time when general audiences for all films had declined. Yet this was a perilous subject to exploit, for public pressure on the film industry to set a wholesome example for youth remained unremitting. Moreover, the accusation that mass culture caused delinquency—especially the "new delinquency" of the postwar period—was the focus of much contemporary attention. If the film industry approached the issue of delinquency, it had to proceed cautiously. It could not present delinquency favorably; hence all stories would have to be set in the moral firmament of the movie Code. Yet to be successful, films had to evoke sympathy from young people who were increasingly intrigued by the growing youth culture of which delinquency seemed to be one variant.

Stanley Kramer's picture, *The Wild One,* released in 1953, stands in transition from the somber realism of "film noir" pessimism and environmentalism to the newer stylized explorations of delinquent culture that characterized the mid-1950s. Shot in dark and realistic black and white, the film stars Marlon Brando and Lee Marvin as rival motorcycle gang leaders who invade a small California town. Brando's character is riven with ambiguity and potential violence—a prominent characteristic of later juvenile delinquency heroes. On the other hand, he is clearly not an adolescent, but not yet an adult either, belonging to a suspended age that seems alienated from any recognizable stage of development. He appears to be tough and brutal, but he is not, nor, ultimately, is he as attractive as he might have been. His character flaws are appealing, but unnerving. This is obvious in the key symbol of the film, the motorcycle trophy which he carries. He has not won it as the townspeople assume; he has stolen it from a motorcycle "scramble." Furthermore, he rejects anything more than a moment's tenderness with the girl he meets. In the end, he rides off alone, leaving her trapped in the small town that his presence has so disrupted and exposed. The empty road on which he travels leads to similar nameless towns; he cannot find whatever it is he is compelled to seek.

Brando's remarkable performance made this film a brilliant triumph. Its moral ambiguity, however, and the very attractiveness of the alienated hero, meant that the producers needed to invoke two film code strategies to protect themselves from controversy. The first of these was an initial disclaimer appearing after the titles: "This is a shocking story. It could never take place in most American towns—but it did in this one. It is a public challenge not to let it happen again." Framing the other end of the film was a speech by a strong moral voice of authority. A sheriff brought in to restore order to the town lectures Brando on the turmoil he has created and then, as a kind of punishment, casts him back onto the lonesome streets.

Aside from Brando's stunning portrayal of the misunderstood and inarticulate antihero, the film did not quite emerge from traditional modes of presenting crime and delinquency: the use of black and white; the musical score with its foreboding big-band sound; the relatively aged performers; and the vague suggestions that Brando and his gang were refugees from urban slums. Furthermore, the reception to the film was not, as some might have predicted, as controversial as what was to come. Of course, there were objections—for example, New Zealand banned the film—but it did not provoke the outrage that the next group of juvenile delinquency films inspired.

5 The film that fundamentally shifted Hollywood's treatment of delinquency was *The Blackboard Jungle*, produced in 1955, and in which traditional elements remained as a backdrop for contemporary action. The movie was shot in black and white and played in a slum high school. But it clearly presented what was to become the driving premise of subsequent delinquency films—the division of American society into conflicting cultures made up of adolescents on one side and adults on the other. In this film the delinquent characters are portrayed as actual teenagers, as high school students. The crimes they commit are, with a few exceptions, crimes of behavior such as defying authority, status crimes, and so on. Of most symbolic importance is the transition in music that occurs in the film. Although it includes jazz numbers by Stan Kenton and Bix Beiderbecke, it is also the first film to feature rock and roll, specifically, "Rock Around the Clock" played by Bill Haley.

The story line follows an old formula of American novels and films. A teacher begins a job at a new school, where he encounters enormous hostility from the students. He stands up to the ringleader of the teenage rowdies, and finally wins over the majority of the students. In itself this is nothing controversial. But *Blackboard Jungle* also depicts the successful defiance of delinquents, who reject authority and terrorize an American high school. Their success and their power, and the ambiguous but attractive picture of their culture, aimed at the heart of the film Code and its commitment to uphold the dignity of figures and institutions of authority. . . .

Following swiftly on this commercial success was *Rebel Without a Cause*, a very different sort of film, and perhaps the most famous and influential of the 1950s juvenile delinquency endeavors. Departing from the somber working-class realism of *Blackboard Jungle*, *Rebel* splashed the problem of middle-class delinquency across America in full color. Moreover, its sympathy lay entirely with adolescents, played by actors James Dean, Natalie Wood, and Sal Mineo, who all live wholly inside the new youth culture. Indeed, this is the substantial message of the film: each parent and figure of authority is grievously at fault for ignoring or otherwise failing youth. The consequence is a rebellion with disastrous results.

Once the script had been developed, shooting began in the spring of 1955, during the height of the delinquency dispute and following fast on the heels of the box-office success of *Blackboard Jungle*. Warner Brothers approved a last minute budget hike to upgrade the film to color. In part this was a response to the box office appeal of the star, James Dean, whose *East of Eden* was released to acclaim in early April.

When it approved the film, the Code Authority issued two warnings. Geoffrey Shurlock wrote to Jack Warner in March 1955: "As you know, we have steadfastly maintained under the requirements of the Code that we should not approve stories of underage boys and girls indulging in either murder or illicit sex." He suggested that the violence in the picture be toned down. Furthermore, he noted: "It is of course vital that there be no inference of a questionable or homosexual relationship between Plato [Sal Mineo] and Jim [James Dean]." A follow-up commentary suggested the need for further changes in the area of violence. For example, Shurlock noted of the fight at the planetarium: "We suggest merely indicating that these high-school boys have tire chains, not showing them flaunting them."

10   Despite these cautions, the film, when it was released, contained substantial violence: the accidental death of one of the teenagers in a "chickie run"; the shooting of another teenager; and Plato's death at the hands of the police. Furthermore, there remained strong echoes of Plato's homosexual interest in Jim.

The film also took a curious, ambiguous position on juvenile delinquency. Overtly, it disapproved, demonstrating the terrible price paid for misbehavior. Yet the film, more than any other thus far, glorified the teenage life-styles it purported to reject. Adult culture is pictured as insecure, insensitive, and blind to the problems of youth. Teenagers, on the other hand, are portrayed as searching for genuine family life, warmth, and security. They choose delinquency in despair of rejection by their parents. Indeed, each of the three young heroes is condemned to search for the emotional fulfillment that adults deny: Dean for the courage his father lacks; Natalie Wood (as his girlfriend) for her father's love; and Plato for a family, which he finds momentarily in Dean and Wood. Instead of being securely set in adult society, each of these values must be constructed outside normal society and inside a new youth-created world. What in other films might have provided a reconciling finale—a voice of authority—becomes, itself, a symbol of alienation. A policeman who befriends Dean is absent at a decisive moment when he could have prevented the tragic ending.

Thus no adults or institutions remain unscathed. The ending, in which adults recognize their own failings, is thus too sudden and contrived to be believable. It is as if the appearance of juvenile delinquency in such a middle-class setting is impossible to explain, too complex and too frightening to be understood in that context.

And also too attractive, for the film pictures delinquent culture as an intrusive, compelling, and dangerous force that invades middle-class homes and institutions. The producers carefully indicated that each family was middle class, although Plato's mother might well be considered wealthier than that. Teenage, delinquent culture, however, has obvious working-class origins, symbolized by souped-up jalopies, levis, and T-shirts that became the standard for youth culture. In fact, when Dean goes out for his fateful "chickie run," he changes into T-shirt and levis from his school clothes. Furthermore, the film presents this delinquent culture without judgment. There is no obvious line drawn between what is teenage culture and what is delinquency. Is delinquency really just misunderstood youth culture? The film never says, thus reflecting public confusion on the same issue.

A second tactic of the filmmakers posed a philosophic problem about youth culture and delinquency. This emerges around the symbol of the planetarium. In the first of two scenes there, Dean's new high school class visits for a lecture and a show. The lecturer ends his presentation abruptly with a frightening suggestion—the explosion of the world and the end of the universe. He concludes: "Man existing alone seems an episode of little consequence." This existential reference precedes the rumble in which Dean is forced to fight his new classmates after they puncture the tires of his car. The meaning is clear: Dean must act to establish an identity which his parents and society refuse to grant him. This is a remarkable translation of the basic premise of contemporary Beat poets, whose solitary search for meaning and self-expression tinged several of the other initial films in this genre also.

Another scene at the planetarium occurs at night, at the end of the film. The police have pursued Plato there after he shoots a member of the gang that has been harassing Dean. Dean follows him into the building, and, in a reprise of the earlier scene, turns on the machine that lights the stars and planets. The two boys discuss the end of the world. Dean empties Plato's gun, and the confused youth then walks out of the building. The police, mistaking his intent, gun him down. Once again tragedy follows a statement about the ultimate meaninglessness of life.

15   By using middle-class delinquency to explore questions of existence, this film undeniably contested the effectiveness of traditional family and community institutions. There is even the hint that Dean, Wood, and Mineo represent the possibility of a new sort of family; but this is only a fleeting suggestion. In the end it is family and community weakness that bring tragedy for which there can be no real solution. Without the strikingly sympathetic performances of Dean, Wood, and Mineo, this picture might have fallen under the weight of its bleak (and pretentious) message. As it was, however, *Rebel Without a Cause* was a box office smash, and Dean's short, but brilliant career was now assured.

As with *Blackboard Jungle*, the MPAA was the focus of furious reaction to the film. Accusations of copycat crimes, particularly for a stabbing in Indiana, Pennsylvania, brought condemnations and petitions against "pictures which depict abnormal or subnormal behavior by the youth of our country and which tend to deprave the morals of young people." The MPAA fought back against this accusation in early 1956 as Arthur DeBra urged an investigation to discover if the incident at the Indiana, Pennsylvania, high school had any relationship to the "juvenile delinquency situation in the school and community." As one writer for the *Christian Science Monitor* put it, "the new Warner Brothers picture will emerge into the growing nationwide concern about the effects on youth of comics, TV, and movies." This prediction was based upon actions already taken by local censors. The Chicago police had ordered cuts in the film, and the city of Milwaukee banned it outright.

On the other hand, much of the response was positive. As *Variety* noted in late 1955, fan letters had poured in to Hollywood "from teenagers who have identified themselves with the characters; from parents who have found the film conveyed a special meaning; and from sociologists and psychiatrists who have paid tribute to the manner in which child-parent misunderstanding is highlighted."

Quite clearly, the film became a milestone for the industry. It established youth culture as a fitting subject for films, and created some of the most pervasive stereotypes that were repeated in later films. These included the tortured, alienated, and misunderstood youth and intolerant parents and authority figures. It did not, however, lead to more subtle explorations of the connections between youth culture and delinquency. If anything, the opposite was true. For one thing, Dean was killed in an auto accident shortly after this enormous success. Furthermore, it was probably the seriousness of *Blackboard Jungle* and *Rebel* that provoked controversy, and the movie industry quickly learned that it could attract teenage audiences without risking the ire of adults if it reduced the dosage of realism. Thus the genre deteriorated into formula films about teenagers, made principally for drive-in audiences who were not particular about the features they saw.

SUGGESTIONS FOR DISCUSSION

1. Gilbert notes that *Rebel Without a Cause* became a "milestone" for the film industry, establishing youth culture as a fitting (and profitable) subject and creating stereotypes of alienated youth and intolerant adults that recurred in later movies. Consider to what extent these stereotypes continue to appear in movies. How would you update their appearance

since the 1950s? List examples of movies that use the conventionalized figures of alienated youth and intolerant adults. What continuity do you see over time? In what ways have the portrayals changed?

2. Gilbert says that by "using middle-class delinquency to explore questions of existence," *Rebel Without a Cause* "contested the effectiveness of traditional family and community institutions." Explain what Gilbert means. Can you think of other films that "contest" family and community institutions?

3. Watch the three films Gilbert discusses — *The Wild One, Blackboard Jungle,* and *Rebel Without a Cause.* Working together with a group of classmates, first summarize Gilbert's discussion of how each film handles the dilemma of evoking viewers' sympathy for young people while in no way presenting delinquency in a favorable light. Next, develop your own analysis of how (or whether) each film creates sympathy for young people in their confrontations with the adult world. To what extent do you agree with Gilbert's line of analysis? Where do you differ with or want to modify his analysis?

SUGGESTED ASSIGNMENT

Pick a film or group of films that in some way characterizes a generation of young people. For example, analyze how *The Graduate* captures something important about youth in the 1960s. Or look at how a cluster of three or four films portrays the "twentysomething" generation of the 1990s. Or you can follow *Newsweek*'s example in "Raging Teen Hormones" and put together a timeline that reveals some trend in youth films. (Notice how the thermometer registers how "hot" the film is.)

Write an analysis of how the film or films represent youth. Do not decide whether the portrayal is accurate, but analyze how it constructs a certain image of youth culture and what might be the significance of the representation.

Here are some suggestions to help you examine how a film represents youth culture:

- *How does the film portray young people?* What in particular marks them as "youth"? Pay particular attention to the characters' clothing, hairstyles, body posture, and ways of speaking.

- *How does the film mark young people generationally?* Are the characters part of a distinctive youth subculture? How would you characterize the group's collective identity? What is the relation of the group to the adult world and its institutions? What intergenerational conflicts figure in the film?

- *How does the film portray a particular historical moment or decade?* What visual clues enable viewers to locate the era of the film? What historical events, if any, enter into the film?

- *How does the sound track contribute to the representation of youth culture that is projected by the film?*

- *How do the stars of the film influence viewers' perceptions of youth culture?* Do they enhance viewers' sympathies? Are the main characters cultural icons like James Dean or Marlon Brando?

FILM CLIP   Hollywood Stars: Brando, Dean, and Monroe

WWW

To learn more about film and contemporary culture, visit www.ablongman.com/george/105

Part of the appeal of Hollywood films is the star system. For movie-goers, the attraction of films is not just the story but the stars who are featured in the leading roles. The star system dates back to the Hollywood studios of the 1920s, 1930s, and 1940s that signed the most prominent actors of the time to exclusive contracts and then developed film projects as vehicles for Spencer Tracy and Katharine Hepburn, Clark Gable, Cary Grant, Humphrey Bogart, and Lana Turner among others. Movie fans began to identify with the actors as much or more than the films, and the star system became a crucial ingredient in the formation of Hollywood's entertainment industry. The Hollywood studios tightly controlled the public image of its stars, going so far as to arrange sham marriages for gay actors such as Rock Hudson. With the breakup of the Hollywood studios and the rise of American independent films in the 1960s, stars are no longer studio properties, and actors such as Tom Cruise, Julia Roberts, and Denzel Washington now have tremendous bargaining power.

We show here pictures of three of the most prominent Hollywood stars of the 1950s: Marlon Brando, James Dean, and Marilyn Monroe. Unlike actors such as Meryl Streep or Robert DeNiro, who are famous for their ability to lose themselves in their roles, each of these stars brought a particular personality to the screen, radiating a sex appeal that seemed to challenge the buttoned-down conservatism

Marlon Brando in *The Wild One* (1953).

Marilyn Monroe in *The Seven Year Itch* (1955).

of the United States in the 1950s. Monroe projected a vulnerable sexuality and a nearly childlike innocence that made her appear to be both a seductress and a "dumb blonde" in need of protection. Brando and Dean, on the other hand, embodied a moody masculinity that suggested rebellion and a cool alienation from mainstream society. In each case, these stars have taken on the status of icons whose images seem to capture something simmering just below the surface of America in the Eisenhower years.

Consider the 1950s films of one of these three stars. Think in particular of the types of roles in which Brando, Dean, or Monroe is cast. What do these roles have in common? What makes them a likely vehicle for the star? What does Brando, Dean, or Monroe bring to the role that seems uniquely their own personality? What is the appeal to film-goers. Here are some of the films you might use:

Marlon Brando: *The Wild One*; *Streetcar Named Desire*; *On the Waterfront*.

James Dean: *Rebel Without a Cause*; *East of Eden*; *Giant*.

Marilyn Monroe: *Some Like It Hot*; *Bus Stop*; *Gentlemen Prefer Blondes*.

Consider, too, the stars of today and what they seem to embody about contemporary culture.

FIELDWORK   Ethnographic Interviews

Music is one of the keys to generational identities. Songs carry the emotional power to define for their listeners what it means to be alive at a particular moment. Singers and musicians evoke generations and decades—Frank Sinatra's emergence as a teen idol in the big band era of the 1940s; Elvis Presley, Little Richard, Buddy Holly, and early rock and roll in the 1950s; the Beatles, Rolling Stones, Bob Dylan, Motown, and the Memphis sound of Aretha Franklin and Otis Redding in the 1960s; the funk of Parliament and War, disco, and punk bands such as the Clash and Sex Pistols in the 1970s; the megastars Bruce Springsteen, Madonna, and Michael Jackson, the rap of Public Enemy and NWA, alternative, and the grunge groups of the 1980s and 1990s.

One way to figure out how people experience their lives as part of a generation is to investigate what music means to them. The fieldwork project in this chapter investigates how people across generations use music daily to create, maintain, or subvert individual and collective identities. The method is the ethnographic interview, a nondirective approach that asks people to explain how they make sense of music in their lives. "Ethnographic" means literally graphing—getting down in the record—the values and practices of the ethnos, the tribe or group.

MY MUSIC

— *Susan D. Craft, Daniel Cavicchi, and Charles Keil*

The following two ethnographic interviews come from the Music in Daily Life Project in the American Studies program at the State University of New York at Buffalo. The project's goal was to use open-ended ethnographic interviews to find out what music means to people and how they integrate music into their lives and identities. Two undergraduate classes conducted the interviews and began with the question "What is music about for you?" (The classes settled on this question "so as not to prejudge the situation" and to give the respondents "room to define music of all kinds in their lives.") Then the interviews were edited, organized by age group, and published in the book *My Music* (1993).

SUGGESTION FOR READING Keep in mind that the interviews you are reading were not scripted but are the result of interviewers' on-the-spot decisions. As you read, notice how the interviewers ask questions and when they ask for more details or redirect the conversation.

EDWARDO

Edwardo is fifteen years old and is enrolled in an auto mechanics program at a vocational high school.

Q: What kind of music do you like to listen to?

A: Basically, I listen to anything. I prefer rap and regular . . . R and B and rock.

Q: What groups do you listen to when you get a choice?

A: When I'm by myself, I listen to rap like Eric B, MC Hammer, and KRS I. People like that. When I'm with my friends, I listen to Ozzie, and Pink Floyd, Iron Maiden, Metallica. You know, groups like that.

Q: Why do you listen to different stuff when you're by yourself? Different than when you're with your friends?

A: Usually when I'm over at their house they have control of the radio, and they don't like to listen to rap that much.

Q: What kind of things do you do when you are listening to music by yourself?

A: I lip-synch it in the mirror. I pretend I'm doing a movie. Kind of embarrassing, but I do that. And I listen to it while I'm in the shower. And . . . that's about all.

Q: Would you like to be a professional musician?

A: Kind of. Yeah.

Q: If you pictured yourself as a musician, how would you picture yourself? What kind of music would you play?

A: I'd probably rap. If I didn't, I'd like to play the saxophone.

Q: When you're walking along, do you ever have a song going through your head? Do you have specific songs that you listen to and, if not, do you ever make up songs?

A: Yes. I rap a lot to myself. I make up rhymes and have one of my friends give it a beat. Sometimes we put it on tape. Sometimes we don't.

Q: Could you give me an example of some of the stuff you have put together on your own?

A: I made up one that goes something like, "Now I have many mikes / stepped on many floors. / Shattered all the windows / knocked down all the doors." That's just a little part of it. This is hard for me. I'm nervous.

Q: So what kind of things do you try to put together in your songs? What kinds of things do you try to talk about in your songs?

A: I make up different stories. Like people running around. Sometimes I talk about drugs and drinking. Most of the time I just brag about myself.

Q: Do you have any brothers and sisters who listen to the same sort of stuff?

A: Yes. My older brother . . . he's the one who got me into rap. We're originally from the Bronx, in New York, and he doesn't listen to anything else. My cousin, he listens to heavy metal but he's kind of switched to late-seventies, early-seventies rock. He listens to Pink Floyd and all them, so I listen with him sometimes. I listen with my friends. That's about all.

Q: How long have you been listening to rap?

A: For about seven or eight years.

Q: What kind of stuff were you listening to before that?

A: Actually, I don't remember. Oh yeah. We used to live in California and I was listening to oldies . . . like the Four Tops and all them. In California . . . the Mexicans down there, they only listen to the oldies and stuff like that.

Q: Why would you say you changed to rap?

A: When I came down here, everything changed. People were listening to different kinds of music and I was, you know, behind times. So I just had to switch to catch up.

Q: So you would say that your friends really influence you and the kind of music you listen to by yourself?

A: Yeah. I would say that.

Q: When you're listening to music by yourself, what kinds of things go through your mind? Are you concentrating on the words or what?

A: Sometimes I think about life, and all the problems I have. Sometimes I just dwell on the lyrics and just listen to the music.

Q: Do you ever use music as a way to change your mood? If you're really depressed, is there a record you put on?

A: No. Usually when I listen to music and it changes me is when I'm bored and I don't have anything to do or I just get that certain urge to listen to music.

STEVE

Steve is fifty-seven years old and works as a salesman. He was interviewed by his daughter.

Q: Dad, what does music do for you?

A: What does music do for me? Well, music relaxes me. In order for me to explain, I have to go back and give you an idea exactly how my whole life was affected by music. For example, when I was five or six years old, my mother and father had come from Poland, so naturally all music played at home was ethnic music. This established my ethnic heritage. I had a love for Polish music. Later on in life, like at Polish weddings, they played mostly Polish music . . . since we lived in Cheektowaga and there is mostly Polish people and a Polish parish. My love for Polish music gave me enjoyment when I was growing up and it carried on all these years to the present time.

But naturally as I got educated in the English language I started going to the movies. I was raised during the Depression and, at that time, the biggest form of escape was musicals . . . people like Dick Powell, Ruby Keeler, Eddie Cantor, Al Jolson, and Shirley Temple. These were big stars of their day and in order to relax and forget your troubles . . . we all went through hard times . . . everybody enjoyed musicals, they were the biggest thing at that time. A lot of musicals were shows from Broadway so, as I was growing up in the Depression and watching movie musicals, I was also getting acquainted with hit tunes that came from Broadway. In that era, Tin Pan Alley was an expression for the place where all these song writers used to write and compose music, and these songs became the hits in the musicals.

Later on these writers went to the movies and it seemed as if every month there was a new hit song that everyone was singing. Some of the writers, like Irving Berlin, Gershwin, Jerome Kern, Harry Warren, and Sammy Kahn . . . some of these songs are the prettiest songs that were ever written. Even though I never played a musical instrument or was a singer, I was like hundreds of thousands of people in my era who loved music. In fact, radio was very popular at that time, so you heard music constantly on the radio, in the musicals, and all my life I could sing a song all the way through, knowing the tune *and knowing the words.*

Later on in life, when we get to W.W. II, music used to inspire patriotism, and also to bring you closer to home when overseas. For example, one place that just meant music was the Stage Door Canteen in Hollywood. All the stars of the movies and musicals used to volunteer their services and entertain everybody. Later on, as these stars went overseas and performed for the G.I.s, I had a chance to see a lot of these stars in person—stars that I really enjoyed, seeing their movies and listening to their music. So it was like bringing home to overseas. Of course, there was a lot of patriotic songs that stirred us . . . we were young . . . say, the Air Force song like "Praise the Lord and Pass the Ammunition." There was sentimental songs like "There'll Be Blue Birds Over the White Cliffs of Dover," "I Heard a Nightingale Sing Over Berkeley Square." But it was actually music that helped you through tough times like W.W. II, the way music helped you feel better during the Depression . . . in days that I was younger.

When I came back from overseas . . . now I'm entering the romantic part of my life, in my early twenties . . . it was the era of the big bands. One of the greatest events in music history were bands like Glenn Miller and Benny Goodman, the Dorsey Brothers and Sammy Kaye . . . big bands were popular at the time you used to go to local Candy Kitchens and play the jukebox, and, just like some of the songs said, it was a wonderful time to be with your friends. Good clean entertainment; you listen to the jukebox, dance on the dance floor.

In the big band era, we get into the popular singers who used to sing with the big bands. They went on their own and the era of the ballads was born, and to me this was my favorite era of music in my life. I'll mention some of the big singers just to give you an idea of what I mean—singers like Bing Crosby, Frank Sinatra, Doris Day, Margaret Whiting, Jo Stafford, and Perry Como.

The time of your life when you meet the "girl of your dreams." I was fortunate that we had the Canadiana. It was just like the Love Boat of its time. They used to have a band, and you used to be able to dance on the dance floor. If they didn't have a dance band that night, they would play records, and you could listen to music riding on the lake at night under the stars and moon. It was unbelievable, that particular part of life. It's a shame the younger people of today couldn't experience, not only the boat, but a lot of the things we went through. We thought it was tough at that time, but it was the music that really made things a lot happier and the

reason why it's so easy for someone like myself to hear a song and just place myself back in time, at exactly where I was. Was I in the Philippines, or Tokyo, or on the boat? What were the songs that were playing when I first met my wife, what were they playing when I was a young recruit in the Air Force? All I have to do is hear the songs and it'll just take me back in time and I will relive a lot of the parts of my life and, of course, you only remember the good parts! (laughing) You don't remember the bad.

Music to me is very important. One thought that I wanted to mention, about going back in time: when I was just five or six years old, my parents, because they were from the old country, played Polish music, so that when I did meet the girl I was going to marry . . . every couple has a favorite song and ours was one that was very popular at that time . . . it was a Polish song to which they put American lyrics. The song was "Tell Me Whose Girl You Are," and I think it was because my wife and I came from a Polish background that Polish music was still a very important part of our life.

Q: What music really did for you was to make you get through bad times and made you think of good things mostly, right?

A: Well, yes, and I would say that music became part of my personality. I use music to not only relax, I use it to relieve tension. About thirty percent of the time I am singing, and it has become part of my personality because it has given me a certain amount of assurance. Not only does it relax me but I think it also bolsters my confidence in being a salesman where you have to always be up. You can't be depressed. Otherwise, you're just going to waste a day. I think music to me is also something that bolsters my spirit.

Q: Does music amplify your mood or does it change your mood? For example, when you're in a depressed mood do you put on something slow or something happy to get you out of that mood?

A: Well, when I was single, if my love life wasn't going right, I used to play sad songs.

Well, I guess like most young kids when their love life isn't going right they turn to sad music. I know that after I'm married and have children and more experience, if I get in a depressed mood then I switch to happier music to change the mood.

SUGGESTIONS FOR DISCUSSION

1. Edwardo's responses to the interviewer's questions are much shorter than Steve's. One senses the pressure that the interviewer must have felt to keep the conversation going. Steve's interview, in contrast, contains an extended statement that is followed by question and answer. Take a second look at the questions that the interviewer asked Steve. What do the purposes of those questions seem to be? Try to get a sense of how and why the interviewer decided to ask particular questions. What alternatives, if any, can you imagine?

2. Notice that the interviewees do not fall easily into one distinct musical subculture. Each talks about a range of music. How do Edwardo and Steve make sense of these various forms of musical expression?

3. Each of the interviewees relates his musical tastes to particular social groups or moments in time. How do they connect music to their relationship with others and/or their memories of the past?

Fieldwork Project

Work with two or three other students on this project. Each group member should interview three people of different ages to get a range of responses across generations. Use the opening question "What is music about for you?" from the Music in Daily Life Project. Tape and transcribe the interview.

As a group, assemble and edit a collection of the interviews and write an introduction that explains the purpose of the interviews and their significance. Refer to "A Note on Interviewing" on the following page.

Editing

An edited interview is not simply the transcribed tape recording. It's important to capture the person's voice, but you also want the interview to be readable. Taped interviews can be filled with pauses, um's and ah's, incomplete or incoherent thoughts, and rambling associations. It is standard practice to "clean up" the interview, as long as doing so does not distort or change the subject's meanings. Cleaning up a transcript may include editing at the sentence level, but you may also leave out some of the taped material if it is irrelevant.

Writing an Introduction

In the introduction to the edited interviews, explain your purpose in asking people about the role that music plays in their lives. Follow this with some observations and interpretations of the results. Remember that the interviews have a limited authority. They don't "prove" anything about the role of music in daily life and the formation of individual or group identity. But they can be suggestive—and you will want to point out how and why.

The Music in Daily Life Project emphasizes the verbs you can use to describe people's relationship to music:

Is this person *finding* music to explore and express an identity or being *invaded* by music to the point of identity diffusion, *using* music to solve personal problems, *consuming* music to fill a void and relieve alienation and boredom, *participating* in musical mysteries to feel fully human, *addicted* to music and evading reality, *orienting* via music to reality?

As you can see, each verb carries a different interpretation.

A NOTE ON INTERVIEWING

- *Choosing subjects.* Choose carefully. The three subjects you choose don't have to be big music buffs, but you will get your best interviews from people who are willing to talk about their likes, dislikes, memories, and associations.

- *Preparing your subject.* Make an appointment for the interview, and be on time. Tell your subject how long you will be spending and why you want this information.

- *Preparing yourself.* Before the interview, make a list of questions you want to ask. Most questions should be open ended—they should not lead to a yes or no response. Just keep in mind that your goal is to listen, so you'll want to give your subject plenty of time to talk.

- *Conducting the interview.* Remember that in many respects, you control the agenda because you scheduled the interview and have determined the questions. The person you interview will be looking for guidance and direction. You are likely to have choices to make during the interview. The guidelines used by the Music in Daily Life Project note the following situation:

  > Somebody says, "I really love Bruce Springsteen and his music, can't help it, I get weepy over 'Born in the USA,' you know? But sometimes I wonder if I haven't just swallowed the hype about his being a working-class hero from New Jersey with the symbolic black guy by his side, you know what I mean?" and then pauses, looking at you for some direction or an answer. A choice to make.

  The choice concerns which thread in the conversation to follow—the person's love for Springsteen or his feeling of being hyped by the working-class hero image. You could do several things at this point in the interview. You could just wait for the person to explain, or you could say, "Tell me a little more about that," and hope the person will decide on which thread to elaborate. Or you could ask a direct question—"Why do you love Springsteen's music so much?" "What makes you weepy about 'Born in the USA'?" "Why do you think you're being hyped?" (Notice that each of these questions involves a choice that may take the interview in a different direction.)

  The point here is that a good interviewer must listen carefully during the interview. The goal is not to dominate but to give the subject some help in developing his or her ideas. Your task as an interviewer is to keep the conversation going.

- *Get permission.* If you plan to use the subject's name in class discussion or a paper, get permission and make arrangements to show your subject what you have written.

MINING THE ARCHIVE   Life Magazine

To learn more about how generations
are portrayed in the media, visit
www.ablongman.com/george/106

During the 1940s and 1950s, *Life* was the most popular general magazine in the United States, with an estimated readership of 20 million. Founded as a weekly in 1936, *Life* was the first American magazine to give a prominent place to the photoessay—visual narratives of the week's news as well as special features about American life and culture. If anything, *Life* taught generations of Americans what events in the world looked like, bringing them the work of such noted photographers as Robert Capa, Margaret Bourke-White, and W. Eugene Smith in photojournalistic accounts of the farm crisis and labor conflicts during the Great Depression and of battlefront situations during World War II.

In another sense, *Life* also taught Americans what the world should look like. After World War II, *Life* regularly featured families in postwar America, ordinary people in their new suburban homes, driving new cars on America's newly built freeway systems to work, school, and church. Perhaps no other source offers such a rich archive of what domestic life was supposed to be in the 1940s and 1950s in these pictorial representations of white, middle-class nuclear families.

To get a sense of how *Life* pictured America in the early postwar period, look up the December 3, 1945, issue at your library and read the news story "U.S. Normalcy: Against the Backdrop of a Troubled World *Life* Inspects an American City at Peace." Published just four months after World War II ended, the article juxtaposed images of international instability (the beginnings of the Cold War, the Nuremburg Trials, and child refugees in war-torn Europe and China) and of domestic turmoil (industrial strikes and unemployment) with the concerns of people in Indianapolis returning "their minds and energies to work, football games, automobile trips, family reunions and all the pleasant trivia of the American way of life."

Most college and public libraries have *Life* in their collection. Take a look through several issues. You will find many family portraits. You could develop various projects from this photojournalistic archive about family values in the postwar period, the role of women as homemakers, representations of teenagers, and the relation of domestic life to the Cold War. Keep in mind that the photoessays on the American family not only provide slices of life from the 1940s and 1950s but they also codify Americans' understanding of the ideal family and the American dream. Remember too that audiences did not read these photoessays on the family in isolation from advertisements and other photoessays. You might want to consider the overall flow of *Life* and how its messages about the family are connected to other messages.

Finally, you might think about why there is no longer a general magazine such as *Life* that claims to picture the "American way of life." The magazine industry today is thriving by attracting specialized readerships based on such interests as computers, skateboarding, mountain biking, and indie rock. The era of such general national magazines as *Life, Look, Colliers*, and the *Saturday Evening Post* has clearly been replaced by niche marketing and subcultural 'zines. What does this proliferation of specialized magazines suggest to you about the current state of American culture?

CHAPTER THREE

Schooling

> I wish first that we should recognize that education is ordinary; that it is, before everything else, the process of giving to the ordinary members of society its full common meanings, and the skills that will enable them to amend these meanings, in the light of their personal and common experience.
>
> —Raymond Williams, *Culture Is Ordinary*

By the time you read this chapter, you will likely have spent a considerable amount of time in school. Most Americans between the ages of five and seventeen or eighteen are full-time students whose daily lives revolve around their schooling. From the moment people enter school until the time they drop out, leave temporarily, graduate from high school, or go on to college, their intellectual and cultural growth is intimately connected to going to school and learning how to be students. Because so much of growing up takes place in them, schools are key agents of acculturation in America, the place where the younger generation not only learns how to read, write, and do mathematics but also gets its upbringing in literature, history, and civics. One of the purposes of all this schooling is to transmit bodies of knowledge from one generation to the next, and classrooms are the place where this intergenerational communication normally occurs, from teacher to student.

Americans have always put a lot of faith in schools to educate the younger generation—to prepare them for the work of the future and to teach them what it means to be an American, a good citizen, and a productive member of society. But it is precisely because Americans put so much faith—and invest so many resources—in schooling that they worry and argue incessantly about what the schools are—or should be—accomplishing. Over the past decade, there has been mounting dissatisfaction with and criticism of the American education system at the elementary, secondary, and college levels. Educational reformers have noted a variety of problems—ranging from declining standardized test scores and the "literacy crisis" to unimaginative teaching, passive learning, and outdated or irrelevant curriculum to skyrocketing college costs and the loss of careers in science, engineering, and mathematics. Critics have called attention to male biases in the curriculum and the neglect of race, ethnicity, and class in the study of history, culture, and literature. Others have argued that the way schools test and reward achievement favors middle-class students over working-class and poor students, whites over blacks, and males over females.

As a student, you are at the center of much of this controversy, and you are in a unique position to comment on schooling in your life and in the lives of others. The purpose of this chapter is to offer you opportunities to read, think, and write about the role of schooling in America today. You are invited to explore the world of schooling to identify how it has influenced you as a student, a learner, and a person. You will be asked in the reading and writing assignments to recall classroom episodes from your past and observe classroom life in the present. You will work your way from examining the everyday practices of schooling to contemplating the mission and function of education in contemporary America. The writers in this chapter will give you an idea of some of the questions educators are currently asking about schooling in America. By engaging in the educational issues raised by the reading and writing assignments, you can begin to develop your own analysis of the role of schooling.

One way to begin is to ask what sounds like a very simple and innocent question: what have you learned in school? The answers, however, may not be simple at all. Consider the formal curriculum you have studied—the subjects you have taken, the teachers who have instructed you, and the knowledge you have acquired. Think about why American schools teach what they do, why academic subjects are organized as they are, and what assumptions about the nature and function of education have shaped the formal curriculum.

The experience of going to school involves more than learning the content of the courses. It is a way of life that shapes the students' sense of themselves and their life chances. Many people remember their first day in school because it marks, quite literally, the transition from home and play to classroom life and the world of schoolwork. The kind of knowledge students acquire when they learn how to be students and go to school forms what educators call the "hidden curriculum." This part of the curriculum is just as structured as the lessons students study in the formal curriculum. The difference is that in the hidden curriculum, the content remains unstated and is acted out in practice. The hidden curriculum, therefore, refers to all the unspoken beliefs and procedures that regulate classroom life—the rules of the game no one writes down but that teachers and students have internalized in their expectations about each other.

Students begin to learn the hidden curriculum in the early grades, when they learn how to sit still, pay attention, raise their hands to be called on, follow directions, perform repetitive tasks, and complete work on time. Students learn what pleases teachers and what doesn't, what they can say to teachers and what they ought to keep to themselves. One of the functions of American schools has been to instill in the younger generation the habits of discipline, punctuality, hard work, and the wise use of time—to teach them, as the old adage goes, that "there is a time for work and a time for play." The hidden curriculum could be described as a training ground where students learn to work for grades and other symbolic rewards, to take tests and believe in their accuracy and fairness.

Examining the hidden curriculum offers a useful way to look at classroom life, in part because it demands that you research, bring into view, and question the kinds of things that take place in school that teachers and students seem to take for granted. Why, for example, is the school day divided as it is, and what is the effect of moving from subject to subject in fifty-minute intervals? Why do students sit in rows? Who has the right to speak in class? Who gets called on by the teacher? Why do teachers ask questions when they already know the answer? You will be asked in the reading and writing assignments to research questions such as these, to bring the hidden curriculum's unstated norms to light, and to assess their effects on students and on the role schooling plays in American culture.

WHAT HIGH SCHOOL IS

— *Theodore R. Sizer*

Theodore R. Sizer has been chair of the Education Department at Brown University; headmaster of Phillips Academy, Andover; and dean of the Graduate School of Education at Harvard University. The following selection is the opening chapter from *Horace's Compromise*, Sizer's book-length study of American high schools. Sizer's book takes a critical look at high schools—at overworked teachers, undermotivated students, and the assembly-line educational practices that process people rather than educate them. Originally published in 1984, Sizer's study was one of a number of national reports that appeared in the 1980s and raised serious questions about the quality of American education. This reading selection looks at how the school day is organized and what it means to students to "take subjects."

SUGGESTION FOR READING   As you read, notice that Sizer gives a full account of Mark's day before stepping back to generalize about its significance. Underline and annotate this selection to indicate where Sizer begins to analyze the meaning of Mark's day and how Sizer goes on to develop a critical analysis of the typical high school day.

1   Mark, sixteen and a genial eleventh-grader, rides a bus to Franklin High School, arriving at 7:25. It is an Assembly Day, so the schedule is adapted to allow for a meeting of the entire school. He hangs out with his friends, first outside school and then inside, by his locker. He carries a pile of textbooks and notebooks; in all, it weighs eight and a half pounds.

From 7:30 to 8:19, with nineteen other students, he is in Room 304 for English class. The

Shakespeare play being read this year by the eleventh grade is *Romeo and Juliet*. The teacher, Ms. Viola, has various students in turn take parts and read out loud. Periodically, she interrupts the (usually halting) recitations to ask whether the thread of the conversation in the play is clear. Mark is entertained by the stumbling readings of some of his classmates. He hopes he will not be asked to be Romeo, particularly if his current steady, Sally, is Juliet. There is a good deal of giggling in class, and much attention paid to who may be called on next. Ms. Viola reminds the class of a test on this part of the play to be given next week.

The bell rings at 8:19. Mark goes to the boys' room, where he sees a classmate who he thinks is a wimp but who constantly tries to be a buddy. Mark avoids the leech by rushing off. On the way, he notices two boys engaged in some sort of transaction, probably over marijuana. He pays them no attention. 8:24. Typing class. The rows of desks that embrace big office machines are almost filled before the bell. Mark is uncomfortable here: typing class is girl country. The teacher constantly threatens what to Mark is a humiliatingly girl future: "Your employer won't like these erasures." The minutes during the period are spent copying a letter from a handbook onto business stationery. Mark struggles to keep from looking at his work; the teacher wants him to watch only the material from which he is copying. Mark is frustrated, uncomfortable, and scared that he will not complete his letter by the class's end, which would be embarrassing.

Nine tenths of the students present at school that day are assembled in the auditorium by the 9:18 bell. The dilatory tenth still stumble in, running down aisles. Annoyed class deans try to get the mob settled. The curtains part; the program is a concert by a student rock group. Their electronic gear flashes under the lights, and the five boys and one girl in the group work hard at being casual. Their movements on stage are studiously at three-quarter time, and they chat with one another as though the tumultuous screaming of

their schoolmates were totally inaudible. The girl balances on a stool; the boys crank up the music. It is very soft rock, the sanitized lyrics surely cleared with the assistant principal. The girl sings, holding the mike close to her mouth, but can scarcely be heard. Her light voice is tentative, and the lyrics indecipherable. The guitars, amplified, are tuneful, however, and the drums are played with energy.

5   The students around Mark—all juniors, since they are seated by class—alternately slouch in their upholstered, hinged seats, talking to one another, or sit forward, leaning on the chair backs in front of them, watching the band. A boy near Mark shouts noisily at the microphone-fondling singer, "Bite it . . . ohhh," and the area around Mark explodes in vulgar male laughter, but quickly subsides. A teacher walks down the aisle. Songs continue, to great applause. Assembly is over at 9:46, two minutes early.

9:53 and biology class. Mark was at a different high school last year and did not take this course there as a tenth-grader. He is in it now, and all but one of his classmates are a year younger than he. He sits on the side, not taking part in the chatter that goes on after the bell. At 9:57, the public address system goes on, with the announcements of the day. After a few words from the principal ("Here's today's cheers and jeers . . ." with a cheer for the winning basketball team and a jeer for the spectators who made a ruckus at the gymnasium), the task is taken over by officers of ASB (Associated Student Bodies). There is an appeal for "bat bunnies." Carnations are for sale by the Girls' League. Miss Indian American is coming. Students are auctioning off their services (background catcalls are heard) to earn money for the prom. Nominees are needed for the ballot for school bachelor and school bachelorette. The announcements end with a "thought for the day. When you throw a little mud, you lose a little ground."

At 10:04 the biology class finally turns to science. The teacher, Mr. Robbins, has placed one of several labeled laboratory specimens—some are pinned in frames, other swim in formaldehyde—on each of the classroom's eight laboratory tables. The three or so students whose chairs circle each of these benches are to study the specimen and make notes about it or drawings of it. After a few minutes each group of three will move to another table. The teacher points out that these specimens are of organisms already studied in previous classes. He says that the period-long test set for the following day will involve observing some of these specimens—then to be without labels—and writing an identifying paragraph on each. Mr. Robbins points out that some of the printed labels ascribe the specimens' names different from those given in the textbook. He explains that biologists often give several names to the same organism.

The class now falls to peering, writing, and quiet talking. Mr. Robbins comes over to Mark, and in whispered words asks him to carry a requisition form for science department materials to the business office. Mark, because of his "older" status, is usually chosen by Robbins for this kind of errand. Robbins gives Mark the form and a green hall pass to show to any teacher who might challenge him, on his way to the office, for being out of a classroom. The errand takes Mark four minutes. Meanwhile Mark's group is hard at work but gets to only three of the specimens before the bell rings at 10:42. As the students surge out, Robbins shouts a reminder about a "double" laboratory period on Thursday.

Between classes one of the seniors asks Mark whether he plans to be a candidate for schoolwide office next year. Mark says no. He starts to explain. The 10:47 bell rings, meaning that he is late for French class.

10   There are fifteen students in Monsieur Bates's language class. He hands out tests taken the day before: "*C'est bien fait, Etienne . . . c'est mieux, Marie . . . Tch, tch, Robert . . .*" Mark notes his C+ and peeks at the A– in front of Susanna, next to him. The class has been assigned seats by M. Bates; Mark resents sitting next to prissy, brainy Susanna. Bates starts by asking a student to read a question and give the correct answer. "*James, question un.*" James

haltingly reads the question and gives an answer that Bates, now speaking English, says is incomplete. In due course: "*Mark, question cinq.*" Mark does his bit, and the sequence goes on, the eight quiz questions and answers filling about twenty minutes of time.

"Turn to page forty-nine. *Maintenant, lisez après moi . . .*" and Bates reads a sentence and has the class echo it. Mark is embarrassed by this and mumbles with a barely audible sound. Others, like Susanna, keep the decibel count up, so Mark can hide. This I-say-you-repeat drill is interrupted once by the public address system, with an announcement about a meeting for the cheerleaders. Bates finishes class, almost precisely at the bell, with a homework assignment. The students are to review these sentences for a brief quiz the following day. Mark takes notes of the assignment, because he knows that tomorrow will be a day of busywork in French class. Much though he dislikes oral drills, they are better than the workbook stuff that Bates hands out. Write, write, write, for Bates to throw away, Mark thinks.

11:36. Down to the cafeteria, talking noisily, hanging out, munching. Getting to Room 104 by 12:17: U.S. history. The teacher is sitting cross-legged on his desk when Mark comes in, heatedly arguing with three students over the fracas that had followed the previous night's basketball game. The teacher, Mr. Suslovic, while agreeing that the spectators from their school certainly were provoked, argues that they should neither have been so obviously obscene in yelling at the opposing cheerleaders nor have allowed Coke cans to be rolled out on the floor. The three students keep saying that "it isn't fair." Apparently they and some others had been assigned "Saturday mornings" (detentions) by the principal for the ruckus.

At 12:34, the argument appears to subside. The uninvolved students, including Mark, are in their seats, chatting amiably. Mr. Suslovic climbs off his desk and starts talking: "We've almost finished this unit, chapters nine and ten. . . ." The students stop chattering among themselves and turn toward Suslovic. Several slouch down in their chairs. Some open notebooks. Most have the five-pound textbook on their desks.

Suslovic lectures on the cattle drives, from north Texas to railroads west of St. Louis. He breaks up this narrative with questions ("Why were the railroad lines laid largely east to west?"), directed at nobody in particular and eventually answered by Suslovic himself. Some students take notes. Mark doesn't. A student walks in the open door, hands Mr. Suslovic a list, and starts whispering with him. Suslovic turns from the class and hears out this messenger. He then asks, "Does anyone know where Maggie Sharp is?" Someone answers, "Sick at home"; someone else says, "I thought I saw her at lunch." Genial consternation. Finally Suslovic tells the messenger, "Sorry, we can't help you," and returns to the class: "Now, where were we?" He goes on for some minutes. The bell rings. Suslovic forgets to give the homework assignment.

15   1:11 and Algebra II. There is a commotion in the hallway: someone's locker is rumored to have been opened by the assistant principal and a narcotics agent. In the five-minute passing time, Mark hears the story three times and three ways. A locker had been broken into by another student. It was Mr. Gregory and a narc. It was the cops, and they did it without Gregory's knowing. Mrs. Ames, the mathematics teacher, has not heard anything about it. Several of the nineteen students try to tell her and start arguing among themselves. "O.K., that's enough." She hands out the day's problem, one sheet to each student. Mark sees with dismay that it is a single, complicated "word" problem about some train that, while traveling at 84 mph, due west, passes a car that was going due east at 55 mph. Mark struggles: Is it $d = rt$ or $t = rd$? The class becomes quiet, writing, while Mrs. Ames writes some additional, short problems on the blackboard. "Time's up." A sigh; most students still writing. A muffled "Shit." Mrs. Ames frowns. "Come on, now." She collects papers, but it takes four minutes for her to corral them all.

"Copy down the problems from the board." A minute passes. "William, try number one." William suggests an approach. Mrs. Ames corrects and cajoles, and William finally gets it right. Mark watches two kids to his right passing notes; he tries to read them but the handwriting is illegible from his distance. He hopes he is not called on, and he isn't. Only three students are asked to puzzle out an answer. The bell rings at 2:00. Mrs. Ames shouts a homework assignment over the resulting hubbub.

Mark leaves his books in his locker. He remembers that he has homework, but figures that he can do it during English class the next day. He knows that there will be an in-class presentation of one of the *Romeo and Juliet* scenes and that he will not be in it. The teacher will not notice his homework writing, or won't do anything about it if she does.

Mark passes various friends heading toward the gym, members of the basketball teams. Like most students, Mark isn't an active school athlete. However, he is associated with the yearbook staff. Although he is not taking "Yearbook" for credit as an English course, he is contributing photographs. Mark takes twenty minutes checking into the yearbook staff's headquarters (the classroom of its faculty adviser) and getting some assignments of pictures from his boss, the senior who is the photography editor. Mark knows that if he pleases his boss and the faculty adviser, he'll take that editor's post for the next year. He'll get English credit for his work then.

After gossiping a bit with the yearbook staff, Mark will leave school by 2:35 and go home. His grocery market bagger's job is from 4:45 to 8:00, the rush hour for the store. He'll have a snack at 4:30, and his mother will save him some supper to eat at 8:30. She will ask whether he has any homework, and he'll tell her no. Tomorrow, and virtually every other tomorrow, will be the same for Mark, save for the lack of the assembly; each period then will be five minutes longer.

20 Most Americans have an uncomplicated vision of what secondary education should be. Their

conception of high school is remarkably uniform across the country, a striking fact, given the size and diversity of the United States and the politically decentralized character of the schools. This uniformity is of several generations' standing. It has, however, two appearances, each quite different from the other, one of words and the other of practice, a world of political rhetoric and Mark's world.

A California high school's general goals, set out in 1979, could serve equally well most of America's high schools, public and private. This school had as its ends:

- Fundamental scholastic achievement . . . to acquire knowledge and share in the traditionally accepted academic fundamentals . . . to develop the ability to make decisions, to solve problems, to reason independently, and to accept responsibility for self-evaluation and continuing self-improvement.
- Career and economic competence
- Citizenship and civil responsibility
- Competence in human and social relations
- Moral and ethical values
- Self-realization and mental and physical health
- Aesthetic awareness
- Cultural diversity

In addition to its optimistic rhetoric, what distinguished this list is its comprehensiveness. The high school is to touch most aspects of an adolescent's existence—mind, body, morals, values, career. No one of these areas is given especial prominence. School people arrogate to themselves an obligation to all.

An example of the wide acceptability of these goals is found in the courts. Forced to present a detailed definition of "thorough and efficient education," elementary as well as secondary, a West Virginia judge sampled the best of conventional wisdom and concluded that there are eight general elements of a thorough and efficient system of education: (a) Literacy, (b) The ability to add, subtract, multiply, and divide numbers, (c) Knowledge of government to the extent the child will be equipped as a citizen to make informed choices among persons and issues that affect his own governance, (d) Self-knowledge and knowledge of his or her total environment to allow the child to intelligently choose life work—to know his or her options, (e) Work-training and advanced academic training as the child may intelligently choose, (f) Recreational pursuits, (g) Interests in all creative arts such as music, theater, literature, and the visual arts, and (h) Social ethics, both behavioral and abstract, to facilitate compatibility with others in this society.

That these eight—now powerfully part of the debate over the purpose and practice of education in West Virginia—are reminiscent of the influential list, "The Seven Cardinal Principles of Secondary Education," promulgated in 1918 by the National Education Association, is no surprise. The rhetoric of high school purpose has been uniform and consistent for decades. Americans agree on the goals for their high schools.

25   That agreement is convenient, but it masks the fact that virtually all the words in these goal statements beg definition. Some schools have labored long to identify specific criteria beyond them; the result has been lists of daunting pseudospecificity and numbing earnestness. However, most leave the words undefined and let the momentum of traditional practice speak for itself. That is why analyzing how Mark spends his time is important: from watching him one uncovers the important purposes of education, the ones that shape practice. Mark's day is similar to that of other high school students across the country, as similar as the rhetoric of one goal statement to others'. Of course, there are variations, but the extent of consistency in the shape of school routine for a large and diverse adolescent population is extraordinary, indicating more graphically than any rhetoric the measure of agreement in America about what one does in high school, and, by implication, what it is for.

The basic organizing structures in schools are familiar. Above all, students are grouped by age (that is, freshman, sophomore, junior, senior), and all are expected to take precisely the same time—around 720 school days over four years, to be precise—to meet the requirements for a diploma. When one is out of his grade level, he can feel odd, as Mark did in his biology class. The goals are the same for all, and the means to achieve them are also similar.

Young males and females are treated remarkably alike; the schools' goals are the same for each gender. In execution, there are differences, as those pressing sex discrimination suits have made educators intensely aware. The students in metalworking classes are mostly male; those in home economics, mostly female. But it is revealing how much less sex discrimination there is in high schools than in other American institutions. For many young women, the most liberated hours of their week are in school.

School is to be like a job: you start in the morning and end in the afternoon, five days a week. You don't get much of a lunch hour, so you go home early, unless you are an athlete or are involved in some special school or extracurricular activity. School is conceived of as the children's workplace, and it takes young people off parents' hands and out of the labor market during prime-time work hours. Not surprisingly, many students see going to school as little more than a dogged necessity. They perceive the day-to-day routine, a Minnesota study reports, as one of "boredom and lethargy." One of the students summarizes: School is "boring, restless, tiresome, puts ya to sleep, tedious, monotonous, pain in the neck."

The school schedule is a series of units of time: the clock is king. The base time block is about fifty minutes in length. Some schools, on what they call modular scheduling, split that fifty-minute block into two or even three pieces. Most schools have double periods for laboratory work, especially in the sciences, or four-hour units for small numbers of students involved in intensive vocational or other work-study programs. The flow of all school activity arises from or is blocked by these time units. "How much time do I have with my kids" is the teacher's key question.

30 Because there are many claims for those fifty-minute blocks, there is little time set aside for rest between them, usually no more than three to ten minutes, depending on how big the school is and, consequently, how far students and teachers have to walk from class to class. As a result, there is a frenetic quality to the school day, a sense of sustained restlessness. For the adolescents, there are frequent changes of room and fellow students, each change giving tempting opportunities for distraction, which are stoutly resisted by teachers. Some schools play soft music during these "passing times," to quiet the multitude, one principal told me.

Many teachers have a chance for a coffee break. Few students do. In some city schools where security is a problem, students must be in class for seven consecutive periods, interrupted by a heavily monitored twenty-minute lunch period for small groups, starting as early as 10:30 a.m. and running to after 1:00 p.m. A high premium is placed on punctuality and on "being where you're supposed to be." Obviously, a low premium is placed on reflection and repose. The student rushes from class to class to collect knowledge. Savoring it, it is implied, is not to be done much in school, nor is such meditation really much admired. The picture that these familial patterns yield is that of an academic supermarket. The purpose of going to school is to pick things up, in an organized and predictable way, the faster the better.

What is supposed to be picked up is remarkably consistent among all sorts of high schools. Most schools specifically mandate three out of every five courses a student selects. Nearly all of these mandates fall into five areas—English, social studies, mathematics, science, and physical education. On the average, English is required to be taken each year, social studies and physical education three out of the four high school years, and mathematics and science one or two years. Trends indicate that in the mid-eighties there is likely to be an increase in the time allocated to these last two subjects. Most students take classes in these four major academic areas beyond the minimum requirements, sometimes in such special areas as journalism and "yearbook," offshoots of English departments.

Press most adults about what high school is for, and you hear these subjects listed. *High school? That's where you learn English and math and that sort of thing.* Ask students, and you get the same answers. High school is to "teach" these "subjects."

What is often absent is any definition of these subjects or any rationale for them. They are just there, labels. Under those labels lie a multitude of things. A great deal of material is supposed to be "covered"; most of these courses are surveys, great sweeps of the stuff of their parent disciplines.

35 While there is often a sequence *within* subjects—algebra before trigonometry, "first-year" French before "second-year" French—there is rarely a coherent relationship or sequence *across* subjects. Even the most logically related matters—reading ability as a precondition for the reading of history books, and certain mathematical concepts or skills before the study of some physics—are only loosely coordinated, if at all. There is little demand for a synthesis of it all; English, mathematics, and the rest are discrete items, to be picked up individually. The incentive for picking them up is largely through tests and, with success at these, in credits earned.

Coverage within subjects is the key priority. If some imaginative teacher makes a proposal to force the marriage of, say, mathematics and physics or to require some culminating challenges to students to use several subjects in the solution of a complex problem, and if this proposal will take "time" away from other things, opposition is usually phrased in terms of what may be thus forgone. If we do that, we'll have to give up colonial history. We won't be able to get to programming. We'll not be able to read *Death of a Salesman*. There isn't time. The protesters usually win out.

The subjects come at a student like Mark in random order, a kaleidoscope of worlds: algebraic formulae to poetry to French verbs to Ping-Pong to the War of the Spanish Succession, all before lunch. Pupils are to pick up these things. Tests measure whether the picking up has been successful.

The lack of connection between stated goals, such as those of the California high school cited earlier, and the goals inherent in school practice is obvious and, curiously, tolerated. Most striking is the gap between statements about "self-realization and mental and physical growth" or "moral and ethical values"—common rhetoric in school documents—and practice. Most physical education programs have neither the time nor the focus really to ensure fitness. Mental health is rarely defined. Neither are ethical values, save at the negative extremes, such as opposition to assault or dishonesty. Nothing in the regimen of a day like Mark's signals direct or implicit teaching in this area. The "schoolboy code" (not ratting on a fellow student) protects the marijuana pusher, and a leech-like associate is shrugged off without concern. The issue of the locker search was pushed aside, as not appropriate for class time.

Most students, like Mark, go to class in groups of twenty to twenty-seven students. The expected attendance in some schools, particularly those in low-income areas, is usually higher, often thirty-five students per class, but high absentee rates push the actual numbers down. About twenty-five per class is an average figure for expected attendance, and the actual numbers are somewhat lower. There are remarkably few students who go to class in groups much larger or smaller than twenty-five.

40 A student such as Mark sees five or six teachers per day; their differing styles and expectations are part of his kaleidoscope. High school staffs are highly specialized; guidance counselors rarely teach mathematics, mathematics teachers rarely teach English, principals rarely do any classroom instruction. Mark, then, is known a little bit by a number of people, each of whom sees him in one specialized situation. No one may know him as a "whole person"—unless he becomes a special problem or has special needs.

Save in extracurricular or coaching situations, such as in athletics, drama, or shop classes, there is little opportunity for sustained conversation between student and teacher. The mode is a one-sentence or two-sentence exchange: *Mark, when was Grover Cleveland president?* Let's see, was 1890 . . . or something . . . wasn't he the one . . . he was elected twice, wasn't he? . . . *Yes . . . Gloria, can you get the dates right?* Dialogue is strikingly absent, and as a result the opportunity of teachers to challenge students' ideas in a systematic and logical way is limited. Given the rushed, full quality of the school day, it can seldom happen. One must infer that careful probing of students' thinking is not a high priority. How one gains (to quote the California school's statement of goals again) "the ability to make decisions, to solve problems, to reason independently, and to accept responsibility for self-evaluation and continuing self-improvement" without being challenged is difficult to imagine. One certainly doesn't learn these things merely from lectures and textbooks.

Most schools are nice places. Mark and his friends enjoy being in theirs. The adults who work in schools generally like adolescents. The academic pressures are limited, and the accommodations to students are substantial. For example, if many members of an English class have jobs after school, the English teacher's expectations for them are adjusted, downward. In a word, school is sensitively accommodating, as long as students are punctual, where they are supposed to be, and minimally dutiful about picking things up from the clutch of courses in which they enroll.

This characterization is not pretty, but it is accurate, and it serves to describe the vast majority of American secondary schools. "Taking subjects" in a systematized, conveyer-belt way is what one does in high school. That this process is, in substantial respects, not related to the rhetorical purposes of education is tolerated by most people, perhaps because they do not really either believe in those ill-defined goals or, in their heart of hearts, believe that schools can or should even try to achieve them. The students are happy taking subjects. The parents are happy, because that's what they did in high school. The rituals, the most important of which is graduation, remain intact. The adolescents are supervised, safely and constructively most of the time, during the morning and afternoon hours, and they are off the labor market. That is what high school is all about.

SUGGESTIONS FOR DISCUSSION

1. The portrait of Mark that begins this selection, as Sizer notes, is a composite blending of several real students and real high schools—"somewhere," Sizer says, "between precise journalism and nonfiction fiction." Sizer's portrait of Mark's school day must appear typical and recognizable for it to be persuasive and credible. Does Sizer achieve the kind of typicality he is trying for? Draw on your own experience and observations in high school to decide whether this is a fair portrait and what, if anything, it leaves out.

2. Sizer says, "Press most adults about what high school is for, and you hear these subjects listed. *High school? That's where you learn English and math and that sort of thing.*" How does Sizer answer his question, what is high school for? How would you answer it? Explain how you would account for differences and similarities between Sizer's answer and your own.

3. Do you agree with Sizer that there is a "lack of connection between stated goals" of high school education and "the goals inherent in school practice?" Sizer gives some examples of stated goals, such as the general goals for California high schools and the goals presented by a West Virginia judge, but he doesn't say what the "goals inherent in school practice" might be. Decide what these unstated goals are and how they determine what actually takes place in the daily routines of American high schools.

SUGGESTIONS FOR WRITING

1. At the end of this selection, Sizer says, " 'Taking subjects' in a systematized, conveyer-belt way is what one does in high school." A few lines later he says, "students are happy taking subjects." Do you agree with Sizer? Are high school students, in your experience, happy "taking subjects," or do they feel something is missing? Write an essay that develops your own position. Begin by summarizing what Sizer views as "conveyer-belt" education. Then explain to what extent and why you agree or disagree with his sense that students are happy "taking subjects."

2. Sizer says, "Most schools are nice. . . . The academic pressures are limited, and the accommodations to students are substantial. For example, if many members of an English class have jobs after school, the English teacher's expectations for them are adjusted, downward." Write an essay that describes the expectations of teachers in the high school you attended and explains what influence those expectations have had on you as a student, a learner, and a person. Take into account whether teachers' expectations varied and whether they held the same expectations for all students.

3. Use Sizer's composite portrait of Mark's school day as a model to write a portrait of a typical day at the high school you attended or your college. You can draw on your own experience and memories, but keep in mind that Sizer's portrait is a made-up character, not a real person. Similarly, in this writing task, you'll need to invent your own typical student and his or her experience of the school day.

LET TEENAGERS TRY ADULTHOOD

— Leon Botstein

Leon Botstein is the president of Bard College and author of *Jefferson's Children: Education and the Promise of American Culture* (1997). The following selection appeared on the Op Ed page of the *New York Times* in May 1999, shortly after the school shootings in Littleton, Colorado. Botstein uses the shootings at Columbine High School to give a sense of urgency to his argument that "American high schools are obsolete and should be abolished." As you will see, however, the case he makes does not depend on the Littleton events alone. In Botstein's view, there are larger reasons for recognizing that high school is a failure not worth reforming.

SUGGESTION FOR READING   Botstein makes his main point—namely that high schools are out of date and should be abolished—in the opening sentence. As you read, mark the reasons he offers to support this position.

1 The national outpouring after the Littleton shootings has forced us to confront something we have suspected for a long time: the American high school is obsolete and should be abolished. In the last month, high school students present and past have come forward with stories about cliques and the artificial intensity of a world defined by insiders and outsiders, in which the insiders hold sway because of superficial definitions of good looks and attractiveness, popularity, and sports prowess.

The team sports of high school dominate more than student culture. A community's loyalty to the high school system is often based on the extent to which varsity teams succeed. High school administrators and faculty members are often former coaches, and the coaches themselves are placed in a separate, untouchable category. The result is that the culture of the inside elite is not contested by the adults in the school. Individuality and dissent are discouraged.

But the rules of high school turn out not to be the rules of life. Often the high school outsider becomes the more successful and admired adult. The definitions of masculinity and femininity go through sufficient transformation to make the game of popularity in high school an embarrassment. No other group of adults young or old is confined to an age-segregated environment, much like a gang in which individuals of the same age group define each other's world. In no workplace, not even in colleges or universities, is there such a narrow segmentation by chronology.

Given the poor quality of recruitment and training for high school teachers, it is no wonder that the curriculum and the enterprise of learning hold so little sway over young people. When puberty meets education and learning in modern America, the victory of puberty masquerading as popular culture and the tyranny of peer groups based on ludicrous values meet little resistance.

5   By the time those who graduate from high school go on to college and realize what really is at stake in becoming an adult, too many opportunities have been lost and too much time has been wasted. Most thoughtful young people suffer the high school environment in silence and in their junior and senior years mark time waiting for college to begin. The Littleton killers, above and beyond the psychological demons that drove them to violence, felt trapped in the artificiality of the high school world and believed it to be real. They engineered their moment of undivided attention and importance in the absence of any confidence that life after high school could have a different meaning.

Adults should face the fact that they don't like adolescents and that they have used high school to isolate the pubescent and hormonally active adolescent away from both the picture-book idealized innocence of childhood and the more accountable world of adulthood. But the primary reason high school doesn't work anymore, if it ever did, is that young people mature substantially earlier in the late 20th century than they did when the high school was invented. For example, the age of first menstruation has dropped at least two years since the beginning of this century, and not surprisingly, the onset of sexual activity has dropped in proportion. An institution intended for children in transition now holds young adults back well beyond the developmental point for which high school was originally designed.

Furthermore, whatever constraints to the presumption of adulthood among young people may have existed decades ago have now fallen away. Information and images, as well as the real and virtual freedom of movement we associate with adulthood, are now accessible to every fifteen- and sixteen-year-old.

Secondary education must be rethought. Elementary school should begin at age four or five and end with the sixth grade. We should entirely abandon the concept of the middle school and junior high school. Beginning with the seventh grade, there should be four years of secondary education that we may call high school. Young people should graduate at sixteen rather than eighteen.

They could then enter the real world, the world of work or national service, in which they would take a place of responsibility alongside older adults in mixed company. They could stay at home and attend junior college, or they could go away to college. For all the faults of college, at least the adults who dominate the world of colleges, the faculty, were selected precisely because they were exceptional and different, not because they were popular. Despite the often cavalier attitude toward teaching in college, at least physicists know their physics, mathematicians know and love their mathematics, and music is taught by musicians, not by graduates of education schools, where the disciplines are subordinated to the study of classroom management.

10   For those sixteen-year-olds who do not want to do any of the above, we might construct new

kinds of institutions, each dedicated to one activity, from science to dance, to which adolescents could devote their energies while working together with professionals in those fields.

At sixteen, young Americans are prepared to be taken seriously and to develop the motivations and interests that will serve them well in adult life. They need to enter a world where they are not in a lunchroom with only their peers, estranged from other age groups and cut off from the game of life as it is really played. There is nothing utopian about this idea; it is immensely practical and efficient, and its implementation is long overdue. We need to face biological and cultural facts and not prolong the life of a flawed institution that is out of date.

SUGGESTIONS FOR DISCUSSION

1. First, make a list of the reasons Botstein gives to support his view that "high school doesn't work anymore." Next, notice that what he calls "the primary reason" appears in paragraph six. Consider why he has organized his reasons in the order they appear. How does the order of reasons lead readers from one point to the next? What assumptions about schooling and American teenagers is Botstein asking readers to share?

2. Both Botstein and Theodore Sizer in the preceding selection, "What High School Is," are highly critical of American high schools. Their critiques, however, are quite different ones. Compare the analyses they offer of American high schools. What in particular do they focus on? Are they looking at the same things and drawing different conclusions, or do their differences begin with the things they are analyzing? How do these differences in perspective set up Botstein to argue for abolishing high school but Sizer to argue for reforming it?

3. Like Botstein, Thomas Hine in "Goths in Tomorrowland" (Chapter 2) is concerned about the alienation of American teenagers from adult society. Read (or reread) the selection from Hine. Compare the perspectives Hine and Botstein offer on the age segregation of American teenagers. What do they see as the larger implications of teenagers' alienation from adult society? Do you share their concern? Explain why or why not. Take into account what, if anything, you can say in favor of the kind of age segregation that takes place in high school.

SUGGESTIONS FOR WRITING

1. Write a letter to the editor of the *New York Times* that responds to Botstein's op-ed piece. You can agree or disagree with his proposal to abolish American high schools or you can provide a different perspective on the issues of schooling he raises. In any case, explain your reasons for agreeing or the significance of the perspective you offer. To get a sense of the tone to use in such a letter and the approach to readers, take a look at some of the letters in a recent edition.

2. Assume that Botstein's plan to restructure American education actually takes place. In the new system, young people will leave secondary school at age sixteen. Some, as Botstein notes, will enter the world of work or national service, while others will go to college. For still others, however, "new kinds of institutions, each dedicated to one activity, from science to dance, to which adolescents could devote their energies while working together with professionals in those fields" will be developed. Develop your own proposal for one of these "new kinds of institutions." Include a rationale that explains why you think the particular activity the institution focuses on is worthwhile, what young people would do, and what the outcome might be.

3. Write an essay that develops your own position on what both Botstein and Thomas Hine write about as the age segregation of young people in high school. First, explain the perspective each offers and the consequences they believe follow from age segregation. Then, explain your own point of view on the issue, indicating whether you think their concern about the alienation of teenagers from adult society is a justifiable one.

CROSSING BOUNDARIES

— Mike Rose

Mike Rose is a professor of education at UCLA. He has worked for the past twenty years teaching and tutoring children and adults from what he calls America's "educational underclass" — working-class children, poorly educated Vietnam vets, underprepared college students, and adults in basic literacy programs. The following selection is from the chapter "Crossing Boundaries" in Rose's award-winning *Lives on the Boundary* (1989). This book is an intensely personal account of Rose's own life growing up in a Los Angeles ghetto and his struggles as an educator to make schooling more accessible to children and adults labeled "remedial," "illiterate," and "intellectually deficient." As the following selection indicates, throughout *Lives on the Boundary*, Rose is especially interested in the "politics and sociology of school failure."

SUGGESTION FOR READING   The following selection is separated into three parts. To help you think about how these parts combine to form a whole (or whether they do), underline and annotate as you read and note the focus of each section and how it provides a commentary on the other sections.

I myself I thank God for the dream to come back to school and to be able to seek the dream I want, because I know this time I will try and make my dream come true.

1   Each semester the staff of the Bay Area literacy program we're about to visit collects samples of their students' writing and makes books for them. You can find an assortment on an old bookshelf by the coordinator's desk. The booklets are simple: mimeographed, faint blue stencil, stapled, dog-eared. There are uneven drawings on the thin paper covers: a bicycle leaning against a tree, the Golden Gate Bridge, an Aubrey Beardsley sketch. The stories are about growing up, raising children, returning—sadly or with anticipation—to hometowns, to Chicago or St. Louis or to a sweep of rural communities in the South. Many of the stories are about work: looking for work, losing work, wanting better work. And many more are about coming back to school. Coming back to school.

Some of these writers haven't been in a classroom in thirty years.

The stories reveal quite a range. Many are no longer than a paragraph, their sentences simple and repetitive, tenuously linked by *and* and *then* and *anyway*. There are lots of grammar and spelling errors and problems with sentence boundaries—in a few essays, periods come where commas should be or where no punctuation is needed at all: "It was hard for me to stay in school because I was allway sick. and that was verry hard for me." Or, "I sound better. now that my boys are grown." Papers of this quality are written, for the most part, by newcomers, people at the end of their first semester. But other papers—quite a few, actually—are competent. They tend to come from those who have received a year or more of instruction. There are still problems with grammar and sentence fragments and with spelling, since the writers are using a wider, more ambitious vocabulary.

Problems like these take longer to clear up, but the writers are getting more adept at rendering their experience in print, at developing a narrative, at framing an illustration, at turning a phrase in written language:

> The kitchen floor was missing some of its tiles and had not been kissed with water and soap for a long time.
>
> The [teacher] looked for a moment, and then said, "All the students wishing to be accounted for, please be seated."
>
> A minute went by, then a tough looking Mexican boy got up, and walked to the teacher with a knife in his hand. When he got to the desk he said, "I'm here teacher! My name is Robert Gomez." With that he put the knife away, and walked over and found a seat.
>
> Back in the jaws of despair, pain, and the ugly scars of the defeated parents he loved. Those jaws he had struggled free of when he had moved out and away when he was eighteen years old.
>
> . . . the wind was howling, angry, whirling.

A few new students also created such moments, indicators of what they'll be able to do as they become more fluent writers, as they develop some control over and confidence in establishing themselves on paper:

> [I used to have] light, really light Brown eyes, like Grasshopper eyes. which is what some peoples used to call me. Grasshopper, or Grasshopper eyes. . . . I decided one Day to catch a Grasshopper. and look at its eye to be sure of the color.
>
> It was early in the morning just before dawn. Big Red, the sun hasn't showed its face in the heaven. The sky had that midnight blue look. The stars losing their shine.

There are about eight or ten of these stapled collections, a hundred and fifty or so essays. Five years' worth. An archive scattered across an old bookcase. There's a folding chair close by. I've been sitting in it for some time now, reading one book, then another, story after story. Losing track. Drifting in and out of lives. Wondering about grasshopper eyes, about segregated schools, wanting to know more about this journey to the West looking for work. Slowly something has been shifting in my perception: the errors—the weird commas and missing letters, the fragments and irregular punctuation—they are ceasing to be slips of the hand and brain. They are becoming part of the stories themselves. They are the only fitting way, it seems, to render dislocation—shacks and field labor and children lost to the inner city—to talk about parents you long for, jobs you can't pin down. Poverty has generated its own damaged script, scars manifest in the spelling of a word.

5   This is the prose of America's underclass. The writers are those who got lost in our schools, who could not escape neighborhoods that narrowed their possibilities, who could not enter the job market in any ascendent way. They are locked into unskilled and semiskilled jobs, live in places that threaten their children, suffer from disorders and handicaps they don't have the money to treat. Some have been unemployed for a long time. But for all that, they remain hopeful, have somehow held onto a deep faith in education. They have come back to school. Ruby, the woman who wrote the passage that opens this section, walks unsteadily to the teacher's desk—the arthritis in her hip goes unchecked—with a paper in her hand. She looks over her shoulder to her friend, Alice: "I ain't givin' up the ship this time," she says and winks, "though, Lord, I might drown with it." The class laughs. They understand.

It is a very iffy thing, this schooling. But the participants put a lot of stock in it. They believe school will help them, and they are very specific about what they want: a high school equivalency, or the ability to earn seven dollars an hour. One wants to move from being a nurse's aide to a licensed vocational nurse, another needs to read and write and compute adequately enough to be self-employed as a car painter and body man. They remind you of how fundamentally important it is—not just to your pocket but to your soul as well—to earn a decent wage, to have a steady job, to be just a little bit in control of your economic life. The goals are specific, modest, but they mean a tremendous amount for the assurance they give to these people that they are still somebody, that they can exercise control. Thus it is that talk of school and a new job brings forth such expansive language, as soaring as any humanist's testament to the glory of the word: "I thank God to be able to seek the dream I want. . . ." For Ruby and her classmates the dream deferred neither dried up like a raisin in the sun, nor has it exploded. It has emerged again— for it is so basic—and it centers on schooling. "I admire and respect knowledge and those that have it are well blessed," writes another student. "My classmates are a swell group because they too have a dream and they too are seeking knowledge and I love them for that."

Sitting in the classroom with Ruby, Alice, and the rest, you think, at times, that you're at a revival meeting. There is so much testifying. Everybody talks and writes about dreams and goals and "doing better for myself." This is powerful, edifying—but something about it, its insistence perhaps, is a little bit discordant. The exuberance becomes jittery, an almost counterphobic boosting and supporting. It is no surprise, then, that it alternates with despair. In their hearts, Ruby and her classmates know how tenuous this is, how many times they've failed before. Somebody says something about falling down. Sally says, "I've felt that too. Not falling down on my legs or knees, but falling down within me." No wonder they sermonize and embrace. It's not just a few bucks more a week that's at stake; literacy, here, is intimately connected with respect, with a sense that they are not beaten, the mastery of print revealing the deepest impulse to survive.

When they entered the program, Ruby and Alice and Sally and all the rest were given several tests, one of which was a traditional reading inventory. The test had a section on comprehension—relatively brief passages followed by multiple-choice questions—and a series of sections that tested particular reading skills: vocabulary, syllabication, phonics, prefixes and roots. The level of the instrument was pretty sophisticated, and the skills it tested are the kind you develop in school: answering multiple-choice questions, working out syllable breaks, knowing Greek and Latin roots, all that. What was interesting about this group of test takers was that—though a few were barely literate—many could read and write well enough to get along, and, in some cases, to help those in their communities who were less skilled. They could read, with fair comprehension, simple news articles, could pay bills, follow up on sales and coupons, deal with school forms for their kids, and help illiterate neighbors in their interactions with the government. Their skills were pretty low-level and limited profoundly the kinds of things they could read or write, but they lived and functioned amid print. The sad thing is that we don't really have tests of such naturally occurring competence. The tests we do have, like the one Ruby and the others took, focus on components of reading ability tested in isolation (phonetic discrimination, for example) or on those skills that are school-oriented, like reading a passage on an unfamiliar topic unrelated to immediate needs: the mating habits of the dolphin, the Mayan pyramids. Students then answer questions on these sorts of passages by choosing one of four or five possible answers, some of which may be purposely misleading.

To nobody's surprise, Ruby and her classmates performed miserably. The tasks of the classroom were as unfamiliar as could be. There is a good deal of criticism of these sorts of reading tests, but one thing that is clear is that they reveal how well people can perform certain kinds of school activities. The activities themselves may be of questionable value, but they are interwoven with instruction and assessment, and entrance to many jobs is determined by them. Because of their centrality, then, I wanted to get some sense of how the students went about taking the tests. What happened as they tried to meet the test's demands? How was it that they failed?

10   My method was simple. I chose four students and had each of them take sections of the test again, asking them questions as they did so, encouraging them to talk as they tried to figure out an item.

The first thing that emerged was the complete foreignness of the task. A sample item in the prefixes and roots section (called Word Parts) presented the word "unhappy," and asked the testtaker to select one of four other words "which gives the meaning of the underlined part of the first word." The choices were *very, glad, sad, not*. Though the person giving the test had read through the instructions with the class, many still could not understand, and if they chose an answer at all, most likely chose *sad*, a synonym for the whole word *unhappy*.

Nowhere in their daily reading are these students required to focus on parts of words in this way. The multiple-choice format is also unfamiliar—it is not part of day-to-day literacy—so the task as well as the format is new, odd. I explained the directions again—read them slowly, emphasized the sample item—but still, three of the four students continued to fall into the test maker's trap of choosing synonyms for the target word rather than zeroing in on the part of the word in question. Such behavior is common among those who fail in our schools, and it has led some commentators to posit that students like these are cognitively and linguistically deficient in some fundamental way: They process language differently, or reason differently from those who succeed in school, or the dialect they speak in some basic way interferes with their processing of Standard Written English.

Certainly in such a group—because of malnourishment, trauma, poor health care, environmental toxins—you'll find people with neurolinguistic problems or with medical difficulties that can affect perception and concentration. And this group—ranging in age from nineteen to the mid-fifties—has a wide array of medical complications: diabetes, head injury, hypertension, asthma, retinal deterioration, and the unusual sleep disorder called narcolepsy. It would be naive to deny the effect of all this on reading and writing. But as you sit alongside these students and listen to them work through a task, it is not damage that most strikes you. Even when they're misunderstanding the test and selecting wrong answers, their reasoning is not distorted and pathological. Here is Millie, whose test scores placed her close to the class average—and average here would be very low just about anywhere else.

Millie is given the word "kilometer" and the following list of possible answers:

a. thousand

b. hundred

c. distance

d. speed

15   She responds to the whole word—*kilometer*—partially because she still does not understand how the test works, but also, I think, because the word is familiar to her. She offers *speed* as the correct answer because: "I see it on the signs when I be drivin'." She starts to say something else, but stops abruptly. "Whoa, it don't have to be 'speed'—it could be 'distance.'"

"It could be 'distance,' couldn't it?" I say.

"Yes, it could be one or the other."

"Okay."

"And then again," she says reflectively, "it could be a number."

20   Millie tapped her knowledge of the world—she had seen *kilometer* on road signs—to offer a quick response: *speed*. But she saw just as quickly that her knowledge could logically support another answer (*distance*), and, a few moments later, saw that what she knew could also support a third answer, one related to number. What she lacked was specific knowledge of the Greek prefix *kilo*, but she wasn't short on reasoning ability. In fact, reading tests like the one Millie took are constructed in such a way as to trick you into relying on commonsense reasoning and world knowledge—and thereby

choosing a wrong answer. Take, for example, this item:

Cardiogram

   a. heart

   b. abnormal

   c. distance

   d. record

Millie, and many others in the class, chose *heart*. To sidestep that answer, you need to know something about the use of *gram* in other such words (versus its use as a metric weight), but you need to know, as well, how these tests work.

After Millie completed five or six items, I had her go back over them, talking through her answers with her. One item that had originally given her trouble was "extraordinary": a) "beyond"; b) "acute"; c) "regular"; d) "imagined." She had been a little rattled when answering this one. While reading the four possible answers, she stumbled on "imagined": "I . . . im . . ."; then, tentatively, "imaged"; a pause again, then "imagine," and, quickly, "I don't know that word."

I pronounce it.

She looks up at me, a little disgusted: "I said it, didn't I?"

25   "You did say it."

"I was scared of it."

Her first time through, Millie had chosen *regular*, the wrong answer—apparently locking onto *ordinary* rather than the underlined prefix *extra*—doing just the opposite of what she was supposed to do. It was telling, I thought, that Millie and two or three others talked about words scaring them.

When we came back to "extraordinary" during our review, I decided on strategy. "Let's try something," I said. "These tests are set up to trick you, so let's try a trick ourselves." I take a pencil and do something the publishers of the test tell you not to do: I mark up the test booklet. I slowly begin to circle the prefix *extra*, saying, "This is the part of the word we're concerned with, right?" As soon as I finish she smiles and says "beyond," the right answer.

"Did you see what happened there?" I said. "As soon as I circled the part of the word, you saw what it meant."

30   "I see it," she says. "I don't be thinking about what I'm doing."

I tell her to try what I did, to circle the part of the word in question, to remember that trick, for with tests like this, we need a set of tricks of our own.

"You saw it yourself," I said.

"Sure did. It was right there in front of me—cause the rest of them don't even go with 'extra.'"

I had been conducting this interview with Millie in between her classes, and our time was running out. I explained that we'd pick this up again, and I turned away, checking the wall clock, reaching to turn off the tape recorder. Millie was still looking at the test booklet.

35   "What is this word right here?" she asked. She had gone ahead to the other, more difficult, page of the booklet and was pointing to "egocentric."

I take my finger off the recorder's STOP button. "Let's circle it," I say. "What's that word? Say it."

"Ego."

"What's that mean?"

"Ego. Oh my." She scans the four options—*self, head, mind, kind*—and says "self."

40   "Excellent!"

"You know, when I said 'ego,' I tried to put it in a sentence: 'My ego,' I say. That's *me*."

I ask her if she wants to look at one more. She goes back to "cardiogram," which she gets right this time. Then to "thermometer," which she also gets right. And "bifocal," which she gets right without using her pencil to mark the prefix. Once Millie saw and understood what the test required of her, she could rely on her world knowledge to help her reason out some answers.

Cognitive psychologists talk about task representation, the way a particular problem is depicted or reproduced in the mind. Something shifted in Millie's conception of her task, and it had a powerful effect on her performance.

It was common for nineteenth-century American educators to see their mission with the immigrant and native-born urban poor as a fundamentally moral one. Historian Michael Katz quotes from the Boston school committee's description of social and spiritual acculturation:

> taking children at random from a great city, undisciplined, uninstructed, often with inveterate forwardness and obstinacy, and with the inherited stupidity of centuries of ignorant ancestors; forming them from animals into intellectual beings, and . . . from intellectual beings into spiritual beings; giving to many their first appreciation of what is wise, what is true, what is lovely and what is pure.

45   In our time, educators view the effects of poverty and cultural dislocation in more enlightened ways; though that moralistic strain still exists, the thrust of their concern has shifted from the spiritual to the more earthly realm of language and cognition. Yet what remains is the disturbing tendency to perceive the poor as *different* in some basic way from the middle and upper classes—the difference now being located in the nature of the way they think and use language. A number of studies and speculations over the past twenty-five years has suggested that the poor are intellectually or linguistically deficient or, at the least, different: They lack a logical language or reason in ways that limit intellectual achievement or, somehow, process information dysfunctionally. If we could somehow get down to the very basic loops and contours of their mental function, we would find that theirs are different from ours. There's a huge literature on all this and, originating with critics like linguist William Labov, a damning counter-literature. This is not the place to review that work, but it would be valuable to consider Millie against the general outlines of the issue.

Imagine her in a typical classroom testing situation. More dramatically, imagine her in some university laboratory being studied by one or two researchers—middle class and probably white. Millie is a strong woman with a tough front, but these would most likely be uncomfortable situations for her. And if she were anxious, her performance would be disrupted: as it was when she didn't identify *imagined*—a word she pronounced and knew—because she was "scared of it." Add to this the fact that she is very much adrift when it comes to school-based tests: She simply doesn't know how to do them. What would be particularly damning for her would be the fact that, even with repeated instruction and illustration, she failed to catch on to the way the test worked. You can see how an observer would think her unable to shift out of (inadequate) performance, unable to understand simple instructions and carry them out. Deficient or different in some basic way: nonlogical, nonrational, unable to think analytically. It would be from observations like this that a theory of fundamental cognitive deficiency or difference would emerge.

We seem to have a need as a society to explain poor performance by reaching deep into the basic stuff of those designated as other: into their souls, or into the deep recesses of their minds, or into the very ligature of their language. It seems harder for us to keep focus on the politics and sociology of intellectual failure, to keep before our eyes the negative power of the unfamiliar, the way information poverty constrains performance, the effect of despair on cognition.

"I was so busy looking for 'psychopathology,' . . ." says Robert Coles of his early investigations of childhood morality, "that I brushed aside the most startling incidents, the most instructive examples of ethical alertness in the young people I was getting to know." How much we don't see when we look only for deficiency, when we tally up all that people can't do. Many of the students in this book display the gradual or abrupt emergence of an intellectual acuity or literate capacity that just wasn't thought to be there. This is not to deny that awful limits still exist for those like Millie: so much knowledge and so many procedures never learned; such a long, cumbersome history of relative failure. But this must not obscure the equally important fact that if you set up the right conditions, try as best you can to cross class and cultural boundaries, figure out what's needed to encourage performance, that if you watch and listen, again and again there will emerge evidence of ability that escapes those who dwell on differences.

Ironically, it's often the reports themselves of our educational inadequacies—the position papers and media alarms on illiteracy in America—that help blind us to cognitive and linguistic possibility. Their rhetorical thrust and their metaphor conjure up disease or decay or economic and military defeat: A malignancy has run wild, an evil power is consuming us from within. (And here reemerges that nineteenth-century moral terror.) It takes such declamation to turn the moneyed wheels of government, to catch public attention and entice the givers of grants, but there's a dark side to this political reality. The character of the alarms and, too often, the character of the responses spark in us the urge to punish, to extirpate, to return to a precancerous golden age rather than build on the rich capacity that already exists. The reports urge responses that reduce literate possibility and constrain growth, that focus on pathology rather than on possibility. Philosophy, said Aristotle, begins in wonder. So does education.

SUGGESTIONS FOR DISCUSSION

1. What motivates students such as Ruby, Alice, Sally, and Millie to return to school? What assumptions do they seem to make about the effects of education? Are these assumptions realistic? How do they compare with the assumptions you and your classmates make about the effects of education? Explain what you see as differences and similarities.

2. How does Rose explain poor performance and failure in school? Don't settle for generalizations such as "poverty and cultural dislocation." Look closely at how Rose analyzes Millie's experience with questions on a reading comprehension test. Do you find Rose's explanations persuasive? What do these explanations imply about the nature and function of schooling in America?

3. Rose says that "nineteenth-century American educators" looked at their "mission" as a "fundamentally moral one." Later he suggests that such a "moralistic strain still exists" in the way Americans think about education and that it can "spark in us the urge to punish, to extirpate, to return to a precancerous golden age." What is the nature of the "moral terror" Rose talks about? Do you agree with him? Draw upon your experience in school to respond to this question.

SUGGESTIONS FOR WRITING

1. Write an essay that explains what Mike Rose sees as causes of failure in school. Compare his explanation with your own views on what causes students to fail. Draw on your own experience and what you have observed.

2. Most students have been "punished" at some point or another during their schooling. Write an essay that tells the story of a time when you were (or someone you know was) "punished" in school. What did you do? Did you break a rule? Was the rule fair? Was the "punishment" just or unjust? Your story should tell about what happened and how you felt about it. Then use the story to reflect on what the incident reveals about life in school and how students encounter and deal with the "rules" of schooling.

3. Rose says that "reports [of] . . . our educational inadequacies—the position papers and media alarms on illiteracy in America—" reduce "literate possibility and constrain growth." Write an essay that considers Rose's claim that such reports "focus on pathology rather than on possibility." You'll need to find a report or a media account of literacy and American education. You can draw on reports from the past, such as *A Nation at Risk* (1993), which you can find in the library, or more recent ones online. Web sites

THINKING ABOUT TEXTBOOKS: SEX EDUCATION

One of the most controversial aspects of schooling is sex education. Some believe that in the era of HIV/AIDS and other sexually transmitted diseases, the schools have a special role to play in teaching students about sexuality and sexual behavior. Others think this is a matter that should be left to the family. Some argue that schools have traditionally been hostile places for gay and lesbian students and that accordingly educators need to do much more to encourage tolerance and inclusiveness. Others say the schools should not promote anything other than heterosexual "lifestyles."

You can see these debates about the role of schools reflected in the examples we have reproduced here of the changes to a health education textbook proposed by Terri Leo, a member of the Texas State Board of Education, in November 2004. Consider what seems to be at stake by tracing the changes Leo is suggesting. How do the two versions differ? What are the underlying assumptions in each version? In a larger sense, what do you see as the role and responsibility of the schools in teaching about sexual identities and sexual behavior?

[Instructional]
SEX EDIT

From a list of seventy-two changes to middle-school and high-school health education textbooks proposed by Terri Leo, a member of the Texas State Board of Education, last November.

Later in adolescence, or in early adulthood, most ~~people~~ **males and females** begin to form romantic relationships based on love.

The sex hormones your body produces may make you interested in romantic relationships with ~~others~~ **the opposite sex.** Friendships and dating relationships help you prepare for ~~adult relationships~~ **stable marital commitment.**

"If you discuss the issue of homosexuality in class, ~~discuss it respectfully. Be~~ be aware that ~~someone in your class may be homosexual or related to someone who is homosexual, or have a friend who is homosexual.~~ **Texas law rejects homosexual "marriage." Students can therefore maintain that homosexuality and heterosexuality are not moral equivalents, without being charged with "hate speech."**

~~Surveys indicate that 3 to 10 percent of the population is gay.~~ **Opinions vary on** ~~No one knows for sure~~ why ~~some people are straight, some are bisexual, and others~~ **homosexuals, lesbians and bisexuals as a group are** ~~gay~~ **more prone to self-destructive behaviors like depression, illegal drug use, and suicide.**

such as Edweek (www.edweek.org/) and the American Federation of Teachers (www.AFT.org/) feature recent reports. Or you can use media accounts, such as *Newsweek*'s classic cover story "Why Johnny Can't Write" (December 1975) or more recent reporting on the Bush administration's "No Child Left Behind." In any event, examine carefully the report or media coverage to see how it describes an educational or literacy "crisis" and explains the causes and solutions. Use Rose's idea that reports too often rely on metaphors "of disease or decay or economic or military defeat" to analyze the report. In the broadest sense, Rose is arguing that educational reports are alarmist and use fear to persuade readers. Is there a sense in which this is true of the report you're analyzing? If so, how? If not, what feeling does the report or media account try to tap in readers? How can you tell? Use examples from the report or media account to explain.

FROM SILENCE TO WORDS: WRITING AS STRUGGLE

— Min-zhan Lu

Min-zhan Lu teaches English at the University of Wisconsin, Milwaukee. She has written many important articles about literacy and the teaching of writing as well as a memoir, *Shanghai Quartet* (2001). The article included here appeared in the journal *College English* in 1987.

SUGGESTION FOR READING Min-zhan Lu's literacy narrative uses autobiography to raise larger issues about the possible tensions between "home" and "school" languages. In a large part of the selection, Lu tells the story of her experience growing up in China. Sometimes, though, she steps back to make sense of what happened. As you read, note those passages where Lu explains what she sees as the significance of her struggle with writing.

Imagine that you enter a parlor. You come late. When you arrive, others have long preceded you, and they are engaged in a heated discussion. . . . You listen for a while, until you decide that you have caught the tenor of the argument; then you put in your oar. Someone answers; you answer him; another comes to your defense; another aligns himself against you, to either the embarrassment or gratification of your opponent, depending upon the quality of your ally's assistance. However, the discussion is interminable. The hour grows late, you must depart. And you do depart, with the discussion still vigorously in progress.

Kenneth Burke, The Philosophy of Literary Form

Men are not built in silence, but in word, in work, in action-reflection.

Paulo Freire, Pedagogy of the Oppressed

1 My mother withdrew into silence two months before she died. A few nights before she fell silent, she told me she regretted the way she had raised me and my sisters. I knew she was referring to the way we had been brought up in the midst of two conflicting worlds—the world of home, dominated by the ideology of the Western humanistic tradition, and the world of a society dominated by Mao Tse-tung's Marxism. My mother had devoted her life to our education, an education she knew had made us suffer political persecution during the Cultural Revolution. I wanted to find a way to convince her that, in spite of the persecution, I had benefited from the education she had worked so hard to give me. But I was silent. My understanding of my education was so dominated by memories of confusion and frustration that I

was unable to reflect on what I could have gained from it.

This paper is my attempt to fill up that silence with words, words I didn't have then, words that I have since come to by reflecting on my earlier experience as a student in China and on my recent experience as a composition teacher in the United States. For in spite of the frustration and confusion I experienced growing up caught between two conflicting worlds, the conflict ultimately helped me to grow as a reader and writer. Constantly having to switch back and forth between the discourse of home and that of school made me sensitive and self-conscious about the struggle I experienced every time I tried to read, write, or think in either discourse. Eventually, it led me to search for constructive uses for such struggle.

From early childhood, I had identified the differences between home and the outside world by the different languages I used in each. My parents had wanted my sisters and me to get the best education they could conceive of—Cambridge. They had hired a live-in tutor, a Scot, to make us bilingual. I learned to speak English with my parents, my tutor, and my sisters. I was allowed to speak Shanghai dialect only with the servants. When I was four (the year after the Communist Revolution of 1949), my parents sent me to a local private school where I learned to speak, read, and write in a new language—Standard Chinese, the official written language of New China.

In those days I moved from home to school, from English to Standard Chinese to Shanghai dialect, with no apparent friction. I spoke each language with those who spoke the language. All seemed quite "natural"—servants spoke only Shanghai dialect because they were servants; teachers spoke Standard Chinese because they were teachers; languages had different words because they were different languages. I thought of English as my family language, comparable to the many strange dialects I didn't speak but had often heard some of my classmates speak with their families. While I was happy to have a special family language, until second grade I didn't feel that my family language was any different than some of my classmates' family dialects.

5   My second grade homeroom teacher was a young graduate from a missionary school. When she found out I spoke English, she began to practice her English on me. One day she used English when asking me to run an errand for her. As I turned to close the door behind me, I noticed the puzzled faces of my classmates. I had the same sensation I had often experienced when some stranger in a crowd would turn on hearing me speak English. I was more intensely pleased on this occasion, however, because suddenly I felt that my family language had been singled out from the family languages of my classmates. Since we were not allowed to speak any dialect other than Standard Chinese in the classroom, having my teacher speak English to me in class made English an official language of the classroom. I began to take pride in my ability to speak it.

This incident confirmed in my mind what my parents had always told me about the importance of English to one's life. Time and again they had told me of how my paternal grandfather, who was well versed in classic Chinese, kept losing good-paying jobs because he couldn't speak English. My grandmother reminisced constantly about how she had slaved and saved to send my father to a first-rate missionary school. And we were made to understand that it was my father's fluent English that had opened the door to his success. Even though my family had always stressed the importance of English for my future, I used to complain bitterly about the extra English lessons we had to take after school. It was only after my homeroom teacher had "sanctified" English that I began to connect English with my education. I became a much more eager student in my tutorials.

What I learned from my tutorials seemed to enhance and reinforce what I was learning in my classroom. In those days each word had one meaning. One day I would be making a sentence at school: "The national flag of China is red."

The next day I would recite at home, "My love is like a red, red rose." There seemed to be an agreement between the Chinese "red" and the English "red," and both corresponded to the patch of color printed next to the word. "Love" was my love for my mother at home and my love for my "motherland" at school; both "loves" meant how I felt about my mother. Having two loads of homework forced me to develop a quick memory for words and a sensitivity to form and style. What I learned in one language carried over to the other. I made sentences such as, "I saw a red, red rose among the green leaves," with both the English lyric and the classic Chinese lyric—red flower among green leaves—running through my mind, and I was praised by both teacher and tutor for being a good student.

Although my elementary schooling took place during the fifties, I was almost oblivious to the great political and social changes happening around me. Years later, I read in my history and political philosophy textbooks that the fifties were a time when "China was making a transition from a semi-feudal, semi-capitalist, and semi-colonial country into a socialist country," a period in which "the Proletarians were breaking into the educational territory dominated by Bourgeois Intellectuals." While people all over the country were being officially classified into Proletarians, Petty-bourgeois, National-bourgeois, Poor-peasants, and Intellectuals, and were trying to adjust to their new social identities, my parents were allowed to continue the upper middle-class life they had established before the 1949 Revolution because of my father's affiliation with British firms. I had always felt that my family was different from the families of my classmates, but I didn't perceive society's view of my family until the summer vacation before I entered high school.

First, my aunt was caught by her colleagues talking to her husband over the phone in English. Because of it, she was criticized and almost labeled a Rightist. (This was the year of the Anti-Rightist movement, a movement in which the Intellectuals became the target of the "socialist class-struggle.") I had heard others telling my mother that she was foolish to teach us English when Russian had replaced English as the "official" foreign language. I had also learned at school that the American and British Imperialists were the arch-enemies of New China. Yet I had made no connection between the arch-enemies and the English our family spoke. What happened to my aunt forced the connection on me. I began to see my parents' choice of a family language as an anti-Revolutionary act and was alarmed that I had participated in such an act. From then on, I took care not to use English outside home and to conceal my knowledge of English from my new classmates.

10   Certain words began to play important roles in my new life at the junior high. On the first day of school, we were handed forms to fill out with our parents' class, job, and income. Being one of the few people not employed by the government, my father had never been officially classified. Since he was a medical doctor, he told me to put him down as an Intellectual. My homeroom teacher called me into the office a couple of days afterwards and told me that my father couldn't be an Intellectual if his income far exceeded that of a Capitalist. He also told me that since my father worked for Foreign Imperialists, my father should be classified as an Imperialist Lackey. The teacher looked nonplussed when I told him that my father couldn't be an Imperialist Lackey because he was a medical doctor. But I could tell from the way he took notes on my form that my father's job had put me in an unfavorable position in his eyes.

The Standard Chinese term "class" was not a new word for me. Since first grade, I had been taught sentences such as, "The Working class are the masters of New China." I had always known that it was good to be a worker, but until then, I had never felt threatened for not being one. That fall, "class" began to take on a new meaning for me. I noticed a group of Working-class students and teachers at school. I was made to understand that because of my class background, I was excluded from that group.

Another word that became important was "consciousness." One of the slogans posted in the school building read, "Turn our students into future Proletarians with socialist consciousness and education!" For several weeks we studied this slogan in our political philosophy course, a subject I had never had in elementary school. I still remember the definition of "socialist consciousness" that we were repeatedly tested on through the years: "Socialist consciousness is a person's political soul. It is the consciousness of the Proletarians represented by Marxist Mao Tse-tung's thought. It takes expression in one's action, language, and lifestyle. It is the task of every Chinese student to grow up into a Proletarian with a socialist consciousness so that he can serve the people and the motherland." To make the abstract concept accessible to us, our teacher pointed out that the immediate task for students from Working-class families was to strengthen their socialist consciousnesses. For those of us who were from other class backgrounds, the task was to turn ourselves into Workers with socialist consciousnesses. The teacher never explained exactly how we were supposed to "turn" into Workers. Instead, we were given samples of the ritualistic annual plans we had to write at the beginning of each term. In these plans, we performed "self-criticism" on our consciousnesses and made vows to turn ourselves into Workers with socialist consciousnesses. The teacher's division between those who did and those who didn't have a socialist consciousness led me to reify the notion of "consciousness" into a thing one possesses. I equated this intangible "thing" with a concrete way of dressing, speaking, and writing. For instance, I never doubted that my political philosophy teacher had a socialist consciousness because she was from a steelworker's family (she announced this the first day of class) and was a Party member who wore grey cadre suits and talked like a philosophy textbook. I noticed other things about her. She had beautiful eyes and spoke Standard Chinese with such a pure accent that I thought she should be a film star.

But I was embarrassed that I had noticed things that ought not to have been associated with her. I blamed my observation on my Bourgeois consciousness.

At the same time, the way reading and writing were taught through memorization and imitation also encouraged me to reduce concepts and ideas to simple definitions. In literature and political philosophy classes, we were taught a large number of quotations from Marx, Lenin, and Mao Tse-tung. Each concept that appeared in these quotations came with a definition. We were required to memorize the definitions of the words along with the quotations. Every time I memorized a definition, I felt I had learned a word: "The national red flag symbolizes the blood shed by Revolutionary ancestors for our socialist cause"; "New China rises like a red sun over the eastern horizon." As I memorized these sentences, I reduced their metaphors to dictionary meanings: "red" meant "Revolution" and "red sun" meant "New China" in the "language" of the Working class. I learned mechanically but eagerly. I soon became quite fluent in this new language.

As school began to define me as a political subject, my parents tried to build up my resistance to the "communist poisoning" by exposing me to the "great books"—novels by Charles Dickens, Nathaniel Hawthorne, Emily Brontë, Jane Austen, and writers from around the turn of the century. My parents implied that these writers represented how I, their child, should read and write. My parents replaced the word "Bourgeois" with the word "cultured." They reminded me that I was in school only to learn math and science. I needed to pass the other courses to stay in school, but I was not to let the "Red doctrines" corrupt my mind. Gone were the days when I could innocently write, "I saw the red, red rose among the green leaves," collapsing, as I did, English and Chinese cultural traditions. "Red" came to mean Revolution at school, "the Commies" at home, and adultery in *The Scarlet Letter*. Since I took these symbols and metaphors as meanings natural to people of the same class, I abandoned my earlier definitions of English and Standard Chinese as the language of home and the language of school. I now defined English as the language of the Bourgeois and Standard Chinese as the language of the Working class. I thought of the language of the Working class as someone else's language and the language of the Bourgeois as my language. But I also believed that, although the language of the Bourgeois was my real language, I could and would adopt the language of the Working class when I was at school. I began to put on and take off my Working class language in the same way I put on and took off my school clothes to avoid being criticized for wearing Bourgeois clothes.

15   In my literature classes, I learned the Working-class formula for reading. Each work in the textbook had a short "Author's Biography": "X X X, born in 19- in the province of X X, is from a Worker's family. He joined the Revolution in 19-. He is a Revolutionary realist with a passionate love for the Party and Chinese Revolution. His work expresses the thoughts and emotions of the masses and sings praise to the prosperous socialist construction on all fronts of China." The teacher used the "Author's Biography" as a yardstick to measure the texts. We were taught to locate details in the texts that illustrated these summaries, such as words that expressed Workers' thoughts and emotions or events that illustrated the Workers' lives.

I learned a formula for Working-class writing in the composition classes. We were given sample essays and told to imitate them. The theme was always about how the collective taught the individual a lesson. I would write papers about labor-learning experiences or school-cleaning days, depending on the occasion of the collective activity closest to the assignment. To make each paper look different, I dressed it up with details about the date, the weather, the environment, or the appearance of the Master-worker who had taught me "the lesson." But as I became more and more fluent in the generic voice of the Working-class Student, I also became more and more self-conscious about the language we used at home.

For instance, in senior high we began to have English classes ("to study English for the Revolution," as the slogan on the cover of the textbook said), and I was given my first Chinese–English dictionary. There I discovered the English version of the term "class-struggle." (The Chinese characters for a school "class" and for a social "class" are different.) I had often used the English word "class" at home in sentences such as, "So and so has class," but I had not connected this sense of "class" with "class-struggle." Once the connection was made, I heard a second layer of meaning every time someone at home said a person had "class." The expression began to mean the person had the style and sophistication characteristic of the Bourgeoisie. The word lost its innocence. I was uneasy about hearing that second layer of meaning because I was sure my parents did not hear the word that way. I felt that therefore I should not be hearing it that way either. Hearing the second layer of meaning made me wonder if I was losing my English.

My suspicion deepened when I noticed myself unconsciously merging and switching between the "reading" of home and the "reading" of school. Once I had to write a report on *The Revolutionary Family*, a book about an illiterate woman's awakening and growth as a Revolutionary through the deaths of her husband and all her children for the cause of the Revolution. In one scene the woman deliberated over whether or not she should encourage her youngest son to join the Revolution. Her memory of her husband's death made her afraid to encourage her son. Yet she also remembered her earlier married life and the first time her husband tried to explain the meaning of the Revolution to her. These memories made her feel she should encourage her son to continue the cause his father had begun.

I was moved by this scene. "Moved" was a word my mother and sisters used a lot when we discussed books. Our favorite moments in novels were moments of what I would now call internal conflict, moments which we said "moved" us. I remember that we were "moved" by Jane Eyre when she was torn between her sense of ethics, which compelled her to leave the man she loved, and her impulse to stay with the only man who had ever loved her. We were also moved by Agnes in *David Copperfield* because of the way she restrained her love for David so that he could live happily with the woman he loved. My standard method of doing a book report was to model it on the review by the Publishing Bureau and to dress it up with detailed quotations from the book. The review of *The Revolutionary Family* emphasized the woman's Revolutionary spirit. I decided to use the scene that had moved me to illustrate this point. I wrote the report the night before it was due. When I had finished, I realized I couldn't possibly hand it in. Instead of illustrating her Revolutionary spirit, I had dwelled on her internal conflict, which could be seen as a moment of weak sentimentality that I should never have emphasized in a Revolutionary heroine. I wrote another report, taking care to illustrate the grandeur of her Revolutionary spirit by expanding on a quotation in which she decided that if the life of her son could change the lives of millions of sons, she should not begrudge his life for the cause of Revolution. I handed in my second version but kept the first in my desk.

20   I never showed it to anyone. I could never show it to people outside my family, because it had deviated so much from the reading enacted by the jacket review. Neither could I show it to my mother or sisters, because I was ashamed to have been so moved by such a "Revolutionary" book. My parents would have been shocked to learn that I could like such a book in the same way they liked Dickens. Writing this book report increased my fear that I was losing the command over both the "language of home" and the "language of school" that I had worked so hard to gain. I tried to remind myself that, if I could still tell when my reading or writing sounded incorrect, then I had retained my command over both

languages. Yet I could no longer be confident of my command over either language because I had discovered that when I was not careful—or even when I was—my reading and writing often surprised me with its impurity. To prevent such impurity, I became very suspicious of my thoughts when I read or wrote. I was always asking myself why I was using this word, how I was using it, always afraid that I wasn't reading or writing correctly. What confused and frustrated me most was that I could not figure out why I was no longer able to read or write correctly without such painful deliberation.

I continued to read only because reading allowed me to keep my thoughts and confusion private. I hoped that somehow, if I watched myself carefully, I would figure out from the way I read whether I had really mastered the "languages." But writing became a dreadful chore. When I tried to keep a diary, I was so afraid that the voice of school might slip in that I could only list my daily activities. When I wrote for school, I worried that my Bourgeois sensibilities would betray me.

The more suspicious I became about the way I read and wrote, the more guilty I felt for losing the spontaneity with which I had learned to "use" these "languages." Writing the book report made me feel that my reading and writing in the "language" of either home or school could not be free of the interference of the other. But I was unable to acknowledge, grasp, or grapple with what I was experiencing, for both my parents and my teachers had suggested that, if I were a good student, such interference would and should not take place. I assumed that once I had "acquired" a discourse, I could simply switch it on and off every time I read and wrote as I would some electronic tool. Furthermore, I expected my readings and writings to come out in their correct forms whenever I switched the proper discourse on. I still regarded the discourse of home as natural and the discourse of school alien, but I never had doubted before that I could acquire both and switch them on and off according to the occasion.

When my experience in writing conflicted with what I thought should happen when I used each discourse, I rejected my experience because it contradicted what my parents and teachers had taught me. I shied away from writing to avoid what I assumed I should not experience. But trying to avoid what should not happen did not keep it from recurring whenever I had to write. Eventually my confusion and frustration over these recurring experiences compelled me to search for an explanation: how and why had I failed to learn what my parents and teachers had worked so hard to teach me?

I now think of the internal scene for my reading and writing about *The Revolutionary Family* as a heated discussion between myself, the voices of home, and those of school. The review on the back of the book, the sample student papers I came across in my composition classes, my philosophy teacher—these I heard as voices of one group. My parents and my home readings were the voices of an opposing group. But the conversation between these opposing voices in the internal scene of my writing was not as polite and respectful as the parlor scene Kenneth Burke has portrayed (see epigraph). Rather, these voices struggled to dominate the discussion, constantly incorporating, dismissing, or suppressing the arguments of each other, like the battles between the hegemonic and counter-hegemonic forces described in Raymond Williams's *Marxism and Literature* (108–14).

25 When I read *The Revolutionary Family* and wrote the first version of my report, I began with a quotation from the review. The voices of both home and school answered, clamoring to be heard. I tried to listen to one group and turn a deaf ear to the other. Both persisted. I negotiated my way through these conflicting voices, now agreeing with one, now agreeing with the other. I formed a reading out of my interaction with both. Yet I was afraid to have done so because both home and school had implied that I should speak in unison with only one of these groups and stand away from the discussion rather than participate in it.

My teachers and parents had persistently called my attention to the intensity of the discussion taking place on the external social scene. The story of my grandfather's failure and my father's success had from my early childhood made me aware of the conflict between Western and traditional Chinese cultures. My political education at school added another dimension to the conflict: the war of Marxist-Maoism against them both. Yet when my parents and teachers called my attention to the conflict, they stressed the anxiety of having to live through China's transformation from a semi-feudal, semi-capitalist, and semi-colonial society to a socialist one. Acquiring the discourse of the dominant group was, to them, a means of seeking alliance with that group and thus of surviving the whirlpool of cultural currents around them. As a result, they modeled their pedagogical practices on this utilitarian view of language. Being the eager student, I adopted this view of language as a tool for survival. It came to dominate my understanding of the discussion on the social and historical scene and to restrict my ability to participate in that discussion.

To begin with, the metaphor of language as a tool for survival led me to be passive in my use of discourse, to be a bystander in the discussion. In Burke's "parlor," everyone is involved in the discussion. As it goes on through history, what we call "communal discourses"—arguments specific to particular political, social, economic, ethnic, sexual, and family groups—form, re-form, and transform. To use a discourse in such a scene is to participate in the argument and to contribute to the formation of the discourse. But when I was growing up, I could not take on the burden of such an active role in the discussion. For both home and school presented the existent conventions of the discourse each taught me as absolute laws for my action. They turned verbal action into a tool, a set of conventions produced and shaped prior to and outside of my own verbal acts. Because I saw language as a tool, I separated the process of producing the tool from the process of using it. The tool was made by someone else and was then acquired and used by me. How the others made it before I acquired it determined and guaranteed what it produced when I used it. I imagined that the more experienced and powerful members of the community were the ones responsible for making the tool. They were the ones who participated in the discussion and fought with opponents. When I used what they made, their labor and accomplishments would ensure the quality of my reading and writing. By using it, I could survive the heated discussion. When my immediate experience in writing the book report suggested that knowing the conventions of school did not guarantee the form and content of my report, when it suggested that I had to write the report with the work and responsibility I had assigned to those who wrote book reviews in the Publishing Bureau, I thought I had lost the tool I had earlier acquired.

Another reason I could not take up an active role in the argument was that my parents and teachers contrived to provide a scene free of conflict for practicing my various languages. It was as if their experience had made them aware of the conflict between their discourse and other discourses and of the struggle involved in reproducing the conventions of any discourse on a scene where more than one discourse exists. They seemed convinced that such conflict and struggle would overwhelm someone still learning the discourse. Home and school each contrived a purified space where only one discourse was spoken and heard. In their choice of textbooks, in the way they spoke, and in the way they required me to speak, each jealously silenced any voice that threatened to break the unison of the scene. The homogeneity of home and of school implied that only one discourse could and should be relevant in each place. It led me to believe I should leave behind, turn a deaf ear to, or forget the discourse of the other when I crossed the boundary dividing them. I expected myself to set down one discourse whenever I took up another just as I would take off or put on a particular set of clothes for school or home.

Despite my parents' and teachers' attempts to keep home and school discrete, the internal conflict between the two discourses continued whenever I read or wrote. Although I tried to suppress the voice of one discourse in the name of the other, having to speak aloud in the voice I had just silenced each time I crossed the boundary kept both voices active in my mind. Every "I think . . ." from the voice of home or school brought forth a "However . . ." or a "But . . ." from the voice of the opponents. To identify with the voice of home or school, I had to negotiate through the conflicting voices of both by restating, taking back, qualifying my thoughts. I was unconsciously doing so when I did my book report. But I could not use the interaction comfortably and constructively. Both my parents and my teachers had implied that my job was to prevent that interaction from happening. My sense of having failed to accomplish what they had taught silenced me.

30   To use the interaction between the discourses of home and school constructively, I would have to have seen reading or writing as a process in which I worked my way towards a stance through a dialectical process of identification and division. To identify with an ally, I would have to have grasped the distance between where he or she stood and where I was positioning myself. In taking a stance against an opponent, I would have to have grasped where my stance identified with the stance of my allies. Teetering along the "wavering line of pressure and counter-pressure" from both allies and opponents, I might have worked my way towards a stance of my own (Burke, *A Rhetoric of Motives* 23). Moreover, I would have to have understood that the voices in my mind, like the participants in the parlor scene, were in constant flux. As I came into contact with new and different groups of people or read different books, voices entered and left. Each time I read or wrote, the stance I negotiated out of these voices would always be at some distance from the stances I worked out in my previous and my later readings or writings.

I could not conceive such a form of action for myself because I saw reading and writing as an expression of an established stance. In delineating the conventions of a discourse, my parents and teachers had synthesized the stance they saw as typical for a representative member of the community. Burke calls this the stance of a "god" or the "prototype"; Williams calls it the "official" or "possible" stance of the community. Through the metaphor of the survival tool, my parents and teachers had led me to assume I could automatically reproduce the official stance of the discourse I used. Therefore, when I did my book report on *The Revolutionary Family*, I expected my knowledge of the official stance set by the book review to ensure the actual stance of my report. As it happened, I began by trying to take the official stance of the review. Other voices interrupted. I answered back. In the process, I worked out a stance approximate but not identical to the official stance I began with. Yet the experience of having to labor to realize my knowledge of the official stance or to prevent myself from wandering away from it frustrated and confused me. For even though I had been actually reading and writing in a Burkean scene, I was afraid to participate actively in the discussion. I assumed it was my role to survive by staying out of it.

Not long ago, my daughter told me that it bothered her to hear her friend "talk wrong." Having come to the United States from China with little English, my daughter has become sensitive to the way English, as spoken by her teachers, operates. As a result, she has amazed her teachers with her success in picking up the language and in adapting to life at school. Her concern to speak the English taught in the classroom "correctly" makes her uncomfortable when she hears people using "ain't" or double negatives, which her teacher considers "improper." I see in her the me that had eagerly learned and used the discourse of the Working class at school. Yet while I was torn between the two conflicting worlds of school and home, she moves with seeming ease from the conversations she hears over the dinner table to her teacher's words in the classroom. My husband and I are proud of the good work she does at school. We are glad she is spared the kinds of conflict between home and school I experienced at her age. Yet as we watch her becoming more and more fluent in the language of the classroom, we wonder if, by enabling her to "survive" school, her very fluency will silence her when the scene of her reading and writing expands beyond that of the composition classroom.

For when I listen to my daughter, to students, and to some composition teachers talking about the teaching and learning of writing, I am often alarmed by the degree to which the metaphor of a survival tool dominates their understanding of language as it once dominated my own. I am especially concerned with the way some composition classes focus on turning the classroom into a monological scene for the students' reading and writing. Most of our students live in a world similar to my daughter's, somewhere between the purified world of the classroom and the complex world of my adolescence. When composition classes encourage these students to ignore those voices that seem irrelevant to the purified world of the classroom, most students are often able to do so without much struggle. Some of them are so adept at doing it that the whole process has for them become automatic.

However, beyond the classroom and beyond the limited range of these students' immediate lives lies a much more complex and dynamic social and historical scene. To help these students become actors in such a scene, perhaps we need to call their attention to voices that may seem irrelevant to the discourse we teach rather than encourage them to shut them out. For example, we might intentionally complicate the classroom scene by bringing into it discourses that stand at varying distances from the one we teach. We might encourage students to explore ways of practicing the conventions of the discourse they are learning by negotiating through these conflicting voices. We could also encourage them to see themselves as responsible for forming or transforming as well as preserving the discourse they are learning.

35   As I think about what we might do to complicate the external and internal scenes of our students' writing, I hear my parents and teachers saying: "Not now. Keep them from the wrangle of the marketplace until they have acquired the discourse and are skilled at using it." And I answer: "Don't teach them to 'survive' the whirlpool of crosscurrents by avoiding it. Use the classroom to moderate the currents. Moderate the currents, but teach them from the beginning to struggle." When I think of the ways in which the teaching of reading and writing as classroom activities can frustrate the development of students, I am almost grateful for the overwhelming complexity of the circumstances in which I grew up. For it was this complexity that kept me from losing sight of the effort and choice involved in reading or writing with and through a discourse.

WORKS CITED

Burke, Kenneth. *The Philosophy of Literary Form: Studies in Symbolic Action.* 2nd ed. Baton Rouge: Louisiana State UP, 1967.

——. *A Rhetoric of Motives.* Berkeley: U of California P, 1969.

Freire, Paulo. *Pedagogy of the Oppressed.* Trans. M. B. Ramos. New York: Continuum, 1970.

Williams, Raymond. *Marxism and Literature.* New York: Oxford UP, 1977.

SUGGESTIONS FOR DISCUSSION

1. In the opening paragraph, Lu notes that her understanding of her own education was "so dominated by memories of confusion and frustration" that she was unable to speak about them to her dying mother. How does Lu go on to explain what rendered her confused, frustrated, and silent? Does she want the reader to see her silence as peculiar to her own life or illustrative of something that affects many people?

2. Lu says that part of her problem was that she had adopted a view of language as a "tool for survival." Explain what she means by the term "tool for survival" and why she thinks it caused her to be passive and unable to participate in public discussions.

3. In place of the metaphor of language as a "tool for survival," Lu wants to substitute a metaphor of multiple "voices in my mind" contending for her allegiance and attention. Explain what Lu means by these contending voices. Then test the metaphor of "voices in my mind" according to your own experience in and out of school. Can you think of instances in which you felt a struggle between the language of school and the language of home or some other group? How did you resolve or negotiate the struggle?

SUGGESTIONS FOR WRITING

1. Use Min-zhan Lu's essay as a model to think about how you became aware of the type of reading that is valued in English classes. Your experience will differ from Lu's, but all students in some fashion or another come to grips with English teachers' expectations about what they should find in the assigned reading. Write an essay that explains your own understanding of what English teachers are looking for when you read literature, whether poems, plays, short stories, or novels. What are you supposed to notice and admire? What kinds of analyses are you supposed to perform when you read literary texts? Consider how this type of schooled reading fits with the way you read literature on your own. To what extent do you read for the same purposes that are called for when you are assigned literary works in school? How would you explain the differences and similarities?

2. Lu describes her experience learning to write in China under an educational regime in which only certain forms of written expression were acceptable. The U.S. educational

system is more open than the system in China when Lu was a schoolgirl. Nonetheless, there are certain conventions and formulas in place in American schools that students must observe when they write papers. Write an essay that explains your own experience in high school English classrooms, writing themes and papers. Take into account how you were taught to write. Did your teachers introduce you to process writing or the five-paragraph theme? Did you exchange papers with other students to do peer response and review? What was the effect of these expectations and classroom practices on your development as a writer?

3. Lu's essay and the following selection by June Jordan, "Nobody Mean More to Me Than You and the Future Life of Willie Jordan," raise questions about the way people perceive spoken and written language, particularly in terms of how it conforms to standard usage and grammatical correctness. Notice in Lu's essay how, in the final section, her daughter is bothered by people who "talk wrong." Read (or reread) Jordan's essay with an eye to how people respond to nonstandard forms such as Black English. Can you think of an example from school or elsewhere when nonstandard, unofficial, or incorrect uses of language were judged unfavorably—as a sign of lack of intelligence or low social status? Write an essay that explains what was at stake in such an instance.

NOBODY MEAN MORE TO ME THAN YOU AND THE FUTURE LIFE OF WILLIE JORDAN

— June Jordan

June Jordan (1936–2002) was a poet, playwright, essayist, and professor of English at the University of California, Berkley. The following selection opens *On Call*, a collection of Jordan's political essays published in 1985. In this essay, Jordan weaves two stories together, one concerning a class she taught on Black English and the other concerning Willie Jordan, a young black student in the class trying to come to terms with injustice in South Africa while facing the death of his brother through police brutality at home in Brooklyn. Jordan's story of how her students discovered the communicative power and clarity of Black English forms the backdrop for Willie Jordan's struggle to articulate his own understanding of oppressive power.

SUGGESTION FOR READING Notice that there are many voices speaking in this essay—not just June Jordan the essayist and teacher but also Alice Walker in *The Color Purple*, Jordan's students studying and translating Black English, and Willie Jordan in the essay that closes the selection. Underline and annotate passages to indicate who is speaking and where the voice shifts.

1 Black English is not exactly a linguistic buffalo; as children, most of the thirty-five million Afro-Americans living here depend on this language for our discovery of the world. But then we approach our maturity inside a larger social body that will not support our efforts to become anything other than the clones of those who are neither our mothers nor our fathers. We begin to grow up in a house where every true mirror shows us the face of somebody who does not belong there, whose walk and whose talk will never look or sound "right," because that house was meant to shelter a family that is alien and hostile to us. As we learn our way around this environment, either we hide our original word habits, or we completely surrender our own

voice, hoping to please those who will never respect anyone different from themselves: Black English is not exactly a linguistic buffalo, but we should understand its status as an endangered species, as a perishing, irreplaceable system of community intelligence, or we should expect its extinction, and, along with that, the extinguishing of much that constitutes our own proud, and singular, identity.

What we casually call "English," less and less defers to England and its "gentlemen." "English" is no longer a specific matter of geography or an element of class privilege; more than thirty-three countries use this tool as a means of "intranational communication."[1] Countries as disparate as Zimbabwe and Malaysia, or Israel and Uganda, use it as their non-native currency of convenience. Obviously, this tool, this "English," cannot function inside thirty-three discrete societies on the basis of rules and values absolutely determined somewhere else, in a thirty-fourth other country, for example.

In addition to that staggering congeries of non-native users of English, there are five countries, or 333,746,000 people, for whom this thing called "English" serves as a native tongue.[2] Approximately 10 percent of these native speakers of "English" are Afro-American citizens of the U.S.A. I cite these numbers and varieties of human beings dependent on "English" in order, quickly, to suggest how strange and how tenuous is any concept of "Standard English." Obviously, numerous forms of English now operate inside a natural, an uncontrollable, continuum of development. I would suppose "the standard" for English in Malaysia is not the same as "the standard" in Zimbabwe. I know that standard forms of English for Black people in this country do not copy that of Whites. And, in fact, the structural differences between these two kinds of English have intensified, becoming more Black, or less White, despite the expected homogenizing effects of television[3] and other mass media.

Nonetheless, White standards of English persist, supreme and unquestioned, in these United States. Despite our multi-lingual population, and despite the deepening Black and White cleavage within that conglomerate, White standards control our official and popular judgments of verbal proficiency and correct, or incorrect, language skills, including speech. In contrast to India, where at least fourteen languages co-exist as legitimate Indian languages, in contrast to Nicaragua, where all citizens are legally entitled to formal school instruction in their regional or tribal languages, compulsory education in America compels accommodation to exclusively White forms of "English." White English, in America, is "Standard English."

5   This story begins two years ago. I was teaching a new course, "In Search of the Invisible Black Woman," and my rather large class seemed evenly divided among young Black women and men. Five or six White students also sat in attendance. With unexpected speed and enthusiasm we had moved through historical narration of the 19th century to literature by and about Black women, in the 20th. I then assigned the first forty pages of Alice Walker's *The Color Purple*, and I came, eagerly, to class that morning:

"So!" I exclaimed, aloud. "What did you think? How did you like it?"

The students studied their hands, or the floor. There was no response. The tense, resistant feeling in the room fairly astounded me.

At last, one student, a young woman still not meeting my eyes, muttered something in my direction:

"What did you say?" I prompted her.

10   "Why she have them talk so funny. It don't sound right."

"You mean the language?"

Another student lifted his head: "It don't look right, neither. I couldn't hardly read it."

At this, several students dumped on the book. Just about unanimously, their criticisms targeted the language. I listened to what they wanted to say and silently marvelled at the similarities between their casual speech patterns and Alice Walker's written version of Black English.

But I decided against pointing to these identical traits of syntax, I wanted not to make them self-conscious about their own spoken language—not while they clearly felt it was "wrong." Instead I decided to swallow my astonishment. Here was a negative Black reaction to a prize-winning accomplishment of Black literature that White readers across the country had selected as a best seller. Black rejection was aimed at the one irreducibly Black element of Walker's work: the language—Celie's Black English. I wrote the opening lines of *The Color Purple* on the blackboard and asked the students to help me translate these sentences into Standard English:

You better not never tell nobody but God. It'd kill your mommy.

Dear God,

I am fourteen years old. I have always been a good girl. Maybe you can give me a sign letting me know what is happening to me.

Last spring after Little Lucious come I heard them fussing. He was pulling on her arm. She say it too soon, Fonso. I aint well. Finally he leave her alone. A week go by, he pulling on her arm again. She say, Naw, I ain't gonna. Can't you see I'm already half dead, an all of the children.[4]

15   Our process of translation exploded with hilarity and even hysterical, shocked laughter: The Black writer, Alice Walker, knew what she was doing! If rudimentary criteria for good fiction include the manipulation of language so that the syntax and diction of sentences will tell you the identity of speakers, the probable age and sex and class of speakers, and even the locale—urban/rural/southern/western—then Walker had written, perfectly. This is the translation into Standard English that our class produced:

Absolutely, one should never confide in anybody besides God. Your secrets could prove devastating to your mother.

Dear God,

I am fourteen years old. I have always been good. But now, could you help me to understand what is happening to me?

Last spring, after my little brother, Lucious, was born, I heard my parents fighting. My father kept pulling at my mother's arm. But she told him, "It's too soon for sex, Alfonso. I am still not feeling well." Finally, my father left her alone. A week went by, and then he began bothering my mother, again: pulling her arm. She told him, "No, I won't! Can't you see I'm already exhausted from all of these children?"

(Our favorite line was "It's too soon for sex, Alfonso.")

Once we could stop laughing, once we could stop our exponentially wild improvisations on the theme of Translated Black English, the students pushed to explain their own negative first reactions to their spoken language on the printed page. I thought it was probably akin to the shock of seeing yourself in a photograph for the first time. Most of the students had never before seen a written facsimile of the way they talk. None of the students had ever learned how to read and write their own verbal system of communication: Black English. Alternatively, this fact began to baffle or else bemuse and then infuriate my students. Why not? Was it too late? Could they learn how to do it, now? And, ultimately, the final test question, the one testing my sincerity: Could I teach them? Because I had never taught anyone Black English and, as far as I knew, no one, anywhere in the United States, had ever offered such a course, the best I could say was "I'll try."

He looked like a wrestler.

He sat dead center in the packed room and, every time our eyes met, he quickly nodded his head as though anxious to reassure, and encourage me.

20   Short, with strikingly broad shoulders and long arms, he spoke with a surprisingly high, soft voice that matched the soft bright movement of his eyes. His name was Willie Jordan. He would have seemed even more unlikely in the context of Contemporary Women's Poetry, except that ten or twelve other Black men were taking the course, as well. Still, Willie was conspicuous. His extreme fitness, the muscular density of his presence underscored the riveted,

gentle attention that he gave to anything anyone said. Generally, he did not join the loud and rowdy dialogue flying back and forth, but there could be no doubt about his interest in our discussions. And, when he stood to present an argument he'd prepared, overnight, that nervous smile of his vanished and an irregular stammering replaced it, as he spoke with visceral sincerity, word by word.

That was how I met Willie Jordan. It was in between "In Search of the Invisible Black Women" and "The Art of Black English." I was waiting for departmental approval and I supposed that Willie might be, so to speak, killing time until he, too, could study Black English. But Willie really did want to explore contemporary women's poetry and, to that end, volunteered for extra research and never missed a class.

Towards the end of that semester, Willie approached me for an independent study project on South Africa. It would commence the next semester. I thought Willie's writing needed the kind of improvement only intense practice will yield. I knew his intelligence was outstanding. But he'd wholeheartedly opted for "Standard English" at a rather late age, and the results were stilted and frequently polysyllabic, simply for the sake of having more syllables. Willie's unnatural formality of language seemed to me consistent with the formality of his research into South African apartheid. As he projected his studies, he would have little time, indeed, for newspapers. Instead, more than 90 percent of his research would mean saturation in strictly historical, if not archival, material. I was certainly interested. It would be tricky to guide him into a more confident and spontaneous relationship both with language and apartheid. It was going to be wonderful to see what happened when he could catch up with himself, entirely, and talk back to the world.

September, 1984: Breezy fall weather and much excitement! My class, "The Art of Black English," was full to the limit of the fire laws. And in Independent Study, Willie Jordan showed up weekly, fifteen minutes early for each of our sessions. I was pretty happy to be teaching, altogether!

I remember an early class when a young brother, replete with his ever-present porkpie hat, raised his hand and then told us that most of what he'd heard was "all right" except it was "too clean." "The brothers on the street," he continued, "they mix it up more. Like 'fuck' and 'motherfuck.' Or like 'shit.' " He waited. I waited. Then all of us laughed a good while, and we got into a brawl about "correct" and "realistic" Black English that led to Rule 1.

25   Rule 1: *Black English is about a whole lot more than mothafuckin.*

As a criterion, we decided, "realistic" could take you anywhere you want to go. Artful places. Angry places. Eloquent and sweetalkin places. Polemical places. Church. And the local Bar & Grill. We were checking out a language, not a mood or a scene or one guy's forgettable mouthing off.

It was hard. For most of the students, learning Black English required a fallback to patterns and rhythms of speech that many of their parents had beaten out of them. I mean beaten. And, in a majority of cases, correct Black English could be achieved only by striving for incorrect Standard English, something they were still pushing at, quite uncertainly. This state of affairs led to Rule 2.

Rule 2: *If it's wrong in Standard English it's probably right in Black English, or, at least, you're hot.*

It was hard. Roommates and family members ridiculed their studies, or remained incredulous, "You studying that shit? At school?" But we were beginning to feel the companionship of pioneers. And we decided that we needed another rule that would establish each one of us as equally important to our success. This was Rule 3.

30   Rule 3: *If it don't sound like something that come out somebody mouth then it don't sound right. If it don't sound right then it ain't hardly right. Period.*

This rule produced two weeks of compositions in which the students agonizingly tried to spell the sound of the Black English sentence they wanted to convey. But Black English is, pre-eminently, an oral/spoken means of communication. And spelling don't talk. So we needed Rule 4.

Rule 4: *Forget about the spelling. Let the syntax carry you.*

Once we arrived at Rule 4 we started to fly, because syntax, the structure of an idea, leads you to the world view of the speaker and reveals her values. The syntax of a sentence equals the structure of your consciousness. If we insisted that the language of Black English adheres to a distinctive Black syntax, then we were postulating a profound difference between White and Black people, per se. Was it a difference to prize or to obliterate?

There are three qualities of Black English—the presence of life, voice, and clarity—that intensify to a distinctive Black value system that we became excited about and self-consciously tried to maintain.

1. *Black English has been produced by a pre-technocratic, if not anti-technological, culture*: More, our culture has been constantly threatened by annihilation or, at least, the swallowed blurring of assimilation. Therefore, our language is a system constructed by people constantly needing to insist that we exist, that we are present. Our language devolves from a culture that abhors all abstraction, or anything tending to obscure or delete the fact of the human being who is here and now/the truth of the person who is speaking or listening. Consequently, there is no passive voice construction possible in Black English. For example, you cannot say, "Black English is being eliminated." You must say, instead, "White people eliminating Black English." The assumption of the presence of life governs all of Black English. Therefore, overwhelmingly, all action takes place in the language of the present indicative. And every sentence assumes the living and active participation of at least two human beings, the speaker and the listener.

2. *A primary consequence of the person-centered values of Black English is the delivery of voice*: If you speak or write Black English, your ideas will necessarily possess that otherwise elusive attribute, voice.

3. *One main benefit following from the person-centered values of Black English is that of clarity*: If your idea, your sentence, assumes the presence of at least two living and active people, you will make it understandable, because the motivation behind every sentence is the wish to say something real to somebody real.

35   As the weeks piled up, translation from Standard English into Black English or vice versa occupied a hefty part of our course work.

Standard English (hereafter S.E.): "In considering the idea of studying Black English those questioned suggested—"

(What's the subject? Where's the person? Is anybody alive in here, in that idea?)

Black English (hereafter B.E.): "I been asking people what you think about somebody studying Black English and they answer me like this:"

But there were interesting limits. You cannot "translate" instances of Standard English preoccupied with abstraction or with nothing/nobody evidently alive, into Black English. That would warp the language into uses antithetical to the guiding perspective of its community of users. Rather you must first change those Standard English sentences, themselves, into ideas consistent with the person-centered assumptions of Black English.

GUIDELINES FOR BLACK ENGLISH

1. *Minimal number of words for every idea:* This is the source for the aphoristic and/or poetic force of the language; eliminate every possible word.

2. *Clarity:* If the sentence is not clear it's not Black English.

3. *Eliminate use of the verb* to be *whenever possible:* This leads to the deployment of more descriptive and, therefore, more precise verbs.

4. *Use* be *or* been *only when you want to describe a chronic, ongoing state of things.*

    He *be* at the office, by 9. (He is always at the office by 9.)

    He *been* with her since forever.

5. *Zero copula:* Always eliminate the verb *to be* whenever it would combine with another verb, in Standard English.

S.E.: She is going out with him.
B.E.: She going out with him.

6. *Eliminate* do *as in:*
   S.E.: What do you think? What do you want?
   B.E.: What you think? What you want?

7. Rules number 3, 4, 5, and 6 provide for the use of the minimal number of verbs per idea and, therefore, greater accuracy in the choice of verb.

8. *In general, if you wish to say something really positive, try to formulate the idea using emphatic negative structure.*
   S.E.: He's fabulous.
   B.E.: He bad.

9. *Use double or triple negatives for dramatic emphasis.*
   S.E.: Tina Turner sings out of this world.
   B.E.: Ain nobody sing like Tina.

10. *Never use the* ed *suffix to indicate the past tense of a verb.*
    S.E.: She closed the door.
    B.E.: She close the door. Or, she have close the door.

11. *Regardless of intentional verb time, only use the third person singular, present indicative, for use of the verb* to have, *as an auxiliary.*
    S.E.: He had his wallet then he lost it.
    B.E.: He have him wallet then he lose it.
    S.E.: We had seen that movie.
    B.E.: We seen that movie. Or, we have see that movie.

12. *Observe a minimal inflection of verbs:* Particularly, never change from the first person singular forms to the third person singular.
    S.E.: Present Tense Forms: He goes to the store.
    B.E.: He go to the store.
    S.E.: Past Tense Forms: He went to the store.
    B.E.: He go to the store. Or, he gone to the store. Or, he been to the store.

13. *The possessive case scarcely ever appears in Black English:* Never use an apostrophe ('s) construction. If you wander into a possessive case component of an idea, then keep logically consistent: ours, his, theirs, mines. But, most likely, if you bump into such a component, you have wandered outside the underlying world view of Black English.
    S.E.: He will take their car tomorrow.
    B.E.: He taking they car tomorrow.

14. *Plurality:* Logical consistency, continued: If the modifier indicates plurality then the noun remains in the singular case.
    S.E.: He ate twelve doughnuts.
    B.E.: He eat twelve doughnut.
    S.E.: She has many books.
    B.E.: She have many book.

15. *Listen for, or invent, special Black English forms of the past tense, such as:* "He losted it. That what she felted." If they are clear and readily understood, then use them.

16. *Do not hesitate to play with words, sometimes inventing them:* e.g. "astropotomous" means huge like a hippo plus astronomical and, therefore, signifies real big.

17. *In Black English, unless you keenly want to underscore the past tense nature of an action, stay in the present tense and rely on the overall context of your ideas for the conveyance of time and sequence.*

18. *Never use the suffix -ly form of an adverb in Black English.*
    S.E.: The rain came down rather quickly.
    B.E.: The rain come down pretty quick.

19. *Never use the indefinite article* an *in Black English.*
    S.E.: He wanted to ride an elephant.
    B.E.: He wanted to ride him a elephant.

20. *Invariant syntax:* in correct Black English it is possible to formulate an imperative, an interrogative, and a simple declarative idea with the same syntax:
    B.E.: You going to the store?
    You going to the store.
    You going to the store!

40   Where was Willie Jordan? We'd reached the mid-term of the semester. Students had formulated Black English guidelines, by consensus, and they were now writing with remarkable beauty, purpose, and enjoyment:

I ain hardly speakin for everybody but myself so understan that.

Kim Parks

Samples from student writings:

Janie have a great big ole hole inside her. Tea Cake the only thing that fit that hole. . . .

That pear tree beautiful to Janie, especial when bees fiddlin with the blossomin pear there growin large and lovely. But personal speakin, the love she get from starin at that tree ain the love what starin back at her in them relationship. (Monica Morris)

Love a big theme in, *They Eye Was Watching God*. Love show people new corners inside theyself. It pull out good stuff and stuff back bad stuff. . . . Joe worship the doing uh his own hand and need other people to worship him too. But he ain't think about Janie that she a person and ought to live like anybody common do. Queen life not for Janie. (Monica Morris)

In both life and writin, Black womens have varietous experience of love that be cold like a iceberg or fiery like a inferno. Passion got for the other partner involve, man or women, seem as shallow, ankle-deep water or the most profoundest abyss. (Constance Evans)

Family love another bond that ain't never break under no pressure. (Constance Evans)

You know it really cold/When the friend you/Always get out the fire/Act like they don't know you/When you in the heat. (Constance Evans)

Big classroom discussion bout love at this time. I never take no class where us have any long arguin for and against for two or three day. New to me and great. I find the class time talkin a million time more interestin than detail bout the book. (Kathy Esseks)

As these examples suggest, Black English no longer limited the students, in any way. In fact, one of them, Philip Garfield, would shortly "translate" a pivotal scene from Ibsen's *A Doll's House*, as his final term paper.

Nora: I didn't gived no shit. I thinked you a asshole back then, too, you make it so hard for me save mines husband life.
Krogstad: Girl, it clear you ain't any idea what you done. You done exact what I once done, and I losed my reputation over it.
Nora: You asks me believe you once act brave save you wife life?
Krogstad: Law care less why you done it.
Nora: Law must suck.
Krogstad: Suck or no, if I wants, judge screw you wid dis paper.
Nora: No way, man. (Philip Garfield)

But where was Willie? Compulsively punctual, and always thoroughly prepared with neat typed compositions, he had disappeared. He failed to show up for our regularly scheduled conference,

and I received neither a note nor a phone call of explanation. A whole week went by. I wondered if Willie had finally been captured by the extremely current happenings in South Africa: passage of a new constitution that did not enfranchise the Black majority, and militant Black South African reaction to that affront. I wondered if he'd been hurt, somewhere. I wondered if the serious workload of weekly readings and writings had overwhelmed him and changed his mind about independent study. Where was Willie Jordan?

One week after the first conference that Willie missed, he called: "Hello, Professor Jordan? This is Willie. I'm sorry I wasn't there last week. But something has come up and I'm pretty upset. I'm sorry but I really can't deal right now."

45   I asked Willie to drop by my office and just let me see that he was okay. He agreed to do that. When I saw him I knew something hideous had happened. Something had hurt him and scared him to the marrow. He was all agitated and stammering and terse and incoherent. At last, his sadly jumbled account let me surmise, as follows: Brooklyn police had murdered his unarmed, twenty-five-year-old brother, Reggie Jordan. Neither Willie nor his elderly parents knew what to do about it. Nobody from the press was interested. His folks had no money. Police ran his family around and around, to no point. And Reggie was really dead. And Willie wanted to fight, but he felt helpless.

With Willie's permission I began to try to secure legal counsel for the Jordan family. Unfortunately, Black victims of police violence are truly numerous, while the resources available to prosecute their killers are truly scarce. A friend of mine at the Center for Constitutional Rights estimated that just the preparatory costs for bringing the cops into court normally approaches $180,000. Unless the execution of Reggie Jordan became a major community cause for organizing and protest, his murder would simply become a statistical item.

Again, with Willie's permission, I contacted every newspaper and media person I could think of. But the Bastone feature article in *The Village Voice* was the only result from that canvassing.

Again, with Willie's permission, I presented the case to my class in Black English. We had talked about the politics of language. We had talked about love and sex and child abuse and men and women. But the murder of Reggie Jordan broke like a hurricane across the room.

There are few "issues" as endemic to Black life as police violence. Most of the students knew and respected and liked Jordan. Many of them came from the very neighborhood where the murder had occurred. All of the students had known somebody close to them who had been killed by police, or had known frightening moments of gratuitous confrontation with the cops. They wanted to do everything at once to avenge death. Number One: They decided to compose a personal statement of condolence to Willie Jordan and his family, written in Black English. Number Two: They decided to compose individual messages to the police, in Black English. These should be prefaced by an explanatory paragraph composed by the entire group. Number Three: These individual messages, with their lead paragraph, should be sent to *Newsday*.

50   The morning after we agreed on these objectives, one of the young women students appeared with an unidentified visitor, who sat through the class, smiling in a peculiar, comfortable way.

Now we had to make more tactical decisions. Because we wanted the messages published, and because we thought it imperative that our outrage be known by the police, the tactical question was this: Should the opening, group paragraph be written in Black English or Standard English?

I have seldom been privy to a discussion with so much heart at the dead beat of it. I will never forget the eloquence, the sudden haltings of speech, the fierce struggle against tears, the furious throwaway, and useless explosions that this question elicited.

That one question contained several others, each of them extraordinarily painful to even

contemplate. How best to serve the memory of Reggie Jordan? Should we use the language of the killer—Standard English—in order to make our ideas acceptable to those controlling the killers? But wouldn't what we had to say be rejected, summarily, if we said it in our own language, the language of the victim, Reggie Jordan? But if we sought to express ourselves by abandoning our language wouldn't that mean our suicide on top of Reggie's murder? But if we expressed ourselves in our own language wouldn't that be suicidal to the wish to communicate with those who, evidently, did not give a damn about us/Reggie/police violence in the Black community?

At the end of one of the longest, most difficult hours of my own life, the students voted, unanimously, to preface their individual messages with a paragraph composed in the language of Reggie Jordan. *"At least we don't give up nothing else. At least we stick to the truth: Be who we been. And stay all the way with Reggie."*

55   It was heartbreaking to proceed, from that point. Everyone in the room realized that our decision in favor of Black English had doomed our writings, even as the distinctive reality of our Black lives always has doomed our efforts to "be who we been" in this country.

I went to the blackboard and took down this paragraph dictated by the class:

You Cops!

We the brother and sister of Willie Jordan, a fellow Stony Brook student who the brother of the dead Reggie Jordan. Reggie, like many brother and sister, he a victim of brutal racist police, October 25, 1984. Us appall, fed up, because that another senseless death what occur in our community. This what we feel, this, from our heart, for we ain't stayin' silent no more.

With the completion of this introduction, nobody said anything. I asked for comments. At this invitation, the unidentified visitor, a young Black man, ceaselessly smiling, raised his hand. He was, it so happens, a rookie cop. He had just joined the force in September and, he said, he thought he should clarify a few things. So he came forward and sprawled easily into a posture of barroom, or fire-side, nostalgia:

"See," Officer Charles enlightened us, "most times when you out on the street and something come down you do one of two things. Over-react or under-react. Now, if you under-react then you can get yourself kilt. And if you over-react then maybe you kill somebody. Fortunately it's about nine times out of ten and you will over-react. So the brother got kilt. And I'm sorry about that, believe me. But what you have to understand is what kilt him: Over-reaction. That's all. Now you talk about Black people and White police but see, now, I'm a cop myself. And (big smile) I'm Black. And just a couple months ago I was on the other side. But it's the same for me. You a cop, you the ultimate authority: the Ultimate Authority. And you on the street, most of the time you can only do one of two things: over-react or under-react. That's all it is with the brother. Over-reaction. Didn't have nothing to do with race."

That morning Officer Charles had the good fortune to escape without being boiled alive. But barely. And I remember the pride of his smile when I read about the fate of Black policemen and other collaborators, in South Africa. I remember him, and I remember the shock and palpable feeling of shame that filled the room. It was as though that foolish, and deadly, young man had just relieved himself of his foolish, and deadly, explanation, face to face with the grief of Reggie Jordan's father and Reggie Jordan's mother. Class ended quietly. I copied the paragraph from the blackboard, collected the individual messages and left to type them up.

60   *Newsday* rejected the piece.

The Village Voice could not find room in their "Letters" section to print the individual messages from the students to the police.

None of the TV news reporters picked up the story.

Nobody raised $180,000 to prosecute the murder of Reggie Jordan.

Reggie Jordan is really dead.

65   I asked Willie Jordan to write an essay pulling together everything important to him from that semester. He was still deeply beside himself with frustration and amazement and loss. This is what he wrote, unedited, and in its entirety:

Throughout the course of this semester I have been researching the effects of oppression and exploitation along racial lines in South Africa and its neighboring countries. I have become aware of South African police brutalization of native Africans beyond the extent of the law, even though the laws themselves are catalyst affliction upon Black men, women and children. Many Africans die each year as a result of the deliberate use of police force to protect the white power structure.

Social control agents in South Africa, such as policemen, are also used to force compliance among citizens through both overt and covert tactics. It is not uncommon to find bold-faced coercion and cold-blooded killings of Blacks by South African police for undetermined and/or inadequate reasons. Perhaps the truth is that the only reasons for this heinous treatment of Blacks rests in racial differences. We should also understand that what is conveyed through the media is not always accurate and may sometimes be construed as the tip of the iceberg at best.

I recently received a painful reminder that racism, poverty, and the abuse of power are global problems which are by no means unique to South Africa. On October 25, 1984 at approximately 3:00 p.m. my brother, Mr. Reginald Jordan, was shot and killed by two New York City policemen from the 75th precinct in the East New York section of Brooklyn. His life ended at the age of twenty-five. Even up to this current point in time the Police Department has failed to provide my family, which consists of five brothers, eight sisters, and two parents, with a plausible reason for Reggie's death. Out of the many stories that were given to my family by the Police Department, not one of them seems to hold water. In fact, I honestly believe that the Police Department's assessment of my brother's murder is nothing short of ABSOLUTE

BULLSHIT, and thus far no evidence had been produced to alter perception of the situation.

Furthermore, I believe that one of three cases may have occurred in this incident. First, Reggie's death may have been the desired outcome of the police officer's action, in which case the killing was premeditated. Or, it was a case of mistaken identity, which clarifies the fact that the two officers who killed my brother and their commanding parties are all grossly incompetent. Or, both of the above cases are correct, i.e., Reggie's murderers intended to kill him and the Police Department behaved insubordinately.

Part of the argument of the officers who shot Reggie was that he had attacked one of them and took his gun. This was their major claim. They also said that only one of them had actually shot Reggie. The facts, however, speak for themselves. According to the Death Certificate and autopsy report, Reggie was shot eight times from point-blank range. The Doctor who performed the autopsy told me himself that two bullets entered the side of my brother's head, four bullets were sprayed into his back, and two bullets struck him in the back of his legs. It is obvious that unnecessary force was used by the police and that it is extremely difficult to shoot someone in his back when he is attacking or approaching you.

After experiencing a situation like this and researching South Africa I believe that to a large degree, justice may only exist as rhetoric. I find it difficult to talk of true justice when the oppression of my people both at home and abroad attests to the fact that inequality and injustice are serious problems whereby Blacks and Third World people are perpetually short-changed by society. Something has to be done about the way in which this world is set up. Although it is a difficult task, we do have the power to make a change.

Willie J. Jordan Jr.
EGL 487, Section 58, November 14, 1984

It is my privilege to dedicate this book to the future life of Willie J. Jordan Jr., August 8, 1985.

NOTES

1. *English Is Spreading, But What Is English?* A presentation by Prof. S. N. Sridhar, Department of Linguistics, SUNY, Stony Brook, April 9, 1985: Dean's Convocation Among the Disciplines.
2. Ibid.
3. *New York Times*, March 15, 1985, Section One, p. 14: Report on Study by Linguists at the University of Pennsylvania.
4. Alice Walker, *The Color Purple* (New York: Harcourt Brace Jovanovich, 1982), p. 11.

SUGGESTIONS FOR DISCUSSION

1. How does June Jordan intertwine the story of her class on Black English and the story of Willie Jordan? Would these stories have the same impact if they were presented separately? What, if anything, does Jordan accomplish by weaving them together?

2. Reread the passages where Jordan's students translate the opening of *The Color Purple* into Standard English and the scene from *A Doll's House* into Black English. Describe the qualities of black expression that get lost in the first case and added in the second.

3. What are the advantages and disadvantages of Jordan's students' decision to write the preface to their individual messages to the police in Black English?

SUGGESTIONS FOR WRITING

1. Write an essay that explains the point June Jordan is making about the relationship between Black English and Standard English and what she thinks ought to be taught in school and why. Compare Jordan's views with your own views on how language should be taught in American schools.

2. Write an essay that explains what you see as the advantages and disadvantages of Jordan's students' decision to compose the introduction to their letters to the police in Black

English. Arrive at your own evaluation of their decision, but before you do, try to explain how and in what sense the decision they had to make was a difficult one.

3. Choose a passage of dialogue in a novel or play you know well in which the speakers are speaking Standard English. Using Phil Garfield's translation of a scene from *A Doll's House* into Black English as a model, translate the passage into some form of nonstandard English—whether the spoken language of your neighborhood, the vernacular of youth culture, or the dialect of a region.

WIRED CULTURE   PowerPoint

To learn more about information design and communications, visit www.ablongman.com/george/107

As Edward R. Tufte notes, PowerPoint™ presentations are "everywhere." They have become a standard feature in business, government, and education. If anything, people have come to expect PowerPoint presentations. It is easy enough to account for PowerPoint's appeal. As a software package that produces and displays slides, PowerPoint has much clearer visual resolution than the old overhead transparencies and is much simpler to use than the old way of making individual slides. To get high-quality visuals, all you have to do is download files or scan in images. It is quite likely that you have seen PowerPoint presentations in your classes, and you may have produced your own PowerPoint presentations. Still, as you will see in the following reading selection, for however ubiquitous PowerPoint has become, visual designers such as Tufte have raised serious questions about how it is used and what it does to the nature of information design and communication.

POWERPOINT IS EVIL

— Edward R. Tufte

Edward R. Tufte is professor emeritus of political science, computer science and statistics, and graphic design at Yale University and the author, designer, and publisher of highly influential books on information design, *The Visual Display of Quantitative Information* (1983), *Envisioning Information* (1990), and *Visual Explanation* (1997). In a recent monograph *The Cognitive Style of PowerPoint*, Tufte develops his analysis and criticism. "PowerPoint Is Evil" was published in *Wired* in September 2003.

SUGGESTION FOR READING   As his title makes abundantly clear, Edward R. Tufte is making a very strong claim about PowerPoint, namely that it is "evil." As you read, consider the evidence Tufte presents, both verbal and visual, to support this claim.

Power Corrupts.

PowerPoint Corrupts Absolutely.

1   Imagine a widely used and expensive prescription drug that promised to make us beautiful but didn't. Instead the drug had frequent, serious side effects: it induced stupidity, turned everyone into bores, wasted time, and degraded the quality and credibility of communication. These side effects would rightly lead to a worldwide product recall.

Yet slideware—computer programs for presentations—is everywhere: in corporate America, in government bureaucracies, even in our schools. Several hundred million copies of Microsoft PowerPoint are churning out trillions of slides each

Military parade, Stalin Square, Budapest, April 4, 1956.

AP/Wide World Photos
Tufte satirizes the totalitarian impact of presentation slideware.

GOOD

Estimates of relative survival rates, by cancer site[12]

	% survival rates and their standard errors			
	5 year	10 year	15 year	20 year
Prostate	98.8 0.4	95.2 0.9	87.1 1.7	81.1 3.0
Thyroid	96.0 0.8	95.8 1.2	94.0 1.6	95.4 2.1
Testis	94.7 1.1	94.0 1.3	91.1 1.8	88.2 2.3
Melanomas	89.0 0.8	86.7 1.1	83.5 1.5	82.8 1.9
Breast	86.4 0.4	78.3 0.6	71.3 0.7	65.0 1.0
Hodgkin's disease	85.1 1.7	79.8 2.0	73.8 2.4	67.1 2.8
Corpus uteri, uterus	84.3 1.0	83.2 1.3	80.8 1.7	79.2 2.0
Urinary, bladder	82.1 1.0	76.2 1.4	70.3 1.9	67.9 2.4
Cervix, uteri	70.5 1.6	64.1 1.8	62.8 2.1	60.0 2.4

Graphi cs Press
A traditional   table :
rich, informative , clear .

BAD

Graphi cs Press
Powe rPoint chartjunk :
smarm y, chaoti c, incoherent .

year. Slideware may help speakers outline their talks, but convenience for the speaker can be punishing to both content and audience. The standard PowerPoint presentation elevates format over content, betraying an attitude of commercialism that turns everything into a sales pitch.

Of course, data-driven meetings are nothing new. Years before today's slideware, presentations at companies such as IBM and in the military used bullet lists shown by overhead projectors. But the format has become ubiquitous under PowerPoint, which was created in 1984 and later acquired by Microsoft. PowerPoint's pushy style seeks to set up a speaker's dominance over the audience. The speaker, after all, is making power points with bullets to followers. Could any metaphor be worse? Voicemail menu systems? Billboards? Television? Stalin?

Particularly disturbing is the adoption of the PowerPoint cognitive style in our schools. Rather than learning to write a report using sentences, children are being taught how to formulate client pitches and infomercials. Elementary school PowerPoint exercises (as seen in teacher guides and in student work posted on the Internet) typically consist of 10 to 20 words and a piece of clip art on each slide in a presentation of three to six slides—a total of perhaps 80 words (15 seconds of silent reading) for a week of work. Students would be better off if the schools simply closed down on those days and everyone went to the Exploratorium or wrote an illustrated essay explaining something.

5   In a business setting, a PowerPoint slide typically shows 40 words, which is about eight seconds' worth of silent reading material. With so little information per slide, many, many slides are needed. Audiences consequently endure a relentless sequentiality, one damn slide after another. When information is stacked in time, it is difficult to understand context and evaluate relationships. Visual reasoning usually works more effectively when relevant information is shown side by side. Often, the more intense the detail, the greater the clarity and understanding. This is especially so for statistical data, where the fundamental analytical act is to make comparisons.

Consider an important and intriguing table of survival rates for those with cancer relative to those without cancer for the same time period. Some 196 numbers and 57 words describe survival rates and their standard errors for 24 cancers.

Applying the PowerPoint templates to this nice, straightforward table yields an analytical disaster. The data explodes into six separate chaotic slides, consuming 2.9 times the area of the table. Everything is wrong with these smarmy, incoherent graphs: the encoded legends, the meaningless color, the logo-type branding. They are uncomparative, indifferent to content and evidence, and so data-starved as to be almost pointless. Chartjunk is a clear sign of statistical stupidity. Poking a finger into the eye of thought, these data graphics would turn into a nasty travesty if used for a serious purpose, such as helping cancer patients assess their survival chances. To sell a product that messes up data with such systematic intensity, Microsoft abandons any pretense of statistical integrity and reasoning.

Presentations largely stand or fall on the quality, relevance, and integrity of the content. If your numbers are boring, then you've got the wrong numbers. If your words or images are not on point, making them dance in color won't make them relevant. Audience boredom is usually a content failure, not a decoration failure.

At a minimum, a presentation format should do no harm. Yet the PowerPoint style routinely disrupts, dominates, and trivializes content. Thus PowerPoint presentations too often resemble a school play—very loud, very slow, and very simple.

10   The practical conclusions are clear. PowerPoint is a competent slide manager and projector. But rather than supplementing a presentation, it has become a substitute for it. Such misuse ignores the most important rule of speaking: respect your audience.

SUGGESTIONS FOR DISCUSSION

1. Visual aids of all sorts, not just PowerPoint presentations but overhead transparencies, slide shows, films, posters, charts, maps, diagrams, and illustrations, have long been a central part of classroom teaching and learning and of textbooks. Consider your own experience with various forms of visual communication in school. What do visual aids make possible for you as a learner? What do you see as their limits?

2. Tufte says that PowerPoint has a particular "cognitive style" that is "disturbing" in schools. How would you define the "cognitive style" Tufte is pointing to here? What does he see as the problems with such a style? Compare Tufte's response with your own experience watching PowerPoint presentations in classes or elsewhere. To what extent does your own experience confirm, refute, or qualify Tufte's point? Consider the examples of "good" and

"bad" information design Tufte offers. How would you distinguish between "good" and "bad" PowerPoint presentations?

3. Consider Tufte's assertion that "PowerPoint's pushy style seeks to set up the speaker's dominance over the audience." Explain what Tufte is getting at here. Take into account how he reinforces his point with the visual satire of the "totalitarian impact of presentation software."

SUGGESTION FOR WRITING

1. Write an essay that compares the "good " and "bad " examples of information design Tufte provides. Explain the criteria Tufte is using to make such a distinction.

2. College and university teaching increasingly makes use of digital communication. Faculty are using PowerPoint, putting course material online, setting up electronic discussion groups, and in some cases running "paperless" classes and teaching online courses. Write an essay that considers the role of digital communication in teaching and learning. Draw on your own experience and what you have observed to explain what you see as the proper role of digital communication in education. What can it do? What are its limits? In your analysis, you might compare online education to older forms such as lectures, seminars, class discussion, and so on.

3. Use Tufte's ideas and your own sense of what PowerPoint can do well and not so well to design your own examples of "good" and "bad" PowerPoint slides. Imagine you are making a presentation to your class on a topic you know a lot about. Explain what makes the "bad" slides "bad" and the "good" ones "good."

PERSPECTIVES — Gender Gap

To learn more about gender roles in math and science, visit www.ablongman.com/george/108

On January 14, 2005, Harvard president Lawrence Summers spoke to a conference on diversifying the workforce in science and engineering, sponsored by the National Bureau of Economic Research. Summers prefaced his remarks by describing them as "some attempts at provocation," and his subsequent exploration of the underrepresentation of women in science and engineering was just that—a provocation that set off a national controversy over his arguments that genetic differences in ability and the choice of family over career are more telling causes of underrepresentation than discrimination against women. In the ensuing debate, no one questioned the facts. There is little question that while the number of women with Ph.D.'s in math and science (and with professional degrees in medicine, law, and business) has increased substantially, to 50 percent or more in many fields, women are still underrepresented on the faculties of colleges and universities and in leadership positions in the professions. The problem here is an interpretive one: how can we explain the gender gap in so many domains of professional life?

Controversy over the gender gap, to be sure, did not begin with Summers' comments. We want to use this controversy rather to present a range of perspectives to help you think about the gender gap not only in universities but also in elementary and secondary classrooms. To this end, we include directions on how to find Summers' talk online, Katha Pollit's response to Summers, and Christina Hoff Sommers' argument that the real gender gap affects boys more than girls.

LAWRENCE SUMMERS' REMARKS AT THE NBER CONFERENCE ON DIVERSIFYING THE SCIENCE AND ENGINEERING WORKFORCE

As noted earlier, Lawrence Summers is president of Harvard University. He is an economist by training and was the Treasury Secretary during the Clinton administration. We had hoped to print here excerpts from his talk at the National Bureau of Economic Research conference on diversifying the science and engineering workforce given in January 2005, but we were not granted permission to do so. Harvard officials told us that the talk was not meant to be a publication but that, out of a commitment to full disclosure, it has been posted at the Harvard Web site.

SUGGESTION FOR READING   As you read, notice how Lawrence Summers defines the problem that needs to be explained. Pay attention especially to the "three broad hypothesis" Summers presents to explain the sources of disparity.

Access Summers's speech at the url given below. If it is not available, you should be able to easily find it using a Google search.

http://www.president.Harvard.edu/speeches/2005/nber.html

SUMMERS OF OUR DISCONTENT

— *Katha Pollitt*

Katha Pollitt is a columnist for the *Nation*. "Summers of Our Discontent" appeared in the magazine's February 21, 2005, issue, just after the story of Lawrence Summers's talk hit the press, before Summers agreed to release his comments to the public.

SUGGESTION FOR READING   As you read, notice the sense of immediacy in Katha Pollitt's column. Consider how she counters much of what Summers said in an effort to shape public opinion as it was forming. Note the reasons she gives to refute Summers.

1   As the saying goes, behind every successful woman is a man who is surprised. Harvard president Larry Summers apparently is that man. A distinguished economist who was Treasury Secretary under Clinton, Summers caused a firestorm on January 14 when, speaking from notes at a conference on academic diversity, he argued that tenured women are rare in math and science for three reasons, which he listed in descending order of importance. One, women choose family commitments over the eighty-hour weeks achievement in those fields requires; two, fewer women than men have the necessary genetic gifts; and three, women are discriminated against. Following standard economic theory, Summers largely discounted discrimination: a first-rate woman rejected by one university would surely be snapped up by a rival. We're back to women's lack of commitment and brainpower.

On campus, Summers has lost big—he has had to apologize, appoint a committee and endure many a hairy eyeball from the faculty, and complaints from furious alumnae like me. In the press, he's done much better: Provocative thinker brought down by PC feminist mob! Women *are* dumber! Steven Pinker says so! The *New York Times* even ran a supportive op-ed by Charles Murray without identifying him as the co-author of *The Bell Curve*, the discredited farrago of racist claptrap. While much was made of MIT biologist Nancy Hopkins walking out of his talk—what about free speech, what about Truth?—we heard little about how Summers, who says he only wanted to spark a discussion, has refused to release his remarks. The bold challenger of campus orthodoxy apparently doesn't want the world to know what he actually said.

Do men have an innate edge in math and science? Perhaps someday we will live in a world free of the gender bias and stereotyping we know exists today both in and out of the classroom, and we will be able to answer that question, if anyone is still asking it. But we know we don't live in a bias-free world now: girls are steered away from math and science from the moment they are born. The interesting fact is that, thanks partly to antidiscrimination laws that have forced open closed doors, they have steadily increased their performance nonetheless. Most of my Radcliffe classmates remember being firmly discouraged from anything to do with numbers or labs; one was flatly told that women couldn't be physicians—at her Harvard med school interview. Today women obtain 48 percent of BAs in math, 57 percent in biology and agricultural science, half of all places in med school, and they are steadily increasing their numbers as finalists in the Intel high school science contest (fifteen out of forty this year, and three out of four in New York City).

Every gain women have made in the past 200 years has been in the face of experts insisting they couldn't do it and didn't really want to. Biology, now trotted out to "prove" women's incapacity for math and science, used to "prove" that they shouldn't go to college at all. As women progress, the proponents of innate inferiority simply adapt their arguments to explain why further advancement is unlikely. But how can we know that in 2005, any more than we knew it in 1905? I'd like to hear those experts explain this instead: the number of tenure offers to women at Harvard has gone down in each of Summers's three years as president, from nine in thirty-six tenures to three in thirty-two. (The year

before his arrival, it was thirteen women out of thirty-six.) Surely women's genes have not deteriorated since 2001?

5   Whatever they may be in theory, in the workplace, biological incapacity and natural preference are the counters used to defend against accusations of discrimination. Summers argues that competition makes discrimination irrational; that wouldn't hold, though, if an entire field is pervaded with discrimination, if there's a consensus that women don't belong there and if female candidates are judged more harshly by all potential employers. It also doesn't work if the threat of competition isn't so credible: it will be a long time before the Ivies feel the heat from Northwestern, which has improved its profile by hiring the first-rate women they foolishly let go. The history of women and minorities in the workplace shows that vigorous enforcement of antidiscrimination law is what drives progress. Moreover, the competition argument can be turned against Summers: after all, given its prestige and wealth, Harvard could "compete" for women with any university on the planet. So why doesn't it?

This brings us to that eighty-hour week and women's domestic "choices." It's a truism that career ladders are based on the traditional male life plan—he knocks himself out in his 20s and 30s while his wife raises the kids, mends his socks and types his papers. If women had been included from the start, the ladder would look rather different—careers might peak later, taking a semester off to have a baby would not blot your copybook, women would not be expected to do huge amounts of academic service work and then be blamed at tenure time for not publishing more. By treating this work culture as fixed, and women as the problem, Summers lets academia off the hook. Yet Harvard, with its $23 billion endowment, doesn't even offer free daycare to grad students.

There's a ton of research on all the subjects raised by Summers—the socialization of girls; conscious and unconscious gender bias in teaching, hiring and promotion; what makes talented females, like Intel finalists, drop out of science at every stage; what makes motherhood so hard to combine with a career. We are past the day when brilliant women could be expected to sit quietly while a powerful man parades his ignorance of that scholarship and of their experience. It is not "provocative" when the president of Harvard justifies his university's lamentable record by recalling that his toddler daughter treated toy trucks like dolls. It's an insult to his audience.

What was his point, anyway? That she'll grow up and flunk calculus? That she'll get a job in a daycare center?

If Summers wants to know why women are underrepresented in math and science, he should do his homework, beginning with Nancy Hopkins's pathbreaking 1999 study of bias against female faculty at MIT. And then he should ask them.

WHERE DO BOYS FIT IN?

— Christina Hoff Sommers

Christina Hoff Sommers, a professor of philosophy, has published a number of books critical of the feminist movement, including *The War Against Boys* (2000), from which this excerpt has been taken. She is responding here to books and reports in the 1980s and 1990s that focused on how girls are "shortchanged" in American education. As you will see, she wants to redefine the gender gap to call attention to the plight of boys rather than of girls.

SUGGESTION FOR READING As you read, notice how Christina Hoff Sommers formulates the problem she is investigating, namely, "where do boys fit in." Consider in particular how she interprets statistical data in government reports.

1 How do boys fit into the "tragedy" of America's "shortchanged" girls? Inevitably, boys are resented, being seen both as the unfairly privileged gender and as obstacles on the path to gender justice for girls. There is an understandable dialectic: the more girls are portrayed as diminished, the more boys are regarded as needing to be taken down a notch and reduced in importance. This perspective on boys and girls is promoted in schools of education, and many a teacher now feels that girls need and deserve special indemnifying consideration. "It is really clear that boys are No. 1 in this society and in most of the world," says Dr. Patricia O'Reilly, professor of education and director of the Gender Equity Center at the University of Cincinnati.

It may be "clear," but it isn't true. If we disregard the girl advocates and look objectively at the relative condition of boys and girls in this country, we find that it is boys, not girls, who are languishing academically. Data from the U.S. Department of Education and from several recent university studies show that far from being shy and demoralized, today's girls outshine boys. Girls get better grades. They have higher educational aspirations. They follow a more rigorous academic program and participate more in the prestigious Advanced Placement (AP) program. This demanding program gives top students the opportunity of taking college-level courses in high school. In 1984, an equal proportion of males and females participated. But according to the United States Department of Education, "Between 1984 and 1996, the number of females who took the examinations rose at a faster rate. . . . In 1996, 144 females compared to 117 males per 1,000 12th graders took AP examinations."

According to the National Center for Education Statistics, slightly more female than male students enroll in high-level math and science courses.

The representation of American girls as apprehensive and academically diminished is not true to the facts. Girls, allegedly so timorous and lacking in confidence, now outnumber boys in student government, in honor societies, on school newspapers, and even in debating clubs. Only in sports are the boys still ahead, and women's groups are targeting the sports gap with a vengeance.

5   At the very time the AAUW was advertising its discovery that girls were subordinates in the schools, the Department of Education published the results of a massive survey showing just the opposite.

Girls read more books. They outperform males on tests of artistic and musical ability. More girls than boys study abroad. More join the Peace Corps. Conversely, more boys than girls are suspended from school. More are held back and more drop out. Boys are three times as likely as girls to be enrolled in special education programs and four times as likely to be diagnosed with attention deficit/hyperactivity disorder.

More boys than girls are involved in crime, alcohol, and drugs. Girls attempt suicide more than boys, but it is boys who actually kill themselves more often. In a typical year (1997), there were 4,493 suicides of young people between the ages of five and twenty-four: 701 females, 3,792 males.

BOYS ARE TRAILING

Quietly, some educators will tell you that it is boys, not girls, who are on the fragile side of the gender gap. In 1997, I met the president of the Board of Education of Atlanta, Georgia. Who is faring better in Atlanta's schools, boys or girls? I asked. "Girls," he replied without hesitating. In what areas? I asked. "Just about any area you can mention." A high school principal from Pennsylvania tells of the condition of boys in his school: "Students who dominate the drop-out list, the suspension list, the failure list and other negative indices of non-achievement in school are males at a wide ratio."

Three years ago, Scarsdale High School in New York State held a gender-equity workshop for its faculty. It was the standard girls-are-being-shortchanged fare, with one notable difference: a male student gave a presentation in which he pointed to evidence suggesting that girls at Scarsdale High were well ahead of boys. David Greene, a social studies teacher, thought the student must be mistaken. But when he and some colleagues analyzed department grading patterns, they saw that the student was right. They found that in Advanced Placement social studies classes, there was little or no difference in grades between boys and girls. But in standard classes, the girls were doing a lot better. Greene also learned from the school's athletic director that its girls' sports teams were far more successful in competition with other schools than the boys' teams were. Of the twelve athletes from Scarsdale High named as All-American in the past ten years, for example, three had been boys, nine girls. Greene came away with a picture flatly at odds with the administrators' preconception: one of ambitious girls and relatively disaffected boys who were willing to settle for mediocrity.

10   Like schools everywhere, Scarsdale High has been strongly influenced by the girl-crisis climate. The belief that girls are systematically deprived prevails on the school's Gender Equity Committee; it is the rationale for the school's offering a special senior elective class on gender equity. Greene has tried gingerly to broach the subject of male underperformance with his colleagues. Many of them concede that in the classes they teach, the girls seem to be doing better than the boys, but they do not see this as part of a larger pattern. After so many years of hearing about the silenced, diminished girls, the suggestion that boys are not doing as well as girls is not taken seriously even by teachers who see it with their own eyes in their own classrooms.

SCHOOL "ENGAGEMENT"

A 1999 Congressional Quarterly Researcher article about male and female academic achievement takes note of a common parental experience: "Daughters want to please their teachers by spending extra time on projects, doing extra credit, making homework as neat as possible. Sons rush through homework assignments and run outside to play, unconcerned about how the teacher will regard the sloppy work." In the technical language of education experts, girls are academically more "engaged." School engagement is a critical measure of student success. The U.S. Department of Education gauges student commitment by the following criteria:

- How much time do students devote to homework each night?

- Do students come to class prepared and ready to learn? (Do they bring books and pencils? Have they completed their homework?)

That boys are less committed to school than girls was already well documented by the Department of Education in the eighties and nineties. Higher percentages of boys than of girls reported they "usually" or "often" come to school without supplies or without having done their homework. Surveys of fourth, eighth, and twelfth grades show girls consistently reporting that they do more homework than boys. By twelfth grade, males are four times as likely as females not to do homework.

Here we have a genuinely worrisome gender gap, with boys well behind girls. It is this gap that should concern educators, parents, school boards, and legislators. Engagement with school is perhaps the single most important predictor of academic success. But boys' weaker commitment is not addressed at the equity seminars and workshops around the country. Instead, the fashionable but spurious self-esteem gap continues to be the prevailing concern—the gap that the AAUW, in its zeal to "know more" about Carol Gilligan's findings, claims to have exposed.

There are some well-tested ways of reengaging boys, improving their study habits, and interesting them in learning and achievement. (I'll discuss what works with boys in later chapters.) But until boys' problems are acknowledged, they cannot be addressed. And until they are addressed, another educational disparity is likely to persist: far more girls than boys go on to college.

THE COLLEGE GAP

15 The U.S. Department of Education reports that in 1996 there were 8.4 million women but only 6.7 million men enrolled in college. It also shows women holding on to and improving this advantage well into the next decade. According to one Department prediction, by 2007 there will be 9.2 million women in college and 6.9 million men.

Girl partisans offer ingenious, self-serving arguments for why the higher enrollment of women in college should not count as an advantage for women. According to feminist essayist Barbara Ehrenreich, "One of the reasons why fewer men are going to college may be because they suspect that they can make a living just as well without a college education; in other words they still have such an advantage over women in the non-professional workforce that they don't require an education."

Ehrenreich is suggesting that a seventeen- or eighteen-year-old boy about to graduate from high school, with no plans for college, may still be better off than the college-bound girl sitting next to him. There may be a handful of enterprising high school students for whom this is true, but for the vast majority of boys a college education allows entrance into the middle class—to say nothing of the personal benefits of a liberal arts education.

In recent years, the economic value of a college education has increased dramatically. An economist at the American Enterprise Institute,

Marvin Kosters, has quantified the trend: "The average wage of a mature adult college graduate was about 25 percent higher in 1978 than the wage of a high school graduate. By 1995, the difference had more than doubled to an average wage of more than 50 percent higher for the college-educated worker."

Someone should have noticed that the boys were lagging behind. The college gap was a genuine and dangerous trend. But at just the time the girls were surpassing the boys in this critical way, the gender activists in the Department of Education, the AAUW, the Wellesley Center, and the Ms. Foundation chose to announce the "shortchanged-girl" crisis. For the next several years, the gender gap in college enrollment continued to widen, but the attention of the American public and government was focused on the nation's "underserved girls."

SUGGESTIONS FOR DISCUSSION

1. Take as a given the gender gap between women and men who receive Ph.D.s in science and engineering and the underrepresentation of women in these fields in American universities. Neither Lawrence Summers nor Katha Pollitt would dispute these facts. How then does each of them explain the disparity between trained women and women in faculty positions? What assumptions does each bring to the argument?

2. Consider Summers's argument about the choices women have to make between family and career. Is it reasonable to think individuals should work eighty hours a week, whether in faculty positions or in the professions of law, medicine, and business, to be successful? What is Pollitt's perspective on this dilemma?

3. As you have seen, Christina Hoff Sommers wants to change the focus of the gender gap discussion. She presents considerable evidence about what is happening to boys in American education. This raises an interesting question: if boys are lagging behind in elementary and secondary education, then why are women underrepresented in high-ranking positions in universities and the professions? How would Summers and Pollitt respond to Sommers? How do such social factors as class, race, and ethnicity enter into this discussion?

SUGGESTIONS FOR WRITING

1. Write an essay that explains the differences between the conclusions of Lawrence Summers and Katha Pollitt. Take into account that they are likely to define the gender gap in the same way, as the disparity between women who receive Ph.D.s in science and engineering and the representation of women on university faculties in these fields. Consider in your essay how each would explain this disparity.

2. Summers describes the work expectations in "high-powered" professions in the university, law, medicine, and business. Write an essay that considers how the expectation to work an eighty-hour week figures in the gender gap.

3. Write an essay in response to Christina Hoff Sommers. Take the data she presents as a given. Do you agree with her interpretation of it? What other perspective might you offer?

SKILLS AND OTHER DILEMMAS OF A PROGRESSIVE BLACK EDUCATOR

— *Lisa Delpit*

Lisa Delpit holds the Benjamin E. Mays Chair of Urban Educational Leadership at Georgia State University and has received the prestigious MacArthur "genius" fellowship and the award for Outstanding Contribution to Education from the Harvard Graduate School of Education. Originally published in the *Harvard Educational Review* in 1986, "Skills and Other Dilemmas of a Progressive Black Educator" began, Delpit says, "as a letter to a University of Alaska colleague to lay out my concerns with the writing project movement and to detail the frustrations many teachers of color felt at being excluded from educational dialogue—in this case, the dialogue about literacy instruction." Delpit's article was an instant classic and is the most recent of the Classic Readings in this edition of *Reading Culture*.

SUGGESTION FOR READING As you read, pay attention to how Delpit identifies the "dilemmas" that are central to this article. Notice in particular how things seem to come to a head at the conference in Philadelphia. When you have finished reading, write a short statement that explains Delpit's "dilemmas" and how she resolves them.

1   Why do the refrains of progressive educational movements seem lacking in the diverse harmonies, the variegated rhythms, and the shades of tone expected in a truly heterogeneous chorus? Why do we hear so little representation from the multicultural voices which comprise the present-day American educational scene?

These questions have surfaced anew as I begin my third year of university "professoring" after having graduated from a prestigious university known for its progressive school of education. My family back in Louisiana is very proud about all of that, but still they find me rather tedious. They say things like, "She just got here and she's locked up in that room with a bunch of papers talking about she's gotta finish some article. I don't know why she bothers to come home." Or, "I didn't ask you about what any research said, what do *you* think?!"

I once shared my family's skepticism of academia. I remember asking myself in the first few months of my graduate school career, "Why is it these theories never seem to be talking about me?" But by graduation time many of my fellow minority students and I had become well trained: we had learned alternate ways of viewing the world, coaxed memories of life in our communities into forms which fit into the categories created by academic researchers and theoreticians, and internalized belief systems that often belied our own experiences.

I learned a lot in graduate school. For one thing I learned that people acquire a new dialect most effectively through interaction with speakers of that dialect, not through being constantly corrected. Of course, when I was growing up, my mother and my teachers in the pre-integration, poor black Catholic school that I attended corrected every other word I uttered in their effort to coerce my Black English into sometimes hypercorrect Standard English forms acceptable to black nuns in Catholic schools. Yet, I learned to speak and write in Standard English.

5   I also learned in graduate school that people learn to write not by being taught "skills" and grammar, but by "writing in meaningful contexts."

In elementary school I diagrammed thousands of sentences, filled in tens of thousands of blanks, and never wrote any text longer than two sentences until I was in the tenth grade of high school. I have been told by my professors that I am a good writer. (One, when told about my poor community and segregated, skill-based schooling, even went so far as to say, "How did you *ever* learn how to write?") By that time I had begun to wonder myself. Never mind that I had learned—and learned well—despite my professors' scathing retroactive assessment of my early education.

But I cannot blame graduate school for all the new beliefs I learned to espouse. I also learned a lot during my progressive undergraduate teacher training. There, as one of the few black education students, I learned that the open classroom was the most "humanizing" of learning environments, that children should be in control of their own learning, and that all children would read when they were ready. Determined to use all that I had learned to benefit black children, I abandoned the cornfields of Ohio, and relocated to an alternative inner-city school in Philadelphia to student-teach.

Located on the border between two communities, our "open-classroom" school deliberately maintained a population of 60 percent poor black kids from "South Philly," and 40 percent well-to-do white kids from "Society Hill." The black kids went to school there because it was their only neighborhood school. The white kids went to school there because their parents had learned the same kinds of things I had learned about education. As a matter of fact, there was a waiting list of white children to get into the school. This was unique in Philadelphia—a predominantly black school with a waiting list of white children. There was no such waiting list of black children.

I apprenticed under a gifted young kindergarten teacher. She had learned the same things that I had learned, so our pairing was most opportune. When I finished my student teaching, the principal asked me to stay on in a full-time position.

The ethos of that school was fascinating. I was one of only a few black teachers, and the other black teachers were mostly older and mostly "traditional." They had not learned the kinds of things I had learned, and the young white teachers sometimes expressed in subtle ways that they thought these teachers were—how to say it—somewhat "repressive." At the very least they were "not structuring learning environments in ways that allowed the children's intellect to flourish": they focused on "skills," they made students sit down at desks, they made students practice handwriting, they corrected oral and written grammar. The subtle, unstated message was, "They just don't realize how smart these kids are."

10   I was an exception to the other black teachers. I socialized with the young white teachers and planned shared classroom experiences with them. I also taught as they did. Many people told me I was a good teacher: I had an open classroom; I had learning stations; I had children write books and stories to share; I provided games and used weaving to teach math and fine motor skills. I threw out all the desks and added carpeted open learning areas. I was doing what I had learned, and it worked. Well, at least it worked for some of the children.

My white students zoomed ahead. They worked hard at the learning stations. They did amazing things with books and writing. My black students played the games; they learned how to weave; and they threw the books around the learning stations. They practiced karate moves on the new carpets. Some of them even learned how to read, but none of them as quickly as my white students. I was doing the same thing for all my kids—what was the problem?

I taught in Philadelphia for six years. Each year my teaching became less like my young white friends' and more like the other black women's who taught at the school. My students practiced handwriting; I wrote on the board; I got some tables to replace some of the thrown-out desks. Each year my teaching moved farther away from what I had learned, even though in many ways I still identified myself as an open-classroom teacher. As my classroom became more "traditional," however, it seemed that my black students steadily improved in their reading and writing. But they still lagged behind. It hurt that I was moving away from what I had learned. It hurt even more that although my colleagues called me a good teacher, I still felt that I had failed in the task that was most important to me—teaching black children and teaching them well. I could not talk about my failure then. It is difficult even now. At least I did not fall into the trap of talking about the parents' failures. I just did not talk about any of it.

In 1977 I left Philadelphia and managed to forget about my quandary for six and a half years—the one and a half years that I spent working in an administrative job in Louisiana and the five years I spent in graduate school. It was easy to forget failure there. My professors told me that everything I had done in Philadelphia was right; that I was right to shun basals; that I was right to think in terms of learner-driven and holistic education; that, indeed, I had been a success in Philadelphia. Of course, it was easy to forget, too, because I could develop new focal points. I could even maintain my political and moral integrity while doing so—graduate school introduced me to all *sorts* of oppressed peoples who needed assistance in the educational realm. There were bilingual speakers of any number of languages; there were new immigrants. And if one were truly creative, there were even whole countries in need of assistance—welcome to the Third World! I could tackle someone else's failures and forget my own.

In graduate school I learned about many more elements of progressive education. It was great. I learned new "holistic" teaching techniques—integrating reading and writing, focusing on meaning rather than form. One of the most popular elements—and one, I should add, which I readily and heartily embraced—was the writing process approach to literacy. I spent a lot of time with writing process people. I learned the

lingo. I focused energy on "fluency" and not on "correctness." I learned that a focus on "skills" would stifle my students' writing. I learned about "fast-writes" and "golden lines" and group process. I went out into the world as a professor of literacy armed with the very latest, research-based and field-tested teaching methods.

15   All went well in my university literacy classes. My student teachers followed my lead and shunned limited "traditional" methods of teaching. They, too, embraced holistic processes and learned to approach writing with an emphasis on fluency and creative expression.

But then I returned to Philadelphia for a conference. I looked up one of my old friends, another black woman who was also a teacher. Cathy had been teaching for years in an alternative high school. Most of the students in her school, and by this time in the entire Philadelphia system, were black. Cathy and I had never taught together but had worked together on many political committees and for many radical causes. We shared a lot of history, *and* a lot of philosophies. In fact, I thought we were probably in agreement on just about everything, especially everything having to do with education. I was astounded to discover our differences.

Cathy invited me to dinner. I talked about my new home, about my research in the South Pacific, and about being a university professor. She brought me up to date on all the gossip about radicals in Philly and on the new committees working against apartheid. Eventually the conversation turned to teaching, as it often does with teachers.

Cathy began talking about the local writing project based, like those in many other areas, on the process approach to writing made popular by the Bay Area Writing Project. She adamantly insisted that it was doing a monumental disservice to black children. I was stunned. I started to defend the program, but then thought better of it, and asked her why she felt so negative about what she had seen.

She had a lot to say. She was particularly adamant about the notion that black children had to learn to be "fluent" in writing—had to feel comfortable about putting pen to paper—before they could be expected to conform to any conventional standards. "These people keep pushing this fluency thing," said Cathy. "What do they think? Our children have no fluency? If they think that, they ought to read some of the rap songs my students write all the time. They might not be writing their school assignments but they sure are writing. Our kids *are* fluent. What they need are the skills that will get them into college. I've got a kid right now—brilliant. But he can't get a score on the SAT that will even get him considered by any halfway decent college. He needs *skills*, not *fluency*. This is just another one of those racist ploys to keep our kids out. White kids learn how to write a decent sentence. Even if they don't teach them in school, their parents make sure they get what they need. But what about our kids? They don't get it at home and they spend all their time in school learning to be *fluent*. I'm sick of this liberal nonsense."

20   I returned to my temporary abode, but found that I had so much to think about that I could not sleep. Cathy had stirred that part of my past I had long avoided. Could her tirade be related to the reasons for my feelings of past failures? Could I have been a pawn, somehow, in some kind of perverse plot against black success? What did those black nuns from my childhood and those black teachers from the school in which I taught understand that my "education" had hidden from me? Had I abrogated my responsibility to teach all of the "skills" my black students were unlikely to get at home or in a more "unstructured" environment? These were painful thoughts.

The next day at the conference I made it my business to talk to some of the people from around the country who were involved in writing process projects. I asked the awkward question about the extent of minority teacher involvement in these endeavors. The most positive answer I received was that writing process projects initially attracted a few black or minority teachers, but they soon dropped out of the pro-

gram. None came back a second year. One thoughtful woman told me she had talked to some of the black teachers about their noninvolvement. She was pained about their response and still could not understand it. They said the whole thing was racist, that the meetings were racist, and that the method itself was racist. They were not able to be specific, she added, but just felt they, and their ideas, were excluded.

I have spent the last few months trying to understand all that I learned in Philadelphia. How could people I so deeply respect hold such completely different views? I could not believe that all the people from whom I had learned could possibly have sinister intentions towards black children. On the other hand, all of those black teachers could not be completely wrong. What was going on?

When I asked another black teacher in another city what she thought of her state's writing project, she replied in a huff, "Oh, you mean the white folks' project." She went on to tell me a tale I have now heard so many times. She had gone to a meeting to learn about a "new" approach to literacy. The group leaders began talking about the need for developing fluency, for first getting anything down on paper, but as soon as this teacher asked when children were to be taught the technical skills of writing standard prose, leaders of the group began to lecture her on the danger of a skills orientation in teaching literacy. She never went back.

In puzzling over these issues, it has begun to dawn on me that many of the teachers of black children have their roots in other communities and do not often have the opportunity to hear the full range of their students' voices. I wonder how many of Philadelphia's teachers know that their black students are prolific and "fluent" writers of rap songs. I wonder how many teachers realize the verbal creativity and fluency black kids express every day on the playgrounds of America as they devise new insults, new rope-jumping chants and new cheers. Even if they did hear them, would they relate them to language fluency?

25   Maybe, just maybe, these writing process teachers are so adamant about developing fluency because they have not really had the opportunity to realize the fluency the kids already possess. They hear only silence, they see only immobile pencils. And maybe the black teachers are so adamant against what they understand to be the writing process approach because they hear their students' voices and see their fluency clearly. They are anxious to move to the next step, the step vital to success in America—the appropriation of the oral and written forms demanded by the mainstream. And they want it to happen quickly. They see no time to waste developing the "fluency" they believe their children already possess. Yes, they are *eager* to teach "skills."

Of course, there is nothing inherent in the writing process approach itself which mitigates against students' acquiring standard literacy skills; many supporters of the approach do indeed concern themselves with the technicalities of writing in their own classrooms. However, writing process advocates often give the impression that they view the direct teaching of skills to be restrictive to the writing process at best, and at worst, politically repressive to students already oppressed by a racist educational system. Black teachers, on the other hand, see the teaching of skills to be essential to their students' survival. It seems as if leaders of the writing process movement find it difficult to develop the vocabulary to discuss the issues in ways in which teachers with differing perspectives can hear them and participate in the dialogue. Progressive white teachers seem to say to their black students, "Let me help you find your voice. I promise not to criticize one note as you search for your own song." But the black teachers say, "I've heard your song loud and clear. Now, I want to teach you to harmonize with the rest of the world." Their insistence on skills is not a negation of their students' intellect, as is often suggested by progressive forces, but an acknowledgment of it: "You know a lot; you can learn more. Do It Now!"

I run a great risk in writing this—the risk that my purpose will be misunderstood; the risk that those who subject black and other minority children to day after day of isolated, meaningless, drilled "subskills" will think themselves vindicated. That is not the point. Were this another paper I would explain what I mean by "skills"—useful and usable knowledge which contributes to a student's ability to communicate effectively in standard, generally acceptable literary forms. And I would explain that I believe that skills are best taught through meaningful communication, best learned in meaningful contexts. I would further explain that skills are a necessary but insufficient aspect of black and minority students' education. Students need technical skills to open doors, but they need to be able to think critically and creatively to participate in meaningful and potentially liberating work inside those doors. Let there be no doubt: a "skilled" minority person who is not also capable of critical analysis becomes the trainable, low-level functionary of the dominant society, simply the grease that keeps the institutions which orchestrate his or her oppression running smoothly. On the other hand, a critical thinker who lacks the "skills" demanded by employers and institutions of higher learning can aspire to financial and social status only within the disenfranchised underworld. Yes, if minority people are to effect the change which will allow them to truly progress we must insist on "skills" *within the context of* critical and creative thinking.

But that is for another paper. The purpose of this one is to defend my fellow minority educators at the same time I seek to reestablish my own place in the progressive educational arena. Too often minority teachers' voices have been hushed: a certain paternalism creeps into the speech of some of our liberal colleagues as they explain that our children must be "given voice." As difficult as it is for our colleagues to hear our children's existing voices, it is often equally difficult for them to hear our own. The consequence is that all too often minority teachers retreat from these "progressive" settings grumbling among themselves, "There they go again." It is vitally important that non-minority educators realize that there is another voice, another reality; that many of the teachers whom they seek to reach have been able to conquer the educational system *because* they received the kind of instruction that their white progressive colleagues are denouncing.

What am I suggesting here? I certainly do not suggest that the writing process approach to literacy development is wrong or that a completely skills-oriented program is right. I suggest, instead, that there is much to be gained from the interaction of the two orientations and that advocates of both approaches have something to say to each other. I further suggest that it is the responsibility of the dominant group members to attempt to hear the other side of the issue; and after hearing, to speak in a modified voice that does not exclude the concerns of their minority colleagues.

30   It is time to look closely at elements of our educational system, particularly those elements we consider progressive; time to see whether there is minority involvement and support, and if not, to ask why; time to reassess what we are doing in public schools and universities to include other voices, other experiences; time to seek the diversity in our educational movements that we talk about seeking in our classrooms. I would advocate that university researchers, school districts, and teachers try to understand the views of their minority colleagues and constituents, and that programs, including the country's many writing projects, target themselves for study. Perhaps ethnographies of various writing projects, with particular attention given to minority participation and nonparticipation, would prove valuable. The key is to understand the variety of meanings available for any human interaction, and not to assume that the voices of the majority speak for all.

I have come to believe that the "open-classroom movement," despite its progressive intentions, faded in large part because it was not able to come to terms with the concerns of poor and minority communities. I truly hope that those who advocate other potentially important programs will do a better job.

SUGGESTIONS FOR DISCUSSION

1. Lisa Delpit seems to be torn between what she has learned in progressive education programs and what she hears from fellow black educators. What exactly is the tension Delpit feels? What seem to be the main issues? What is the significance of these issues for teaching and educational policy?

2. Delpit acknowledges that she runs a "great risk" of being misunderstood. What does she worry readers might misunderstand? What does she do to reduce the risk of misunderstanding?

3. It is likely that you and your classmates have had experience with both a "writing process" approach and a "skills-oriented" approach to literacy development. Drawing on your own experiences, what do you see as the strengths and weaknesses of each approach? Consider Delpit's case for their interaction. What would this interaction look like concretely?

SUGGESTIONS FOR WRITING

1. Write an analysis of the differing claims of process and skills that set up Delpit's "dilemmas." Your task here is not to side with one or the other approach but to identify and explain their underlying assumptions. Consider, on the one hand, what writing process advocates must assume to hold that teaching skills directly restricts individual development and is politically repressive. On the other hand, consider what the black teachers

Delpit talks to must assume to think that the indirect teaching of writing process advocates is at best "liberal nonsense" and at worst racist. What is dividing the two groups? What is at stake in this division?

2. Assume, as Delpit does, that "skills are best taught through meaningful communication, best learned in meaningful contexts." This sounds sensibly balanced but remains somewhat abstract, the subject, as Delpit says, of another paper. Write an essay that takes on this work of developing more fully and more concretely how skills might best be taught and learned. First, explain what the issue of skills is, as Delpit sees it. Then invent an assignment or two for a high school or college writing class that integrates the learning of skills into a meaningful context. Identify the skill you want to teach and how you tie it to critical and creative thinking.

3. Delpit says that black teachers "see the teaching of skills to be essential to their students' survival." The positive spin that Delpit gives here to the idea of survival differs considerably from Min-Zhan Lu's sense that "the metaphor of language as a tool for survival led me to be passive in my use of discourse, to be a bystander in the discussion." Write an essay that compares their differing uses of the term *survival*. Do they mean the same thing by the term or do their conceptions differ? What might explain why one invests the term with positive, enabling qualities while the other makes it a limiting condition? What do you see as the significance of these differing uses?

VISUAL CULTURE   Picturing Schooldays

To learn more about historical and contemporary school rooms, visit www.ablongman.com/george/109

Visual images of teachers and children can be found in many places and put to many uses. A photograph of a one-room schoolhouse, for example, recaptures the early days of American schooling and summons up nostalgia for tight-knit communities of the past. By the same token, Norman Rockwell's paintings of school scenes summon up pictures of lost innocence—a time when students were well behaved and learned the three R's from strict but benevolent teachers. More recently, images of school have been used to illustrate the plight of American education, to argue for uniforms or dress codes, and to advertise new educational products.

Viewing images of schooling releases fond and not-so-fond emotional associations. Nearly everyone can remember what it was like to be in school and what their relationships were like with teachers and peers. The way people make sense of images of schooling, however, depends on more than just their personal experience. The composition of the images also provides cues about how to respond to them.

This section investigates the composition of photographs of school—to see how the pictures represent teachers and students and to examine their relationship to each other and to the institution of schooling. In particular, the section looks at how the composition of photographs uses vectors to establish relationships among the people in a photograph and perspective to establish the viewer's attitude toward what the photo represents.

Vectors

When viewers look at visual images of schooling, such as the photographs assembled here, they turn these images into a story about what the people are doing and what their relationship is to each other. Because the photograph itself is a still shot, it can't record action that occurs over time. Accordingly, viewers have to fill in the story themselves based on their familiarity with the scene pictured and the cues they take from the photograph.

To see how the composition of a photograph enables the viewer to fill in the story, look at how the people and things in the photo are connected by vectors, or the diagonal lines a viewer's eyes follow from one element of the photograph to another.

Take, for example, the first photograph—Francis Benjamin Johnston's picture of schoolchildren at the Hampton Institute saluting the American flag. The viewer recognizes the flag salute right away because it is such a familiar part of schooling and civic life. What may be puzzling is why the students' arms are outstretched in salute. The outstretched arm—or Roman salute—was the conventional way of saluting the flag until World War II, when it was changed because it reminded people of the Nazi salute to Hitler. But the photograph also contains visual cues that enable the viewer to recognize this familiar gesture. Notice in the schematic drawing how the outstretched arms and eyelines of the schoolchildren create a vector that connects them to the image of the flag and cues viewers to the interaction taking place.

Francis Benjamin Johnston, "Pledging Allegiance."

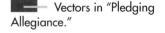

Vectors in "Pledging Allegiance."

Wallace Kirkland, "Jane Addams Reading at Hull House, Chicago, 1930s."

Perspective

Perspective is the angle of sight—or point of view—that a photograph offers a viewer. Viewers' attitudes toward what is represented in a photograph will vary depending on perspective.

1. **Frontal** angle promotes a high level of involvement and the sense that viewers are directly engaged with the image.

2. **Oblique** angle gives viewers a sense of detachment, as though they are simply looking on as a bystander.

3. **High** angle, in which the camera looks down on the people in the photo, gives the viewer a sense of power.

4. **Low** angle, in which the camera looks up, makes the people in the photo seem powerful.

SUGGESTIONS FOR DISCUSSION

1. Francis Benjamin Johnston's photograph of the schoolchildren saluting the flag at Hampton Institute can be an unsettling one that may provoke mixed feelings. How is the viewer to respond to the photo? How do the outstretched arms, and their now unavoidable association with the Hitler salute, influence the viewer's attitude to the photograph? Is the viewer being asked to admire the students' patriotism and the sense of order depicted, or does the image cast the students as victims of an authoritarian system? Could both, in some sense, be true? How does the fact that the students are African Americans at an all-black school in the time of segregated education enter into your response?

2. Notice how the children are grouped in the photo "Jane Addams Reading at Hull House." What do these groupings suggest about the children's relationship to each other and to

Make sense of our times.

The New York Times

Expect the World®
nytimes.com

©1956 SEPS: The Curtis Publishing Co., Agent.
Advertisement Copyright ©2001 The New York Times.

the teacher? Follow the eyelines in the photo. What vectors connect the participants, and what story do they tell? Compare the vectors in this photo with those in the classroom photo at the opening of the chapter. Notice too how the frontal perspective in the photo of Jane Addams compares to the oblique angle in the classroom photo. What effects on viewers' attitudes and involvement are these differing angles likely to have?

3. The ad from the November 9, 2001, *New York Times* updates Norman Rockwell's fondly nostalgic painting of an idealized American classroom by overlaying a map of Afghanistan on a blackboard of birthday messages the children have written to their teacher Miss Jones. The *New York Times* designer uses this combination of Rockwell's innocent American past and the breaking news of the U.S. invasion of Afghanistan as the visual counterpoint to the ad's message: "Make sense of our times. Expect the World." Consider how the low angle of Rockwell's painting positions viewers to look up at the teacher. Notice how this compares to the high angle of the photo in the chapter's opening that looks down into the classroom.

SUGGESTED ASSIGNMENT

What photographic image could tell the story of your classroom and the prevailing relationships among the students and between the teacher and the students? For this project, work in a group with two or three other students to take a photograph of your classroom.

When composing a photographic image, consider the following questions. How would students and the teacher be distributed and grouped in space? What vectors, or eyelines, would connect them? How would you want to position the viewer in relation to the classroom? How would you frame a shot that creates the point of view and angle of sight that you want for the viewer?

When you have decided on the shot you want, take the picture. This may involve posing students and the teacher in particular ways or asking them to do certain things. Everyone in class needs to cooperate on this project—whether you are taking the picture or being its subject.

When all the groups have developed the photos, bring them to class and discuss to what extent they portray different and similar stories. Identify the main vectors in each and how they establish the key relationships among the participants. Consider, too, how the photos create points of view and degrees of involvement on the viewer's part.

FILM CLIP

Reading and Writing About Film: Reviews, Histories, Criticism

To read and write more about film, visit
www.ablongman.com/george/110

Understanding films involves more than just watching movies. For film buffs, fans, academics, and people in the entertainment industry, there is a wealth of material to read—from the movie reviews that appear in daily newspapers to industry information in *Variety* and other publications to popular books on the Hollywood history and theoretical articles on film studies. Given the sheer volume of writing about film, it can be helpful to sort these writings into categories, to look at the various genres of writing about film in order to identify the purposes they embody and the interests they serve. Here we consider three common genres of writing about film:

- **Reviews.** Reviews offer description and evaluation of recently released films. Most daily newspapers and many magazines have film reviewers on staff. The reviews of a film create what is called its critical reception. Sometime reviewers agree about the merits of a film but often they are divided in their views. Of course, the reviewers' opinions may or may not match the popularity of a particular film, and in some cases films that have come to be considered "classics" received negative or lukewarm reviews.

    An interesting exercise is to compare the reviews of a recent film that appear in, say, the *New York Times*, the *Washington Post*, the *New Yorker*, and the *Nation*. The question to ask here concerns the various and variable criteria each reviewer brings to his or her review and how these assumptions about film lead to particular judgments.

- **Histories.** Another way to learn about movies is to read histories of film. You can find everything from histories of the Hollywood film industry to histories of Italian cinema to histories of particular types of film such as westerns, musicals, or thrillers. One of the benefits of understanding film history is that you can see the evolution of the medium, the contributions of leading filmmakers, and the influence of past films on the present. Histories, as the term implies, are most often arranged chronologically to trace developments in film. These histories can lead you to watch older films and think about the role they play in the evolution of filmmaking. They are particularly valuable in research projects to analyze, say, how film noir reflected the anxieties of the Cold War of the 1950s (see Jon Tuska's *Dark Cinema: American Film Noir in Cultural Perspective*) or how independent filmmakers challenged the Hollywood studios in the 1970s (see Gene Biskind's *Easy Riders, Raging Bulls*).

    You can design your own historical research project by putting together a bibliography of books and articles about a topic that interests you, such as how films in the 1930s represented the hopes and fears of ordinary Americans during the Great Depression, or the French New Wave of François Truffaut, Jean-Luc Godard, Agnes Varda, Alain Resnais, Jean-Pierre Melville, and others.

- **Criticism.** Film criticism offers more specialized analyses of particular aspects of filmmaking. Typically, film criticism begins with a sense of an issue. What is the contribution of a particular director? How do viewers watch films? How do films represent particular groups of people? How do films reflect social understandings of sexuality? You can find studies of individual directors, such as Alfred Hitchcock or Stanley Kubrick or Orson Welles. There are also studies of how films position their viewers, such as Laura Mulvey's classic essay "Visual Pleasure and Narrative Cinema," and bell hooks's writings about how films represent African Americans in *Black Looks*.

    To get a sense of the range of issues and topics film critics write about, browse through leading film journals like *Film Quarterly*, *Sight and Sound*, and *Screen*. See, for example, the special supplement in the September 1992 *Sight and Sound* on the New Queer Cinema of Gus Van Sant, Todd Haynes, Greg Araki, and others.

FIELDWORK — Classroom Observation

Most students know that being successful in school means understanding what teachers value and what they expect from students. This is sometimes called "psyching out" a teacher, and students learn to be good at it. They do this by evaluating the formal requirements of the course (e.g., reading assignments, labs, homework, tests, papers), by observing what takes place in the classroom (e.g., lectures, discussion, films, group work), and by learning the teacher's personality and eccentricities.

The purpose of this project is to investigate what it takes to be successful in a course in which you are enrolled and to draw some conclusions about the nature of teaching and learning. The method used is participant/observation. You are asked, in effect, to observe yourself, your teacher, and other students and to take detailed notes on what you do in and out of class.

Several weeks will be needed for this project so that you can accumulate a sufficient amount of entries in your field log to make your observations reliable and conclusions possible.

Field Log

As a participant–observer, you need to keep a field log on the classes, reading assignments, papers, exams, sections or labs, study groups, and informal conversations outside of class.

Background

When you start this project, write a statement that summarizes what you know about the course at this time. Ask yourself the following questions:

1. *Why are you taking the class?* To fulfill a requirement, for personal interest, for some other motivation?

2. *Read the syllabus:* How does it describe the content of the course and what you will learn? What are the assignments? How will the course grade be determined?

3. *Describe the format of the class:* What size is the class? In what kind of room does it meet? Does it look like it will be mostly lecture, discussion, a combination of the two, something else? Keep track of attendance patterns. Note where students sit to see if patterns develop.

4. *From what you can tell so far, what will you need to do to get the grade you want?*

Field Notes

Field notes consist of the observations you record during and outside the class. Use these questions:

1. *Where do you sit in class?* Why?

2. *How do you actually spend your time in class?* Taking notes, doodling, engaging in class discussion, looking around, writing notes to other students, daydreaming, talking to other students, working on something for another class, reading a newspaper or magazine?

3. *What does the teacher do in class?* Is it the same thing every day or does it change? How does the teacher run the class? Do individual class meetings have a routine

format? Is there a set schedule (e.g., lecture Monday, discussion Wednesday, film Friday)? Who talks?

4. *What do other students do?*

5. *What do you do outside the classroom?* Keep track of the time devoted to various activities: reading assignments, reviewing or rewriting notes, studying for tests (alone or with others), attending lab sessions or section meetings, doing research, writing papers, meeting with the teacher or assistant, talking informally with other students about the class, and so on.

Analysis

Review your notes and look for patterns and key points. Here are some questions to consider:

1. *Compare what you know now about the course with what you wrote earlier in your field log:* Have your responses changed? Does the course syllabus give an accurate forecast of what to expect, or have you become aware in other ways of the "real" requirements of the class? Have you changed your mind about the grade you think you might get?

2. *What kinds of patterns emerge from notes on what you do in class?* Do you do the same thing in every class meeting, or does your activity vary? Have you changed what you do in class consciously? If so, why?

3. *Has the work returned to you so far (homework, tests, quizzes, papers, etc.) confirmed or revised what you thought it would take to do well in the course?* What have you learned about the teacher's expectations and preferences?

4. *How does the work you do outside the classroom figure in?* Could you skip class and still do well? Do you do all the work or only certain assignments? Do you have a system for deciding what to do and not do? If so, how did you develop it? Do you meet with or talk to the teacher, the teaching assistant, or other students about the class?

5. *What patterns emerge from your observations of other students?*

6. *What are the main differences and similarities in the courses you have observed?* What is their significance?

Writing the Report

For this project, use a version of the standard format for reports.

Introduction

Explain what you are investigating and the purpose of your research. Identify the class you observed, its enrollment, usual attendance, course requirements, and any other pertinent information. You can help readers by summarizing this information in a diagram that accompanies your Introduction. (See Table 3.1.)

Method

Explain how you gathered data.

Observations

Summarize key points from your field log to establish patterns and to characterize your participation in the course. (See the sample observations in "Cross-Curricular Underlife," below.)

Conclusions

Derive inferences and generalizations from your observations. (See the sample conclusions in "Cross-Curricular Underlife," below.)

OBSERVATIONS AND CONCLUSIONS FROM "CROSS-CURRICULAR UNDERLIFE: A COLLABORATIVE REPORT ON WAYS WITH ACADEMIC WORDS"

— *Worth Anderson, Cynthia Best, Alycia Black, John Hurst, Brandt Miller, and Susan Miller*

The following examples of a report's Observations and Conclusions sections come from a longer article written by a group of undergraduates at the University of Utah in an independent study course under the direction of Susan Miller, a faculty member in English and a prominent writing theorist. Following an introductory section, the article consists of observations and conclusions written by the various members of the research group.

SAMPLE OBSERVATIONS

Art History

On the first day of class, the professor urged us all to drop, said she was willing to dispense drop cards to everyone, launched into a lecture that filled the time, handed out a syllabus, and reminded us that it was not too late to drop. I promptly named her "Madame Battleaxe."

It got worse. She was the embodiment of objectivist theories: "There are these facts. They constitute Truth. I will speak. You will listen. You will emerge with Truth." She spoke quickly, had some funky uses for the word "sensuous." I take notes very poorly, so I just sat and listened. A friend who sat beside me and played stenographer was frustrated by this, but for me I did better by just listening.

I realized that I was having trouble memorizing dates on pictures, so I went to see her. We got to talking about Charles V, and amazingly, I liked her. She reassured me about the test, and explained how highly she valued coherent writing, composed with an eye to history. I decided that she considered herself a historian, so her audience values would be in that community.

After our meeting, I was far more tolerant of her in class. On the midterm and final I wrote much more than anyone else, and emerged both times with the top grade. Serving up what she wanted worked.

Sociology

The teacher basically taught lecture one day—film one day—lecture one day. . . . I believe that it's good to develop a routine, but not a rut! At first people groaned when they found out we were going to be watching another film. Once the students realized how the class would be taught, they began walking out during the films and lectures. One day I counted twenty-two people who walked out during a film. Later, the students developed a different routine. They would come to class and stay only if there was a film (so they could answer the test questions). But they would leave if the teacher was lecturing because they felt they could get more from reading the book.

The teacher lectured from an outline of key words on the overhead projector. Several people commented that his lectures were hard to follow, but I thought they weren't too difficult because he followed the book. In fact, at times he read straight from it! The professor had the habit of leaning on the lectern while he lectured and placing his hand on his chin. (It almost covered his mouth!) One day I observed, "Five people walked out of the lecture early. I assume from the time that had elapsed that it was after they'd copied the outline. I noticed people who simply copied the outline of key words and then just sat there in a kind of stupor."

Descriptions of Courses Observed

Student	Course Title	Enrollment and % Usual Attendance	Course Requirements and Student Interpretations of Them (MC = Multiple Choice)
Worth	Anthropology	90 (60%)	Pass 2 MC midterms = take notes, attend, study notes; 1-pg. extra credit paper.
	Common Medicines	150 (90%)	2 MC tests: drug names, uses = memorize, memorize; good notes are critical; final cramming will not do here.
	International Studies: Africa	55 (90%)	4 short ans. tests; 6-pg. paper. Study ugly stuff like population distribution.
	Art History	100 (95%)	Midterm and Final, both essay. Memorize names and dates; concepts not a problem.
Cynthia	Anthropology	76 (60%)	Read for weekly quizzes, watch films, pass MC midterm and final. 1-pg. book review for extra credit.
	Intellectual Trad. of the West (Medieval)	25 (90%)	Write 4 papers, essay midterm and final. Read, attend.
	Sociology	400 (50%)	3 MC tests. Read, take notes, watch films.
Alycia	Intellectual Trad. of the West (Medieval)	25 (80%)	1 paper; midterm, final with take-home essay. 150–200 pp./wk. reading.
	Critical Literature	22 (60–75%)	3 papers; response ¶s. 15–60 min. reading/night to practice analyzing.
	Law	20 (95%)	10 1-page papers; research on topic about church and state
John	Astronomy	105 (60%)	MC tests. Attend, read text, extra credit for 1000-word report.
	Psychology	155 (70–75%)	MC tests. Attend, read text, extra credit for being a subject in dept. experiments.
	Basic Acting II	9 (100%)	Perform 2 scenes, one monologue; attend 3 plays, review 2 of them.
Brandt	Calculus	35 (80%)	Problem sets. Take notes; geometrically interpret concepts; review and keep up.
	Chemistry	450 (70%)	Problem sets and MC test; read to get high grades on tests.
	History of Science	20 (97%)	Essay midterm and final; paper. Take notes & refer to them when reading; research final paper (use Wr. 210 skills); do well on final by catching up.

In such a large class I noticed diverse student behaviors. One day during the film, as I counted the twelve people who left early, the girl to my left did homework for another class, the guy in front of me ate yogurt, and the guy to my right organized his Franklin Day Planner. I rarely took notes on the films because they were irrelevant, but some people took notes anyway. One girl's notes consisted of "Boring . . . Big Time!"

Calculus

I would go early to hear students discuss assignments and compare solutions to take-home quizzes, but this seemed almost a formality rather than a concern over concepts. When the professor began to work rapidly on the board, the lead flew across my notebook. She may not be exceptionally exciting, but unless you pay attention, you get lost fast. There was only moderate interaction between students and instructor by way of questions. Amazingly few questions are raised about such complex material.

There were several overlapping communities of student interaction in this class. Although it was a small class, there were many students whose names I didn't know, and could barely recognize by sight. I think this was because math is an independent discipline. You only need to interact with a few students to find the right answer. I took notes the whole time. After class, I would talk to students who could explain concepts like double integration a little better than what I had understood.

Math is a very sequential subject. When I had had trouble understanding the last assignment, I knew it would only compound with a new one. Today's concepts would be based on what we learned yesterday, which was based on the day before. Students had a tough time when they hadn't been here. Dr. A. covers the new material by relating it to yesterday's material, which makes it easier. Dr. A. becomes a narrator for the strange mathematical figures that appear on the board.

When Dr. A. explained what kind of questions there would be on tests, she sometimes let us use a "cheat sheet," so we knew it would be hard. I would meet with other students to study.

SAMPLE CONCLUSIONS

A.

In ITW, I learned both on my own and in class. I learned as I read the assignments alone, and then my knowledge was expanded when the professor expounded on the material. Sections of this course are taught by teachers from different disciplines, so students who take more than one part of the sequence learn about ideas and about professors' specific fields. This section was actually "taught." The history professor who taught it connected ideas to historical background. But in Sociology, I learned the most from the text. The instructor's lectures were helpful, but I gained very little from the films. Ironically though, I preferred the films to the lectures. As I wrote one day, "I enjoyed the film simply because I didn't have to listen to another lecture." Anthropology was not "taught." The professor simply spouted facts each day. In considering where the learning occurred here, I've decided I learned most from the text. The films were informative and very helpful, but they were never shown at the right times. I really struggled with the professor's lectures, yet I learned from my notes because that's the only place that certain material was given.

School is a contract between a student and a teacher. Each must share a mutual respect for the other for learning to occur. In my liberal education courses, the teachers were not as concerned about the classes as they should have been. I got the impression that these teachers were being punished. They were bored because the material was so fundamental to their disciplines. But to the students, the material is new. If the professor shows excitement and projects a positive attitude, students will tend to be more interested in learning. Large classes require more effort from both students and teachers.

B.

Generally, the crucial part of learning in any classroom is digging up what the professor expects. I find that all classes require exceptional note-taking and analytical reading. Not all classes "require" attendance; in some I learn more from reading than from going to class. Poorly attended classes are those where the professor reads the text and gives no additional information. Well-attended classes are taught by professors who enjoy the subject and make the students feel comfortable with it.

Although most of the students' learning must be done outside of class, an attitude toward learning is developed in the classroom. The professor's role is crucial because the students will be as active as the teacher is. Many of my peers say that the average student counts on having at least one "blow-off" class. If a teacher is strict, the students will make greater efforts and follow the teacher's guidelines. If a teacher is dull and doesn't include fun tidbits or allow us to express varying views, the students will find the material dull and difficult to study. But if the professor is excited, encourages us to voice different opinions, and interacts with us, the students will be excited about the subject and have an easier time.

MINING THE ARCHIVE   Textbooks from the Past

A Doll for Jane

"Hello, Father," said Dick.

"Jane will have a birthday soon.

Please get a new doll for Jane.

Get a baby doll that talks.

Please get a doll that talks."

15

One way to get a sense of schooling in an earlier time is to take a look at that period's textbooks. Two of the most famous and popular series were designed to teach reading: *McGuffey's Eclectic Readers*, used by millions of American children during the nineteenth century, and the Dick and Jane primers, used from the 1930s to the 1960s. Each series offers a fascinating view of how elementary school students learned to read as well as the kinds of social values transmitted through the reading lessons. On the one hand, the McGuffey readers were anthologies of essays, poems, speeches, and stories filled with moral advice, patriotic ideas, and religious instruction. Heavily didactic in tone, the content of the readers was meant to be morally uplifting. The Dick and Jane readers, on the other hand, created a child's world of fun and surprise. Dick and Jane, along with their little sister, Sally, dog, Spot, and kitten, Puff, lived in an American dream of white picket-fenced suburban homes, loving parents, laughter, and security. Most college and large public libraries will have copies of *McGuffey's Eclectic Reader* and some will have Dick and Jane readers as well. You can also find selections from the two textbook series in Elliot J. Gorn, ed., *The McGuffey Readers: Selections from the 1879 Edition* (Boston: Bedford, 1998), and Carol Kismaric and Marvin Heiferman, *Growing Up with Dick and Jane: Learning and Living the American Dream* (San Francisco: Collins Publishers, 1996). Researching these textbooks can lead to writing projects that focus on a range of topics. Below are a few examples.

To learn more about the history of textbooks, visit www.ablongman.com/george/111

- Nineteenth-century reading instruction
- The Protestant middle-class values of the McGuffey readers
- Gender stereotypes in Dick and Jane
- The postwar American dream in the Dick and Jane primers

CHAPTER FOUR

Images

In no other form of society in history has there been such a concentration of images, such a density of visual messages.
—John Berger, *Ways of Seeing*

It is in fact hard to get the camera to tell the truth.
—James Agee, *A Way of Seeing. Photographs by Helen Levitt*

New York, c. 1940. © Helen Levitt. Courtesy Laurence Miller Gallery, New York

We are surrounded daily by the visual message. On billboards, in magazines, on television, in film and video, on our computer screens, and in nearly every public and private space, images of all sorts compete for our attention. They carry messages from corporate advertisers, nonprofit organizations, public and private institutions, and friends and family, and they ask us to buy, to give, to believe, to subscribe, to respond, to understand, to act.

The image that conveys a message is hardly a new phenomenon. For centuries the images people created—paintings, drawings, designs, sketches, icons—did not simply decorate the insides of caves, temples, churches, palaces, and the like but they also recorded family and community history; taught lessons in religion, culture, and politics; and even gave directions to locations.

New to the experience of the image are the vast numbers and many kinds of images available and the ease with which they may be reproduced, copied, parodied, and reconstructed. Also new is the aggressive nature of the image. Unless we purposefully isolate ourselves from the industrial world, it is difficult to avoid a continuous onslaught of visual communication.

Advertisers depend on people automatically recognizing the message-laden images that they see as they speed down the highway, surf through TV channels, or flip through a magazine. Some images are effective simply because they have been around for so long. A full-color photo of a cowboy silhouetted on a horse at sunset is likely going to call to mind the Marlboro Man, whether or not it is in an ad for cigarettes. These images can almost speak for themselves, and advertisers do not need many words to convey the accompanying message—the Marlboro ad often includes only the product's name and the obligatory FDA warning.

As you read this chapter, you will be asked to look at and read such messages— messages that rely on pictures or graphics more than on words to carry meaning. Many of the images we will discuss here are taken from print ads so that you have easy access to images you can study carefully for long periods of time. However, the power of the image to convey messages is not at all limited to print advertising. Television, film, photographs, music videos, web pages, even the very layout of the page all signal an increased demand for all of us to become active readers and producers of visual text.

The language of images is much like verbal language. To relay meaning, visual language depends on familiarity, patterns of use, composition, references to other images, and the context in which the image appears. Like verbal language, visual language does not convey simply one stable message to everyone who reads it. Meaning depends on the reader as well as the text. Still, the most quickly read messages are often those that carry with them expressions of common cultural ideas or ideals—images that act as a kind of cultural shorthand.

We begin our discussion, then, with an illustration of that cultural shorthand. See the "America: Open for Business" graphic reproduced here. The graphic uses a simple design depicting the U.S. flag with shopping bag handles attached to the top.

Even without the words, most readers are likely to understand that this is a statement about what the United States stands for. The flag, as a common symbol for America, sends that message. Many readers will also recognize this as a shopping bag with an American flag motif. The text works to anchor a meaning for the shopping bag handles on the flag, but that meaning is not entirely a stable one. In other words, not everyone will read this graphic in the same way. However, if you know about the events leading to the creation of this graphic, you are likely to read in it a more complex message than if you see it without knowing that context.

"America: Open for Business" was created in the aftermath of the September 11, 2001, attacks on the World Trade Center. Here is how Craig Frazier, the graphic designer who created this image, explains what he was trying to say with it:

> As I sat in sunny California so insulated from the disaster, feeling its national impact, I wondered what I could do. Unfortunately, the American economy is

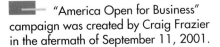 "America Open for Business" campaign was created by Craig Frazier in the aftermath of September 11, 2001.

directly connected to our emotional state of mind, and the national gloom of this attack threatens to be far-reaching and long-lasting. I wanted to create an image that says, "We aren't shutting down because we are American." I am not in any way denying the grief of so many, and the fact that many businesses are not open any more. I am trying to create a sense of community in an effort to lift our heads and carry on. This poster stands to unite the local coffee shop on the corner with the national chain on the opposite corner, and the patrons of both. Ultimately, everyone can do something.

Frazier is relying on the reader's ability to read this poster by using a cultural short-hand that combines the flag with the reference to shopping in the context of 9/11.

What the cultural shorthand cannot control is the additional meaning that readers are able to generate with an image such as this one. Though Frazier clearly wanted to make a positive statement about American strength in the face of tragedy, a reader who is not persuaded that shopping is a positive virtue is likely to see something very different in the graphic. Both the reader Frazier is aiming at and the reader he is not aiming at are likely to understand the intended message, but their response to that message would vary depending on differences in gender, politics, social status, ethnicity, or economic background. Visual meaning, like all meaning, is dependent on both the message being sent and the receiver of that message.

Focusing on the importance of the visual does not mean ignoring the written text. Many images, such as the "America: Open for Business" poster, rely on pictures combined with words to carry meaning, even when the words are few. In Frazier's design or the ad for Coach bags that we reproduce here, words serve to anchor the image to a particular message. Frazier's asks readers to support American business. The Coach ad, not as directly but just as assuredly, asks readers to buy Coach bags. And yet, words can also complicate readers' responses.

A Coach ad associates Sitting Bull's great great great granddaughter with the Coach binocular bag.

On its own, the visual image in the Coach ad is simple and commonplace: The attractive young woman posed in a rugged yet beautiful setting with her dog and her Coach bag is likely meant to associate the product with those things that are appealing in the image. At the same time, the **ad copy** (what is written in the ad about the product) asks the reader to associate the product with more than natural beauty or rugged independence. The copy identifies the young woman as Jacqueline Brown-Smith, the great-great-great-granddaughter of Sitting Bull, the famous Hunkpapa Sioux who resisted being placed on a reservation and whose name continues to call forth the image of Indian people as profoundly independent.

Such identification gives this image a cultural significance. That is, once the woman is identified as the direct descendant of Sitting Bull, the reader is no longer looking at her but through her to her great-great-great-grandfather. Jacqueline Brown-Smith is thereby assigned special significance because of her relation to Sitting Bull. After discovering who she is, the reader is likely to look again at the image, which has now taken on a different meaning. Naturally, the Coach bag is likely to pick up some of that meaning. In this ad, the bag is called "An American Legacy" like, the reader must assume, Sitting Bull's legacy represented here in the image of his great-great-great-granddaughter.

This particular campaign includes ads using the descendants of other luminaries such as Albert Einstein, Jesse Owens, Gene Kelly, and George Washington to suggest that Coach represents intelligence, endurance, priceless quality, good taste, and status. The bag Brown-Smith is carrying is a binocular case, which links her (and, by extension, her great-great-great-grandfather) to the natural world—to a rugged existence with an uptown taste.

Of course, readers might also find meanings in this ad, as in any ad, that the advertiser did not intend. They might question the appropriateness of using Sitting Bull—a man who clearly stood in opposition to U.S. government policies—to sell an expensive bag to what has become a consumer culture. Advertisers are aware of that possibility, which is why they carefully control where they place their ads so that they can pitch ads differently to different groups of people.

Advertisers take advantage of cultural meanings every time they present an image as if it were representative of what everyone desires or understands. Take, for example, the Jeep ad reprinted here. This ad uses a very simple design—the placement of one image above the other—to convey a complex message. By placing the peace symbol ("International Symbol for Peace") above the word Jeep ("International Symbol for Freedom"), the advertiser is asking us to connect one with the other.

When we talk about the arrangement of images in relation to one another, we are describing the **visual syntax** of the ad. In other words, the images are arranged in such a way as to convey meaning. Cartoons, for example, use a sequencing of images to suggest an event unfolding over time. The Jeep ad simply juxtaposes one image above the other so that we might see a connection between the two images.

This particular ad has the potential to reach several kinds of readers because of the cultural meanings the two images already carry. The peace symbol and the word *Jeep* are each depicted as if they could be worn on leather laces around the neck, so the retro look of the peace symbol might appeal to current fashion. The peace symbol continues to evoke a strong emotional response from those who were young during the Vietnam War, so the message is one that could elicit memories of youth and freedom from that generation. In addition, the Jeep is a vehicle that was made popular particularly during World War II, the war Studs Terkel and others have called

INTERNATIONAL SYMBOL FOR PEACE.

Jeep

INTERNATIONAL SYMBOL FOR FREEDOM.

Jeep
THERE'S ONLY ONE

A Jeep ad associates the international peace symbol with the Jeep logo.

the last "good war." The Jeep name as an "international symbol for freedom" can, then, even appeal to a generation not entirely in sympathy with the peace movement of the 1960s or the retro look of the next generation.

In fact, the fewer words an ad such as this uses, the more likely it will allow for several different readings—many of which will be positive and all of which will call up something of the reader's memories or desires or associations. Finally, with the statement "There's only one Jeep," the ad seems to acknowledge the possibility that there may be many responses to this juxtapositioning, but that there is only one product that can evoke all of those responses. Advertisers naturally hope that those associations eventually will lead readers to think of and then purchase the product after they have seen the ad.

On their own and depending on the person, readers might still question the association of the peace symbol with the Jeep or wonder how the peace symbol could have changed from a political statement of the 1960s to a fashion statement of the 1990s. Such a reading, though, would threaten to interrupt the primary purpose of the ad, which is to sell Jeep cars and trucks. That kind of reading is certainly possible, but it must be done consciously. Most ads function at a subconscious, even visceral level. They call on feelings and loyalties and fears and desires—responses most people do not take much time to question.

Other kinds of visual images do the same: logos for sports teams, poster campaigns, graffiti, news photos, and family albums, for example. Some images are purely functional and wholly visual; many of them are multinational signs that tell a great deal in a simple design: the icons that instruct viewers to buckle their seat belts on planes, not to smoke in public places, and which restroom door to walk through.

As you look at and consider the visual messages around you, remember that you don't have to be mindless consumers of visual culture. You are a producer as well, and you can make your own visual messages. One thing that bothers many people when they look at ads is the assuredness with which advertisers sell lifestyles and attempt to create new interests. Knowing that most people let ads go by without reading them closely, some activists write over ads to attract the public's attention to the alternative or oppositional readings possible in an ad campaign. You will find some of those rewrites in this chapter, in the feature "Visual Essay: Rewriting the Image," where you will have the opportunity to do some rewrites of your own.

While many rewrites comment on advertising or art tastes, others simply take advantage of familiar images to make new statements. Take, for example, the cover

The January 3, 2005 issue of *The Nation* featured a Dorothea Lange photo of Florence Thompson.

on the January 3, 2005, issue of the *Nation* magazine. Cover designers took the extremely popular Depression-era Dorothea Lange photograph of Florence Thompson, often called "Migrant Madonna," to comment on current economic conditions. They relied on their readers recognizing this as a reference to the Great Depression. They updated the clothing just slightly and added a Wal-Mart employee's badge to the outfit. In that way, the image carries much of the message or theme of the magazine's January 2005 issue.

Throughout this chapter, you will be asked to read images in the same way you read any text—for meaning and for how those images connect to the world around you. As well, you will be given the chance to create visual messages of your own. The first step is to notice and collect examples of the visual messages that are a routine part of your day. As you begin to develop projects of your own, your collection should become more focused and purposeful, but you should always have as many choices to draw from as possible, so don't limit yourself too soon. Look for patterns, similarities, and images that surprise you. You could find that you have already been doing much of this work automatically, just by looking at the world around you.

IN THE SHADOW OF THE IMAGE

— *Stuart Ewen and Elizabeth Ewen*

Stuart Ewen and Elizabeth Ewen have each written several books and articles on the history and meaning of popular culture. Cultural scholar Stuart Ewen's work includes *All Consuming Images: The Politics of Style in Contemporary Culture* and *Captains of Consciousness*. Historian Elizabeth Ewen's work includes *Immigrant Women in the Land of Dollars* (1985). *Channels of Desire* (1982), from which the following selection is taken, is their first full-length collaboration. The Ewens argue that much of what Americans understand about self-image is actually a reflection of mass-media images. As this essay illustrates, today's culture is one living "in the shadow of the image," whether the image is present in advertising, news reporting, or popular television and film. Everywhere people go, they see images created for mass consumption but aimed at individuals. Sometimes consciously but mostly not, people measure their looks, their moods, their success or lack of it against the appearances that surround them daily.

SUGGESTION FOR READING This series of vignettes describes the daily, often unconscious encounters Americans have with popular culture and especially with commercial images. As you read each vignette, take note of the effects these encounters seem to have on the characters the Ewens have created. If you begin to lose track of what is going on in this selection, skip to the final four paragraphs where the point of the vignettes is explained, then go back and reread individual sections.

1   Maria Aguilar was born twenty-seven years ago near Mayagüez, on the island of Puerto Rico. Her family had lived off the land for generations. Today she sits in a rattling IRT subway car, speeding through the iron-and-rock guts of Manhattan. She sits on the train, her ears dazed by the loud outcry of wheels against tracks. Surrounded by a galaxy of unknown fellow strangers, she looks up at a long strip of colorful signboards placed high above the bobbing heads of the others. All the posters call for her attention.

Looking down at her, a blond-haired lady cabdriver leans out of her driver's side window. Here is the famed philosopher of this strange urban world, and a woman she can talk to. The tough-wise eyes of the cabby combine with a youthful beauty, speaking to Maria Aguilar directly:

Estoy sentada 12 horas al dia.
Lo último que necesito son hemorroides.
(I sit for twelve hours a day. The last thing I
need are hemorrhoids.)

Under this candid testimonial lies a package
of Preparation H ointment, and the promise
"*Alivia dolores y picasonas. Y ayuda a reducir la
hinchazón.*" (Relieves pain and itching. And
helps reduce swelling.) As her mind's eye takes
it all in, the train sweeps into Maria's stop. She
gets out; climbs the stairs to the street; walks to
work where she will spend her day sitting on a
stool in a small garment factory, sewing hems on
pretty dresses.

Every day, while Benny Doyle drives his
Mustang to work along State Road Number 20,
he passes a giant billboard along the shoulder.
The billboard is selling whisky and features a
woman in a black velvet dress stretching across
its brilliant canvas.

5   As Benny Doyle downshifts by, the lounging
beauty looks out to him. Day after day he sees
her here. The first time he wasn't sure, but now
he's convinced that her eyes are following him.

The morning sun shines on the red-tan forehead of Bill O'Conner as he drinks espresso on
his sun deck, alongside the ocean cliffs of La
Jolla, California. Turning through the daily
paper, he reads a story about Zimbabwe.

"Rhodesia," he thinks to himself.

The story argues that a large number of
Africans in Zimbabwe are fearful about black
majority rule, and are concerned over a white
exodus. Two black hotel workers are quoted by
the article. Bill puts this, as a fact, into his
mind.

Later that day, over a business lunch, he
repeats the story to five white business associates, sitting at the restaurant table. They share a
superior laugh over the ineptitude of black
African political rule. Three more tellings, children of the first, take place over the next four
days. These are spoken by two of Bill O'Conner's

luncheon companions; passed on to still others
in the supposed voice of political wisdom.

10   Barbara and John Marsh get into their
seven-year-old Dodge pickup and drive twenty-
three miles to the nearest Sears in Cedar Rapids.
After years of breakdowns and months of hesitation they've decided to buy a new washing
machine. They come to Sears because it is there,
and because they believe that their new Sears
machine will be steady and reliable. The
Marshes will pay for their purchase for the next
year or so.

Barbara's great-grandfather, Elijah Simmons,
had purchased a cream-separator from Sears,
Roebuck in 1897 and he swore by it.

When the clock-radio sprang the morning
affront upon him, Archie Bishop rolled resent-
fully out of his crumpled bed and trudged slowly
to the john. A few moments later he was unconsciously squeezing toothpaste out of a mess of
red and white Colgate packaging. A dozen
scrubs of the mouth and he expectorated a
white, minty glob into the basin.

Still groggy, he turned on the hot water,
slapping occasional palmfuls onto his gray face.

A can of Noxzema shave cream sat on the
edge of the sink, a film of crud and whiskers
across its once neat label. Archie reached for the
bomb and filled his left hand with a white
creamy mound, then spread it over his beard. He
shaved, then looked with resignation at the regular collection of cuts on his neck.

15   Stepping into a shower, he soaped up with
a soap that promised to wake him up. Groggily,
he then grabbed a bottle of Clairol Herbal
Essence Shampoo. He turned the tablet-shaped
bottle to its back label, carefully reading the
"Directions."

"Wet hair."

He wet his hair.

"Lather."

He lathered.

20   "Rinse."

He rinsed.

"Repeat if necessary."

Not sure whether it was altogether necessary, he repeated the process according to directions.

Late in the evening, Maria Aguilar stepped back in the subway train, heading home to the Bronx after a long and tiring day. This time, a poster told her that "The Pain Stops Here!"

25   She barely noticed, but later she would swallow two New Extra Strength Bufferin tablets with a glass of water from a rusty tap.

Two cockroaches in cartoon form leer out onto the street from a wall advertisement. The man cockroach is drawn like a hipster, wearing shades and a cockroach zoot-suit. He strolls hand-in-hand with a lady cockroach, who is dressed like a floozy and blushing beet-red. Caught in the midst of their cockroach-rendezvous, they step sinfully into a Black Flag Roach Motel. Beneath them, in Spanish, the words:

Las Cucarachas entran . . . pero non pueden salir.
(In the English version: Cockroaches check in . . . but they don't check out.)

The roaches are trapped; sin is punished. Salvation is gauged by one's ability to live roach-free. The sinners of the earth shall be inundated by roaches. Moral tales and insects encourage passersby to rid their houses of sin. In their homes, sometimes, people wonder whether God has forsaken them.

Beverly Jackson sits at a metal and tan Formica table and looks through the *New York Post*. She is bombarded by a catalog of horror. Children are mutilated . . . subway riders attacked. . . . Fanatics are marauding and noble despots lie in bloody heaps. Occasionally someone steps off the crime-infested streets to claim a million dollars in lottery winnings.

Beverly Jackson's skin crawls; she feels a knot encircling her lungs. She is beset by immobility, hopelessness, depression.

30   Slowly she walks over to her sixth-floor window, gazing out into the sooty afternoon. From the empty street below, Beverly Jackson imagines a crowd yelling "Jump! . . . Jump!"

Between 1957 and 1966 Frank Miller saw a dozen John Wayne movies, countless other westerns and war dramas. In 1969 he led a charge up a hill without a name in Southeast Asia. No one followed; he took a bullet in the chest.

Today he sits in a chair and doesn't get up. He feels that images betrayed him, and now he camps out across from the White House while another movie star cuts benefits for veterans. In the morning newspaper he reads of a massive weapons buildup taking place.

Gina Concepcion now comes to school wearing the Jordache look. All this has been made possible by weeks and weeks of after-school employment at a supermarket checkout counter. Now, each morning, she tugs the decorative denim over her young legs, sucking in her lean belly to close the snaps.

These pants are expensive compared to the "no-name" brands, but they're worth it, she reasons. They fit better, and she fits better.

35   The theater marquee, stretching out over a crumbling, garbage-strewn sidewalk, announced "The Decline of Western Civilization." At the ticket window a smaller sign read "All seats $5.00."

It was ten in the morning and Joyce Hopkins stood before a mirror next to her bed. Her interview at General Public Utilities, Nuclear Division, was only four hours away and all she could think was "What to wear?"

A half hour later Joyce stood again before the mirror, wearing a slip and stockings. On the bed, next to her, lay a two-foot-high mountain of discarded options. Mocking the title of a recent bestseller, which she hadn't read, she said aloud to herself, "Dress for Success. . . . What do they like?"

At one o'clock she walked out the door wearing a brownish tweed jacket; a cream-colored Qiana blouse, full-cut with a tied collar; a dark beige skirt, fairly straight and hemmed (by Maria Aguilar) two inches below the knee; shear fawn stockings, and simple but elegant reddish-brown pumps on her feet. Her hair was to the shoulder, her look tawny.

When she got the job she thanked her friend Millie, a middle manager, for the tip not to wear pants.

40   Joe Davis stood at the endless conveyor, placing caps on a round-the-clock parade of automobile radiators. His nose and eyes burned. His ears buzzed in the din. In a furtive moment he looked up and to the right. On the plant wall was a large yellow sign with THINK! printed on it in bold type. Joe turned back quickly to the radiator caps.

Fifty years earlier, in another factory, in another state, Joe's grandfather, Nat Davis, had looked up and seen another sign:

A Clean Machine Runs Better.
Your Body Is a Machine.
KEEP IT CLEAN.

Though he tried and tried, Joe Davis' grandfather was never able to get the dirt out from under his nails. Neither could his great-grandfather, who couldn't read.

In 1952 Mary Bird left her family in Charleston to earn money as a maid in a Philadelphia suburb. She earned thirty-five dollars a week, plus room and board, in a dingy retreat of a ranch-style tract house.

Twenty-eight years later she sits on a bus, heading toward her small room in North Philly. Across from her, on an advertising poster, a sumptuous meal is displayed. Golden fried chicken, green beans glistening with butter and flecked by pimento, and a fluffy cloud of rice fill the greater part of a calico-patterned dinner plate. Next to the plate sit a steaming boat of gravy, and an icy drink in an amber tumbler. The plate is on a quilted blue placemat, flanked by a thick linen napkin and colonial silverware.

45   As Mary Bird's hungers are aroused, the wording on the placard instructs her: "Come Home to Carolina."

Shopping List
paper towels
milk
eggs
rice crispies
chicken
snacks for kids (twinkies, chips, etc.)
potatoes
coke, ginger ale, plain soda
cheer
brillo
peanut butter
bread
ragu (2 jars)
spaghetti
saran wrap
salad
get cleaning, bank, must pay electric!!!

On his way to Nina's house, Sidney passed an ad for Smirnoff vodka. A sultry beauty with wet hair and beads of moisture on her smooth, tanned face looked out at him. "Try a Main Squeeze." For a teenage boy the invitation transcended the arena of drink; he felt a quick throb-pulse at the base of his belly and his step quickened.

In October of 1957, at the age of two and a half, Aaron Stone was watching television. Suddenly, from the black screen, there leaped a circus clown, selling children's vitamins, and yelling "Hi! boys and girls!" He ran, terrified, from the room, screaming.

For years after, Aaron watched television in perpetual fear that the vitamin clown would reappear. Slowly his family assured him that the television was just a mechanical box and couldn't really hurt him, that the vitamin clown was harmless.

50   Today, as an adult, Aaron Stone takes vitamins, is ambivalent about clowns, and watches television, although there are occasional moments of anxiety.

These are some of the facts of our lives; disparate moments, disconnected, dissociated. Meaningless moments. Random incidents. Memory traces. Each is an unplanned encounter, part of day-to-day existence. Viewed alone, each by itself, such spaces of our lives seem insignificant, trivial. They are the decisions and reveries of survival; the stuff of small talk; the chance preoccupations of our eyes and minds in a world of images—soon forgotten.

Viewed together, however, as an ensemble, an integrated panorama of social life, human activity, hope and despair, images and information, another tale unfolds from these vignettes. They reveal a pattern of life, the structures of perception.

As familiar moments in American life, all of these events bear the footprints of a history that weighs upon us, but is largely untold. We live and breathe an atmosphere where mass images are everywhere in evidence; mass produced, mass distributed. In the streets, in our homes, among a crowd, or alone, they speak to us, overwhelm our vision. Their presence, their messages are given; unavoidable. Though their history is still relatively short, their prehistory is, for the most part, forgotten, unimaginable.

The history that unites the seemingly random routines of daily life is one that embraces the rise of an industrial consumer society. It involves explosive interactions between modernity and old ways of life. It includes the proliferation, over days and decades, of a wide, repeatable vernacular of commercial images and ideas. This history spells new patterns of social, productive, and political life.

SUGGESTIONS FOR DISCUSSION

1. Although many of the vignettes describe the effects of ad images on so much of the public, others, such as the story of Bill O'Conner, the story of the roach motel, and the story of Joe Davis, suggest something about the way information and even cultural attitudes are passed along or processed. Reread those sections and others like them and discuss what kind of information you unconsciously process in your daily life. In your discussion, take into account such things as the choices you make in what to wear, what to take when you have a cold, how to act around others, what to believe about political issues, and the like.

2. The grocery list intersperses generic items such as paper towels with name brands that represent generics (such as Brillo for scouring pads). Consider the products you buy that are brand name. How would you say your own or your family's buying habits are influenced by what appears in newspapers, on television, on billboards, or on bus-stop ads? To what extent do you think those habits are influenced by loyalty or habit, like the Marshes' purchase of a new Sears washing machine?

3. Near the end of this selection, the Ewens write, "As familiar moments in American life, all of these events bear the footprints of a history that weighs upon us, but is largely untold." After rereading this series of events, discuss what the authors mean by such a sweeping statement. Do you see that statement illustrated or not in the observations you have made about the way you and the people you know respond to living "in the shadow of the image"?

SUGGESTIONS FOR WRITING

1. Write a series of vignettes about the daily encounters that you, your friends, and your family have with ad images. Pay attention to how the Ewens structure their piece. The vignettes lead to a summary statement in which the Ewens briefly explain what such a

sequence of encounters might mean for them. Include a statement that draws your reader away from the vignettes and sums up the stories with a commentary on your daily encounters with visual messages of all sorts.

2. Make a list of images that you see on most days. The list might include posters, billboards, commercials, magazine and newspaper ads, cartoons, road signs, family and news photos, and shop-window displays. Write an essay in which you describe the kinds of images

SUGGESTIONS FOR READING ADVERTISING

As you read and write about ads in this chapter, you can start by asking fairly simple questions:

1. What is the product being sold, and what is that product used for?

2. What does the ad promise? What claim does the ad make about the product?

3. What visuals are used in the ad? Do they illustrate the product claim or promise, or do they associate the product with something else—for example, a lifestyle or a celebrity?

4. Who is the target audience? Who is likely to buy the product? Is age or gender an important issue for the ad or the product? Is cost an issue? How can you tell?

5. Where does the ad appear? If it is a magazine or newspaper ad, who reads that publication? If it is a billboard, where is it placed? Who is likely to be the target audience for that publication or location?

6. How are people depicted in the ad image? Do they conform to or break with stereotypes?

7. Can you identify the cultural significance of this product? Is it a product that has been around for several generations? Is it associated with a particular idea or ideal about American culture or family life? Is it new to the market and suddenly popular with teens or young children? Does the ad refer to current events in the news or to popular films or media events?

8. Is this ad more text than image or more image than text? In other words, does the advertiser think the audience wants more information about the product, or is the audience one that will more likely be persuaded by the visual appeal of the ad? Typically, ads in electronics equipment magazines will give readers quite a bit of text—the details of the equipment—suggesting that advertisers are assuming the readers are an audience that knows something about the product and are looking for specific features. Ads for clothing, cosmetics, soap products, cigarettes, and the like rarely provide much information beyond the product name, the product claim—"softer, younger-looking skin"—and the advertising image.

9. Does the ad look familiar to you? Does it remind you of other ads or other media? If it does, what is that association?

you encounter daily and what those images seem to be asking of you or telling you about the way people should look or act or feel.

3. Near the end of this selection, the Ewens write, "The history that unites the seemingly random routines of daily life is one that embraces the rise of an industrial consumer society. It involves explosive interactions between modernity and old ways of life. It includes the proliferation, over days and decades, of a wide, repeatable vernacular of commercial images and ideas. This history spells new patterns of social, productive, and political life." Write an explanation of what you understand the authors to be saying in that statement. Provide examples from your own experience or reading that help make the meaning clear for your readers.

THE IRON MAIDEN: HOW ADVERTISING PORTRAYS WOMEN

Michael F. Jacobson and Laurie Anne Mazur

Michael F. Jacobson is founder of the Center for the Study of Commercialism and has served as executive director of the Center for Science in the Public Interest. Laurie Ann Mazur is a writer and consultant to nonprofit organizations who has written widely on environment and population issues. "The Iron Maiden" originally appeared in 1995 as a part of *Sexism and Sexuality in Advertising*, their book-length analysis of representations of women in advertising.

SUGGESTION FOR READING Before you read this selection, page through a number of women's magazines, paying close attention to how women are represented in the advertisements. Write a brief description of the ideal of female beauty as depicted in these magazines. Bring your description and a group of 5–10 sample ads to class with you for discussion.

1 Fourteen year-old Lisa arranges herself in the mirror—tightening her stomach, sucking in her cheeks, puffing her lips into an approximation of a seductive pout. It's no use, she thinks, as she glances down at the open magazine on her dresser table. I'll never look like the women in the ads. She flips through the pages, studying the beautiful women with their slender hips, flawless skin, and silky hair. Well, maybe if I lost twenty pounds, she thinks, pinching her baby-fat tummy with an acid feeling of despair. Or if I had the right clothes and makeup . . .

Everywhere we turn, advertisements tell us what it means to be a desirable man or woman. For a man, the message is manifold: he must be powerful, rich, confident, athletic. For a woman, the messages all share a common theme: She must be "beautiful." Advertising, of course, did not invent the notion that women should be valued as ornaments; women have always been measured against cultural ideals of beauty. But advertising has joined forces with sexism to make images of the beauty ideal more pervasive, and more unattainable, than ever before.

In her 1991 book *The Beauty Myth*, Naomi Wolf compares the contemporary ideal of beauty to the Iron Maiden, a medieval torture device that enclosed its victims in a spike-lined box painted with a woman's image. Like the Iron Maiden, the beauty ideal enforces conformity to a single, rigid shape. And both cause suffering—even death—in their victims.

The current Iron Maiden smiles at us from the pages of *Vogue* magazine. She's a seventeen-year-old professional model, weighing just 120 pounds on a willowy 5'10" frame. Her eyes are a deep violet-blue, her teeth pearly white. She has no wrinkles, blemishes—or even pores, for that matter. As media critic Jean Kilbourne observes in *Still Killing Us Softly*, her ground-breaking film about images of women in advertising, "The ideal cannot be achieved; it is inhuman in its flawlessness. And it is the only standard of beauty—and worth—for women in this culture."[1]

5   The flawlessness of the Iron Maiden is, in fact, an illusion created by makeup artists, photographers, and photo re-touchers. Each image is painstakingly worked over: Teeth and eyeballs are bleached white; blemishes, wrinkles, and stray hairs are airbrushed away. According to Louis Grubb, a leading New York re-toucher, "Almost every photograph you see for a national advertiser these days has been worked on by a re-toucher to some degree. . . . Fundamentally, our job is to correct the basic deficiencies in the original photograph or, in effect, to improve upon the appearance of reality."[2] In some cases, a picture is actually an amalgam of body parts of several different models—a mouth from this one, arms from that one, and legs from a third.[3] By inviting women to compare their unimproved reality with the Iron Maiden's airbrushed perfection, advertising erodes self-esteem, then offers to sell it back—for a price.

The price is high. It includes the staggering sums we spend each year to change our appearance: $33 billion on weight loss;[4] $7 billion on cosmetics; $300 million on cosmetic surgery.[5] It includes women's lives and health, which are lost to self-imposed starvation and complications from silicone breast implants. And it includes the impossible-to-measure cost of lost self-regard and limited personal horizons.

THE BEAUTY CONTEST OF LIFE

Ads instruct us to assume a self-conscious perspective; to view our physical selves through the censorious eyes of others. To those of us who grew up in the consumer culture, intense self-scrutiny has become an automatic reflex. But this reflex is not God-given; it is the product of decades of deliberate marketing effort. Since the birth of the modern advertising industry in the 1920s, marketers have sought to foster insecurity in consumers. One advertiser, writing in the trade journal *Printer's Ink* in 1926, noted that effective ads must "make [the viewer] self-conscious about matter of course things such as enlarged nose pores, bad breath." Another commented that "advertising helps to keep the masses dissatisfied with their mode of life, discontented with the ugly things around them. Satisfied customers are not as profitable as discontented ones."[6]

Advertisers in the 1920s did everything they could to create profitably discontented customers. Their ads depicted a hostile world peopled with critical strangers who would fasten on some part of one's anatomy and deliver a negative judgment. "The Eyes of Men . . . The Eyes of Women judge Your Loveliness Every Day," warned an ad for Camay soap. "You can hardly glance out the window, much less walk in town but that some inquiring eye searches you and your skin. This is the Beauty Contest of Life." For women, of course, participation in this contest was compulsory.

In the 1920s, before Americans had learned to dread ring-around-the-collar and halitosis, blunt instruments were needed to instill the self-consciousness that would eventually fuel the consumer culture. Perhaps because today's audiences are more predisposed to self-examination, contemporary ads can afford to be more subtle. Nonetheless, the Beauty Contest of Life continues. "We'll make a non-competitive suit when they make a non-competitive beach," reads the copy of an ad for Speedo bathing suits.

10   Countless ads reinforce insecurity by asking women to view their faces and bodies as an ensemble of discrete parts, each in need of a major overhaul. An ad for foundation garments depicts two disembodied backsides and promises "New improved fannies." "If your hair isn't beautiful," warns a shampoo ad, "the rest hardly matters." Another demands to know: "Why aren't your feet as sexy as the rest of you?"

And an ad for Dep styling products suggests that we beautify our hair in order to counteract our other glaring flaws: "Your breasts may be too big, too saggy, too pert, too flat, too full, too far apart," the copy reads, "but . . . at least you can have your hair the way you want it."

The psychological costs of advertising induced self-consciousness are difficult to quantify. For most women, they include an endless self-scrutiny that is tiresome at best and paralyzing at worst. As Susan Brownmiller writes in *Femininity*, her classic treatise on the feminine ideal, "Because she is forced to concentrate on the minutiae of her bodily parts, a woman is never free of self-consciousness. She is never quite satisfied, and never secure, for desperate, unending absorption in the drive for perfect appearance—call it feminine vanity—is the ultimate restriction on freedom of mind."[7]

Men also lose out in a culture dominated by Iron Maiden imagery; advertising encourages men to measure their girlfriends and wives against a virtually unattainable ideal, perpetuating frustration among both genders. Wolf says that ads don't sell sex, they sell sexual discontent.

Sexual discontent fuels the engines of the consumer culture. The ideal bodies presented in the ads invite comparison to ourselves and our mates, and in the likely event that the comparison is unfavorable to us, the ads suggest we attain the ideal by buying another product. According to Wolf, "Consumer culture is best supported by markets made up of sexual clones, men who want objects and women who want to be objects, and the object desired ever-changing, disposable, and dictated by the market."[8]

THE THINNING OF THE IRON MAIDEN

Women come in an endless array of shapes and sizes, but you'd never know it from looking at ads. In every generation, advertisers issue a new paradigm of female perfection. The very rigidity of the ideal guarantees that most women will fall outside of it, creating a gap between what women are and what they learn they should be.

This gap is very lucrative for the purveyors of commercialized beauty.

15   In the portrayal of women's bodies, the gap has never been wider. The slender reigning ideal provides a stark contrast to the rounder curves of most women's bodies. As an adaptation to the physical demands of childbearing, women's bodies typically have a fat content of around 25 percent, as opposed to 15 percent in men. For much of human history, this characteristic was admired, sought after, and celebrated in the arts. But the twentieth century has seen a steady chipping away at the ideal female figure. A generation ago, according to Naomi Wolf, a typical model weighed 8 percent less than the average woman; more recently she weighs 23 percent less. Most models are now thinner than 95 percent of the female population.[9]

In the early 1990s, the fashion industry promoted the "waif look," epitomized by Calvin Klein's young supermodel Kate Moss. At 5'7" and an estimated 100 pounds, "Moss looks as if a strong blast from a blow dryer would waft her away," according to *People* magazine.[10] Marcelle d'Argy, editor of *British Cosmopolitan*, called fashion photos of Moss "hideous and tragic. If I had a daughter who looked like that, I would take her to see a doctor."[11] As the gap between ideal and reality has widened, women's self-esteem has fallen into the void. A 1984 *Glamour* magazine survey of 33,000 women found that 75 percent of respondents aged eighteen to thirty-five thought they were fat, although only 25 percent were medically overweight. Even 45 percent of the underweight women believed they were fat. Weight was virtually an obsession for many of the *Glamour* respondents, who chose "losing 10–15 pounds" as their most cherished goal in life.[12] Another study in Boston found that fifth-, sixth-, and ninth-graders were much more critical of their body shape after looking at fashion advertising.[13]

Although the glorification of slenderness is sometimes defended in the interests of health, for most women it is anything but healthy. Almost 40 percent of women who smoke say they do so to maintain their weight; one-quarter of those will die of a disease caused by smoking.[14] In one scientific study, researchers found that women's magazines contained ten times as many advertisements and articles promoting weight loss as men's magazines—corresponding exactly to the ratio of eating disorders in women versus men.[15] And recent studies have suggested that it may sometimes be healthier to be overweight than to repeatedly gain and lose weight through "yo-yo dieting."

Surrounded by ads that depict the Iron Maiden as a stick figure, few women can eat in peace. On any given day, "25 percent of American women are dieting, and another 50 percent are finishing, breaking, or starting diets."[16] The *Glamour* survey found that "50 percent of respondents used diet pills, 27 percent used liquid formula diets, 18 percent used diuretics, 45 percent fasted, 18 percent used laxatives, and 15 percent engaged in self-induced vomiting." While women have purged and starved themselves, the diet industry has grown fat.[17]

The cycle of self-loathing and dieting begins early. In a survey of 494 middle-class San Francisco schoolgirls, more than half thought they were fat, yet only 15 percent were medically overweight. And pre-adolescent dieting has increased "exponentially" in recent years according to Vivian Meehan, president of the National Association of Anorexia Nervosa and Associated Disorders.[18]

20   The Iron Maiden may be a stick figure, but she is often endowed with a pair of gravity-defying breasts. The laws of physics dictate that large breasts eventually droop downward, but the breasts depicted in ads are typically high, firm, and round—a shape that is only attainable by very young or surgically altered women. This, too, takes its toll on women's self-esteem. In 1973, *Psychology Today* reported that one quarter of American women were unhappy with the size or shape of their breasts. By 1986, a similar study found that number had risen to one-third.[19] Tragically, millions of women sacrifice their health—and even their lives—to conform

to the shape of the Iron Maiden. Roughly 80 percent of the 150,000 women who have breast implant surgery each year do so for cosmetic reasons, most often to enlarge their breasts.[20] Recent revelations, which came to light despite suppression by implant-maker Dow Corning, suggest that silicone implants may cause immune-system disorders and death. In response, the Food and Drug Administration has sharply limited implants.

"YOU'VE GOT TO BE YOUNG AND BEAUTIFUL IF YOU WANT TO BE LOVED"

The Iron Maiden is not shaped like most women. Moreover, she never ages; she is merely replaced with a newer, younger model. Why? A recent TV commercial for *Nike* and *Foot Locker* puts it succinctly: "You've got to be young and beautiful if you want to be loved."

Although *Adweek's Marketing Week* reports an increased demand for "older" models (defined by the advertising industry as women in their late twenties), most professional models are considered over the hill by the time they're twenty-four.[21]

If older women manage to make it into ads at all, visible signs of age are retouched out of their photographs. Naomi Wolf invites us to imagine a parallel—say, if all photographs of blacks in advertising were routinely lightened. "That would be making the same value judgment about blackness that this tampering makes about the value of female life: that less is more," she writes.[22]

Innumerable ads reinforce—and prey on—women's fear of aging. For example, Jean Kilbourne cites an ad headlined "My husband is seeing a younger woman these days . . . Me!" Kilbourne notes that "the ad wouldn't work if there wasn't the fear that, if she didn't use the product, he would in fact replace her with a younger woman."[23]

25   Seeking to forestall the inevitable, women spend an estimated $20 billion worldwide each year on skin-care products that promise to eliminate wrinkles and retard aging. Yet even some

marketers of these products privately admit that they are worthless. Buddy Wedderburn, a biochemist for Unilever, confessed that "the effect of rubbing collagen onto the skin is negligible. . . . I don't know of anything that gets into these areas—certainly nothing that will stop wrinkles."[24] In his exposé, *The Skin Game: The International Beauty Business Brutally Exposed*, Gerald McKnight called the skin-care industry "a massive con . . . a sweetly disguised form of commercial robbery."[25]

Fear of aging also fuels the booming cosmetic-surgery business. Despite the expense and danger, thousands of women submit to the knife in order to preserve the appearance of youth. Although it may be derided as narcissistic, the choice to undergo surgery may seem to be a rational one in a culture where advertisers and media "disappear" older women—with a retoucher's brush or simple exclusion.

LITTLE MISS MAKEUP

Girls and teenagers are perhaps most vulnerable to beauty-industry propaganda. For them, advertising is a window into adult life, a lesson in what it means to be a woman. And lacking the sophistication of their older sisters and mothers, girls are less likely to distinguish between fact and advertising fiction.

Marketers increasingly target the lucrative teen and preadolescent market with ads for beauty products. And they are having an effect: Female teens spend an average of $506 per year on cosmetics and beauty salon visits. Most wear makeup by the time they are thirteen, and 26 percent wear perfume every day.[26] Ever younger girls are being fitted for miniature Iron Maidens: Christian Dior makes bras and panties with lace and ruffles for preschoolers.[27] One toymaker produces a Little Miss Makeup doll, which looks like a five- or six-year-old girl. When water is applied, the doll sprouts eyebrows, colored eyelids, fingernails, tinted lips, and a heart-shaped beauty mark.[28]

Sexualized images of little girls may have dangerous implications in a world where 450,000 American children were reported as victims of sexual abuse in 1993.[29] It also robs girls of their brief freedom from the constraints of the beauty imperative; they have little chance to develop a sense of bodily self-worth and integrity before beginning to compare themselves to the airbrushed young beauties in *Seventeen*.

If little girls are presented as sex objects, grown women are depicted as children. A classic example is an ad that ran in the 1970s for Love's Baby Soft cosmetics. The ad featured a grown woman in a little girl dress, licking a lollipop and hiking up her short skirt next to phallic-shaped bottles of Love's Baby Soft. The tag line read, "Because innocence is sexier than you think." And an ad for Cutex lipstick shows a cartoon of a woman' s bright red lips with a pacifier stuck in them, and the caption "lipstick that makes your lips baby soft." Such ads, says Kilbourne, "send out a powerful sexual message at the same time they deny it, which is exactly what the ads are telling women to do. The real message is 'don't be a mature sexual being, stay like a little girl'—passive, powerless, and dependent."[30]

WOMEN'S MAGAZINES AND THE IRON MAIDEN

Advertising's images of the Iron Maiden are everywhere, but women's magazines deserve a special mention for promoting their commercialized beauty ideal. These magazines, so widely read that they are nicknamed "cash cows" in the publishing trade, have a nearly symbiotic relationship with advertisers. Gloria Steinem, describing *Ms.* magazine's largely unsuccessful attempts to attract ad revenue (before that magazine went ad-free), explains that advertisers for women's products demand "supportive editorial atmosphere," that is, "clothing advertisers expect to be surrounded by fashion spreads (especially ones that credit their designers); and shampoo, fragrance, and beauty products in general usually insist on positive editorial coverage of beauty subjects."

Advertisers influence the content of virtually all media, but their stranglehold over women's magazines is especially unyielding. Steinem notes, "If *Time* and *Newsweek* had to lavish praise on cars in general and credit GM in particular to get GM ads, there would be a scandal—maybe even a criminal investigation. When women's magazines from *Seventeen* to *Lear's* praise beauty products in general and credit Revlon in particular to get ads, it's just business as usual."[31]

Women's magazines are the manifestos of Iron Maidenhood, typically running "objective" editorial copy that touts the products advertised in their pages. These ads too narrowly define the acceptable contours of female shape and appearance. And although women s magazines increasingly publish articles on explicitly feminist themes, their ties to advertisers prevent them from challenging the sacred Iron Maiden. For example, Steinem tells of the time *Ms.* published an exclusive cover story about Soviet women exiled for publishing underground feminist books. This journalistic coup won *Ms.* a Front Page Award but lost it an advertising account with Revlon. "Why?" asks Steinem, "Because the Soviet women on our cover [were] not wearing makeup."[32]

THE KITCHEN AND THE BEDROOM: LIMITED VIEWS OF WOMEN

Clearly, ads present unrealistic images of women's faces and bodies. Just as insidiously, they present highly circumscribed views of women's lives. One study of magazine ads from 1960 to 1979—a time when women entered the workforce in unprecedented numbers—found that ads failed to depict a significant increase in women's employment outside the home. The study also noted that women in ads were apt to be portrayed in traditional female roles: cooking, cleaning, caring for children."[33] And a more recent survey of Canadian broadcast ads concluded that men were far more likely than women to be presented as experts or authorities.[34]

35   A quarter-century after the rebirth of the women's movement, women in ads are still depicted as housewives obsessed with ring-around-the-collar and spots on the dishes. If they do work outside the home, they are presented as super-moms who cook, clean, take care of the kids, then slip into something sexy—all with the help of Brand X. (Some ads parrot the slogans of the women's movement while their content explicitly refutes them.). . .

Ads that show working women usually focus on their appearance and sexual availability. An ad for Hennessy cognac depicts an after-hours office scene: While a man talks on the phone, a female co-worker in a low-cut blouse seductively hands him a drink. The Maidenform woman disembarks from an airplane, briefcase in hand; her businesslike raincoat blows open to reveal lingerie. Women's work is trivialized, as in an ad declaring that "Phoebe chose to work, not because she had to, but because it gave her a place to wear her Braeburn sweaters."

To be fair, there have been modest improvements in advertising's portrayal of women since the 1970s. And recently, women have been appointed to high-level positions at some of the nation's leading ad agencies. Although the industry is still heavily dominated by men, the ascension of women to top jobs is prompting some agencies to reevaluate their messages to women.[35]

But ads have a long way to go. Until ads depict women in a realistic way, women will continue to measure themselves against an inhuman ideal. And until they are released from the rigid confines of the Iron Maiden, women will continue to seek commercial remedies for imaginary flaws. . . .

Men's bodies, too, are no longer immune from exploitation in advertising. Recent years have seen a veritable deluge of beefcake photos in ads glorifying men's muscled torsos, backs, and thighs. Often aimed at women, who make the majority of consumer purchases, these ads are the mirror image of "T & A." Typical of the genre is an ad for Cool Water cologne, which features the torso of a water-sprayed nude male basking in the sun. A Calvin Klein ad supplement to *Vanity Fair* contained no less than twenty-seven bare-chested and two bare-bottomed men, two bare-bottomed and four top-less women. In a 1994 Hyundai television commercial, two women coyly estimate men's physical endowment, based on the car they drive. While assuming that men in fancy cars are lacking elsewhere, the women are dearly impressed by the Hyundai driver: "Wonder what he's got under the hood."

40   "Women are recognizing that they like men's bodies," Judith Langer, head of a market research firm, told the *New York Times*. "It used to be that men offered power and women offered beauty. Now men have to be on their toes and in shape. They can't allow themselves to go to pot."[36] Not surprisingly, many men feel uneasy about being held to the standard presented in the ads—as women have been for generations. Women's unclothed bodies have proliferated in ads and other media, but male nudity has historically remained off-limits. Interestingly, much outcry about sex in advertising has accompanied the crossing of this sacred line. For example, a *New York Times* article entitled "Has Madison Avenue Gone Too Far?" cites ten examples of sexually suggestive ads, all of which featured male models.[37] Exhibiting a similar double standard, *Sports Illustrated* editors refused to run a 1993 Adidas ad that featured a Canadian soccer team of naked men squatting and covering their genitalia with soccer balls, trophies, and their hands.[38] *Sports Illustrated* is far less prudish when it comes to the annual swimsuit issue, which flaunts nubile women in tiny bikinis. Ubiquitous images of women's bodies seem somehow natural in a culture that sanctions the objectification of women; subjecting male anatomy to the same cold, critical gaze is going "too far."

NOTES

1. Jean Kilbourne, *Still Killing Us Softly*, film distributed by Cambridge Documentary Films, Cambridge, Mass., 1987.

2. Quoted in Stuart Ewen, *All Consuming Images: The Politics of Style in Contemporary Culture* (New York: Basic Books, 1988), p. 87.

3. Ibid.

4. Molly O'Neill, "Diet Companies Ask U.S. for Uniform Rules on Ads," *New York Times*, August 25, 1992.

5. Figures given are for both men and women. Naomi Wolf, *The Beauty Myth: How Images of Beauty Are Used Against Women* (New York: William Morrow, 1991), p. 17; Elaine Brumberg, *Save Your Money, Save Your Face* (New York: Harper & Row, 1987), p. xiii.

6. Quoted in Stuart Ewen, *Captains of Consciousness: Advertising and the Social Roots of Consumer Culture* (New York: McGraw-Hill, 1976), p. 39.

7. Susan Brownmiller, *Femininity* (New York: Fawcett Columbine, 1984), p. 51.

8. Ibid., p. 144.

9. Wolf, *The Beauty Myth*, p. 184. Wolf does not specify the years being compared. It is worth noting that the prevalence of overweight among adult women remained fairly constant from 1960 to 1980, but then rose by one-third during the 1980s (Robert J. Kuczmarski et al., "Increasing Prevalence of Overweight Among U.S. Adults," *Journal of the American Medical Association* 272, July 20, 1994, p. 205).

10. Louise Lague and Alison Lynne, "How Thin Is Too Thin?" *People Magazine*, September 20, 1993, p. 74.

11. Quoted in ibid.

12. S. C. Wooley, "Feeling Fat in a Thin Society," *Glamour*, February 1984, p. 198.

13. Alison Bass, " 'Anorexic Marketing' Faces Boycott," *Boston Globe*, April 2 5, 1994, p. 1.

14. Wolf, *The Beauty Myth*, p. 229.

15. Arnold E. Andersen and Lisa Di Domenico, "Diets Shape Content of Popular Male and Female Magazines: A Dose-Response Relationship to the Incidence of Eating Disorders?" *International Journal of Eating Disorders* 11, no. 3, 1992, pp. 283–287.

16. Wolf, *The Beauty Myth*, p. 185.

17. Wooley, "Feeling Fat in a Thin Society.

18. Wolf, *The Beauty Myth*, p. 215.

19. Ibid., p. 248.

20. Lena Williams, "Woman's Image in a Mirror: Who Defines What She Sees?" *New York Times*, February 6, 1992, p. A1.

21. Cara Appelbaum, "Beyond the Blonde Bombshell," *Adweek's Marketing Week*, June 3, 1991.

22. Wolf, *The Beauty Myth*, p. 83.

23. Kilbourne, *Still Killing Us Softly*.

24. Quoted in Wolf, *The Beauty Myth*, p. 110.

25. Gerald McKnight, *The Skin Game: The International Beauty Business Brutally Exposed* (London: Sedgwick & Jackson, 1989), p. 20.

26. Cara Appelbaum, "Thirteen Going on Twenty-one," *Adweek's Marketing Week*, March 11, 1991.

27. Media Watch (Santa Cruz, Calif., Media Watch), Fall 1990, p. 2.

28. Wolf, *The Beauty Myth*, p. 215.

29. Karen McCurdy and Deborah Darol "Current Trends in Child Abuse Reporting and Fatalities: The Results of the 1993 Annual Fifty State Survey," working paper no. 808, the National Center on Child Abuse Prevention Research, a program of the National Committee to Prevent Child Abuse, Chicago, Ill., April 1994, pp. 3, 7.

30. Kilbourne, *Still Killing Us Softly*.

31. Gloria Steinem, "Sex, Lies, and Advertising," *Ms.*, July–August 1990, p. 19.

32. Ibid., p. 23.

33. England and Gardner, "How Advertising Portrays Men and Women," p. 2.

34. Canadian Advertising Foundation, "Sex Role Stereotyping Guidelines," July 24, 1987.

35. Kim Foltz, "Women Deflate Some Adland Images," *New York Times*, November 17, 1991.

36. Stuart Elliott, "Looking at Male Bodies," *New York Times*, December 15, 1991, sec. 3, p. 6.

37. Elliott, "Has Madison Avenue Gone Too Far?"

38. Anne Swardson, "The Shoe's on the Other Foot?" *Washington Post*, June 30, 1993.

SUGGESTIONS FOR DISCUSSION

1. Share the ads you collected and the description of ideal beauty in women's magazine advertisements that you wrote in preparation for this reading with a group of your classmates. What did each of your group members identify as the ideal portrayed in the ads? In what ways do your descriptions differ? Which ads do not seem to correspond to the ideal?

2. Jacobson and Mazur write that the ideal represented in ads is not only stereotypical and unreal, but actually unhealthy—even dangerous. How is the danger manifest in the women and girls you know? To what extent do you think women are able to ignore or reject the ideal represented in these ads?

3. What is the ideal male represented in advertising? In what ways does the male ideal correspond to what Jacobson and Mazur say about the female ideal?

SUGGESTIONS FOR WRITING

1. Choose three to four prominent women's magazines. These magazines should be aimed at different age groups, ethnicities, and interest groups. If you can, it is best to look at the most recent six months of the magazines. If not, look at the most recent issue of each magazine. After you have collected the magazines, survey the advertising in each very carefully, noting how women are depicted in the ads. Write an essay in which you respond to Jacobson and Mazur using the material you have collected. In what ways do the ads you have collected reinforce their argument? In what ways do they depart from that argument? What argument could you make about representations of women in current women's magazine advertising? Remember that Jacobson and Mazur were writing in 1995. Your task is to update their argument.

2. With a group of two or three classmates, develop an argument for changing the way women are depicted in advertisements. You might, for example, choose a particular product and pitch an idea for an ad campaign that breaks with the stereotype but that is just as appealing as current advertising that relies on sexist portrayals. Present your ad campaign idea to the class using mock-ads to illustrate your new image.

3. Write a response to Jacobson and Mazur's claim that sexist images of women are just as damaging to men as they are to women. How might that be the case, or not? Do you accept their argument? What would you add to that discussion?

*To learn more about gender
and advertising, visit
www.ablongman.com/george/112*

VISUAL ESSAY

Reading the Gaze—Gender Roles in Advertising

Much discussion over the years has drawn the public's attention to the image of women in advertising, and yet men have also been objectified in popular advertising. This Visual Essay illustrates how advertisers use what is called *the gaze* to establish a relationship between the reader and the person represented in the image. Though theorists first began talking about the gaze in reference to images of women, even a quick survey of today's ads will turn up images that subject both men and women to the gaze. The ads reprinted here offer a good illustration of how sophisticated advertisers can be as they both reinforce and challenge gender stereotypes.

As you examine images of men and women in advertising, notice that the way you as a viewer are being asked to relate to the person in the picture is often signaled by whether the person in the image is looking at or away from the camera (or you, as the imaginary viewer).

When the person in the image looks at you directly and at close range, a different message is sent than when the person is depicted looking down, away from, or beyond your gaze. Some images show the model only from behind, as if an imaginary viewer is looking at the model but the model is unaware of that intrusion (as in a lingerie or cologne ad). In that case, the viewer holds power over the model. It's almost as if the viewer is watching from a hidden place.

In *Reading Images: The Grammar of Visual Design* (Routledge, 1996), Gunther Kress and Theo van Leeuwen describe the position of the subject in an image as portraying either an offer or a demand. They explain the difference between the two in this way (pp. 122–124):

> There is, then, a fundamental difference between pictures from which represented participants look directly at the viewer's eyes and pictures in which this is not the case. When represented participants look at the viewer, vectors, formed by participants' eyelines, connect the participants with the viewer. Contact is established, even if it is only on an imaginary level. . . . [This representation] creates a visual form of direct address. It acknowledges the viewers explicitly, addressing them with a visual "you." . . . It is for this reason we have called this kind of image a "demand": the participant's gaze (and the gesture, if present) demands something from the viewer, demands that the viewer enter into some kind of imaginary relation with him or her. Exactly what kind of relation is then signified by other means, for instance by the facial expression of the represented participants. They may smile, in which case the viewer is asked to enter into a relation of social affinity with them; they may stare at the viewer with cold disdain, in which case the viewer is asked to relate to them, perhaps, as an inferior relates to a superior; they may seductively pout at the viewer, in which case the viewer is asked to desire them. The same applies to gestures. A hand can point at the viewer, in a visual "Hey, you there, I mean you," or invite the viewer to come closer, or hold the

viewer at bay with a defensive gesture as if to say: stay away from me. In each case the image wants something from the viewers—wants them to do something (come closer, stay at a distance) or to form a pseudo-social bond of a particular kind with the represented participant. . . .

Other pictures address us indirectly. Here the viewer is not object but subject of the look, and the represented participant is the object of the viewer's dispassionate scrutiny. No contact is made. The viewer's role is that of the invisible onlooker . . . we have called this kind of image an "offer"—it "offers" the represented participants to the viewer as items of information, objects of contemplation, impersonally, as though they were specimens in a display case.

As you examine the collection of images reproduced here, keep in mind how the man or woman in each image looks at or away from the viewer. (To learn more about vectors, review "Visual Culture: Picturing Schooldays" in Chapter 3.)

SUGGESTIONS FOR DISCUSSION

1. With a group of your classmates, look carefully at the ads reproduced here, paying particular attention to the manner in which each model is posed looking at or away from the viewer. Which models seem to be individuals? Which seem to be types? What kind of relationship, as Kress and van Leeuwen describe it, is each image setting up with the viewer? How is that relationship likely to change if the viewer is a man or a woman? What else, besides the viewer's gender, might determine the viewer's relationship to these images?

2. Paying attention to the way the gaze is used is one important way of determining the viewer's relationship to the subject of the image, but it is not the only way. Writing about the way men and women are depicted in art and advertising, scholar John Berger once declared, "Men act. Women appear." By that, Berger meant that, even when posing nude or partially nude, men appear strong and active whereas women typically appear submissive or acted upon. Look again at the ads reprinted here. To what extent does Berger's observation hold true for these images?

3. How do the ads in this Visual Essay both break with and conform to typical stereotypes? How does the gaze figure into these stereotypes?

SUGGESTIONS FOR WRITING

1. This Visual Essay is quite obviously about gender stereotypes in advertising and how those stereotypes are signaled by the way the model relates to (looks at or away from) the viewer. In general, the concept of the gaze asks readers to pay attention to how the subject of an image is treated—whether that subject seems to be an individual or just a body. Write an essay in which you imagine the models in these ads reversed. That is, how would the ice cream ad change if the model were looking at you? Would a nude male model looking at you change the ad even more? The aim of your essay is to examine the effect of both gender and visual treatment of gender.

2. After examining this Visual Essay, consider what it is saying about sexuality and gender and determine what is left out or what you would want to say if you were asked to create a visual essay depicting the image of sexuality in advertising.

   Once you have decided what you would add or change, revise this Visual Essay with images you find in several different sources. You might, for example, decide to remake this essay as one solely focused on either women or men and stereotypes of sexuality.

   Or you might want to consider how the message changes depending on who is reading the ads or how the camera "treats" the model being represented. Is there a distancing between the viewer and the model? Does the model look at you straight on? What is the effect of that look? Does the model do anything in the ad or is he or she just an object to be looked at? Look for advertising that breaks with the common stereotype.

   Once you have created your revision of this Visual Essay, write a one-page explanation for what you found and why you revised the essay in the way you did.

3. Media analyst Jean Kilbourne has written, "The aspect of advertising most in need of analysis and change is the portrayal of women," and certainly Jacobson and Mazur would seem to agree with that. Some readers, however, think that claim is much too narrow. For this essay, begin collecting ads that focus on other stereotypes. Consider images of men, race, ethnicity, success, poverty, age, family, athletes, and so on. Once you have chosen a topic, collect as many as ten to twenty images. Collecting will be easier if, after you have looked through several magazines or watched commercials, you decide on a focus. For example, you might focus on the changing image of men in advertising. Or

you might decide that, though there appears to be a change in the way men are depicted, that change is superficial and not much of a change at all. Sometimes it is easier to write about the stereotype when you find an image that breaks with that stereotype, so don't ignore images that at first do not seem to fit your argument. As you explain the stereotype of the group you have chosen, refer to the ads you have collected as examples of the points you want to make. Your position will be stronger if you can also refer to other places where the stereotype is common—in television sitcoms or Hollywood films, for example. You do not need to argue that women are not stereotyped or that there is no longer any need to pay attention to female stereotyping.

VISUAL ESSAY   Rewriting the Image

WWW

To learn more about Adbusters, visit
www.ablongman.com/george/113

Advertising doesn't just create "images," it constructs differences between men and women, which operate under the assumption that they reflect a universal timeless truth. And so it is never merely a case of a good image versus a bad image. Looking itself has to be rewritten. . . .

It is time for some interventions in the belly of the beast.

There are many methods for upsetting the echelons of imagery. There is no one perfect way to intervene, not when the gospel of perfection is the very text being tampered with. From critiques to billboard activism, the creation of alternative imagery to boycotts and protests, strategic intervention is needed on all fronts. Humor and the unexpected are always good tools for deconstructing the codes the advertising world operates under.

—*Katherine Dodds, writing in* Adbusters Magazine

Writing over, remaking, or talking back to an image is a tactic that has been around for a long time. Look, for example, at Marcel Duchamp's remake of Leonardo's *Mona Lisa*. The Da Vinci portrait had been held up for so long as a masterpiece of Renaissance art that Duchamp, trying to change the way people see the classics, did the unthinkable: he painted a mustache on the *Mona Lisa* (well, actually, on a reproduction of the *Mona Lisa*). It was, it could be argued, one of the most effective acts of graffiti ever created. It shocked many in the art world and those who considered the masterpieces sacred, and it made the public laugh. At the same time, it also made a statement about how art had to change, new voices had to be heard, and new images had to be accepted.

In the same way, the Canadian-based organization Adbusters advocates rewriting ads that represent unhealthy products, products that promote stereotypes, and products that exploit workers. In the article from which Katherine Dodds's statement is taken, she writes of the importance of this act of taking control of advertising images, many of which you have read and written about in this chapter.

Sometimes, though, a rewrite isn't meant to change attitudes or attack stereotypes at all. Sometimes a rewrite is simply necessary, in a world so thick with images, if anyone is ever to say something new, or to revise the ways people see each other, or even to laugh at themselves. Rewriting the image can be activism, as Dodds suggests, but it can also be a way of understanding how images function so that people aren't simply consumers but are also producers of the image.

Of course, if people are going to complain about what's produced out there, then the best way to change it is to change it.

SUGGESTION FOR READING

Because parody depends on knowledge of the original to make its point, the message that results from the parody or rewriting threatens to change one's response to the original. Duchamp, for example, certainly wanted to change the way viewers saw the *Mona Lisa*. As you look at the images here, make notes for yourself on how the rewrite makes you rethink the original image.

Mona Lisa, by Leonardo da Vinci, 1503–1506.

L.H.O.O.Q., by Marcel Duchamp, 1930.

L.H.O.O.Q. by Marcel Duchamp, 1930. © 2005 Artists Rights Society (ARS), New York/ADAGP, Paris/Succession.

The Grand Odalisque, by Jean Auguste Dominique Ingres, 1814.

Guerrilla Girls' poster displayed on New York City buses.

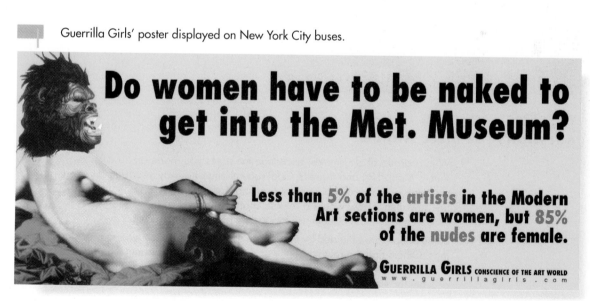

Courtesy of Nirvana L.L.C.

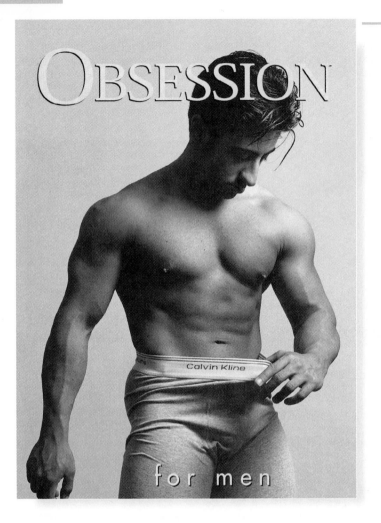

Adbusters' spoof ad.

SUGGESTIONS FOR DISCUSSION

1. With a group of classmates, exchange the notes you made on how the rewrites of Da Vinci's *Mona Lisa* and Ingres's *Odalisque* change the way you read the original. With your group, make a list of popular paintings, advertisements, or photographs that could be "rewritten." How would a rewrite change those images? What images would your group consider "out of bounds" for parody or satire of this sort? Why?

2. Some people are offended by the images that are the result of writing over classic paintings. Others find the rewrites funny or powerful statements about the originals. What is your response to the Guerrilla Girls' rewrite of Ingres's *Odalisque*? How would you account for your response?

3. With a group of your classmates, choose a popular image to rewrite or parody. Present your rewrite to the class, and explain what your group wanted to accomplish with the image that you created.

SUGGESTIONS FOR WRITING

1. Choose an advertisement or series of ads that illustrates Dodds's statement that advertising "constructs differences between men and women, which operate under the assumption that they reflect a universal timeless truth." Write a brief explanation of what Dodds means, then use your ad or ads to explain how, as Dodds suggests, "Looking itself has to be rewritten." To do that, write over the ads, creating a parody, or explain what a reader needs to understand to look at these images differently.

2. When you rewrite an advertisement as Adbusters suggests, your purpose usually is to bring to the surface the oppositional readings that are possible in any ad image. In the Adbuster ad, for example, the word *Obsession* is taken literally and applied to consumers of Calvin Klein ads. In that way, the ad takes on a powerful new meaning. Find an ad image that you would like to rewrite, and redo the image in a way that clearly draws on the original yet brings to the surface a new and oppositional reading of the original.

3. Choose any kind of image—on a T-shirt, poster, cereal box, magazine cover, commercial, famous painting, cover from a textbook or novel. Rewrite the image so that you bring an alternate reading of that image to the surface or so that you create an entirely new meaning. One T-shirt rewrite that has become a popular tourist souvenir, for example, is the shirt that reads, "My parents went to Paris and all I got was this lousy T-shirt." It's a rewrite because it acknowledges the habit of buying souvenir T-shirts as gifts to placate family and friends left at home. As well, Duchamp's rewrite of *Mona Lisa* only makes its point if you think *Mona Lisa* is a great work of art that shouldn't be changed. To make your own rewrite, you will have to understand the original message, so pay attention to how the image conveys the meaning it carries at this time, and use the original to create your own image. The image you choose and the meaning you make with that image depend on your interests and on the interests of your intended audience. For whom are you making this image? Classmates? Parents? A "general audience" of readers in a particular age group?

VISUAL ESSAY   Public Health Messages

Public health campaigns take several forms, with messages that appear everywhere from billboards and subway posters to newspaper and magazine ads to public service announcements on radio and television. Like advertising, public health messages are intended to persuade readers, viewers, and listeners to do something. In the case of public health publicity, however, the pitch is not to buy a product but to live a healthy lifestyle—to eat a balanced diet, stop smoking, drink in moderation, avoid drugs, exercise regularly, use a condom, immunize your kids, or have annual checkups.

Like advertising, public health publicity uses images that readers and viewers will recognize immediately to get its message across. The "be sexy" Candie's Foundation ad on page 228, for example, uses a male model who looks like he could just as easily be in a fashion advertisement. This message ran in the magazine *Elle Girl*, the teen version of the upscale fashion magazine *Elle*, and obviously assumes that

young people want to be sexy. It's an ad that argues for teen abstinence rather than safe sex while it draws from all of the codes of sultriness and sexuality these readers would be familiar with from ads in the same magazine.

As is true in all advertising, agencies designing public health messages face decisions about how to sell the message: should the publicity emphasize the negative consequences of unhealthy behavior or the positive benefits of a healthy lifestyle?

Some of the most interesting cases of how public health messages use images can be found in publicity concerning sexually transmitted diseases (STDs). This Visual Essay includes three examples:

- The two posters "Worst of the Three" and "She May Look Clean" were directed at men in the military during World War II.
- The third example, "Roses Have Thorns", is the cover of a recent pamphlet for teens on STDs.

SUGGESTION FOR READING

Before you read, look around your campus—in the dorms, the commons, the health service, any place where you are likely to find STD health messages—and bring examples of those (or take notes and bring descriptions of them) to class for your discussion.

SUGGESTIONS FOR DISCUSSION

1. The first two posters were part of a World War II campaign to stem the spread of syphilis and gonorrhea—the most widespread STDs, or venereal diseases (VD)—among allied forces. Notice how each poster portrays women. In the first, a female death figure representing VD is accompanied by Hitler of Nazi Germany and Hirohito of Japan. What assumptions do these posters seem to make about the role of women in spreading STDs? What assumptions do they seem to make about male sexual behavior?

2. Consider the cover of the pamphlet on STDs. It uses a familiar image of romantic love, the rose. How do the public health messages use these familiar images to get their point across? To what extent do the messages emphasize negative consequences or positive benefits?

3. Share the public health messages you collected in preparation for this assignment. How would you describe them? Do they conform to or break with the images of men and women and sexuality that you see in this visual essay? To what extent are some of the older attitudes preserved in newer messages? To what extent do newer messages break with those older themes and warnings? How effective are these newer messages?

SUGGESTIONS FOR WRITING

1. Work with two other classmates. Assemble several public health messages on STDs. (Your campus health center is a good resource, but also notice messages posted around campus or in other public places.) Analyze the kinds of images that appear in the public health publicity. Do your examples use familiar images? If so, are they used in expected or unexpected ways? Do the images seem to transmit messages about negative consequences or positive benefits (or some combination of the two)? How effective do you think the publicity is, given its intended audience? Prepare a report that explains your findings.

2. Design your own public health publicity. Choose any topic you find interesting and important (e.g., smoking, drugs, diet, exercise, STDs, alcohol). Decide on your intended audience—college students, teenagers, pregnant women, new mothers. Fashion your message so that it speaks to the particular audience you have in mind. Choose carefully the image or images that can best convey your message.

3. Examine the public health images reprinted here. Each is designed to appeal to a specific audience at a specific time. Choose one of these images for an analysis of how the ad targets that audience and what images, ideals, or ideas the ad takes advantage of from popular culture to create that message.

WHEN YOU MEET ESTELLA SMART, YOU BEEN MET!

— *Vertamae Smart-Grosvenor*

Vertamae Smart-Grosvenor describes herself as a "poet, culinary anthropologist and writer." She has written books and numerous essays, poems, and articles for national magazines and newspapers, including the *New York Times*, the *Washington Post*, *Redbook*, and *Ebony*. Her autobiographical cookbook *Vibration Cooking or the Travel Notes of a Geechee Girl* was first published in 1970 and reissued in 1986 and again in 1992. For several years, she was a commentator on NPR's *All Things Considered* and served as host of their documentary series *Horizons*. The following essay appeared in 1994 in the Deborah Willis collection *Picturing Us: African American Identity in Photography*.

SUGGESTION FOR READING   Smart-Grosvenor's essay uses a photograph of her grandmother to prompt memories about the grandmother and about growing up. Most of the memories she has of those people and times are not in pictures, though she tells us she wishes she did have photographs of some of them. Before you read, think of a family story or a person in your family's past you wish you had a picture of.

1   If family stories were photographs, I'd need a small museum to house them, but a shoe box could hold all the photos I have of my family. Devastation by fire was a common occurrence in the wooden-frame houses where my family lived in rural South Carolina—besides which, photo opportunities were few and far between. Few photos survived.

Memories are our photos. The family history is told in stories; and I mean those Geechee people tell some stories!

I would do the hucklebuck in Macy's window for a photo of my great-grandfather Mott. They say he was a seven-feet-tall African man who could jump so high that his heels clicked three times before he came down. And they say his voice was so powerful that when he called "quitting time" you could hear him on plantations in the next county.

Not too long ago a bank was running TV spots called "First Americans." The idea was to talk about a person in your family who was or did something unusual and succeeded. I submitted Granddaddy Mott's name. He was a first American, and succeeded in spite of bitter southern oppression to live to be ninety-five years old.

5   I never heard from the bank. I'm convinced it's because I didn't have a photo.

On the other hand, I do have a picture of my grandmother, and it is one of my most treasured possessions.

Estella Smart was my grandmother on my father's side. I could say she was my paternal grandmother, but I like the way they say it back home.

For sure the picture was taken in Philadelphia where my grandmother, like many other southern blacks, migrated in the forties in search of a better life.

And I believe it was taken in the 1100 block of Girard Avenue. On visits to my grandmother I remember seeing a studio there, where on the weekend a steady stream of southern migrants came, eager to have the camera catch their likeness, to send home so everybody could see how well they were doing in the promised land.

10   Like most of the southern arrivals, my grandmother worked as a domestic when she first came to Philadelphia.

She hated it.

"I can't stand cleaning my own house, so you know I didn't want to clean nobody else's!"

Estella Smart.

So she worked as a domestic by day, and at night went to school to learn factory sewing, eventually getting the factory job she held until she retired in the sixties.

They say that children don't know that their lives or family circumstances are weird or different. To them that's what it is. I'm not sure that's always true. I knew straightaway my grandmother was different.

15 She just didn't or wouldn't do things the way everybody did, and it didn't seem to bother her. But it bothered almost everybody else. They had

moved north to better themselves, and one of the first ways to do that was to get rid of those country ways, and Geechees were the *country-est* of all country people, the butt of numerous jokes. It was painful to be called "a bad-talking rice eater."

But Estella Smart wasn't about to get rid of nothing that was worth keeping. She continued to eat her rice every day, say "goober" for peanut, "kiver" for cover, "britches" for pants, and any other Geechee thing she wanted.

"They can ki-ki [a Gullah word meaning gossip] this and ki-ki that about me as much as they please, I'll talk about them on my knees," she said.

"Hit'a sin and a shame."

"Going to the market with a homemade basket, instead of shopping bag like everybody else, up here."

20   "Ain't hit the truth!"

"Did you see what she was wearing?"

"Lord knows hit's a shame."

"She make 'em!"

"Think she is something! She ain't no better than nobody else."

25   "There's was a way to act and that's all there is to it!"

It wasn't only the way she acted, it was her presence.

Langston Hughes must have had her in mind when he wrote, "There are people (you've probably noted it also) who have the unconscious faculty of making the world spin around themselves, throb and expand, contract and go dizzy."

But magic is threatening and, for many, a little Estella Smart went a long way. Those who knew her when would always allow with a certain edge in their voice, "She always been like that."

Estella, or Telly, as she was called, was the youngest of eight children born to Sam and Rina Myers, in the Atlantic coastal city of Port Royal, South Carolina. Her parents were former slaves. She used to tell me, "Many days us shed tears of sorrow" when we talked about slavery time.

30   According to family legend, young Telly was "oomanish"—meaning she was sassy.

She married twenty-four-year-old Cleveland Smart, a wheelwright, when she was fourteen. And as family legend has it, Mr. Smart had his hands full.

His independent and strong-willed bride didn't "act right." For one thing, she balked at working by the sun in the fields with her husband as most wives were expected to do, and did. Cleveland Smart went to see his father-in-law and asked him to do something with this peculiar-acting bride. But Sam Myers couldn't help him.

"Us never could do nuthin wid Telly, she just don't take no tea for the fever. Takes after her grandmama who she named for, and they couldn't do nuthin wid her either. Now if you don't want Telly bring her home. And anyhow we didn't name her to be no mule."

Cleveland Smart kept his bride and they had five children. Now according to some more legend, Estella birthed all five by herself without a midwife. I don't know if it's true, but if you ever met Estella Smart you would believe it could be true.

35   There is a lot of mystery surrounding Cleveland Smart's life. They say he was a big black man. "A saltwater African" who was adopted. By whom, and from whom? They say the Smarts lived in the swamp in a house surrounded by a moat and that they had a safe in the house. Why?

Still I would love to see a photograph of Cleveland Smart. Legend is he was a dreamer. . . . When Cleveland Smart dreamt something and told you this and that was going to happen, it did!

When my mother was "that way" he had a dream and told her she would have a girl and to name her Verta.

Well to make a very long story short, Mama did have a girl and a boy, so it looked like Cleveland Smart's dream didn't come true. But the baby boy died, and of course they named me Verta. Still I could never understand why they did, because Gullah people pronounce v's like w's and everybody called me "Werta."

I couldn't call Estella Smart "Grandmama," like I called my other grandmother. I was to call her "Mother Dear," which came out sounding like "Mudear." This was alright around other Geechees, but as I got older and integrated with blacks from other places, I was, as they say, "too shame to say it." But Estella Smart didn't have no shame around "siddy" blacks or white folks. She was confident and self-assured around everybody.

40 In 1970, when my first book came out, she came to the book party in New York. A slightly drunk and very condescending white man came up to her and said, "Haven't I met you before?"

"If you had met me you would have know it, cause when you meet Estella Smart, you've been met!"

I think that is the quality I admire most about my grandmother, her sense of self. Where did she get it? It certainly wasn't easy for an eccentric Geechee woman with a second-grade education. . . . I asked her about it, but she didn't think "sense of self" was something people could give you.

"Yes," I would say, "but it's not easy in these hard times." She would look at me with her eyes the color of iced tea and say, "If colored people didn't have hard times, they wouldn't have no times, so keep your eyes on the prize and git on up and keep yourself to yourself."

I also admire the way Estella Smart took on the challenge of living in Philadelphia, a woman apart from Carolina. She and the others who came to the city from the country were real urban pioneers.

45 I have no idea how old my grandmother was at the time the photograph was taken. She always said, "A woman who will tell her age will tell anything."

I didn't discover her age until she died in 1985, a week before her hundredth birthday.

Now that I know her age, I think of what it must have been to go from cooking in a fireplace to a gas stove, from kerosene lamps to electric lights, and from driving a horse and buggy to driving a car. Unbeknownst to the family, Estella Smart took driving lessons. I was in high school the day she asked us to come with her outside the house. We did and she stepped into the car and drove off.

Estella Smart was not an easy grandmother to have. She had little patience, and not the greatest sense of humor. Saturdays, when other children were going to the movies, I was at her house helping her clean and sew. I had to bring my own lunch because she didn't cook.

She never remembered birthdays and didn't give Christmas presents. But I was enchanted by her.

50 My favorite memories of Mudear are of the good times we had in Atlantic City.

She would take me to Atlantic City to "catch the sea breeze and bathe in the salt water, cause we come from saltwater people."

We didn't have money to rent a room, so we undressed on the beach.

Estella Smart looked normal until she peeled off her clothes down to the two-piece bathing suit made of cretonne-print upholstery fabric that she had made. Then she was a mermaid.

She would swim way out on her back. The lifeguards would blow their whistles. She kept on swimming.

55 The lifeguards would look scared, afraid they might have to swim out that far to get her. But they never did.

When they would blow the whistle, folks would crowd around as folks will and ask, "What happened?"

Once someone asked me, "Who is that woman out there?"

"That's no woman," I said, "That's Mudear riding the waves."

60 For a picture of that I would do the huckle-buck naked in Macy's window.

SUGGESTIONS FOR DISCUSSION

1. With a group of your classmates, share a story you wish you had a picture of. What makes some people or events in families special enough so that we want to look at them later in a photograph? What photographs do people generally want to keep? Why?

2. Twice in this piece, Smart-Grosvenor writes about a particular person, "I would do the hucklebuck in Macy's window for a photo." What is she saying here? What is so important about having a photograph?

3. Smart-Grosvenor writes that "a little Estella Smart went a long way." Look at the photograph and then reread Smart-Grosvenor's description of Estella Smart. What of her character comes through in this photograph? How would you describe this woman? What makes this a memorable photograph?

SUGGESTIONS FOR WRITING

1. In many ways, this essay is about more than Vertamae Smart-Grosvenor's photo of her grandmother. It is also about what photos reveal about people—what photo portraits tell us. Choose a photo portrait that you find compelling. It might be a photo of a famous person like Malcolm X or Ida B. Wells or Martin Luther King Jr., for example. Examine the portrait carefully. What does the portrait seem to reveal about the person? Is there something trustworthy in the face? A sadness? Wisdom? A sense of humor? How do you know? Write an essay in which you read that portrait for what it seems to convey.

2. Choose a photograph from your family or from a time and place of your childhood. Write an essay that, like Smart-Grosvenor's, uses the photograph as a starting point for what was important about that person or place or time.

3. Make a photo essay of your own family history and write an accompanying essay in which you explain what absolutely has to be included, what is left out, and what stories photos can tell about the people in our lives?

WIRED CULTURE   Photographic Truth in a Digital Age

WWW

To learn more digital photography,
visit
www.ablongman.com/george/114

From the very invention of photography in the nineteenth century, the photograph has been at the center of a debate over accuracy or what some have called the "truth value" of the photograph. After all, it seems logical that when a photographer points a camera at a subject and takes a picture, there isn't much between the eye of the photographer and the subject of the photograph but the camera lens itself. Photographs have, in fact, been at the center of forensic evidence in trials for many years, even though most people know that photographs can be manipulated, subjects can be posed, events can be staged. The fact is that most photographs—especially of the sort used in courtrooms—simply *look* real and so carry strong truth value.

That reliance on photographic truth has, however, begun to disappear with the emergence of digital photography and image manipulation software such as Adobe Photo Shop, iPhoto, and others like them. As Brian Bergstein's report reprinted here suggests, that change is having a particularly crucial impact on the courts.

DIGITAL PHOTOGRAPHY POSES THORNY ISSUES FOR JUSTICE SYSTEM

Brian Bergstein

Brian Bergstein is business and technology reporter for the Associated Press. This article originally appeared in *USA Today* in February 2004.

SUGGESTION FOR READING Bergstein's article is a news report on the implications of digital technology for the use of photography as evidence in the courtroom. As you read, keep track of the distinction critics are making between film photography and digital photography, in terms of either's reliability to show what actually happened.

1 When Victor Reyes went on trial for murder last year, the technology that fingered him was supposed to be a star witness.

Police in Florida had used software known as More Hits to determine that a smudged handprint they had found on duct tape wrapped around a body—but originally couldn't decipher—implicated Reyes in the 1996 killing.

The judge let prosecutors introduce More Hits' digital enhancement. But the defense called it "junk science," and had an art professor testify that the process resembled how Adobe Photoshop can be used to make trick-photo illustrations.

Reyes was acquitted.

5 Jurors said they based their decision mainly on the notion that the print didn't prove Reyes was the killer—not on the legitimacy of More Hits' method. And a Florida appeals court later ruled that More Hits' technology—used by 215 U.S. police departments—is acceptable.

Still, some defense attorneys learned a lesson: get more aggressive about challenging digitally generated evidence.

"Now whenever you hear the word enhancement, an antenna goes up," said Hilliard Moldof, a Florida defense attorney who is questioning digitally enhanced fingerprints in two cases.

Or in the words of Mary DeFusco, head of training for the Philadelphia public defender's office: "I thought digital was better, but apparently it's not. We're definitely going to take a look at it."

As more police departments abandon chemically processed film in favor of digital photography, the technology could be confounding for the justice system.

10 Film images are subject to darkroom tricks, but because digital pictures are merely bits of data, manipulating them is much easier.

And although willful evidence manipulation is rare, forensic specialists acknowledge that a poorly trained examiner incorrectly using computer enhancement programs can unwittingly introduce errors.

"What you can do in a darkroom is 2% of what Photoshop is capable of doing," said Larry Meyer, former head of photography for State Farm Insurance Co.

Courts have consistently allowed digital photographs and enhancement techniques. But some observers say such methods should endure a more thorough examination, as have technologies such as DNA analysis.

"There have been relatively few challenges to the use of digital technology as evidence and in most of them the courts have looked at them in a fairly superficial way," said Edwin Imwinkelried, an evidence expert at the University of California–Davis law school.

15 Concerns about the impeachability of digital photographs are one reason many police departments have been hesitant to ditch film for crime scene photographs and forensic analysis.

In fact, some people who train law enforcement agencies in photography estimate that only

25 to 30% of U.S. police departments have gone digital—despite the huge cost benefits of no longer having to buy film and the ease with which digital pictures can be captured and disseminated.

The police department in Santa Clara, Calif., bought 30 digital cameras recently but is holding off on giving them to detectives and technicians until the department specifies ways to lock away the original photos as evidence "so there can be no question that anything was changed," said Sharon Hoehn, an analyst for the department.

SUGGESTIONS FOR DISCUSSION

1. What distinctions do critics make between film and digital photography, in terms of each one's ability to "tell the truth"? How legitimate is that distinction?

2. This article opens with a case in which the defendant was acquitted on the basis of objections to digitally enhanced evidence. In your reading, did you have the impression that the defendant was actually guilty or that the evidence was unfairly manipulated? What would you say is Bergstein's position on this matter? What in the article indicates that position?

3. To what extent is the notion of "photographic truth" legitimate—either for digital or film photographs?

SUGGESTIONS FOR WRITING

1. Write a response to Bergstein's article and take a position on whether or not digital photography and accompanying enhancement programs should be allowed as evidence in court. In your response, address the notion of photography—digital as well as film—as evidence.

2. In 1900, Kodak introduced a small, handheld camera they called the Brownie. It sold for $1, was marketed for children, and was even given out free as a Kodak promotion to spread the word of this new photographic technology. With the Brownie came the birth of the snapshot—the informal, inexpensive photo that anyone could take and have developed. Before the widespread use of handheld cameras, photography was in the hands of experts, and family photos tended to be posed studio photos. On its site, http://www.kodak.com/US/en/corp/features/brownieCam/, Kodak writes, "This small, simple box launched a new industry, and forever changed the way we communicate. Photojournalism. The motion picture industry. Medical x-rays. Satellite imaging. The Internet. Every technology we use to communicate with pictures can trace its ancestry to that first black box." Write an essay in which you argue the importance of the introduction of inexpensive and widely available digital cameras and technology for the next generation of visual communication and simple family snapshots.

3. At the heart of the courtroom controversy is the long-held notion that photographs have what has sometimes been called a higher "truth value" than other visual media like painting, for example. Photography has typically *seemed* more real—closer to the world as we see it around us. Digital photography, with its photo manipulation programs, *seems* less trustworthy. Write an essay in which you examine the truth value of different visual media, including digital photography. Can a painting be closer to the truth than a photograph? Can an enhanced digital image be more real than an un-enhanced film image? How real is television news or documentary film? In your essay, refer back to the courtroom argument as a way of framing your comments.

A WAY OF SEEING: AN INTRODUCTION TO THE PHOTOGRAPHS OF HELEN LEVITT

— James Agee

American writer James Agee (1909–1953) worked as a journalist, playwright, and novelist, but he is perhaps best remembered today for his collaboration with Walker Evans in the 1941 publication *Let Us Now Praise Famous Men*, which combined Evans's photos of southern share-croppers with Agee's observations on the lives of the people he and Evans met and lived with in the summer of 1936. In 1946, Agee teamed up with photographer Helen Levitt, who had, since the mid-1930s, been photographing the street life in New York City, and especially in Spanish Harlem. Together, they planned the collection of photos they called *A Way of Seeing*, from which the photos here are reprinted. In 2002, Levitt published *Crosstown: Photographs by Helen Levitt*, a major retrospective of her documentary work.

SUGGESTION FOR READING As you read, keep in mind that Agee is both introducing Levitt as a photographer and artist and developing an argument for photography as an uncompromising visual record and as a fine art form. Keep track, by underlining/highlighting and annotating this passage, of how Agee makes that argument.

1 The mind and the spirit are constantly formed by, and as constantly form, the senses, and misuse or neglect the senses only at grave peril to every possibility of wisdom and well-being. The busiest and most abundant of the senses is that of sight. The sense of sight has been served and illuminated by the visual arts for as long, almost, as we have been human. For a little over a hundred years, it has also been served by the camera. Well used, the camera is unique in its power to develop and to delight our ability to see. Ill or indifferently used, it is unique in its power to defile and to destroy that ability. It is clear enough by now to most people that "the camera never lies" is a foolish saying. Yet it is doubtful whether most people realize how extraordinarily slippery a liar the camera is. The camera is just a machine, which records with impressive and as a rule very cruel faithfulness, precisely what is in the eye, mind, spirit, and skill of its operator to make it record. Since relatively few of its operators are notably well endowed in any of these respects, save perhaps in technical skill, the results are, generally, disheartening. It is probably well on the conservative side to estimate that during the past ten to fifteen years the camera has destroyed a thousand pairs of eyes, corrupted ten thousand, and seriously deceived a hundred thousand, for every one pair that it has opened, and taught.

It is in fact hard to get the camera to tell the truth; yet it can be made to, in many ways and on many levels. Some of the best photographs we are ever likely to see are innocent domestic snapshots, city postcards, and news and scientific photographs. If we know how, moreover, we can enjoy and learn a great deal from essentially untrue photographs, such as studio portraits, movie romances, or the national and class types apotheosized in ads for life insurance and feminine hygiene. It is a good deal harder to tell the truth, in this medium, as in all others, at the level of perception and discipline on which an artist works, and the attempt to be "artistic" or, just as bad, to combine "artistry" with something that pays better, has harmed countless

New York, c. 1942.

photographs for every one it has helped, and is harming more all the time. During the century that the camera has been available, relatively few people have tried to use it at all consistently as an artist might, and of these very few indeed could by any stretch of courtesy be called good artists. Among these few, Helen Levitt is one of a handful who have to be described as good artists, not loosely, or arrogantly, or promotively, but simply because no other description will do.

In every other art which draws directly on the actual world, the actual is transformed by the artist's creative intelligence, into a new and different kind of reality: aesthetic reality. In the kind of photography we are talking about here, the actual is not at all transformed; it is reflected and recorded, within the limits of the camera, with all possible accuracy. The artist's task is not to alter the world as the eye sees it into a world of aesthetic reality, but to perceive the aesthetic reality within the actual world, and to make an undisturbed and faithful record of the instant in which this movement of creativeness achieves its most expressive crystallization. Through his eye and through his instrument the artist has, thus, a leverage upon the materials of existence which is unique, opening to him a universe which has never before been so directly or so purely available to artists, and requiring of his creative intelligence and of his skill, perceptions and disciplines no less deep than those required in any other act of aesthetic creation, though very differently deprived, and enriched.

The kind of beauty he records may be so monumentally static, as it is in much of the work of Mathew Brady, Eugène Atget, and Walker Evans, that the undeveloped eye is too casual and wandering to recognize it. Or it may be so filled with movement, so fluid and so transient, as it is in much of the work of Henri Cartier-Bresson and of Miss Levitt, that the undeveloped eye is too slow and too generalized to foresee and to isolate the most illuminating moment. It would be mistaken to suppose that any of the best photography is come at by intellection; it is, like all art, essentially the result of an intuitive process, drawing on all that the artist *is* rather than on anything he thinks, far less theorizes

© Helen Levitt. Courtesy Laurence Miller Gallery, New York

New York, c. 1942.

about. But it seems quite natural, though none of the artists can have made any choice in the matter, that the static work is generally the richest in meditativeness, in mentality, in attentiveness to the wonder of materials and of objects, and in complex multiplicity of attitudes of perception, whereas the volatile work is richest in emotion; and that, though both kinds, at their best, are poetic in a very high degree, the static work has a kind of Homeric or Tolstoyan nobility, as in Brady's photographs, or a kind of Joycean denseness, insight and complexity resolved in its bitter purity, as in the work of Evans; whereas the best of the volatile work is nearly always lyrical.

5   It is remarkable, I think, that so little of this lyrical work has been done; it is perhaps no less remarkable that, like nearly all good photographic art, the little that has been done has been so narrowly distributed and so little appreciated. For it is, after all, the simplest and most direct way of seeing the everyday world, the most nearly related to the elastic, casual and subjective way in which we ordinarily look around us. One would accordingly suppose that, better than any other kind of photography, it could bring pleasure, could illuminate and enhance our ability to see what is before us and to enjoy what we see, and could relate all that we see to the purification and healing of our emotions and of our spirit, which in our time are beguiled with such unprecedented dangerousness towards sickness and atrophy.

I do not at all well understand the reasons for the failure, but a few possibilities may be worth mentioning in passing. For a long time the camera was too slow, large, and conspicuous to work in the fleeting and half-secret world which is most abundant in lyrical qualities. More recently it has become all but impossible, even for those who had it in the first place, to maintain intact and uncomplicated the simple liveliness of soul and of talent without which true lyrical work cannot be done. As small, quick, foolproof cameras became generally available, moreover, the camera has been used so much and so flabbily by so many people that it

has acted as a sort of contraceptive on the ability to see. And more recently, as the appetite for looking at photographs has grown, and has linked itself with the worship of "facts," and as a prodigious apparatus has been developed for feeding this appetite, the camera has been used professionally, a hundred times to one, in ways which could only condition and freeze the visual standards of a great majority of people at a relatively low grade.

As a further effect of this freezing and standardization, photographers who really have eyes, and who dare to call their eyes their own, and who do not care to modify them towards this standardized, acceptable style, have found it virtually impossible to get their work before most of those who might enjoy it; or to earn, through such work, the food, clothing, shelter, leisure, and equipment which would make the continuance of that work possible. Almost no photographer whose work is preeminently worth looking at has managed to produce more than a small fraction of the work he was capable of, and the work, as a rule, has remained virtually unknown except to a few friends and fellow artists. This is true to a great extent, of course, of artists who work in any field. Yet distinctions, standards, and assumptions exist and have existed for centuries which guarantee a good poet or painter or composer an audience, if generally a small one; and these are not yet formed in relation to photographs. In its broad design, however, this is a familiar predicament, as old as art itself, and as tiresome at least, one may assume, to the artists who suffer the consequences as to the nonartists to whom it is just a weary cliché. I don't propose to discuss who, if anyone, is to blame, being all the less interested in such discussion because I don't think anyone is to blame. I mention it at all only because I presume that the distinction between faithfulness to one's own perceptions and a readiness to modify them for the sake of popularity and self-support is still to be taken seriously among civilized human beings; and because it helps, in its way, to place and evaluate Miss Levitt's work.

At least a dozen of Helen Levitt's photographs seem to me as beautiful, perceptive, satisfying,

Helen Levitt. Courtesy Laurence Miller Gallery, New York

New York, c. 1940.

and enduring as any lyrical work that I know. In their general quality and coherence, moreover, the photographs as a whole body, as a book, seem to me to combine into a unified view of the world, an uninsistent but irrefutable manifesto of a way of seeing, and in a gentle and wholly unpretentious way, a major poetic work. Most of these photographs are about as near the pure spontaneity of true folk art as the artist, aware of himself as such, can come; and an absolute minimum of intellection, of technical finesse, or of any kind of direction or interference on the part of the artist as artist stands between the substance and the emotion and their communication.

It is of absolute importance, of course, that all of these photographs are "real" records; that the photographer did not in any way prepare, meddle with, or try to improve on any one of them. But this is not so important of itself as, in so many of them, unretouched reality is shown transcending itself. Some, to be sure, are so perfectly simple, warm and direct in their understanding of a face or of an emotion that they are likely to mean a great deal to anyone who cares much for human beings: it would be hard to imagine anyone who would not be touched by all that is shown—by all that so beautifully took place in the unimagined world.

SUGGESTIONS FOR DISCUSSION

1. What does Agee mean when he says that the camera is a "slippery liar" and that it "is in fact hard to get the camera to tell the truth"?

2. Agee writes that most art transforms the real world into a new kind of reality. Helen Levitt's photography does not transform. Instead, the actual "is reflected and recorded, within the limits of the camera, with all possible accuracy. The artist's task is not to alter the world . . . but to perceive the aesthetic reality within the actual world." What does he mean by that? In what ways do the photos reproduced here not transform the actual but find the beauty in what is already there?

3. Choose one of the photographs reproduced here and, with a group of your classmates, discuss what the photo shows. What are the relationships between the people in the photo, for example? How do you know? What is the position of the viewer? What do you think is happening in the photograph?

SUGGESTIONS FOR WRITING

1. Agee writes, "In their general quality and coherence, moreover, the photographs as a whole body, as a book, seem to me to combine into a unified view of the world, an uninsistent but irrefutable manifesto of a way of seeing." In preparation for this writing, reread the selection excerpted here and spend some time looking at the photographs reproduced from this collection. In a brief (two to three page) response, explain what that "way of seeing" is. How would you describe the world Helen Levitt depicts here? What other choices might a documentary photographer make that would change the view of the world that Levitt gives here?

2. In *Camera Lucida,* Roland Barthes's book-length study of how photographs convey meaning, he writes that there is always some detail, something special in a good photograph that makes us take notice, that arouses our curiosity, and that gives the photograph its power over us. He called that detail the "punctum" and said it might be as simple as a missing shoe or as complicated as the way the subject of the photograph looks at the camera or the association a viewer has with the subject of the photo. Whatever the detail, it is what makes us wonder or laugh or cry or simply want to keep looking at the image.

    Choose one of Levitt's photographs or a photo that has always captured your imagination, and in a brief analysis, explain what detail makes this a powerful or interesting photograph for you.

3. As Agee says, the camera can be brutal and it can be kind. It is a technology that depends very much on who is looking through the lens when the picture is taken. For this assignment, you need a camera—even a single-use disposable camera will do. Choose a place, a group of people, or an event and make a series of photographs that conveys your own "way of seeing" that subject.

    Arrange your photographs in a notebook and write an introduction to the photos. You will have to make choices. Not every photo you take will be worth putting in your book. Use the introduction to examine the nature of amateur photography today or to explain the challenge of using the camera to present what you want others to know about a place or group of people, for example. What you say is up to you and will be determined by the subject you choose and the pictures you get, so wait until you have compiled your collection before you write your introduction.

    This is an assignment that will take time. You will have to choose a subject, take the pictures, get the pictures developed, and write your introductory essay. Don't count on one-hour photo services because they are not always reliable and don't develop all types of film in one hour. If you have access to a digital camera, you can get your images immediately, but make sure you have access to a computer and printer that is compatible with your equipment before you commit yourself to digital work.

FILM CLIP — Storyboarding: Editing and Camera Work

By the time a film is ready for an audience, it has gone through a number of pre-production jobs that include casting, scripting, designing sets and costumes, and more. In terms of editing and deciding on how the camera will tell the story, some of the most useful pre-production strategies happen at what is called the *storyboarding* stage.

A storyboard is basically a shot-by-shot schematic plan of what will be included in the camera frame. In storyboarding, shots are sketched out in advance and in sequence, like a comic strip, so that the director can begin editing even before the camera crew begins filming.

Storyboarding can also be a useful way to isolate what is important in a scene and what role the camera plays in conveying that. Look, for example, at a storyboard we have created from the film *Love Actually*. In this 36-second scene, Jamie (played by Colin Firth), a mystery writer, has left London having discovered his girlfriend with his brother. He has gone to a country house in France where he intends to spend his time alone, writing his next book and, presumably, getting over his girlfriend.

The scene is clearly intended to visually convey his disappointment and loneliness. It begins in a darkened room. Jamie (Firth) gradually moves around the room, opening windows and doors to let shafts of light in until the entire room is lit and visible. In the process, we also get what's called an *establishing shot*, a shot showing the house from the outside to let viewers know that Jamie is no longer in London and is now somewhere in a beautiful and quiet country-house setting.

In our storyboard, each panel represents a separate shot, numbered in the sequence in which it occurs on film. (Numbers with a letter indicate a continuation of a shot.) We have also identified what type of shot it is—how close the camera is to the subject. For more on camera distance, see Chapter 1. Also see "Camera Work and Editing: Some Useful Terms," below.

Key to Abbreviations

CU—Close-up

MCU—Medium close-up

ECU—Extreme close-up

POV—Point of view (this means the audience is seeing the shot from the point of view of the character in the scene—in this case, from Jamie's point of view).

LS—Long shot

MLS—Medium long shot

ELS—Extreme long shot

CU (POV)—Close-up point of view shot

Arrows drawn in the sketch indicate movement.

1. MCU. Jamie opening shutters, letting light into totally dark room. (4 sec.)

2. MS. Jamie turns and continues back into the room to open doors and let more light in. (4 sec.)

3. CU (POV) of angel cut-out in shutter. We can barely see hints of the green outside. Everything surrounding the cut-out is black. Only a slit of the shutter opening shows light as the shutter opens. (1 sec.)

3a. CU (POV) of window opening onto LS (POV) of sunlight on pond and trees outside. (1 sec.)

4. LS (Establishing shot) of country house. Jamie barely visible opening doors to the outside. (3 sec.)

5. MLS (Interior shot). Jamie stands looking out the door and then turns to walk behind desk. (4 sec.)

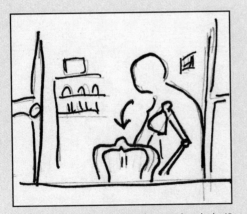

6. MS. Jamie slowly sitting down at his desk. (2 sec.)

6a. MS. Jamie seated at desk in front of typewriter. Turns head to look around and think. Camera has pulled back slightly. (5 sec.)

6b. MS. Camera has pulled back more, revealing more of the desk and the room. Jamie is behind the typewriter, settled and, after a pause, says, "Alone again. [pause] Naturally." (5 sec.)

SUGGESTED ASSIGNMENT

Make a storyboard. Choose a film that interests you for one reason or another. You might enjoy the characters or find the action interesting or the story especially entertaining. Once you have chosen the film, isolate one scene to storyboard.

Remember that each separate shot gets a single panel, so you might want to choose a scene that is brief enough for you to storyboard but also important to the story or character development or theme as a whole.

Storyboarding is generally done before the film is shot, so you might find it a bit tricky when you begin this process. You will have to watch the scene several times, and it is best if you can start and pause or forward slowly through the scene. Time each shot and the scene as a whole.

Once you have completed your storyboard, present it to the class. In your presentation, spend some time addressing the following questions:

- Why did you choose this scene?
- What is the establishing shot of the scene (the shot that tells you where you are)?
- What is the focus or meaning of the scene and how is that indicated in the camera work?
- What is in the frame? What is left out but suggested?
- What or who is the most important element of the scene? How does the camera work indicate that?

CAMERA WORK AND EDITING: SOME USEFUL TERMS

Camera angle—the angle of view in relation to the subject being filmed; the perspective of the viewer shifts depending on whether the camera shoots at a low angle, a high angle, or level with the subject.

Camera distance—the apparent distance of the camera from the frame; in an extreme long shot, the person in the frame is just visible; a long shot brings the person in closer view but the background still predominates the frame; in a medium long shot the figure is framed from about knees up and there is less background visible in the frame; a medium shot frames the body from about waist up; medium close-up, from about chest up; a close-up shot is primarily the head or face that fills the frame; extreme close-up shot moves in on a small part of the body—the eye or mouth, for example.

Editing—the process of joining a series of shots to make scenes and then of moving from shot to shot or scene to scene.

Establishing shot—usually a long shot at the beginning of a film that establishes context for upcoming scenes.

Fade—the gradual disappearance of one image. To fade out, the image ends in black screen. To fade in, an image appears gradually onscreen.

Framing—the space of the film image; what the viewer sees through the camera's frame.

Montage—transitional sequences of a quick series of shots, often to suggest the passage of time or to establish a particular theme.

Off-screen space—the space not visible but assumed outside the frame.

Scene—a unit of film composed of a number of shots, usually a completed episode in the storyline.

Shot/reverse shot—often used during dialogue when the camera shoots one actor then shoots the second actor in the opposite space speaking or looking back in the direction of the first shot.

Shot—an unedited strip of film from the time the camera starts until it stops.

Two-shot—a medium shot that features two actors in the same frame.

FIELDWORK

Taking Inventory of Images

We began this chapter by asserting that visual messages surround us and are so ubiquitous that we barely even notice how many we read in our daily routine. Several of the authors in this chapter have said much the same. In our assignment suggestions, we have asked you to look for and keep track of the visuals you see during your normal daily routine. As you might already have realized, that is a big job because the visual messages that surround us have increased significantly over the years and because most of us are so used to those signs, we take them for granted.

Fieldwork is meant to be more thorough and careful in detailing what is actually out there than a personal journal might be. For this project, you should join with a work group of three or four of your classmates. Your aim will be to get as accurate a count as you can of the number and types of visuals that are typically available in a particular place—in your classroom building, in designated areas of the campus, or in the local town or city where you are doing your work, for example. In other words, you are testing the premise of this chapter by doing fieldwork of your own.

When you have completed your count, write up your report, including schematic diagrams of the area each group member examined and where visuals occurred in those areas. You might also want to indicate on your diagram where the highest concentration of visuals occurred. Present your report to the class.

To be as representative as possible, each member of your group should choose a different part of the building, campus, town, or other location you have chosen for this project.

The space should be strictly limited. For example, if you were to focus on downtown, one member of your group should examine one block of the main street; another can work with a side street; a third might look at a local shopping spot. If you were to focus on your campus, ask different members of the group to focus on different buildings or different, clearly defined areas. Elect one person in the group to coordinate assignments, keep the project focused, and check the group's work for consistency.

1. Begin by surveying the area and noting down every visual message that you see—posters, icons for restrooms or to give directions, television monitors, artwork, etc.
2. Count the number of visual messages in your assigned area.
3. Identify the different media used to make or project the visual messages in the area. (*Media* refers to the technology used to create the message—television, digital display, neon, print, painting, etc.)

For your report:

1. Describe the area your group studied, making sure to indicate how you divided that area among group members. You should also indicate when you visited your site and how long your count took.

2. Provide the total number of visuals in the site as well as the different types or media, the places that held the highest concentration of visuals, and the places with the lowest concentration.

3. Explain, if you can, why different areas have more or fewer visuals.

4. When you present your findings to the class, provide examples of the different types of visuals (you can take digital photos or provide sketches) and project them so the entire class can see your samples.

For more information on writing up a report, see Chapter 2, Classroom Observation.

To learn more about culture and communication, visit www.ablongman.com/george/116

MINING THE ARCHIVE   Advertising Through the Ages

VIGILANCE IS THE PRICE OF BEAUTY

"Mum" is the word!

The Alluring Charm of a Dainty Woman

A simple precaution

An important use

"Mum" prevents all body odors

SPECIAL OFFER COUPON

Locate old copies of any popular magazine. *Good Housekeeping*, for example, began publication in January 1900, so it represents a full century of magazine design. You'll see a dramatic change, especially in advertising design, over these years.

How do the claims of older ads compare with claims in today's advertisements for the same products?

Once you have found several ads ranging from the early to the mid to the late twentieth century and now the twenty-first century, write a report on your findings, comparing the ad copy (written text) of older ads with current advertising. What role do pictoral elements play in those older ads?

How would you describe the change in design over the years? This kind of report is easier to write if you choose one type of product for a focus—for example, cosmetics, bath soaps, laundry detergent, cigarettes.

If you don't have access to a good library, you can find a stockpile of ads from newspapers and magazines between 1911 and 1955 at Duke University's Ad*Access Project. This project is housed in the Rare Book, Manuscript, and Special Collections room at the Duke University Library and can be accessed on the Internet at **http://scriptorium. lib.duke.edu/adaccess.** The site also includes useful information about copyright and fair use policies for using images for your class projects.

Style

Courtesy of Nirvana L.L.C.

© 1998 Nirvana Under License to CBD Visionary Inc.

The rhythm is so dynamic that a "slice of life" seen from a cafe terrace is a spectacle. The most diverse elements collide and jostle one another there. The interplay of contrasts is so violent that there is always exaggeration in the effect you glimpse.

On the boulevards two men are carrying some immense gilded letters in a handcart; the effect is so unexpected that everyone stops and listens. *There is the origin of the modern spectacle.* The shock of the surprise effect.

Objects, lights, the colors that used to be fixed and restrained have become alive and mobile.

—Fernand Leger

In societies dominated by modern conditions of production, life is presented as an immense accumulation of spectacles. Everything that was directly lived has receded into a representation.

—Guy Debord

Americans live in a style-conscious culture—even elementary school children know the difference between Air Jordans and the cheaper imitations. By the time they enter junior high school, most American adolescents are already highly skilled at distinguishing between brand names. They are learning to recognize the difference, say, between the Gap and Wal-Mart, between the Pottery Barn and Sears, between a Ford Taurus and a BMW. And, of course, they are also learning that these differences *make a difference.*

The point is more than the importance of being able to recognize brand names, though this is certainly of great interest to consumers and manufacturers alike. The real lesson young Americans learn is that they live in a world where it matters what brand of clothes or furniture or car they buy. It matters what style of music they listen to, how they wear their hair, whether they're tatooed or pierced, and what kind of food they like to eat. Even mundane personal belongings—everyday-use objects from staplers to toothbrushes to laptop computers—matter too.

All of these things matter because the styles we follow and products we use send messages about who we are. They're part of the identity kits we all put together to make up a self.

In many ways, it seems that such a concern for personal style and the appearance of objects is shallow and trivial. After all, what does it really matter whether someone's clothes or music or CD player or computer is at the cutting edge of style? Why should anyone care? One reason is that style is a guide to economic and social class in America. Style identifies. Whether consciously or unconsciously, we make judgments about people based on their appearance and their style. Simply by growing up in American culture, we acquire a sense of the style appropriate to different walks of life—how, for example, a high school teacher, a business executive, a truck driver, or a rock star ought to look.

Style communicates messages about economic and social class precisely because we share with others cultural codes that define what's normal and expected. For example, we expect wealthy professionals in metropolitan areas to be museum members, go to the opera, and enjoy gourmet food and fine wine. On the other hand, we are likely to expect that working-class men in the Midwest drink beer, listen to classic rock or country and western, and support their local pro football team. This doesn't mean that everyone in a particular social group conforms to these cultural codes. What it does indicate, however, is that style carries cultural meanings that go far beyond individual likes and dislikes.

Style, in other words, is linked to the way of life that identifies groups of people, cultures, and subcultures. If the styles we adopt seem to be freely taken personal choices, they are contained nonetheless in a larger system of cultural codes that organize the way we think about identity, social status, prestige, good (and bad) taste, tradition, and innovation. The role of food is a good example. On the one hand, the style of food people eat can reaffirm their ties to the ethnicity and traditions of their ancestors, as has been the case for generations of Italian Americans, Chinese Americans, Mexican Americans, and others in the United States. On the other hand, food may serve as the basis for a break with the lifestyle of one's upbringing and a new identification with a different group of people, as may be the case when people become vegetarians or convert to Islam and stop eating pork. Think of it this way: it would be nearly unimaginable to have the countercultural styles of hippies, punks, grunge, and goths without also having a recognized mainstream cultural code that can be rejected, parodied, violated, or otherwise rebelled against.

Fashion designers, graphic designers, and product designers understand this intimate connection between style and identity. They design everything from corporate logos and brand trademarks to the latest style of jeans and athletic shoes to computers and cars. Their job is to match styles to people's identities and, at the same time, to create styles that offer people new identities. But in spite of all these outside influences, people still make choices about what they wear, the products they use, the music they listen to, the way they decorate their living space, and so on, that matches their own personal style of life.

This chapter looks not only at the professional designers whose work floods the contemporary marketplace, both also at rebel designers, such as the punks of the 1970s and 1980s who created a whole new style and cultural identity out of mainstream objects.

STYLE IN REVOLT: REVOLTING STYLE

— Dick Hebdige

Dick Hebdige is a lecturer in communication at Goldsmith College, University of London. The following selection comes from *Subculture: The Meaning of Style* (1979), in which he examines the political and cultural importance of postwar British youth cultures, including the punk movement. In this excerpt, Hebdige looks at how the punks used style as a tool of disruption and revolt. This selection is also an introduction to the Visual Essay that follows, "Graphic Design in Rock Culture."

SUGGESTION FOR READING   As you read, notice the range of evidence Hebdige brings forward to characterize the style of punk culture. Underline/highlight as many different examples of punk style as you can find. Notice too how the final paragraph on graphic design and typography serves as an introduction to the graphic style of the rock posters and T-shirts in the Visual Essay.

Nothing was holy to us. Our movement was neither mystical, communistic nor anarchistic. All of these movements had some sort of programme, but ours was completely nihilistic. We spat on everything, including ourselves. Our symbol was nothingness, a vacuum, a void.

George Grosz on Dada

We're so pretty, oh so pretty . . . vac-unt.

The Sex Pistols

1   Although it was often directly offensive (T-shirts covered in swear words) and threatening (terrorist/guerilla outfits) punk style was defined principally through the violence of its cut ups. Like Duchamp's ready mades—manufactured objects which qualified as art because he chose to call them such, the most unremarkable and inappropriate items—a pin, a plastic clothes peg, a television component, a razor blade, a tampon—could be brought within the province of punk (un)fashion. Anything within or without reason could be turned into part of what Vivien Westwood called "confrontation dressing" so long as the rupture between "natural" and constructed context was clearly visible (i.e., the rule would seem to be: if the cap doesn't fit, wear it).

Objects borrowed from the most sordid of contexts found a place in the punks' ensembles: lavatory chains were draped in graceful arcs across chests encased in plastic bin-liners. Safety pins were taken out of their domestic "utility" context and worn as gruesome ornaments through the cheek, ear or lip. "Cheap" trashy fabrics (PVC, plastic, lurex, etc.) in vulgar designs (e.g., mock leopard skin) and "nasty" colours, long discarded by the quality end of the fashion industry as obsolete kitsch, were salvaged by the punks and turned into garments (fly boy drainpipes, "common" mini-skirts) which offered self-conscious commentaries on the notions of modernity and taste. Conventional ideas of prettiness were jettisoned along with the traditional feminine lore of cosmetics. Contrary to the advice of every woman's magazine, make-up for both boys and girls was worn to be seen. Faces became abstract portraits: sharply observed and meticulously executed studies in alienation. Hair was obviously dyed (hay yellow, jet black, or bright orange with tufts of green or bleached in question marks), and T-shirts and trousers told the story of their own construction with multiple zips and outside seams clearly displayed. Similarly, fragments of school uniform (white brinylon shirts, school ties) were symbolically defiled (the shirts covered in graffiti, or fake blood; the ties left undone) and juxtaposed against leather drains or shocking pink mohair tops. The perverse and the abnormal were valued intrinsically. In particular, the illicit iconography of sexual fetishism was used to predictable effect. Rapist masks and rubber wear, leather bodices and fishnet stockings, implausibly pointed stiletto heeled shoes, the whole paraphernalia of bondage—the belts, straps and chains—were exhumed from the boudoir, closet and the pornographic film and placed on the street where they retained their forbidden connotations. Some young punks even donned the dirty raincoat—that most prosaic symbol of sexual "kinkiness"—and hence expressed their deviance in suitably proletarian terms.

Of course, punk did more than upset the wardrobe. It undermined every relevant discourse. Thus dancing, usually an involving and expressive medium in British rock and mainstream pop cultures, was turned into a dumbshow of blank robotics. Punk dances bore absolutely no relation to the desultory frugs and clinches which Geoff Mungham describes as intrinsic to the respectable working-class ritual of Saturday night at the Top Rank or Mecca.[1] Indeed, overt displays of heterosexual interest were generally regarded with contempt and suspicion (who let the BOF/wimp[2] in?) and conventional courtship patterns found no place on the floor in dances like the pogo, the pose and the robot. Though the pose did allow for a minimum sociability (i.e., it could involve two people) the "couple" were generally of the same sex and physical contact was ruled out of court as the relationship depicted in the dance was a "professional" one. One participant would strike a suitable cliché fashion pose while the other would fall into a classic "Bailey" crouch to snap an imaginary picture. The pogo forebade even this much interaction, though admittedly there was always a good deal of masculine jostling in front of the stage. In fact the pogo was a caricature—a reductio ad absurdum of all the solo dance styles associated with rock music. It resembled the "anti dancing" of the "Leapniks" which Melly describes in connection with the trad boom (Melly, 1972). The same abbreviated gestures—leaping into the air, hands clenched to the sides, to head an imaginary ball—were repeated without variation in time to the strict mechanical rhythms of the music. In contrast to the hippies' languid, free-form dancing, and the "idiot dancing" of the heavy metal rockers, the pogo made improvisation redundant: the only variations were imposed by changes in the tempo of the music—fast numbers being "interpreted" with manic abandon in the form of frantic on-the-spots, while the slower ones were pogoed with a detachment bordering on the catatonic.

The robot, a refinement witnessed only at the most exclusive punk gatherings, was both more "expressive" and less "spontaneous" within the very narrow range such terms acquired in punk usage. It consisted of barely perceptible twitches of the head and hands or more extravagant lurches (Frankenstein's first steps?) which were abruptly halted at random points. The resulting pose was held for several moments, even minutes, and the whole sequence was as suddenly, as unaccountably, resumed and re-enacted. Some zealous punks carried things one step further and choreographed whole evenings, turning themselves for a matter of hours, like Gilbert and George,[3] into automata, living sculptures.

5 The music was similarly distinguished from mainstream rock and pop. It was uniformly basic and direct in its appeal, whether through intention or lack of expertise. If the latter, then the

punks certainly made a virtue of necessity ("We want to be amateurs"—Johnny Rotten). Typically, a barrage of guitars with the volume and treble turned to maximum accompanied by the occasional saxophone would pursue relentless (un)melodic lines against a turbulent background of cacophonous drumming and screamed vocals. Johnny Rotten succinctly defined punk's position on harmonics: "We're into chaos not music."

The names of the groups (the Unwanted, the Rejects, the Sex Pistols, the Clash, the Worst, etc.) and the titles of the songs: "Belsen Was a Gas," "If You Don't Want to Fuck Me, Fuck Off," "I Wanna Be Sick on You," reflected the tendency towards willful desecration and the voluntary assumption of outcast status which characterized the whole punk movement. Such tactics were, to adapt Levi-Strauss's famous phrase, "things to whiten mother's hair with." In the early days at least, these "garage bands" could dispense with musical pretensions and substitute, in the traditional romantic terminology, "passion" for "technique," the language of the common man for the arcane posturings of the existing élite, the now familiar armoury of frontal attacks for the bourgeois notion of entertainment or the classical concept of "high art."

It was in the performance arena that punk groups posed the clearest threat to law and order. Certainly, they succeeded in subverting the conventions of concert and nightclub entertainment. Most significantly, they attempted both physically and in terms of lyrics and life-style to move closer to their audiences. This in itself is by no means unique: the boundary between artist and audience has often stood as a metaphor in revolutionary aesthetics (Brecht, the surrealists, Dada, Marcuse, etc.) for that larger and more intransigent barrier which separates art and the dream from reality and life under capitalism.[4] The stages of those venues secure enough to host "new wave" acts were regularly invaded by hordes of punks, and if the management refused to tolerate such blatant disregard for ballroom etiquette, then the groups and their followers could be drawn closer together in a communion of spittle and mutual abuse. At the Rainbow Theatre in May 1977 as the Clash played

"White Riot," chairs were ripped out and thrown at the stage. Meanwhile, every performance, however apocalyptic, offered palpable evidence that things could change, indeed were changing: that performance itself was a possibility no authentic punk should discount. Examples abounded in the music press of "ordinary fans" (Siouxsie of Siouxsie and the Banshees, Sid Vicious of the Sex Pistols, Mark P of Sniffin Glue, Jordan of the Ants) who had made the symbolic crossing from the dance floor to the stage. Even the humbler positions in the rock hierarchy could provide an attractive alternative to the drudgery of manual labour, office work or a youth on the dole. The Finchley Boys, for instance, were reputedly taken off the football terraces by the Stranglers and employed as roadies.

If these "success stories" were, as we have seen, subject to a certain amount of "skewed" interpretation in the press, then there were innovations in other areas which made opposition to dominant definitions possible. Most notably, there was an attempt, the first by a predominantly working-class youth culture, to provide an alternative critical space within the subculture itself to counteract the hostile or at least ideologically inflected coverage which punk was receiving in the media. The existence of an alternative punk press demonstrated that it was not only clothes or music that could be immediately and cheaply produced from the limited resources at hand. The fanzines (*Sniffin Glue*, *Ripped and Torn*, etc.) were journals edited by an individual or a group, consisting of reviews, editorials and interviews with prominent punks, produced on a small scale as cheaply as possible, stapled together and distributed through a small number of sympathetic retail outlets.

The language in which the various manifestoes were framed was determinedly "working class" (i.e., it was liberally peppered with swear words) and typing errors and grammatical mistakes, misspellings and jumbled pagination were left uncorrected in the final proof. Those corrections and crossings out that were made before publication were left to be deciphered by the reader. The overwhelming impression was one of urgency and immediacy, of a paper produced in indecent haste, of memos from the front line.

10   This inevitably made for a strident button-holing type of prose which, like the music it described, was difficult to "take in" in any quantity. Occasionally a written, more abstract item—what Harvey Garfinkel (the American ethnomethodologist) might call an "aid to sluggish imaginations"—might creep in. For instance, *Sniffin Glue*, the first fanzine and the one which achieved the highest circulation, contained perhaps the single most inspired item of propaganda produced by the subculture—the definitive statement of punk's do-it-yourself philosophy—a diagram showing three finger positions on the neck of a guitar over the caption: "Here's one chord, here's two more, now form your own band."

Even the graphics and typography used on record covers and fanzines were homologous with punk's subterranean and anarchic style. The two typographic models were graffiti which was translated into a flowing "spray can" script, and the ransom note in which individual letters cut up from a variety of sources (newspapers, etc.) in different type faces were pasted together to form an anonymous message. The Sex Pistols' "God Save the Queen" sleeve (later turned into T-shirts, posters, etc.) for instance incorporated both styles: the roughly assembled legend was pasted across the Queen's eyes and mouth which were further disfigured by those black bars used in pulp detective magazines to conceal identity (i.e., they connote crime or scandal). Finally, the process of ironic self abasement which characterized the subculture was extended to the name "punk" itself which, with its derisory connotations of "mean and petty villainy," "rotten," "worthless," etc., was generally preferred by hardcore members of the subculture to the more neutral "new wave."[5]

NOTES

1. In his P.O. account of the Saturday night dance in an industrial town, Mungham (1976) shows how the constricted quality of working-class life is carried over into the ballroom in the form of courtship rituals, masculine paranoia and an atmosphere of sullenly repressed sexuality. He paints a gloomy picture of joyless evenings spent in the desperate pursuit of "booze and birds" (or "blokes and a romantic bus-ride home") in a controlled setting where "spontaneity is regarded by managers and their staff—principally the bouncers—as the potential hand-maiden of rebellion".

2. BOF = Boring Old Fart. Wimp = "wet."

3. Gilbert and George mounted their first exhibition in 1970 when, clad in identical conservative suits, with metallized hands and faces, a glove, a stick and a tape recorder, they won critical acclaim by performing a series of carefully controlled and endlessly repeated movements on a dais while miming to Flanagan and Allen's "Underneath the Arches." Other pieces with titles like "Lost Day" and "Normal Boredom" have since been performed at a variety of major art galleries throughout the world.

4. Of course, rock music had always threatened to dissolve these categories, and rock performances were popularly associated with all forms of riot and disorder—from the slashing of cinema seats by teddy boys through Beatlemania to the hippy happenings and festivals where freedom was expressed less aggressively in nudity, drug taking and general "spontaneity." However, punk represented a new departure.

5. The word "punk," like the black American "funk" and "superbad," would seem to form part of that "special language of fantasy and alienation" which Charles Winick describes (1959), "in which values are reversed and in which 'terrible' is a description of excellence." See also Wolfe (1969) where he describes the "cruising" scene in Los Angeles in the mid-60s—a subculture of custom-built cars, sweatshirts and "high-piled, perfect coiffure" where "rank" was a term of approval: Rank! Rank is just the natural outgrowth of Rotten . . . Roth and Schorsch grew up in the Rotten Era of Los Angeles teenagers. The idea was to have a completely rotten attitude towards the adult world, meaning, in the long run, the whole established status structure, the whole system of people organizing their lives around a job, fitting into the social structure embracing the whole community. The idea in Rotten was to drop out of conventional status competition into the smaller netherworld of Rotten Teenagers and start one's own league.

WORKS CITED

Melly, G. (1972). *Revolt into Style*. Penguin.

Mungham, G. (1976). "Youth in Pursuit of Itself." In G. Mungham and G. Pearson (eds.), *Working Class Youth Culture*. Routledge & Kegan Paul.

Winick, C. (1959). "The Uses of Drugs by Jazz Musicians." *Social Problems* 7, no. 3, Winter.

Wolfe, T. (1969). *The Pump House Gang*. Bantam.

Graphic Design in Rock Culture

This Visual Essay gathers artifacts from rock culture—a poster, an album cover, an AC/DC T-shirt, and a Nasa rave flyer. (See also the Nirvana decal at the beginning of the chapter.) We have tried to choose examples of distinctive styles, including the psychedelic '60s, punk, heavy metal, grunge, and dance. As you look through the various visual artifacts, consider the defining graphic style of each example. What does the graphic style seem to express about a particular style or movement in rock culture? What visual elements does it use?

NEVER MIND THE BOLLOCKS

HERE'S THE

SeX PisTOLS

Design: Michael Szabo; Art Direction: DB + Scotto

SUGGESTIONS FOR DISCUSSION

1. Make a list of the examples of punk style you underlined or highlighted while reading Hebdige's "Style in Revolt" article. Work with others in class to construct a table that starts with general categories (clothes, music, dancing, etc.) and then fill in the first column with examples from the punk movement. Add further columns on youth styles and subcultures since the punks. Name the subcultural style and give examples.

	PUNKS	GRUNGE	HIP HOP, ETC.
Clothes			
Dancing			
Music			

2. Hebdige's work is primarily about British punks in the late 1970s, though punk style still has an influence on fashion, music, and graphics. If Hebdige were writing a book on American and/or British youth subcultures in the late 1990s and 2000s that are in revolt against the dominant culture, what groups and styles might he focus on (or would he find any at all)? What is the nature of the revolt? How is it expressed stylistically?

3. It is possible to present here only a few examples of "Graphic Design in Rock Culture." To add to the Visual Essay, bring your own examples of posters, fanzines, T-shirts, and album covers to class. Be prepared to explain what your examples signify about a particular style in rock culture. Consider the visual elements—the style of font, the layout, images, and whether any aspects of the design are borrowed and recycled.

SUGGESTIONS FOR WRITING

1. Use the table you constructed to identify an example of subcultural or group style that interests you. Pick a particular example—clothes, music, dancing, graphics, and so on— to serve as the topic of an essay. In the essay, explain who the group or subculture is and then show how the example you've chosen illustrates some central meaning about the group's style.

2. As Hebdige explains, punks used common objects and forms of dress in ways that departed from their originally intended uses to create new meanings. This kind of cultural recycling, however, is by no means limited to the punks. Others have recycled old styles to produce retro looks that are often both ironic and nostalgic. Write an essay about a group or style that recycles fashions and objects. Explain how the recycling creates new meanings for older styles.

3. Use Hebdige's analysis of punk graphics and typography as a model to analyze the graphic design of a visual artifact from rock culture. Use any of the examples in the Visual Essay or others you've brought to class or found on your own.

Theme Parties

People like to dress in costumes—to go trick or treating on Halloween and to go to costume parties. There are interesting questions to ask about why we like to put on costumes and masks and to change our identities, if only briefly. What is it about costumes that is so appealing? How do costumes take us out of our ordinary, day-to-day lives and transform us into other kinds of beings? What is the social function of parties that gather together people wearing costumes? These questions are the backdrop for a certain kind of party where individuals dress up according to themes— *Star Trek* parties (where people dress up as their favorite character), punk parties (where people spike their hair and put on spiked belts and ripped pants), and 1950s martini parties (where everyone puts on the fashions of the time and listens to Frank Sinatra).

Such theme parties are, for the most part, simply good fun, and they have become a part of the college students' repertoire of popular entertainment. The two following readings, however, focus on theme parties that are more problematic—and that raise further questions about why people put on costumes. As you will see, the first reading focuses on the controversy that arose when Britain's Prince Harry wore a Nazi costume to a " colonial or native" party in England. The second reading is a commentary on theme parties in the United States—in this case the "ghetto parties" staged by high school and college students.

THE VERY NASTY PARTY

— *Mark Lawson*

Mark Lawson is a columnist for the British newspaper the *Guardian* and the author of the novels *Enough Is Enough or the Emergency Government* (2003) and *Going Out Live* (2002). What appears here is an excerpt from "The Very Nasty Party," his column in the *Guardian* in 2005.

SUGGESTION FOR READING In many ways, the title of Mark Lawson's column in the *Guardian* tells the story: it was a "very nasty party." As you read, notice what exactly makes the "colonial or native" party "nasty" in Lawson's view.

— Britain's Prince Harry in Nazi uniform.

1 It may be some consolation to the Prince of Wales that it could have been worse. The owner of Maud's Cotswold Costumes told the Sun that Prince Harry looked at SS costumes but "to be honest they all come in small sizes and there was no way any of them would have fitted him." So the prince's father can be grateful that he inherited his mother's height because the third in line to the throne was forced to settle for a lower Nazi rank.

Various defenders of the swastika prince have suggested that he has suffered enough criticism, and, while I think he deserves at least a few more days of burning ears, there's another aspect of the matter to be considered.

Every so often, something happens—an investigative documentary, a social worker's report into the murder of a child—that lifts up the British carpet to show the stamped-down filth. This is such a moment. While Harry's costume was shocking, it seems equally astonishing that, in 2005, there is a section of society in which it is not considered odd for a teenager to throw a party with the theme of "colonial or native" and at which, according to some reports, young male guests blacked up their faces. The implication of much coverage is that Harry misjudged the party mood, but perhaps he merely took the nasty theme to its logical conclusion.

Equally perplexing is the revelation of the range available at Maud's Cotswold Costumes. Given that the Nazi kit was presumably not stocked just in case a prince of the realm wished to perpetrate a monstrous moral gaffe, the question arises of just who would hire it in normal circumstances. This calculation is made more complicated by the owner's quoted claim that the SS outfits "all come in small sizes."

5 Unless school theatre clubs or amateur dramatics groups for people of restricted growth are constantly putting on productions of Colditz throughout Gloucestershire, then it must be assumed that fancy-dress parties at which people wear Nazi uniforms are common in middle England, and that the chaps favouring this rig tend to be quite little. (This would be historically consistent, as few of the leading figures in the

actual Nazi party were at risk of banging their heads on the ceiling.)

There has been some attempt by friends of Harry and the monarchy to mount what might be called the Mel Brooks defence. This line suggests that some confusion over matters of taste is understandable when one of the West End's hottest tickets is a musical in which the swastika is camply treated as a kind of drag. As the only reviewer in Britain who disliked The Producers (worried by the spectacle of an audience whooping at dancers in Nazi insignia), I have some sympathy with this view, but the musical's fans argue that Brooks is inoculated against the possibility of offence by being Jewish. Unless something lies in the royal bloodline beyond even the most lurid internet rumours, Prince Harry can hardly claim this exculpation.

But, if Harry Windsor has made a large miscalculation, Tony Blair may also have made a significant slip on this issue. The need to give the head of state's grandson a dressing down for dressing up was a tricky moment for the prime minister. Throughout his eight years in office, almost all his public pronouncements on prominent Britons have demanded praise of the recently dead. Even when he had cause to attack (Brown, Cook, Mandelson, etc), he has generally resisted for tactical reasons.

So he had no easy template to follow when calculating the government's response to Prince Harry's Germanic pantomime. Unable to say "he is the people's Nazi" or "this is no time for sound-bites, but I see the badge of history on his shoulder," Blair seems to have panicked and sent Lord Falconer on to Question Time to put foam on the fire: youthful enthusiasm, all woken up with regrets in our time and so on.

This was a continuation of Blair's long-time policy of supporting the monarchy wherever possible in order to give signals of moderation to middle England and the tabloids. But, on this occasion, the populist approach may well have been to box Harry's ears. The sight of the most famous British 20-year-old outside the Premiership wearing a Nazi armband was surely—please, hopefully—shocking to most people.

10   In calling for a fuller apology, Michael Howard may for once have outwitted Blair in a publicity game—although, as the most prominent Jewish politician in recent British history, he may also have cause for deep worry about the social subculture inadvertently revealed by the row. For, at the risk of political stereotype, do you think it likely that the kind of people whose kids have "colonial or native" parties fitted out by shops that stock SS costumes tend to be Labour or Liberal Democrat voters?

MISTAKEN IDENTITY:
THE PERILS OF THEME PARTIES

— *Shana Pearlman*

Shana Peterson was an undergraduate major in English and Modern Studies in 1999 when "Mistaken Identities: The Perils of Theme Parties" was published in the *Declaration*, a student weekly tabloid of opinion at the University of Virginia. As you will see, she addresses the question of "ghetto parties" on college campuses, where students dress up as "pimps" and "hos."

SUGGESTION   As you read, consider why Shana Pearlman has responded to "ghetto parties" with a "mix-
FOR READING   ture of horror and incredulity." Notice how she cites Eric Lott's analysis of the dependence of "cultural definitions of whiteness" on "cultural definitions of blackness."

1 Ah, the Greek system at the University. It's controversial and oft-debated from the outside looking in, but inside it is a pretty sweet deal. Life in the fraternities and sororities is as easy and simple as Chef Boyardee ravioli, as carefree as Leave It to Beaver, as comfortable as American Eagle pajamas. What these students really need, however, is a good party from time to time; as social organizations, the parties are what define fraternities and sororities. The form those parties take (the formal, semi-formal, and themed mixer) define them as well. What these parties provide is a chance to step outside normal, everyday life for an evening; how they provide that opportunity can sometimes take strange and disturbing twists and turns.

The web magazine Salon (www.salon-magazine.com) recently ran an article about a controversial party that took place among the Greek community at Dartmouth College. Last year something called a "ghetto party" was sponsored by several fraternities and sororities there, sending the participants "scurrying for Afro wigs, toy handguns, and crimping irons." When word of this party leaked to the larger community it caused quite a stink. There was an almost daily flurry of protests, demonstrations, and letters to the editor, according to the student newspaper The Dartmouth. African-American and Asian-American applicants to the Ivy League school dropped by 75 percent and 25 percent respectively; op-ed columnists hastened to blame the decrease on a hostile racial environment exemplified by events like the ghetto party.

I read about these happenings with a mixture of growing horror and incredulity. I was once in a sorority myself (before it was recolonized because its sisters weren't WASPy enough—but that's another story) and remembered that we too sponsored a "ghetto party." When we asked our social chair how one dressed for such a party, she blithely replied, "Oh, you know, track bottoms, sports bras, bandannas, a bottle of Colt 45 in your hand—pretty much like your average crack ho." During my

"research" for this piece I happened across the Sigma Sigma Sigma web page and discovered in their pictures section a cheery little photograph entitled "Straight Out of Compton." Compton, for those of you who may not know, is a lower-class African-American neighborhood in Los Angeles, made famous by gangsta rap. In the picture are five white girls and one Asian girl at some sort of restaurant or bar, all wearing matching track bottoms, bandannas and sports bras and revealing a bit of tummy for an appreciative male who appears in the picture. It seems "ghetto parties" are a somewhat ordinary occurrence in the Greek system. Do they make only me grimace? Why isn't everyone else's stomach turning?

I realize that at this university the Greek and non-Greek communities are relatively separated and that neither really cares to know what goes on in the other. But just as fraternities and sororities care how they appear in print (and no doubt one or two will write to opine, "But other organizations have offensive parties too!"), we should all think about the way we choose to portray others. It's very easy to pick out an image or two to represent a culture for the purposes of dress-up, but what does that do to true members of a culture? What does it do to the people who appropriate that culture? What is the cultural significance if upper-middle-class white girls dress up as though they were "from the ghetto?"

5 The rules for a ghetto party for women mean that you are to dress as though you were a "crack ho," as though you came from Compton. But Compton is not just a symbol you find in gangsta rap, it's a real neighborhood where people live. What does it mean to equate "Compton," the neighborhood, with "crack ho," the image familiar from countless music videos? Does it imply that all working-class African-American women who live in Compton are "hos"? And since a woman from Compton can so easily be reduced to a costume and a drink, does that imply that ALL working-class African-American women can so easily be reduced? And

if we follow that argument, we all know what that makes the male audience for which the women are dressing up. What does it mean when nice white boys take on the role of pimp? Considering the way the fraternities broker the Greek social scheme, and sororities live or die on being able to attract enough fraternities to have a full mixer schedule, it doesn't seem too far off the mark.

Whether or not the Greek system ought to be faulted for its lack of ethnic diversity isn't clear. What is clear is that it is largely white. Professor Eric Lott of the English Department has made a case for cultural definitions of whiteness being dependent on cultural definitions of blackness. White needs black as something against which it is identified. Lott uses examples such as minstrel shows and Al Jolson to demonstrate how this has happened throughout American history; the white aping of black culture sets whiteness apart while conversely demonstrating a curious dependence upon and solidarity with

it. The trouble is that in practical terms, minstrel shows were racist and employed negative racial stereotypes for entertainment. The same politics are at work in ghetto parties. White girls and boys dress up according to popular African-American images to underscore their whiteness, yet they are racist and misogynist. Representations of African Americans in popular culture are few and far between—the ones that prevail are often those that are the most suspect. Yet in order to use blackness to define whiteness, those are the images that have to be used.

This article won't stop ghetto parties, nor will it cause protests on the Lawn to occur. What I hope it will do is bring about awareness of how we represent other people. This kind of exchange shouldn't be simply behind closed doors; it's important to understand the appeal behind being a ho or a pimp. In other words, we had better know what we mean when we say we're "Straight Out of Compton" via the manicured lawns and freshly scrubbed Jeeps of sweet suburbia.

SUGGESTIONS FOR DISCUSSION

1. Think about the costumes you have worn at various points in the past. What was the occasion? What costume did you wear? In what sense did wearing the costume amount to a change of identity, if only briefly? Compare your experience to that of your classmates. What generalizations can you draw about the social function of putting on costumes?

2. The title of Mark Lawson's column announces his theme—it was a "very nasty party." Why does he think so? What, exactly, is in question about "colonial or native" parties? Consider the photo from the party reproduced here.

3. "Ghetto parties" have become commonplace events for high school and college students. Do a Google search to find photos from "ghetto parties." What do you make of this cultural phenomenon? What is Shana Pearlman's evaluation? Consider her discussion of the relationship between "whiteness" and "blackness" in American culture.

SUGGESTIONS FOR WRITING

1. Write an essay that looks at your own experience dressing up in costumes. Consider the occasion that called on you to wear a costume and your choice of costume. Why did you choose the costume? Consider also the costumes other people wore. What do you see as the meaning of dressing up in this occasion?

2. Consider Mark Lawson's report that Maud's Cotswold Costumes apparently had a number of Nazi costumes to rent. Why would anyone want to dress up in a Nazi costume? Presumably neither Prince Harry nor most of those who rent Nazi costumes are supporters of Hitler and Nazism. Write an essay that explains the significance of dressing up in Nazi gear.

3. Write a response to Shana Pearlman's column on "ghetto parties." First, you need to summarize briefly her position. You may agree or disagree with her, extend one of the points she makes, or develop your own analysis. Your task here, whatever writing strategy you choose, is to make sense of the "ghetto parties" phenomenon and what it tells us about contemporary American culture.

AXLE OF EVIL
America's Twisted Love Affair with Sociopathic Cars

— Gregg Easterbrook

Gregg Easterbrook's "Axle of Evil," which appeared in the January 20, 2003, issue of the *New Republic*, is a lengthy review of Keith Bradsher's *High and Mighty: SUVs—The World's Most Dangerous Vehicles and How They Got That Way*. Easterbrook is lavish in his praise of the book, saying that it "belongs on the same shelf as Ralph Nader's *Unsafe at Any Speed* and Ida Tarbell's *The History of Standard Oil*, chronicles of the dangerous interaction of corporate perfidy and regulatory breakdown." The following is the fourth section of the review, where Easterbrook discusses the meaning of Sport Utility Vehicle (SUV) style and design.

SUGGESTION FOR READING   As you read, notice how Gregg Easterbrook identifies two distinct appeals of SUVs: "sociopathy and fantasy." Consider how he provides evidence from *High and Mighty* and elsewhere to support his analysis.

1   "They tend to be people who are insecure and vain. They are frequently nervous about their marriages and uncomfortable about parenthood. They often lack confidence in their driving skills. Above all, they are apt to be self-centered and self-absorbed, with little interest in their neighbors." This is Bradsher's summary of the auto industry's own marketing research about SUV buyers, and he adduces numerous on-the-record comments from auto-marketing gurus to back this up. One such wise man, named Clotaire Rapaille, tells the Big Three that people buy SUVs "because they want to look as menacing as possible." It is perhaps not startling that rather than trying to alter these buyer proclivities, the manufacturers of SUVs have tried to encourage them. There are lots of self-centered and self-absorbed people with little interest in their neighbors. Somebody finally made a class of vehicles designed to bring out the worst in them.

Many SUVs, such as the Durango, have been consciously engineered to look as threatening as possible, with auto companies using focus groups and other techniques documented in *High and Mighty* to determine which features and styling cues suggest an anti-social message and then zeroing in on them. The styling goal for the oversized Dodge Ram megapickup was "a vehicle that would make other motorists want to get out of your way." Cadillac markets the Escalade with photography staged to make it appear to be an armored combat vehicle, over the huge-type sell line YIELD.

Bradsher asserts that Rapaille, who will not drive an SUV himself owing to the danger of rollover, has been an influential force in encouraging Detroit to make SUVs and light pickups heavier and nastier-looking, arguing that selfish modern buyers think they can cut off other drivers more easily in wheels that seem threatening. Certainly not all large cars are marketed with a hostile message. Minivans, which though also large are far safer, more fuel efficient, and lower-polluting than SUVs and pickups, are marketed with an emphasis on positive values: caring for children, arriving safely, offering rides to the softball game. SUVs and pickups are sold by appealing to belligerence, and what you promote is often what you get.

One hostility-intensification feature is the "grill guard" that SUV manufacturers promote. Grill guards, useful mainly for pushing oryx out of the road in Namibia, have no application under normal driving conditions. But they make SUVs look angrier, especially when viewed through a rearview mirror. (The grotesque new General Motors Hummer H2 offers a cage of steel in front of the grill for an additional $525.) Grill guards also increase the chance that an SUV will kill someone in an accident. As with so many other aspects of the SUV, the addition of the grill guards is unregulated—though standard cars, for which there are strict bumper rules, are not supposed to have metal grill guards.

5   In addition to marketing hostility, SUV manufacturers assiduously promote the fiction that the true purpose of the SUV is a romantic off-road adventure to the far reaches of nowhere. Just as sports-car manufacturers show their products boldly barreling around the corners of country roads with no other cars anywhere in sight, SUV ads feature these vehicles climbing pristine hillsides, perching atop natural wonders, fording rough and beautiful streams, or racing through magnificent canyons. There is never anybody or anything in the scene except the sovereign SUV, which seems to have all of creation to itself. Often the advertisements are computer-generated productions in which an SUV is digitally spliced into a natural scene because the vehicle is not in fact capable of getting to these farthest reaches of sublimity.

All automakers are guilty of advancing the fiction that SUVs are intended for off-road adventures, but nothing surpasses in romantic deception Ford's "No Boundaries" campaign for the company's Explorer, Expedition, and Excursion

SUVs, in which it is suggested that these vehicles are used primarily to support kayaking, Himalayan ascents, and Peruvian anthropology. The earth-crushing Excursion weighs four tons, versus one and a half tons for the typical car. Ford's website gives the length and height of the Excursion down to tenths of an inch, but says nothing about its weight.

The marketing of SUVs as if they had something to do with the outdoors plainly appeals to aging boomers who fancy themselves adventurous and free-spirited while living tame suburban lives. If the overwhelming majority of traveling boomers never stray far from their hotels, millions still wish to maintain the illusion that they might. Bradsher reports that one of Daimler-Chrysler's chief SUV designers convinced the company that what counted was not how SUVs were actually used but "the fantasy of what [the buyer] might want to do during a vacation, and the ability to show friends and other motorists that they really were the bold people they liked to see themselves as." That SUVs are becoming popular with young buyers suggests that the daydream has multi-generational appeal.

The outdoor-adventure illusion of SUVs makes these vehicles worse in a nefarious way that relates to their treatment in the media. *High and Mighty* includes an intriguing discussion on the role of the press in auto sales. For consumer items such as soft drinks, studies show that buyers make choices based 90 percent on advertising and promotion ("paid media," in corporate terms) and just 10 percent on what newspapers and magazines say ("free media"). When it comes to cars, by contrast, people tend to read up: studies show that only 20 percent of the buyer's decision is based on promotion, with the rest coming from what buyers read and hear from the "free media." It is reassuring to learn that the power of the press still exists somewhere; but when it comes to SUVs, this power is consistently misused.

The automotive writers in newspapers and the many "buff books"—*Car & Driver, Road & Track*, and the rest—tend to review SUVs by focusing on their off-road prowess. Auto writers drive these machines up hills, across boulders, and through deserts, and then analyze the fine points of four-wheel-drive performance. (Bradsher describes a hilarious SUV-introduction junket in which writers were given a succession of washed and polished new Fords to drive like lunatics through a wilderness area, while they were followed everywhere by chefs, wine stewards, and a huge trailer that contained marble bathrooms for the Ford executives.) This form of rating is wildly irrelevant to the actual uses of these vehicles. But in order to be assured of good off-road ratings, General Motors, Daimler-Chrysler, and Ford beef up the suspensions, the frame rails, and the horsepower of their SUV models, rendering them more wasteful and more dangerous in the conditions under which they are actually used.

10   Auto writers and buff books rarely discuss SUV safety or gas mileage, not wanting to upset advertising buyers or alter their own obsequious, handout-based relationship with Detroit. The *Washington Post* recently offered an instance beyond parody. Its auto writer, Warren Brown, penned a love poem to the new General Motors Hummer H2, the most offensive SUV yet devised. Skipping the fact that the Hummer is a leather-lined luxury toy (heated seats, nine Bose speakers) being marketed to affluent suburbanites, Brown deliriously proclaimed that the Hummer is what Jesus would drive. Its size and its profligacy are justified, Brown said, because "if you are a missionary like some of my friends," you could use a Hummer "to bring loads of food and medical supplies" to the poor. But verily I tell you that no car on the road will allow its driver to pass through the eye of a needle less easily than a Hummer.

The SUV's combination of sociopathy and fantasy has reached its preposterous culmination in this vehicle, which is based on the military Humvee, originally designed to carry infantry and machine guns. The Hummer gets ten miles per gallon, meaning that its annual greenhouse-gas emissions triple those of a car, and it weighs nearly three tons. (Still another loophole: if an SUV grows heavy enough, like the Hummer, the manufacturer does not have to report its fuel mileage to the EPA.) Hummers are even longer and higher than standard large SUVs, but *Consumer Guide* recently warned of the vehicle's "limited cargo room" and "cramped" seats, evidence of poor design. (The mid-size Nissan Maxima, which weighs less than half as much as a Hummer, has more front legroom.) The Hummer cannot park without straddling spaces. Its owner would be out of his or her mind to take this $52,000 bauble off the interstate, though of course the advertising features the usual postcard scenes of the noble outdoors. (In my favorite, a Hummer is racing across a glacier.) Do I need to tell you that Arnold Schwarzenegger persuaded General Motors to offer the civilian Hummer, endorsed it, and purchased the first one? The Hummer screams to the world the words that stand as one of Schwarzenegger's signature achievements as an actor: "Fuck you, asshole!" Maybe this class of vehicles should be called FUVs.

VISUAL ESSAY   American Car Culture

To learn more about car culture, visit
www.ablongman.com/george/117

There is no question that SUVs have become wildly popular in the United States and, increasingly, throughout the world. Gregg Easterbrook offers some reasons to explain their appeal, but there is certainly more to say about Americans' long-standing love affair with cars. The following images offer opportunities to think about the role cars play in American life, what they say about us as individuals and as a society, and what inferences we draw from the cars other people drive. We present a Hummer H2, a Mini Cooper, and Polo Garza's 1956 customized Chevy lowrider.

A Hummer.

A Mini Cooper.

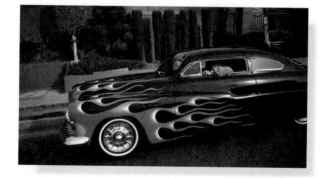

A Low-rider.

SUGGESTIONS FOR DISCUSSION

1. Review the argument that Greg Easterbrook makes about the appeal of SUVs, based in part on Keith Bradsher's *High and Mighty*. Imagine how SUV owners might respond (whether you agree or not). How might they defend their decisions to buy SUVs? How do the underlying assumptions differ?

2. Consider the three images of cars presented here. What do the design and style of each car seem to signify? What inferences do you draw about the identities of people who own each type of car?

3. Cars are no doubt one of the most important possessions of many Americans. Why is this so? What role do cars play in the lives of individuals? What role do they play in American culture?

SUGGESTIONS FOR WRITING

1. As you are probably aware, there is a debate about SUVs. Do a bit of research on what people are saying about SUVs. You could, for example, read the complete text of Easterbrook's review in the January 20, 2003, issue of *New Republic*, consult Bradsher's book *High and Mighty*, and visit the Ultimate Poseur Sport Utility Page on the Web as good statements of the anti-SUV position. In turn you can find various sources that defend SUVs against these criticisms, such as the SUV Owners page. Write an essay that analyzes the debate. You can, of course, align yourself with one side or the other, but take as your main task reviewing the debate and explaining what is at stake in the various views of SUVs.

2. Pick a particular model or type of car and write an essay that explains what the car's design and style signify. You can use one of the images here of the Hummer, Mini Cooper, and the 1956 Chevy. You do not have to limit yourself to new cars. You might pick, for example, a van painted in psychedelic colors with Grateful Dead stickers or a customized low rider or an old Volkswagen bug someone has kept on the road. In any case, consider what the car tells you about its owner's identity and social status.

3. Write an essay that presents your views about American car culture. Consider, for example, why cars play such a central role in individuals' lives and in the society as a whole. What emotional ties do people have to their cars? What do these ties reveal about their values?

WIRED CULTURE   iPods

To learn more about iPods and communications, visit www.ablongman.com/george/118

Portable music players started in 1979 with the Sony Walkman, the first pocket-sized cassette player. By 1999, Sony had sold a staggering 186 million Walkmen. In the mid-1980s, Sony, along with competing brands, added portable CD players, but it was the appearance of MP3 players in the late 1990s that really revolutionized the portable music scene by enabling listeners to download and store music files. Instead of playing one cassette or CD at a time, the new portable players could hold thousands of songs. By 2005, Apple's iPod had captured the portable music player market. Launched in 2001, the iPod sold 1.4 million units in the first two years. In the following year, the number of iPod owners jumped to over 20 million. Such success raises a number of interesting questions about the design of the iPod, how it appeals to consumers, and how it has worked its way into their lives. The following two readings offer different approaches. As you will see, Rob Walker focuses on the design of the iPod, while Andrew Sullivan looks at how people use iPods and the consequences.

THE AURA

▰— *Rob Walker*

Rob Walker writes a weekly feature about product design, "Consumed," for the New York Times Magazine. "The Aura" is an excerpt from a longer article on the iPod, "The Guts of a New Machine," that appeared in the magazine in 2003.

SUGGESTION FOR READING   Notice how Rob Walker quotes a number of sources about the popularity and appeal of the iPod. As you read, note each source and consider how they add up in this selection to an over-all impression of the iPod's design.

1 Two years ago this month, Apple Computer released a small, sleek-looking device it called the iPod. A digital music player, it weighed just 6.5 ounces and held about 1,000 songs. There were small MP3 players around at the time, and there were players that could hold a lot of music. But if the crucial equation is "largest number of songs" divided by "smallest physical space," the iPod seemed untouchable. And yet the initial reaction was mixed: the thing cost $400, so much more than existing digital players that it prompted one online skeptic to suggest that the name might be an acronym for "Idiots Price Our Devices." This line of complaint called to mind the Newton, Apple's pen-based personal organizer that was ahead of its time but carried a bloated price tag to its doom.

Since then, however, about 1.4 million iPods have been sold. (It has been updated twice and now comes in three versions, all of which improved on the original's songs-per-space ratio, and are priced at $300, $400 and $500, the most expensive holding 10,000 songs.) For the months of July and August, the iPod claimed the No. 1 spot in the MP3 player market both in terms of unit share (31 percent) and revenue share (56 percent), by Apple's reckoning. It is now Apple's highest-volume product. "It's something that's as big a brand to Apple as the Mac," is how Philip Schiller, Apple's senior vice president of worldwide product marketing, puts it. "And that's a pretty big deal."

Of course, as anyone who knows the basic outline of Apple's history is aware, there is no guarantee that today's innovation leader will not be copycatted and undersold into tomorrow's niche player. Apple's recent and highly publicized move to make the iPod and its related software, iTunes, available to users of Windows-based computers is widely seen as a sign that the company is trying to avoid that fate this time around. But it may happen anyway. The history of innovation is the history of innovation being imitated, iterated and often overtaken.

Whether the iPod achieves truly mass scale—like, say, the cassette-tape Walkman, which sold an astonishing 186 million units in its first 20 years of existence—it certainly qualifies as a hit and as a genuine breakthrough. It has popped up on "Saturday Night Live," in a 50 Cent video, on Oprah Winfrey's list of her "favorite things," and in recurring "what's on your iPod" gimmicks in several magazines. It is, in short, an icon. A handful of familiar clichés have made the rounds to explain this—it's about ease of use, it's about Apple's great sense of design. But what does that really mean? "Most people make the mistake of thinking design is what it looks like," says Steve Jobs, Apple's C.E.O. "People think it's this veneer—that the designers are handed this box and told, 'Make it look good!' That's not what we think design is. It's not just what it looks like and feels like. Design is how it works."

THE AURA

5 If you want to understand why a product has become an icon, you of course want to talk to the people who dreamed it up and made it. And you want to talk to the design experts and the

technology pros and the professors and the gurus. But what you really want to do is talk to Andrew Andrew. Andrew Andrew is a "highly diversified company" made of two personable young men, each named Andrew. They dress identically and seem to agree on everything; they say, among other things, that they have traveled from the future "to set things on the right course for tomorrow." They require interviewers to sign a form agreeing not to reveal any differences between Andrew and Andrew, because to do so might undermine the Andrew Andrew brand—and since this request is more interesting than whatever those differences might be, interviewers sign it.

Among other things, they do some fashion design and they are DJ's who "spin" on iPods, setting up participatory events called iParties. Thus they've probably seen more people interact with the player than anyone who doesn't work for Apple. More important, they put an incredible amount of thought into what they buy, and why: in a world where, for better or worse, aesthetics is a business, they are not just consumers but consumption artists. So Andrew remembers exactly where he was when he first encountered the iPod: 14th Street near Ninth Avenue in New York City. He was with Andrew, of course. A friend showed it to them. Andrew held the device in his hand. The main control on the iPod is a scroll wheel: you spin it with your thumb to navigate the long list of songs (or artists or genres), touch a button to pick a track and use the wheel again to adjust the volume. The other Andrew also tried it out. "When you do the volume for the first time, that's the key moment," says Andrew. "We knew: we had to have one." (Well, two.)

Before you even get to the surface of the iPod, you encounter what could be called its aura. The commercial version of an aura is a brand, and while Apple may be a niche player in the computer market, the fanatical brand loyalty of its customers is legendary. A journalist, Leander Kahney, has even written a book about it, "The Cult of Mac," to be published in the spring. As he points out, that base has supported the company with a faith in its will to innovate—even during stretches when it hasn't. Apple is also a giant in the world of industrial design. The candy-colored look of the iMac has been so widely copied that it's now a visual cliché.

But the iPod is making an even bigger impression. Bruce Claxton, who is the current president of the Industrial Designers Society of America and a senior designer at Motorola, calls the device emblematic of a shift toward products that are "an antidote to the hyper lifestyle," which might be symbolized by hand-held devices that bristle with buttons and controls that seem to promise a million functions if you only had time to figure them all out. "People are seeking out products that are not just simple to use but a joy to use." Moby, the recording artist, has been a high-profile iPod booster since the product's debut. "The kind of insidious revolutionary quality of the iPod," he says, "is that it's so elegant and logical, it becomes part of your life so quickly that you can't remember what it was like beforehand."

Tuesday nights, Andrew Andrew's iParty happens at a club called APT on the spooky, far western end of 13th Street. They show up at about 10 in matching sweat jackets and sneakers, matching eyeglasses, matching haircuts. They connect their matching iPods to a modest Gemini mixer that they've fitted with a white front panel to make it look more iPodish. The iPods sit on either side of the mixer, on their backs, so they look like tiny turntables. Andrew Andrew change into matching lab coats and ties. They hand out long song lists to patrons, who take a number and, when called, are invited up to program a seven-minute set. At around midnight, the actor Elijah Wood (Frodo) has turned up and is permitted to plug his own iPod into Andrew Andrew's system. His set includes a Squarepusher song.

10   Between songs at APT, each Andrew analyzed the iPod. In talking about how hard it was, at first, to believe that so much music could be stuffed into such a tiny object, they came back to the scroll wheel as the key to the product's initial seductiveness. "It really

bridged the gap," Andrew observed, "between fantasy and reality."

The idea of innovation, particularly techno-logical innovation, has a kind of aura around it, too. Imagine the lone genius, sheltered from the storm of short-term commercial demands in a research lab somewhere, whose tinkering produces a sudden and momentous breakthrough. Or maybe we think innovation begins with an epiphany, a sudden vision of the future. Either way, we think of that one thing, the lightning bolt that jolted all the other pieces into place. The Walkman came about because a Sony executive wanted a high-quality but small stereo tape player to listen to on long flights. A small recorder was modified, with the recording pieces removed and stereo circuitry added. That was February 1979, and within six months the product was on the market.

The iPod's history is comparatively free of lightning-bolt moments. Apple was not ahead of the curve in recognizing the power of music in digital form. It was practically the last computer maker to equip its machines with CD burners. It trailed others in creating jukebox software for storing and organizing music collections on computers. And various portable digital music players were already on the market before the iPod was even an idea. Back when Napster was inspiring a

million self-styled visionaries to predict the end of music as we know it, Apple was focused on the relationship between computers and video. The company had, back in the 1990's, invented a technology called FireWire, which is basically a tool for moving data between digital devices—in large quantities, very quickly. Apple licensed this technology to various Japanese consumer electronics companies (which used it in digital camcorders and players) and eventually started adding FireWire ports to iMacs and creating video editing software. This led to programs called iMovie, then iPhoto and then a conceptual view of the home computer as a "digital hub" that would complement a range of devices. Finally, in January 2001, iTunes was added to the mix.

And although the next step sounds pro-saic—we make software that lets you organize the music on your computer, so maybe we should make one of those things that lets you take it with you—it was also something new. There were companies that made jukebox software, and companies that made portable players, but nobody made both. What this meant is not that the iPod could do more, but that it would do less. This is what led to what Jonathan Ive, Apple's vice president of industrial design, calls the iPod's "overt simplicity." And this, per-versely, is the most exciting thing about it.

SOCIETY IS DEAD: WE HAVE RETREATED INTO THE iWORLD

—*Andrew Sullivan*

Andrew Sullivan has served as editor of the *New Republic* and contributes to periodicals such as the *New York Times* and the *Times* (London). "Society Is Dead: We Have Retreated Into the iWorld" appeared in the *Sunday Times* (London) in 2005.

SUGGESTION FOR READING   Notice how Andrew Sullivan draws on his personal experience to generalize about the uses and effects of the iPod and other new technologies. As you read, consider Sullivan's reasoning about cause and effect.

1   I was visiting New York last week and noticed something I'd never thought I'd say about the city. Yes, nightlife is pretty much

dead (and I'm in no way the first to notice that). But daylife—that insane mishmash of yells, chatter, clatter, hustle and chutzpah that makes New York the urban equivalent of methamphetamine—was also a little different. It was quieter.

Manhattan's downtown is now a Disney-like string of malls, riverside parks and pretty upper-middle-class villages. But there was something else. And as I looked across the throngs on the pavements, I began to see why.

There were little white wires hanging down from their ears, or tucked into pockets, purses or jackets. The eyes were a little vacant. Each was in his or her own musical world, walking to their soundtrack, stars in their own music video, almost oblivious to the world around them. These are the iPod people.

Even without the white wires you can tell who they are. They walk down the street in their own MP3 cocoon, bumping into others, deaf to small social cues, shutting out anyone not in their bubble.

5   Every now and again some start unconsciously emitting strange tuneless squawks, like a badly tuned radio, and their fingers snap or their arms twitch to some strange soundless rhythm. When others say "Excuse me" there's no response. "Hi," ditto. It's strange to be among so many people and hear so little. Except that each one is hearing so much.

Yes, I might as well own up. I'm one of them. I witnessed the glazed New York looks through my own glazed pupils, my white wires peeping out of my ears. I joined the cult a few years ago: the sect of the little white box worshippers.

Every now and again I go to church—those huge, luminous Apple stores, pews in the rear, the clerics in their monastic uniforms all bustling around or sitting behind the "Genius Bars," like priests waiting to hear confessions.

Others began, as I did, with a Walkman—and then a kind of clunkier MP3 player. But the sleekness of the iPod won me over. Unlike other models it gave me my entire music collection to rearrange as I saw fit—on the fly, in my pocket.

What was once an occasional musical diversion became a compulsive obsession. Now I have my iTunes in my iMac for my iPod in my iWorld. It's Narcissus heaven: we've finally put the "i" into Me.

10   And, like all addictive cults, it's spreading. There are now 22m iPod owners in the United States and Apple is becoming a mass-market company for the first time.

Walk through any airport in the United States these days and you will see person after person gliding through the social ether as if on autopilot. Get on a subway and you're surrounded by a bunch of Stepford commuters staring into mid-space as if anaesthetised by technology. Don't ask, don't tell, don't overhear, don't observe. Just tune in and tune out.

It wouldn't be so worrying if it weren't part of something even bigger. Americans are beginning to narrow their lives.

You get your news from your favourite blogs, the ones that won't challenge your view of the world. You tune into a satellite radio service that also aims directly at a small market—for new age fanatics, liberal talk or Christian rock. Television is all cable. Culture is all subculture. Your cell phones can receive e-mail feeds of your favourite blogger's latest thoughts—seconds after he has posted them—get sports scores for your team or stock quotes of your portfolio.

Technology has given us a universe entirely for ourselves—where the serendipity of meeting a new stranger, hearing a piece of music we would never choose for ourselves or an opinion that might force us to change our mind about something are all effectively banished. Atomisation by little white boxes and cell phones. Society without the social. Others who are chosen—not met at random. Human beings have never lived like this before. Yes, we have always had homes, retreats or places where we went to relax, unwind or shut out the world.

15   But we didn't walk around the world like hermit crabs with our isolation surgically attached.

Music was once the preserve of the living room or the concert hall. It was sometimes solitary but it was primarily a shared experience, something that brought people together, gave them the comfort of knowing that others too understood the pleasure of a Brahms symphony or that Beatles album.

But music is as atomised now as living is. And it's secret. That bloke next to you on the bus could be listening to heavy metal or a Gregorian chant. You'll never know. And so, bit by bit, you'll never really know him. And by his white wires, he is indicating he doesn't really want to know you.

What do we get from this? The awareness of more music, more often. The chance to slip away for a while from everydayness, to give our lives its own soundtrack, to still the monotony of the commute, to listen more closely and carefully to music that can lift you up and keep you going.

We become masters of our own interests, more connected to people like us over the internet, more instantly in touch with anything we want, need or think we want and think we need. Ever tried a Stairmaster in silence? But what are we missing? That hilarious shard of an overheard conversation that stays with you all day; the child whose chatter on the pavement takes you back to your early memories; birdsong; weather; accents; the laughter of others. And those thoughts that come not by filling your head with selected diversion, but by allowing your mind to wander aimlessly through the regular background noise of human and mechanical life.

20   External stimulation can crowd out the interior mind. Even the boredom that we flee has its uses. We are forced to find our own means to overcome it.

And so we enrich our life from within, rather than from white wires. It's hard to give up, though, isn't it.

Not so long ago I was on a trip and realised I had left my iPod behind. Panic. But then something else. I noticed the rhythms of others again, the sound of the airplane, the opinions of the taxi driver, the small social cues that had been obscured before. I noticed how others related to each other. And I felt just a little bit connected again and a little more aware.

Try it. There's a world out there. And it has a soundtrack all its own.

SUGGESTIONS FOR DISCUSSION

1. Rob Walker opens with the question of understanding why a product such as the iPod has become an icon. What does he mean by "icon"? What other products might be considered icons? How does the design of the product contribute to its iconic status?

2. Both Walker and Andrew Sullivan offer explanations for the popularity and appeal of the iPod. Compare the reasons they give? To what extent do they overlap? Are there important differences, whether they are implicit or explicit?

3. Sullivan sees the iPod as a retreat from sociability and shared experience. Does this seem a reasonable conclusion? Consider the evidence he gives. How do you think Walker would respond to Sullivan's argument?

SUGGESTIONS FOR WRITING

1. Write an essay on a product that has, in one way or another, become an icon. You will need to explain what the term "icon" means. Consider what the iconic status of the product reveals about contemporary American culture and the lifestyles of the people who use the product.

2. As Sullivan suggests, there are other ways to listen to music besides the iPod. Write an essay that compares the iPod to one or more other systems for playing music, such as CD players, boom boxes, and the radio. Consider the effects. Do some systems seem to enhance sociability or promote atomization?

3. To explain the appeal of the iPod, Walker quotes Moby's remark that the "insidious revolutionary quality of the iPod is that . . . it becomes a part of your life so quickly that you can't remember what it was like beforehand." Write an essay on a product that insinuated itself into people's lives in this manner. Take into account what it was like before the product and after. Explain the reasons for the shift.

PERSPECTIVES   Branding

Branding has become one of the pervasive features of the contemporary cultural landscape. Nowadays, brand names don't just appear in the places they always have, such as packages, labels, stores, billboards, and advertisements. The world in which we live appears to be branded. Stadiums and arenas no longer have names such as Candlestick Park or the Boston Garden. Now they're called 3Com Park and the Fleet Center. The uniforms of college and professional athletes not only identify the players by displaying their numbers but they identify which company—for example, Nike or Reebok—has the team franchise by displaying its brand. And people who once simply wore brand-name clothes are now walking advertisements for several companies, branded by the name and logo on their shirts, shoes, sweaters, caps, and other clothing.

All of this branding has caused a good deal of controversy. We present two selections to explore the terms of the controversy: an excerpt from the opening chapter of Naomi Klein's *No Logo* and a response to Klein that appeared in the British magazine the *Economist*.

NO LOGO

— *Naomi Klein*

Naomi Klein is a journalist and anticorporate activist. She is a regular columnist for the *Globe and Mail*, Canada's national newspaper; the British *Guardian*; and the weekly U.S. magazine *In These Times*. *No Logo* (2002), the book in which this selection appeared, connects the branding phenomenon to the way multinational corporations operate in a global economy and to the anticorporate activism that has emerged in recent years.

SUGGESTION FOR READING Notice how Naomi Klein develops the idea of branding as a corporate strategy. When you've finished reading the selection, write a short explanation of what Klein means by the term *branding*.

As a private person, I have a passion for landscape, and I have never seen one improved by a billboard. Where every prospect pleases, man is at his vilest when he erects a billboard. When I retire from Madison Avenue, I am going to start a secret society of masked vigilantes who will travel around the world on silent motor bicycles, chopping down posters at the dark of the moon. How many juries will convict us when we are caught in these acts of beneficent citizenship?

—*David Ogilvy, founder of the Ogilvy & Mather advertising agency,* in Confessions of an Advertising Man, *1963*

1   The astronomical growth in the wealth and cultural influence of multinational corporations over the last fifteen years can arguably be traced back to a single, seemingly innocuous idea developed by management theorists in the mid-1980s: that successful corporations must primarily produce brands, as opposed to products.

Until that time, although it was understood in the corporate world that bolstering one's brand name was important, the primary concern of every solid manufacturer was the production of goods. This idea was the very gospel of the machine age. An editorial that appeared in *Fortune* magazine in 1938, for instance, argued that the reason the American economy had yet to recover from the Depression was that America had lost sight of the importance of making *things*:

> This is the proposition that the basic and irreversible function of an industrial economy is *the making of things*; that the more things it makes the bigger will be the income, whether dollar or real; and hence that the key to those lost recuperative powers lies . . . in the factory where the lathes and the drills and the fires and the hammers are. It is in the factory and on the land and under the land that purchasing power *originates* [italics theirs].

And for the longest time, the making of things remained, at least in principle, the heart of all industrialized economies. But by the eighties, pushed along by that decade's recession, some of the most powerful manufacturers in the world had begun to falter. A consensus emerged that corporations were bloated, oversized; they owned too much, employed too many people, and were weighed down with *too many things*. The very process of producing—running one's own factories, being responsible for tens of thousands of full-time, permanent employees—began to look less like the route to success and more like a clunky liability.

At around this same time a new kind of corporation began to rival the traditional all-American manufacturers for market share; these were the Nikes and Microsofts, and later, the Tommy Hilfigers and Intels. These pioneers made the bold claim that producing goods was only an incidental part of their operations, and that thanks to recent victories in trade liberalization and labor-law reform, they were able to have their products made for them by contractors, many of them overseas. What these companies produced primarily were not things, they said, but *images* of their brands. Their real work lay not in manufacturing but in marketing. This formula, needless to say, has proved enormously profitable, and its success has companies competing in a race toward weightlessness: whoever owns the least, has the fewest employees on the payroll and produces the most powerful images, as opposed to products, wins the race.

5   And so the wave of mergers in the corporate world over the last few years is a deceptive phenomenon: it only *looks* as if the giants, by joining forces, are getting bigger and bigger. The true key to understanding these shifts is to realize that in several crucial ways—not their profits, of course—these merged companies are actually shrinking. Their apparent bigness is simply the most effective route toward their real goal: divestment of the world of things.

Since many of today's best-known manufacturers no longer produce products and advertise them, but rather buy products and "brand" them, these companies are forever on the prowl for creative new ways to build and strengthen their brand images. Manufacturing products may require drills, furnaces, hammers and the like, but creating a brand calls for a completely different set of tools and materials. It requires an endless parade of brand extensions, continuously renewed imagery for marketing and, most of all, fresh new spaces to disseminate the brand's idea of itself. In this section of the book, I'll look at how, in ways both insidious and overt, this corporate obsession with brand identity is waging a war on public and individual space: on public institutions such as schools, on youthful identities, on the concept of nationality and on the possibilities for unmarketed space.

THE BEGINNING OF THE BRAND

It's helpful to go back briefly and look at where the idea of branding first began. Though the words are often used interchangeably, branding and advertising are not the same process. Advertising any given product is only one part of branding's grand plan, as are sponsorship and logo licensing. Think of the brand as the core meaning of the modern corporation, and of the advertisement as one vehicle used to convey that meaning to the world.

The first mass-marketing campaigns, starting in the second half of the nineteenth century, had more to do with advertising than with branding as we understand it today. Faced with a range of recently invented products—the radio, phonograph, car, light bulb and so on—advertisers had more pressing tasks than creating a brand identity for any given corporation; first, they had to change the way people lived their lives. Ads had to inform consumers about the existence of some new invention, then convince them that their lives would be better if they used, for example, cars instead of wagons, telephones instead of mail and electric light instead of oil lamps. Many of these new products bore brand names—some of which are still around today—but these were almost incidental. These products were themselves news; that was almost advertisement enough.

The first brand-based products appeared at around the same time as the invention-based ads, largely because of another relatively recent innovation: the factory. When goods began to be produced in factories, not only were entirely new products being introduced but old products—even basic staples—were appearing in strikingly new forms. What made early branding efforts different from more straightforward salesmanship was that the market was now being flooded with uniform mass-produced products that were virtually indistinguishable from one another. Competitive branding became a necessity of the machine age—within a context of manufactured sameness, image based difference had to be manufactured along with the product.

10   So the role of advertising changed from delivering product news bulletins to building an image around a particular brand-name version of a product. The first task of branding was to bestow proper names on generic goods such as sugar, flour, soap and cereal, which had previously been scooped out of barrels by local shopkeepers. In the 1880s, corporate logos were introduced to mass-produced products like Campbell's Soup, H.J. Heinz pickles and Quaker Oats cereal. As design historians and theorists Ellen Lupton and J. Abbott Miller note, logos were tailored to evoke familiarity and folksiness, in an effort to counteract the new and unsettling anonymity of packaged goods. "Familiar personalities such as Dr. Brown, Uncle Ben, Aunt Jemima, and Old Grand-Dad came to replace the shopkeeper, who was traditionally responsible for measuring bulk foods for customers and acting as an advocate for products . . . a nationwide vocabulary of brand names replaced the small local shopkeeper as the interface between consumer and product." After the product names and characters had been established, advertising gave them a venue to speak directly to would-be consumers. The corporate "personality," uniquely named, packaged and advertised, had arrived.

For the most part, the ad campaigns at the end of the nineteenth century and the start of the twentieth used a set of rigid, pseudoscientific formulas: rivals were never mentioned, ad copy used declarative statements only and headlines had to be large, with lots of white space—according to one turn-of-the-century adman, "an advertisement should be big enough to make an impression but not any bigger than the thing advertised."

But there were those in the industry who understood that advertising wasn't just scientific; it was also spiritual. Brands could conjure a feeling—think of Aunt Jemima's comforting presence—but not only that, entire corporations could themselves embody a meaning of their own. In the early twenties, legendary adman Bruce Barton turned General Motors into a metaphor for the American family, "something personal, warm and human," while GE was not so much the name of the faceless General

Electric Company as, in Barton's words, "the initials of a friend." In 1923 Barton said that the role of advertising was to help corporations find their soul. The son of a preacher, he drew on his religious upbringing for uplifting messages: "I like to think of advertising as something big, something splendid, something which goes deep down into an institution and gets hold of the soul of it . . . . Institutions have souls, just as men and nations have souls," he told GM president Pierre du Pont. General Motors ads began to tell stories about the people who drove its cars—the preacher, the pharmacist or the country doctor who, thanks to his trusty GM, arrived "at the bedside of a dying child" just in time "to bring it back to life."

By the end of the 1940s, there was a burgeoning awareness that a brand wasn't just a mascot or a catchphrase or a picture printed on the label of a company's product; the company as a whole could have a brand identity or a "corporate consciousness," as this ephemeral quality was termed at the time. As this idea evolved, the adman ceased to see himself as a pitchman and instead saw himself as "the philosopher-king of commercial culture," in the words of ad critic Randall Rothberg. The search for the true meaning of brands—or the "brand essence," as it is often called—gradually took the agencies away from individual products and their attributes and toward a psychological/anthropological examination of what brands mean to the culture and to people's lives. This was seen to be of crucial importance, since corporations may manufacture products, but what consumers buy are brands.

It took several decades for the manufacturing world to adjust to this shift. It clung to the idea that its core business was still production and that branding was an important add-on. Then came the brand equity mania of the eighties, the defining moment of which arrived in 1988 when Philip Morris purchased Kraft for $12.6 billion—six times what the company was worth on paper. The price difference, apparently, was the cost of the word "Kraft." Of course Wall Street was aware that decades of

marketing and brand bolstering added value to a company over and above its assets and total annual sales. But with the Kraft purchase, a huge dollar value had been assigned to something that had previously been abstract and unquantifiable—a brand name. This was spectacular news for the ad world, which was now able to make the claim that advertising spending was more than just a sales strategy: it was an investment in cold hard equity. The more you spend, the more your company is worth. Not surprisingly, this led to a considerable increase in spending on advertising. More important, it sparked a renewed interest in puffing up brand identities, a project that involved far more than a few billboards and TV spots. It was about pushing the envelope in sponsorship deals, dreaming up new areas in which to "extend" the brand, as well as perpetually probing the zeitgeist to ensure that the "essence" selected for one's brand would resonate karmically with its target market. For reasons that will be explored in the rest of this chapter, this radical shift in corporate philosophy has sent manufacturers on a cultural feeding frenzy as they seize upon every corner of unmarketed landscape in search of the oxygen needed to inflate their brands. In the process, virtually nothing has been left unbranded. That's quite an impressive feat, considering that as recently as 1993 Wall Street had pronounced the brand dead, or as good as dead.

THE BRAND'S DEATH (RUMORS OF WHICH HAD BEEN GREATLY EXAGGERATED)

15 On April 2, 1993, advertising itself was called into question by the very brands the industry had been building, in some cases, for over two centuries. That day is known in marketing circles as "Marlboro Friday," and it refers to a sudden announcement from Philip Morris that it would slash the price of Marlboro cigarettes by 20 percent in an attempt to compete with bargain brands that were eating into its market. The pundits went nuts, announcing in frenzied unison that not only was Marlboro dead, all brand

names were dead. The reasoning was that if a "prestige" brand like Marlboro, whose image had been carefully groomed, preened and enhanced with more than a billion advertising dollars, was desperate enough to compete with no-names, then clearly the whole concept of branding had lost its currency. The public had seen the advertising, and the public didn't care. The Marlboro Man, after all, was not any old campaign; launched in 1954, it was the longest-running ad campaign in history. It was a legend. If the Marlboro Man had crashed, well, then, brand equity had crashed as well. The implication that Americans were suddenly thinking for themselves en masse reverberated through Wall Street. The same day Philip Morris announced its price cut, stock prices nose-dived for all the household brands: Heinz, Quaker Oats, Coca-Cola, PepsiCo, Procter and Gamble and RJR Nabisco. Philip Morris's own stock took the worst beating.

Bob Stanojev, national director of consumer products marketing for Ernst and Young, explained the logic behind Wall Street's panic: "If one or two powerhouse consumer products companies start to cut prices for good, there's going to be an avalanche. Welcome to the value generation."

Yes, it was one of those moments of overstated instant consensus, but it was not entirely without cause. Marlboro had always sold itself on the strength of its iconic image marketing, not on anything so prosaic as its price. As we now know, the Marlboro Man survived the price wars without sustaining too much damage. At the time, however, Wall Street saw Philip Morris's decision as symbolic of a sea change. The price cut was an admission that Marlboro's name was no longer sufficient to sustain the flagship position, which in a context where image is equity meant that Marlboro had blinked. And when Marlboro—one of the quintessential global brands—blinks, it raises questions about branding that reach beyond Wall Street, and way beyond Philip Morris.

The panic of Marlboro Friday was not a reaction to a single incident. Rather, it was the culmination of years of escalating anxiety in the face of some rather dramatic shifts in consumer habits that were seen to be eroding the market share of household-name brands, from Tide to Kraft. Bargain-conscious shoppers, hit hard by the recession, were starting to pay more attention to price than to the prestige bestowed on their products by the yuppie ad campaigns of the 1980s. The public was suffering from a bad case of what is known in the industry as "brand blindness."

Study after study showed that baby boomers, blind to the alluring images of advertising and deaf to the empty promises of celebrity spokespersons, were breaking their life-long brand loyalties and choosing to feed their families with private-label brands from the supermarket—claiming, heretically, that they couldn't tell the difference. From the beginning of the recession to 1993, Loblaw's President's Choice line, Wal-Mart's Great Value and Marks and Spencer's St. Michael prepared foods had nearly doubled their market share in North America and Europe. The computer market, meanwhile, was flooded by inexpensive clones, causing IBM to slash its prices and otherwise impale itself. It appeared to be a return to the proverbial shopkeeper dishing out generic goods from the barrel in a prebranded era.

THE BRANDS BOUNCE BACK

20   There were some brands that were watching from the sidelines as Wall Street declared the death of the brand. Funny, they must have thought, we don't feel dead.

Just as the admen had predicted at the beginning of the recession, the companies that exited the downturn running were the ones who opted for marketing over value every time: Nike, Apple, the Body Shop, Calvin Klein, Disney, Levi's and Starbucks. Not only were these brands doing just fine, thank you very much, but the act of branding was becoming a larger and larger focus of their businesses. For these companies, the ostensible product was mere filler for the real production: the brand. They integrated the idea of branding into the very fabric of their companies. Their corporate cultures were so tight and cloistered that to outsiders they appeared to be a cross between fraternity house, religious cult and sanitarium. Everything was an ad for the brand: bizarre lexicons for describing employees (partners, baristas, team players, crew members), company chants, superstar CEOs, fanatical attention to design consistency, a propensity for monument-building, and New Age mission statements. Unlike classic household brand names, such as Tide and Marlboro, these logos weren't losing their currency, they were in the midst of breaking every barrier in the marketing world—becoming cultural accessories and lifestyle philosophers. These companies didn't wear their image like a cheap shirt—their image was so integrated with their business that other people wore it as *their* shirt. And when the brands crashed, these companies didn't even notice—they were branded to the bone.

So the real legacy of Marlboro Friday is that it simultaneously brought the two most significant developments in nineties marketing and consumerism into sharp focus: the deeply unhip big-box bargain stores that provide the essentials of life and monopolize a disproportionate share of the market (Wal-Mart et al.) and the extra-premium "attitude" brands that provide the essentials of lifestyle and monopolize ever-expanding stretches of cultural space (Nike et al.). The way these two tiers of consumerism developed would have a profound impact on the economy in the years to come. When overall ad expenditures took a nosedive in 1991, Nike and Reebok were busy playing advertising chicken, with each company increasing its budget to outspend the other. In 1991 alone, Reebok upped its ad spending by 71.9 percent, while Nike pumped an extra 24.6 percent into its already soaring ad budget, bringing the company's total spending on marketing to a staggering $250 million annually. Far from worrying about competing on price, the sneaker pimps were designing ever more intricate and pseudoscientific air pockets, and driving up prices by signing star athletes to colossal

sponsorship deals. The fetish strategy seemed to be working fine: in the six years prior to 1993, Nike had gone from a $750 million company to a $4 billion one and Phil Knight's Beaverton, Oregon, company emerged from the recession with profits 900 percent higher than when it began.

Benetton and Calvin Klein, meanwhile, were also upping their spending on lifestyle marketing, using ads to associate their lines with risque art and progressive politics. Clothes barely appeared in these high-concept advertisements, let alone prices. Even more abstract was Absolut Vodka, which for some years now had been developing a marketing strategy in which its product disappeared and its brand was nothing but a blank bottle-shaped space that could be filled with whatever content a particular audience most wanted from its brands: intellectual in *Harper's*, futuristic in *Wired*, alternative in *Spin*, loud and proud in *Out* and "Absolut Centerfold" in *Playboy*. The brand reinvented itself as a cultural sponge, soaking up and morphing to its surroundings.

Saturn, too, came out of nowhere in October 1990 when GM launched a car built not out of steel and rubber but out of New Age spirituality and seventies feminism. After the car had been on the market a few years, the company held a "homecoming" weekend for Saturn owners, during which they could visit the auto plant and have a cookout with the people who made their cars. As the Saturn ads boasted at the time, "44,000 people spent their vacations with us, at a car plant." It was as if Aunt Jemima had come to life and invited you over to her house for dinner.

25   In 1993, the year the Marlboro Man was temporarily hobbled by "brand-blind" consumers, Microsoft made its striking debut on *Advertising Age*'s list of the top 200 ad spenders—the very same year that Apple computer increased its marketing budget by 30 percent after already making branding history with its Orwellian takeoff ad launch during the 1984 Super Bowl. Like Saturn, both companies

were selling a hip new relationship to the machine that left Big Blue IBM looking as clunky and menacing as the now-dead Cold War.

And then there were the companies that had always understood that they were selling brands before product. Coke, Pepsi, McDonald's, Burger King and Disney weren't fazed by the brand crisis, opting instead to escalate the brand war, especially since they had their eyes firmly fixed on global expansion. They were joined in this project by a wave of sophisticated producer/retailers who hit full stride in the late eighties and early nineties. The Gap, Ikea and the Body Shop were spreading like wildfire during this period, masterfully transforming the generic into the brand-specific, largely through bold, carefully branded packaging and the promotion of an "experiential" shopping environment. The Body Shop had been a presence in Britain since the seventies, but it wasn't until 1988 that it began sprouting like a green weed on every street corner in the U.S. Even during the darkest years of the recession, the company opened between forty and fifty American stores a year. Most baffling of all to Wall Street, it pulled off the expansion without spending a dime on advertising. Who needed billboards and magazine ads when retail outlets were three-dimensional advertisements for an ethical and ecological approach to cosmetics? The Body Shop was all brand.

The Starbucks coffee chain, meanwhile, was also expanding during this period without laying out much in advertising; instead, it was spinning off its name into a wide range of branded projects: Starbucks airline coffee, office coffee, coffee ice cream, coffee beer. Starbucks seemed to understand brand names at a level even deeper than Madison Avenue, incorporating marketing into every fiber of its corporate concept—from the chain's strategic association with books, blues and jazz to its Euro-latte lingo. What the success of both the Body Shop and Starbucks showed was how far the branding project had come in moving beyond splashing one's logo on a billboard. Here were two companies that had

fostered powerful identities by making their brand concept into a virus and sending it out into the culture via a variety of channels: cultural sponsorship, political controversy, the consumer experience and brand extensions. Direct advertising, in this context, was viewed as a rather clumsy intrusion into a much more organic approach to image building.

Scott Bedbury, Starbucks' vice president of marketing, openly recognized that "consumers don't truly believe there's a huge difference between products," which is why brands must "establish emotional ties" with their customers through "the Starbucks Experience." The people who line up for Starbucks, writes CEO Howard Shultz, aren't just there for the coffee. "It's the romance of the coffee experience, the feeling of warmth and community people get in Starbucks stores."

Interestingly, before moving to Starbucks, Bedbury was head of marketing at Nike, where he oversaw the launch of the "Just Do It!" slogan, among other watershed branding moments. In the following passage, he explains the common techniques used to infuse the two very different brands with meaning:

> Nike, for example, is leveraging the deep emotional connection that people have with sports and fitness. With Starbucks, we see how coffee has woven itself into the fabric of people's lives, and that's our opportunity for emotional leverage. . . . A great brand raises the bar—it adds a greater sense of purpose to the experience, whether it's the challenge to do your best in sports and fitness or the affirmation that the cup of coffee you're drinking really matters.

30   This was the secret, it seemed, of all the success stories of the late eighties and early nineties. The lesson of Marlboro Friday was that there never really was a brand crisis—only brands that had crises of confidence. The brands would be okay, Wall Street concluded, so long as they believed fervently in the principles of branding and never, ever blinked. Overnight, "Brands, not products!" became the rallying cry for a marketing renaissance led by a new breed of companies

that saw themselves as "meaning brokers" instead of product producers. What was changing was the idea of what—in both advertising and branding—was being sold. The old paradigm had it that all marketing was selling a product. In the new model, however, the product always takes a back seat to the real product, the brand, and the selling of the brand acquired an extra component that can only be described as spiritual. Advertising is about hawking product. Branding, in its truest and most advanced incarnations, is about corporate transcendence.

It may sound flaky, but that's precisely the point. On Marlboro Friday, a line was drawn in the sand between the lowly price slashers and the high-concept brand builders. The brand builders conquered and a new consensus was born: the products that will flourish in the future will be the ones presented not as "commodities" but as concepts: the brand as experience, as lifestyle.

Ever since, a select group of corporations has been attempting to free itself from the corporeal world of commodities, manufacturing and products to exist on another plane. Anyone can manufacture a product, they reason (and as the success of private-label brands during the recession proved, anyone did). Such menial tasks, therefore, can and should be farmed out to contractors and subcontractors whose only concern is filling the order on time and under budget (ideally in the Third World, where labor is dirt cheap, laws are lax and tax breaks come by the bushel). Headquarters, meanwhile, is free to focus on the real business at hand—creating a corporate mythology powerful enough to infuse meaning into these raw objects just by signing its name.

The corporate world has always had a deep New Age streak, fed—it has become clear—by a profound need that could not be met simply by trading widgets for cash. But when branding captured the corporate imagination, New Age vision quests took center stage. As Nike CEO Phil Knight explains, "For years we thought of ourselves as a production-oriented company,

meaning we put all our emphasis on designing and manufacturing the product. But now we understand that the most important thing we do is market the product. We've come around to saying that Nike is a marketing-oriented company, and the product is our most important marketing tool." This project has since been taken to an even more advanced level with the emergence of on-line corporate giants such as Amazon.com. It is on-line that the purest brands are being built: liberated from the real-world burdens of stores and product manufacturing, these brands are free to soar, less as the disseminators of goods or services than as collective hallucinations.

Tom Peters, who has long coddled the inner flake in many a hard-nosed CEO, latched on to the branding craze as the secret to financial success, separating the transcendental logos and the earthbound products into two distinct categories of companies. "The top half—Coca-Cola, Microsoft, Disney, and so on—are pure 'players' in brainware. The bottom half [Ford and GM] are still lumpy-object purveyors, though automobiles are much 'smarter' than they used to be," Peters writes in *The Circle of Innovation* (1997), an ode to the power of marketing over production.

35 When Levi's began to lose market share in the late nineties, the trend was widely attributed to the company's failure—despite lavish ad spending—to transcend its products and become a free-standing meaning. "Maybe one of Levi's problems is that it has no Cola," speculated Jennifer Steinhauer in *The New York Times*. "It has no denim-toned house paint. Levi makes what is essentially a commodity: blue jeans. Its ads may evoke rugged outdoorsmanship, but Levi hasn't promoted any particular life style to sell other products."

In this high-stakes new context, the cutting-edge ad agencies no longer sold companies on individual campaigns but on their ability to act as "brand stewards": identifying, articulating and protecting the corporate soul. Not surprisingly, this spelled good news for the U.S. advertising industry, which in 1994 saw a spending increase of 8.6 percent over the previous year. In one year, the ad industry went from a near crisis to another "best year yet." And that was only the beginning of triumphs to come. By 1997, corporate advertising, defined as "ads that position a corporation, its values, its personality and character" were up 18 percent from the year before.

With this wave of brand mania has come a new breed of businessman, one who will proudly inform you that Brand X is not a product but a way of life, an attitude, a set of values, a look, an idea. And it sounds really great—way better than that Brand X is a screwdriver, or a hamburger chain, or a pair of jeans, or even a very successful line of running shoes. Nike, Phil Knight announced in the late eighties, is "a sports company"; its mission is not to sell shoes but to "enhance people's lives through sports and fitness" and to keep "the magic of sports alive." Company president-cum-sneaker-shaman Tom Clark explains that "the inspiration of sports allows us to rebirth ourselves constantly."

Reports of such "brand vision" epiphanies began surfacing from all corners. "Polaroid's problem," diagnosed the chairman of its advertising agency, John Hegarty, "was that they kept thinking of themselves as a camera. But the '[brand] vision' process taught us something: Polaroid is not a camera—it's a social lubricant." IBM isn't selling computers, it's selling business "solutions." Swatch is not about watches, it is about the idea of time. At Diesel Jeans, owner Renzo Rosso told *Paper* magazine, "We don't sell a product, we sell a style of life. I think we have created a movement. . . . The Diesel concept is everything. It's the way to live, it's the way to wear, it's the way to do something." And as Body Shop founder Anita Roddick explained to me, her stores aren't about what they sell, they are the conveyers of a grand idea—a political philosophy about women, the environment and ethical business. "I just use the company that I surprisingly created as a success—it shouldn't have been like this, it wasn't meant to be like this—to stand on the products to shout out on these issues," Roddick says.

The famous late graphic designer Tibor Kalman summed up the shifting role of the brand this way: "The original notion of the brand was quality, but now brand is a stylistic badge of courage."

40   The idea of selling the courageous message of a brand, as opposed to a product, intoxicated these CEOs, providing as it did an opportunity for seemingly limitless expansion. After all, if a brand was not a product, it could be anything! And nobody embraced branding theory with more evangelical zeal than Richard Branson, whose Virgin Group has branded joint ventures in everything from music to bridal gowns to airlines to cola to financial services. Branson refers derisively to the "stilted Anglo-Saxon view of consumers," which holds that a name should be associated with a product like sneakers or soft drinks, and opts instead for "the Asian 'trick'" of the *keiretsus* (a Japanese term meaning a network of linked corporations). The idea, he explains, is to "build brands not around products but around reputation. The great Asian names imply quality, price and innovation rather than a specific item. I call these 'attribute' brands: They do not relate directly to one product—such as a Mars bar or a Coca-Cola—but instead to a set of values."

Tommy Hilfiger, meanwhile, is less in the business of manufacturing clothes than he is in the business of signing his name. The company is run entirely through licensing agreements, with Hilfiger commissioning all its products from a group of other companies: Jockey International makes Hilfiger underwear, Pepe Jeans London makes Hilfiger jeans, Oxford Industries make Tommy shirts, the Stride Rite Corporation makes its footwear. What does Tommy Hilfiger manufacture? Nothing at all.

So passé had products become in the age of lifestyle branding that by the late nineties, newer companies like Lush cosmetics and Old Navy clothing began playing with the idea of old-style commodities as a source of retro marketing imagery. The Lush chain serves up its face masks and moisturizers out of refrigerated stainless-steel bowls, spooned into plastic containers with grocery-store labels. Old Navy showcases its shrink-wrapped T-shirts and sweatshirts in deli-style chrome refrigerators, as if they were meat or cheese. When you are a pure, concept-driven brand, the aesthetics of raw product can prove as "authentic" as loft living.

And lest the branding business be dismissed as the playground of trendy consumer items such as sneakers, jeans and New Age beverages, think again. Caterpillar, best known for building tractors and busting unions, has barreled into the branding business, launching the Cat accessories line: boots, back-packs, hats and anything else calling out for a postindustrial *je ne sais quoi.* Intel Corp., which makes computer parts no one sees and few understand, transformed its processors into a fetish brand with TV ads featuring line workers in funky metallic space suits dancing to "Shake Your Groove Thing." The Intel mascots proved so popular that the company has sold hundreds of thousands of bean-filled dolls modeled on the shimmery dancing technicians. Little wonder, then, that when asked about the company's decision to diversify its products, the senior vice president for sales and marketing, Paul S. Otellini, replied that Intel is "like Coke. One brand, many different products."

And if Caterpillar and Intel can brand, surely anyone can.

45 There is, in fact, a new strain in marketing theory that holds that even the lowliest natural resources, barely processed, can develop brand identities, thus giving way to hefty premium-price markups. In an essay appropriately titled "How to Brand Sand," advertising executives Sam Hill, Jack McGrath and Sandeep Dayal team up to tell the corporate world that with the right marketing plan, nobody has to stay stuck in the stuff business. "Based on extensive research, we would argue that you can indeed brand not only sand, but also wheat, beef, brick, metals, concrete, chemicals, corn grits and an endless variety of commodities traditionally considered immune to the process."

Over the past six years, spooked by the near-death experience of Marlboro Friday, global corporations have leaped on the brand-wagon with what can only be described as a religious fervor. Never again would the corporate world stoop to praying at the altar of the commodity market. From now on they would worship only graven media images. Or to quote Tom Peters, the brand man himself: "Brand! Brand!! Brand!!! That's the message . . . for the late '90s and beyond."

WHO'S WEARING THE TROUSERS?

— *The Economist*

> *The Economist* is a leading weekly business and news magazine in the United Kingdom. This "Special Report" on brands appeared in the September 8, 2002, issue, not long after Naomi Klein's *No Logo* was published.

SUGGESTION FOR READING   As you read, notice first how *The Economist* characterizes the "antibranding" argument in Klein's *No Logo.* Then consider how the magazine responds to the criticism of branding.

1 Brands are in the dock, accused of all sorts of mischief, from threatening our health and destroying our environment to corrupting our children. Brands are so powerful, it is alleged, that they seduce us to look alike, eat alike and be alike. At the same time, they are spiritually empty, gradually (and almost subliminally) undermining our moral values.

This grim picture has been popularised by a glut of anti-branding books, ranging from Eric

Schlosser's "Fast Food Nation" and Robert Frank's "Luxury Fever" to "The World Is Not for Sale" by François Dufour and José Bové—a French farmer who is best known for vandalising a McDonald's restaurant. The argument has, however, been most forcefully articulated in Naomi Klein's book "No Logo: Taking Aim at the Brand Bullies."

Not since Vance Packard's 1957 classic "The Hidden Persuaders" has one book stirred up so much antipathy to marketing. Its author has become the spokesman for a worldwide movement against multinationals and their insidious brands. Britain's *Times* newspaper rated her one of the world's most influential people under 35. Published in at least seven languages, "No Logo" has touched a universal nerve.

Its argument runs something like this. In the new global economy, brands represent a huge portion of the value of a company and, increasingly, its biggest source of profits. So companies are switching from producing products to marketing aspirations, images and lifestyles. They are trying to become weightless, shedding physical assets by shifting production from their own factories in the first world to other people's in the third.

5   These image mongers offer "a Barbie world for adults" says Ms Klein, integrating their brands so fully into our lives that they cocoon us in a "brandscape." No space is untouched: schools, sports stars and even youth identity are all being co-opted by brands. "Powerful brands no longer just advertise in a magazine, they control its content," says Ms Klein.

Now they are the target of a backlash. A new generation of activists is rising up and attacking, not governments or ideologies but brands, directly and often violently. Coca-Cola, Wal-Mart and McDonald's have been rounded on over issues ranging from racism to child labour to advertising in schools.

LESS A PRODUCT, MORE A WAY OF LIFE

In one sense it is easy to understand why Ms Klein and her camp feel as they do. The word "brand" is everywhere, to the point where Disney chairman Michael Eisner calls the term "overused, sterile and unimaginative." Products, people, countries and companies are all racing to turn themselves into brands—to make their image more likeable and understandable. British Airways did it. Target and Tesco are doing it, while people from Martha Stewart to Madonna are branding themselves. Britain tried to become a brand with its "Cool Britannia" slogan, and Wally Olins, a corporate-identity consultant and co-founder of Wolff Olins, a consultancy, even wants to have a crack at branding the European Union.

At the very least, Ms Klein overstates the case. Brands are not as powerful as their opponents allege, nor is the public as easily manipulated. The reality is more complicated. Indeed, many of the established brands that top the league tables are in trouble, losing customer loyalty and value. Annual tables of the world's top ten brands used to change very little from year to year. Names such as Kellogg's, Kodak, Marlboro and Nescafé appeared with almost monotonous regularity. Now, none of these names is in the top ten. Kellogg's, second less than a decade ago, languishes at 39th in the latest league table produced by Interbrand, a brand consultancy.

Of the 74 brands that appear in the top 100 rankings in both of the past two years, 41 declined in value between 2000 and 2001, while the combined value of the 74 fell by $49 billion—to an estimated $852 billion, a drop of more than 5%. Brands fall from grace and newer, nimbler ones replace them.

10   Meanwhile, consumers have become more fickle. A study of American lifestyles by DDB, an advertising agency, found that the percentage of consumers between the ages of 20 and 29 who said that they stuck to well-known brands fell from 66% in 1975 to 59% in 2000. The bigger surprise, though, was that the percentage in the 60–69 age bracket who said that they remained loyal to well-known brands fell over the same period, from 86% to 59%. It is not only the young who flit from brand to brand. Every age group, it seems, is more or less equally disloyal. The result is that many of the world's biggest

brands are struggling. If they are making more and more noise, it is out of desperation.

As they move from merely validating products to encapsulating whole lifestyles, brands are evolving a growing social dimension. In the developed world, they are seen by some to have expanded into the vacuum left by the decline of organised religion. But this has made brands—and the multinationals that are increasingly identified with them—not more powerful, but more vulnerable. Consumers will tolerate a lousy product for far longer than they will tolerate a lousy lifestyle.

BRANDS PAST

Historically, building a brand was rather simple. A logo was a straightforward guarantee of quality and consistency, or it was a signal that a product was something new. For that, consumers were, quite rationally, prepared to pay a premium. "Brands were the first piece of consumer protection," says Jeremy Bullmore, a long-time director of J. Walter Thompson, an advertising agency. "You knew where to go if you had a complaint." Even the central planners in the old Soviet Union had to establish "production marks" to stop manufacturers cutting corners on quality.

Brands also helped consumers to buy efficiently. As Unilever's chairman Niall FitzGerald points out: "A brand is a storehouse of trust. That matters more and more as choices multiply. People want to simplify their lives."

This implicit trade-off was efficient and profitable for companies too. Building a brand nationally required little more than an occasional advertisement on a handful of television or radio stations showing how the product tasted better or drove faster. There was little regulation. It was easy for brands such as Coca-Cola, Kodak and Marlboro to become hugely powerful. Because shopping was still a local business and competition limited, a successful brand could maintain its lead and high prices for years. A strong brand acted as an effective barrier to entry for others.

15   In western markets, over time, brand building became much trickier. As standards of man-

ufacturing rose, it became harder for firms to differentiate on quality alone and so to charge a premium price. This was particularly true of packaged goods like food: branded manufacturers lost market share to retailers' own brands, which consumers learned to trust.

Nor were traditional branded products any longer the only choice in town. As shoppers became more mobile and discovered more places to buy, including online websites, they switched products more often. Brands now face competition from the most unexpected quarters, says Rita Clifton, chief executive of Interbrand: "If you were a soap-powder company years ago, your competition would come from the same industry and probably the same country. Now it could be anyone. Who'd have thought that Virgin would sell mobile phones, Versace run hotels or Tesco sell banking services?"

Even truly innovative products can no longer expect to keep the market to themselves for long. Gillette spent $750m and seven years developing its three-bladed Mach 3 men's razor, for which it charged a fat premium. But only months later it was trumped by Asda, a British supermarket that came out with its own version for a fraction of the price.

Consumers are now bombarded with choices. They are "commercials veterans," inundated with up to 1,500 pitches a day. Far from being gullible and easily manipulated, they are cynical about marketing and less responsive to entreaties to buy. "Consumers are like roaches," say Jonathan Bond and Richard Kirshenbaum in their book "Under the Radar—Talking to Today's Cynical Consumer." "We spray them with marketing, and for a time it works. Then, inevitably, they develop an immunity, a resistance."

Some of the most cynical consumers, say the authors, are the young. Nearly half of all American college students have taken marketing courses and "know the enemy." For them, "shooting down advertising has become a kind of sport."

20   Consumers are also harder to reach. They are busier, more distracted and have more media

to choose from. And they lead lives that are more complicated and less predictable. A detergent can no longer count on its core consumer being a white housewife. Against this background, it has never been harder to develop or even just sustain a brand. Coca-Cola, Gillette and Nike are prominent examples of the many that are struggling to increase volumes, raise prices and boost margins.

MARKETING MISTAKES

Marketers have to take some of the blame. While consumers have changed beyond recognition, marketing has not. Elliott Ettenberg, author of a forthcoming book on the decline of marketing says: "Everything else has been reinvented—distribution, new product development, the supply chain. But marketing is stuck in the past." Even in America, home to nine of the world's ten most valuable brands, it can be a shockingly old-fashioned business. Marketing theory is still largely based on the days when Procter & Gamble's brands dominated America, and its advertising agencies wrote the rules. Those rules focused on the product and where to sell it, not the customer.

The new marketing approach is to build a brand not a product—to sell a lifestyle or a personality, to appeal to emotions. But this requires a far greater understanding of human psychology. It is a much harder task than describing the virtues of a product.

Sweden's Absolut Vodka, one of the world's biggest spirits brands, demonstrates this well. Its clever, simple ads featuring its now famous clear bottle were dreamt up long before the vodka was fermented. Goran Lundqvist, the company's president, says that Absolut's wit, rather than its taste, is the reason for the spirit's success: "Absolut is a personality," he claims. "We like certain people, but some people are just more fun and interesting." Other products have also succeeded in touching the emotions. Fans of Ben & Jerry's ice cream, for example, think that it is hip for its ethical stance, while many Harley Davidson owners are literally in love with their machines.

The trouble is that most marketers have to struggle to create such feelings for their brands. Many firms, most notably banks, mistake inertia for liking. Others, such as Coca-Cola and McDonald's, complacent from past success, find it difficult to admit that their customers are drifting away to newer offerings. Yet others, panicking that they need to do something, reinvent themselves and unwittingly lose the essence of their appeal. Old-fashioned market-research methods help explain such mistakes. Focus groups, for example, are poor at rooting out the real reasons why people like brands, but they are still heavily used.

The attempt by brands to adopt a social component—to embrace a lifestyle—is giving consumers a lever to influence the behaviour of the companies that stand behind them. The "No Logo" proponents are correct that brands are a conduit through which influence flows between companies and consumers. But far more often, it is consumers that dictate to companies and ultimately decide their fate, rather than the other way round. Think of the failure of such high-profile product launches as "New Coke"; the disastrous effect on Hoover of a badly-designed sales promotion in Britain a few years ago; or the boycott of genetically modified foods by Europe's consumers.

The Internet also provides some telling examples. Dotcoms such as Webvan and Kozmo were lauded for the speed with which they built their brands. Unconstrained by the need to make profits, however, such companies built customer loyalty artificially. Once business reality returned, they were revealed as unsustainable promises. Consumers, it turned out, were not gullible. As Mr Olins says: "Is the brand immoral, can it get us to do things we don't want to? No. When we like a brand we manifest our loyalty in cash. If we don't like it, we walk away. Customers are in charge."

LEVERS FOR LIFTING STANDARDS

The truth is that people like brands. They not only simplify choices and guarantee quality, but they add fun and interest. "In technocratic and colourless times, brands bring warmth, familiarity and trust," says Peter Brabeck, boss of Nestlé. They also have a cultish quality that creates a sense of belonging. "In an irreligious world, brands provide us with beliefs," says Mr Olins. "They define who we are and signal our affiliations."

Jim McDowell, head of marketing at BMW North America, says that when young people visit a 3Com-sponsored baseball stadium or a Continental Airlines' hockey arena, they realise that "some of the best things they have ever experienced have come through brands."

Since brands and their corporate parents are becoming ever more entwined—both in the public perception and commercial reality—it follows that consumers can increasingly influence the behaviour of companies. Arrogance, greed and hypocrisy are swiftly punished. Popular outrage forced Shell to retreat over the scrapping of its Brent Spar oil platform and its activities in Nigeria. Nike has had to revamp its whole supply chain after being accused of running sweatshops.

30   Even mighty Coca-Cola has been humbled. Told of a contamination incident in Belgium, its then-boss, Doug Ivester, is said to have dismissed it with the comment: "Where the fuck is Belgium?" A few months later, after a mishandled public-relations exercise that cost Coke sales across Europe, he was fired. "It is absurd to say that brands can be too powerful," concludes Interbrand's Ms Clifton. "Brands are the ultimate accountable institution. If people fall out of love with your brand, you go out of business."

This ultimately makes brands highly effective tools through which to bring about change. Rafael Gomez, professor of marketing at the London School of Economics, points out that companies like Nike have been forced to invest heavily in improving their manufacturing standards in order to protect their brands. World Bank studies show that brands have been a boon for developing economies, because it is the branded multinationals that pay the best wages and have the best working conditions. Those countries that are more open to trade and foreign investment, such as the Asian tigers, have shown faster increases in living standards than relatively closed countries such as much of Africa.

Brands of the future will have to stand not only for product quality and a desirable image. They will also have to signal something wholesome about the company behind the brand. "The next big thing in brands is social responsibility," says Mr Olins. "It will be clever to say there is nothing different about our product or price, but we behave well." Far from being evil, brands are becoming an effective weapon for holding even the largest global corporations to account. If we do not use them for that purpose, as Mr Olins puts it, "we are lazy and indifferent and we deserve what we get."

Fittingly, brands will then have come full circle. The founders of some of the world's oldest—Hershey, Disney, Cadbury and Boots, for example—devoted their lives and company profits to social improvements, to building spacious towns, better schools and bigger hospitals. The difference in the future will be that it will be consumers, not philanthropists, who will dictate the social agenda.

SUGGESTIONS FOR DISCUSSION

1. Compare the explanations of the term *branding* that you and your classmates wrote in response to the excerpt from Naomi Klein's *No Logo*. What exactly does Klein mean? What examples and evidence does she provide to illustrate her meaning? What assumptions does she seem to be making?

2. Consider how *The Economist* article characterizes Klein's "antibranding" point of view. Do you think it's a fair and comprehensive explanation? What, if anything, does it leave out? What are the main points of difference *The Economist* presents to distinguish its view from Klein's? What assumptions does the magazine seem to be making?

3. Branding attempts to distinguish products that are largely indistinguishable by creating a brand style. Consider similar products, such as Pepsi and Coca Cola, Nike and Reebok, or Nissan Sentra and Toyota Corolla. How do advertising, packaging, logos, slogans, and other features distinguish one brand style from the other?

SUGGESTIONS FOR WRITING

1. Write an essay about your personal relationship to brands. Pick a particular brand to focus your writing. Take seriously the point that Klein and marketing people make about the way brands identify not just a product but, as Klein puts it, a "way of life, an attitude, a set of values, a look, an idea." How does a particular brand of goods you wear, use, or otherwise consume project a lifestyle? How does the brand influence your own sense of identity? What attitudes does it have for you?

2. There are clearly significant differences in the way Naomi Klein and *The Economist* think about brands. Write an essay that locates your own thinking in relation to what they have written. First, summarize the two points of view. Then analyze what you see as the main differences and the assumptions behind these differences. Finally, explain what you think.

3. Write an essay that analyzes the brand style of two similar products. Consider advertising, packaging, logos, slogans, and other elements of branding that attempt to distinguish one product from the other.

FILM CLIP

Makeup and Costumes: Monsters and the Middle Ages

To learn more about costumes and drama, visit www.ablongman.com/george/119

The style of a film depends in part on makeup artists and costume designers who work closely with directors and actors to give a movie its particular look. The work of makeup artists ranges from highlighting the natural features of a film star to changing altogether actors' appearances to fit the characters they portray. In the era of black-and-white filmmaking, movies favored stars such as Katharine Hepburn and Lauren Bacall whose angular faces and prominent cheekbones caught the light and cast lovely shadows. With the advent of color, the emphasis shifted to the glowing complexion of Marilyn Monroe, Grace Kelly, and Kim Novak. The job of the makeup artist, in either case, was to prepare these stars to face the camera by accentuating the telling features. At the same time, makeup artists have also created totally new faces for actors, making them seem older or younger and, in the case of horror films, turning normal people into vampires, werewolves, mummies, or other monsters.

One way to think about the work of makeup artists is to look at how they have created film monsters. To do this, you might trace the various film versions of Dracula, Frankenstein, or the Phantom of the Opera. In turn, you could compare these classic film monsters to more recent menaces such as Freddy Krueger of a *Nightmare on Elm Street* or Jason of the *Friday the 13th* series.

Costuming plays a key role in enabling moviegoers to visualize the identities of actors and the historical period a film recreates. In some cases, such as the *Godfather* trilogy, *Malcolm X*, *Titanic*, or *Gangs of New York*, costume design creates a sense of authenticity about the time in which the film is set. In other cases, costuming seems to be a comment on an actor's character, such as the disheveled look of Jeff Bridges in a bathrobe in *The Big Lebowski* or the cool style of George Clooney and the rest of the cast in *Ocean's Eleven* and *Ocean's Twelve*.

From such extravaganzas as *Gone With the Wind* in 1939 to *Vanity Fair* in 2004, Hollywood has produced many costume dramas. One of the historical periods Hollywood keeps coming back to is the Middle Ages—the era of knights, chivalry, and romance. To think about the work of costume designers, you could examine a number of films that portray the Middle Ages, such as the *Knights of the Round Table* (1953), *El Cid* (1961), *Lion in Winter* (1968), *Monty Python and the Holy Grail* (1975), *Excalibur* (1981), *The Return of Martin Guerre* (1984), *Braveheart* (1995), and *King Arthur* (2004).

VISUAL ESSAY

Sweet-Talking Spaghetti Sauce:
How to Read a Label

— *Tibor Kalman*

Tibor Kalman (1949–1999) was an important and influential graphic designer who worked on everything from the redevelopment of Times Square in New York to Talking Heads' record jackets. The following Visual Essay on the design of labels on spaghetti sauce jars appeared in a special edition of the *New York Times Magazine*, "The Shock of the Familiar," about design in contemporary society. As the *New York Times Magazine* says, "We asked the designer Tibor Kalman . . . to pretend he was pitching these labels to various manufacturers. We wanted to know how he thought they would have tried to sell the designs, as well as to get a view of the messages the labels are trying to communicate."

SUGGESTION FOR READING   As you read, notice that Tibor Kalman looks first at the message that the label sends and then at the market that the message addresses. Consider how the design of the labels sets up a relationship between message and market.

Caslon   *William Caslon (1692-1766) designed the typeface named after him at his foundry in England. This variation was digitalized by Matthew Carter in 1994*

80

Message: Sweet-Talking Spaghetti Sauce

How to really read a label. By Tibor Kalman

Photographs by Davies + Starr

W

SUPER

ITALIAN STYLE
MEATLESS
SPAGHETTI SAUCE

NET WT. 30 OZ. (1 LB. 14 OZ.) 850 g

Aunt Millie's
THERE'S A LOT OF LITTLE ITALY IN EVERY JAR

100%
NATURAL
PASTA
SAUCE

HOMEMADE
FLAVOR
SINCE 1946

◇ TRADITIONAL ◇
TOMATO & HERBS

CLASSICO
DI NAPOLI

TOMATO & BASIL

PASTA SAUCE   NET WT. 26 OZ. (1 LB. 10 OZ.)

SUPER A

"Good morning, gents. I am interested in conveying the favorable price-quantity ratio of Super A meatless sauce. Our serving-suggestion photo (a pound of spaghetti, a pound of sauce, a fork and a knife) represents an inexpensive, nutritious meal for a very, very large, very, very hungry individual."
MARKET: Thrifty, large, hungry people, all ages

AUNT MILLIE'S

"Just look at this picture of Aunt Millie. Can you imagine anyone sweeter, purer, more Italian? And we got 'Little Italy,' 'homemade' and '1946' right on the label. What else could you want?"
MARKET: Mama's boys, proud, older Italian-Americans

CLASSICO

"The Classico typeface is right here. We antiqued it to make sure it looks really old. We have the antique tomato drawing, the Amish jar engineer-made. The jar is square, to suggest that people used to put up their own tomatoes in them. And it only took 175 focus groups to get us to this label design."
MARKET: Upscale types 25 to 49 who enjoy fake antique furniture

hen you think about it, sauce is mostly sauce. It's the label that makes the difference. A multimillion-dollar business, packaging is the most lucrative form of design work in the United States. We asked the designer Tibor Kalman (shown below the jars) to pretend he was pitching these labels to various manufacturers. We wanted to know how he thought they would have tried to sell the designs, as well as to get a view of the messages the labels are trying to communicate.

VICTORIA

"Mama mia! What do we have here? We have the typeface from the old grocery in Palermo. The gondola picture from the wall of an old bar in Calabria. Traditionalist, but Venetian. Very romantic."

MARKET: 65-plus Sicilian-born Italian-Americans

MILLINA'S FINEST

"We got Mama, fields, a nice basket of tomatoes, fat free, sun-dried tomatoes, organic. The whole shebang. Perfect for people who want the best but have no idea what the best is."

MARKET: Collegiate 18- to 49-ers who need a lot of "benefits" in their sauce.

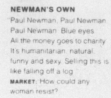

NEWMAN'S OWN

"Paul Newman, Paul Newman, Paul Newman. Blue eyes. All the money goes to charity. It's humanitarian, natural, funny and sexy. Selling this is like falling off a log."

MARKET: How could any woman resist?

HUNT'S OLD COUNTRY

"Guys. We gotta make a sauce for guys. So I got some good old Picket Fence Gothic type, with cracked paint and all. Very barbecue. Thought the guys would appreciate these bodacious tomatoes."

MARKET: West of New York, east of Los Angeles. 50-plus guys, weighing 250-plus pounds.

SUGGESTIONS FOR DISCUSSION

1. Tibor Kalman first uses the voice of an advertising pitchman to describe the message in the label. (The pitch appears in quotes.) What visual features of the labels does he seem to notice? He then identifies the market targeted by the message, but without explicitly explaining how the connection works. Fill in that connection. Why would particular labels appeal to particular segments of the spaghetti sauce market?

2. The market in the United States is saturated with similar products. Spaghetti sauce is just one example. Notice that Kalman is interested in how the visual styles of labels differ, but he doesn't mention anything about whether there are consequential differences among the products themselves. In your experience, when there is a range of competing products, do the products themselves differ, or are the differences mainly in the labeling?

3. Work in a group with three or four other students and pick a product you're familiar with that has competing brands. Bring at least four examples of the product to class to make a presentation. Follow Kalman's example, and explain the message on the label and the market that is targeted.

SUGGESTIONS FOR WRITING

1. Using Tibor Kalman's Visual Essay as a guide, write your own essay on the visual design of spaghetti sauce jars. Make explicit how the advertising pitch connects to the targeted audience. Pick two or three jar labels, and explain how the visual design is related to a particular part of the market.

2. Follow Kalman's example and do a visual essay on the labels of several similar products. Use at least three or four examples. Give the advertising pitch in quotes, and then indicate the targeted audience.

3. Design a label for a product. Accompany the design with a written explanation or an oral presentation (depending on what your teacher asks for) of the message on the label and the market you've targeted. Think here in terms of how to distinguish what is basically the same product from other products of the same type.

CLASSIC READING

THE FACE OF GARBO

— Roland Barthes

Roland Barthes (1915–1980) was a professor at the College de France in Paris and one of the most influential cultural and literary critics of the twentieth century. The following selection, "The Face of Garbo," comes from *Mythologies*, a collection of essays Barthes wrote and published in French periodicals in the 1950s. "The starting point" of these essays, as Barthes says, was "a feeling of impatience at the sight of 'naturalness' with which newspapers, art, and common sense constantly dress up a reality which, even though it is the one we live in, is undoubtedly determined by history." Barthes was interested in analyzing such commonplaces as toys, food, wrestling, striptease, detergents, and, as you can see in this brief essay, the faces of movie stars to investigate how their taken-for-granted presence in everyday life shapes the style and sensibility of French culture.

SUGGESTION FOR READING   Greta Garbo was one of the greatest screen actresses of the 1930s and 1940s, appearing in such Hollywood classics as *Queen Christina*, *Ninotchka*, and *Camille*. As you read, notice how Roland Barthes sets up terms to describe the beauty of her face—as part of a "moment in cinema" when film actors still plunged audiences "into the deepest ecstasy" and as the reconciliation of "two iconographic ages" and the "passage from awe to charm."

Greta Garbo.

1 Garbo still belongs to that moment in cinema when capturing the human face still plunged audiences into the deepest ecstasy, when one literally lost oneself in a human image as one would in a philtre, when the face represented a kind of absolute state of the flesh, which could be neither reached nor renounced. A few years earlier the face of Valentino was causing suicides; that of Garbo still partakes of the same rule of Courtly Love, where the flesh gives rise to mystical feelings of perdition.

It is indeed an admirable face-object. In *Queen Christina*, a film which has again been shown in Paris in the last few years, the make-up has the snowy thickness of a mask: it is not a painted face, but one set in plaster, protected by the surface of the colour, not by its lineaments. Amid all this snow at once fragile and compact, the eyes alone, black like strange soft flesh, but not in the least expressive, are two faintly tremulous wounds. In spite of its extreme beauty, this face, not drawn but sculpted in something smooth and friable, that is, at once perfect and ephemeral, comes to resemble the flour-white complexion of Charlie Chaplin, the dark vegetation of his eyes, his totem-like countenance.

Now the temptation of the absolute mask (the mask of antiquity, for instance) perhaps implies less the theme of the secret (as is the case with Italian half mask) than that of an archetype of the human face. Garbo offered to one's gaze a sort of Platonic Idea of the human creature, which explains why her face is almost sexually undefined, without however leaving one in doubt. It is true that this film (in which Queen Christina is by turns a woman and a young cavalier) lends itself to this lack of differentiation; but Garbo does not perform in it any feat of transvestism; she is always herself, and carries without pretence, under her crown or her wide-brimmed hats, the same snowy solitary face. The name given to her, *the Divine*, probably aimed to convey less a superlative state of beauty than the essence of her corporeal person, descended from a heaven where all things are formed and perfected in the clearest light. She herself knew this: how many actresses have consented to let the crowd see the ominous maturing of their beauty. Not she, however; the essence was not to be degraded, her face was not to have any reality except that of its perfection, which was intellectual even more than formal. The Essence became gradually obscured, progressively veiled with dark glasses, broad hats and exiles: but it never deteriorated.

And yet, in this deified face, something sharper than a mask is looming: a kind of voluntary and therefore human relation between the curve of the nostrils and the arch of the eyebrows; a rare, individual function relating two regions of the face. A mask is but a sum of lines; a face, on the contrary, is above all their thematic harmony. Garbo's face represents this fragile moment when the cinema is about to draw an existential from an essential beauty, when the archetype leans towards the fascination of mortal faces, when the clarity of the flesh as essence yields its place to a lyricism of Woman.

5   Viewed as a transition the face of Garbo reconciles two iconographic ages, it assures the passage from awe to charm. As is well known, we are today at the other pole of this evolution: the face of Audrey Hepburn, for instance, is individualized, not only because of its peculiar thematics (woman as child, woman as kitten) but also because of her person, of an almost unique specification of the face, which has nothing of the essence left in it, but is constituted by an infinite complexity of morphological functions. As a language, Garbo's singularity was of the order of the concept, that of Audrey Hepburn is of the order of the substance. The face of Garbo is an Idea, that of Hepburn, an Event.

SUGGESTIONS FOR DISCUSSION

1. Roland Barthes raises the question of why certain film stars are considered "beautiful." Who are the film stars you and your classmates consider "beautiful"? What, if anything, do they have in common with Greta Garbo? How does their beauty differ? How would you explain these differences?

2. Barthes says that "Garbo offered to one's gaze a sort of Platonic Idea of the human creature." What does he mean by this?

3. Barthes says that the face of Garbo marks a kind of transition from "awe to charm" and compares Garbo to Audrey Hepburn, the popular Hollywood actress of the 1950s and 1960s. What does he mean by this comparison? In what sense is the face of Garbo "an Idea" and that of Hepburn "an Event." (To answer this question, it may be helpful to look online for images of both Greta Garbo and Audrey Hepburn.)

SUGGESTIONS FOR WRITING

1. Write an essay that begins by explaining Barthes's analysis of the "face of Garbo." He is very brief and only suggestive about his ideas. Consider the assumptions he is making and how his line of analysis applies to current film stars.

2. Do some research on Greta Garbo to respond to Barthes's essay. Do you think he provides a useful interpretation? What would you add, revise, or argue about?

3. Barthes is certainly correct to assume that every age has its own notion of feminine beauty. He does not, however, say much about how these images of beauty function in society or what effect they have on women and men. Write an essay that takes up this issue.

MINING THE ARCHIVE   Race and Branding

Chief Wahoo thru the years

The Cleveland Indians have used various forms of Chief Wahoo as their logo since 1915, and the current version since 1992.

1920s   1930s   1940s   1950s-90s

To learn more about branding, visit
www.ablongman.com/george/120

The history of branding by companies and sports teams in the United States is deeply implicated in the racial politics of the nation. Companies have for years used images of African Americans such as Aunt Jemima and Uncle Ben as familiar and reassuring symbols of product quality, and critics have argued that these representations perpetuate racial stereotypes of blacks as cooks and servants to whites. A similar issue has arisen about the use of Native American nicknames and logos of professional baseball and football teams—the Cleveland Indians, the Atlanta Braves, the Washington Redskins, and the Kansas City Chiefs. Do these images invoke a powerful identity for their teams as warriors, or do they contribute to the myth of Native Americans as a savage, vanishing race? In recent years, several high schools and colleges have changed their nicknames and logos. There are several archival sources you can consult. To find out more about the representation of African Americans in branding, check out *Aunt Jemima, Uncle Ben, and Rastus: Blacks in Advertising, Yesterday, Today, and Tomorrow* by Marilyn Kern-Foxworth; on Aunt Jemima, see *Slave in a Box* by M. M. Manring. It is possible that your own college or high school or one nearby has a Native American nickname and logo. If that is the case, research the original decision to name the school teams and any stylistic changes that occur over time, as you can see here in the evolution of the Cleveland Indians' "mascot," Chief Wahoo.

Public Space

Walker Evans, © The Walker Evans Archive, The Metropolitan Museum of Art.

In wildness, is the preservation of the world.

—Henry David Thoreau

When you go up to the city, you better have some cash, 'cause the people in the city don't mess around with trash.

—Traditional blues lyric

One way of examining how a culture lives and what it values is to look at its public spaces—its streets, parks, sports arenas, shopping malls, museums—all those places where people gather to do business and play and loiter. Such spaces are abundant in countrysides and suburbs as well as in cities. Megamalls and fast food restaurants line the highway system as a result of urban sprawl, and in small towns and rural areas, the fairgrounds, town halls, county arenas, and churches still function as public gathering spots. In fact, even America's wilderness areas have become places where the public gathers, where tourists travel to catch a glimpse of the Grand Canyon, to picnic in Yellowstone, and to hike in the Adirondacks.

Most public spaces are designed simply to be functional, which is why much of what you see every day is remarkable only for its similarity to nearly everything else you see. Office buildings that seem to pop up from the pavement overnight look like every other office building in the city. The new wing of a local hospital looks tacked on to the old wing as a high-rise box of rooms and corridors. One grocery store looks like all the others, schools look like schools, and doctors' offices look like doctors' offices. A popular motel chain even tried for a while to capitalize on its across-the-continent sameness—Holiday Inn ads promised "no surprises," apparently assuming that most Americans are uncomfortable with anything too different. Perhaps that is why it is so easy to take most public spaces for granted. It is only when a place looks distinctive—newer, flashier, stranger—that most visitors stop to look. In a world crowded with so much to look at, it takes an effort, a real spectacle, to get the public's attention.

It is easy to think of the most famous or infamous public spaces in contemporary America as constituting spectacle above all else. From the Mall of America to Epcot Center, each new public space seems to be vying to be the biggest and most expensive. Such spaces compete for attention, inviting visitors to look, to linger, and to buy. These public spaces turned spectacle characterize at least one impulse in a consumer economy—the impulse to sell.

Of course, our interest in public space has to do with more than appearance. To say a space is public is to suggest it belongs to everyone—a space for a community, not simply for private use. Yet more and more spaces that at first seem to be open to the public aren't at all public in the strictest sense. Malls, for example, are often credited with becoming the new "town square," but a town square is clearly a public space where people in the community do have certain rights, such as the right to free speech. Malls are private property. You cannot distribute campaign literature or any other kinds of materials without the permission of mall owners, and many of those owners are very careful about letting anyone into their space who might seem to threaten business by diverting the public's attention from the stores to political issues. So even though a mall might invite a Senior Mall Walker's Club to come and exercise before stores open for business, that is not the same as walking out your door and taking your morning jog through the neighborhood. The mall owners can rescind the invitation at any time and bar from the property anyone they feel interferes with business.

Even public streets are not so free to the public as we might imagine. In recent years, demonstrators at both Republican and Democratic national conventions have found themselves segregated into small groups, many quite far from the convention site, as city officials attempt to control the unexpected. Officials of the St. Patrick's Day Parade in New York City have fought for years to ban gays from having a visible presence in that event. Throughout the United States, town squares, plazas, and shop fronts are purposely designed to keep people from being able to sit and chat or rest comfortably, so that loiterers, street people, groups of teenagers, and anyone without a "purpose" to be there won't be tempted to hang around.

What's more, the tension between public use of public space and private land ownership is a serious one, especially when it comes to wilderness land holdings. In the West, cattle ranchers fight attempts to limit their access to or increase usage fees on grazing land within national parks. The debate over whether or not to open the Black Hills to more gold mining is an ongoing one. Throughout the country, the national park system has moved forward with privatizing many of its services. Consequently, parks have been changing in response to revenue generated by those new businesses. In other words, it is a contradiction: Americans want public spaces but value private use. It is a conflict that is not easily resolved.

That conflict was never more apparent than in the debate over what to do with the site of the former World Trade Center in New York City in the aftermath of the September 11, 2001, attacks that leveled those two buildings. Because this was the site of a tragedy for thousands of Americans, many people think that any new construction certainly has to memorialize the victims. However, the spot is also what has been come to be called "prime commercial real estate," owned not by the city or the nation, but by entrepreneurs who want to capitalize on its value. Plans have been made for a memorial, yet any new construction will certainly remain the center of conflict between private rights and public use for many years to come.

The very design of our cities, towns, subdivisions, and planned communities can reflect the concerns and struggles of the culture at large. For example, the gap between rich and poor is apparent not only in people's income (or lack of income) but also in the breakdown of public services and the disrepair of buildings and roads in poorer parts of town. If you live in the city, the suburbs, or the country, have visited historical monuments, spent time in New York or Los Angeles, attended a ball game, watched a parade, shopped in a mall, eaten in a fast food restaurant, or simply attended a church bazaar or school dance, you already know a good deal about how public space is organized in contemporary America, and you probably make more judgments about public spaces than you think.

One way to look at public space is to recall the first impressions you had of places you have seen. As you explore these memories, you may begin to understand how you form your own judgments of places. For many people across the United States, public space means open land, wilderness holdings, national parks, and other lands held by the government in the public trust. For others, public space is the space on city streets.

Though the work in this chapter begins with observation and memory, you will have the opportunity to do fieldwork, collect and examine images of public space, and offer your own assessments of the way people use the spaces they inhabit. What you write depends on what you have already experienced and what you already think about the topic. Take time, then, at the beginning of your reading to mine your memory about public spaces.

THE CENTER OF THE UNIVERSE

— Tina McElroy Ansa

Tina McElroy Ansa is a journalist, novelist, and teacher who grew up in middle Georgia in the 1950s hearing, she says, her grandfather's stories on the porch of her family home and strangers' stories downtown in her father's juke joint. Her first novel, *Baby of the Family* (2002), was listed by the state of Georgia as one of the twenty-five books every Georgian should read. Her articles and op-ed pieces have appeared in a number of newspapers and magazines across the country, including the *Los Angeles Times*, the *Atlanta Constitution*, *Ms. Magazine*, and *Essence*. "The Center of the Universe" (2003) is about Ansa's memories of growing up in Macon, Georgia. In it she raises the question of place and belonging—especially for African Americans growing up in the South.

**SUGGESTION
FOR READING** Before you read, write a brief description of what you would call Small-Town America in the 1950s. Think about where you get the impression of what that place should look like, what the people are like, and whether or not you believe this place really ever existed.

1   On the way home from school one day when I was seven or eight years old—a black child growing up in Macon, Georgia, in the 1950s—my father, Walter McElroy, took me to a huge fountain in a city park. At the edge of the fountain, he pointed to the water and said very seriously, "That is the exact center of Georgia."

It was a momentous revelation for me. Since that instant, I have always thought of myself being at the center of my universe, enveloped in the world around me. From that day, I have imagined myself standing at that fountain surrounded by my African American community of Pleasant Hill, in my hometown of Macon, in middle Georgia, with the muddy Ocmulgee River running nearby, with the entire state of Georgia around me, then all of the southeastern section of the continental United States, then the country, the Western Hemisphere, then the world.

The image has always made me feel safe. Sheltered by my surroundings, enveloped in the arms of "family" of one kind or another, mostly southern family. That is how I see myself, a southerner.

For some folks, my discussing my southernness makes them downright uncomfortable. I mean really, the very idea, a black person, an African American over the age of thirty-five, going on and on about the South and her place in it as if she weren't aware of the region, its past, and all it stands for.

5   Doesn't she know history? she seems to think. And she's a writer, too. It's almost embarrassing.

As if a black person does not belong in the South, to the South. In a couple of decades of moving up and down the United States' eastern seaboard, I found there was no place else I *did belong.*

Of course I know the region's history, I want to tell folks looking askance at me. I know it because I am a part of the history. My parents were part of that history. And their parents were part of it.

My father's people came from Wrightsville, in the south-central part of the state. They were farming people, like most black people at the turn of the twentieth century. At that time, black folks owned nearly twenty million acres of farmland in the United States. When my father's father, Frank, left the farm nearly one hundred years ago for the city of Macon and work on the M-D-S— the Macon-Dublin-Savannah train line, which connected those three Georgia cities—his brother Isadore (whom we called "Uncle Sunshine") and his family remained there on the farm. As a child, when my parents, two older brothers and two older sisters, and I piled into our green woodie station wagon and left the "city" for a few days in summer to visit the "country," it was to Uncle Sunshine's farm we went.

My mother's people—the Lees—were also from middle Georgia. But they were "city people," they were not farmers. They were schoolteachers and tradespeople and semiprofessionals. Everyone in town knew my great-grandfather as "Pat, the barber." All I have to do now is say that name to make my mother smile with nostalgia and begin telling me stories surrounding the antique red leather barbershop chair that sat on my great-aunt's back porch for decades. Patrick Lee's maiden daughter, Elizabeth, not only took over her father's barbershop when he died in the 1930s. She also taught folks in middle Georgia from the cradle to the grave. During the day, she led her own private kindergarten class. During the evenings, she taught illiterate adults to read. "All I want to do is learn to read the Bible," they would tell her. She always chuckled: "Lord, some of the most difficult words and concepts in the world are in the Bible."

10   In childhood, I always thought of her as just a stern religious old maid who didn't even drink Coca-Colas or take aspirin because they were "dope" or let you sleep in any bed in her house past sunup lest you get "the big head." I thank the Holy Spirit that she and I both lived long enough for me to see her for the extraordinary African American woman that she was. She was one of the reasons my mother loved reading and passed that love on to her children.

Today, every word I write, I write on a computer atop the old pedal-motored Singer sewing machine console that once sat in Auntie's bedroom.

It is no wonder that in my childhood family house—a big old brick two-story house with an attic and basement—there were books everywhere: in the bedrooms, the bathroom, the living room, and the kitchen. When I was a child, the joke in our family was to shove a copy of the tiny Macon telephone book under the door of the bathroom when someone hollered out for some new reading material. Whenever that happened to me, I happily sat there with my legs dangling off the toilet and amused myself by reading that phone book, looking up my friends' numbers and addresses, coming upon interesting names, making up stories about the people and streets I encountered there.

When I was growing up, I thought the entire world was made up of stories. My mother gossiping on the phone was to my ear my mother weaving stories. The tales of love and woe that I overheard from the customers at my father's juke joints and liquor store down on Broadway and Mulberry Street, as I sat at the end of the bar in my Catholic school uniform doing my homework, were to me stories. My grandfather Walter McElroy's ghost stories of cats wearing diamond rings sticking their hands into blazing campfires. My Baptist great-auntie Elizabeth Lee relating how she always wanted to go to the Holy Land but had no intention of crossing any water to get there. My mother telling me over and over as she whipped up batter for one of her light-as-air,

sweet-as-mother's-love desserts how she made her first cake when she was only seven.

I draw sustenance from these stories, in the same way I draw nourishment from knowing that my father's people farmed land right up the road in Wrightsville, Georgia. In my southern mind, I can see Uncle Sunshine drawing his bony mule under the hot shade of a tall Georgia pine and wiping his brow when I gaze at the pine trees around my house. I never cross a railroad track without recalling my grandfather's years with the M-D-S line and the first time my father put me on the famed "Nancy Hanks" train for a trip to Savannah by myself. After my father handed me over to the care of the train's porters, they asked, pointing to my father's retreating back, "Who was that boy?" I replied indignantly, "That's no boy! That's my daddy!" The black men looked at each other and just beamed. Then proceeded to getting me cold Coca-Colas and sneaking me sandwiches from the whites-only dining car. For the rest of the four-hour trip, they treated me like a princess, heaping on me the loving attention usually thought of as the preserve of little white girls traveling on the southern train system. In fact, they treated me better. They treated me like family.

15   Family. As a writer, a novelist, it is all that I write about. My first novel, *Baby of the Family*, is not just about my retaining that special place of the last born in my household. It is also about the ties, the connections, the stories, the food, the rituals, the seasons, the minutiae that go into forming the family unit.

Like all of us, I carry my childhood with me.

No matter where I go or in what time zone I find myself, at eleven o'clock Eastern Standard Time Sunday mornings, I think of St. Peter Claver Church sitting at the top of Pleasant Hill and the sacrament of the Eucharist being celebrated there. Sunday morning mass in my childhood parish is still the quintessential Sunday morning to me. Just as that fountain in the middle of Tatnall Square Park is the primary bellwether for my place in the universe.

When I write, I still envision myself standing at that fountain surrounded by my family, my community, my hometown, my state, my country, and the world.

From time to time, my mother will wistfully remind some old friend of hers who asks about me, "Tina doesn't live in Macon anymore."

20   My Mama is right. I *don't* live in Macon anymore.

Macon lives in me.

SUGGESTIONS FOR DISCUSSION

1. At the beginning of her essay, Ansa poses a problem for her readers: why would an African American love the South? After all, the history of that region should make it very difficult for any African American to want to claim it as home. What is her response to that question?

2. With a group of your classmates, share the piece you wrote before you read this essay. What does each person in your group identify as the idealized place that has been called "Small-Town America"? What are the characteristics of that place? How do the descriptions differ? What do they have in common? To what extent do individuals' experiences growing up today and in different places influence their impressions of Small-Town America as it has been idealized?

3. "Family," writes Ansa. "As a writer, a novelist, it is all that I write about." This essay is certainly a story about family, but it is also about place. What role does place play in the childhood that Ansa says she carries with her?

SUGGESTIONS FOR WRITING

1. Write your own description of how you do or do not carry the place or places where you grew up with you. What role do those early places in your life play in the way you think people should live or what you think towns or cities should look like? What role do popular media play in the way most of us envision a good place (and its opposite) for living or raising children?

2. Write a response to Ansa's defense of her love of the South—especially southern Georgia, a place that has a particularly harsh history for African Americans.

3. Most readers would say that Ansa's description of small-town Georgia in the 1950s is an idealized one. Write an essay in which you examine this essay as an extension of the media or idealized image of U.S. small towns in the 1950s. What makes Ansa's description seem idealized? What about it strikes you as real?

SHOPPING FOR PLEASURE: MALLS, POWER, AND RESISTANCE

— *John Fiske*

John Fiske is a professor of communication at the University of Wisconsin–Madison. He is among the many scholars today who make use of the artifacts of daily life to interpret modern culture. For Fiske, as well as others engaging in cultural studies, the analysis of popular culture can help reveal how a society produces meaning from its social experience. The following selection, taken from *Reading the Popular* and written in 1989, demonstrates how phenomena we take for granted in our everyday lives, such as shopping malls, are a part of that cultural production of meaning.

SUGGESTION
FOR READING Notice as you read that Fiske makes reference to other studies from which he has drawn ideas, interpretations, and information. He uses those references to give scholarly weight to his argument and to acknowledge his use of others' work in building his own interpretation. If you are not familiar with the names (he usually uses last names only), don't let that stop your reading. The context in which the name is used can usually give you enough information to allow you to continue. As you read, underline passages in which Fiske distinguishes his own view from that of those other scholars.

1   Shopping malls are cathedrals of consumption—a glib phrase that I regret the instant it slides off my pen. The metaphor of consumerism as a religion, in which commodities become the icons of worship and the rituals of exchanging money for goods become a secular equivalent of holy communion, is simply too glib to be helpful, and too attractive to those whose intentions, whether they be moral or political, are to expose the evils and limitations of bourgeois materialism. And yet the metaphor is both attractive and common precisely because it does convey and construct a knowledge of consumerism; it does point to one set of "truths," however carefully selected a set.

Truths compete in a political arena, and the truths that the consumerism-as-contemporary-religion strives to suppress are those that deny the difference between the tenor and vehicle of the metaphor. Metaphor always works within that tense area within which the forces of similarity and difference collide, and aligns itself with those of similarity. Metaphor constructs similarity out of difference, and when a metaphor becomes a cliché, as the shopping mall-cathedral one has, then a resisting reading must align itself with the differences rather than the similarities, for clichés become clichés only because of their centrality to common sense: the cliché helps to construct the commonality of common sense.

So, the differences: the religious congregation is powerless, led like sheep through the rituals and meanings, forced to "buy" the truth on offer, all the truth, not selective bits of it. Where the interests of the Authority on High differ from those of the Congregation down Low, the congregation has no power to negotiate, to discriminate: all accommodations are made by the powerless, subjugated to the great truth. In the U.S. marketplace, 90 percent of new products fail to find sufficient buyers to survive (Schudson 1984), despite advertising, promotions, and all the persuasive techniques of the priests of consumption. In Australia, Sinclair (1987) puts the new product failure rate at 80 percent—such statistics are obviously best-guesstimates: what matters is that the failure rate is high. The power of consumer discrimination evidenced here has no equivalent in the congregation: no religion could tolerate a rejection rate of 80 or 90 percent of what it has to offer.

Religion may act as a helpful metaphor when our aim is to investigate the power of consumerism; when, however, our focus shifts to the power of the consumer, it is counter-productive. . . . Shopping is the crisis of consumerism: it is where the art and tricks of the weak can inflict most damage on, and exert most power over, the strategic interests of the powerful. The shopping mall that is seen as the terrain of guerrilla warfare looks quite different from the one constructed by the metaphor of religion.

5   Pressdee (1986), in his study of unemployed youth in the South Australian town of Elizabeth, paints a clear picture of both sides in this war. The ideological practices that serve the interests of the powerful are exposed in his analysis of the local mall's promotional slogan, which appears

in the form of a free ticket: "Your ticket to a better shopping world: ADMITS EVERYONE." He comments:

> The words "your" and "everyone" are working to socially level out class distinction and, in doing so, overlook the city's two working class groups, those who have work and those who do not. The word "admits" with a connotation of having to have or be someone to gain admittance is cancelled out by the word "everyone"—there are no conditions of admittance; everyone is equal and can come in.

This pseudoticket to consumerism denies the basic function of a ticket—to discriminate between those who possess one and those who do not—in a precise moment of the ideological work of bourgeois capitalism with its denial of class difference, and therefore of the inevitability of class struggle. The equality of "everyone" is, of course, an equality attainable only by those with purchasing power: those without are defined out of existence, as working-class interests (derived from class *difference*) are defined out of existence by bourgeois ideology. "The ticket to a better shopping world does not say 'Admits everyone with at least some money to spend'. . . ; money and the problems associated with getting it conveniently disappear in the official discourse" (Pressdee 1986: 10–11).

Pressdee then uses a variation of the religious metaphor to sum up the "official" messages of the mall:

> The images presented in the personal invitation to all in Elizabeth is then that of the cargo cult. Before us a lightshaft beamïs down from space, which contains the signs of the "future"; "Target", "Venture"—gifts wrapped; a table set for two. But beamed down from space they may as well be, because . . . this imagery can be viewed as reinforcing denial of the production process—goods are merely beamed to earth. The politics of their production and consumption disappear.

Yet his study showed that 80 percent of unemployed young people visited the mall at least once a week, and nearly 100 percent of young unemployed women were regular visitors. He comments on these uninvited guests:

> For young people, especially the unemployed, there has been a congregating within these cathedrals of capitalism, where desires are created and fulfilled and the production of commodities, the very activity that they are barred from, is itself celebrated on the altar of consumerism. Young people, cut off from normal consumer power, are invading the space of those with consumer power. (p. 13)

Pressdee's shift from the religious metaphor to one of warfare signals his shift of focus from the powerful to the disempowered.

Thursday nights, which in Australia are the only ones on which stores stay open late, have become the high points of shopping, when the malls are at their most crowded and the cash registers ring up their profits most busily, and it is on Thursday nights that the youth "invasion" of consumer territory is most aggressive. Pressdee (1986) describes this invasion vividly:

> Thursday nights vibrate with youth, eager to show themselves:—it belongs to them, they have possessed it. This cultural response is neither spectacular nor based upon consumerism itself. Nor does it revolve around artifacts or dress, but rather around the possession of space, or to be more precise the possession of consumer space where their very presence challenges, offends and resists.

> Hundreds of young people pour into the centre every Thursday night, with three or four hundred being present at any one time. They parade for several hours, not buying, but presenting, visually, all the contradictions of employment and unemployment, taking up their natural public space that brings both life and yet confronts the market place. Security men patrol all night aided by several police patrols, hip guns visible and radios in use, bringing a new understanding to law and order.

> Groups of young people are continually evicted from this opulent and warm environment, fights appear, drugs seem plentiful,

alcohol is brought in, in various guises and packages. The police close in on a group of young women, their drink is tested. Satisfied that it is only coca-cola they are moved on and out. Not wanted. Shopkeepers and shoppers complain. The security guards become agitated and begin to question all those seen drinking out of cans or bottles who are under 20, in the belief that they must contain alcohol. They appear frightened, totally outnumbered by young people as they continue their job in keeping the tills ringing and the passage to the altar both free and safe. (p. 14)

10   Pressdee coins the term "proletarian shopping" (p. 16) to describe this window shopping with no intention to buy. The youths consumed images and space instead of commodities, a kind of sensuous consumption that did not create profits. The positive pleasure of parading up and down, of offending "real" consumers and the agents of law and order, of asserting their difference within, and different use of, the cathedral of consumerism became an oppositional cultural practice.

The youths were "tricksters" in de Certeau's terms—they pleasurably exploited their knowledge of the official "rules of the game" in order to identify where these rules could be mocked, inverted, and thus used to free those they were designed to discipline. De Certeau (1984) points to the central importance of the "trickster" and the "guileful ruse" throughout peasant and folk cultures. Tricks and ruses are the art of the weak that enables them to exploit their understanding of the rules of the system, and to turn it to their advantage. They are a refusal to be subjugated:

The actual order of things is precisely what "popular" tactics turn to their own ends, without any illusion that it will change any time soon. Though elsewhere it is exploited by a dominant power . . . here order is tricked by an art. (de Certeau 1984: 26)

This trickery is evidence of "an ethics of tenacity (countless ways of refusing to accord the established order the status of a law, a meaning or a fatality)" (p. 26).

Shopping malls are open invitations to trickery and tenacity. The youths who turn them into their meeting places, or who trick the security guards by putting alcohol into some, but only some, soda cans, are not actually behaving any differently from lunch hour window shoppers who browse through the stores, trying on goods, consuming and playing with images, with no intention to buy. In extreme weather people exploit the controlled climate of the malls for their own pleasure—mothers take children to play in their air-conditioned comfort in hot summers, and in winter older people use their concourses for daily walks. Indeed, some malls now have notices welcoming "mall walkers," and a few have even provided exercise areas set up with equipment and instructions so that the walkers can exercise more than their legs.

Of course, the mall owners are not entirely disinterested or altruistic here—they hope that some of the "tricky" users of the mall will become real economic consumers, but they have no control over who will, how many will, how often, or how profitably. One boutique owner told me that she estimated that 1 in 30 browsers actually bought something. Shopping malls are where the strategy of the powerful is most vulnerable to the tactical raids of the weak.

REFERENCES

De Certeau, M. (1984). *The Practice of Everyday Life*. Berkeley: University of California Press.

Pressdee, M. (1986). "Agony or Ecstasy: Broken Transitions and the New Social State of Working-Class Youth in Australia." Occasional Papers, S. Australian Centre for Youth Studies, S.A. College of A.E., Magill, S. Australia.

Schudson, M. (1984). *Advertising: The Uneasy Persuasion*. New York: Basic Books.

Sinclair, J. (1987). *Images Incorporated: Advertising as Industry and Ideology*. London: Croom Helm.

SUGGESTIONS FOR DISCUSSION

1. Why does Fiske challenge the cathedral metaphor as a useful one for analyzing the place of malls in today's culture? How is the mall of today like the great cathedrals of the past? How does the metaphor of the mall as a place of warfare work in Fiske's analysis?

2. What do you think Fiske means when he says, "The equality of 'everyone' is, of course, an equality attainable only by those with purchasing power; those without are defined out of existence"?

3. Fiske has based most of what he says on his observations of malls in Australia. How would you describe mall culture in America?

SUGGESTIONS FOR WRITING

1. As we mentioned in the Suggestion for Reading in this selection, the Fiske essay could be difficult to follow because he relies heavily on others' writing as well as his own observations. Begin your work with Fiske by making sure that you know what he is arguing. To get at his argument, write a one-page summary of Fiske's interpretation of mall culture. Share your summary with a group of your classmates. As you read others' summaries, take note of ideas or details they noticed that you did not notice. Once you have finished your discussion, come to a consensus on what your group considers Fiske's most important assertions.

2. Review the opening two paragraphs of Fiske's essay. In that passage, he offers his readers a metaphor and then suggests that there are always problems with any metaphor. It can be a tough passage because it takes in more than just the metaphor of the mall, but it also suggests the problem with that metaphor and the problems with metaphors in general. Still, these early paragraphs contain important information for a reader to understand. Write a one-paragraph paraphrase of those opening paragraphs. (In a paraphrase, you restate using your own words from a portion of a text. This kind of exercise can be useful in helping you to make sure that you understand what you are reading and can apply it to other things, like examining the usefulness of the metaphors that Fiske offers. If you were to use your paraphrase in an essay, you would have to make sure that you acknowledge your source and give information about where you found the material. However, you would not use quotation marks around a paraphrase because you are using your language, not the language of the writer.)

3. Fiske's analysis of mall culture focuses attention away from the store owners and mall managers who make the rules and hope to profit from their investments. Instead, Fiske pays attention to how people use the mall. He writes, "Shopping malls are open invitations to trickery and tenacity. The youths who turn them into their meeting places, or who trick the security guards by putting alcohol into some, but only some, soda cans, are not actually behaving any differently from lunch hour shoppers who browse through the stores, trying on goods, consuming and playing with images, with no intention to buy." Choose another public space that people use for their own purposes rather than or in addition to the purpose for which it was designed, and write an essay that explains what it is about the place that lends itself to "trickery and tenacity," as Fiske says malls do. For this essay, rely on your own recollection of and experience with the place for your analysis. Remember to bring in events you have witnessed or things you and your friends or family have done in that place. You can also draw on Fiske's analysis of the way the public uses mall space to help you understand and explain the way the public uses the place you have chosen. If you wrote summaries and the paraphrase suggested above, you will find those helpful as resources for your own use of Fiske.

WOODRUFF PARK AND THE SEARCH FOR COMMON GROUND

— Murphy Davis

Murphy Davis is cofounder of the Open Door Community, a group of men and women living in community to work with Atlanta's homeless and with prison inmates in Georgia. Along with providing meals, showers, clothing, and a safe space to gather, the Open Door also participates in political action and advocacy meant to address city projects and local legislation that unfairly targets people living in the streets. The article reprinted here originally appeared in 1996 in *Hospitality*, the Open Door newspaper. In it, Davis argues that the city's multimillion dollar attempts to keep homeless people out of a downtown park have actually made the park unfriendly to everyone and eliminated one more common ground in Atlanta.

SUGGESTION FOR READING   Davis's analysis of the Woodruff Park project argues that a space designed to keep some people out is a space that will keep everyone out. As you read, underline and annotate those passages where she makes that argument clear.

1   Woodruff Park is a 1.7-acre tract of land in the center of downtown Atlanta. Like many other valuable pieces of real estate in American history, it has become the subject of hot debate, quiet deals, great expenditure of funds—both public and private—and has seemed to require, along the way, a military presence to secure its function for those who hold the power and intend to define the park's use.

The park, formerly known as Central City Park, most recently emerged from behind a curtain of chain link with a five-million-dollar facelift. This new park is, more than anything else, a spot to look at. It is not a public gathering place: indeed, there is no area of the park that encourages gathering, conversation, play, human exchange, or interrelatedness of any kind.

While the old park never seemed like a spectacular place to me, its walkways were wide and spacious, lined with benches and grass. People walked to and through, stopped and talked together, waved to, and even hassled, one another. But it was at least somewhat inviting, friendly, and spacious.

The new park is mostly an expanse of concrete, stone, and some grass. The walkway is narrow and has a greatly reduced number of benches (all of these face in the same direction).

The benches, of course, are a crucial symbol of reality.

5   In 1993 we won one of the only (narrowly defined) major political victories in the history of our political action and advocacy. We tested the city ordinance that prohibited lying on a city park bench (or against a tree). In two actions in September and October of 1993, twelve of our number were arrested and went to jail for "slouching" or lying on the benches of Woodruff Park. The city council rescinded the law. Amazing.

Exactly one year later, the park was closed for a five-million-dollar renovation. Nimrod Long, whose firm was paid three hundred thousand dollars for a new design, was frank. He said that they were charged with the mission of creating a park that would be inhospitable to homeless people. This, of course, must include park benches with armrests spaced so that it is impossible to lie down.

Well, we can be proud of the fact that they darn well did their job. This park clearly does not invite homeless people to gather. Trouble is, if we mandate a public space inhospitable to any one group of people, we end with a public space that is inhospitable to everybody.

Woodruff Park is unfriendly space. This is not, for instance, a place you would think to bring children to play. There is no play equipment, no bathroom, no drinking fountain, no convivial space for parents to gather while the children play, and it simply is not clear whether or not the grass is an inviting space to run and tumble.

Gone are the wraparound-bench tree planters that invited long chess games and spontaneous lunch gatherings. What is left is a narrow walkway, a relocated *Phoenix* statue (the post–Civil War image of Atlanta rising out of the ashes), a huge, very expensive thirty-foot cascading waterfall, and a stretch of grass. The grass will be nice if people are allowed to sit for picnics, naps, and conversation. But it will not do to replace the benches, especially for the elderly, the disabled, people in business attire, or for anybody when the weather is wet or cold. Neither will it do if the powers that be decide, as they did with the old park, that people cannot sit or play or walk or lie down on the grass. In fact, in the old park they installed what our street friends call "pneumonia grass"—sprinklers buried invisibly that come on without warning, drenching anyone who might be unwittingly sitting or sleeping.

10   The park is intended to be, as Mayor Campbell proudly proclaimed at the opening ceremony, "a beautiful place to look at," which seems a gross concession to the suburban mentality that controls our city. Downtown Atlanta is designed more to entertain tourists and suburbanites who want to drive through, with doors locked and windows rolled up, than to foster an urban life and culture. In addition, you might be led to question Mayor Campbell's sense of beauty.

Perhaps the opening ceremony was somewhat premature, and more trees, shrubs, and plantings are yet to come. But for now there is much less greenery. From the northeast corner the park looks like a fortress. And when the water is turned off, the "cascading waterfall" actually resembles the exposed, barnacle-encrusted, pocked, and rusted hull of an aging battleship. Beautiful this place is not.

It could be that this "battleship," this lifeless wall, is indeed a fitting monument for the center of Atlanta. The city government and controlling business interests have pursued a course of destruction in the central city for several generations now, displacing people seen as undesirable. When these policies of removal began in the 1950s, it was clear that race was the motivating factor. The powers in Atlanta did not want African American people in the downtown business district. So neighborhoods were broken up and gave way to interstate highways; housing was destroyed, little shops and businesses were forced out, and a stadium, a civic center, and countless parking lots rolled over the poor. These practices, which began thirty years ago, resulted in much of the poverty and homelessness in the African American population we see in our city today.

This pattern of destruction has been repeated, and there is little beauty, culture, or humanity left. What we have instead is precisely what the powers say they want: a "sanitized zone," "vagrant-free," and deserted enough to appear safe, devoid of the color of a rich, urban culture whose life has never been antiseptic, colorless, cold, and heartless.

Eight years ago, the rebirth of Underground Atlanta brought a similar enthusiasm for displacement and destruction to this current renovation of Woodruff Park.

15   Plaza Park, once a lively place filled with street vendors, preachers, homeless folks, and pedestrians on their way to the Five Points MARTA station, was razed to make way for the cement, light tower, glitz, and security guards at Underground. A large number of people made homeless by the destruction of their neighborhoods were once again displaced from Plaza Park.

Within a stone's throw of Woodruff Park, thousands of units of single-room occupancy housing have been demolished since the late 1970s. These SROs were places where many who would now like to rest in the park could have lived, and where some of them probably did at one time. Where was the outcry when the Avon and Capital Hotels were destroyed and replaced with parking decks? Where were the protests when the Francis Hotel was closed, mysteriously burned, and replaced with John Portman's latest gleaming tower? Where now is the outcry from any Atlanta government or business leader for housing for Atlanta's homeless? Their silence is deafening. Instead, editorials and columns whine, "City Doesn't Belong Just to Bums and Winos"; countless city laws have been thrown in place to empower police to hound the homeless and to move them from one corner to the next, and the next.

Now we see this same forced removal in Atlanta's Olympic zeal. Hundreds of public housing units were lost as Techwood Homes was torn down to make room for dormitories for Olympic athletes. Where did all those people go? Why is housing for transient Olympic visitors more important than homes for the people of Atlanta?

Additional examples abound. Seventy-two acres of a low-income, mixed-use area (with shelters, labor pools, day-care centers, small businesses, and ware-houses) are now being plowed under to make way for Centennial Olympic Park and to clear this space of undesirable elements. The area, so that no one would question its removal, was labeled a "cancer" by the former head of the Atlanta Chamber of Commerce. But the lost housing has not been replaced, businesses have folded, and shops and restaurants have nowhere to relocate. Of the seventy-two acres, twenty-five will remain after the Olympics as space for a park, at an estimated cost of fifty million dollars. The space will be given, not to the city, but to the state of Georgia for management and control. Why? Could the reason be to up the ante and to make any infraction there a state offense rather than a violation of municipal laws? The rest of the acreage will be developed as commercial property, and if past patterns remain the same, African American people and businesses that were displaced will not find a welcome. The park and surroundings are being redeveloped, not because Atlanta wants to cultivate public space, but because the world is coming to town, and Atlanta wants a clean façade; the "garbage" will be swept under a rug temporarily.

How do these decisions about public space and policy get made? As a citizen of Atlanta, I have no recollection of being asked for my opinion. Whose park is Woodruff Park? Like most of the important decisions about Atlanta's life and future, this was one more deal cut by the powers in a back room. There was never any public discussion, debate, conversation, or exchange about the park. Why does this autocratic method of decision making exist in a democratic society? The answer seems clear: including everyone in a discussion about the use and regulation of public space might not bring the desired results for those who already have so much and who stand to gain much more. Atlanta is in fact one of the poorest cities in the United States, but the super glitz we put forward is a thin, often convincing, veneer for the rest of the world. If the real poverty were known, would the world come to Atlanta to fill Billy Payne's pockets? Could the world of Coke continue to deceive the world, or would we all realize that the veneer covers an ugly, rat-infested, festering bleakness?

20   How can we have a truly beautiful, friendly city that welcomes all people, without regard for race or economic status? We can all agree that nobody likes to be assailed by an "aggressive panhandler." But why do we like to be, or allow ourselves to be, assailed by the pages of a respectable newspaper, which refers to the poor in epithets laced with strong racist implications? While the columnists complain bitterly about their loathing for the poor and homeless, where is the public outrage and protest that people in Atlanta do not have the food, medical care, housing, and good work they need to sustain life? Instead, we dismiss these poor folk as mere trash to be moved around and pushed out of sight and mind.

The task for those of us who love the city is to transform Woodruff Park into a beautiful, friendly space. Welcoming hospitality cannot be found through another design firm, or with an army of bulldozers. We need to move in with play equipment, music, chairs and benches, picnic tables and blankets, and then all the people of the world can come to celebrate the true urban culture of Atlanta. We need to put up bathrooms and drinking fountains right away. Woodruff Park could yet become a welcoming space for the women and men and boys and girls of the city. Can't you see the rich and poor, the Black and white, the homeless and well-housed, dancing and laughing and clapping their hands to the music of Blind Willie McTell, while the smell of smoked ribs wafts on the breeze, and children swing high enough to touch the sky, as the old folks play a hand of dominoes? Who knows? Such a party could inspire us to build a city with housing, justice, and care for all of its people.

SUGGESTIONS FOR DISCUSSION

1. Murphy Davis provides several examples of "urban renewal" meant to spruce up the city for business and prepare for visitors. Make a list of those examples. What arguments does she make for her claim that the real effect of these changes is to eliminate public space?

2. Basic to Davis's argument is her belief that the homeless have as much right to gather in public spaces as anyone in a city. How do you respond to that? Why should anyone care if a public space is unfriendly to homeless people?

3. In her argument, Davis writes, "Trouble is, if we mandate a public space inhospitable to any one group of people, we end with a public space that is inhospitable to everybody." What public spaces do you know about that seem to be natural gathering places for people? What are they like? What would make them unfriendly to everybody?

SUGGESTIONS FOR WRITING

1. City planners apparently believe that any place that has a lot of homeless people is going to keep others away. Create a "mental" map of your home town, your campus, or any place you have lived long enough to know pretty well. Start with a real map of the place and identify four kinds of areas: areas where you will not go, areas you consider "ethnic," areas of conflict, and areas you would call "normal." After you have completed that map, write a key for it and explain what identifies each of these areas as safe or not safe, comfortable or uncomfortable, foreign or familiar.

2. Once you have completed your mental map and key, examine what you have written and write a response to your mental map and key that explores how others might read your map. What in your background or experience makes some places seem normal to you and others out of bounds? How might the people who live in those areas describe your "normal" spaces?

3. Write a descriptive analysis of a public space you consider friendly to all kinds of people. Who hangs out there? What do they do? Are there structures in place to keep the homeless away? If so, what are those structures like?

SIGNS FROM THE HEART: CALIFORNIA CHICANO MURALS

Eva Sperling Cockcroft and Holly Barnet-Sánchez

In his full-length work on Chicano culture in Los Angeles (*Anything but Mexican: Chicanos in Contemporary Los Angeles*), Rodolfo Acuña writes that "no space in East Lost Angeles is left unused or unmarked." For Acuña, Chicano or Latino culture has claimed, if not always the physical space, at least interpretive space—signs and images that mark a place as belonging to a certain group or person. Interpretive space is claimed in East Los Angeles primarily through the Los Angeles mural movement, which was begun in the 1960s, carried on today under the direction of the Social and Public Arts Resource Center (SPARC), and headed by artist and activist Judy Baca. In the following selection, artists Eva Cockcroft and Holly Barnet-Sánchez write of the origins of the mural movement in Los Angeles. Their essay appeared in 1993 in the book *Signs from the Heart: California Chicano Murals.*

This selection consists of portions of an introduction to a collection of essays about California Chicano murals. The authors set the mural movement in the larger context of public art throughout history as a way of explaining what murals have meant in the past and what they have come to mean today. After you read this selection, write a brief outline that traces the rise and fall of murals from high art to popular statement as described by Cockcroft and Barnet-Sánchez.

1 A truly "public" art provides society with the symbolic representation of collective beliefs as well as a continuing re-affirmation of the collective sense of self. Paintings on walls, or "murals" as they are commonly called, are perhaps the quintessential public art in this regard. Since before the cave paintings at Altamira some 15,000 years before Christ, wall paintings have served as a way of communicating collective visions within a community of people. During the Renaissance in Italy, considered by many to be the golden age of Western Art, murals were regarded as the highest form in the hierarchy of painting. They served to illustrate the religious lessons of the church and to embody the new Humanism of the period through artistic innovations like perspective and naturalistic anatomy.

After the Mexican Revolution of 1910–1917, murals again served as the artistic vehicle for educating a largely illiterate populace about the ideals of the new society and the virtues and evils of the past. As part of a re-evaluation of their cultural identity by Mexican-Americans during the Chicano movement for civil rights and social justice that began in the mid-1960s, murals again provided an important organizing tool and a means for the reclamation of their specific cultural heritage.

The desire by people for beauty and meaning in their lives is fundamental to their identity as human beings. Some form of art, therefore, has existed in every society throughout history. Before the development of a significant private picture market in Seventeenth Century Holland, most art was public, commissioned by royalty, clergy, or powerful citizens for the greater glory of their country, church, or city and placed in public spaces. However, after the Industrial Revolution and the development of modern capitalism with its stress on financial rather than social values, the art world system as we know it today with galleries, critics, and museums gradually developed. More and more, art became a luxury object to be enjoyed and traded like any other commodity. The break-up of the stable structures of feudal society and the fluidity and dynamism of post-Industrial society was reflected symbolically in art by the disruption of naturalistic space and the experimentation characteristic of Modernism.

Modernism has been a mixed blessing for art and artists. Along with a new freedom for innovation and the opportunity to express an individual vision that resulted from the loss of direct control by patrons of artistic production, artists experienced a sense of alienation from the materialistic values of capitalism, loss of a feeling of clearly defined social utility, and the freedom to starve. This unstable class situation and perception of isolation from society was expressed in the attitude of the bohemian *avant garde* artist who scorns both the crass commercialism of the bourgeoisie and the

La Familia, detail from *Chicano Time Trip* by East Los Streetscapers (Wayne Alaniz Healy and David Rivas Botello), 1977. 18' × 26' panel (total mural is 18' × 90'). Lincoln Heights, East Los Angeles. City Wide Mural Project.

unsophisticated tastes of the working class, creating work exclusively for the appreciation of a new aristocracy of taste. Especially in the United States of the 1960s, for most people art had become an irrelevant and mysterious thing enjoyed only by a small educated elite.

5   When muralism emerged again as an important art movement in Mexico during the 1920s, the murals served as a way of creating a new national consciousness—a role quite similar to that of the religious murals of the Renaissance although directed toward a different form of social cohesion. Unlike the murals of the Italian Renaissance which expressed the commonly held beliefs of both rulers and masses, the Mexican murals portrayed the ideology of a worker, peasant, and middle class revolution against the former ruling class: capitalists, clergy, and foreign interests. Since that time in the eyes of many, contemporary muralism has been identified with poor people, revolution, and communism. This association has been a major factor in changing muralism's rank within the hierarchy of the "fine arts" from the highest to the

lowest. Once the favored art of popes and potentates, murals, especially Mexican-style narrative murals, now considered a "poor people's art," have fallen to a level of only marginal acceptance within the art world.

The three great Mexican artists whose names have become almost synonymous with that mural renaissance, Diego Rivera, Jose Clemente Orozco, and David Alfaro Siqueiros, were all influenced by stylistic currents in European modernism—Cubism, Expressionism, and Futurism—but they used these stylistic innovations to create a new socially motivated realism. Rather than continuing to use the naturalistic pictorial space of Renaissance murals, the Mexicans explored new forms of composition. Rivera used a collage-like discontinuous space which juxtaposed elements of different sizes; Orozco employed non-naturalistic brushwork, distorted forms, and exaggerated light and dark, while Siqueiros added expressive uses of perspective with extreme foreshortening that made forms burst right out of the wall. The stylistic innovations of the Mexicans have provided the basis for a modern mural language and most contemporary muralism is based to some extent or another on the Mexican model. The Mexican precedent has been especially important in the United States for the social realist muralists of the Works Progress Administration (WPA) and Treasury Section programs of the New Deal period and the contemporary mural movement that began in the late 1960s.

More than 2500 murals were painted with government sponsorship during the New Deal period in the United States. By the beginning of World War II however, support for social realist painting, and muralism in general, had ended. During the Cold War period that followed, realistic painting became identified with totalitarian systems like that of the Soviet Union, while abstraction, especially New York–style Abstract Expressionism, was seen as symbolizing individual freedom in *avant garde* art circles. By the early 1960s, only the various kinds of abstract art from the geometric to the bio-morphic were even considered to really be art. Endorsed by critics and the New York museums, abstraction was promulgated abroad as the International Style and considered to be "universal"—in much the same way as straight-nosed, straight-haired blondes were considered to be the "universal" ideal of beauty. Those who differed or complained were dismissed as ignorant, uncultured, or anti-American.

The concept of a "universal" ideal of beauty was closely related to the "melting pot" theory, then taught in schools, which held that all the different immigrants, races and national groups which composed the population of the United States could be assimilated into a single homogeneous "American." This theory ignored the existence of separate cultural enclaves within the United States as well as blatant discrimination and racism. It also ignored the complex dialectic between isolation and assimilation and the problem of identity for people like the Mexican-Americans of California who were neither wholly "American" nor "Mexican" but a new, unique, and constantly changing composite variously

called "American of Mexican descent," "Mexican-American," Latino or Hispanic. In the 1960s the term "Chicano" with its populist origins was adopted by socially conscious youth as a form of positive self-identification for Mexican-Americans. Its use became a form of political statement in and of itself.[1]

The dialectic between assimilation and separatism can be seen in the history of Los Angeles, for example, first founded in 1781 as a part of New Spain. In spite of constant pressure for assimilation including job discrimination and compulsory use of English in the schools, the Mexican-American population was able to maintain a culture sufficiently distinct so that, as historian Juan Gómez-Quiñones has frequently argued, a city within a city can be defined. This separate culture continues to exist as a distinct entity within the dominant culture, even though it is now approximately 150 years since Los Angeles was acquired by the United States. This situation, by itself, tends to discredit the melting pot concept.

10   The Civil Rights Movement, known among Mexican-Americans as the Chicano Movement or *el movimiento*, fought against the idea of a "universal" culture, a single ideal of beauty and order. It re-examined the common assumption that European or Western ideas represented the pinnacle of "civilization," while everything else, from the thought of Confucius to Peruvian portrait vases, was second-rate, too exotic, or "primitive." The emphasis placed by Civil Rights leaders on self-definition and cultural pride sparked a revision of standard histories to include the previously unrecognized accomplishments of women and minorities as well as a re-examination of the standard school curriculum. Along with the demonstrations, strikes, and marches of the political movement came an explosion of cultural expression.

As was the case after the Mexican Revolution, the Civil Rights Movement inspired a revival of muralism. However, this new mural movement differed in many important ways from the Mexican one. It was not sponsored by a successful revolutionary government, but came out of the struggle by the people themselves against the *status quo*. Instead of well-funded projects in government buildings, these new murals were located in the *barrios* and ghettos of the inner cities, where oppressed people lived. They served as an inspiration for struggle, a way of reclaiming a cultural heritage, or even as a means of developing self-pride. Perhaps most significantly, these murals were not the expression of an individual vision. Artists encouraged local residents to join them in discussing the content, and often, in doing the actual painting. For the first time, techniques were developed that would allow non-artists working with a professional to design and paint their own murals. This element of community participation, the placement of murals on exterior walls in the community itself, and the philosophy of community input, that is, the right of a community to decide on what kind of art it wants, characterized the new muralism.

Nowhere did the community-based mural movement take firmer root than in the Chicano communities of California. With the Mexican mural tradition as part of their heritage, murals were a particularly congenial form for Chicano artists to express the collective vision of their community. The mild climate and low, stuccoed buildings provided favorable physical conditions, and, within a few years, California had more murals than any other region of the country. As home to the largest concentration of Mexicans and people of Mexican ancestry anywhere outside of Mexico City, Los Angeles became the site of the largest concentration of Chicano murals in the United States. Estimates range from one thousand to fifteen hundred separate works painted between 1969 and the present. The Social and Public Art Resource Center's "California Chicano Mural Archive" compiled in 1984 documents close to 1000 mural projects throughout the state in slide form.

Because Chicano artists were consciously searching to identify the images that represented their shared experience they were continually led back to the *barrio*. It became the site for "finding" the symbols, forms, colors, and narratives that would assist them in the redefinition of their communities. Not interested in perpetuating the Hollywood notion that art was primarily an avenue of escape from reality, Chicano artists sought to use their art to create a dialogue of demystification through which the Chicano community could evolve toward cultural liberation. To this end, murals and posters became an ubiquitous element of the *barrioscape*. According to Ybarra-Frausto, they publicly represented the reclamation of individual Chicano minds and hearts through the acknowledgement and celebration of their community's identity through the creation of an art of resistance.

Prior to the Chicano movement, U.S. Mexicans were defined externally through a series of derogatory stereotypes with total assimilation as the only way to break out of the situation of social marginalization. Art that integrated elements of U.S. Mexican or *barrio* culture was also denigrated as "folk" art and not considered seriously. The explosion of Chicano culture and murals as a result of the political movement, provided new recognition and value for Chicano art which weakened the old barriers. According to Sánchez-Tranquilino, this experience allowed artists to figuratively break through the wall that confined artists either to the *barrio* or to unqualified assimilation. It gave them the confidence to explore new artistic forms and a new relationship to the dominant society.

NOTE

1. Throughout this book several terms are used to identify Americans of Mexican descent: "Mexican-Americans," "U.S. Mexicans," and "Chicanos." Each carries specific meanings and they are not used interchangeably. "Mexican-American" is primarily a post World War II development in regular use until the politicization of *el movimiento*, the Chicano civil rights movement of the 1960s and 1970s. Its use acknowledges with pride the Mexican heritage which was hidden by an earlier, less appropriate term, "Spanish-American." However, its hyphenated construction implies a level of

equality in status between the Mexican and the American which in actuality belies the unequal treatment of Americans of Mexican descent within United States society.

U.S. Mexican is a term developed by essayist Marcos Sánchez-Tranquilino to replace the term Mexican-American with one that represents both more generally and clearly all Mexicans within the United States whether their families were here prior to annexation in 1848, have been here for generations, or for only two days. In other words, it represents all Mexicans living within U.S. borders regardless of residence or citizenship status.

The most basic definition of the term Chicano was made by journalist Ruben Salazar in 1970: "A Chicano is a Mexican-American who does not have an Anglo image of himself." It is a term of self-definition that denotes politicization.

SUGGESTIONS FOR DISCUSSION

1. Throughout this selection, Cockcroft and Barnet-Sánchez remind their readers that, though mural painting might have been considered high art in earlier periods when it was funded by church or state, by the time the Chicano mural movement had come to California, these highly realistic, working-class, public wall paintings were no longer valued by the art world. Instead, the mural movement became a part of the *barrioscape*—a sign of Chicano culture and a statement about Chicano politics. How do Cockcroft and Barnet-Sánchez explain the fall of murals from high to low in the art world? Why do you think artists or art collectors care whether or not such public art is considered "high culture"? How would you differentiate "art" from "wall paintings"?

2. One of the roles that the Chicano mural movement has played, according to this selection, has been to challenge universal standards of beauty. How do Cockcroft and Barnet-Sánchez define this "universal" standard? What do they see as its relation to the "melting pot"? With a group of your classmates, look at the mural reprinted in this selection, and explain how it offers a challenge to that standard.

3. The introduction to this selection notes that Chicano murals have claimed an "interpretive space" in Los Angeles. As Cockcroft and Barnet-Sánchez write, these murals "publicly represented the reclamation of individual Chicano minds and hearts through the acknowledgment and celebration of their community's identity through the creation of an art of resistance." Why do you think it might be important for a group such as the one described here to claim a space through art or signs or language or music (i.e., interpretive space)? In what ways do other groups or people that you know claim interpretive space?

SUGGESTIONS FOR WRITING

1. Write an essay in which you discuss how a knowledge of the mural movement, as it is described in the selection above, either changes or reinforces the impression that you have of Los Angeles from television and film portrayals of that place.

2. Write an essay that examines why it might be important for marginalized groups to claim interpretive space through images or signs such as the mural movement. Do you know of any similar strategies to the mural movement that other groups use to claim interpretive space? Draw on your reading on Los Angeles and the mural movement to help you with this writing. You might also draw on experiences in your own town, city, or school to help you explain the need for those who feel like outsiders to claim interpretive space with images or signs.

3. Cockcroft and Barnet-Sánchez write, "Prior to the Chicano movement, U.S. Mexicans were defined externally through a series of derogatory stereotypes." Watch a film that includes or deals with Latinos in the United States (for example, *Selena, Mi Familia, The Bronze Screen,* or *A Walk in the Clouds*) and write an essay in which you address that

comment. In what ways do the characters and their situations break with the familiar stereotypes? In what ways are those stereotypes perpetuated? Before you begin your essay (and even before you begin watching one of these films), make a list of familiar stereotypes. If you are unsure of the common Latino stereotypes, ask classmates, friends, and family to help you.

WIRED CULTURE   Cell Phone Space

To learn more about technology and public space, visit www.ablongman.com/george/121

By all accounts the invention of the cell phone has changed the shape of public space. What we once thought was a private moment is now quite public, and the public at large is not liking it much. A 2004 MIT survey reported that cell phones beat out alarm clocks as being the invention people hate the most but cannot live without. A similar survey conducted in 2005 at the University of Michigan indicates that 60 percent of cell phone users indicate that public use of cell phones has become a nuisance.

CELL PHONE ETIQUETTE: SHUT UP, ALREADY!

— *Annie Nakao*

Annie Nakao has been a staff writer for the *San Francisco Chronicle* and *Examiner* and a Knight fellow at Stanford University. She received a daily news reporting award from the National Association of Black Journalists for her series on the academic achievement of black middle-class students. The article reprinted here appeared in the *Chronicle* on August 8, 2004.

SUGGESTION FOR READING In her column, Nakao quotes one source as saying, "cell phones have changed what public spaces mean in America." Before you read, spend some time in a public space and keep track of how often you see people talking on cell phones. How present is the cell phone in the spaces where you spend your time?

1 Oakland chiropractor Sallie MacNeill chuckled when she read the sign at the No Sweat Cafe in Helena, Mont.: "Please check your guns and your phones at the door." She'd just sat down and settled in when her cell phone rang.

"Everybody in the place was giving me dirty looks," MacNeill recalls sheepishly. "I picked it up—it was my husband calling from California—spoke briefly and hung up. Then I apologized, saying, 'I'm an out-of-towner.' "

Now, MacNeill, a quietly cheery sort, would hardly qualify as a cell phone lout—she doesn't even use up the measly 200 minutes on her monthly plan. But increasingly, abject apology

and shame seem to be the price paid by those whose trilling phones happen to eviscerate the public space of our restaurants, theaters and buses.

It's as it should be, asserts Ed Moose of San Francisco's North Beach institution Moose's restaurant, where each table sports a discreet note card, adorned with a cartoon of the restaurant's antlered mascot, that says, "No Cell Phones, Please."

5 "There's ringing all around you and there's no place to hide," says Moose. "But we're a little refuge."

For now, anyway.

With more than half of Americans owning cell phones, the cacophony of wireless communications has turned public protocol on its head and unleashed a backlash from bystanders who complain that they're being subjected to not just infernal ringing but also shocking second-hand intimacies, banal chatter and just plain rudeness.

"Our personal space is being severely endangered," said Larry Magid, a Bay Area syndicated technology columnist. "We're getting to the point where people are getting pissed off."

In fact, cell phones, he says, are becoming the cigarettes of our day.

10   "I don't care if someone wants to smoke, but I don't want to breathe your smoke," Magid says. "In the same way, I don't care if you want to yell at your boyfriend, but I don't want to be brought into it."

Truth be told, Magid, who's a media commentator on call, admits to having his own phone on 24/7.

"It buzzes," he says. "I'll whisper into it and walk out. But you feel bad. People give you dirty looks, and rightfully so. I know I'm doing something rude."

At least he admits it.

According to Sprint's first-ever survey on cell phone etiquette last month, 80 percent of those queried said people were less courteous on their cell phones today than five years ago. Yet 97 percent of respondents also felt they themselves were "very courteous" or "somewhat courteous."

15   "If we looked in the mirror, we'd take a more active role in curing this behavior, or misbehavior," says Jacqueline Whitmore, founder of the Protocol School in Palm Beach, Fla.

To underscore the fact that cell phone pique is now on the wireless industry's radar, July was noted as National Cell Phone Courtesy Month.

Why would the mobile phone industry care? After all, with only a 58 percent market penetration, untold corporate millions—mostly from women who now make up the majority of American cell phone users—are yet to be made in a country that lags far behind Europe and Asia in per-capita cell phone sales.

Maybe it's a sense of urgency radiating from an annoyed public that has had it up to here. In New York City, it's already illegal to use cell phones during public performances. Maybe they're thinking they'd better act now, before cell phone users, like smokers, are banished to skulking outside doorways.

It's all about responsibility, explains Delly Tamer, chief executive and president of LetsTalk, a San Francisco online wireless retailer.

20   "We are more than a company that wants to sell cell phones," says Tamer. "We all have to be more socially responsible or we will turn our streets, restaurants and public places into cacophony."

Some would swear it's already happening as technology uproots what Rutgers University communications Professor James E. Katz calls "our normative order."

"Cell phones certainly have dramatically changed what public spaces mean in America, and what it's like to be in them," says Katz, co-editor of the book "Perpetual Contact: Mobile Communication, Private Talk, Public Performance."

Wireless technology has done so by altering social norms.

"It used to be extremely weird and disturbing to see people walking down the street, talking on their mobile phones," Katz says. "Non-users used to stop and gawk and discuss how strange that was. That's disappeared as a subject of comment."

25   But social tensions created by cell phones haven't.

"There's a basic problem with mobile phones in terms of the way it affects people around the user," Katz says, whose book notes that predictably, those who don't own cell phones tend to be more annoyed.

For some people, listening to cell phone chatter is highly disturbing.

"For others, they're able to insulate themselves from it," Katz says. "The question of manners is very important. Some people are exceedingly concerned about the comfort of others around them. Some people are exceedingly insensitive to that. Cell phones are handy and, in some ways, a compelling way for people to administer to their personal needs. So if you're disinclined to respect feelings of those around you, then the mobile phone acts to incite that insensitivity further."

And people—rude or otherwise—are busily administering to their personal needs. Consider the results of LetsTalk's 2003 national survey on cell phone etiquette:

- 61 percent said using a cell phone in a supermarket is acceptable.

- 53 percent said it was fine to use a cell phone on public transit.

- Far fewer respondents—29 percent—approved of using a cell phone in a restaurant; only 3 percent approved of it in movies or at a theater.

- The approval rate for cell phone use in cars has plummeted from a high of 76 percent in 2001, but slightly less than half of respondents still think it's acceptable to carry on a wireless conversation while driving.

30   The most intriguing finding: 62 percent found it OK to gab on cell phones in rest rooms. In 2001, only 39 percent did.

"That one puzzles me," Tamer says. "Perhaps they have some privacy, so they relax and yak away."

Apparently so, according to Brawny Matt, the code name of a volunteer from Boston who "spies" on rude cell phone users for CellManners.com:

"One day I went to the men's bathroom. There are two urinals, and our VP of information science was at one of them, so I took the other.

"The VP said, 'Hello.' "

35   "I paused, taken aback a little, and replied, 'Hello.' "

"He continued. 'Yeah. OK. No.' "

"At that point, I leaned back and peeked over to his side of the 'modesty panel.' Yes, he was having a cell phone conversation while urinating.

"The very next day, I used the bathroom again. One of our engineers came in yakking away on his cell phone, and saddled up to a urinal. . . . I was tempted to take his phone and tell the other party, 'Did you know he pees while talking to you?' "

From San Francisco, fellow CellManners.com spy Bucky Dialtone reports that he and a friend were enjoying their shrimp and spring rolls at a Thai restaurant when a woman plopped down at the next table, dialed up her cell and began droning on in a loud voice about how a rude driver had kept her from parking.

40   "After 15 minutes . . . she was still on the phone with the same person, although her conversation had taken a turn toward her trip to the market. Fascinating, huh? I could take it no longer. 'Excuse me, ma'am,' I asked. 'Could you please take your conversation outside or to the rest room?'

" 'Uhh (disgustedly, as if I were a lesser being), no,' was her reply. I was stunned, although after I confronted her, she did speak more quietly."

Carol Page, a Boston-area writer, created the Web site after an incident in which she took out her phone in a Harvard Square movie theater to check her messages.

"I thought I was going to be drawn and quartered," she recalls. "When the mere appearance of a cell phone causes a near war in a movie theater, I began to see the problem.

"People abuse cell phones so much, it's become a moral issue," Page says. "For one thing, they yell their heads off. Then they get very defensive when they're told about it. Something about having your cell phone behavior criticized bends people out of shape. Then there's ringing. You're dipping into some dim sum and all of a sudden, the cell phone goes off. And what people are forced to overhear, like the results of somebody's colonoscopy. The health stuff's nasty."

45   Not that she's anti-cell phone, she says.

Page's Web site has "Saved by the Cell" stories about heroic cell phone users.

"Cell phones are useful things," she said. "But they didn't come with a set of instructions."

SUGGESTIONS FOR DISCUSSION

1. As we indicated above, the cell phone has quickly become people's least favorite invention, though many think they can't do without one. What accounts for this attitude? How do the people you know use their cell phones? How do you use yours? When would you say it is legitimate to have a private cell phone conversation in a public space?

2. Nakao quotes one of her sources as saying that cell phones are becoming the cigarettes of our day. In what ways does that analogy work (or not)?

3. How have cell phones "changed what public space means in America"?

SUGGESTIONS FOR WRITING

1. Spend one day keeping track of how often you see cell phones used in public, who is using them, what kinds of conversations they are having (if you can hear without having to move closer to listen in), where they are using their phones, and whether or not the phones interrupt other public activities—church, school, sports events, theater, movies, etc. Write up your findings and report them to the class. In your report, indicate how much of the use you witnessed seemed inappropriate or intrusive.

2. Go to the Internet site CellManners.com, which promotes itself as a site for "Promoting civility between cell phone users and the people around them." This is how the site describes its purpose: "Make no mistake about it—a new set of manners is exactly what's needed. Usually well-behaved people often forget their manners when they're around cell phones, whether they're using them or someone else is. The common is frequently left out of common sense when it comes to mobile technology. We're calling for a truce in the Cell Wars. And we're inviting you to join us—in the Forum—in a meaningful, well-mannered discussion about Cell Manners. Have you stopped to consider that your morning cell phone conversation might be interfering with much needed sleep by a fellow passenger on the bus? Read the letter from a tired commuter in the Forum. Just how much quiet can people reasonably expect in a public place? When is it OK, if ever, to have the ringer on your cell phone turned on? Is it possible to ask somebody to mind his/her manners without an unpleasant incident? How do you do it? . . . Help us create a 21st century manifesto of manners for mobile technology. Let's turn down not only the noise, but also the stress levels of daily living and protect our ability to use cell phones responsibly."

    Read several of the stories archived on the site—both those stories that complain of cell phone abuse and those that praise cell phone technology for saving lives. Write a response to CellManners.com in which you respond to the site's call for a manifesto to the dilemma of cell phone use as a public nuisance.

3. Write an essay in which you respond to the comment that cell phones have redefined public space in America. In your essay consider how that might be the case. Where do you see that change happening?

PERSPECTIVES

Public Roadsides, Private Grief: Roadside Memorials and Public Policy

To learn more about public memorials, visit www.ablongman.com/george/122

Most of us have seen them along the highways and along back roads as we drive across the country: roadside crosses, wreathes, and other memorials marking the sites of fatal accidents. Every now and then, the roadside memorial features a grouping of crosses, each with the name of a victim, certainly a site where several people died. Most people don't stop to read these handmade memorials. They have become a part of the landscape in this country where thousands of drivers and passengers are killed on highways every year. It might seem odd, then, that what is essentially a private expression of grief could be at the heart of a controversy. After all, what does it matter if someone wants to erect a memorial to a lost loved one?

The problem is that roadside memorials are placed on what is essentially public land—the state and local road system—and that alone puts them at the center of a dispute over what rights any of us have to place signs of any sort on public roads and highways and whether or not religious icons can be placed freely on public roads (most memorials are small wooden crosses, though some are elaborate shrines and some are large, sturdy structures).

These memorials are also at the center of cultural tradition for many people, especially those in the southwest regions of the country. Writer Rudolfo Anaya explains the origins of roadside memorials, called *descansos* in the Southwest:

> The first descansos were resting places where those who carried the coffin from the church to the camposanto paused to rest. In the old villages of New Mexico, high in the Sangre de Cristo Mountains or along the river valleys, the coffin was shouldered by four or six men.
>
> Led by the priest or preacher and followed by mourning women dressed in black, the procession made its way from the church to the cemetery. The rough hewn pine of the coffin cut into the shoulders of the men. If the camposanto was far from the church, the men grew tired and they paused to rest, lowering the coffin and placing it on the ground. The place where they rested was the descanso.
>
> The priest prayed; the wailing of the women filled the air; there was time to contemplate death. Perhaps someone would break a sprig of juniper and bury it in the ground to mark the spot, or place wild flowers in the ground. Perhaps someone would take two small branches of piñon and tie them together with a leather thong, then plant the cross in the ground.
>
> Rested, the men would shoulder the coffin again, lift the heavy load, and the procession would continue. With time, the descansos from the church to the cemetery would become resting spots. . . .
>
> Time touches everything with change. The old descanso became the new as the age of the automobile came to the provinces of New Mexico. How slow and soft and deeper seemed the time of our grandfathers. Horses or mules drew the wagons. "Voy a preparar el carro de vestia," my grandfather would say. I remember the sound of his words, the ceremony of his harnessing the horses.

Yes, there have always been accidents, a wagon would turn over, a man would die. But the journeys of our grandfathers were slow, there was time to contemplate the relationship of life and death. Now time moves fast, cars and trucks race like demons on the highways, there is little time to contemplate. Death comes quickly, and often it comes to our young. Time has transformed the way we die, but time cannot transform the shadow of death.

I remember very well the impact of the car on the people of the llano and the villages of my river valley. I remember because I had a glimpse of the old way, the way of my grandfather, and as a child I saw the entry of the automobile.

One word describes the change for me: violence. The cuentos of the people became filled with tales of car wrecks, someone burned by gasoline while cleaning a carburetor, someone crippled for life in an accident. The crosses along the country roads increased. Violent death had come with the new age. Yes, there was utility, the ease of transportation, but at a price. Pause and look at the cross on the side of the road, dear traveler, and remember the price we pay.

From "Introduction/Dios da y Dios quita," in *Descansos: An Interrupted Journey*, by Rudolfo Anaya, Juan Estevan Arellano, and Denise Chavez (Del Norte, 1995).

As you read the following two articles on the debate over roadside memorials, keep in mind the complexity of this issue, one that touches private pain, public land rights, cultural traditions, separation of church and state, and even free speech issues.

ROADSIDE CROSSES: CENTURIES-OLD TRADITION CAN STIR CONTROVERSY

— *L. Anne Newell*

Anne Newell is a staff reporter for the *Arizona Daily Star*. The following story was printed in the *Star* on Tuesday, September 3, 2002.

SUGGESTION FOR READING   Before you read, look up the Department of Transportation regulations for your state on roadside memorials or crosses.

1   It used to be that Michael Sanchez didn't think a lot about the eight white crosses standing near his family's house.

They'd been there since his family moved to the neighborhood in 1998, like silent soldiers, a lingering memory of a car collision that killed eight people, five of them children.

Then Sanchez's father died in February in a car accident at Interstate 10 and Palo Verde Road. The family put a cross there.

"I think they're really important," Sanchez, 18, says now. "It's a memorial for people to know what happened."

5   Roadways across the country are dotted with crosses and other markers. It's at least a centuries-old tradition, a Tucson folklorist said— a way for the living to remember those they have lost and a religious ceremony for some, to mark the holy spot where a soul has left a body.

But they're not without controversy. One such memorial is the focus of a court battle in Colorado. And officials across the country are finding different ways to handle the markers.

Tucson folklorist Jim Griffith said the memorials began in Arizona in the Catholic community for people who died without having the chance to be absolved of sin.

They lined trails in their early days, and passers-by would stop, light a candle or say a prayer, Griffith said.

In 1783, the bishop of Sonora asked Spanish military authorities to forbid the practice because it discouraged other settlers, Griffith said. It was forbidden, he said, but it didn't stop.

10   The state Highway Patrol used white crosses in the 1940s and 1950s to mark the places motorists died, Griffith said. It has stopped the practice, but the markers continue to be placed by others.

"There still are people who take these as an indication they should say a prayer for the repose of the people who died there," he said.

In New Mexico, where people have made grave markers out of flowers, pumpkins, tin cans and other materials since Spanish rule, memorials are protected as "traditional cultural properties" through the Historic Preservation Division.

Last year, roadside memorials, also known as descansos (resting places), crucitas and memorias, were banned as traffic hazards in North Carolina.

California memorials are "discreetly removed" as road hazards, except when a victim was killed by a drunken driver who is convicted. Then, the state will erect a sign for $1,000.

15   In Florida, the state will put up a nondenominational marker for free, upon request.

In West Virginia, memorials are protected by a 2000 statute and can remain indefinitely if registered with the state.

And in Idaho last year, legislators replaced a program under which gold stars were placed at accident sites with a policy allowing roadside memorials.

Arizona traffic officials say they don't mind the memorials—if they aren't permanent and don't cause traffic hazards or impede road maintenance.

"There's really not a law or a written policy," said Walt Gray, a state Transportation Department spokesman. "Our general policy is we leave them there."

20   Crews will even move a memorial rather than remove it.

"We recognize that it's something important to the families for their closure," Gray said.

Michael Graham, spokesman for the city's Transportation Department, and Carol Anton, in community relations in the county Transportation Department, said their agencies' stances are similar. They just ask people to be cautious in erecting the signs.

"This is a very sensitive issue," Graham said. "People are mourning, and they need an opportunity to mourn."

That opportunity has led to a court battle in Colorado.

25   Brian Rector, 18, died in March 1998 when his Ford Escort was hit by a semi.

After the cremation and funeral, a family friend took some 2-by-4s and paint and fashioned a 3-foot-tall white cross, inscribing it "Son, Brother, Friend."

Relatives added flowers and small angel figurines.

"Because we don't have a cemetery plot to go to," Rector's mother, Deena Breeden, said, "we definitely want to keep up the memorial forever."

A driver who often passed Rector's memorial and others disagreed—and took action one night in April 2000.

30   A state trooper saw Rodney Lyle Scott's truck on the side of the road with its hazard lights on. A collection of flowers and wooden crosses was in the bed.

Scott told the trooper he was "cleaning up the interstate." Thinking Scott had permission, the trooper let him go.

Soon, the Breedens and other families noticed their memorials missing and complained. They found a sympathetic ear at the office of Adams County District Attorney Robert Grant.

Scott, identified through his license number taken by the trooper, was charged with "desecration of a venerated object" and faced the possibility of six months in jail and a $750 fine.

"I had gone through a lot of personal turmoil myself," Scott said. "I didn't appreciate somebody else throwing their hurt and sorrow out for the public view, as if it was more important than someone else's."

35 Denver attorney Bob Tiernan, a member of the Madison, Wis.-based Freedom From Religion Foundation, offered to represent Scott for free.

The memorials "are using public property to endorse religion," Tiernan said. "It's a violation of the U.S. Constitution, as far as I'm concerned, and it's a serious distraction."

In April 2001, Tiernan won acquittal for Scott when a judge ruled the Rector memorial was "discarded refuse" and "unlawful advertising" under the law, not a venerated object.

The district attorney appealed and said he'll take the case to the state Supreme Court.

The memorials, he said, "are to venerate the life and passing of the person involved in the fatal accident, and at the same time serve the public purpose in getting people to slow down."

40 The Breedens were allowed to put a memorial back up—its cross removed, they said, to keep from offending anyone—without receiving a citation.

Michael Oscar Sanchez was 43 when he was thrown from his truck in February as it rolled across I-10 near Palo Verde.

He'd been eastbound on I-10 when he veered off the road, scraping along a guardrail for nearly 100 feet. He overcorrected, driving across the eastbound lanes and into the median, where his truck rolled and he was thrown outside. The vehicle flipped once and came to rest in the westbound lanes.

A white cross memorializes the spot now, marked with his name, birth date and death date.

"I think they should leave it there," Sanchez's son said as he stood outside his family's home, about 50 feet from the large collection of crosses at West Corona and South San Fernando roads.

45 Other memorials dot the streets in this South Side neighborhood. They mark the roads on the Tohono O'odham Reservation. And, increasingly, they're appearing all around Tucson, in various forms.

The one near the Sanchez house marks where Carlos Manuel Peralta ran a stop sign going about 65 mph in 1997, plowing into a minivan and killing eight members of two families. Peralta was sentenced to more than 200 years in prison.

It was one of the worst car crashes in Tucson's history. Neighbors have maintained the memorial since, and the victims' relatives still visit it. Stuffed animals, dried and silk flowers, and a rock border mark the spot, which Sanchez says he thinks of differently now.

But the Pima Community College freshman—who's studying administrative justice—doesn't think every state should be as lenient as Arizona.

He suggests standards for states where the memorials are being challenged.

50 "I think it should be a state-by-state decision," he said. "If it distracts someone, I don't think it should be there."

Joe Villa Jr., who raced out of his home to help the victims of the 1997 crash and whose family keeps watch over the memorial with other neighbors, said it's important to the neighborhood and the relatives of the victims.

"I think it shows a lot of people what can happen when you drink and do drugs and don't pay attention to the road signs," he said. "It's important for the family, too. They can leave a remembrance. They bring flowers or something. The spirits went to God in this spot."

MEMORIALS CAUSE CONTROVERSY

— *Jeff Burlew*

Jeff Burlew is a staff writer for the *Tallahassee Democrat*. This story appeared in that paper in November 2003. In it, Burlew reports on one memorial cross that sparked new regulations on all roadside markers in Florida.

SUGGESTION FOR READING As you read, underline and annotate the arguments each side uses in the controversy over roadside memorials.

1   After James H. "Jim" Ward Jr. was killed in a crash at Gum and Aenon Church roads, his family placed an 8-foot wooden cross near the scene to remember him.

Ward, 45, died March 18, 2002, when a Leon County school bus ran a stop sign in foggy weather and crashed into his pickup truck. Family members put up the custom-made cross in July 2002.

But about a year after the cross went up, the county's public works department took it down and placed it in storage because of complaints from a nearby business owner.

And last month, county commissioners unanimously approved a new memorial-marker policy that bans homemade crosses from county roadways. Under the policy, the county will erect round memorial markers at a family's request that say "Drive Safely" and list the crash victim's name.

5   Ward's widow, Lynn Ward of Greensboro, is upset by the removal of the cross and the new policy on roadside memorials. She said she got permission from the county and others before putting up the cross.

"I feel this is very unfair because our cross was up before this new policy came into effect," she wrote in a letter to the Democrat. "Does this mean others will have to fear that their cross will be taken down too. After all, what is it hurting to put up a cross in memory of someone you loved and lost."

Jeanie Lewis, owner of Jeanie's Beauty Salon, said she didn't object when the Ward family called and asked to put up a cross in front of her business. She and her husband, Larry, were among the first on the scene the morning of the crash.

But Lewis said the cross was too big and blocked her own business sign. She complained to the county and asked Commissioner Jane Sauls, who represents her district, for help.

"It was a beautiful cross, but it just needed to be somewhere else," Lewis said. "I've been here for 27 years. Why should I be blocked?"

10   County officials said they tried to be sensitive to the Ward family in handling the cross issue. And they said the policy was needed because homemade memorials can interfere with maintenance of the right of way and even pose dangers for motorists and mourners. They based their policy and the markers themselves on the Florida Department of Transportation's policy and signs.

"We want a way to honor those people that have lost their lives and do it in a way that doesn't obstruct signs or even your vision on the right of way," Sauls said. "We really looked at it as a positive thing."

The markers are 15 inches in diameter and stand about 3½ feet high. None has gone up yet because no one has asked for one, according to Dale Walker, the county's road superintendent. The signs cost the county about $100 to make and install but are offered to the public for free.

The policy states that all homemade memorials along county-maintained roads will be removed immediately, although both state and county officials said road crews don't aggressively look for them.

Family members or friends with family permission can ask the county to put up the new markers, which the county will maintain for a year. They must reapply after a year to keep them up.

15   This isn't the first time government policies over memorial markers have led to controversy. In 1997, the state decided against moving forward with a policy that would have replaced homemade memorials along state-maintained roads with white crosses, which also symbolize safety.

After atheist and Jewish groups complained about the crosses, the state came up with the round "Drive Safely" signs. Since then, more than 1,800 memorial signs have gone up across the state, according to DOT spokesman Dick Kane.

"I think it's been very successful for the families out there who want to memorialize their loved ones," Kane said, adding that the memorials also remind motorists to use caution behind the wheel.

But Ward and others said the county and state memorial signs are impersonal. The families of two boys killed in a 1988 crash on U.S. Highway 27 put up crosses on private property to remember them. Marsha Long, whose son, Stevie, died in the crash, said the round signs don't convey the same message as crosses.

"What is a little round circle sticking in the ground?" she asked. "It means nothing. If you see a cross, you know something happened."

20   Some, however, are happy to see roadside crosses go. Dan DeWiest contacted the Democrat recently to complain about two crosses placed off Apalachee Parkway near an entrance to Wal-Mart.

"While I believe in the freedom of religious expression," he wrote in an e-mail, "I don't think that [it] is fair to promote one religion over any other religion on public property."

Ward, however, still is hoping the county will let her put up the cross. Her attorney, J. C. O'Steen, said the family would rather not take legal action but hasn't ruled it out. Ward wrote that crosses should be allowed if they make grieving families feel better.

"Everyone should realize that it's not always someone else facing a tragedy," she wrote. "Sometimes, it's you."

SUGGESTIONS FOR DISCUSSION

1. With a group of your classmates, summarize the issues at the center of this dispute. In what way might the issues be different for one part of the country than for another?

2. Rudolfo Anaya makes it clear that, though these memorials are Catholic in origin, they also are a part of the culture of Mexicans and Indians who have lived in the Southwest for many generations. To what extent, then, should the memorials (and the disputes surrounding them) be thought of in terms of separation of church and state?

3. What rights do you think any of us should have to place memorials or any sort of personal sign on public roadways?

SUGGESTIONS FOR WRITING

1. The removal of any roadside memorial is obviously a very delicate matter. After all, they mark places where people have lost their lives and where families have lost loved ones. On the other hand, state highway workers, citizens who do not believe religious symbols are appropriate in public spaces, and business owners like the owner of Jeanie's Beauty Salon in Tallahassee do have legitimate concerns. Write an essay in which you explain the complexities of this controversy. Don't settle for a "who is right?" argument, and don't try to settle the dispute. Instead, explain the dimensions of this debate.

2. Colorado, like many states, prohibits roadside memorials. In Georgia, the only memorials allowed are those sponsored by Mothers Against Drunk Driving. Other states offer state designed warnings against dangerous driving instead of homemade crosses and shrines to mark the place of a fatal accident. All of this sounds very reasonable, but you might have already noticed that when writers write about these memorials, they often begin with the story of a person killed on the roadway. Write your own proposal for how to address the concerns of the many sides of this dispute. For example, how do you memorialize an individual and follow state guidelines for road maintenance? Or, how do you respect cultural traditions but honor the separation of church and state?

3. With camera or sketchbook in hand, take a drive along your own local highways and take pictures of, sketch, or write a description of the roadside memorials you see. Which ones might be seen as a driving hazard? Do any of these memorials tell the story of what happened in that place? Are any maintained regularly? If you hadn't been looking for them, would you have noticed most of them? After you have finished your survey, report your findings to the class. Add to your report the local or state regulations on roadside

memorials. Are the regulations being followed? If not, why not? Are there personal messages besides memorials (graffiti, artwork, signs of all sorts) displayed along the roadways that are clearly not official? What are they?

CLASSIC READING

THE USES OF SIDEWALKS—SAFETY

Jane Jacobs

Jane Jacobs had no formal training in urban development and completed no college degree. Yet *The Death and Life of Great American Cities*, her classic 1961 study of how people live in cities from which this selection is taken, has become a catalyst for many organizations opposed to suburban sprawl and what is known as the gentrification of older, lower-income neighborhoods.

SUGGESTION FOR READING   Jacobs writes of city streets people feel safe on and those people don't feel safe on. Before you read, write a description of the kind of street you think is a safe one and the kind of street that seems less safe when you are in a city you don't know well.

1   Streets in cities serve many purposes besides carrying vehicles, and city sidewalks—the pedestrian parts of the streets—serve many purposes besides carrying pedestrians. These uses are bound up with circulation but are not identical with it and in their own right they are at least as basic as circulation to the proper workings of cities.

A city sidewalk by itself is nothing. It is an abstraction. It means something only in conjunction with the buildings and other uses that border it, or border other sidewalks very near it. The same might be said of streets, in the sense that they serve other purposes besides carrying wheeled traffic in their middles. Streets and their sidewalks, the main public places of a city, are its most vital organs. Think of a city and what comes to mind? Its streets. If a city's streets look interesting, the city looks interesting; if they look dull, the city looks dull.

More than that, and here we get down to the first problem, if a city's streets are safe from barbarism and fear, the city is thereby tolerably safe from barbarism and fear. When people say that a city, or a part of it, is dangerous or is a jungle what they mean primarily is that they do not feel safe on the sidewalks.

But sidewalks and those who use them are not passive beneficiaries of safety or helpless victims of danger. Sidewalks, their bordering uses, and their users, are active participants in the drama of civilization versus barbarism in cities. To keep the city safe is a fundamental task of a city's streets and its sidewalks.

5   This task is totally unlike any service that sidewalks and streets in little towns or true suburbs are called upon to do. Great cities are not like towns, only larger. They are not like suburbs, only denser. They differ from towns and suburbs in basic ways, and one of these is that cities are, by definition, full of strangers. To any one person, strangers are far more common in big cities than acquaintances. More common not just in places of public assembly, but more common at a man's own doorstep. Even residents who live near each other are strangers, and must

be, because of the sheer number of people in small geographical compass.

The bedrock attribute of a successful city district is that a person must feel personally safe and secure on the street among all these strangers. He must not feel automatically menaced by them. A city district that fails in this respect also does badly in other ways and lays up for itself, and for its city at large, mountain on mountain of trouble.

Today barbarism has taken over many city streets, or people fear it has, which comes to much the same thing in the end. "I live in a lovely, quiet residential area," says a friend of mine who is hunting another place to live. "The only disturbing sound at night is the occasional scream of someone being mugged." It does not take many incidents of violence on a city street, or in a city district, to make people fear the streets. And as they fear them, they use them less, which makes the streets still more unsafe.

To be sure, there are people with hobgoblins in their heads, and such people will never feel safe no matter what the objective circumstances are. But this is a different matter from the fear that besets normally prudent, tolerant and cheerful people who show nothing more than common sense in refusing to venture after dark—or in a few places, by day—into streets where they may well be assaulted, unseen or unrescued until too late.

The barbarism and the real, not imagined, insecurity that gives rise to such fears cannot be tagged a problem of the slums. The problem is most serious, in fact, in genteel-looking "quiet residential areas" like that my friend was leaving.

10   It cannot be tagged as a problem of older parts of cities. The problem reaches its most baffling dimensions in some examples of rebuilt parts of cities, including supposedly the best examples of rebuilding, such as middle-income projects. The police precinct captain of a nationally admired project of this kind (admired by planners and lenders) has recently admonished residents not only about hanging around outdoors after dark but has urged them never to answer their doors without knowing the caller. Life here has much in common with life for the three little pigs or the seven little kids of the nursery thrillers. The problem of sidewalk and doorstep insecurity is as serious in cities which have made conscientious efforts at rebuilding as it is in those cities that have lagged. Nor is it illuminating to tag minority groups, or the poor, or the outcast with responsibility for city danger. There are immense variations in the degree of civilization and safety found among such groups and among the city areas where they live. Some of the safest sidewalks in New York City, for example, at any time of day or night, are those along which poor people or minority groups live. And some of the most dangerous are in streets occupied by the same kinds of people. All this can also be said of other cities.

Deep and complicated social ills must lie behind delinquency and crime, in suburbs and towns as well as in great cities. This book will not go into speculation on the deeper reasons. It is sufficient, at this point, to say that if we are to maintain a city society that can diagnose and keep abreast of deeper social problems, the starting point must be, in any case, to strengthen whatever workable forces for maintaining safety and civilization do exist—in the cities we do have. To build city districts that are custom made for easy crime is idiotic. Yet that is what we do.

The first thing to understand is that the public peace—the sidewalk and street peace—of cities is not kept primarily by the police, necessary as police are. It is kept primarily by an intricate, almost unconscious, network of voluntary controls and standards among the people themselves, and enforced by the people themselves. In some city areas—older public housing projects and streets with very high population turnover are often conspicuous examples—the keeping of public sidewalk law and order is left almost entirely to the police and special guards. Such places are jungles. No amount of police can enforce civilization where the normal, casual enforcement of it has broken down.

The second thing to understand is that the problem of insecurity cannot be solved by spreading people out more thinly, trading the characteristics of cities for the characteristics of suburbs. If this could solve danger on the city streets, then Los Angeles should be a safe city because superficially Los Angeles is almost all suburban. It has virtually no districts compact enough to qualify as dense city areas. Yet Los Angeles cannot, any more than any other great city, evade the truth that, being a city, it *is* composed of strangers not all of whom are nice. Los Angeles' crime figures are flabbergasting. Among the seventeen standard metropolitan areas with populations over a million, Los Angeles stands so pre-eminent in crime that it is in a category by itself. And this is markedly true of crimes associated with personal attack, the crimes that make people fear the streets.

Los Angeles, for example, has a forcible rape rate (1958 figures) of 31.9 per 100,000 population, more than twice as high as either of the next two cities, which happen to be St. Louis and Philadelphia; three times as high as the rate of 10.1 for Chicago, and more than four times as high as the rate of 7.4 for New York.

15   In aggravated assault, Los Angeles has a rate of 185, compared with 149.5 for Baltimore and 139.2 for St. Louis (the two next highest), and with 90.9 for New York and 79 for Chicago.

The overall Los Angeles rate for major crimes is 2,507.6 per 100,000 people, far ahead of St. Louis and Houston, which come next with 1,634.5 and 1,541.1, and of New York and Chicago, which have rates of 1,145.3 and 943.5.

The reasons for Los Angeles' high crime rates are undoubtedly complex, and at least in part obscure. But of this we can be sure: thinning out a city does not insure safety from crime and fear of crime. This is one of the conclusions that can be drawn within individual cities too, where pseudosuburbs or superannuated suburbs are ideally suited to rape, muggings, beatings, holdups and the like.

Here we come up against an all-important question about any city street: How much easy opportunity does it offer to crime? It may be that there is some absolute amount of crime in a given city, which will find an outlet somehow (I do not believe this). Whether this is so or not, different kinds of city streets garner radically different shares of barbarism and fear of barbarism.

Some city streets afford no opportunity to street barbarism. The streets of the North End of Boston are outstanding examples. They are probably as safe as any place on earth in this respect. Although most of the North End's residents are Italian or of Italian descent, the district's streets are also heavily and constantly used by people of every race and background. Some of the strangers from outside work in or close to the district; some come to shop and stroll; many, including members of minority groups who have inherited dangerous districts previously abandoned by others, make a point of cashing their paychecks in North End stores and immediately making their big weekly purchases in streets where they know they will not be parted from their money between the getting and the spending.

20   Frank Havey, director of the North End Union, the local settlement house, says, "I have been here in the North End twenty-eight years, and in all that time I have never heard of a single case of rape, mugging, molestation of a child or other street crime of that sort in the district. And if there had been any, I would have heard of it even if it did not reach the papers." Half a dozen times or so in the past three decades, says Havey, would-be molesters have made an attempt at luring a child or, late at night, attacking a woman. In every such case the try was thwarted by passers-by, by kibitzers from windows, or shopkeepers.

Meantime, in the Elm Hill Avenue section of Roxbury, a part of inner Boston that is suburban in superficial character, street assaults and the ever present possibility of more street assaults with no kibitzers to protect the victims, induce prudent people to stay off the sidewalks at night. Not surprisingly, for this and other reasons that are related (dispiritedness and dullness), most of

Roxbury has run down. It has become a place to leave.

I do not wish to single out Roxbury or its once fine Elm Hill Avenue section especially as a vulnerable area; its disabilities, and especially its Great Blight of Dullness, are all too common in other cities too. But differences like these in public safety within the same city are worth noting. The Elm Hill Avenue section's basic troubles are not owing to a criminal or a discriminated against or a poverty-stricken population. Its troubles stem from the fact that it is physically quite unable to function safely and with related vitality as a city district.

Even within supposedly similar parts of supposedly similar places, drastic differences in public safety exist. An incident at Washington Houses, a public housing project in New York, illustrates this point. A tenants' group at this project, struggling to establish itself, held some outdoor ceremonies in mid-December 1958, and put up three Christmas trees. The chief tree, so cumbersome it was a problem to transport, erect, and trim, went into the project's inner "street," a landscaped central mall and promenade. The other two trees, each less than six feet tall and easy to carry, went on two small fringe plots at the outer corners of the project where it abuts a busy avenue and lively cross streets of the old city. The first night, the large tree and all its trimmings were stolen. The two smaller trees remained intact, lights, ornaments and all, until they were taken down at New Year's. "The place where the tree was stolen, which is *theoretically* the most safe and sheltered place in the project, is the same place that is unsafe for people too, especially children," says a social worker who had been helping the tenants' group. "People are no safer in that mall than the Christmas tree. On the other hand, the place where the other trees were safe, where the project is just one corner out of four, happens to be safe for people."

This is something everyone already knows: A well-used city street is apt to be a safe street.

A deserted city street is apt to be unsafe. But how does this work, really? And what makes a city street well used or shunned? Why is the sidewalk mall in Washington Houses, which is supposed to be an attraction, shunned? Why are the sidewalks of the old city just to its west not shunned? What about streets that are busy part of the time and then empty abruptly?

25   A city street equipped to handle strangers, and to make a safety asset, in itself, out of the presence of strangers, as the streets of successful city neighborhoods always do, must have three main qualities:

First, there must be a clear demarcation between what is public space and what is private space. Public and private spaces cannot ooze into each other as they do typically in suburban settings or in projects.

Second, there must be eyes upon the street, eyes belonging to those we might call the natural proprietors of the street. The buildings on a street equipped to handle strangers and to insure the safety of both residents and strangers, must be oriented to the street. They cannot turn their backs or blank sides on it and leave it blind.

And third, the sidewalk must have users on it fairly continuously, both to add to the number of effective eyes on the street and to induce the people in buildings along the street to watch the sidewalks in sufficient numbers. Nobody enjoys sitting on a stoop or looking out a window at an empty street. Almost nobody does such a thing. Large numbers of people entertain themselves, off and on, by watching street activity.

In settlements that are smaller and simpler than big cities, controls on acceptable public behavior, if not on crime, seem to operate with greater or lesser success through a web of reputation, gossip, approval, disapproval and sanctions, all of which are powerful if people know each other and word travels. But a city's streets, which must control not only the behavior of the people of the city but also of visitors from suburbs and towns who want to have a big time away from the gossip and sanctions at home, have to operate by more direct, straightforward methods. It is a wonder cities have solved such an inherently difficult problem at all. And yet in many streets they do it magnificently.

30   It is futile to try to evade the issue of unsafe city streets by attempting to make some other features of a locality, say interior courtyards, or sheltered play spaces, safe instead. By definition again, the streets of a city must do most of the job of handling strangers for this is where strangers come and go. The streets must not only defend the city against predatory strangers, they must protect the many, many peaceable and well-meaning strangers who use them, insuring their safety too as they pass through. Moreover, no normal person can spend his life in some artificial haven, and this includes children. Everyone must use the streets.

On the surface, we seem to have here some simple aims: To try to secure streets where the public space is unequivocally public, physically unmixed with private or with nothing-at-all space, so that the area needing surveillance has clear and practicable limits; and to see that these public street spaces have eyes on them as continuously as possible.

But it is not so simple to achieve these objects, especially the latter. You can't make people use streets they have no reason to use. You can't make people watch streets they do not want to watch. Safety on the streets by surveillance and mutual policing of one another sounds grim, but in real life it is not grim. The safety of the street works best, most casually, and with least frequent taint of hostility or suspicion precisely where people are using and most enjoying the city streets voluntarily and are least conscious, normally, that they are policing.

The basic requisite for such surveillance is a substantial quantity of stores and other public places sprinkled along the sidewalks of a district; enterprises and public places that are used by evening and night must be among them especially. Stores, bars and restaurants, as the chief examples, work in several different and complex ways to abet sidewalk safety.

First, they give people—both residents and strangers—concrete reasons for using the sidewalks on which these enterprises face.

35   Second, they draw people along the sidewalks past places which have no attractions to public use in themselves but which become traveled and peopled as routes to somewhere else; this influence does not carry very far geographically, so enterprises must be frequent in a city district if they are to populate with walkers those other stretches of street that lack public places along the sidewalk. Moreover, there should be many different kinds of enterprises, to give people reasons for crisscrossing paths.

Third, storekeepers and other small businessmen are typically strong proponents of peace and order themselves; they hate broken windows and holdups; they hate having customers made nervous about safety. They are great street watchers and sidewalk guardians if present in sufficient numbers.

Fourth, the activity generated by people on errands, or people aiming for food or drink, is itself an attraction to still other people.

This last point, that the sight of people attracts still other people, is something that city planners and city architectural designers seem to find incomprehensible. They operate on the premise that city people seek the sight of emptiness, obvious order and quiet. Nothing could be less true. People's love of watching activity and other people is constantly evident in cities everywhere. This trait reaches an almost ludicrous extreme on upper Broadway in New York, where the street is divided by a narrow central mall, right in the middle of traffic. At the cross-street intersections of this long north-south mall, benches have been placed behind big concrete buffers and on any day when the weather is even barely tolerable these benches are filled with people at block after block after block, watching the pedestrians who cross the mall in front of them, watching the traffic, watching the people on the busy sidewalks, watching each other. Eventually Broadway reaches Columbia University and Barnard College, one to the right, the other to the left. Here all is obvious order and quiet. No more stores, no more activity generated by the stores, almost no more pedestrians crossing—and no more watchers. The benches are there but they go empty in even the finest weather. I have tried them and can see why. No place could be more boring. Even the students of these institutions shun the solitude. They are doing their outdoor loitering, outdoor homework and general street watching on the steps overlooking the busiest campus crossing.

It is just so on city streets elsewhere. A lively street always has both its users and pure watchers. Last year I was on such a street in the Lower East Side of Manhattan, waiting for a bus. I had not been there longer than a minute, barely long enough to begin taking in the street's activity of errand goers, children playing, and loiterers on the stoops, when my attention was attracted by a woman who opened a window on the third floor of a tenement across the street and vigorously yoo-hooed at me. When I caught on that she wanted my attention and responded, she shouted down, "The bus doesn't run here on Saturdays!" Then by a combination of shouts and pantomime she directed me around the corner. This woman was one of thousands upon thousands of people in New York who casually take care of the streets. They notice strangers. They observe everything going on. If they need to take action, whether to direct a stranger waiting in the wrong place or to call the police, they do so. Action usually requires, to be sure, a certain self-assurance about the actor's proprietorship of the street and the support he will get if necessary, matters which will be gone into later in this book. But even more fundamental than the action and necessary to the action, is the watching itself.

40   Not everyone in cities helps to take care of the streets, and many a city resident or city worker is unaware of why his neighborhood is safe. The other day an incident occurred on the street where I live, and it interested me because of this point.

My block of the street, I must explain, is a small one, but it contains a remarkable range of buildings, varying from several vintages of tenements to three- and four-story houses that have been converted into low-rent flats with stores on the ground floor, or returned to single-family use like ours. Across the street there used to be mostly four-story brick tenements with stores below. But twelve years ago several buildings, from the corner to the middle of the block, were converted into one building with elevator apartments of small size and high rents.

The incident that attracted my attention was a suppressed struggle going on between a man and a little girl of eight or nine years old. The man seemed to be trying to get the girl to go with him. By turns he was directing a cajoling attention to her, and then assuming an air of nonchalance. The girl was making herself rigid, as children do when they resist, against the wall of one of the tenements across the street.

As I watched from our second-floor window, making up my mind how to intervene if it seemed advisable, I saw it was not going to be necessary. From the butcher shop beneath the tenement had emerged the woman who, with her husband, runs the shop; she was standing within earshot of the man, her arms folded and a look of determination on her face. Joe Cornacchia, who with his sons-in-law keeps the delicatessen, emerged about the same moment and stood solidly to the other side. Several heads poked out of the tenement windows above, one was withdrawn quickly and its owner reappeared a moment later in the doorway behind the man. Two men from the bar next to the butcher shop came to the doorway and waited. On my side of the street, I saw that the locksmith, the fruit man and the laundry proprietor had all come out of their shops and that the scene was also being surveyed from a number of windows besides ours. That man did not know it, but he was surrounded. Nobody was going to allow a little girl to be dragged off, even if nobody knew who she was.

I am sorry—sorry purely for dramatic purposes—to have to report that the little girl turned out to be the man's daughter.

45   Throughout the duration of the little drama, perhaps five minutes in all, no eyes appeared in the windows of the high-rent, small-apartment building. It was the only building of which this was true. When we first moved to our block, I used to anticipate happily that perhaps soon all the buildings would be rehabilitated like that one. I know better now, and can only anticipate with gloom and foreboding the recent news that exactly this transformation is scheduled for the rest of the block frontage adjoining the high-rent building. The high-rent tenants, most of whom are so transient we cannot even keep track of their faces (some, according to the storekeepers, live on beans and bread and spend their sojourn looking for a place to live where all their money will not go for rent) have not the remotest idea of who takes care of their street, or how. A city neighborhood can absorb and protect a substantial number of these birds of passage, as our neighborhood does. But if and when the neighborhood finally *becomes* them, they will gradually find the streets less secure, they will be vaguely mystified about it, and if things get bad enough they will drift away to another neighborhood which is mysteriously safer.

In some rich city neighborhoods, where there is little do-it-yourself surveillance, such as residential Park Avenue or upper Fifth Avenue in New York, street watchers are hired. The monotonous sidewalks of residential Park Avenue, for example, are surprisingly little used; their putative users are populating, instead, the interesting store-, bar- and restaurant-filled sidewalks of Lexington Avenue and Madison Avenue to east and west, and the cross streets leading to these. A network of doormen and superintendents, of delivery boys and nursemaids, a form of hired neighborhood, keeps residential Park Avenue supplied with eyes. At night, with the security of the doormen as a bulwark, dog walkers safely venture forth and supplement the doormen. But this street is so blank of built-in eyes, so devoid

of concrete reasons for using or watching it instead of turning the first corner off of it, that if its rents were to slip below the point where they could support a plentiful hired neighborhood of doormen and elevator men, it would undoubtedly become a woefully dangerous street.

Once a street is well equipped to handle strangers, once it has both a good, effective demarcation between private and public spaces and has a basic supply of activity and eyes, the more strangers the merrier.

Strangers become an enormous asset on the street on which I live, and the spurs off it, particularly at night when safety assets are most needed. We are fortunate enough, on the street, to be gifted not only with a locally supported bar and another around the corner, but also with a famous bar that draws continuous troops of strangers from adjoining neighborhoods and even from out of town. It is famous because the poet Dylan Thomas used to go there, and mentioned it in his writing. This bar, indeed, works two distinct shifts. In the morning and early afternoon it is a social gathering place for the old community of Irish longshoremen and other craftsmen in the area, as it always was. But beginning in midafternoon it takes on a different life, more like a college bull session with beer, combined with a literary cocktail party, and this continues until the early hours of the morning. On a cold winter's night, as you pass the White Horse, and the doors open, a solid wave of conversation and animation surges out and hits you; very warming. The comings and goings from this bar do much to keep our street reasonably populated until three in the morning, and it is a street always safe to come home to. The only instance I know of a beating in our street occurred in the dead hours between the closing of the bar and dawn. The beating was halted by one of our neighbors who saw it from his window and, unconsciously certain that even at night he was part of a web of strong street law and order, intervened.

A friend of mine lives on a street uptown where a church youth and community center, with many night dances and other activities, performs the same service for his street that the White Horse bar does for ours. Orthodox planning is much imbued with puritanical and Utopian conceptions of how people should spend their free time, and in planning, these moralisms on people's private lives are deeply confused with concepts about the workings of cities. In maintaining city street civilization, the White Horse bar and the church-sponsored youth center, different as they undoubtedly are, perform much the same public street civilizing service. There is not only room in cities for such differences and many more in taste, purpose and interest of occupation; cities also have a need for people with all these differences in taste and proclivity. The preferences of Utopians, and of other compulsive managers of other people's leisure, for one kind of legal enterprise over others is worse than irrelevant for cities. It is harmful. The greater and more plentiful the range of all legitimate interests (in the strictly legal sense) that city streets and their enterprises can satisfy, the better for the streets and for the safety and civilization of the city.

50   Bars, and indeed all commerce, have a bad name in many city districts precisely because they do draw strangers, and the strangers do not work out as an asset at all.

This sad circumstance is especially true in the dispirited gray belts of great cities and in once fashionable or at least once solid inner residential areas gone into decline. Because these neighborhoods are so dangerous, and the streets typically so dark, it is commonly believed that their trouble may be insufficient street lighting. Good lighting is important, but darkness alone does not account for the gray areas' deep, functional sickness, the Great Blight of Dullness.

SUGGESTIONS FOR DISCUSSION

1. Jacobs writes that most urban designers think an empty space—one in which there is nowhere to sit or gather in groups—is a place that looks safe to the people in a city. Her argument is that people feel safe in spaces where others gather, where shopkeepers and neighbors pay attention to what goes on in the streets. How does her description of safe streets compare with the description you wrote before you read? Would you revise your description after reading Jacobs?

2. What does Jacobs mean when she writes, "A city sidewalk by itself is nothing. It is an abstraction. It means something only in conjunction with the buildings and other uses that border it, or border other sidewalks near it."

3. What point is Jacobs making with her story of the "suppressed struggle going on between a man and a little girl of eight or nine years old" that she witnesses on the street below her window?

SUGGESTIONS FOR WRITING

1. One of the features that distinguishes country from city is the sidewalk. The countryside does not have sidewalks. Small towns have sidewalks, but suburbs often do not, or the sidewalks are limited to small areas in subdivisions or at the front of malls, schools, and other public buildings. Write an essay in which you discuss your own experience of sidewalks as a gathering place. Did they function for you, your family, and your friends in the same way Jacobs noticed that they functioned in cities in the early 1960s?

2. Jacobs writes that cities are distinguished from towns and suburbs because "they are, by definition, full of strangers." Moreover, a sidewalk should be a place where all of these

strangers feel safe with one another. Write of a time when you found yourself in a place surrounded by strangers—a large campus, a city, a mall, for example. Explain what made that place feel safe, or not. Draw on Jacobs's discussion of safety in public places where it is useful.

3. In "Shopping for Pleasure: Malls, Power, and Resistance" and in "Woodruff Park and the Search for Common Ground," John Fiske and Murphy Davis write of spaces that have been strictly regulated and ordered to keep some people away from others and to make sure that the users of these public spaces behave themselves or keep to themselves. Jacobs's discussion of "natural proprietors of the street" who keep an eye on things would suggest that one of the problems with trying to police people's use of space, as mall owners and Atlanta city planners have tried to do, is that it simply does not work. Instead, it discourages community use of a place, and encourages illegal uses of the place. Jacobs also points out that a successful neighborhood has a "clear demarcation between what is public space and what is private space." The two cannot "ooze into one another."

Choose a space on your campus or in your town or city that you consider unattractive, uncomfortable, even dangerous to some extent. What gives it that feeling? What measures have been taken to make it a safer or more comfortable place? Write a letter to local or school officials recommending changes that you believe will improve the space for people to use it. Draw on the work of Jane Jacobs, Murphy Davis, and John Fiske where it seems helpful in your recommendation.

VISUAL CULTURE   The Troubled Landscape

To learn more about landscape and the environment visit www.ablongman.com/george/123

Most of us have taken pictures of the places where we grew up or visited on vacation. The fact that Ansel Adams's landscape photographs of the West continue to be extremely popular—as calendar art, in museum retrospectives, as posters, and more—is a tribute to the beauty of those photographs and, perhaps, to the hopefulness of Adams's audience. Americans like to think of the land as something beautiful and free. Landscape photography, hearkening as it does back to the great landscape paintings that came before it, has traditionally captured that sort of beauty. It very typically pictures an uninhabited land, one unmarred by human presence, unchanged by time. The very nature of landscape art, then, is to picture the ideal.

It is that convention of picturing the ideal that has led landscape photographers like Robert Adams and Richard Misrach to recreate this genre in an attempt to capture both beauty and the ravages of industrialization. Landscape in the context of growing industry, environmental health hazards, and the loss of the land as free and open space shares the haunting beauty of traditional landscapes at the same time that it reveals the reality of living with waste.

With the following essay by Jason Berry and the Richard Misrach photos that accompany it, we invite you to reconsider your notion of what landscape photography can be, especially in a land troubled by chemical spills, air and water pollution, and urban sprawl.

CANCER ALLEY: THE POISONING OF THE AMERICAN SOUTH

— Jason Berry—with photographs by Richard Misrach

Jason Berry is a freelance investigative reporter based in New Orleans. Richard Misrach has photographed the American desert for much of his career. His beautiful, startling photographs of such images as nuclear waste in a strikingly beautiful landscape can be both powerful and frightening. Like photographer Robert Adams before him, Misrach rarely photographs an untouched landscape. The photographs here appeared in *Aperture* no. 162 (Winter 2001) along with Berry's essay "Cancer Alley."

SUGGESTION FOR READING In the library, look up the issue of the magazine *Aperture* (Winter 2001) where this essay and photographs originally appeared. Spend some time looking at all of the Misrach photographs that accompany the article. Berry also mentions Misrach's Desert Cantos photographs and the photographs of Clarence Laughlin. Look at those in the library or online, as well, so that you have a good notion of what Berry is talking about when you come to those sections of the article.

1   "Baton Rouge was clothed in flowers, like a bride—no, much more so; like a greenhouse. For we were in the absolute South now," wrote Mark Twain of the vistas from a riverboat in his 1883 classic *Life on the Mississippi.* "From Baton Rouge to New Orleans," he continued, "the great sugar-plantations border both sides of the river all the way, and stretch their league-wide levels back to the dim forest of bearded cypress in the rear. The broad river lying between the two rows becomes a sort of spacious street."

Twain caught the ninety-mile river corridor between the old Capitol and New Orleans at a poignant moment. Plantations still harvested profits in cotton and sugarcane; the black field workers, no longer slaves, were sharecroppers or virtual serfs. The river flowed through a land riddled with injustice. Yet there was beauty in the waterway and surrounding landscape, and beauty—although burdened with an unsavory history—in those old houses of "the absolute South," with their porticoes and pillared balconies.

By the 1940s, when Clarence John Laughlin trained his lens upon the area, some of the mansions had been torn down and others lay in ruins. The wrecked buildings riveted his eye as much as the several dozen that were still pre-served (then starting to shift from farming to tourist sites, which most remain today). A haunting sense of loss suffuses the black-and-white surrealism in Laughlin's remarkable book *Ghosts Along the Mississippi.*

Between the time of Twain's reportage and Laughlin's elegiac photographs from the mid-twentieth century, oil and petrochemical producers bought up vast pieces of land along the river and began grafting an industrial economy over the old agricultural estates. The refineries and plants—like the derricks that dot the Cajun prairie and the oil-production platforms in Louisiana coastal waters off the Gulf of Mexico—boosted the economies of communities once mired in poverty. The downside has been a political mentality blind to the ravages of pollution.

ORIGINS OF CANCER ALLEY

5   Standard Oil opened a refinery in 1909 on the fringes of Baton Rouge. In 1929 Governor Huey P. Long erected the new Capitol, a thirty-four-story Art Deco tower near the Standard plant. Today that political temple stands out in high relief from the expanded grid of pumping stacks and smoke clouds where Exxon (Standard's successor) functions like a city-within-the-city.

The Capitol and the massive oil complex issuing pungent clouds have melded into an awesome symbol of Louisiana politics: pollution as the price of power.

Providence Plantation, which dated to the 1720s, was in the river town of Des Allemands, and on its grounds was a massive tree known as the Locke Breaux Live Oak, which was 36 feet around and 101 feet high, with a limb span of 172 feet. That majestic tree, estimated to be over three hundred years old, died from exposure to pollution in 1968: the new owner of its site, Hooker Chemical, had it cut up and removed.

The human toll has been even more harsh.

By the 1980s, according to the Louisiana Office of Conservation, thousands of oil-waste pits, many leaching toxic chemicals, were scattered across Louisiana; hundreds of them were seeping into areas of the fertile rice belt in Cajun country. As awareness spread about groundwater contamination and diseases in communities along the river's industrial corridor, activists began calling the area "Cancer Alley."

Although Louisiana ranks in the top 10 percent of states in terms of its cancer mortality rate, petrochemical interests dismiss the term "Cancer Alley" as factually unsupported, a provocation. Black irony coats their charge.

10   The Louisiana Chemical Association provided base funding for the state Tumor Registry, which assembles the data on cancers. The registry is undertaken by a division of the Louisiana State University Medical Center, which is a beneficiary of donations from polluting industries. Louisiana's Tumor Registry, unlike those in most other states, offers no reliable data on incidences of childhood cancer, or incidences by parish (county), or incidences on a yearly basis. It reports trends only in larger geographic groupings; as a result, disease clusters cannot be pinpointed. Rare forms of cancer can't be tracked geographically. Much information gathered by physicians who treat cancer patients is anecdotal.

And that, in the opinion of Dr. Patricia Williams, is just the way business and petrochemical lobbyists want it. "Without reliable data, no one can link disease patterns to pollution," says Williams, who is herself a professor at the LSU Medical School, and is at the forefront of attempts to change the system.

"We're being denied the raw data and it's unconscionable," says Williams. "Embryonic tumors are not being reported as they are diagnosed. Raw data, by parish, would allow prevention programs. If you see a particular trend of brain cancers, you could begin to sort out what's going on. . . . The same [holds true] with cancer clusters."

Despite the state's history of being at or near the top of statistical lists in categories of toxic emissions, plaintiff attorneys have a great deal of trouble getting medical data to prove the impact of pollution in a given community.

Like Clarence John Laughlin before him, Richard Misrach captures the tones of a culture in spiritual twilight—clinging to a past beauty in the old mansions and icons of Catholicism—now facing a darkness brought about by big oil. Misrach's use of color sets him apart from Laughlin stylistically, as does his striking sense of juxtapositions: the petrochemical specters shadowing fields, ponds, buildings, cemeteries, and basketball courts. Misrach's commitment to discovering the ravaged landscape, while conceptually similar to Laughlin's, is rooted in the land itself. His long-term exploration of the American West and its defilement, the epic "Desert Cantos," are relentlessly straightforward. The "Bravo 20" series of the late 1980s—photographs of Nevada's disturbingly stunning bombing ranges—allow the terrain to create its own dark metaphors. Misrach's work reveals the primary emblems and moods of these frightening landscapes; the Louisiana images are thus as mysterious as they are horrific.

CITIZENS TAKE A STAND

15 Clarence Laughlin was a romantic who saw industry in symbolic terms—machine against man. In 1980, he took a firm stand at a news conference in New Orleans, lashing out against

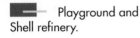 Playground and Shell refinery.

(Untitled), Norco, Louisiana, 1998 from "Cancer Alley" © Richard Misrach.

a plan to put the world's largest toxic-waste incinerator next to the historic Houmas House plantation, in Ascension Parish, midway along the river corridor south of Baton Rouge. A California-based company called Industrial Tank (I.T.) had begun with a $350,000 grant from the state government in Baton Rouge for a site feasibility study. I.T. recommended the construction of a massive disposal complex on a piece of land that was a proven flood plain, below sea level, in an already congested industrial road fronting the Mississippi River. In a move that reeked of corrupt politics, state officials then awarded I.T. the necessary permits to build the complex—whose feasibility I.T. had just been paid to assess. (In fact, the company had put money down on the land before it even got the permits.)

Reports soon surfaced that I.T. had pollution problems at its California sites, and was utterly inexperienced in managing a project of the scope envisioned in Louisiana. A citizens' group filed suit against I.T. and the state. In 1984, the state Supreme Court threw out the permits, killing the project. By then, activists were challenging industry over other conflicts.

DYNAMICS OF CHANGE

Amos Favorite, a seventy-eight-year-old black man, is now retired after many years in the union at Ormet Aluminum. Favorite grew up speaking the Creole French patois in the town of Vacherie, where Fats Domino was born. He remembers when ponds were blue. As a teenager he moved to nearby Geismar, where he has lived ever since.

"This was a good place to live at one time," says Favorite. "All the meat was wild game. I was raised on rabbits, squirrels, and deer." He hated work in the fields, however, and when he came home from infantry in World War II, Favorite bought a dozen acres of Geismar plantation, which was being sold off at thirty-five dollars an acre. The town is named for the family that owned the estate. Favorite's nine children grew up on his acreage; one of his sons was building

Holy Rosary Cemetery and Union Carbide complex.
Holy Rosary Cemetery and Union Carbide Complex, Taft, Louisiana, 1998 from "Cancer Alley" © Richard Misrach.

a handsome two story house next door to Amos Favorite's this past August.

One of his daughters, artist Malika Favorite, was the first black child to desegregate the local white school. Because of that, two KKK members tried to dynamite the family home. Before they could set the charge, Amos Favorite took his shotgun and started blasting. "I gave 'em the red ass, yes I did," he laughs. "They went runnin' to the sheriff, but that sheriff didn't do nothin' to me."

20   That was in 1968. A few years later, Favorite began to realize that people were getting sick from wells that drew water from the local aquifer, and he started speaking out against Ascension Parish's sacred cow: industry. BASF, the largest chemical company in the world, and Vulcan, which produces perchloroethylene (the chemical that goes into dry cleaning fluid) have plants in the area.

Despite opposition from management at thirteen major plants in Geismar, including BASF and Vulcan, Favorite won support from union members in those industries for his attempt to establish a public water system and separate district for Geismar. Favorite found a valuable ally in Willie Fontenot, the environmental investigator in the state attorney general's office. Fontenot has made a career of helping communities organize and gather research against polluters and unresponsive state agencies.

"The local government in Ascension had failed to provide adequate water," says Fontenot. "Amos Favorite and the Labor Neighbor project [a cross section of activists from various walks of life] broke the impasse and got the Baton Rouge water company to extend piping and set up a distribution system in Ascension to supplant the old private wells. . . . It was a pretty big victory for a ragtag citizens' group."

The most recent "ragtag" victory came in the town of Convent, where a company called Shintech wanted to build a huge chemical plant in an area of low-income black residents. Tulane University's Environmental Law Clinic helped the citizens challenge the state's operating permits, citing new EPA standards to guard against environmental racism. Shintech pulled out, and found another site, rather than risk being the first major test case of EPA's guidelines. The law clinic took a pounding from Governor Mike Foster and the State Supreme Court, which issued a ruling that severely restricts law students from working with community groups on environmental cases.

The people who live and work in this region of the Mississippi take a long view of their struggle. "The pendulum is going to swing," says Dr. Williams, who lives in LaPlace, twenty miles upriver from New Orleans. "Pollution is such a problem that people are becoming aware of cancers in their friends. They're becoming suspicious. Ten or fifteen years from now, what has happened to big tobacco companies is going to happen to industries that are polluting here." A surge of civil-damage suits against industry is inevitable, she predicts, "because there has been such a concerted effort to conceal what's happened."

SUGGESTIONS FOR DISCUSSION

1. With a group of your classmates, look carefully at Misrach's photos of "Cancer Alley" and then offer a reading of them as "geography, autobiography, and metaphor."

2. Berry writes, "Misrach's work reveals the primary emblems and moods of these frightening landscapes; the Louisiana images are thus as mysterious as they are horrific." Most of Misrach's photos are also quite beautiful. What does Misrach achieve in finding beauty in this pollution? Is there a way in which the beautiful can undercut the history of abuse that Berry writes of?

3. One way to examine photos like the ones Misrach takes is to look for what they are saying about the place they depict. In photos detailing pollution or the consequences of heavy industry, there is the implication that the scene should (or did) appear different before the impact of industrial waste. In other words, we have the sense that either something is missing or that something is very out of line—like the photo of Holy Rosary cemetery with Union Carbide as a backdrop. How do you read this photograph? What is the metaphor—the meaning outside the photo?

SUGGESTED ASSIGNMENT

Photographer Robert Adams once wrote that we rely on landscape photography "to make intelligible to us what we already know." Make your own photographic record of a specific landscape as it has been affected by industry or development. Once you have completed your project, write a reflection in which you examine your photographs in terms of the truths they tell about the landscape and the way it is changing. In your reflection, consider what the photographs reveal that "we already know" but that is often hidden in calendar or postcard landscape photography.

<table>
<tr><td>

FILM CLIP

</td><td>

Analyzing Set Design: Cities in Decay

</td></tr>
</table>

To learn more about cities
in decay, visit
www.ablongman.com/george/124

For many filmmakers, set design plays as important a role in conveying the meaning, tone, and symbolic action of a film as does the story, acting, and camera work. Whether you are looking at the classic haunted castle and dark corridors of a horror film or the too-clean attempt at realism in small-town dramas, set design is one key to understanding what the filmmaker is getting at.

The film dystopia is an especially rich genre for analyzing set design. Contrary to a utopian vision that presents an impossibly ideal world, the dystopian world often seems impossibly broken. It is an image of a future world gone mad.

From Fritz Lang's 1927 classic *Metropolis* to Ridley Scott's 1982 *Blade Runner* to Frank Miller's 2005 film adaptation of his graphic novel *Sin City*, the dystopic world is often an urban setting that has much in common with the city as we know it, though just a bit off. *The Eternal Sunshine of the Spotless Mind*, for example, looks more like our world than the Los Angeles of *Blade Runner*, and yet both are dystopias. On the other hand, the setting of *The Truman Show* seems to be a perfect little town until Truman discovers that he is not living in that world at all.

Choose one of the films listed here or another urban dystopia. Watch the film, paying particular attention to the film's set design. You can use the following questions to help you focus your analysis:

- ■ Where is the film set?
- ■ How would you describe the world in which the film takes place?
- ■ To what extent is the set realistic? To what extent is it imaginary?
- ■ What does the dystopic setting of this film say about the world we are currently living in?
- ■ How does the setting contribute to the overall theme or storyline of the film?
- ■ What features of the film's future world are recognizable to you so that that could be in any city or town today? What effect does that familiarity have for you as an audience to either accept or reject the world of the film?

Film Suggestions

Blade Runner

Metropolis

Eternal Sunshine of the Spotless Mind

Sin City

Brazil

Demolition Man

The Terminator

Observing the Uses of Public Space

In 1980 William Whyte published findings from nearly a decade of fieldwork in the streets of New York City which sought to reveal what Whyte called "the behavior of ordinary people on city streets." To do that, Whyte, as the director of the New York Street Life Project, set up teams of observers, used time-lapse photography to monitor activity in the streets, and mapped the spaces to see if the design of the space might influence how people use that space.

One of Whyte's most basic, though important discoveries in this study had to do with why people gather in some places and not in others. After observing people in several plazas similar in most respects except in the number of people who tended to hang around each space, Whyte's team came to this conclusion:

> *People tend to sit most where there are places to sit.*
>
> This may not strike you as an intellectual bombshell, and, now that I look back on our study, I wonder why it was not more apparent to us from the beginning. Sitting space, to be sure, is only one of the many variables, and, without a control situation as a measure, one cannot be sure of cause and effect. But sitting space is most certainly prerequisite. The most attractive fountains, the most striking designs, cannot induce people to come and sit if there is no place to sit.
>
> From *The Social Life of Small Urban Spaces*.

Whyte discovered that it didn't matter much whether there were actual chairs and benches. It just mattered if there were places to sit—even low walls with room to sit were enough to encourage people to hang around.

In her article "Woodruff Park and the Search for Common Ground," which appears earlier in this chapter, Murphy Davis writes that a space designed to be unfriendly to some people is a space that will end up being unfriendly to everyone. Whyte's studies seem to support her conclusion.

The Project

The purpose of your fieldwork project is to find a space where people do hang out—a campus common area, a public park, etc.—and study how people use the space and what in the space actually invites people to sit and stay.

With a group of your classmates, make at least three visits—at different times of the day—to see how well the space is suited for gathering. Who hangs out there? How do they spend their time? Where do they sit? How long do they stay? When you have completed your project, present your observations to the class, making sure you focus on your conclusions about why this space is a popular one for gathering or just hanging out. Detail the features your group observed that make the space inviting and easy to rest or spend time in.

Mapping the Space

When you begin your observation, sketch a map of the space. Note the layout of the place. How large is the space? What kind of furniture, if any, is available for sitting? How is the furniture arranged? Can it be moved? How do people enter the space? Make any important notes about the way the space is arranged on this map. If there is no furniture, where do people sit? How comfortable is the space for gathering or finding privacy?

If you reproduce your map on a transparency or put it in a program that will project images, you can use your sketch as a visual when you present your findings to the class.

Watching People

Begin by keeping as accurate a count of people as you can. Don't try to get too much information or guess at too much. Note how long people stay and where they sit. Your aim here is to get as accurate a picture as possible of how many people use the space, how easy it is for them to sit, where they sit, and for how long. Make sure you include the details of these observations in your report.

For more information on writing a report from fieldwork observations, review instructions on writing a report in the fieldwork assignment in Chapter 3 (see pages 192–193).

MINING THE ARCHIVE   Take a Walking Tour

To learn more about public space organizations, visit www.ablongman.com/george/125

We normally think of an archive as a collection of papers or documents. Yet a city, town, or national park area can also function as a kind of archive—a place where you will find sites of historic, political, or cultural importance.

Certainly one of the best ways to learn about a public space and its archival potential is to take a walking tour. Cities, towns, local and national parks, botanical gardens, museums, campuses, cemeteries, and historical buildings across this country have walking tours designed to show visitors the history of the place; the best places to shop; popular restaurants; homes of poets, artists, and politicians; little-known places of historic interest; and more. These tours usually include a step-by-step guide to the places on the tour, an easy-to-follow map, and a thumbnail description of the importance of each stop.

Begin this project by locating several sample walking tours. Most travel guides in local bookstores and public libraries will include walking tours. For example, Frommer's guide to San Francisco includes a walking tour of Chinatown. *The Eyewitness Travel Guide to New York* includes walking tours of Greenwich Village, Lower Manhattan, and the Upper East Side. There are even alternative walking tours such as Bruce Kayton's *Radical Walking Tours of New York City*, whose maps include the homes of leftists, anarchists, and radicals who are often left out of the commercial guides or chamber of commerce maps designed for most tourists.

Bring the walking tours you have located to class for a general discussion of what walking tours include, what they leave out, and how they identify public space.

A good walking tour should have the following:

- A focus or theme.
- A clear map.
- A brief description of each stop on the tour.
- Information about how to get there, how long the tour will take, and what difficulties a walker might encounter.

Hampton's Historic "Ring"

A Walking/Riding Tour of Hampton's Old Town Center

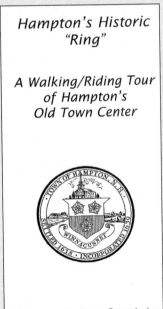

Hampton Heritage Commission
100 Winnacunnet Road
Hampton, NH 03842

Displayed here are portions of a walking tour of historic Hampton, New Hampshire. Study the map and entries we have selected from the guide's description of each stop. When you have a good sense of what a walking tour entails, make a walking tour of a place you know well. Be sure to draw a clear map and time the walk. Give your tour a theme or focus. Your tour can focus on people, places, events, whatever ties the place together as a historical resource. You can even create an underground tour—of campus dorms or the library or the place where you grew up—that, like Bruce Kayton's *Radical Walking Tours of New York City*, highlights the people, places, and events in the history of that city not considered mainstream or not usually shown to visitors.

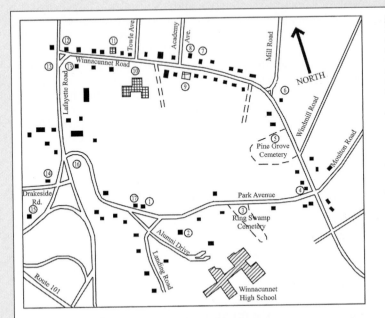

The Ring, which encompasses roughly the area now bounded by Park Avenue and Winnacunnet and Lafayette Roads, is the original center of the town of Hampton. The Ring consisted of the Meeting-house Green and the house lots of the early settlers surrounding it.

Point 1 *The Meeting House Green. Site of the first four meetinghouses and the first Hampton Academy building. The center of town activities from 1638 to the early 19th century. Founders' Park, in the triangle, was established in 1925 to honor the early Hampton families.*

Point 2 *Emery-Jackson House House, 47 Park Avenue. Home of two 18th-century physicians, Clement Jackson and Anthony Emery.*

Point 3 *Ring Swamp Cemetery, opened in 1799. The second town cemetery with iron gates made by a local blacksmith, Enoch Young.*

Point 4 *Enoch Young's House, 86 Park Avenue. The house dates to the early nineteenth century.*

Point 5 *Pine Grove Cemetery, before 1654. This is the oldest public cemetery in the state, where most townsmen were buried before 1800. The oldest stone still standing dates to the late 17th century.*

Point 6 *188 Winnacunnet Road. Site of the Morris Hobbs house, where the newly-formed Congregational Society met 1796-97, after separation from the town church and before their meetinghouse was built.*

Point 7 Site of the 1797 Congregational meetinghouse, later the town hall. The old building burned in 1949.

Point 8 Hampton District Courthouse. The building was the old Centre School, built in 1873, one of four grammar schools in town. This, the only one to still stand, was moved here in 1922 and raised on a high basement to house the fire department in the cellar.

Point 9 Congregational Church, 1844. The chapel was added in 1873. This was the first Congregational meetinghouse not to have been owned by the town.

Point 10 Centre School, 1922. This has been the site of a school since the 18th century.

Point 11 Baptist Church, 1834. The Baptist Society was formed in 1817, the second religious society in the town. This is now the oldest church building in Hampton.

Point 12 The site where George Whitfield, the great English evangelist, preached in 1740, sparking a religious revival in the area.

Point 13 The sites of the Toppan houses, facing each other across Lafayette Rd. The Toppan family was prominent in Hampton for over a century as merchants, lawyers, politicians, and historians. Christopher Toppan donated the site for the 1797 meetinghouse, and a descendant gave the land for the present Hampton Academy.

Point 14 The David Towle House, built in the mid-18th century in North Hampton and moved to this site in the 19th century.

Point 15 The General Jonathan Moulton House, 1769. The only high-style Georgian house in Hampton, this house has been the focus of a number of ghost stories and tales of dealings with the Devil.

Point 16. Rand's Hill (now part of Park Avenue). The site of Hampton's earliest tavern, operated by Robert Tuck, and supposedly the site of the home of the accused witch Goody Cole.

Point 17 Site of the Samuel Harden house. The Tuck Museum stands on the land which the town allowed to Samuel Harden, a War of 1812 veteran. He was the town sexton for decades.

CHAPTER SEVEN

Storytelling

Experience which is passed on from mouth to mouth is the source from which all storytellers have drawn. And among those who have written down the tales, it is the great ones whose written version differs least from the speech of the many nameless storytellers.

—Walter Benjamin,
The Storyteller

"Why to think of it, we're in the same tale still! It's going on. Don't the great tales never end?"

"No, they never end as tales," said Frodo. "But the people in them come, and go when their part's ended. Our part will end later—or sooner."

—J. R. R. Tolkein,
The Two Towers

Richard Hutchings/PhotoEdit, Inc.

One of the pleasures of listening to stories is suspending disbelief and entering into the imaginary world that storytelling creates. It doesn't matter so much whether the story is true or if it could have happened. What matters is that listeners know their feelings and their responses to a story are real. When people hear the words "Once upon a time . . . " at the beginning of a fairy tale (or Jason's footsteps in the *Friday the 13th* horror flicks), they know they are entering a world that could never happen, yet this knowledge does not stop them from trying on, at least temporarily, the version of reality (or unreality) that the story offers.

Storytelling is a persistent form of popular entertainment, whether people tell ghost stories around a campfire or watch the electronic glow of a television set. Every culture has its own storytelling tradition of myths, legends, epics, fables, animal stories, fairy tales, and romances. Listeners take delight in the mythic powers of their heroes, laugh at the comic predicaments clowns and tricksters get themselves into, and feel awe—and sometimes terror—when they hear stories of unseen worlds and the supernatural. In every storytelling tradition, there is a repertoire of stock characters and plots that listeners recognize immediately—and know how to respond to through laughter, tears, excitement, fear, and grief.

But the fact that people everywhere, in all known cultures, tell stories only raises a series of questions we will ask you to explore in this chapter. We will be asking you to recall stories from the past and present to think about the functions storytelling performs, the occasions on which stories are told, and the people who tell stories. The reading and writing assignments in this chapter will ask you to look at some of the stories circulating in contemporary America. We will be asking you to explore the familiar stories that you hear from family and friends, read in novels and comic books, or watch in the movies to see what these stories can tell you about the culture that you are living in and the kinds of knowledge the imaginary worlds of storytelling transmit.

One of the key functions of storytelling, aside from entertaining listeners, is a pedagogical one. Stories teach. As one of the oldest forms of human communication, stories are important ways young people learn about the world and what their culture values. In traditional societies, stories were passed along from generation to generation orally. The elders were responsible for initiating young people into the lore of the tribe. In many respects, the same is true today, in the mass-mediated world of contemporary America. To be an adult and a full member of society means knowing the stories a particular culture tells about the world and about itself.

What's more, the kinds of stories people tell teach them as much about who they want to be and how they want to live as about who they are now. The stories uncover fears and desires. They comfort and disturb. Even the fantasy worlds people create look amazingly like the real world they live in—only much better—with heroes who know what to do and villains so evil it's impossible not to know they are the bad guys. Storytelling is, then, as much about understanding and reordering the world as it is about entertaining.

In addition to the stories you read and watch, we will be asking you to recall the stories that you tell in the course of casual conversation, when you explain what happened over the weekend or pass along the latest gossip, political controversy, or scandal. People love to tell and listen to stories about politicians, celebrities, and professional athletes—who is dating whom, who is getting divorced, who is checking into a drug or alcohol abuse clinic, who is under investigation for what. These kinds of stories—personal anecdotes, gossip, bits and pieces of the evening news—may seem so trivial that they don't really merit the title of storytelling. But although telling and listening to these stories may appear to be no more than a way to pass the time with family, neighbors, coworkers, and friends, in fact this type of storytelling performs a useful social function within local communities. As people tell and listen to stories, perhaps without fully recognizing it, they are working out their own attitudes and evaluations of a wide range of social realities, from relations between the sexes to politics.

If you have seen such popular television and film genres as family sitcoms, hospital dramas, soap operas, action adventure stories, science fiction, mysteries, westerns, and slasher flicks, you already know about many of the conventions of storytelling. In each, the cast of characters is a familiar one: interracial cop teams, superheroes, cyberpunks, urban vigilantes, gangsters, android terminators, martial arts masters, hard-boiled private eyes, cowboys, swinging singles, career women, men behaving badly, dumb parents, and precocious kids. These popular figures inhabit fictional worlds—the western frontier, the criminal underworld, interstellar space, the mean streets of the city, the middle-class homes of the suburbs—where they are working out the aspirations and anxieties of average people while dealing with whichever conflict threatens to overturn their/our world.

RED SKY IN THE MORNING

— *Patricia Hampl*

Patricia Hampl is Regents' Professor at the University of Minnesota, where she teaches creative writing. She is a poet and memoirist, a writer who tells stories of her own life. She teaches in Minneapolis and lives in St. Paul, where she has spent most of her life. In 1990, she was awarded a prestigious MacArthur Fellowship in part for her first book-length memoir, *A Romantic Education* (1981). "Red Sky in the Morning" appeared in *I Could Tell You Stories* (1999), Hampl's collection of essays devoted to memoir.

SUGGESTION FOR READING

Although many people associate storytelling with fiction, most of us have also experienced the long tradition of storytelling that is characteristic of family or town stories, stories that recall local or family history and the people that made up that history. In her brief essay on memoir, Hampl raises the question of what kinds of incidents, people, or memories make it into the family stories we tell. Before you read, think about a story you remember an adult in your life telling—one you would be willing to share with others. Write about why that story stays with you. Is the story about family? About the person who told it? About how people treat one another? Why do you think it is worth remembering or not?

1 Years ago, in another life, I woke to look out the smeared window of a Greyhound bus I had been riding all night, and in the still-dark morning of a small Missouri river town where the driver had made a scheduled stop at a grimy diner, I saw below me a stout middle-aged woman in a flowered housedress turn and kiss full on the mouth a godlike young man with golden curls. But I've got that wrong: *he* was kissing *her*. Passionately, without regard for the world and its incomprehension. He had abandoned himself to his love, and she, stolid, matronly, received this adoration with simple grandeur, like a socialist-realist statue of a woman taking up sheaves of wheat.

Their ages dictated that he must be her son, but I had just come out of the cramped, ruinous half sleep of a night on a Greyhound and I was clairvoyant: This was that thing called love. The morning light cracked blood red along the river.

Of course, when she lumbered onto the bus a moment later, lurching forward with her two bulging bags, she chose the empty aisle seat next to me as her own. She pitched one bag onto the overhead rack, and then heaved herself into the seat as if she were used to hoisting sacks of potatoes onto the flatbed of a pickup. She held the other bag on her lap, and leaned toward the window. The beautiful boy was blowing kisses. He couldn't see where she was in the dark interior, so he blew kisses up and down the side of the bus, gazing ardently at the blank windows. "Pardon me," the woman said without looking at me, and leaned over, bag and all, to rap the glass. Her beautiful boy ran back to our window and kissed and kissed, and finally hugged himself, shutting his eyes in an ecstatic pantomime of love-sweet-love. She smiled and waved back.

Then the bus was moving. She slumped back in her seat, and I turned to her. I suppose I looked transfixed. As our eyes met she said, "Everybody thinks he's my son. But he's not. He's my husband." She let that sink in. She was a farm woman with hands that could have been a man's; I was a university student, hair down to my waist. It was long ago, as I said, in another life. It was even another life for the country. The Vietnam War was the time we were living through, and I was traveling, as I did every three weeks, to visit my boyfriend who was in a federal prison. "Draft dodger," my brother said. "Draft resister," I piously retorted. I had never been kissed the way this woman had been kissed. I was living in a tattered corner of a romantic idyll, the one where the hero is willing to suffer for his beliefs. I was the girlfriend. I lived on pride, not love.

5   My neighbor patted her short cap of hair, and settled in for the long haul as we pulled onto the highway along the river, heading south. "We been married five years and we're happy," she said with a penetrating satisfaction, the satisfaction that passeth understanding. "Oh," she let out a profound sigh as if she mined her truths from the bountiful, bulky earth, "Oh, I could tell you stories." She put her arms snugly around her bag, gazed off for a moment, apparently made pensive by her remark. Then she closed her eyes and fell asleep.

I looked out the window smudged by my nose which had been pressed against it at the bus stop to see the face of true love reveal itself.

Beyond the bus the sky, instead of becoming paler with the dawn, drew itself out of a black line along the Mississippi into an alarming red flare. It was very beautiful. The old caution—*Red sky in the morning, sailor take warning*—darted through my mind and fell away. Remember this, I remember telling myself, hang on to this. I could feel it all skittering away, whatever conjunction of beauty and improbability I had stumbled upon.

It is hard to describe the indelible bittersweetness of that moment. Which is why, no doubt, it had to be remembered. The very word—*Remember!*—spiraled up like a snake out of a basket, a magic catch in its sound, the doubling of the m—*re memmemem*—setting up a low murmur full of inchoate associations as if a loved voice were speaking into my ear alone, occultly.

Whether it was the unguarded face of love, or the red gash down the middle of the warring country I was traveling through, or this exhausted farm woman's promise of untold tales that bewitched me, I couldn't say. Over it all rose and remains only the injunction to remember. This, the most impossible command we lay upon ourselves, claimed me and then perversely disappeared, trailing an illusive silken tissue of meaning, without giving a story, refusing to leave me in peace.

Because everyone "has" a memoir, we all have a stake in how such stories are told. For we do not, after all, simply *have* experience; we are entrusted with it. We must do something—make something—with it. A story, we sense, is the only possible habitation for the burden of our witnessing.

10   The tantalizing formula of my companion on the Greyhound—*oh, I could tell you stories*—is the memoirist's opening line, but it has none of the delicious promise of the storyteller's "Once upon a time . . . " In fact, it is a perverse statement. The woman on the bus told me nothing—she fell asleep and escaped to her dreams. For the little sentence inaugurates nothing, and leads nowhere after its *dot dot dot* of expectation. Whatever

experience lies tangled within its seductive promise remains forever balled up in the woolly impossibility of telling the-truth-the-whole-truth of a life, any life.

Memoirists, unlike fiction writers, do not really want to "tell a story." They want to tell it *all*—the all of personal experience, of consciousness itself. That includes a story, but also the whole expanding universe of sensation and thought that flows beyond the confines of narrative and proves every life to be not only an isolated story line but a bit of the cosmos, spinning and streaming into the great, ungraspable pattern of existence. Memoirists wish to tell their mind, not their story.

The wistfulness implicit in that conditional verb—*I could tell*—conveys an urge more primitive than a storyteller's search for an audience. It betrays not a loneliness for someone who will listen but a hopelessness about language itself and a sad recognition of its limitations. How much reality can subject-verb-object bear on the frail shoulders of the sentence? The sigh within the statement is more like this: I could tell you stories—if only stories could tell what I have in me to tell.

For this reason, autobiographical writing is bedeviled. It is caught in a self which must become a world—and not, please, a narcissistic world. The memoir, once considered a marginal literary form, has emerged in the past decade as the signature genre of the age. "The triumph of memoir is now established fact," James Atlas trumpeted in a cover story on "The Age of the Literary Memoir" in the *New York Times Magazine.* "Fiction," he claimed, "isn't delivering the news. Memoir is."

With its "triumph," the memoir has, of course, not denied the truth and necessity of fiction. In fact, it leans heavily on novelistic assumptions. But the contemporary memoir has reaf-firmed the primacy of the first person voice in American imaginative writing established by Whitman's "Song of Myself." Maybe a reader's love of memoir is less an intrusive lust for confession than a hankering for the intimacy of this first-person voice, the deeply satisfying sense of being spoken to privately. More than a story, we want a voice speaking softly, urgently, in our ear. Which is to say, to our heart. That voice carries its implacable command, the ancient murmur that called out to me in the middle of the country in the middle of a war—remember, remember (*I dare you, I tempt you*).

15 Looking out the Greyhound window that red morning all those years ago, I saw the improbable face of love. But even more puzzling was the cryptic remark of the beloved as she sat next to me. I think of her more often than makes sense. Though he was the beauty, she is the one who comes back. How faint his golden curls have become (he also had a smile, crooked and charming, but I can only remember the idea of it—the image is gone). It is she, stout and unbeautiful, wearing her flowery cotton housedress with a zipper down the middle, who has taken up residence with her canny eye and her acceptance of adoration. To be loved like that, loved improbably: of course, she had stories to tell. She took it for granted in some unapologetic way, like being born to wealth. Take the money and run.

But that moment before she fell asleep, when she looked pensive, the red morning rising over the Mississippi, was a wistful moment. *I could tell you stories*—but she could not. What she had to tell was too big, too much, too *something*, for her to place in the small shrine that a story is.

When we met—if what happened between us was a meeting—I felt nothing had ever happened to me and nothing ever would. I didn't understand that riding this filthy Greyhound down the middle of bloodied America in the middle of a mutinous war was itself a story and that something *was* happening to me. I thought if something was happening to anybody around me it was happening to people like my boyfriend: They were the heroes, according to the lights that shined for me then. I was just riding shotgun in my own life. I could not have imagined containing, as the farm woman slumped next to me did, the sheer narrative bulk to say, "I could tell you stories," and then drifting off with the secret heaviness of experience into the silence where stories live their real lives, crumbling into the loss we call remembrance.

The boastful little declaration, pathetically conditional (not "I'll tell you a story" but "I could") wavered wistfully for an instant between us. The stranger's remark, launched in the dark of the Greyhound, floated across the human landscape like the lingering tone of a struck bell from a village church, and joined all the silence that ever was, as I turned my face to the window where the world was rushing by along the slow river.

SUGGESTIONS FOR DISCUSSION

1. With a group of your classmates, retell the parts of Hampl's story that you remember best. Why did they stick out for you? Compare what you remember to what others remember. How does each group member's memory of the story differ? How does Hampl characterize herself in this story? What details from the story serve to build that characterization for you?

2. Near the end of her anecdote, Hampl writes, "Remember this, I remember telling myself, hang on to this." What is it about this incident/this woman that she believes is important enough to remember? What, for example, is the point of Hampl telling the story of the woman and her husband?

3. In the middle of this essay Hampl writes, "Because everyone 'has' a memoir, we all have a stake in how such stories are told. For we do not, after all, simply *have* experience; we are entrusted with it. We must do something—make something—with it. A story, we sense, is the only possible habitation for the burden of our witnessing." What does she mean by that? How is the story you wrote down before you read Hampl part of a memoir?

SUGGESTIONS FOR WRITING

1. On one level, "Red Sky in the Morning" is a simple memory piece—memoir. In it, the author recounts a chance meeting with a woman whose words—"*I could tell you stories*"—haunt her. On a more important level, this essay and the story within it is about storytelling. Write an essay in which you explain the nature of storytelling as Hampl's story reveals it. Why, for example, does she remember the woman better than anything else? What is it that she did not understand then (as she tells us near the end of the essay) that she now understands better—about herself, about storytelling, about expectations? You might want to use the woman's words—"*I could tell you stories*"—as a focus for your essay.

2. Within the story of the woman and her husband is the story of Hampl, her boyfriend, and the temper of the times—a country at war. Write an essay in which you explain the importance of that background for the story. Besides being the reason for Hampl's bus trip, what other purpose does that story serve? Keep in mind the several places in the essay where Hampl explains what a memoirist does. For example, "Memoirists wish to tell their mind, not their story." Use that and other statements like it to help frame your essay.

3. Write your own story from the story you wrote before you read Hampl's essay. Keep in mind Hampl's notion that stories are things we are entrusted with. To make them useful for others, we must shape them. Tell your story so that it is meaningful for others outside your circle of family and friends. Remember that your story should "tell your mind," not your story.

"THE HOOK" AND OTHER TEENAGE HORRORS

— *Jan Harold Brunvand*

Jan Harold Brunvand is a folklorist and professor emeritus of English at the University of Utah. " 'The Hook' and Other Teenage Horrors" is a chapter from Brunvand's book *The Vanishing Hitchhiker: American Urban Legends and Their Meaning* (1981). In *The Vanishing Hitchhiker* and its two sequels, *The Choking Doberman* (1986) and *The Mexican Pet* (1988), Brunvand has gathered examples of contemporary storytelling—strange, scary, funny, macabre, and embarrassing tales storytellers relate as true accounts of real-life experience. Brunvand calls these stories "urban legends" because they are, by and large, set in contemporary America and, like all legends, are alleged to be about real people and real events. These legends, often about someone that the narrator knows or the "friend of a friend," are passed on by word of mouth, forming an oral tradition in the midst of America's print and media culture. As Brunvand says, urban legends "survive by being as lively and 'factual' as the television evening news, and, like the daily newscasts, they tend to concern deaths, injuries, kidnappings, tragedies, and scandals." Stories such as "The Hook" are told and are believed—or at least are believable—as "human interest" stories that capture some of the fears and anxieties of contemporary America.

SUGGESTION FOR READING   As a folklorist, Brunvand is interested in interpreting urban legends as well as in gathering them. As you read through " 'The Hook' and Other Teenage Horrors," underline and annotate the passages where Brunvand offers his own interpretations or those of other folklore scholars.

GROWING UP SCARED

1   People of all ages love a good scare. Early childlore is full of semiserious spooky stories and ghastly threats, while the more sophisticated black humor of Little Willies, Bloody Marys, Dead Babies, and other cycles of sick jokes enters a bit later. Among the favorite readings at school are Edgar Allan Poe's blood-soaked tales, and favorite stories at summer camp tell of maniacal ax-murderers and deformed giants lurking in the dark forest to ambush unwary Scouts. Halloween spook houses and Hollywood horror films cater to the same wish to push the level of tolerable fright as far as possible.

The ingredients of horror fiction change little through time, but the style of such stories does develop, even in oral tradition. In their early teens young Americans apparently reject the overdramatic and unbelievable juvenile "scaries" and adopt a new lore of more plausible tales with realistic settings. That is, they begin to enjoy urban legends, especially those dealing with "folks" like themselves—dating couples, students, and baby-sitters—who are subjected to grueling ordeals and horrible threats.

One consistent theme in these teenage horrors is that as the adolescent moves out from home into the larger world, the world's dangers may close in on him or her. Therefore, although the immediate purpose of many of these legends is to produce a good scare, they also serve to deliver a warning: Watch out! This could happen to you! Furthermore, the horror tales often contain thinly-disguised sexual themes which are, perhaps, implicit in the nature of such plot situations as parking in a lovers' lane or baby-sitting (playing house) in a strange home. These sexual elements furnish both a measure of further entertainment and definite cautionary notices about the world's actual dangers. Thus, from the teenagers' own major fears, concerns, and experiences, spring their favorite "true" oral stories.

The chief current example of this genre of urban legend—one that is even older, more popular, and more widespread than "The Boyfriend's Death"—is the one usually called "The Hook."

"THE HOOK"

5 On Tuesday, November 8, 1960, the day when Americans went to the polls to elect John F. Kennedy as their thirty-fifth president, thousands of people must have read the following letter from a teenager in the popular newspaper column written by Abigail Van Buren:

> Dear Abby: If you are interested in teenagers, you will print this story. I don't know whether it's true or not, but it doesn't matter because it served its purpose for me:
>
> A fellow and his date pulled into their favorite "lovers' lane" to listen to the radio and do a little necking. The music was interrupted by an announcer who said there was an escaped convict in the area who had served time for rape and robbery. He was described as having a hook instead of a right hand. The couple became frightened and drove away. When the boy took his girl home, he went around to open the car door for her. Then he saw—a hook on the door handle! I don't think I will ever park to make out as long as I live. I hope this does the same for other kids.
>
> Jeanette

This juicy story seems to have emerged in the late 1950s, sharing some common themes with "The Death Car" and "The Vanishing Hitchhiker" and then . . . influencing "The Boyfriend's Death" as that legend developed in the early 1960s. The story of "The Hook" (or "The Hookman") really needed no national press report to give it life or credibility, because the teenage oral-tradition underground had done the job well enough long before the election day of 1960. Teenagers all over the country knew about "The Hook" by 1959, and like other modern legends the basic plot was elaborated with details and became highly localized.

One of my own students, originally from Kansas, provided this specific account of where the event supposedly occurred:

> Outside of "Mac" [McPherson, Kansas], about seven miles out towards Lindsborg, north on old highway 81 is an old road called "Hookman's Road." It's a curved road, a traditional parking

spot for the kids. When I was growing up it [the legend] was popular, and that was back in the '60's, and it was old then.

Another student told a version of the story that she had heard from her baby-sitter in Albuquerque in 1960:

> over the radio came an announcement that a crazed killer with a hook in place of a hand had escaped from the local insane asylum. The girl got scared and begged the boy to take her home. He got mad and stepped on the gas and roared off. When they got to her house, he got out and went around to the other side of the car to let her out. There on the door handle was a bloody hook.

But these two students were told, after arriving in Salt Lake City, that it had actually occurred *here* in Memory Grove, a well-wooded city park. "Oh, no," a local student in the class insisted. "This couple was parked outside of Salt Lake City *in a mountain canyon* one night, and . . . " It turned out that virtually every student in the class knew the story as adapted in some way to their hometowns.

Other folklorists have reported collecting "The Hook" in Maryland, Wisconsin, Indiana, Illinois, Kansas, Texas, Arkansas, Oregon, and Canada. Some of the informants' comments echo Dear Abby's correspondent in testifying to the story's effect (to discourage parking) even when its truth was suspect. The student said, "I believe that it *could* happen, and this makes it seem real," or "I don't really [believe it], but it's pretty scary; I sort of hope it didn't happen."

10 Part of the great appeal of "The Hook"—one of the most popular adolescent scare stories—must lie in the tidiness of the plot. Everything fits. On the other hand, the lack of loose ends would seem to be excellent testimony to the story's near impossibility. After all, what are the odds that a convicted criminal or crazed maniac would be fitted with a hook for a missing hand, that this same threatening figure would show up precisely when a radio warning had been broadcast of his escape, and that the couple would

drive away rapidly just at the instant the hook-man put his hook through the door handle? Besides, why wouldn't he try to open the door with his good hand, and how is it that the boy—furious at the interruption of their lovemaking—is still willing to go around politely to open the girl's door when they get home? Too much, too much—but it makes a great story.

In an adolescent novel titled *Dinky Hocker Shoots Smack!*, M. E. Kerr captured the way teenagers often react to such legends—with cool acceptance that it might have happened, and that's good enough:

> She told Tucker this long story about a one-armed man who was hanging around a lovers' lane in Prospect Park [Brooklyn]. There were rumors that he tried to get in the cars and carry off the girls. He banged on the windshields with his hooked wooden arm and frothed at the mouth. He only said two words: *bloody murder*; and his voice was high and hoarse.
>
> Dinky claimed this girl who went to St. Marie's was up in Prospect Park one night with a boyfriend. The girl and her boyfriend began discussing the one-armed man while they were parked. They both got frightened and decided to leave. The boy dropped the girl off at her house, and drove home. When he got out of his car, he found this hook attached to his door handle.
>
> Dinky said, "They must have driven off just as he was about to open the door."
>
> "I thought you weren't interested in the bizarre, anymore," Tucker said.
>
> "It's a true story."
>
> "It's still bizarre."

A key detail lacking in the *Dinky Hocker* version, however, is the boyfriend's frustrated anger resulting in their leaving the scene in a great hurry. Almost invariably the boy guns the motor and roars away: " . . . so he revs up the car and he goes torquing out of there." Or, "The boy floored the gas pedal and zoomed away," or "Her boyfriend was annoyed and the car screeched off. . . ." While this behavior is essential to explain the sudden sharp force that tears loose the maniac's hook, it is also a reminder of the original sexual purpose of the parking, at

least on the boy's part. While Linda Dégh saw "the natural dread of the handicapped," and "the boy's disappointment and suddenly recognized fear as an adequate explanation for the jump start of the car," folklorist Alan Dundes disagreed, mainly because of the curtailed sex quest in the plot.

Dundes, taking a Freudian line, interpreted the hook itself as a phallic symbol which penetrates the girl's door handle (or bumps seductively against her window) but which is torn off (symbolic of castration) when the car starts abruptly. Girls who tell the story, Dundes suggests, "are not afraid of what a man lacks, but of what he has"; a date who is "all hands" may really want to "get his hooks into her." Only the girl's winding up the window or insisting upon going home at once saves her, and the date has to "pull out fast" before he begins to act like a sex maniac himself. The radio—turned on originally for soft, romantic background music—introduces instead "the consciencelike voice from society," a warning that the girl heeds and the boy usually scorns. Dundes concluded that this popular legend "reflects a very real dating practice, one which produces anxiety . . . particularly for girls."

"THE KILLER IN THE BACKSEAT"

A similar urban legend also involves cars and an unseen potential assailant; this time a man threatens a woman who is driving alone at night. The following version of "The Killer in the Backseat" was contributed in 1967 by a University of Utah student who had heard other versions set in Denver and Aurora, Colorado:

> A woman living in the city [i.e., Salt Lake City] was visiting some friends in Ogden. When she got into her car in front of this friend's house, she noticed that a car started up right behind her car. It was about 2:00 in the morning, and there weren't any other cars on the road. After she had driven to the highway, she began to think that this car was following her. Some of the time he would drive up real close to her car, but he wouldn't ever pass. She was really scared to

death and kept speeding to try to get away from him.

When she got to Salt Lake, she started running stop lights to get away from him, but he would run right through them too. So when she got to her driveway she pulled in really fast, and this guy pulled in right behind her. She just laid on the horn, and her husband came running out. Just then, the guy jumped out of the car, and her husband ran over and said, "What the hell's goin' on here?" So he grabbed the guy, and his wife said, "This man's followed me all the way from Ogden." The man said, "I followed your wife because I was going to work, and as I got into my car, I noticed when I turned my lights on, a man's head bob down in her back seat." So the husband went over to her backseat, opened the door, and pulled this guy from out of the backseat.

15   This legend first appeared in print in 1968 in another version, also—coincidentally—set in Ogden, Utah, but collected at Indiana University, Bloomington. (This shows how the presence of folklorists in a locality will influence the apparent distribution patterns of folk material.) Twenty further texts have surfaced at Indiana University with, as usual, plenty of variations and localizations. In many instances the pursuing driver keeps flashing his headlights between the high and low beam in order to restrain the assailant who is popping up and threatening to attack the driver. Sometimes the pursuer is a burly truck driver or other tough-looking character, and in several of the stories the supposed would-be attacker (the pursuing rescuer) is specifically said to be a black man. (Both motifs clearly show white middle class fears of minorities or of groups believed to be socially inferior.)

In a more imaginative set of these legends the person who spots the dangerous man in back is a gas station attendant who pretends that a ten dollar bill offered by the woman driver in payment for gas is counterfeit. With this ruse he gets her safely away from her car before calling the police. In another version of the story, a passing motorist sharply warns the woman driver to roll up her window and follow him, driving in

exactly the same manner he does. She obeys, speeding and weaving along the highway, until a suspected assailant—usually carrying an ax—is thrown from his perch on the roof of her car.

"THE BABY-SITTER AND THE MAN UPSTAIRS"

Just as a lone woman may unwittingly be endangered by a hidden man while she is driving at night, a younger one may face the same hazard in a strange home. The horror legend of "The Baby-sitter and the Man Upstairs," similar in structure to "The Killer in the Backseat," is possibly a later variation of the same story relocated to fit teenagers' other direct experiences. This standard version is from a fourteen-year-old Canadian boy (1973):

There was this baby-sitter that was in Montreal baby-sitting for three children in a big house. She was watching TV when suddenly the phone rang. The children were all in bed. She picked up the phone and heard this guy on the other end laughing hysterically. She asked him what it was that he wanted, but he wouldn't answer and then hung up. She worried about it for a while, but then thought nothing more of it and went back to watching the movie.

Everything was fine until about fifteen minutes later when the phone rang again. She picked it up and heard the same voice laughing hysterically at her, and then hung up. At this point she became really worried and phoned the operator to tell her what had been happening. The operator told her to calm down and that if he called again to try and keep him on the line as long as possible and she would try to trace the call.

Again about fifteen minutes later the guy called back and laughed hysterically at her. She asked him why he was doing this, but he just kept laughing at her. He hung up and about five seconds later the operator called. She told the girl to get out of the house at once because the person who was calling was calling from the upstairs extension. She slammed down the phone and just as she was turning to leave she saw the man coming down the stairs laughing hysterically with a bloody butcher knife in his hand and meaning to kill her. She ran out onto the street but he didn't follow. She called the police and they came and caught the man, and discovered that he had murdered all the children.

The storyteller added that he had heard the story from a friend whose brother's girlfriend was the baby-sitter involved.

By now it should come as no surprise to learn that the same story had been collected two years earlier (1971) some 1500 miles southwest of Montreal, in Austin, Texas, and also in Bloomington, Indiana, in 1973 in a college dormitory. These three published versions are only samples from the wide distribution of the story in folk tradition. Their similarities and differences provide another classic case of folklore's variation within traditional boundaries. In all three legend texts the hour is late and the baby-sitter is watching television. Two of the callers make threatening statements, while one merely laughs. In all versions the man calls three times at regular intervals before the girl calls the operator, then once more afterwards. In both American texts the operator herself calls the police, and in the Indiana story she commands "Get out of the house immediately; don't go upstairs; don't do anything; just leave the house. When you get out there, there will be policemen outside and they'll take care of it." (One is reminded of the rescuers' orders not to look back at the car in "The Boyfriend's Death.") The Texas telephone operator in common with the Canadian one gives the situation away by adding, "The phone call traces to the upstairs." The murder of the child or children (one, two, or three of them—no pattern) is specified in the American versions: in Texas they are "chopped into little bitty pieces"; in Indiana, "torn to bits." All of the storytellers played up the spookiness of the situation—details that would be familiar to anyone who has ever baby-sat—a strange house, a television show, an unexpected phone call, frightening sounds or threats, the abrupt orders from the operator, and finally the shocking realization at the end that (as in "The Killer in the Backseat") the caller had been there in the house (or behind her) all the time.

The technical problems of calling another telephone from an extension of the same number, or the actual procedures of call-tracing, do not seem to worry the storytellers.

Folklorist Sue Samuelson, who examined hundreds of unpublished "Man Upstairs" stories filed in American folklore archives, concluded that the telephone is the most important and emotionally-loaded item in the plot: the assailant is harassing his victim through the device that is her own favorite means of communication. Baby-sitting, Samuelson points out, is an important socializing experience for young women, allowing them to practice their future roles, imposed on them in a male-dominated society, as homemakers and mothers. Significantly, the threatening male figure is upstairs—on top of and in control of the girl—as men have traditionally been in the sexual relationship. In killing the children who were in her care, the man brings on the most catastrophic failure any mother can suffer. Another contributing factor in the story is that the baby-sitter herself is too intent on watching television to realize that the children are being murdered upstairs. Thus, the tale is not just another scary story, but conveys a stern admonition to young women to adhere to society's traditional values.

20   Occasionally these firmly believed horror legends are transformed from ghastly mysteries to almost comical adventures. The following Arizona version of "The Baby-sitter and the Man Upstairs," collected in 1976, is a good example:

It was August 8, 1969. She was going to baby-sit at the Smiths who had two children, ages five and seven. She had just put the children to bed and went back to the living room to watch TV.

The phone began to ring; she went to answer it; the man on the other end said, "I'm upstairs with the children; you'd better come up."

She hung the phone up immediately, scared to death. She decided that it must be a prank phone call; again she went to watch TV. The phone rang again; she went to answer it, this time more scared than last.

The man said, "I'm upstairs with the children," and described them in detail. So she hung up the phone, not knowing what to do. Should I call the police? Instead she decided, "I'll call the operator. They can trace these phone calls." She called the operator, and the operator said that she would try and do what she could. Approximately ten minutes later the phone rang again; this time she was shaking.

She answered the phone and the man again said, "I'm upstairs with the children; you'd better come quick!" She tried to stay on the phone as long as she could so that the operator could trace the call; this time the man hung up.

She called back, and the operator said, "Run out of the house; the man is on the extension."

She didn't quite know what to do; should she go and get the children? "No," she said, "he's up there; if I go and get the children, I'll be killed too!!" She ran next door to the neighbor's house and called the police. The sirens came— there must have been at least ten police cars. They went inside the house, ran upstairs, and found not a man, but a seven-year-old child who was sitting next to the phone with a tape recorder. Later they found that a boy down the street had told this young boy to do this next time he had a baby-sitter. You see the boy didn't like his parents going out, and he didn't like having baby-sitters. So he felt this was the only way he could get rid of them. The boys [sic] don't have baby-sitters anymore; now they go to the nursery school.

"THE ROOMMATE'S DEATH"

Another especially popular example of the American adolescent shocker story is the widely known legend of "The Roommate's Death." It shares several themes with other urban legends. As in "The Killer in the Backseat" and "The Baby-sitter and the Man Upstairs," it is usually a lone woman in the story who is threatened—or thinks she is—by a strange man. As in "The Hook" and "The Boyfriend's Death," the assailant is often said to be an escaped criminal or a maniac. Finally, as in the latter legend, the actual commission of the crime is never described; only the resulting mutilated corpse is.

The scratching sounds outside the girl's place of refuge are an additional element of suspense. Here is a version told by a University of Kansas student in 1965 set in Corbin Hall, a freshman women's dormitory there:

> These two girls in Corbin had stayed late over Christmas vacation. One of them had to wait for a later train, and the other wanted to go to a fraternity party given that night of vacation. The dorm assistant was in her room—sacked out. They waited and waited for the intercom, and then they heard this knocking and knocking outside in front of the dorm. So the girl thought it was her date and she went down. But she didn't come back and she didn't come back. So real late that night this other girl heard a scratching and gasping down the hall. She couldn't lock the door, so she locked herself in the closet. In the morning she let herself out and her roommate had had her throat cut, and if the other girl had opened the door earlier, she [the dead roommate] would have been saved.

At all the campuses where the story is told the reasons for the girls' remaining alone in the dorm vary, but they are always realistic and plausible. The girls' homes may be too far away for them to visit during vacation, such as in Hawaii or a foreign country. In some cases they wanted to avoid a campus meeting or other obligation. What separates the two roommates may be either that one goes out for food, or to answer the door, or to use the rest room. The girl who is left behind may hear the scratching noise either at her room door or at the closet door, if she hides there. Sometimes her hair turns white or gray overnight from the shock of the experience (an old folk motif). The implication in the story is that some maniac is after her (as is suspected about the pursuer in "The Killer in the Backseat"); but the truth is that her own roommate needs help, and she might have supplied it had she only acted more decisively when the noises were first heard. Usually some special emphasis is put on the victim's fingernails, scratched to bloody stumps by her desperate efforts to signal for help.

A story told by a California teenager, remembered from about 1964, seems to combine motifs of "The Baby-sitter and the Man Upstairs" with "The Roommate's Death." The text is unusually detailed with names and the circumstances of the crime:

Linda accepted a baby-sitting job for a wealthy family who lived in a two-story home up in the hills for whom she had never baby-sat for before. Linda was rather hesitant as the house was rather isolated and so she asked a girlfriend, Sharon, to go along with her, promising Sharon half of the baby-sitting fee she would earn. Sharon accepted Linda's offer and the two girls went up to the big two-storey house.

The night was an especially dark and windy one and rain was threatening. All went well for the girls as they read stories aloud to the three little boys they were sitting for and they had no problem putting the boys to bed in the upstairs part of the house. When this was done, the girls settled down to watching television.

It was not long before the telephone rang. Linda answered the telephone, only to hear the heavy breathing of the caller on the other end. She attempted to elicit a response from the caller but he merely hung up. Thinking little of it and not wanting to panic Sharon, Linda went back to watching her television program, remarking that the caller had dialed a wrong number. Upon receiving the second call at which time the caller first engaged in a bit of heavy breathing and then instructed them to check on the children, the two girls became frightened and decided to call the operator for assistance. The operator instructed the girls to keep the caller on the line as long as possible should he call again so that she might be able to trace the call. The operator would check back with them.

The two girls then decided between themselves that one should stay downstairs to answer the phone. It was Sharon who volunteered to go upstairs. Shortly, the telephone rang again and Linda did as the operator had instructed her. Within a few minutes, the operator called back telling Linda to leave the house immediately with her friend because she had traced the calls to the upstairs phone.

Linda immediately hung up the telephone and proceeded to run to the stairway to call Sharon. She then heard a thumping sound coming from the stairway and when she approached the stairs she saw her friend dragging herself down the stairs by her chin, all of her limbs severed from her body. The three boys also lay dead upstairs in their beds.

Once again, the Indiana University Folklore Archive has provided the best published report on variants of "The Roommate's Death," Linda Dégh's summary of thirty-one texts and several subtypes and related plots collected since 1961. The most significant feature, according to her report, is the frequent appearance of a male rescuer at the end of the story. In one version, for example, two girls are left behind alone in the dorm by their roommate when she goes downstairs for food; they hear noises, and so stay in their room all night without opening the door. Finally the mailman comes around the next morning, and they call him from the window:

The mailman came in the front door and went up the stairs, and told the girls to stay in their room, that everything was all right but that they were to stay in their rooms [sic]. But the girls didn't listen to him cause he had said it was all right, so they came out into the hall. When they opened the door, they saw the girlfriend on the floor with a hatchet in her head.

In other Indiana texts the helpful male is a handyman, a milkman, or the brother of one of the roommates.

According to folklorist Beverly Crane, the male-female characters are only one pair of a series of significant opposites, which also includes home and away, intellectual versus emotional behavior, life and death, and several others. A male is needed to resolve the female's uncertainty—motivated by her emotional fear—about how to act in a new situation. Another male has mutilated and killed her roommate with a blow to her head, "the one part of the body with which women are not supposed to compete." The girls, Crane suggested, are doubly out of place in the beginning, having left the haven of home to engage in intellectual pursuits, and having remained alone in the campus dormitory instead of rejoining the family on a holiday. Ironically, the injured girl must use her fingernails, intended to be long, lovely, feminine adornments, in order to scratch for help. But because her roommate fails to investigate the sound, the victim dies, her once pretty nails now bloody stumps. Crane concluded this ingenious interpretation with these generalizations:

> The points of value implicit in this narrative are then twofold. If women wish to depend on traditional attitudes and responses they had best stay in a place where these attitudes and responses are best able to protect them. If, however, women do choose to venture into the realm of equality with men, they must become less dependent, more self-sufficient, more confident in their own abilities, and, above all, more willing to assume responsibility for themselves and others.

One might not expect to find women's liberation messages embedded in the spooky stories told by teenagers, but Beverly Crane's case is plausible and well argued. Furthermore, it is not at all unusual to find up-to-date social commentary in other modern folklore—witness the many religious and sexual jokes and legends circulated by people who would not openly criticize a church or the traditional social mores. Folklore does not just purvey the old codes of morality and behavior; it can also absorb newer ideas. What needs to be done to analyze this is to collect what Alan Dundes calls "oral-literary criticism," the informants' own comments about their lore. How clearly would the girls who tell these stories perceive—or even accept—the messages extrapolated by scholars? And a related question: Have any stories with clear liberationist themes replaced older ones cautioning young women to stay home, be good, and—next best—be careful, and call a man if they need help?

SUGGESTIONS FOR DISCUSSION

1. Brunvand suggests that teenagers tell horror stories not only "to produce a good scare" but also "to deliver a warning" about the "world's actual dangers." To what extent do you think the stories in " 'The Hook' " serve as cautionary tales? Do you think they would be heard and understood in different ways by male and female listeners?

2. Do you find Beverly Crane's interpretation of "The Roommate's Death" persuasive? How would you answer the question Brunvand poses at the end of this selection?

3. Work together with classmates to create your own collection of urban legends. Which of the stories in this selection or similar types of stories have you heard before? Where, when, and from whom did you hear a particular story? How were the details of the story adapted to local conditions? Did the narrator and the listeners seem to believe the story? What did the narrator and the listeners seem to feel were the most important meanings of the story? What fears, concerns, or experiences does the story seem to reflect?

SUGGESTIONS FOR WRITING

1. Jan Harold Brunvand begins this selection with the statement, "People of all ages love a good scare." Write an essay that explains why people enjoy being scared by ghost stories, horror films, and thrillers. Compare the horror story with another kind of storytelling, such as fairy tales or adventure stories. Or begin with the kinds of stories that scare you but that you read or watch anyway. What is it that draws you to them? What kinds of stories did you and your friends tell to scare each other as you were growing up? What did you like about the experience of sharing scary stories?

2. Reread " 'The Hook' and Other Teenage Horrors," and notice the interpretations of the stories you have marked. Pick one of the interpretations that you find particularly inter-

esting or striking. Write an essay in which you summarize the interpretation and explain why it seems adequate or inadequate. Are there alternative interpretations that you would offer?

3. Use the individual stories and commentaries in this selection ("The Hook," "The Killer in the Backseat," "The Baby-Sitter and the Man Upstairs," and "The Roommate's Death") as a model to recreate and comment on an urban legend you have heard. Set the scene of the storytelling—where, when, and who told it—and then give an account of the story. Follow this with a commentary of your own that interprets the dominant theme of the story.

I HEARD IT THROUGH THE GRAPEVINE

— Patricia A. Turner

Patricia A. Turner is currently vice provost of undergraduate studies and professor of folklore in the Department of African-American and African Studies at the University of California, Davis. Her work includes the book-length study of images of African Americans *Ceramic Uncles and Celluloid Mammies: Black Images and Their Influence on Culture* (1994), *Whispers on the Color Line: Rumor and Race in America* (2001) with Gary Alan Fine, and *I Heard It Through the Grapevine: Rumor in African-American Culture* (1993), from which the following selection has been excerpted. Turner's work takes its start from Brunvand's claim in his introduction to *The Vanishing Hitchhiker* that urban legends are "an integral part of white Anglo-American culture." Turner traces African American contemporary legends and rumors to the earliest slave ships and argues that the stories emerging from that experience, and from periods of racial discord since, function as a tool of resistance for the African Americans who tell them.

SUGGESTION FOR READING Like Brunvand, Turner recounts rumors and contemporary legends that are horrifying but somehow believable. Where Brunvand would emphasize the role of urban legends to keep sexually active teens aware of potential dangers surrounding their activities, Turner argues that African American rumors are linked to racial strife and arise from actual horrors that African Americans have faced since the beginnings of the slave trade. After you have read this selection, write a short response in which you compare the kinds of stories popular in African American traditions with the urban legends Brunvand collects. In what ways are they similar? In what ways are they specific to the African American experience in this country?

1   I was teaching Introduction to Black Literature at the University of Massachusetts at Boston in February 1986. Like most folklorists, I rely on folk material for examples in even my nonfolklore courses. After telling the students about the popular contemporary legend known as the Kentucky Fried Rat, Wayne, an intelligent young African-American, raised his hand to say, "Oh well, I guess that's like what they say about eating at Church's Chicken—you know the Klan owns it and they do something to the chicken so that when black men eat there they become sterile. Except that I guess it isn't really like the one about the Kentucky Fried Rat because it is true about Church's. I know because a friend of mine saw the story on '60 Minutes.' " Several other black students nodded in silent agreement; the white students looked at them in rapt disbelief, while the remaining black students seemed to be making a mental note not to eat at Church's. After class I sprinted to my office and began calling folklore colleagues. No professional folklorists

(all white) had heard any version of the Church's text, but throughout the remainder of the day I was able to collect several variations from black students and black members of the university staff.

Several months later, as I was finishing an article on the Church's cycle, I found myself discussing it with another class. An African-American student raised her hand and said, "Well, if you don't believe that one, you probably don't believe that the FBI was responsible for the deaths of all those children in Atlanta. I heard that they were taking the bodies to the Centers for Disease Control in Atlanta to perform interferon experiments on them." As I began research on *that* story, also unknown to my white colleagues, I confirmed my earlier suspicions that these contemporary texts were not mere ephemera lacking in historical antecedents. Indeed, a provocative corpus of related material can be traced back to the early sixteenth century, when white Europeans began to have regular contact with sub-Saharan Africa. I realized that this discourse was sufficiently rich to explore in book-length form.

A white colleague familiar with my work on the Church's and Atlanta Child Killer stories then pointed out that the increasingly common claim that the AIDS virus was the product of an anti-black conspiracy fit the pattern of my research. And in early 1989 I was querying a black studies class about the Church's item when one student raised her hand and said, "I don't know about the Klan owning Church's, but I do know that they are supposed to own Troop clothing." Other African-American students expressed agreement, while white students sat perplexed by this unfamiliar news. With this text the students had a real advantage over me because I had never even heard of the popular line of clothing apparently marketed quite aggressively to young black consumers.

I was convinced that these items fit into the category dubbed by folklorists as "urban" or "contemporary legend." Interestingly enough, Jan Harold Brunvand, a prolific writer on urban

legend, referred to such stories as "an integral part of *white* [emphasis added] Anglo-American culture and are told and believed by some of the most sophisticated 'folk' of modern society—young people, urbanites, and the well-educated." The fact that no in-depth investigation of the texts that circulate among African-Americans has been conducted is not surprising. Most folklorists are white, and they have not discovered the black urban legend tradition.

5   The following is a representative sampling of rumors known to many African-Americans from all over the United States during this era:

Text #1: Church's [fast food chicken franchise] is owned by the Ku Klux Klan [KKK], and they put something in it to make black men sterile.

Text #2: I remember hearing that the killings [of twenty-eight African-Americans] in Atlanta were related to genocide of the black race. The FBI [Federal Bureau of Investigation] was responsible and using the bodies for interferon research.

Text #3: I have heard that U.S. scientists created AIDS in a laboratory (possibly as a weapon to use against enemy in the event of war), and they needed to test the virus, so they go to Africa, as they [Africans] are expendable, introduce the disease, and then are unable to control its spread to Europeans and Americans.

Text #4: Troop [a popular brand of athletic wear] is owned by the Ku Klux Klan. They are using the money they make from the products to finance the lawsuit that they lost to the black woman whose son was killed by the Klan.

Text #5: Reebok is made in South Africa. All of the money they make off of those shoes goes to support whites in South Africa.

Text #6: The production and mass distribution of drugs is an attempt by the white man to keep blacks who are striving to better themselves from making it in the world. So many blacks take drugs in order to find release and escape from the problems they face in life. By taking drugs, blacks are killing themselves, and by selling them they are bringing about the imminent destruction of their race. Overall, the white man has conspired to wipe out the black population by using them [blacks] to destroy themselves.

Text #7: Tropical Fantasy [a fruit-flavored soft drink] is made by the KKK. There is a special ingredient in it that makes black men sterile.

CONTAMINATION

Let us now look at texts in which the conspiracy in question is intended specifically to contaminate blacks in a physical way, either directly or indirectly. The majority of people who spoke with me about the Church's rumor, for example, allege much more than a simple KKK plot to capitalize monetarily on a product preferred by African-Americans. The first informant who shared the item told me, "They're doing something to the chicken so that when black men eat it, they become sterile," and this comment accusing the KKK of imposing a sinister form of ethnic birth control pervades my fieldwork. The same motif dominates the Tropical Fantasy cycle. Many informants who claim that the FBI was responsible for the Atlanta child murders elaborate by reporting that the bodies were taken to the Centers for Disease Control in Atlanta for biological experiments. A college-aged African-American female said, "I remember hearing that the killings in Atlanta were related to the genocide of the black race. The FBI was responsible and using the bodies for interferon during research." (Interferon is an antiviral glycoprotein produced by human cells exposed to a virus; according to certain research reports of the late 1970s and early 1980s, the scientific community was well on its way to testing it so that it could be marketed as a genuine "miracle drug.")

In some folk items, contamination is a much more prominent motif than conspiracy. Growing public awareness of the threat implicit in the acquired immune deficiency syndrome (AIDS) epidemic caused various contemporary legends to arise connecting this fatal, sexually transmitted disease with an ethnically based contamination plot. Some informants, for instance, claimed that AIDS was developed from experiments having to do with disease, chemical, or germ warfare. These experiments were supposedly conducted in Haiti or West Africa, populations that the experimenters (usually identified as some group affiliated with "the government") perceived to be expendable. As one informant reported, "The United States government was developing germ warfare when it got out of control. AIDS was the project, and they tried it out in Africa first to see if it would work. It did." Others claim even more heinous motives, saying that the disease was developed for the express purpose of limiting the growth of third world populations. A New England–born thirty-nine-year-old African-American female offered this succinct version: "AIDS originated in Africa by the [U.S.] government in that it was a conspiracy to kill off a lot of black people."

Dangerous Chicken

Approximately half of my informants claimed that the Klan's goal in its ownership of Church's was to put something (spices, drugs) into the chicken (either into the batter or flour coating, or, by injections, directly into the chicken) that would cause sterility in black male eaters. Similar aims and tactics were true of the Tropical Fantasy conspiracy. This motif contains the specificity and narrative closure that folklorists often find in contemporary legend texts. However, the other texts I collected lacked any such closure. Most informants used the present tense and described the contamination as an ongoing, relatively unfocused conspiracy. Typical of the comments I collected was, "I heard that the Klan owns Church's chicken and has been lacing the batter with a spermicide." Several people suggested that the KKK's goal was to "make blacks infertile." Thus both men and women have something to fear. One black female informant claimed that eating the chicken "makes something go wrong with pregnant black women so that their children come out retarded."

Typically, food contamination rumors and contemporary legends are associated either with instances of accidental, incidental contamination (the Kentucky Fried Rat, the mouse in the Coke bottle) or with premeditated food substitution, ostensibly for the purpose of increasing the company's profit ("wormburgers," the use of dog food on fast food pizzas). In the latter case, the company is not trying to hurt its customers, but rather to decrease costs through the use of socially distasteful but essentially safe ingredients. In the Church's rumor, by contrast, greed is not stated as a strong motive for the Klan. Although a few informants contributed versions that lacked any contamination motif, maintaining merely that the KKK owned the company, not a single informant speculated on how much money the Klan could make by selling fast food fried chicken to African-Americans. The white supremacist organization's goal, simply put, was to implement domestic genocide.

10   To those outside the rumor's public, the mechanism of contamination makes the accusation seem highly implausible. I encountered very few white informants who were familiar with the rumor. Upon hearing a summary, most responded by asking, "How is this mysterious substance supposed to distinguish between white male eaters and black male eaters?" When this question is posed to blacks, a common explanation is that most Church's franchises are located in black neighborhoods. Similarly, those who believe the Tropical Fantasy rumors note that the beverage is sold in inner-city ma-and-pa grocery stores, not at downtown soda counters. Hence, the KKK runs very little risk of sterilizing white male consumers. Other informants suggest that a substance has been discovered that impedes the production of sperm in black males but is harmless when consumed by whites.

When the Church's rumor surfaced in San Diego in 1984, Congressman Jim Bates arranged to have the Food and Drug Administration test the chicken using gas chromatography and mass spectrometry. After finding no evidence of foreign materials, an assistant of Bates together with two West Coast Church's officials held a press conference to share their findings with the public. Tropical Fantasy was tested in 1991. A female informant told me that the Klan had probably "fixed things up with the FDA" so that the test on Church's would come out negative. Although I performed no scientific investigation of the chicken myself, I queried University of Massachusetts biologists and chemists about the possibility of such tampering. They maintained that there is no known tasteless, odorless substance that could be disguised in the chicken that would result in sterilization with no discernible side effects. I asked a black male student who overheard one of these conversations if he still believed the rumor. He said he did not. I asked him if he would patronize the nearby Church's. He said he would not.

To better understand the appeal of the contamination motif in the Church's and Tropical Fantasy rumors, it is useful to look at a very similar rumor. In speculating on just how the alleged sterilization agent in the chicken could function, none of my informants made any specific reference to the "ethnic weapon." This is the label that the U.S. intelligence community applied to rumors alleging that government scientists had developed a substance that could kill blacks but leave whites unharmed. These rumors, which appeared in leftist publications in the mid-1980s, caused great concern for the United States Information Agency (USIA). However, officials charged with exploring the reports drew no connections between them and other items of folk belief concerning people of color; rather, they claimed that the Soviet Union had designed and disseminated the rumors. In a publication familiarizing members of Congress with the scope of communist propaganda activity, the agency introduced the segment on the ethnic weapon thus:

Since at least 1980, the Soviet press has been circulating claims that the United States is conducting research on or has developed a so-called "ethnic weapon," which would kill only non-whites. The Soviet media typically also charges that the South Africans—or less frequently the Israelis—are supposedly collaborating with the United States in this research. The Soviet goal in this campaign seems clear: to make it appear as if the United States and its alleged collaborators are pursuing racist, genocidal policies.

 The Soviet charge is absurd on the face of it. Even if the U.S. government wanted to produce such a weapon, it would make no sense to do so, given the multi-ethnic composition of the American population and the armed forces. The only plausible group that would want to produce such a weapon would be unregenerate white supremacists—a portrait of the U.S. government that Soviet disinformation specialists apparently want their audiences to believe.

These comments are followed by various statements by scientific authorities explaining why such a substance could not be developed, as well as forty-five references in left-wing and communist publications to the U.S. government's role in the development of such a weapon.

Because none of my over two hundred Church's and Tropical Fantasy informants mentioned the "ethnic weapon" by name, I can only conclude that this rumor was not embraced by the African-American population. Whether communist-inspired journalists actually planted the rumor or simply reported one that was gaining popularity is less relevant, in my view, than the fact that the item did not capture the African-American imagination. Why did a rumor alleging the KKK's malevolent involvement in a fast food company find more acceptance than one claiming the government was manufacturing a weapon for racial genocide?

In the various left-wing print references cited in the USIA pamphlet, the so-called ethnic weapon is either a perfected substance or one still under development. Except in one item linking it to the AIDS virus, there are no hints that the weapon has been deployed. Nor are there any real indications of how, when, or why it

would be used. The threat is in its mere existence—in the possibility that the U.S. government might want to have such a weapon, in the fact that it could not be used in a clandestine manner, and in the fact that the potential victims have no control over its implementation. In the Church's and Tropical Fantasy texts, by contrast, a form of random deployment is at work. Any African-American who chances to eat at Church's or sip a Tropical Fantasy soft drink is a potential victim. Yet in these cases, people can avoid victimization by refusing to purchase the product. The Church's and Tropical Fantasy rumors, in short, give people some control over their fate, whereas the ethnic weapon texts do not.

15   The other primary difference between the Church's rumor—as well as the other contamination rumors—and the ethnic weapon item resides in the mode of contamination. With the ethnic weapon, there is no clue as to how the victims will be infected with the deadly substance or what modus operandi will govern the weapon's use. In the other items, however, the contamination is more specifically rendered: poisoned food or soft drinks, postmortem intrusions, and sexual intercourse are concrete threats. In short, rumors that contain specific physical consequences are more likely to seize the interest of a public than ambiguous, unspecific ones.

With motifs pinpointing a particular company, a known antiblack conspiratorial group, a familiar prepared food, and a detrimental outcome, the Church's rumor contains all of the nuances the ethnic weapon rumor lacks. Because a person can do something about the threat contained in the Church's item simply by not patronizing the restaurant, it is ultimately a much less ominous rumor. No informants who professed belief in the Church's story believed themselves to have been sterilized permanently because they consumed the chicken before they heard the item. No one said anything like, "It's too late for me now." Instead they merely observed, "So I haven't eaten any since."

Like other folk groups, African-Americans assign food and its preparation symbolic importance; food choice is part of the ordering process by which humans endow the environment with meaning and feeling. At first glance, a fast food chain that provides decent, familiar foods at a friendly price is offering a fair service and product. But by removing the preparation of an ethnic food from the home kitchens most strongly identified with it, the Church's corporation unwittingly intruded on sacred territory.

Ethnic foods, as a rule, are prepared and consumed by the very people who have created the dishes or by descendants who have had the recipes handed down to them. On special occasions or in special settings, these foods are shared with outsiders eager to participate in "equal opportunity eating." Church's created a new, public context for the sharing of what had thus far been considered communal foods—and foods, moreover, that carried with them strong symbolic associations. Nor are these associations necessarily positive. American popular culture has long perpetuated a stereotype in which blacks are portrayed as inordinately fond of foods that can be eaten without utensils, such as fried chicken and watermelon. Given this background, it is not surprising that blacks wish to approach these foods, particularly when offered outside the home, cautiously. The anthropologist Mary Douglas has pointed out that people with a minority status in their society are often suspicious of cooked foods as well as protective of the body's orifices: "If we treat ritual protection of bodily orifices as a symbol of social preoccupations about exits and entrances," she writes, "the purity of cooked food becomes important. I suggest that food is not likely to be polluting at all unless the external boundaries of the social system are under pressure."

The popularity of the Church's rumor indicates that the black community perceives itself as vulnerable to the hostile desires of the majority population, which, it seems, will stop at nothing to inhibit the growth of the minority population—including the use of polluted food to weaken individual sexual capacity. In this case, indeed, the threat to fertility comes from a source that employs the name of the very religious structure presumed by the black community to offer the most safety: the church.

20 The key to understanding the item's popularity, however, resides in the power it bestowed upon its public to seize control over a perceived threat to all African-American people. In the spring of 1990, an African-American female Californian discussed it as if it were ancient history. She recalled first hearing it "a long time ago," and concluded her commentary by stating, with obvious satisfaction, "A lot of these Church's have closed up now." Like many other informants who used similar closing motifs, she believed that a battle had been "won."

SUGGESTIONS FOR DISCUSSION

1. With a group of your classmates, compare the responses you each wrote to this selection. As a group, discuss how the rumors Turner recounts compare with the urban legends Brunvand collects. In what ways are they similar? How do they differ?

2. Examine the list of "Texts" Turner provides. Which of these stories have you heard before? Are there versions of the stories circulating today outside the African American community? Why might these remain within African American rumor circles? How might they change for a different audience?

3. Why does one of Turner's informants believe that the "battle" against Church's Chicken "has been won"? What is the battle? How was it won?

SUGGESTIONS FOR WRITING

1. In her introduction to *I Heard It Through the Grapevine*, Turner argues that African American contemporary legends and rumors go beyond teenage scare stories to function as

"tools of resistance" in the African American community. Once a conspiracy story is circulated widely, the conspiracy can no longer be carried out because too many people know about it. Write an essay in which you examine how stories of contamination or KKK conspiracy function as tools of resistance. In your discussion, consider how the power shifts to the teller of the story as it is circulated through a community.

2. Turner makes it clear that African American rumors, like all urban legends, begin with a seed of truth. In Brunvand's stories, you can see how adult worries over teenage sexuality, for example, can feed into the perpetuation of stories such as "The Hook" or all of those baby-sitter stories. Turner's stories, however, connect with fears of genocide and racism. Write an essay in which you compare the kinds of stories Brunvand tells with the stories Turner tells. Is one more believable than another? More serious? More likely to be taken as fact by only some groups and not others? Why? What makes a rumor or legend believable to some and not to others?

3. Retell a contamination story—either a food story or a disease story (like AIDS or the ebola virus, for example). If you don't know one, ask friends, family members, or adults in your life. Write the story with as much detail as you can, including any variations you have heard or are able to find. Note where you heard the story, who told it, and how much of the story you find believable. After reviewing both Brunvand and Turner, explain the function the story seems to have either to warn hearers or to blame someone or a part of the population for the contamination. How would you explain the popularity of the story?

THE AMAZING ADVENTURES OF KAVALIER AND CLAY

▬— *Michael Chabon*

Michael Chabon's *Amazing Adventures of Kavalier and Clay*, from which this selection is taken, won the 2001 Pulitzer Prize for fiction. In it, Chabon tells the tale of two young men breaking into the comic book business just as superheroes such as Superman, Batman, Aquaman, and others are coming on the scene. Chabon's novel opens in 1939 with the story of Josef Kavelier's escape from Nazi-occupied Prague. He makes it to New York, where he meets his cousin Sammy Klayman, a would-be comic book writer working for a novelty company that sells items such as fart cushions and fake vomit. Together, Sammy and Joe create the Escapist, a superhero to rival Superman. Since writing *Kavalier and Clay*, Chabon has written a series of comics based on Sammy and Joe's super-hero, the Escapist.

SUGGESTION FOR READING The chapter excerpted here begins immediately after Sammy has convinced his boss to let him and Joe create their own comic book superhero. As you read, highlight/underline and annotate those places in the story where Sammy and Joe name the qualities their superhero must have as well as the qualities they reject as overdone, improbable, or just too silly. Keep in mind the superhero stories you already know—Superman, Batman, Spiderman, Wonder Woman, and others who remain popular in comic books, cartoons, and movies.

1 The first official meeting of their partnership was convened outside the Kramler Building, in a nimbus compounded of the boys' exhalations and of subterranean steam purling up from a grate in the pavement.

"This is good," Joe said.

"I know."

"He said *yes*," Joe reminded his cousin, who stood patting idly with one hand at the front of his overcoat and a panicked expression on his face, as though worried that he had left something important behind in Anapol's office.

"Yes, he did. He said yes."

"Sammy." Joe reached out and grabbed Sammy's wandering hand, arresting it in its search of his pockets and collar and tie. "This is *good*."

"Yes, this is good, god damn it. I just hope to God we can *do* it."

Joe let go of Sammy's hand, shocked by this expression of sudden doubt. He had been completely taken in by Sammy's bold application of the Science of Opportunity. The whole morning, the rattling ride through the flickering darkness under the East River, the updraft of Klaxons and rising office blocks that had carried them out of the subway station, the ten thousand men and women who immediately surrounded them, the ringing telephones and gum-snapping chitchat of the clerks and secretaries in Sheldon Anapol's office, the sly and harried bulk of Anapol himself, the talk of sales figures and competition and cashing in big, all this had conformed so closely to Joe's movie-derived notions of life in America that if an airplane were now to land on Twenty-fifth Street and disgorge a dozen bathing-suit-clad Fairies of Democracy come to award him the presidency of General Motors, a contract with Warner Bros., and a penthouse on Fifth Avenue with a swimming pool in the living room, he would have greeted this, too, with the same dreamlike unsurprise. It had not occurred to him until now to consider that his cousin's display of bold entrepreneurial confidence might have been entirely bluff, that it was 8°C and he had neither hat nor gloves, that his stomach was as empty as his billfold, and that he and Sammy were nothing more than a couple of callow young men in thrall to a rash and dubious promise.

"But I have belief in you," Joe said. "I trust you."

"That's good to hear."

"I mean it."

"I wish I knew why."

"Because," said Joe. "I don't have any choice."

"Oh ho."

"I need money," Joe said, and then tried adding, "god *damn* it."

"Money." The word seemed to have a restorative effect on Sammy, snapping him out of his daze. "Right. Okay. First of all, we need horses."

"Horses?"

"Arms. Guys."

"Artists."

"How about we just call them 'guys' for right now?"

"Do you know where we can find some?"

Sammy thought for a moment. "I believe I do," he said. "Come on."

They set off in a direction that Joe decided was probably west. As they walked Sammy seemed to get lost quickly in his own reflections. Joe tried to imagine the train of his cousin's thoughts, but the particulars of the task at hand were not clear to him, and after a while he gave up and just kept pace. Sammy's gait was deliberate and crooked, and Joe found it a challenge to keep from getting ahead. There was a humming sound everywhere that he attributed first to the circulation of his own blood in his ears before he realized that it was the sound produced by Twenty-fifth Street itself, by a hundred sewing machines in a sweat-shop overhead, exhaust grilles at the back of a warehouse, the trains rolling deep beneath the black surface of the street. Joe gave up trying to think like, trust, or believe in his cousin and just walked, head abuzz, toward the Hudson River, stunned by the novelty of exile.

"Who is he?" Sammy said at last, as they were crossing a broad street which a sign identified, improbably somehow, as Sixth Avenue. Sixth Avenue! The Hudson River!

"Who is he," Joe said.

"Who is he, and what does he do?"

"He flies."

Sammy shook his head. "Superman flies."

"So ours does not?"

30   "I just think I'd . . . "

"To be original."

"If we can. Try to do it without flying, at least. No flying, no strength of a hundred men, no bulletproof skin."

"Okay," Joe said. The humming seemed to recede a little. "And some others, they do what?"

"Well, Batman—"

35   "He flies, like a bat."

"No, he doesn't fly."

"But he is blind."

"No, he only dresses like a bat. He has no batlike qualities at all. He uses his fists."

"That sounds dull."

40   "Actually, it's spooky. You'd like it."

"Maybe another animal."

"Uh, well, yeah. Okay. A hawk. Hawkman."

"Hawk, yes, okay. But that one must fly."

"Yeah, you're right. Scratch the bird family. The, uh, the Fox. The Shark."

45   "A swimming one."

"Maybe a swimming one. Actually, no, I know a guy works in the Chesler shop, he said they're already doing a guy who swims. For Timely."

"A lion?"

"Lion. The Lion. Lionman."

"He could be strong. He roars very loud."

50   "He has a super roar."

"It strikes fear."

"It breaks dishes."

"The bad guys go deaf."

They laughed. Joe stopped laughing.

55   "I think we have to be serious," he said.

"You're right," said Sammy. "The Lion, I don't know. Lions are lazy. How about the Tiger. Tigerman. No, no. Tigers are killers. Shit. Let's see."

They began to go through the rolls of the animal kingdom, concentrating naturally on the predators: Catman, Wolfman, the Owl, the Panther, the Black Bear. They considered the primates: the Monkey, Gorillaman, the Gibbon, the Ape, the Mandrill with his multicolored

wonder ass that he used to bedazzle opponents.

"Be serious," Joe chided again.

"I'm sorry, I'm sorry. Look, forget animals. Everybody's going to be thinking of animals. In two months, I'm telling you, by the time our guy hits the stands, there's going to be guys running around dressed like every damn animal in the zoo. Birds. Bugs. Underwater guys. And I'll bet you anything there's going to be five guys who are really strong, and invulnerable, and can fly."

60   "If he goes as fast as the light," Joe suggested.

"Yeah, I guess it's good to be fast."

"Or if he can make a thing burn up. If he can—listen! If he can, you know. Shoot the fire, with his eyes!"

"His eyeballs would melt."

"Then with his hands. Or, yes, he turns into a fire!"

65   "Timely's doing that already, too. They got the fire guy and the water guy."

"He turns into *ice*. He makes the ice everywhere."

"Crushed or cubes?"

"Not good?"

Sammy shook his head. "Ice," he said. "I don't see a lot of stories in ice."

70   "He turns into electricity?" Joe tried. "He turns into acid?"

"He turns into gravy. He turns into an enormous hat. Look, stop. Stop. Just stop."

They stopped in the middle of the sidewalk, between Sixth and Seventh avenues, and that was when Sam Clay experienced a moment of global vision, one which he would afterward come to view as the one undeniable brush against the diaphanous, dollar-colored hem of the Angel of New York to be vouchsafed to him in his lifetime.

"This is not the question," he said. "If he's like a cat or a spider or a fucking wolverine, if he's huge, if he's tiny, if he can shoot flames or ice or death rays or Vat 69, if he turns into fire or water or stone or India rubber. He could be a Martian, he could be a ghost, he could be a god or a demon or a wizard or monster. Okay? It doesn't *matter*, because right now, see, at this very moment, we have a bandwagon rolling, I'm telling you. Every little skinny guy like me in New York who believes there's life on Alpha Centauri and got the shit kicked out of him in school and can smell a dollar is out there right this minute trying to jump onto it, walking around with a pencil in his shirt pocket, saying, 'He's like a falcon, no, he's like a tornado, no, he's like a goddamned wiener dog.' Okay?"

"Okay."

75   "And no matter what we come up with, and how we dress him, some other character with the same shtick, with the same style of boots and the same little doodad on his chest, is already out there, or is coming out tomorrow, or is going to be knocked off from our guy inside a week and a half."

Joe listened patiently, awaiting the point of this peroration, but Sammy seemed to have lost the thread. Joe followed his cousin's gaze along the sidewalk but saw only a pair of what looked to be British sailors lighting their cigarettes off a single shielded match.

"So . . . " Sammy said. "So . . . "

"So that is not the question," Joe prompted.

"That's what I'm saying."

80   "Continue."

They kept walking.

"How? is not the question. What? is not the question," Sammy said.

"The question is why."

"The question is *why*.

85   "Why," Joe repeated.

"Why is he doing it?"

"Doing what?"

"Dressing up like a monkey or an ice cube or a can of fucking corn."

"To fight the crime, isn't it?"

90   "Well, yes, to fight crime. To fight evil. But that's all any of these guys are doing. That's as far as they ever go. They just . . . you know, it's the right thing to do, so they do it. How interesting is that?"

"I see."

"Only Batman, you know . . . see, yeah, that's good. That's what makes Batman good, and not dull at all, even though he's just a guy who dresses up like a bat and beats people up."

"What is the reason for Batman? The why?"

"His parents were killed, see? In cold blood. Right in front of his eyes, when he was a kid. By a robber."

95   "It's revenge."

"That's *interesting*," Sammy said. "See?"

"And he was driven mad."

"Well . . . "

"And that's why he puts on the bat's clothes."

100   "Actually, they don't go so far as to say that," Sammy said. "But I guess it's there between the lines."

"So, we need to figure out what is the why."

" 'What is the why,' " Sammy agreed.

"Flattop."

Joe looked up and saw a young man standing in front of them. He was short-waisted and plump, and his face, except for a pair of big black spectacles, was swaddled and all but invisible in an elaborate confection of scarf and hat and earflaps.

105   "Julius," Sammy said. "This is Joe. Joe, this is a friend from the neighborhood, Julie Glovsky."

Joe held out his hand. Julie studied it a moment, then extended his own small hand. He had on a black woolen greatcoat, a fur-lined leather cap with mammoth earflaps, and too-short green corduroy trousers.

"This guy's brother is the one I told you about," Sammy told Joe. "Making good money in comics. What are you doing here?"

Somewhere deep within his wrappings, Julie Glovsky shrugged. "I need to see my brother."

"Isn't that remarkable, we need to see him, too."

110   "Yeah? Why's that?" Julie Glovsky shuddered. "Only tell me fast before my nuts fall off."

"Would that be from cold or, you know, atrophy?"

"Funny."

"I am funny."

"Unfortunately not in the sense of 'humorous.'"

115   "Funny," Sammy said.

"I am funny. What's your idea?"

"Why don't you come to work for me?"

"For you? Doing what? Selling shoestrings? We still got a box of them at my house. My mom uses them to sew up chickens."

"Not shoelaces. My boss, you know, Sheldon Anapol?"

120   "How would I know him?"

"Nevertheless, he is my boss. He's going into business with his brother-in-law, Jack Ashkenazy, who you also do not know, but who publishes *Racy Science, Racy Combat*, et cetera. They're going to do comic books, see, and they're looking for talent."

"What?" Julie poked his tortoise face out from the shadows of its woolen shell. "Do you think they might hire *me*?"

"They will if I tell them to," said Sammy. "Seeing as how I'm the art director in chief."

Joe looked at Sammy and raised an eyebrow. Sammy shrugged.

125   "Joe and I, here, we're putting together the first title right now. It's going to be all adventure heroes. All in costumes," he said, extemporizing now. "You know, like Superman. Batman. The Blue Beetle. That type of thing."

"Tights, like."

"That's it. Tights. Masks. Big muscles. It's going to be called *Masked Man Comics*," he continued. "Joe and I've got the lead feature all taken care of, but we need backup stuff. Think you could come up with something?"

"Shit, Flattop, yes. You bet."

"What about your brother?"

130   "Sure, he's always looking for more work. They got him doing *Romeo Rabbit* for thirty dollars a week."

"Okay, then, he's hired, too. You're both hired, on one condition."

"What's that?"

"We need a place to work," said Sammy.

"Come on then," said Julie. "I guess we can work at the Rathole." He leaned toward Sammy as they started off, lowering his voice. The tall skinny kid with the big nose had fallen a few steps behind them to light a cigarette. "Who the hell *is* that guy?"

135   "This?" Sammy said. He took hold of the kid's elbow and tugged him forward as though bringing him out onstage to take a deserved bow. He reached up to grab a handful of the kid's hair and gave it a tug, just kind of rocking his head from side to side while holding on to his hair, grinning at him. Had Joe been a young woman, Julie Glovsky might almost have been inclined to think that Sammy was sweet on her. "This is my *partner*."

SUGGESTIONS FOR DISCUSSION

1. Make a list of the superheroes you know about. What are their special powers? What are their attributes? How do they dress? What is their motivation (the "why")?

2. What problems do Sammy and Joe encounter as they try to create their own original superhero?

3. Film critic A. O. Scott has written that the hero in much fantasy fiction is the outsider—the orphan, the marginalized. In what ways do the superheroes you know of fall into that category?

SUGGESTIONS FOR WRITING

1. As they walk and talk, Sammy tells Joe, "How? is not the question? What? is not the question. The question is *why*." To make a superhero that people will care about, Sammy and Joe have to find his motivation. From the list of superheroes you have generated, choose one and write about that character's motivation. Find out your hero's "origin story," the story of the character's beginnings and how super powers came to be. Why does the

character do whatever it is that he or she does? Does this character's motivation match the motivation of other superheroes you know about? How might readers or viewers respond to that motivation?

2. Write an essay in which you explain why today—this moment in history—is either a good time or a bad time for books and movies about superheroes. What is it about the superhero story that would or would not connect with current events, the mood of the time, and today's audience?

3. In a review article about fantasy stories and popular film, A. O. Scott writes that the central characters in fantasies are archetypal, "following a convention so deep it seems to be encoded in the human storytelling gene, orphans summoned out of obscurity to undertake a journey into the heart of evil that will also be a voyage of self-discovery." Once Sammy and Joe do finally settle on their superhero, they also create an orphan hero—one who is able to fight Hitler and the Nazis. Create a superhero for today. What would he or she look like? What would be the "why?"

WIRED CULTURE   Video Games and Storytelling

To learn more about video games
and stories, visit
www.ablongman.com/george/126

Although the earliest video games remained frozen in the world of Pac Man and other computer dexterity games, they were always at least loosely tied to the world of storytelling. After all, if you have to rescue the victim, shoot the enemy, or find your way into the castle, you are a part of a story. With role-playing games and games like the *Sims*, which ask players to create the entire world of the game, storytelling becomes an even more vital component. The selection below, by Tom Loftus, reviews the next step in video game storytelling: bringing emotions into games so that the story has more depth and comes closer, Loftus argues, to the storytelling we are used to in films and television drama.

BRINGING EMOTIONS TO VIDEO GAMES

— Tom Loftus

Tom Loftus is a science and technology columnist for MSNBC.com. The article reprinted here appeared on MSBNC.com on February 17, 2004. In it, Loftus writes about the potential of the newest video games to go beyond mere storytelling and actually create characters and situations that are close to film experiences.

SUGGESTION
FOR READING Before you read, write a brief account of your own experience with video games and their storytelling possibilities. If you don't play video games or aren't familiar with many games, write about your current knowledge of or attitude toward video games.

1 Imagine this video game scenario: Assigned to rescue the embattled squad you've fought with for the past 10 hours, you fail miserably. You have nothing to show save for a torn piece of clothing, bloody at the edges. As the soundtrack reaches its crescendo and the words "Game Over" materialize over the mists of Planet X, it's not frustration you feel, but

regret, sadness, even, for those brave soldiers you left behind.

Sound familiar? Probably not. When it comes to emotions, most games touch our simpler instincts: Keypad-throwing anger at missing a jump in "Ratchet and Clank" or an "I-Feel-Good-Uh" triumph of scoring a touchdown in "Madden 2004."

A game that can evoke complex emotions–longing, despair, empathy–is the holy grail for some in the industry. Not only would it open gaming to a true mass audience, but it would confirm their vision of interactive entertainment as the greatest story-telling medium since the invention of film.

FINDING THAT MAGICAL BALANCE

Before film became art—no "Gigli" jokes, please—it was spectacle. It took decades for filmmakers to mine their medium for a library of techniques capable of evoking emotion and telling a good story; techniques like camera angles, editing and acting to the camera.

5   "When you think about where our medium is and if you could apply it to film, then games are still in the pre-'Citizen Kane' era," said Neil Young, vice president at game publishing power house Electronic Arts.

"We are just beginning to understand the pace," said Young. "When we started, the pace was 'Space Invaders.' Then came CD-ROMs and everything was start and stop. We're only now getting comfortable."

Although, to push the film theme a little further, the industry has experienced several "Birth of a Nation" moments with titles like the Japanese sci-fi series "Final Fantasy," "The Sims" and a little known, but influential, game for Playstation 2 called "Ico."

While "Final Fantasy" relied on linear storytelling akin to that in films to evoke emotion, "The Sims" was an anomaly. It had no "story." In fact, the digital dollhouse where players led their sims through a number of real-world scenarios was barely a game. But the act of controlling the life of a sim allowed players to insert their own emotional story. Its interactivity made it emotional.

"Ico" was something different: a traditional jump and puzzle game where the player controls a boy condemned to death by his village for being born with tiny horns. The game play itself was repetitive, but it managed to weave an emotional subplot with a skill rarely seen in the genre. When you discover that the boy's mortal enemies are actually the ghosts of other little horned boys killed by villagers the surprise carries an emotional punch. The hero is fighting his own kind.

GIVE 'EM SOMEONE TO ROOT FOR

10   Games like "Ico" where interactivity and emotion are deftly melded gives hope to Warren Spector, the legendary game designer whose credits include "Ultima Underworld," "Wing Commander" and "Deus Ex."

"We almost never get at joy, sorrow, ambivalence, caring. I hate that," Spector said. "If I can get away with not putting a virtual gun—commercially speaking—in a game I would do it in a heartbeat."

While "Deus Ex" is loaded with more weaponry than an NRA picnic, it also forces players to make decisions that then have serious repercussions on game play. Deciding what groups to fight on the verge of the apocalypse can be emotionally gripping.

That kind of experience is the future of emotion-laden games, according to game consultant David Freeman. "It will be no more an option than it is now of becoming emotionally involved than with a film like 'The Lord of the Rings.' "

An evangelist of sorts for making games emotionally resonant, Freeman thinks he has the answer. It's called "Emotioneering," several hundred writing techniques that he has devised and taken on the road to clients like Atari, Vivendi and Ubisoft.

15   "Most game designers started as programmers, testers and sometimes visual artists," said

Freeman. "So none of these people have a background in sophisticated story telling."

Freeman, who also lectures about screenwriting, incorporates standard film advice (avoid cliches, use symbols, create complex characters) with tips specific to the interactive experience: How to inspire players to root for non-player characters and how and when to let the game be "saved" without interrupting its flow.

"It's not just a matter of having a compelling story, it's a matter of having characters that you can identify with," he said. "It's a matter of having the player go on the emotional journey."

LIFE: THE GAME

But writing, no matter how emotionally evocative, only goes so far, according to Michael Mateas, a professor of artificial intelligence and entertainment at the Georgia Institute of Technology. When games introduce an emotionally poignant moment, technology should be ready to back it up.

For example, Mateas said, take the "Grand Theft Auto" episode where the player is asked by a crime boss to kill his wife. What would happen if the player decided not to carry out the mission and maybe befriend the wife? "Though the game suggests this possibility," he said, "there's no way for you to act on it. No way to have complex interactions with characters."

20   A game that attempts to evoke complex emotions must eventually utilize "some serious advances in game AI," he said.

For the last four years Mateas and Andrew Stern, a veteran of the early artificial intelligence hit "Petz," have been working on "Facade," an "interactive drama" that uses natural speech recognition and a level of artificial intelligence never seen in gaming. The player interacts, via natural speech, with an arguing couple.

To deliver realism, Mateas and Stern had to literally break the story down into what they call "beats" or specific behaviors built for a particular situation. "Facade" serves up these beats based on moment-by-moment interactions as well as what happened before so that the unfolding actions and dialogue form a dramatic story arc. The end result is an experience that's much more open-ended than that found in games hardwired with the typical design tree approach. "We've blown up the tree," said Stern.

"Facade" could represent a new step in gaming. Its artificial intelligence could be adapted by other genres, bringing a new realism to games. And as the technology improves, what's to stop what Stern calls "new genres of interactive experiences, such as interactive love stories, family dramas and virtual friends."

MAKING GAMES CRY

Or perhaps the emotional games of the future will involve players' emotions affecting the game and not the other way around.

25   Jon Sykes, a lecturer in Computer Game Design and Human-Computer Interaction at Glasgow Caledonian University, has been studying how digital recreations of real-life spots reputed to be haunted can have an emotional effect on people. What if, Sykes asked, the emotions some of his test subjects felt could be channeled back into the simulation? A haunted house game, for example, could trigger the appearance of ghosts based not on what the player does, but how he or she feels.

Some of his colleagues have rigged up a crude experiment: A fighting game called "Zen Warrior" where the finishing move must be executed in what Sykes calls a "Zen-like state of inner calm." The "inner calm" is measured simply by the pressure applied to a keypad button, but the implications are endless.

"We may look back at this time of video gaming and see it as very primitive," said Sykes. "You don't know about the benefits until you have it."

THE FUTURE

So what will these new games look like? A first-person shooter with "Mystic River"-like performances? Interactive dramas where it's possible to form deep friendships with virtual characters? Will consoles of the future come shrink-wrapped with emotional biofeedback devices?

It's still hard to say. But Spector, at least, is ready to make an ultimatum.

30 "Finding ways to broaden range of emotions you can experience and express in games is the future of games as far as I'm concerned," Spector said. "If it turns out I'm wrong, I'm going to open a bookstore."

SUGGESTIONS FOR DISCUSSION

1. With a group of your classmates, describe your favorite video games. Which games definitely have a storyline? How active are the players in creating that storyline? Is it necessary to have a story in a game for it to be a good game to play?

2. Loftus describes the newest video games as being like the earliest films. What does he mean by that? What games do you know that seem to have filmlike qualities?

3. What advantage or disadvantage do you see in a game that can recreate or create emotion?

SUGGESTIONS FOR WRITING

1. With a group of three or four classmates, review a video game in terms of its appeal as a storytelling game and as a game that evokes or avoids emotion. In your review, make sure you compare the game to others created around the same time and aimed at some of the same audience. What makes the game popular (or not)? What makes it innovative (or not)? Present your review, with sample clips from the game, to the class.

2. Many popular films and television programs have generated video games. *Matrix*, *Lord of the Rings*, *Star Wars*, *CSI*, even *ER* all have generated companion video games. Choose one of these and familiarize yourself with both the original and the video game. Write an essay on the game in which you examine how much the game has benefited from what Loftus in his article calls "emotioneering." In other words, how much of the game picks up not just the action but the inter-relationships and emotions of the characters from the story?

3. Although it is common today to create a video game from a film or television story, it is less common (though becoming more frequent) to do the opposite—create a film from a video game. *Lara Croft: Tomb Raider* is one of the first video games to become a movie. Watch the film and familiarize yourself with the game (both can be rented at film rental firms). Write an essay in which you examine what the film storyline and characters retain from the original game. What changes? What can you identify in a game like *Tomb Raider* that seems to lend itself easily to popular film? (If you cannot locate *Tomb Raider*, look for other video games that have become films.)

PERSPECTIVES Film Reviews: The Case of *Spider-Man 2*

One of the most frequently read genres of writing today is the film review. Moviegoers consult reviews online, in magazines, on television, and in regular reviewers' columns in both national and local newspapers. When a story as popular as *Spider-Man* is filmed, reviewers are compelled to write about how well or badly the filmmaker did the job. Though some thought he was an unlikely hero, Spider-Man has been one of Marvel's most popular superheroes since his 1962 debut. It makes sense, then, that director Sam Raimi's two recent film adaptations of the story and its character have demanded the attention of critics from all ranks. In a simple Internet search for reviews of *Spider-Man 2* (2004), you will find more than 200 reviews.

The reviews we have reprinted here represent some of the most common themes that reviewers touched on when they saw *Spider-Man 2*. As you will notice, these film reviewers are especially interested in how well Sam Raimi adapted Marvel's comic-book superhero and how close actor Tobey Maguire came to portraying the "real" Spider-Man. Most reviewers of this film also paid attention to how well the movie did as a sequel to the first film.

Before you read, watch both *Spider-Man* and *Spider-Man 2*. They are widely available on DVD and video. Also, read about Spider-Man's origin story. You will find that information using a simple Internet search, or you can go directly to Marvel's Web site. Spider-Man's story is also available as part of the special feature materials on the *Spider-Man* DVD.

SPIDER-MAN 2

— *Todd Gilchrist*

Todd Gilchrist is a regular film reviewer for FilmStew.com. In their link to Gilchrist's review, the Internet film site Rottentomatoes.com wrote on June 30, 2004: "Even though the Rotten Tomatoes approval rating for Sam Raimi's sequel is hovering around 95%, critic Todd Gilchrist feels compelled to take a slightly contrarian view."

SUGGESTION FOR READING   As you read, note in the margins how Gilchrist contrasts *Spider-Man 2* with *Spider-Man*. What does he dislike about the sequel?

1   Sometimes, film criticism boils down to the merits of a single, solitary on screen moment, be it as a lynchpin of compelling storytelling, an embodiment of a movie's overall message or its ability to evoke sentiment from the audience. Then again, there are other times when one must pore over the entire fabric of a film, theoretical magnifying glass in hand, to scrutinize each sequence, portrayal and plot point with an empiricist's attention to detail.

Ironically, it's this second approach that I felt I had to take with Sam Raimi's *Spider-Man 2*, an engaging if uneven film that treads heavily in its predecessor's footsteps and doesn't quite seem to keep the same kind of single-minded path as its predecessor. Rather, Raimi pulls out all the stops in the face of his best opportunity yet to explore the kinetic visual worlds of *Evil Dead* and the fertile emotional territory of *A Simple Plan*, and ultimately loses his once firm grasp on Stan Lee's indelible material.

Since the first *Spider-Man*, which it must be noted I declared the best comic book adaptation of all time, it seems that both a whole lot and nothing at all has happened at the same time. Peter Parker (Tobey Maguire), once sharing a house with his Aunt May (Rosemary Harris), and then later, an apartment with best pal Harry Osborn (James Franco), now lives alone in a rundown New York tenement, scurrying from one low-paying job to another. Though he tries to balance the disparate responsibilities in his life, most notably the seemingly endless necessity for web-slinging, Peter only finds his life swinging further and further out of control.

His lifelong love, Mary Jane Watson (Kirsten Dunst), tires of his unreliability and moves on to a better life in Manhattan, where she lands a job as a cosmetics model as well as a suitor who is no less than the son of his adversarial boss J. Jonah Jameson (J. K. Simmons). Harry still blames Spider-Man for his father's death and vows to avenge him, but has focused his energies on developing a new power source based on the research of a renowned scientist named Otto Octavius (Alfred Molina), whom Peter respects. When Octavius' experiment goes horribly awry, fusing massive tentacles to his back and overriding control of his better judgment, Spider-Man is called into action once again, just as his powers mysteriously begin to wane.

5   All of these elements weave together to form a captivating narrative tapestry, juxtaposing Peter's numerous neglected relationships and responsibilities with his foundering Spider powers and creating a portrait of a hero who's more human than super. Raimi's cameras, never more free than they are here, leap into the midst of the action with the same abandon as in his *Evil Dead* films, but this time gain the added emotional weight of storytelling that's as invigorating as the visuals. Like all sequels should, the film elevates the stakes—and the scale—of the film's physical and emotional actions, imbuing the characters with added dimensions that build on the first film while evoking past struggles and introducing compelling new ones.

At the same time, the script and editing occasionally leave a little to be desired; plot developments that would have been referenced in passing in the first film are labored upon so heavily in *Spider-Man 2* that I felt compelled to stand up in my seat during the screening and shout out, 'Okay! We get it!' In particular, Peter's continuing struggle with the death of Uncle Ben receives the brunt of the film's over-attentive screenwriting (by *Wonder Boys* scribe Michael Chabon, Alvin Sargent and a host of others), as does his evolving definition of what it means to be a hero.

In one scene, Aunt May delivers a crucial speech about how necessary heroes like Spider-Man are to the world, and her dialogue runs so long I began to wonder if the filmmakers were going to run subtitles at the bottom of the screen that explained, 'NOW PETER IS CONSIDERING BECOMING SPIDER-MAN AGAIN,' since they chose to underscore his dilemma with such egregiously long rhetoric.

Other scenes simply play too long for their relative value, such as a throwaway gag where Peter, too frazzled to use his powers, takes an elevator to the top of a building instead of scaling it from the outside. Although Hal Sparks fans (*Talk Soup, Queer as Folk*) will be happy to see him riding with Spidey, the scene again goes on a good thirty seconds after the joke has been established, and drags down the flow of the picture.

Similarly, Peter shares a piece of cake with Ursula (Mageina Tovah), his landlord's daughter, for the purposes of introducing nary a crumb of new information. The scene could have been a tender moment shared between two outcasts, leavened by some task her father demanded of her as he decides what life to lead, but its appearance towards the end of the film disrupts the momentum of the Doc Ock storyline and leaves the audience without a comfortable sense of focus as the film hurtles towards its dramatic conclusion.

10   Fans of the '70s *Spider-Man* books will find much to enjoy in this sequel; it owes a greater debt to those storylines than to any other decade in the superhero's existence, and in a way, pays homage as much to the movies of that era as it does Stan Lee's pulp fiction. The conflicts are more serious, more pronounced and, in the end, less satisfyingly resolved, which works for a serial tome like a comic but doesn't quite satisfy when it comes to wrapping up a $200 million film that opens mid-summer and aims to capture the popcorn-gorging throngs.

It's a shortcoming I guess that can be overlooked if you're one of those who defines the movie's quality by snapshots of greatness, an overriding emotional weight or simply some moment that makes your spider-sense tingle (like Mary Jane's final line of dialogue).

Originally, I'd planned to see the film a second time before writing this review, to see if I felt the same way about it with all of my attention focused on what *is* there rather than what I expected. My anticipation for *Spider-Man 2* was admittedly high and it's possible I hoped for too great an accomplishment from Raimi, and got something not worse but merely different.

Still, *Spider-Man 2* remains in many ways the benchmark by which all future "event" movies should be judged; if all of them could be as carefully introspective and yet breathtakingly exciting as much of this film is, I'd have far less to complain about once the summer heat dried up and the final tallies of good and bad had been compiled.

At the same time, its glaring flaws distract from what might have become the placeholder for the new best comic book film ever, and instead give it residence as a close second. All in all, it's a pretty great film, but not so great that I can throw away my magnifying glass just yet.

SPIDER-MAN 2

— *Roger Ebert*

Roger Ebert has served as film critic for the *Chicago Sun-Times* since 1967. He was the first recipient of the Pulitzer Prize for film criticism (1975) and for several years appeared with co-host Gene Siskel on PBS's *At the Movies*. He is the author of several books on cinema, including *A Kiss Is Still a Kiss* (1984). This review was published in the *Sun-Times* on June 30, 2004. It is also available on Ebert's Web site, rogerebert.com.

SUGGESTION FOR READING Ebert writes in this review that Raimi's *Spider-Man 2* is "what a superhero movie should be"; it "demonstrates what's wrong with a lot of other superhero epics." Follow that line of argument throughout as you underline/highlight and annotate this review.

1 Now this is what a superhero movie should be. "Spider-Man 2" believes in its story in the same way serious comic readers believe, when the adventures on the page express their own dreams and wishes. It's not camp and it's not nostalgia, it's not wall-to-wall special effects and it's not pickled in angst. It's simply and poignantly a realization that being Spider-Man is a burden that Peter Parker is not entirely willing to bear.

The movie demonstrates what's wrong with a lot of other superhero epics: they focus on the superpowers, and short-change the humans behind them. (Has anyone ever been more boring, for instance, than Clark Kent or Bruce Wayne?)

"Spider-Man 2" is the best superhero movie since the modern genre was launched with "Superman" (1978). It succeeds by being true to the insight that allowed Marvel Comics to upturn decades of comic-book tradition: Readers could identify more completely with heroes like themselves than with remote godlike paragons. Peter Parker was an insecure high school student, in grade trouble, inarticulate in love, unready to assume the responsibilities that came with his unexpected superpowers. It wasn't that Spider-Man could swing from skyscrapers that won over his readers; it was that he fretted about personal problems in the thought balloons above his Spidey face mask.

Parker (Tobey Maguire) is in college now, studying physics at Columbia, more helplessly in love than ever with Mary Jane Watson (Kirsten Dunst). He's on the edge of a breakdown: he's lost his job as a pizza deliveryman, Aunt May faces foreclosure on her mortgage, he's missing classes, the colors run together when he washes his Spider-Man suit at the Laundromat, and after his web-spinning ability inexplicably seems to fade, he throws away his beloved uniform in despair. When a bum tries to sell the discarded Spidey suit to Jonah Jameson, editor of the Daily Bugle, Jameson offers him $50. The bum says he could do better on eBay. Has it come to this?

5   I was disappointed by the original "Spider-Man" (2002), and surprised to find this film working from the first frame. Sam Raimi, the director of both pictures, this time seems to know exactly what he should do, and never steps wrong in a film that effortlessly combines special effects and a human story, keeping its parallel plots alive and moving. One of the keys to the movie's success must be the contribution of novelist Michael Chabon to the screenplay; Chabon understands in his bones what comic books are, and why. His inspired 2000 novel The Amazing Adventures of Kavalier and Clay chronicles the birth of a 1940s comic book superhero and the young men who created him; he worked on the screen story that fed into Alvin Sargent's screenplay.

The seasons in a superhero's life are charted by the villains he faces (it is the same with James Bond). "Spider-Man 2" gives Spider-Man an enemy with a good nature that is overcome by evil. Peter Parker admires the famous Dr. Otto Octavius (Alfred Molina), whose laboratory on the banks of the East River houses an experiment that will either prove that fusion can work as a cheap source of energy, or vaporize Manhattan. To handle the dangerous materials of his experiments, Octavius devises four powerful tentacles that are fused to his spine and have a cyber-intelligence of their own; a chip at the top of his spine prevents them from overriding his orders, but when the chip is destroyed, the gentle scientist is transformed into Doc Ock, a fearsome fusion of man and machine, who can climb skyscraper walls by driving his tentacles through concrete and bricks. We hear him coming, hammering his way toward us like the drums of hell.

Peter Parker, meanwhile, has vowed that he cannot allow himself to love Mary Jane, because her life would be in danger from Spider-Man's enemies. She has finally given up on Peter, who is always standing her up; she announces her engagement to no less than an astronaut. Peter has heart-to-hearts with her and with Aunt May (Rosemary Harris), who is given full screen time and not reduced to an obligatory cameo. And he has to deal with his friend Harry Osborn (James Franco), who likes Peter but hates Spider-Man, blaming him for the death of his father (a k a the Green Goblin, although much is unknown to the son).

There are special effects, and then there are special effects. In the first movie I thought Spider-Man seemed to move with all the realism of a character in a cartoon. This time, as he swings from one skyscraper to another, he has more weight and dimension, and Raimi is able to seamlessly match the CGI and the human actors. The special-effects triumph in the film is the work on Doc Ock's four robotic tentacles, which move with an uncanny life, reacting and responding, doing double takes, becoming characters on their own.

Watching Raimi and his writers cut between the story threads, I savored classical workmanship: the film gives full weight to all of its elements, keeps them alive, is constructed with such skill that we care all the way through. In a lesser movie from this genre, we usually perk up for the action scenes but wade grimly through the dialogue. Here both stay alive, and the dialogue is more about emotion, love and values, less about long-winded explanations of the inexplicable (it's kind of neat that Spider-Man never does find out why his web-throwing ability sometimes fails him).

10   Tobey Maguire almost didn't sign for the sequel, complaining of back pain; Jake Gyllenhaal, another gifted actor, was reportedly in the wings. But if Maguire hadn't returned (along with Spidey's throwaway line about his aching back), we would never have known how good he could be in this role.

Dunst is valuable, too, bringing depth and heart to a girlfriend role that in lesser movies would be conventional. When she kisses her astronaut boyfriend upside-down, it's one of those perfect moments that rewards fans of the whole saga; we don't need to be told she's remembering her only kiss from Spider-Man.

There are moviegoers who make a point of missing superhero movies, and I can't blame them, although I confess to a weakness for the genre. I liked both of the "Crow" movies, and "Daredevil," "The Hulk" and "X2," but not enough to recommend them to friends who don't like or understand comic books. "Spider-Man 2" is in another category: It's a real movie, full-blooded and smart, with qualities even for those who have no idea who Stan Lee is. It's a superhero movie for people who don't go to superhero movies, and for those who do, it's the one they've been yearning for.

SUGGESTIONS FOR DISCUSSION

1. With a group of your classmates, examine the way Gilchrist and Ebert each describe the film *Spider-Man 2* in their reviews. What does each of these reviewers focus on as his primary reason for either liking or not liking the film? What, if anything, do both reviewers miss about the film that your group would add in any review of *Spider-Man 2*.

2. With a group of your classmates, compare the notes you took on each of these reviews. How do they differ? In what ways are they similar? Where do they agree about the film? What criteria does each group member use to make his or her judgments?

3. Roger Ebert writes that *Spider-Man 2* is "the best superhero movie since the modern genre was launched with *Superman* (1978)." He admits that he did not care much for the first of Raimi's two films (*Spider-Man*). Todd Gilchrist, by contrast, writes that the first *Spider-Man* was "the best comic book adaptation of all time." What criteria do these two critics use for their judgments of the film. What does each see as a strength of the film they deem "best" that they do not see in the other film? What does each seem to value in a film adaptation of a popular comic-book superhero story?

SUGGESTIONS FOR WRITING

1. Which of these reviewers comes closest to your assessment of the two *Spider-Man* films? What would you add? Where would you disagree? Write your own review of the two films, drawing on the comments of these three film critics when you find it useful.

2. Notice that these critics cover some of the same ground for judging the film. For example, they each note whether or not the film seems a faithful adaptation of the original comic-book story and character. They point to the screenwriters and director as being responsible for that element of the film. They each make it a point to talk about character development and acting. They write about how well the story moves, how complicated the plot is, and how (even in fantasy) believable the visuals are. Write an essay in which you examine the criteria these critics use for their reviews. In what ways are they similar? Where do they differ? When does personal preference or personal taste come (some people like this kind of movie; others don't) into play?

3. Choose a film currently popular and write your own review. Pay attention to the story, the characters, and how convincing the acting and the action sequences (if there are action sequences) are. Can you identify what makes this a popular film? Is it the way the story is told? The way it looks? The acting? Does the subject of the movie appeal to a specific audience or age group, or does it have a broader audience appeal? Does the film draw on interests, concerns, fears, or desires that seem current to you? What is your recommendation to classmates? Should they see this movie or pass this one up? (For more information on film reviews, refer to the Film Clip feature in Chapter 3.)

CLASSIC READING

THE GANGSTER AS TRAGIC HERO

— Robert Warshow

Robert Warshow was a film critic and one of the first American intellectuals to write seriously about popular culture. The following essay, "The Gangster as Tragic Hero," is taken from his book *The Immediate Experience*, published posthumously in 1962. (Warshow died in 1955.) The essay, though brief, is considered by many to be a classic example of film criticism and cultural analysis. Since the 1950s, when Warshow was writing, any number of gangster films have appeared: *Bonnie and Clyde*, the famous *Godfather* trilogy, *Goodfellas*, a remake of *Scarface* (starring Al Pacino this time), a film version of the TV show *The Untouchables*, black gangster films such as *New Jack City*. On television, HBO's series *The Sopranos*, *Wired*, and *Deadwood* all draw large and loyal audiences.

SUGGESTION FOR READING As you read, keep the title of the essay—"The Gangster as Tragic Hero"—in mind. Underline/highlight and annotate passages in the essay where Warshow explains what makes gangsters tragic figures.

1   America, as a social and political organization, is committed to a cheerful view of life. It could not be otherwise. The sense of tragedy is a luxury of aristocratic societies, where the fate of the individual is not conceived of as having a direct and legitimate political importance, being determined by a fixed and supra-political—that is, non-controversial—moral order or fate. Modern equalitarian societies, however, whether democratic or authoritarian in their political forms, always base themselves on the claim that they are making life happier; the avowed function of the modern state, at least in its ultimate terms, is not only to regulate social relations, but also to determine the quality and the possibilities of human life in general. Happiness thus becomes the chief political issue—in a sense, the only political issue—and for that reason it can never be treated as an issue at all. If an American or a Russian is unhappy, it implies a certain reprobation of his society, and therefore, by a logic of which we can all recognize the necessity, it becomes an obligation of citizenship to be cheerful; if the authorities find it necessary, the citizen may even be compelled to make a public display of his cheerfulness on important occasions, just as he may be conscripted into the army in time of war.

Naturally, this civic responsibility rests more strongly upon the organs of mass culture. The individual citizen may still be permitted his private unhappiness so long as it does not take on political significance, the extent of this tolerance being determined by how large an area of private life the society can accommodate. But every production of mass culture is a public act and must conform with accepted notions of the public good. Nobody seriously questions the principle that it is the function of mass culture to maintain public morale, and certainly nobody in the mass audience objects to having his morale maintained.[1] At a time when the normal condition of the citizen is a state of anxiety, euphoria spreads over our culture like the broad smile of an idiot. In terms of attitudes towards life, there is very little difference between a "happy" movie like *Good News*, which ignores death and suffering, and a "sad" movie like *A Tree Grows in Brooklyn*, which uses death and suffering as incidents in the service of a higher optimism.

But, whatever its effectiveness as a source of consolation and a means of pressure for maintaining "positive" social attitudes, this optimism is fundamentally satisfying to no one, not even to those who would be most disoriented without its support. Even within the area of mass culture, there always exists a current of opposition, seeking to express by whatever means are available to it that sense of desperation and inevitable failure which optimism itself helps to create. Most often, this opposition is confined to rudimentary or semiliterate forms: in mob politics and journalism, for example, or in certain kinds of religious enthusiasm. When it does enter the field of art, it is likely to be disguised or attenuated: in an unspecific form of expression like jazz, in the basically harmless nihilism of the Marx Brothers, in the continually reasserted strain of hopelessness that often seems to be the real meaning of the soap opera. The gangster film is remarkable in that it fills the need for disguise (though not sufficiently to avoid arousing uneasiness) without requiring any serious distortion. From its beginnings, it has been a consistent and astonishingly complete presentation of the modern sense of tragedy.[2]

In its initial character, the gangster film is simply one example of the movies' constant tendency to create fixed dramatic patterns that can be repeated indefinitely with a reasonable expectation of profit. One gangster film follows another as one musical or one Western follows another. But this rigidity is not necessarily opposed to the requirements of art. There have been very successful types of art in the past which developed such specific and detailed conventions as almost to make individual examples of the type interchangeable. This is true, for example, of Elizabethan revenge tragedy and Restoration comedy.

5   For such a type to be successful means that its conventions have imposed themselves upon the general consciousness and become the accepted vehicles of a particular set of attitudes and a particular aesthetic effect. One goes to any individual example of the type with very definite expectations, and originality is to be welcomed only in the degree that it intensifies the expected experience without fundamentally altering it. Moreover, the relationship between the conventions which go to make up such a type and the real experience of its audience or the real facts of whatever situation it pretends to describe is of only secondary importance and does not determine its aesthetic force. It is only in an ultimate sense that the type appeals to its audience's experience of reality; much more immediately, it appeals to previous experience of the type itself: it creates its own field of reference.

Thus the importance of the gangster film, and the nature and intensity of its emotional and aesthetic impact, cannot be measured in terms of the place of the gangster himself or the importance of the problem of crime in American life. Those European movie-goers who think there is a gangster on every corner in New York are certainly deceived, but defenders of the "positive" side of American culture are equally deceived if they think it relevant to point out that most Americans have never seen a gangster. What matters is that the experience of the gangster *as an experience of art* is universal to Americans. There is almost nothing we understand better or react to more readily or with quicker intelligence. The Western film, though it seems never to diminish in popularity, is for most of us no more than the folklore of the past, familiar and understandable only because it has been repeated so often. The gangster film comes much closer. In ways that we do not easily or willingly define, the gangster speaks for us, expressing that part of the American psyche which rejects the qualities and the demands of modern life, which rejects "Americanism" itself.

The gangster is the man of the city, with the city's language and knowledge, with its queer and dishonest skills and its terrible daring, carrying his life in his hands like a placard, like a club. For everyone else, there is at least the theoretical possibility of another world—in that happier American culture which the gangster denies, the city does not really exist; it is only a more crowded and more brightly lit country—but for the gangster there is only the city; he must inhabit it in order to personify it: not the real city, but that dangerous and sad city of the imagination which is so much more important, which is the modern world. And the gangster—though there are real gangsters—is also, and primarily, a creature of the imagination. The real city, one might say, produces only criminals; the imaginary city produces the gangster: he is what we want to be and what we are afraid we may become.

Thrown into the crowd without background or advantages, with only those ambiguous skills which the rest of us—the real people of the real city—can only pretend to have, the gangster is required to make his way, to make his life and impose it on others. Usually, when we come upon him, he has already made his choice or the choice has already been made for him, it doesn't matter which: we are not permitted to ask whether at some point he could have chosen to be something else than what he is.

The gangster's activity is actually a form of rational enterprise, involving fairly definite goals and various techniques for achieving them. But this rationality is usually no more than a vague background; we know, perhaps, that the gangster sells liquor or that he operates a numbers racket; often we are not given even that much information. So his activity becomes a kind of pure criminality: he hurts people. Certainly our response to the gangster film is most consistently and most universally a response to sadism; we gain the double satisfaction of participating vicariously in the gangster's sadism and then seeing it turned against the gangster himself.

10   But on another level the quality of irrational brutality and the quality of rational enterprise become one. Since we do not see the rational and routine aspects of the gangster's behavior, the practice of brutality—the quality of unmixed criminality—becomes the totality of his career. At the same time, we are always conscious that the whole meaning of this career is a drive for success: the typical gangster film presents a steady upward progress followed by a very precipitate fall. Thus brutality itself becomes at once the means to success and the content of success—a success that is defined in its most general terms, not as accomplishment or specific gain, but simply as the unlimited possibility of aggression. (In the same way, film presentations of businessmen tend to make it appear that they achieve their success by talking on the telephone and holding conferences and that success *is* talking on the telephone and holding conferences.)

From this point of view, the initial contact between the film and its audience is an agreed conception of human life: that man is a being with the possibilities of success or failure. This principal, too, belongs to the city; one must emerge from the crowd or else one is nothing. On that basis, the necessity of the action is established, and it progresses by inalterable paths to the point where the gangster lies dead and the principal has been modified: there is really only one possibility—failure. The final meaning of the city is anonymity and death.

In the opening scene of *Scarface*, we are shown a successful man; we know he is successful because he has just given a party of opulent proportions and because he is called Big Louie. Through some monstrous lack of caution, he permits himself to be alone for a few moments. We understand from this immediately that he is about to be killed. No convention of the gangster film is more strongly established than this: it is dangerous to be alone. And yet the very conditions of success make it impossible not to be alone, for success is always the establishment of an *individual* preeminence that must be imposed on others, in whom it automatically arouses hatred; the successful man is an outlaw. The gangster's whole life is an effort to assert himself as an individual, to draw himself out of the crowd, and he always dies *because* he is an individual; the final bullet thrusts him back, makes him, after all, a failure. "Mother of God," says the dying Little Caesar, "Is this the end of

Rico?"—speaking of himself thus in the third person because what has been brought low is not the undifferentiated *man*, but the individual with a name, the gangster, the success; even to himself he is a creature of the imagination. (T. S. Eliot has pointed out that a number of Shakespeare's tragic heroes have this trick of looking at themselves dramatically; their true identify, the thing that is destroyed when they die, is something outside themselves—not a man, but a style of life, a kind of meaning.)

At bottom, the gangster is doomed because he is under the obligation to succeed, not because the means he employs are unlawful. In the deeper layers of the modern consciousness, *all* means are unlawful, every attempt to succeed is an act of aggression, leaving one alone and guilty and defenseless among enemies: one is *punished* for success. This is our intolerable dilemma: that failure is a kind of death and success is evil and dangerous, is—ultimately—impossible. The effect of the gangster film is to embody this dilemma in the person of the gangster and resolve it by his death. The dilemma is resolved because it is *his* death, not ours. We are safe; for the moment, we can acquiesce in our failure, we can choose to fail.

NOTES

1. In her testimony before the House Committee on Un-American Activities, Mrs. Leila Rogers said that the movie *None But the Lonely Heart* was un-American because it was gloomy. Like so much else that was said during the unhappy investigation of Hollywood, this statement was at once stupid and illuminating. One knew immediately what Mrs. Rogers was talking about; she had simply been insensitive enough to carry her philistinism to its conclusion.

2. Efforts have been made from time to time to bring the gangster film into line with the prevailing optimism and social constructiveness of our culture; *Kiss of Death* is a recent example. These efforts are usually unsuccessful; the reasons for their lack of success are interesting in themselves, but I shall not be able to discuss them here.

SUGGESTIONS FOR DISCUSSION

1. Warshow says that the gangster film is "a consistent and astonishingly complete presentation of the modern sense of tragedy." What does Warshow mean by tragedy here? In what sense are gangster films tragic? Pick a gangster film or two that you are familiar with and see if they fit Warshow's definition of tragedy. Does Warshow's definition hold? How might it be updated?

2. Warshow says that for the gangster, "the whole meaning of [his] career is a drive for success." What does he mean by this statement? What does "success" mean in this context? What do gangster films have to tell about the American dream of success?

3. Warshow begins the essay by saying that "it is the function of mass culture to maintain public morale" and to "conform with accepted notions of public good." Think about some of the movies you have seen recently. To what extent does Warshow's statement seem valid? Consider the benefits and limits of America's commitment to what Warshow calls "a cheerful view of life."

SUGGESTIONS FOR WRITING

1. According to Warshow, gangsters are more attractive figures than the "good guys." Why is this so? Write an essay that explains why the gangster—or any other hero who lives outside the law—is such a popular figure in the American imagination.

2. Use Warshow's definition of tragedy to analyze a film or TV show featuring the gangster as a tragic hero. Films that feature gangster-hero types range from the recent and campy *Kill Bill* (volumes I and II) to more traditional stories like the 1970s bio-pic *Bonnie and Clyde*. Does the film or television character actually meet the criteria Warshow sets up? How does seeing the gangster as a tragic hero influence the way viewers respond to the story?

3. Think of other films besides gangster movies that have a tragic ending for the main character or characters (such as *Titanic, American Beauty, Vanilla Sky,* or *American History X*). Pick one whose tragic end represents something interesting and important about the limits of American culture. Write an essay that explains the tragedy in the film. What were the main character or characters striving to do? Why was their tragic end inevitable? What does this tragic end tell about American culture?

VISUAL CULTURE   The Graphic Novel: Reader Participation

To learn more about storytelling, visit www.ablongman.com/george/127

Although storytelling is usually considered an oral or written form, people have been telling stories with pictures—making visual narratives—since ancient times. Prehistoric cave paintings tell hunting stories or detail rituals. Medieval church murals and windows narrate the lives of saints. Even today, many modes of storytelling are visual ones. Obviously, television and film carry much of the story through pictures, but still pictures—cartoons, comic books, children's books, and much print advertisement—depend on visual sequencing and arrangement to move the narrative (the story) along. With very little dialogue, the reader must follow the logic of the panel sequence.

Graphic novels work because readers fill in the information that is not expressly drawn or written in the panels. For example, in the second panel of the story reprinted here, Marjane Satrapi tells us that she is in the picture, although we cannot see her because she has been cut off. We see only a bit of her veil. Satrapi is depending here on the reader's ability to put her into the picture, especially since she gives us a complete drawing of herself in the panel before. In this way, the reader relies on both the sequencing of the two panels (panel 1 with a complete drawing of Satrapi as a child, followed by panel 2 with Satrapi cut off but identified as being "in" the picture) and the reader's ability to imagine outside the panel to fill in the image. That is how *reader participation* works in comics and in graphic novels.

The following excerpts are from Marjane Satrapi's autobiographical graphic novel *Persepolis: The Story of a Childhood.* This graphic novel works very much like a visual memoir, drawing on the conventions of comics and visual narrative to tell a young girl's story of growing up in Iran during the Islamic revolution there. In what follows, we have reprinted Satrapi's introductory essay that sets the scene and historic context for this memoir and "The Veil," the opening chapter of *Persepolis.*

THE VEIL

— *Marjane Satrapi*

Marjane Satrapi was born in 1969 in Rasht, Iran. She grew up in Tehran, where she studied at the Lycée Française before leaving for Vienna and going to Strasbourg to study illustration. She has written several children's books, and her illustrations appear in newspapers and magazines throughout the world, including the *New Yorker* and the *New York Times*. *Persepolis*, a memoir of growing up in Iran during the Islamic revolution, was first published in 2000. Satrapi has called it an autobiographical novel in graphic novel form. This excerpt, "The Veil," is the opening chapter in *Persepolis*.

SUGGESTION FOR READING In an exploratory writing, write what you already know about or think about Iran, the Islamic revolution there, and/or the Islamic practice of requiring women to wear the veil.

1   In the second millennium B.C., while the Elam nation was developing a civilization alongside Babylon, Indo-European invaders gave their name to the immense Iranian plateau where they settled. The word "Iran" was derived from "Ayryana Vaejo," which means "the origin of the Aryans." These people were semi-nomads whose descendants were the Medes and the Persians. The Medes founded the first Iranian nation in the seventh century B.C.; it was later destroyed by Cyrus the Great. He established what became one of the largest empires of the ancient world, the Persian Empire, in the sixth century B.C. Iran was referred to as Persia—its Greek name—until 1935 when Reza Shah, the father of the last Shah of Iran, asked everyone to call the country Iran.

Iran was rich. Because of its wealth and its geographic location, it invited attacks: from Alexander the Great, from its Arab neighbors to the west, from Turkish and Mongolian conquerors, Iran was often subject to foreign domination. Yet the Persian language and culture withstood these invasions. The invaders assimilated into this strong culture, and in some ways they became Iranians themselves.

In the twentieth century, Iran entered a new phase. Reza Shah decided to modernize and westernize the country, but meanwhile a fresh source of wealth was discovered: oil. And with the oil came another invasion. The West, particularly Great Britain, wielded a strong influence on the Iranian economy. During the Second World War, the British, Soviets, and Americans asked Reza Shah to ally himself with them against Germany. But Reza Shah, who sympathized with the Germans, declared Iran a neutral zone. So the Allies invaded and occupied Iran. Reza Shah was sent into exile and was succeeded by his son, Mohammad Reza Pahlavi, who was known simply as the Shah.

In 1951, Mohammed Mossadeq, then prime minister of Iran, nationalized the oil industry. In retaliation, Great Britain organized an embargo on all exports of oil from Iran. In 1953, the CIA, with the help of British intelligence, organised a coup against him. Mossadeq was overthrown and the Shah, who had earlier escaped from the country, returned to power. The Shah stayed on the throne until 1979, when he fled Iran to escape the Islamic revolution.

5   Since then, this old and great civilization has been discussed mostly in connection with fundamentalism, fanaticism, and terrorism. As an Iranian who has lived more than half of my life in Iran, I know that this image is far from the truth. This is why writing *Persepolis* was so important to me. I believe that an entire nation should not be judged by the wrongdoings of a few extremists. I also don't want those Iranians who lost their lives in prisons defending freedom, who died in the war against Iraq, who suffered under various repressive regimes, or who were forced to leave their families and flee their homeland to be forgotten.

One can forgive but one should never forget.

Marjane Satrapi
Paris, September 2002

SUGGESTIONS FOR DISCUSSION

1. How much do you already know about the Islamic revolution in Iran? How does that previous knowledge help you read this visual narrative?

2. The basis of all visual sequencing is the reader's ability to connect the actions or characters of one image to the actions or characters of the image that follows it. That is how comics tell stories. If a character is shown in one panel with his hand on a doorknob and in the next greeting someone at an open door, we assume the character opened the door to find this visitor on the other side. We don't see the door open, but the logic of the sequence tells us what the action is. Look carefully at the selection from *Persepolis* reprinted here. Notice, for example, that Satrapi takes advantage of the reader's ability to fill in information that is not actually in the picture when she tells us that she is in her school picture with her friends but we cannot see her because she is cut off. Discuss with a group of your classmates other places in this excerpt where the reader must fill in the action from the few details, our assumptions about what must be outside the frame, or the sequence of the panels.

3. In her introduction to *Persepolis*, Marjane Satrapi writes that the old and great civilization that was Iran is, from the outside, seen "mostly in connection with fundamentalism, fanaticism, and terrorism. As an Iranian who has lived more than half of my life in Iran, I know that this image is far from the truth. This is why writing *Persepolis* was so important to me." With a group of your classmates, discuss the images you each have or preconceptions you each have about Iran and the Middle East in general. How does this graphic memoir figure into the way you think of Iran? Does it shift perception at all? What difference might it make if this story were told from the point of view of an adult in the family?

SUGGESTED ASSIGNMENT

Drawing from a well-known short story, play, short novel, or film, create your own graphic novel. Or make your own graphic memoir by telling a story in your life using the techniques of a graphic novel. You do not have to be an artist to make a visual narrative. Use computer programs such as PowerPoint to arrange clip art, use photographs arranged in a sequence, cut images from magazines, or make your own drawings or paintings that you arrange in a sequence to tell a story.

- Choose a story that you have read and liked and that seems to lend itself well to being told in pictures. Your might even choose one of the Urban Legends you read about earlier in this chapter. ("The Killer in the Backseat" would make a good visual narrative, for example.)

- If you are writing your own story, reread Patricia Hampl's essay on memoir reprinted earlier in this chapter. A memoir must be about something more than just the story. It should, as Hampl suggest, tell your mind, not just the story. Satrapi, for example, is telling a story about a people. Her part in the story is interesting and sometimes funny and sometimes sad, but it is not a story about her. It is a story about everything around her.

- Write the story down. Write down the basics of the story. Make sure you write out the parts of the story that you believe are crucial to telling this story well. If you are working with a novel, you very likely can only work with one chapter rather than the entire novel. Decide which chapter is key for understanding the story.

- Make a list of the key scenes in your story. Your visual narrative cannot convey every detail in the story, so you have to decide which parts of the story make for good visual narration. What can you show? Decide on the number of scenes. Choose scenes that are crucial for telling the story and that have good potential for visual impact.

■ Arrange your scenes. On paper (or in a computer program with storyboard capabilities), make a storyboard such as the storyboard reproduced on pages 245–246. Fill in your storyboard with general sketches or notes on what scenes must go in each space. Sequencing is important in the way you tell your story, so pay attention to the order of your scenes.

■ Present the completed story to your classmates. Be sure that you can project the story in a computer program or on transparencies so that the entire class can see clearly. In your presentation, talk about what choices you had to make to turn a written story into a graphic novel. Use the following questions to guide your preparations for the presentation:

What does the story gain when you change it from the written version to the visual?

What does it lose?

What in the original story seemed to lend itself to being told as a graphic novel?

What roles do color, line, and sequence play in telling the story?

When did you have to use dialogue, caption, and sounds?

When could you rely on image and sequence alone to tell the story?

FILM CLIP Book to Film: The Adaptation

To learn more about film adaptations, visit www.ablongman.com/george/128

One of the comments most of us have heard about film adaptations of books is: "The movie is never as good as the book." What that statement usually means is that the reader misses both the experience of reading the book and the events (and sometimes whole plotlines and characters) as they are portrayed in the book.

A good film adaptation, however, is not a faithful rendering of the pages of a novel, short story, or play. Storytelling in film is different because the medium is different. For one thing, film depends on the visual to make many of the connections that are spelled out in a book. Popular film also has difficulty if a story contains too many plotlines that threaten to distract or confuse viewers. When the very popular *Lord of the Rings* trilogy was adapted into three films by Peter Jackson, Fran Walsh, and Phillipa Boyens, each film was over three hours long, and their extended DVD editions run over four hours. But these films did not come close to reproducing everything in the three novels. Most films are limited to just about two hours, so time constraints will affect the way a book is adapted into film. Moreover, production companies want to make movies that appeal to the widest audiences possible, so popular films are often driven to maintain a faster pace than many novels.

If you think of film adaptations of books as interpretations of those stories rather than faithful renderings of what is on the page, then you have a notion of what it means to translate a story from a book onto screen. The filmmaker and scriptwriters are forced to make choices about what they can leave in and what must go. Jackson, for example, has talked of his interpretation of *The Lord of the Rings* as being "Frodo-centric," meaning that the scriptwriting team cut from the storyline anything that did not directly relate to Frodo and his mission. Other filmmakers do much the same. They make a decision about how to interpret events of a novel, play or short story, and that interpretation shapes the way the film is written, acted, shot, and edited.

Watch a film adaptation of a novel, short story, play, or comic book or graphic novel, and write an essay in which you examine the way the film interprets the original. You can write this sort of essay doing one of the following:

- Choose a story that has been filmed more than once (*Pride and Prejudice, David Copperfield, Sense and Sensibility, The Importance of Being Earnest, Hamlet, Jane Eyre, Wuthering Heights, Frankenstein,* or *Dracula,* for example) and compare two film interpretations of the work. What does each emphasize? What does each cut? Is anything added? What is the purpose of the cut or the addition?

- Choose a novel, short story, comic book, or play that you know well and like. Watch a film adaptation of that piece of literature. How does the filmmaker interpret characters, important events, setting, and central themes or conflicts? Write an essay in which you examine the film interpretation of the written work. *Lord of the Rings, Harry Potter, The Hitchhiker's Guide to the Galaxy, Do Androids Dream of Electric Sheep?* (filmed as *Blade Runner*), *Sin City,* and *The Road to Perdition* are all popular stories that have been interpreted through film.

- Choose a film version of a novel, short story, play, or comic book that has been remade so that it is changed for very new audiences. For example, *Clueless* is a reworking of the novel and many film versions of Jane Austen's *Emma. Bridget Jones' Diary* and the recent Bollywood film *Bride and Prejudice* are both rewritings of *Pride and Prejudice. Apocalypse Now* is a rewriting of *Heart of Darkness. Forbidden Planet* and *Prospero's Books* are reworkings of Shakespeare's *The Tempest.* Write an essay in which you examine the update as an interpretation of the original. What does it emphasize? What does it change? What does the story gain in the update? What do you think is lost?

FIELDWORK
Writing a Questionnaire

Everyone has strong preferences when it comes to what they like to read, what they hate, what they think is too sappy or gory or outright boring. And, since everyone knows what they like and why they like it, it's often difficult to imagine other people's preferences. Who reads those romance novels? What is the audience for cyberfiction? Does anybody, outside of English teachers, still read *Silas Marner* for pleasure?

One way to find out what people like to read is, quite simply, to ask them. For this assignment, you will be doing just that by designing and distributing a questionnaire that asks people what they read for pleasure and how their reading tastes have changed over the years.

Design this questionnaire either on your own, with a small group of classmates, or even as an entire class. If you do it on your own, try to get fifteen to twenty-five responses. If you work with a small group, each person should get ten responses to compile a fairly large sampling. If the entire class uses the same questionnaire, each person can get ten responses and have a substantial amount of information to sort through.

Even if you have only twenty-five responses to your questionnaire, you will have more than your own and your classmates' impressions from which to draw. That kind of information can help you broaden your own response and begin to account for the differences as well as the similarities that you see around you.

Suggestions for Designing a Questionnaire

1. *Make it brief and readable.* It is best to limit your questionnaire to one page. The simpler it seems to your audience members, the more likely they will be to fill it out. Make it readable as well. Don't try to crowd too many questions on the page or make instructions complicated. There should be plenty of white space, and the language should be simple and direct.

2. *Write different kinds of questions to get different kinds of answers.* The kind of questions that you ask will determine the kind of information you receive. If you ask questions that can be answered with a yes or a no, then you will likely get more responses but less specific information. If you ask people to write quite a bit, you won't get as many participants and might have trouble summarizing your findings.

3. *Decide who will answer your questionnaire.* If you want to know what a certain age group is reading—middle school or high school or college age students, for example—target that audience.

   You might, however, want to know what older adults are reading and how their reading interests have changed over the years.

   Or you might want to know what women read or what men read.

   You could also ask about a certain kind of reading. Stephen King says that people love a good scare, but not everyone does, just as not everyone is fond of romance novels or stories about superheroes or fantasy and science fiction. You can create one kind of questionnaire to focus on a particular kind of story—such as science fiction—and try to get at what it is in those stories that appeals to the audience.

It's probably best that you decide as a class or as a group what information you hope to get from your questionnaire. The sample questionnaire below is adapted from Janice Radway's *Reading the Romance*, a study of women whose favorite reading for pleasure is the romance novel.

Sample Questionnaire

1. At what age did you begin reading for pleasure?
   a. _____ 5–10
   b. _____ 11–20
   c. _____ 21–30
   d. _____ 31 or above

2. Age today:
   a. _____ 18–21
   b. _____ 22–30
   c. _____ 31–45
   d. _____ 46–55
   e. _____ over 55

3. What kinds of books did you read for pleasure when you were a teenager?
   a. _____ biography
   b. _____ historical fiction
   c. _____ romances
   d. _____ westerns
   e. _____ mysteries
   f. _____ comic books

g. _____ sports stories

h. _____ other (specify)

4. What kind of book do you read for pleasure now?

a. _____ biography

b. _____ historical fiction

c. _____ romances

d. _____ westerns

e. _____ mysteries

f. _____ comic books

g. _____ sports stories

h. _____ other (specify)

5. What kinds of books do you never read for pleasure?

a. _____ biography

b. _____ historical fiction

c. _____ romances

d. _____ westerns

e. _____ mysteries

f. _____ comic books

g. _____ sports stories

h. _____ other (specify)

6. What book or story have you read most recently for pleasure?

Remember that your questionnaire should be designed to answer the questions you and your classmates have about reading for pleasure. Some or all of these questions might be useful, but be sure to target your audience, decide on what you want to know, and ask questions that can get at that information.

Report on Your Findings

Once you have completed your questionnaire, report your findings to the rest of the class. Write a report, give a presentation, or design a chart or graph that visually illustrates your findings.

MINING THE ARCHIVE   Comic Strips and Comic Books

To learn more about digital story sites, visit www.ablongman.com/george/129

Comic strips started to appear in daily newspapers and the Sunday papers in the late 1890s and early 1900s, establishing a new medium of storytelling that brings together three key ingredients: a narrative sequence of pictures, speech balloons, and a regular cast of characters. The Yellow Kid (1895)—a bald, gap-toothed street urchin dressed in a yellow nightshirt—became the first comic-strip celebrity, followed by the Katzenjammer Kids (1897), Happy Hooligan (1900), Mutt and Jeff (1907), and Krazy Kat (1910).

Examples of these early joke-a-day gag strips that anticipate Pogo (1949), Peanuts (1950), Doonesbury (1970), Cathy (1976), and Dilbert (1989) are in Robert C. Harvey's books, *The Art of the Funnies: An Aesthetic History* (1994) and *Children of the Yellow Kid: The Evolution of the American Comic Strip* (1998). The Web site Krazy Kat Daily Strips at rrnet.com/-nakamura/soba/kat/day/ contains thirty enlargements of Krazy Kat strips. As you look at old comic strips, consider how the narrative sequencing from panel to panel sets up the humor and how cartooning styles give the characters their particular identities.

You can also find examples in Harvey's two books of detective and adventure themes in comic strips such as Dick Tracy (1931), Terry and the Pirates (1934), Prince Valiant (1937), and Steve Canyon (1947), as well as domestic sitcoms such

as Bringing Up Father (1913), Gasoline Alley (1918), Little Orphan Annie (1924), and Blondie (1930).

In the 1930s, the narrative techniques of the comic strip found a new outlet in comic books. In 1938, Superman—the first of the great comic-book heroes—made his appearance, followed quickly by Batman, Green Lantern, Wonder Woman, Captain America, and Plastic Man. You can find examples of these super-heroes in Jules Feiffer's *The Great Comic Book Heroes* (1965) and Robert C. Harvey's *The Art of the Comic Book: An Aesthetic History* (1996). Comic books offer opportunities to think about how the integration of the visual and the verbal has created new narrative possibilities in graphic storytelling.

Work

Lewis W. Hine, Courtesy George Eastman House

Never leave that to tomorrow, which you can do today.

—Benjamin Franklin, *Poor Richard's Almanac*

I'm goin' . . . where they hung the jerk who invented work on the Big Rock Candy Mountain.

—Harry McClintock

Historically, Americans have had a love/hate relationship with their jobs. That may be due partially to something typically called the "Protestant work ethic," a philosophy of living that has formed a part of this nation's character from the first European settlements. According to this ethic, "Idle hands are the devil's workshop." The contrast between fruitful labor and wasteful leisure is one the

Puritans brought with them as they traveled to the New World to explore and to settle in this country. Its message is a simple (and simplistic) one: success is the reward for diligence; failure is the consequence of idleness.

Of course, success and failure are never so easily explained away, but a cultural myth—even one as readily dispelled as this one—is difficult to ignore. For many American workers, getting a good job and keeping it is a measure of success. Losing it, for whatever reason, means failure. Workers who lose their jobs might well have been fired through no fault of their own, but the suspicion often remains that those let go somehow deserved dismissal.

Our identities are formed, in many respects, by the jobs that we hold or want to hold. From the time children start school, parents and teachers ask them what they want to be when they grow up. By adulthood, we are expected to have a "career"—a job that will support a family, provide opportunities for professional advancement, buy leisure time, perhaps contribute to community well-being, signal status, and be fulfilling, all at once.

Even though many workers know that their jobs are subject to the whims of the marketplace, researchers are finding that the workplace has become a sanctuary from the tensions of home life, or a second neighborhood where friendships are forged, jokes are traded, and identities are formed. Work as a home away from home continues to be a popular theme for television series that place sitcoms and dramas—shows such as *ER*, *CSI*, or *24*—in what has been called the "work-family" setting. On television, the work-family is a group of people in the workplace who substitute for the home family. It is a formula that began with the old *Mary Tyler Moore Show* and has grown in popularity ever since. That these work-family shows are so popular might indicate some of the public's fascination with and hopes for the world of work.

Work has historically been a site of struggle as well as a home away from home. Management and labor have often been at odds over such issues as the forty-hour week, the minimum wage, child labor regulations, health and safety issues, and the rights of workers to organize. Disputes that may have been settled for American workers in the first half of the twentieth century have now reemerged as global struggles, with companies outsourcing (or "off-shoring") their labor to countries where sweatshop conditions and lower wages are commonplace. In the past decade, consumers have begun to demand more information about where their clothing is made and under what conditions it was produced. That may be why Students United Against Sweatshops has become the fastest growing, most powerful campus movement since 1960s protests. This grassroots opposition to sweatshops indicates that American students care very much about working conditions both inside and outside their country's borders.

Throughout this chapter, you will be asked to think and write about the role that work plays in American culture. You will need to think about your own work experiences, how work has been represented in this culture, how workers have interpreted their own work environments, and what can be learned by researching current labor and marketplace issues.

Work, as you will see, is rarely just as simple as a place to go to earn a paycheck. Workers' identities are often tied to the work that they do or the work that they would like to do. We may not continue to believe in the simple logic of the Protestant work ethic, but this is a culture concerned at some level with the dignity of work. It is that concern for dignity and fair play that comes into nearly every discussion about work.

THE FIRST JOB

— Sandra Cisneros

Sandra Cisneros was born in Chicago, the daughter of a Mexican father and a Mexican American mother. She has been a poet in the schools, a teacher for high school dropouts, and an arts administrator. Cisneros is the author of *My Wicked Ways* (1987), a volume of poetry; two collections of short stories—*The House on Mango Street* (1985), from which the following selection has been excerpted, and *Woman Hollering Creek* (1991)—and the novel *Caramelo* (2002).

SUGGESTION FOR READING   Write a brief description of a time when you found yourself in a situation that was uncomfortable—a place where you did not know what to expect. After you have read Cisneros's story, use your own memory piece to help you focus on what the event that she writes of means to you.

1   It wasn't as if I didn't want to work. I did. I had even gone to the social security office the month before to get my social security number. I needed money. The Catholic high school cost a lot, and Papa said nobody went to public school unless you wanted to turn out bad. I thought I'd find an easy job, the kind other kids had, working in the dime store or maybe a hotdog stand. And though I hadn't started looking yet, I thought I might the week after next. But when I came home that afternoon, all wet because Tito had pushed me into the open water hydrant—only I had sort of let him—Mama called me in the kitchen before I could even go and change, and Aunt Lala was sitting there drinking her coffee with a spoon. Aunt Lala said she had found a job for me at the Peter Pan Photo Finishers on North Broadway where she worked and how old was I and to show up tomorrow saying I was one year older and that was that.

So the next morning I put on the navy blue dress that made me look older and borrowed money for lunch and bus fare because Aunt Lala said I wouldn't get paid 'til the next Friday and I went in and saw the boss of the Peter Pan Photo Finishers on North Broadway where Aunt Lala worked and lied about my age like she told me to and sure enough I started that same day.

In my job I had to wear white gloves. I was supposed to match negatives with their prints, just look at the picture and look for the same one on the negative strip, put it in the envelope, and do the next one. That's all. I didn't know where these envelopes were coming from or where they were going. I just did what I was told.

It was real easy and I guess I wouldn't have minded it except that you got tired after a while and I didn't know if I could sit down or not, and then I started sitting down only when the two ladies next to me did. After a while they started to laugh and came up to me and said I could sit when I wanted to and I said I knew.

5   When lunch time came I was scared to eat alone in the company lunchroom with all those men and ladies looking, so I ate real fast standing in one of the washroom stalls and had lots of time left over so I went back to work early. But then break time came and not knowing where else to go I went into the coatroom because there was a bench there.

I guess it was time for the night shift or middle shift to arrive because a few people came in and punched the time clock and an older Oriental man said hello and we talked for a while about my just starting and he said we could be friends and next time to go in the lunchroom and sit with him and I felt better. He had nice eyes and I didn't feel so nervous anymore. Then he asked if I knew what day it was and when I said I didn't he said it was his

birthday and would I please give him a birthday kiss. I thought I would because he was so
old and just as I was about to put my lips on

his cheek, he grabs my face with both hands
and kisses me hard on the mouth and doesn't
let go.

SUGGESTIONS FOR DISCUSSION

1. Why does the narrator say, "It wasn't as if I didn't want to work"? How would you describe her motivations for getting a job, and how would you explain the situation in which she finds herself?

2. Compare the event that you wrote about before you read this story with the events that your classmates wrote about. Do they have anything in common with what the narrator experienced? How typical do you think an experience like hers is?

3. Why do you think the older man thought he could get away with his actions? Would anything comparable to this have happened to her had she been a young man?

SUGGESTIONS FOR WRITING

1. As a reader, you may understand or relate to stories because they touch upon something that you already have experienced or an emotion that you have felt. Cisneros's story about a young woman's first day on a new job describes a brief and confusing encounter with an adult world of which she had no prior knowledge. In an exploratory piece of writing, examine the narrator's response to this world of work and human interaction using your own experiences in the working world or in situations that seemed out of your control. Even if you have experienced nothing like this, you probably have a reaction to or an understanding of how the young woman in this story felt. Use this writing to explain that reaction and how you think it is evoked in the story.

2. Reread Cisneros and notice how abruptly Cisneros's story ends and especially how the attitude of the narrator shifts so suddenly in that last paragraph. Write an explanation of how that sudden shift changes the story. How does that ending affect the way that you understand what this story is about?

3. Tell a story about one of the first jobs you ever held (whether it was a paying job or just some new responsibility that you were asked to take on in the family, the community, your peer group, an organization, or for school or church). Try to convey what the job meant to you and how you did or didn't fit into this new world. Choose a moment that sticks with you because it seemed to represent your entire experience with the world of work or the world of adults. In preparation for this writing, spend some time listing jobs you did and jotting memories of people, places, and events connected to those jobs. Notice how Cisneros manages to tell a great deal about why she began working, about the workplace, and about the event that concludes this story in a short piece of writing. Before you begin composing your story, reread Cisneros to see how the form of her narrative might help you to plan your own.

ALABANZA: IN PRAISE OF LOCAL 100

— Martín Espada

Martín Espada is a poet, essayist, and translator. His collection *Alabanza: New and Selected Poems (1982–2002)*, from which we have taken the title poem, appeared in 2003. It was awarded the Paterson Award for Sustained Literary Achievement and was named an American Library Association Notable Book of the year. An earlier collection of Espada's work, *Imagine the Angels of Bread* (1996), won an American Book Award. *Rebellion Is the Circle of a Lover's Hands* (1990) received the Paterson Poetry Prize and a PEN/Revson Fellowship. Other awards include the Robert Creeley Award and two NEA Fellowships. His poems have appeared in the *New York Times Book Review, Harper's*, the *Nation*, and *The Best American Poetry*. Much of his writing arises from his Puerto Rican heritage and his work experiences, ranging from bouncer to tenant lawyer. He is also the editor of *Poetry Like Bread: Poets of the Political Imagination* from Curbstone Press. Espada is a professor in the Department of English at the University of Massachusetts, Amherst, where he teaches creative writing, Latino poetry, and the work of Pablo Neruda. Espada is also a lawyer who has acted as an advocate for the Latino community and for immigrants.

The word *alabanza* is Spanish for "praise" and comes from the Latin *alabar*, meaning "to celebrate with words." This poem is dedicated to the forty-three members of Local 100 of the Hotel Employees and Restaurant Employees union who were working in the Windows on the World restaurant that sat at the top of the World Trade Center and were killed when that building was attacked on September 11, 2001.

SUGGESTION FOR READING This poem functions, in part, as a eulogy to the restaurant workers who died in the World Trade Center. Before you read, look up the term *eulogy.*

For the 43 members of Hotel Employees and Restaurant Employees Local 100, working at the Windows on the World restaurant, who lost their lives in the attack on the World Trade Center

---

Alabanza. Praise the cook with a shaven head
and a tattoo on his shoulder that said Oye,
a blue-eyed Puerto Rican with people from
    Fajardo,
the harbor of pirates centuries ago.
Praise the lighthouse in Fajardo, candle
glimmering white to worship the dark saint of
    the sea.
Alabanza. Praise the cook's yellow Pirates cap
worn in the name of Roberto Clemente, his
    plane
that flamed into the ocean loaded with cans for
    Nicaragua,
for all the mouths chewing the ash of
    earthquakes

Alabanza. Praise the kitchen radio, dial clicked
even before the dial on the oven, so that music
    and Spanish
rose before bread. Praise the bread. *Alabanza*.

Praise Manhattan from a hundred and seven
    flights up,

like Atlantis glimpsed through the windows of
    an ancient aquarium.
Praise the great windows where immigrants
    from the kitchen
could squint and almost see their world, hear
    the chant of nations:
Ecuador, México, Republica Dominicana,
Haiti, Yemen, Ghana, Bangladesh.
Alabanza. Praise the kitchen in the morning,
where the gas burned blue on every stove
and exhaust fans fired their diminutive
    propellers,
hands cracked eggs with quick thumbs
or sliced open cartons to build an altar of cans.
Alabanza. Praise the busboy's music, the
    chime-chime
of his dishes and silverware in the tub.
Alabanza. Praise the dish-dog, the dishwasher
who worked that morning because another
    dishwasher
could not stop coughing, or because he needed
    overtime
to pile the sacks of rice and beans for a family
floating away on some Caribbean island
    plagued by frogs.

Alabanza. Praise the waitress who heard the
    radio in the kitchen

and sang to herself about a man gone.
    Alabanza.

After the thunder wilder than thunder,
after the shudder deep in the glass of the great
    windows,
after the radio stopped singing like a tree full of
    terrified frogs,
after night burst the dam of day and flooded
    the kitchen,
for a time the stoves glowed in darkness like
    the lighthouse in Fajardo,
like a cook's soul. Soul I say, even if the dead
    cannot tell us
about the bristles of God's beard because God
    has no face,

soul I say, to name the smoke-beings flung in
    constellations
across the night sky of this city and cities to
    come.
Alabanza I say, even if God has no face.

Alabanza. When the war began, from
    Manhattan and Kabul
two constellations of smoke rose and drifted to
    each other,
mingling in icy air, and one said with an
    Afghan tongue:
Teach me to dance. We have no music
    here.
And the other said with a Spanish tongue:
I will teach you. Music is all we have.

SUGGESTIONS FOR DISCUSSION

1. In what ways does this poem function as a eulogy, as you understand the term? In what ways does it function as a political statement about what kinds of work are valued in America and what kinds tend to be somewhat invisible?

2. With a group of your classmates, discuss what each stanza of this poem tells you about the people working in the World Trade Center restaurant.

3. Reread the final stanza of this poem. It might be clear that, in Kabul where a war has begun, workers would feel that there is no music—nothing beautiful. Why, though, would immigrant workers in the United States feel that the only thing they have is music?

SUGGESTIONS FOR WRITING

1. Paraphrase this poem so that someone who doesn't read much poetry would be able to understand what it is saying. A paraphrase is a rewriting of the original in your own words.

2. In an interview with PBS, Martín Espada spoke of one reason to call attention to the restaurant workers of Local 100: "when we think of these buildings, the WTC, these were, after all, office buildings in Manhattan. And a shadow army passes through every office building in Manhattan, making those buildings run and providing what we need. What could be more basic than food, than feeding us? That is what those food service workers were doing that very morning." For one day, keep a record of the hidden tasks, and the people who do them, that make your day the way it is. Your list might include food service workers, computer systems administrators, janitors and housekeepers, power plant workers, and more. You won't be able to list them all, but do your best. Then write an essay in which you explain how much of your daily life depends on a "hidden army" of workers.

3. This poem is about individuals who lost their lives in a terrible tragedy, but it is also about low-wage jobs that go primarily to immigrants in this country, many of whom speak little or no English and have connections to other countries and other cultures. Write an essay in which you examine how these workers are depicted in the poem. Who are they? What do they care about? What connects them to each other and to the world as a whole? How does the last stanza of the poem characterize them and their living and working situations?

THE DILBERT PRINCIPLE

— *Scott Adams*

Scott Adams received his MBA from the University of California at Berkeley and worked for several years in a cubicle in the offices of Pacific Bell in northern California before he quit to devote all his time to the Dilbert comic strip. The article included here originally appeared in the *Wall Street Journal* on May 22, 1995. It got a huge response, which led to the publication of Adams's book of the same title. In August 1996, *Newsweek* published a cover story on Adams and his newly published book, *The Dilbert Principle*, reporting that the comic character had moved "from cult status to mass phenomenon," as *The Dilbert Principle* moved to number one on the *New York Times* best-seller list shortly after it was published. Office workers all over the United States were clipping Dilbert strips because Dilbert's office life seemed so much like their own. That closeness to reality is partially due to the fact that Adams gets many of his ideas from readers who send him stories of their workplaces via e-mail.

SUGGESTION FOR READING When you read this piece, you may have to remind yourself that, though there is much in it that strikes office workers as real, its purpose is to be humorous. Some might call it serious humor, but it is humor nonetheless. Humor (especially satire) historically has been one way to comment on the shortcomings of modern society. Take note of what strikes you as funny but painfully true.

1 I use a lot of "bad boss" themes in my syndicated cartoon strip "Dilbert." I'll never run out of material. I get at least two hundred e-mail messages a day, mostly from people who are complaining about their own clueless managers. Here are some of my favorite stories, all allegedly true:

- A vice president insists that the company's new battery-powered product be equipped with a light that comes on to tell you when the power is off.

- An employee suggests setting priorities so the company will know how to apply its limited resources. The manager's response: "Why can't we concentrate our resources across the board?"

- A manager wants to find and fix software bugs more quickly. He offers an incentive plan: $20 for each bug the Quality Assurance people find and $20 for each bug the programmers fix. (These are the same programmers who create the bugs.) Result: An

underground economy in "bugs" springs up instantly. The plan is rethought after one employee nets $1,700 the first week.

Stories like these prompted me to do the first annual Dilbert Survey to find out what management practices were most annoying to employees. The choices included the usual suspects: Quality, Empowerment, Reengineering, and the like. But the number-one vote-getter in this highly unscientific survey was "Idiots Promoted to Management."

This seemed like a subtle change from the old concept by which capable workers were promoted until they reached their level of incompetence—best described as the "Peter Principle." Now, apparently, the incompetent workers are promoted directly to management without ever passing through the temporary competence stage.

When I entered the workforce in 1979, the Peter Principle described management pretty well. Now I think we'd all like to return to those Golden Years when you had a boss who was once good at something.

5   I get all nostalgic when I think about it. Back then, we all had hopes of being promoted beyond our levels of competence. Every worker had a shot at someday personally navigating the company into the tar pits while reaping large bonuses and stock options. It was a time when inflation meant everybody got an annual raise; a

time when we freely admitted that the customers didn't matter. It was a time of joy.

We didn't appreciate it then, but the much underrated Peter Principle always provided us with a boss who understood what we did for a living. Granted, he made consistently bad decisions—after all he had no management skills. But at least they were the informed decisions of a seasoned veteran from the trenches.

Example
   Boss: "When I had your job I could drive a three-inch rod through a metal casing with one motion. If you're late again I'll do the same thing to your head."

Nitpickers found lots of problems with the Peter Principle, but on the whole it worked. Lately, however, the Peter Principle has given way to the "Dilbert Principle." The basic concept of the Dilbert Principle is that the most ineffective workers are systematically moved to the place where they can do the least damage: management.

This has not proved to be the winning strategy that you might think.

Maybe we should learn something from nature. In the wild, the weakest moose is hunted down and killed by dingo dogs, thus ensuring survival of the fittest. This is a harsh system—especially for the dingo dogs who have to fly all the way from Australia. But nature's process is a good one; everybody agrees, except perhaps for the dingo dogs and the moose in question . . . and the flight attendants. But the point is that we'd all be better off if the least competent managers were being eaten by dingo dogs instead of writing Mission Statements.

10   It seems as if we've turned nature's rules upside down. We systematically identify and promote the people who have the least skills. The usual business rationalization for promoting idiots (the Dilbert Principle in a nutshell) is something along the lines of "Well, he can't write code, he can't design a network, and he doesn't have any sales skill. But he has very good hair . . . "

If nature started organizing itself like a modern business, you'd see, for example, a band of mountain gorillas led by an "alpha" squirrel. And it wouldn't be the most skilled squirrel; it would be the squirrel nobody wanted to hang around with.

I can see the other squirrels gathered around an old stump saying stuff like "If I hear him say, 'I like nuts' one more time, I'm going to kill him." The gorillas, overhearing this conversation, lumber down from the mist and promote the unpopular squirrel. The remaining squirrels are assigned to Quality Teams as punishment.

You may be wondering if you fit the description of a Dilbert Principle manager. Here's a little test:

1. Do you believe that anything you don't understand must be easy to do?

2. Do you feel the need to explain in great detail why "profit" is the difference between income and expense?

3. Do you think employees should schedule funerals only during holidays?

4. Are the following words a form of communication or gibberish:

   The Business Services Leadership Team will enhance the organization in order to continue on the journey toward a Market Facing Organization (MFO) model. To that end, we are consolidating the Object Management for Business Services into a cross strata team.

5. When people stare at you in disbelief do you repeat what you just said, only louder and more slowly?

Now give yourself one point for each question you answered with the letter "B." If your score is greater than zero, congratulations—there are stock options in your future.

15   (The language in question four is from an actual company memo.)

SUGGESTIONS FOR DISCUSSION

1. How would you explain the popularity of Dilbert? Does it appeal to people who have never done office work? Why? Why not?

2. Scott Adams gets many of his ideas from office workers who e-mail him real situations and real memos. With two or three of your classmates, make a list of absurdities from your own experience with bureaucracy that you would send to Adams.

3. Scott Adams's humor is much like the humor in Matt Groening (his Hell series) or Gary Larson's Far Side. Bring to class a comic strip that uses satire or dark humor to make you laugh. What is it about these strips that makes you laugh even when they make you cringe?

SUGGESTIONS FOR WRITING

1. In his introduction to *Working*, Studs Terkel writes that his book, as it is about work, "is, by its very nature, about violence—to the spirit as well as to the body. It is about ulcers as well as accidents, about shouting matches as well as fistfights. . . . To survive the day is triumph enough for the walking wounded among the great many of us." In the years

it took Terkel to assemble the stories of the men and women in his collection, he had reached the conclusion that the real drive of most workers was for a job that gave them "daily meaning as well as daily bread." No matter the work people do, they want to believe that it is for something more than the paycheck. That doesn't mean that the paycheck is inconsequential, but it does mean that it matters to most folks how they spend their time making that pay. Write an essay in which you explain how Dilbert addresses the question of what the workplace ought to be about as opposed to what it actually is about.

2. Write about a time when you found yourself caught up in the sort of bureaucracy that Scott Adams uses as the basis for his satire of the workplace—perhaps a situation where none of the employees quite knew what the job they were assigned was supposed to be. How did you handle it? In what ways was it typical of that workplace or that organization?

3. In a *Newsweek* cover story on *The Dilbert Principle*, *Newsweek* reporters write of "the suppressed rage of workers who tolerate abuses and absurdities in a marketplace leaned-and-meaned to Wall Street's specifications. Reading Dilbert allows them, in some small way, to strike back, or at least to experience a pleasant catharsis by identifying the nature of the beast: a general yet pervasive sense of idiocy in corporate America that is seldom dealt with by the captains of industry who have great hair and offices with doors." Write an essay in which you offer a possible explanation for how reading Dilbert helps abused workers strike back or how humor, graffiti, or any underground type of activity can help people in what seems like a repressive system feel as if they have some control.

NICKEL-AND-DIMED: ON (NOT) GETTING BY IN AMERICA

— *Barbara Ehrenreich*

Barbara Ehrenreich is a contributing editor of *Harper's Magazine*, a regular contributor to the *Nation*, and the author of a dozen books, including *Fear of Falling: The Inner Life of the Middle Class* (1989), which was nominated for a National Book Critics Award. The following excerpts, taken from a longer essay detailing Ehrenreich's experiment living the life of a minimum-wage laborer, originally appeared in *Harper's* (January 1999) and appeared as a book-length study under the same title in 2001.

SUGGESTION FOR READING Throughout her narrative, Ehrenreich uses figures from such sources as the Department of Housing and Urban Development, the Economic Policy Institute, and the National Coalition for the Homeless to support her discussion of how difficult it is for anyone to live on the wages paid in most service jobs. It will help you keep track of Ehrenreich's argument if you keep those reports in mind as you read.

1 At the beginning of June 1998 I leave behind everything that normally soothes the ego and sustains the body—home, career, companion, reputation, ATM card—for a plunge into the low-wage workforce. There, I become another, occupationally much diminished "Barbara Ehrenreich"—depicted on job-application forms as a divorced homemaker whose sole work experience consists of housekeeping in a few private homes. I am terrified, at the beginning, of

being unmasked for what I am: a middle-class journalist setting out to explore the world that welfare mothers are entering, at the rate of approximately 50,000 a month, as welfare reform kicks in. Happily, though, my fears turn out to be entirely unwarranted: during a month of poverty and toil, my name goes unnoticed and for the most part unuttered. In this parallel universe where my father never got out of the mines and I never got through college, I am "baby," "honey," "blondie," and, most commonly, "girl."

My first task is to find a place to live. I figure that if I can earn $7 an hour—which, from the want ads, seems doable—I can afford to spend $500 on rent, or maybe, with severe economies, $600. In the Key West area, where I live, this pretty much confines me to flophouses and trailer homes—like the one, a pleasing fifteen-minute drive from town, that has no air-conditioning, no screens, no fans, no television, and, by way of diversion, only the challenge of evading the landlord's Doberman pinscher. The big problem with this place, though, is the rent, which at $675 a month is well beyond my reach. All right, Key West is expensive. But so is New York City, or the Bay Area, or Jackson Hole, or Telluride, or Boston, or any other place where tourists and the wealthy compete for living space with the people who clean their toilets and fry their hash browns.[1] Still, it is a shock to realize that "trailer trash" has become, for me, a demographic category to aspire to.

So I decide to make the common trade-off between affordability and convenience, and go for a $500-a-month efficiency thirty miles up a two-lane highway from the employment opportunities of Key West, meaning forty-five minutes if there's no road construction and I don't get caught behind some sun-dazed Canadian tourists. I hate the drive, along a roadside studded with white crosses commemorating the more effective head-on collisions, but it's a sweet little place—a cabin, more or less, set in the swampy back yard of the converted mobile home where my landlord, an affable TV repairman, lives with his bartender girlfriend.

Anthropologically speaking, a bustling trailer park would be preferable, but here I have a gleaming white floor and a firm mattress, and the few resident bugs are easily vanquished.

Besides, I am not doing this for the anthropology. My aim is nothing so mistily subjective as to "experience poverty" or find out how it "really feels" to be a long-term low-wage worker. I've had enough unchosen encounters with poverty and the world of low-wage work to know it's not a place you want to visit for touristic purposes; it just smells too much like fear. And with all my real-life assets—bank account, IRA, health insurance, multiroom home—waiting indulgently in the background, I am, of course, thoroughly insulated from the terrors that afflict the genuinely poor.

5   No, this is a purely objective, scientific sort of mission. The humanitarian rationale for welfare reform—as opposed to the more punitive and stingy impulses that may actually have motivated it—is that work will lift poor women out of poverty while simultaneously inflating their self-esteem and hence their future value in the labor market. Thus, whatever the hassles involved in finding child care, transportation, etc., the transition from welfare to work will end happily, in greater prosperity for all. Now there are many problems with this comforting prediction, such as the fact that the economy will inevitably undergo a downturn, eliminating many jobs. Even without a downturn, the influx of a million former welfare recipients into the low-wage labor market could depress wages by as much as 11.9 percent, according to the Economic Policy Institute (EPI) in Washington, D.C.

But is it really possible to make a living on the kinds of jobs currently available to unskilled people? Mathematically, the answer is no, as can be shown by taking $6 to $7 an hour, perhaps subtracting a dollar or two an hour for child care, multiplying by 160 hours a month, and comparing the result to the prevailing rents. According to the National Coalition for the Homeless, for example, in 1998 it took, on average nationwide, an hourly wage of $8.89 to afford a one-bedroom apartment, and the Preamble Center for Public Policy estimates that the odds against a typical welfare recipient's landing a job at such a "living wage" are about 97 to 1. If these numbers are right, low-wage work is not a solution to poverty and possibly not even to homelessness.

It may seem excessive to put this proposition to an experimental test. As certain family members keep unhelpfully reminding me, the viability of low-wage work could be tested, after a fashion, without ever leaving my study. I could just pay myself $7 an hour for eight hours a day, charge myself for room and board, and total up the numbers after a month. Why leave the people and work that I love? But I am an experimental scientist by training. In that business, you don't just sit at a desk and theorize; you plunge into the everyday chaos of nature, where surprises lurk in the most mundane measurements. Maybe, when I got into it, I would discover some hidden economies in the world of the low-wage worker. After all, if 30 percent of the workforce toils for less than $8 an hour, according to the EPI, they may have found some tricks as yet unknown to me. Maybe—who knows?—I would even be able to detect in myself the bracing psychological effects of getting out of the house, as promised by the welfare wonks at places like the Heritage Foundation. Or, on the other hand, maybe there would be unexpected costs—physical, mental, or financial—to throw off all my calculations. Ideally, I should do this with two small children in tow, that being the welfare average, but mine are grown and no one is willing to lend me theirs for a month-long vacation in penury. So this is not the perfect experiment, just a test of the best possible case: an unencumbered woman, smart and even strong, attempting to live more or less off the land.

On the morning of my first full day of job searching, I take a red pen to the want ads, which are auspiciously numerous. Everyone in Key West's booming "hospitality industry" seems to be looking for someone like me—trainable, flexible, and with suitably humble expectations as to pay. I know I possess certain traits that might be advantageous—I'm white and, I like to think, well-spoken and poised—but I decide on two rules: One, I cannot use any skills derived from my education or usual work—not that there are a lot of want ads for satirical essayists anyway. Two, I have to take the best-paid job that is offered me and of course do my best to hold it; no Marxist rants or sneaking off to read novels in the ladies' room. In addition, I rule out various occupations for one reason or another: Hotel front-desk clerk, for example, which to my surprise is regarded as unskilled and pays around $7 an hour, gets eliminated because it involves standing in one spot for eight hours a day. Waitressing is similarly something I'd like to avoid, because I remember it leaving me bone tired when I was eighteen, and I'm decades of varicosities and back pain beyond that now. Telemarketing, one of the first refuges of the suddenly indigent, can be dismissed on grounds of personality. This leaves certain supermarket jobs, such as deli clerk, or housekeeping in Key West's thousands of hotel and guest rooms. Housekeeping is especially appealing, for reasons both atavistic and practical: it's what my mother did before I came along, and it can't be too different from what I've been doing part-time, in my own home, all my life.

So I put on what I take to be a respectful-looking outfit of ironed Bermuda shorts and scooped-neck T-shirt and set out for a tour of the local hotels and supermarkets. Best Western, Econo Lodge, and Ho Jo's all let me fill out application forms, and these are, to my relief, interested in little more than whether I am a legal resident of the United States and have committed any felonies. My next stop is Winn-Dixie, the supermarket, which turns out to have a particularly onerous application process, featuring a fifteen-minute "interview" by computer since, apparently, no human on the premises is deemed capable of representing the corporate point of view. I am conducted to a large room decorated with posters illustrating how to look "professional" (it helps to be white and, if female, permed) and warning of the slick promises that union organizers might try to tempt me with. The interview is multiple choice: Do I have anything, such as child-care problems, that might make it hard for me to get to work on time? Do I think safety on the job is the responsibility of management? Then, popping up cunningly out of the blue: How many dollars' worth of stolen goods have I purchased in the last year? Would I turn in a fellow employee if I caught him stealing? Finally, "Are you an honest person?"

10   Apparently, I ace the interview, because I am told that all I have to do is show up in some doctor's office tomorrow for a urine test. This seems to be a fairly general rule: if you want to stack Cheerio boxes or vacuum hotel rooms in chemically fascist America, you have to be willing to squat down and pee in front of some health worker (who has no doubt had to do the same thing herself). The wages Winn-Dixie is offering—$6 and a couple of dimes to start with—are not enough, I decide, to compensate for this indignity.[2]

I lunch at Wendy's, where $4.99 gets you unlimited refills at the Mexican part of the Superbar, a comforting surfeit of refried beans and "cheese sauce." A teenage employee, seeing me studying the want ads, kindly offers me an application form, which I fill out, though here, too, the pay is just $6 and change an hour. Then it's off for a round of the locally owned inns and guesthouses. At "The Palms," let's call it, a bouncy manager actually takes me around to see the rooms and meet the existing housekeepers, who, I note with satisfaction, look pretty much like me—faded ex-hippie types in shorts with long hair pulled back in braids. Mostly, though, no one speaks to me or even looks at me except to proffer an application form. At my last stop, a palatial B&B, I wait twenty minutes to meet "Max," only to be told that there are no jobs now but there should be one soon, since "nobody lasts more than a couple of weeks." (Because none of the people I talked to knew I was a reporter, I have changed their names to protect their privacy and, in some cases perhaps, their jobs.)

Three days go by like this, and, to my chagrin, no one out of the approximately twenty places I've applied calls me for an interview. I had been vain enough to worry about coming across as too educated for the jobs I sought, but no one even seems interested in finding out how overqualified I am. Only later will I realize that the want ads are not a reliable measure of the actual jobs available at any particular time. They are, as I should have guessed from Max's comment, the employers' insurance policy against the relentless turnover of the low-wage workforce. Most of the big hotels run ads almost continually, just to build a supply of applicants to replace the current workers as they drift away or are fired, so finding a job is just a matter of being at the right place at the right time and flexible enough to take whatever is being offered that day. This finally happens to me at one of the big discount hotel chains, where I go, as usual, for housekeeping and am sent, instead, to try out as a waitress at the attached "family restaurant," a dismal spot with a counter and about thirty tables that looks out on a parking garage and features such tempting fare as "Pollish [sic] sausage and BBQ sauce" on 95-degree days. Philip, the dapper young West Indian who introduces himself as the manager, interviews me with about as much enthusiasm as if he were a clerk processing me for Medicare, the principal questions being what shifts can I work and when can I start. I mutter something about being woefully out of practice as a waitress, but he's already on to the uniform: I'm to show up tomorrow wearing black slacks and black shoes; he'll provide the rust-colored polo shirt with HEARTHSIDE embroidered on it, though I might want to wear my own shirt to get to work, ha ha. At the word "tomorrow," something between fear and indignation rises in my chest. I want to say, "Thank you for your time, sir, but this is just an experiment, you know, not my actual life."

So begins my career at the Hearthside, I shall call it, one small profit center within a global discount hotel chain, where for two weeks

I work from 2:00 till 10:00 P.M. for $2.43 an hour plus tips.[3] In some futile bid for gentility, the management has barred employees from using the front door, so my first day I enter through the kitchen, where a red-faced man with shoulder-length blond hair is throwing frozen steaks against the wall and yelling, "Fuck this shit!" "That's just Jack," explains Gail, the wiry middle-aged waitress who is assigned to train me. "He's on the rag again"—a condition occasioned, in this instance, by the fact that the cook on the morning shift had forgotten to thaw out the steaks. For the next eight hours, I run after the agile Gail, absorbing bits of instruction along with fragments of personal tragedy. All food must be trayed, and the reason she's so tired today is that she woke up in a cold sweat thinking of her boyfriend, who killed himself recently in an upstate prison. No refills on lemonade. And the reason he was in prison is that a few DUIs caught up with him, that's all, could have happened to anyone. Carry the creamers to the table in a monkey bowl, never in your hand. And after he was gone she spent several months living in her truck, peeing in a plastic pee bottle and reading by candlelight at night, but you can't live in a truck in the summer, since you need to have the windows down, which means anything can get in, from mosquitoes on up.

At least Gail put to rest any fears I had of appearing overqualified. From the first day on, I find that of all the things I have left behind, such as home and identity, what I miss the most is competence. Not that I have ever felt utterly competent in the writing business, in which one day's success augurs nothing at all for the next. But in my writing life, I at least have some notion of procedure: do the research, make the outline, rough out a draft, etc. As a server, though, I am beset by requests like bees: more iced tea here, ketchup over there, a to-go box for table fourteen, and where are the high chairs, anyway? Of the twenty-seven tables, up to six are usually mine at any time, though on slow afternoons or if Gail is off, I sometimes have the whole place to

myself. There is the touch-screen computer-ordering system to master, which is, I suppose, meant to minimize server-cook contact, but in practice requires constant verbal fine-tuning: "That's gravy on the mashed, okay? None on the meatloaf," and so forth—while the cook scowls as if I were inventing these refinements just to torment him. Plus, something I had forgotten in the years since I was eighteen: about a third of a server's job is "side work" that's invisible to customers—sweeping, scrubbing, slicing, refilling, and restocking. If it isn't all done, every little bit of it, you're going to face the 6:00 P.M. dinner rush defenseless and probably go down in flames. I screw up dozens of times at the beginning, sustained in my shame entirely by Gail's support—"It's okay, baby, everyone does that sometime"—because, to my total surprise and despite the scientific detachment I am doing my best to maintain, I care.

15   You might imagine, from a comfortable distance, that people who live, year in and year out, on $6 to $10 an hour have discovered some survival stratagems unknown to the middle class. But no. It's not hard to get my co-workers to talk about their living situations, because housing, in almost every case, is the principal source of disruption in their lives, the first thing they fill you in on when they arrive for their shifts. After a week, I have compiled the following survey:

■ Gail is sharing a room in a well-known downtown flophouse for which she and a roommate pay about $250 a week. Her roommate, a male friend, has begun hitting on her, driving her nuts, but the rent would be impossible alone.

■ Claude, the Haitian cook, is desperate to get out of the two-room apartment he shares with his girlfriend and two other, unrelated, people. As far as I can determine, the other Haitian men (most of whom only speak Creole) live in similarly crowded situations.

■ Annette, a twenty-year-old server who is six months pregnant and has been abandoned by her boyfriend, lives with her mother, a postal clerk.

- Marianne and her boyfriend are paying $170 a week for a one-person trailer.

- Jack, who is, at $10 an hour, the wealthiest of us, lives in the trailer he owns, paying only the $400-a-month lot fee.

- The other white cook, Andy, lives on his dry-docked boat, which, as far as I can tell from his loving descriptions, can't be more than twenty feet long. He offers to take me out on it, once it's repaired, but the offer comes with inquiries as to my marital status, so I do not follow up on it.

- Tina and her husband are paying $60 a night for a double room in a Days Inn. This is because they have no car and the Days Inn is within walking distance of the Hearthside. When Marianne, one of the breakfast servers, is tossed out of her trailer for subletting (which is against the trailer-park rules), she leaves her boyfriend and moves in with Tina and her husband.

- Joan, who had fooled me with her numerous and tasteful outfits (hostesses wear their own clothes), lives in a van she parks behind a shopping center at night and showers in Tina's motel room. The clothes are from thrift shops.[4]

When I moved out of the trailer park, I gave the key to number 46 to Gail and arranged for my deposit to be transferred to her. She told me that Joan is still living in her van and that Stu had been fired from the Hearthside. I never found out what happened to George.

In one month, I had earned approximately $1,040 and spent $517 on food, gas, toiletries, laundry, phone, and utilities. If I had remained in my $500 efficiency, I would have been able to pay the rent and have $22 left over (which is $78 less than the cash I had in my pocket at the start of one month). During this time I bought no clothing except for the required slacks and no prescription drugs or medical care (I did finally buy some vitamin B to compensate for the lack

of vegetables in my diet). Perhaps I could have saved a little on food if I had gotten to a super-market more often, instead of convenience stores, but it should be noted that I lost almost four pounds in four weeks, on a diet weighted heavily toward burgers and fries.

How former welfare recipients and single mothers will (and do) survive in the low-wage workforce, I cannot imagine. Maybe they will figure out how to condense their lives—including child-raising, laundry, romance, and meals—into the couple of hours between full-time jobs. Maybe they will take up residence in their vehicles, if they have one. All I know is that I couldn't hold two jobs and I couldn't make enough money to live on with one. And I had advantages unthinkable to many of the long-term poor—health, stamina, a working car, and no children to care for and support. Certainly nothing in my experience contradicts the conclusion of Kathryn Edin and Laura Lein, in their recent book *Making Ends Meet: How Single Mothers Survive Welfare and Low-Wage Work*, that low-wage work actually involves more hardship and deprivation than life at the mercy of the welfare state. In the coming months and years, economic conditions for the working poor are bound to worsen, even without the almost inevitable recession. As mentioned earlier, the influx of former welfare recipients into the low-skilled workforce will have a depressing effect on both wages and the number of jobs available. A general economic downturn will only enhance these effects, and the working poor will of course be facing it without the slight, but nonetheless often saving, protection of welfare as a backup.

The thinking behind welfare reform was that even the humblest jobs are morally uplifting and psychologically buoying. In reality they are likely to be fraught with insult and stress. But I did discover one redeeming feature of the most abject low-wage work—the camaraderie of people who are, in almost all cases, far too smart and funny and caring for the work they do and the wages they're paid. The hope, of course, is that someday these people will come to know what they're worth, and take appropriate action.

NOTES

1. According to the Department of Housing and Urban Development, the "fair-market rent" for an efficiency is $551 here in Monroe County, Florida. A comparable rent in the five boroughs of New York City is $704; in San Francisco, $713; and in the heart of Silicon Valley, $808. The fair-market rent for an area is defined as the amount that would be needed to pay rent plus utilities for "privately owned, decent, safe, and sanitary rental housing of a modest (non-luxury) nature with suitable amenities."

2. According to the *Monthly Labor Review* (November 1996), 28 percent of work sites surveyed in the service industry conduct drug tests (corporate workplaces have much higher rates), and the incidence of testing has risen markedly since the Eighties. The rate of testing is highest in the South (56 percent of work sites polled), with the Midwest in second place (50 percent). The drug most likely to be detected—marijuana, which can be detected in urine for weeks—is also the most innocuous, while heroin and cocaine are generally undetectable three days after use. Prospective employees sometimes try to cheat the tests by consuming excessive amounts of liquids and taking diuretics and even masking substances available through the Internet.

3. According to the Fair Labor Standards Act, employers are not required to pay "tipped employees," such as restaurant servers, more than $2.13 an hour in direct wages. However, if the sum of tips plus $2.13 an hour falls below the minimum wage, or $5.15 an hour, the employer is required to make up the difference. This fact was not mentioned by managers or otherwise publicized at either of the restaurants where I worked.

4. I could find no statistics on the number of employed people living in cars or vans, but according to the National Coalition for the Homeless's 1997 report, "Myths and Facts About Homelessness," nearly one in five homeless people (in twenty-nine cities across the nation) is employed in a full- or part-time job.

SUGGESTIONS FOR DISCUSSION

1. Ehrenreich tells the story of her own experience and of the lives of people she encountered during her experiment. She also makes an argument using both her story and the studies and reports she cites. With a group of your classmates, summarize Ehrenreich's argument. What in the argument depends on her stories of individuals and what depends on the broader reports and studies?

2. Recently one fast-food chain ran advertisements that depicted jobs at its restaurants as "starter jobs." In these commercials, employees are shown making shakes, handing food out the drive-up window, or ringing up an order while the voice-over says that one is a future aerospace engineer, and another is a future CEO of a multimillion-dollar corporation. Why might a successful fast-food chain bother to make what is clearly an image-building advertisement? Why focus on the future of its employees?

3. How does Ehrenreich's discussion of the workplace touch on the descriptions of work in Dilbert's world?

SUGGESTIONS FOR WRITING

1. Make a list of service-sector jobs you are familiar with—because you have held them or have frequented a business that depends on them (fast-food restaurants, motels, bars, for example). Write an essay in which you examine to what extent Ehrenreich's experience working in the service sector rings true for you. How does your own experience (or lack of experience) with these kinds of jobs influence your reading?

2. Ehrenreich writes that she does not expect to "experience poverty" because she is aware that she can always go back to her middle-class lifestyle when things get tough or when she tires of this life. In addition, she admits that friends have pointed out that if she just wants to prove that it is extremely difficult to live on minimum-wage work, she can do

that easily enough on paper. Given that Ehrenreich knows she does not have to do the experiment, write an assessment of what she accomplished by posing as an out-of-work, down-on-her-luck single woman.

3. Throughout this chapter, several of the writers have suggested that work has to be about more than just bringing home a paycheck. Ehrenreich's experience trying to live on low pay for long hours suggests that the pay takes priority when there is so little of it. Write an essay in which you consider the conditions that must be in place for a job to mean more than the paycheck. Whether the paycheck is large or small might not be the most important element for some workers.

WIRED CULTURE   Business in Bangalore

According to a Reuters report, December 2004 marked the first time in thirty years that the median salary for an electrical engineer in the United States dropped. That report cited the recent practice of "offshoring" high-skill technology jobs to take advantage of the lower wages in overseas markets. In the articles that follow, Thomas L. Friedman and David Moberg explore the implications of offshoring made possible by advances in high-speed digital technology.

THE GREAT INDIAN DREAM

— Thomas L. Friedman

Thomas L. Friedman is a columnist for the *New York Times*. In that position he has won three Pulitzer Prizes for commentary. He is the author of *From Beirut to Jerusalem* (1989), which won the National Book Award for nonfiction, and *The Lexus and the Olive Tree* (2000), which won an Overseas Press Club award. His latest book, *The World Is Flat: A Brief History of the Twenty-first Century* (2005), argues that globalization and the digital revolution have essentially leveled the playing field so that developing nations now can compete successfully in the global market and even change the balance of economic power. "The Great Indian Dream" first appeared in Friedman's *New York Times* column on March 11, 2004. In it, Friedman credits the free market, globalization, and the digital revolution for changing the economic outlook of places like Bangalore, India.

SUGGESTION FOR READING   In this column, Friedman argues that Bangalore's recent success in the marketplace can be traced to good timing, hard work, talent, and luck. Highlight/underline and annotate those places in the column where he explains that argument.

1 Nine years ago, as Japan was beating America's brains out in the auto industry, I wrote a column about playing a computer geography game with my daughter, then 9 years old. I was trying to help her with a clue that clearly pointed to Detroit, so I asked her, "Where are cars made?" And she answered, "Japan." Ouch.

Well, I was reminded of that story while visiting an Indian software design firm in Bangalore, Global Edge. The company's marketing manager, Rajesh Rao, told me he had just made a cold call to the vice president for engineering of a U.S. company, trying to drum up business. As soon as Mr. Rao introduced himself as calling from an Indian software firm, the U.S. executive said to him, "Namaste"—a common Hindi greeting. Said Mr. Rao: "A few years ago nobody in America wanted to talk to us. Now they are eager." And a few even know how to say hi in proper Hindu fashion. So now I wonder: if I have a granddaughter one day; and I tell her I'm going to India, will she say, "Grandpa, is that where software comes from?"

Driving around Bangalore you might think so. The Pizza Hut billboard shows a steaming pizza under the headline "Gigabites of Taste!" Some traffic signs are sponsored by Texas Instruments. And when you tee off on the first hole at Bangalore's KGA golf course, your playing partner points at two new glass-and-steel buildings in the distance and says: "Aim at either Microsoft or I.B.M."

How did India, in 15 years, go from being a synonym for massive poverty to the brainy country that is going to take all our best jobs? Answer: good timing, hard work, talent and luck.

5   The good timing starts with India's decision in 1991 to shuck off decades of socialism and move toward a free-market economy with a focus on foreign trade. This made it possible for Indians who wanted to succeed at innovation to stay at home, not go to the West. This, in turn, enabled India to harvest a lot of its natural assets for the age of globalization.

One such asset was Indian culture's strong emphasis on education and the widely held belief here that the greatest thing any son or daughter could do was to become a doctor or an engineer, which created a huge pool of potential software technicians. Second, by accident of history and the British occupation of India, most of those engineers were educated in English and could easily communicate with Silicon Valley. India was also neatly on the other side of the world from America, so U.S.

designers could work during the day and e-mail their output to their Indian subcontractors in the evening. The Indians would then work on it for all of their day and e-mail it back. Presto: the 24-hour workday.

Also, this was the age of globalization, and the countries that succeed best at globalization are those that are best at "glocalization"—taking the best global innovations, styles and practices and melding them with their own culture, so they don't feel overwhelmed. India has been naturally glocalizing for thousands of years.

Then add some luck. The dot-com bubble led to a huge overinvestment in undersea fiber-optic cables, which made it dirt-cheap to transfer data, projects or phone calls to far-flung places like India, where Indian techies could work on them for much lower wages than U.S. workers. Finally, there was Y2K. So many companies feared that their computers would melt down because of the Year 2000 glitch they needed software programmers to go through and recode them. Who had large numbers of programmers to do that cheaply? India. That was how a lot of Indian software firms got their first outsourced jobs.

So if you are worried about outsourcing, I've got good news and bad news. The good news is that a unique techno-cultural-economic perfect storm came together in the early 1990's to make India a formidable competitor and partner for certain U.S. jobs—and there are not a lot of other Indias out there. The bad news, from a competition point of view, is that there are 555 million Indians under the age of 25, and a lot of them want a piece of "The Great Indian Dream," which is a lot like the American version.

10   As one Indian exec put it to me: The Americans' self-image that this tech thing was their private preserve is over. This is a wake-up call for U.S. workers to redouble their efforts at education and research. If they do that, he said, it will spur "a whole new cycle of innovation, and we'll both win. If we each pull down our shutters, we will both lose."

SUGGESTIONS FOR DISCUSSION

1. Friedman argues that part of India's success is due to "glocalization." From what you have read here, what is "glocalization"? How has India been "naturally glocalizing for years," as Friedman claims?

2. Friedman opens with an anecdote about his daughter, who had identified Japan rather than Detroit as the place where cars are made. He ends by asking if his granddaughter will one day identify India as "where software comes from." What is Friedman's attitude toward this shift in economic power and identification? What in the article indicates that attitude?

3. In what ways is Friedman's column a warning that "The Great Indian Dream" looks a lot like the Great American Dream? Why might that be a problem for the United States?

HIGH-TECH HIJACK: CORPORATIONS RAMP UP OFFSHORING OF IT SERVICE JOBS

David Moberg

David Moberg is a senior editor for *In These Times*, where he has been on staff since 1976, covering the labor movement. In 2003, Moberg received the Max Steinbock Award from the International Labor Communications Association and, in 1993, a Project Censored Award for his coverage of labor issues. His writing has also appeared in the *Nation*, the *New York Times*, the *Chicago Tribune*, and the *Boston Globe* and many other national publications. "High-tech Hijack" appeared in the January 2005 issue of *In These Times*.

SUGGESTION FOR READING   As you read, keep in mind how Friedman interprets the phenomenon of offshoring in the previous reading. Note in the margins where Friedman and Moberg share similar concerns on this issue. Where do they depart?

1 Stephen Gentry had worked as a programmer for Boeing for 15 years before he was laid off in July 2003. His last project was training his replacements, software engineers from India. They were working in Seattle on temporary visas before returning home to do Gentry's job at Infosys, one of India's leading subcontractors of information technology (IT) services.

Eighteen months later, Gentry, 52, who earned a computer sciences degree while working as a construction worker, still hasn't found a job. "American corporations," he says, "are so greedy and cutthroat-oriented they don't care about me, you or anybody else except their bottom line."

Gentry is not alone. The offshoring of work once done by Americans is growing rapidly. Over the past few years, corporations have shifted roughly a half million business service and IT jobs, many highly skilled, to developing countries. This has kept high-tech unemployment up, driven down wages, sparked widespread job anxieties, depressed support for free trade and generated a political backlash.

Elite apologists for globalization had long assured workers that they had a secure future with a college degree and a service job, especially anything computer-related. Now fewer Americans share the blind faith that the market will supply new and better jobs, as corporations cut costs by sending work—ranging from customer services to reading X-rays—to countries like India, where wages are often one-tenth the level in the United States.

5   Nobody knows precisely how many high-tech service jobs have been moved offshore. The number is still much less than the number of manufacturing jobs moved overseas, but future prospects are grim. Multinational companies are speeding up plans either to outsource more jobs to overseas contractors—including both U.S. multinationals and fast-growing foreign firms like Infosys—or to set up their own offshore service operations. IDC, a private IT research firm, predicts that IT offshoring will increase by more than 500 percent by 2007, and, according to the company's senior vice president for research, Frank Gens, China—now moving into services—"represents a wild card that could well accelerate the U.S. offshoring trend." Forrester Research predicts 3.3 million service jobs—a third of them in the highest-paying fifth of the job market—will go overseas by 2015. And a University of California Berkeley study estimates that that 14 million service jobs are vulnerable.

"If you work behind a computer screen, your job is up for grabs," says Sanjay Kumar, former CEO of Computer Associates, a leading management software company.

END OF THE LINE

Offshoring service work is the latest chapter in the history of capitalist reorganization of work. Early capitalists subdivided and routinized tasks so they could be performed by less-skilled—and lower-paid—workers. With digitization of information and standardization of software, the strategies behind dividing the manufacture of widgets can be applied to bytes of information relating to insurance claims, financial accounting, tax preparation, and hundreds of other tasks.

This new division of work meshes with two other growing trends: first, outsourcing, or subcontracting, of tasks to other companies, including even core tasks like manufacturing and design of products and, second, the shift of production overseas. Manufacturing was the first to go global, but with the expansion of high-speed Internet links and plummeting international telecommunication costs, the stage was set for offshoring services.

Multinational service corporations had long expected to globalize, mainly by setting up foreign branches to provide services. A few, like General Electric and American Express, began using technical and service workers in low-wage countries to cut costs for their own global operations or, later, to provide services for other companies. Now a wide range of multinationals can digitally fragment their work, outsourcing to many different worldwide suppliers in a search for the lowest cost. Consultants—many with a financial stake in outsourcing services—promoted offshoring as the wave of the future.

10   Over the past decade, companies in developing countries have become major offshoring players as well. Indian software companies in particular expanded by taking advantage of tens of thousands of English-speaking Indian engineers, who had worked in the United States on temporary visas, to develop a skilled workforce and knowledge of American business. Their reputation for good, cheap work was boosted by the surge of contracts to fix Y2K software problems. Meanwhile, Indian universities have been churning out thousands of graduates, and the government relaxed controls on foreign businesses and service exporters.

WINNERS AND LOSERS

Offshoring services hasn't always been as smooth or as cheap as promised, but companies have prospered. An Institute for Policy Studies/United for a Fair Economy study found that executive pay for the 50 largest outsourcers of service jobs increased dramatically in 2003 to 28 percent above the average for large-company CEOs.

But will offshoring be good for everyone else? Here's the pro-offshoring argument: Businesses that offshore jobs will save money, cut prices, expand sales, make more profit and then reinvest in new, high value-added, high-skilled jobs—if only redundant workers will just retrain themselves. But that scenario has its skeptics. Marcus Courtney, president of WashTech, an IT local of the Communications Workers, asks, "Everybody assumes they'll reinvest here, but why wouldn't they reinvest where it's cheaper?" Indeed, Philip Mattera of the Corporate Research Project reports that venture capitalists now ask IT start-up companies to present their offshoring strategy.

High-level American IT jobs are still growing. However, overall IT employment declined in recent years even after corporate IT spending rebounded. The threat of offshoring has also depressed IT wages, and college IT enrollment is dropping. Meanwhile, offshore firms are moving higher up the services skill ladder.

SILICON CEILING

Most new U.S. jobs, according to the Economic Policy Institute (EPI), are not steps up: they pay 21 percent less on average than job-losing industries. Six of the 10 occupations that the Bureau of Labor Statistics forecasts will provide the largest number of new jobs through 2012 require no college education and typically pay low wages. Foreign investment—contrary to hype about "insourcing" of jobs to the United States—is no solution. Foreign investors have mainly acquired existing U.S. companies, according to EPI, resulting in a net loss of jobs and a rising trade deficit, while generating a measly 25,000 jobs a year from new enterprises. And stirring up a hornet's nest among economists, Nobel Prize winner Paul Samuelson last summer pointed out that the U.S. economy could end up losing, not winning, from expanded free trade if low-wage foreign competitors drive down the price of products where the United States theoretically has a comparative advantage. That seems increasingly possible.

WHAT'S THE SOLUTION?

15 In the short run, legislation has been introduced at the state and federal level to restrict outsourcing of public jobs, tighten tech visa controls, increase disclosure of offshoring, ensure privacy of information and otherwise regulate offshoring of services. But such legislation, while useful, would have limited effect. Meanwhile, two Indian union leaders recently toured the United States, advocating transnational labor action to raise labor standards in India—call centers can be oppressive operations—and slow offshoring. But tech and business service workers are largely unorganized in both countries.

The U.S. government could spur new job creation by increasing scientific research funding (which Bush is cutting) and linking corporate use of federal research to investment in the United States. It could also expand trade adjustment to cover now-excluded service workers and provide all displaced workers more comprehensive education (which Bush opposes).

In the long run, however, workers and communities must win a greater voice in corporate strategic decisions through federal reform of corporate governance, shifting of more of the financial burden from displaced workers and their communities to corporations, collective bargaining and putting pressure on pension funds. Pension funds and corporate reformers should also try to reduce Wall Street's focus on short-run profits. And any national economic benefits from globalization must be shared with everyone—such as through universal health care, improved pensions and higher service sector wages—not hoarded by a tiny elite.

The crisis looming from the massive offshoring of the service industry may make these currently utopian notions politically feasible—and a matter of practical national survival.

SUGGESTIONS FOR DISCUSSION

1. Notice that Friedman tells this story from the point of view of Bangalore's gain. Moberg tells it from the point of view of American workers. How does this change the way you read the story of globalization in the digital revolution?

2. Low-tech jobs have been outsourced for many years now. Is high-tech, high-skill job out-sourcing (offshoring) more serious? Why?

3. Where in Moberg's article does he seem to be saying much the same thing Friedman is saying? In what ways do they part company on this issue of offshoring?

SUGGESTIONS FOR WRITING

1. Write a synthesis of the arguments in Friedman's and Moberg's articles. In your synthesis, make sure you lay out the basic arguments, note where the two seem to have common ground, and point out where the two depart. What, in the end, is the issue at stake in this discussion?

2. Write an analysis of the two articles in which you examine how the discussion changes depending on whose point of view you write from. Friedman clearly writes from the point of view of the corporation—in particular, the offshore corporation—while Moberg writes from the point of view of U.S. workers in high-tech industry.

3. Write an essay in which you speculate about how this digital revolution leading to off-shoring high-tech jobs will affect you and your peers preparing for careers right now. When it is useful, refer to Friedman and Moberg's discussions on the topic.

PERSPECTIVES   Sweatshop Economy

To learn more about outsourcing, visit
www.ablongman.com/george/130

It has become a commonplace today to talk of a global marketplace and to express concern over what some call "outsourcing" and others call "exporting jobs" to countries where wages are low and unionization difficult. No industry has been criticized more for this practice than the fashion industry. Organizations such as the National Labor Committee, Students United Against Sweatshops, Global Exchange, and UNITE have organized boycotts and demonstrations against companies that profit on sweatshop labor. United Students Against Sweatshop Labor has been a particularly powerful voice in its efforts to force colleges and universities to stop buying school logo clothing that has been produced in sweatshops.

For some critics, the answer to sweatshop economy is simple: boycott sweatshop goods. Others, however, argue that sweatshops have become a crucial part of the economy base in developing countries. They say that $1 a day might not seem like much to Americans, but it is a good wage to workers in East Asia.

The two articles that follow do not see the issue as such a simple dichotomy. Both acknowledge that all workers deserve a decent wage, but they differ markedly in how they would define decent wages and in what to do about companies that rely on sweatshop labor.

TWO CHEERS FOR SWEATSHOPS

— *Nicholas D. Kristof and Sheryl WuDunn*

Nicholas Kristof and Sheryl WuDunn won the 1990 Pulitzer Prize for international reporting for their *New York Times* stories on the Tiananmen democracy movement in China. Kristof has been the *Times* bureau chief in Hong Kong, Beijing, and Tokyo. WuDunn has served as a foreign correspondent in Beijing and Tokyo. The following article was excerpted in the *New York Times Magazine* (September 24, 2000) from their book *Thunder from the East: Portrait of a Rising Asia.*

SUGGESTION FOR READING   In their article, Kristof and WuDunn are careful to explain that they came to their position on sweatshops after many years of living in Asia and interviewing Asian workers. As you read, take note of how they make their argument for not boycotting sweatshops despite the low wages and bad conditions that they do acknowledge.

1   It was breakfast time, and the food stand in the village in northeastern Thailand was crowded. Maesubin Sisoipha, the middle-aged woman cooking the food, was friendly, her portions large and the price right. For the equivalent of about 5 cents, she offered a huge green mango leaf filled with rice, fish paste and fried beetles. It was a hearty breakfast, if one didn't mind the odd antenna left sticking in one's teeth.

One of the half-dozen men and women sitting on a bench eating was a sinewy, bare-chested laborer in his late 30's named Mongkol Latlakorn. It was a hot, lazy day, and so we started chatting idly about the food and, eventually, our families. Mongkol mentioned that his daughter, Darin, was 15, and his voice softened as he spoke of her. She was beautiful and smart, and her father's hopes rested on her.

"Is she in school?" we asked.

"Oh, no," Mongkol said, his eyes sparkling with amusement. "She's working in a factory in Bangkok. She's making clothing for export to America." He explained that she was paid $2 a day for a nine-hour shift, six days a week.

5   "It's dangerous work," Mongkol added. "Twice the needles went right through her hands. But the managers bandaged up her hands, and both times she got better again and went back to work."

"How terrible," we murmured sympathetically.

Mongkol looked up, puzzled. "It's good pay," he said. "I hope she can keep that job. There's all this talk about factories closing now, and she said there are rumors that her factory might close. I hope that doesn't happen. I don't know what she would do then."

He was not, of course, indifferent to his daughter's suffering; he simply had a different perspective from ours—not only when it came to food but also when it came to what constituted desirable work.

Nothing captures the difference in mind-set between East and West more than attitudes toward sweatshops. Nike and other American companies have been hammered in the Western press over the last decade for producing shoes, toys and other products in grim little factories with dismal conditions. Protests against sweatshops and the dark forces of globalization that they seem to represent have become common at meetings of the World Bank and the World Trade Organization and, this month, at a World Economic Forum in Australia, livening up the scene for Olympic athletes arriving for the competition. Yet sweatshops that seem brutal from the vantage point of an American sitting in his living room can appear tantalizing to a Thai laborer getting by on beetles.

10   Fourteen years ago, we moved to Asia and began reporting there. Like most Westerners, we arrived in the region outraged at sweatshops. In time, though, we came to accept the view supported by most Asians: that the campaign against sweatshops risks harming the very people it is intended to help. For beneath their grime, sweatshops are a clear sign of the industrial revolution that is beginning to reshape Asia.

This is not to praise sweatshops. Some managers are brutal in the way they house workers in firetraps, expose children to dangerous chemicals, deny bathroom breaks, demand sexual favors, force people to work double shifts or dismiss anyone who tries to organize a union. Agitation for improved safety conditions can be helpful, just as it was in 19th-century Europe. But Asian workers would be aghast at the idea of American consumers boycotting certain toys or clothing in protest. The simplest way to help the poorest Asians would be to buy more from sweatshops, not less.

On our first extended trip to China, in 1987, we traveled to the Pearl River delta in the south of the country. There we visited several factories, including one in the boomtown of Dongguan, where about 100 female workers sat at workbenches stitching together bits of leather to make purses for a Hong Kong company. We chatted with several women as their fingers flew over their work and asked about their hours.

"I start at about 6:30, after breakfast, and go until about 7 p.m.," explained one shy teenage girl. "We break for lunch, and I take half an hour off then."

"You do this six days a week?"

15 "Oh, no. Every day."

"Seven days a week?"

"Yes." She laughed at our surprise. "But then I take a week or two off at Chinese New Year to go back to my village."

The others we talked to all seemed to regard it as a plus that the factory allowed them to work long hours. Indeed, some had sought out this factory precisely because it offered them the chance to earn more.

"It's actually pretty annoying how hard they want to work," said the factory manager, a Hong Kong man. "It means we have to worry about security and have a supervisor around almost constantly."

20 It sounded pretty dreadful, and it was. We and other journalists wrote about the problems of child labor and oppressive conditions in both China and South Korea. But, looking back, our worries were excessive. Those sweatshops tended to generate the wealth to solve the problems they created. If Americans had reacted to the horror stories in the 1980's by curbing imports of those sweatshop products, then neither southern China nor South Korea would have registered as much progress as they have today.

The truth is, those grim factories in Dongguan and the rest of southern China contributed to a remarkable explosion of wealth. In the years since our first conversations there, we've returned many times to Dongguan and the surrounding towns and seen the transformation. Wages have risen from about $50 a month to $250 a month or more today. Factory conditions have improved as businesses have scrambled to attract and keep the best laborers. A private housing market has emerged, and video arcades and computer schools have opened to cater to workers with rising incomes. A hint of a middle class has appeared—as has China's closest thing to a Western-style independent newspaper, Southern Weekend.

Partly because of these tens of thousands of sweatshops, China's economy has become one of the hottest in the world. Indeed, if China's 30 provinces were counted as individual countries, then the 20 fastest-growing countries in the world between 1978 and 1995 would all have been Chinese. When Britain launched the Industrial Revolution in the late 18th century, it took 58 years for per capita output to double. In China, per capita output has been doubling every 10 years.

In fact, the most vibrant parts of Asia are nearly all in what might be called the Sweatshop Belt, from China and South Korea to Malaysia, Indonesia and even Bangladesh and India. Today these sweatshop countries control about one-quarter of the global economy. As the industrial revolution spreads through China and India, there are good reasons to think that Asia will continue to pick up speed. Some World Bank forecasts show Asia's share of global gross domestic product rising to 55 to 60 percent by about 2025—roughly the West's share at its peak half a century ago. The sweatshops have helped lay the groundwork for a historic economic realignment that is putting Asia back on its feet. Countries are rebounding from the economic crisis of 1997–98 and the sweatshops—seen by Westerners as evidence of moribund economies—actually reflect an industrial revolution that is raising living standards in the East.

Of course, it may sound silly to say that sweatshops offer a route to prosperity, when wages in the poorest countries are sometimes less than $1 a day. Still, for an impoverished Indonesian or Bangladeshi woman with a handful of kids who would otherwise drop out of school and risk dying of mundane diseases like diarrhea, $1 or $2 a day can be a life-transforming wage.

25   This was made abundantly clear in Cambodia, when we met a 40-year-old woman named Nhem Yen, who told us why she moved to an area with particularly lethal malaria. "We needed to eat," she said. "And here there is wood, so we thought we could cut it and sell it."

But then Nhem Yen's daughter and son-in-law both died of malaria, leaving her with two grandchildren and five children of her own. With just one mosquito net, she had to choose which children would sleep protected and which would sleep exposed.

In Cambodia, a large mosquito net costs $5. If there had been a sweatshop in the area, however harsh or dangerous, Nhem Yen would have leapt at the chance to work in it, to earn enough to buy a net big enough to cover all her children.

For all the misery they can engender, sweatshops at least offer a precarious escape from the poverty that is the developing world's greatest problem. Over the past 50 years, countries like India resisted foreign exploitation, while countries that started at a similar economic level—like Taiwan and South Korea—accepted sweatshops as the price of development. Today there can be no doubt about which approach worked better. Taiwan and South Korea are modern countries with low rates of infant mortality and high levels of education; in contrast, every year 3.1 million Indian children die before the age of 5, mostly from diseases of poverty like diarrhea.

The effect of American pressure on sweatshops is complicated. While it clearly improves conditions at factories that produce branded merchandise for companies like Nike, it also raises labor costs across the board. That encourages less well established companies to mechanize and to reduce the number of employees needed. The upshot is to help people who currently have jobs in Nike plants but to risk jobs for others. The only thing a country like Cambodia has to offer is terribly cheap wages; if companies are scolded for paying those wages, they will shift their manufacturing to marginally richer areas like Malaysia or Mexico.

30   Sweatshop monitors do have a useful role. They can compel factories to improve safety. They can also call attention to the impact of sweatshops on the environment. The greatest downside of industrialization is not exploitation of workers but toxic air and water. In Asia each year, three million people die from the effects of pollution. The factories springing up throughout the region are far more likely to kill people through the chemicals they expel than through terrible working conditions.

By focusing on these issues, by working closely with organizations and news media in foreign countries, sweatshops can be improved. But refusing to buy sweatshop products risks making Americans feel good while harming those we are trying to help. As a Chinese proverb goes, "First comes the bitterness, then there is sweetness and wealth and honor for 10,000 years."

PENNIES AN HOUR AND NO WAY UP

— Tom Hayden and Charles Kernaghan

Tom Hayden is a writer, former California state senator, and longtime activist. Charles Kernaghan is director of the National Labor Committee (NLC) in New York City. The NLC is an independent, nonprofit human-rights organization focused on the protection of worker rights.

Kernaghan has led fact-finding missions to Central America and the Caribbean, recently bringing a delegation of U.S. university students to investigate working condition in the free-trade zones. He and the NLC have also hosted U.S. tours of workers from Honduras, El Salvador, Haiti, and China. This article first appeared on the *New York Times* op-ed page on July 6, 2002.

SUGGESTION FOR READING As you read, note those places in their argument where Hayden and Kernaghan touch upon the same issues Kristof and WuDunn use in their discussion of sweatshop economy. Notice where they seem to agree and where their positions differ.

1   In last week's meeting in Canada, the Group of Eight industrial nations grappled with the question of how to better economic conditions in poor nations. One powerful means would be to improve the conditions of workers in sweatshops. Two billion people in the world make less than two American dollars a day. As voters and consumers of sweatshop products, Americans can make a difference in ending the miserable conditions under which these people work.

Some argue that sweatshops are simply a step up a ladder toward the next generation's success: the garment worker at her loom is carrying out some objective law of development, or the young girl making toys for our children is breaking out of male-dominated feudalism. This line of thinking recalls the mythic rise of our immigrant ancestors to the middle class and beyond.

But the real story of those white ethnic ancestors was hardly a smooth ride up the escalator. Life in New York was better than oppression abroad, but people worked 16 hours a day for paltry wages, lived in cellars with raw sewage, died of starvation and fever and were crowded into tenements. Their misery shocked reformers like Jacob Riis and Charles Dickens. They fought their way out—marched for economic justice, built unions, voted and finally forced the Gilded Age to become the New Deal.

Today young, mostly female workers in Bangladesh, a Muslim country that is the fourth-largest garment producer for the United States market, are paid an average of 1.6 cents for each baseball cap with a Harvard logo that they sew. The caps retail at the Harvard bookstore for $17, which means the garment workers, who often are younger than the Harvard students, are being paid a tenth of 1 percent of the cap's price in the market. Also in Bangladesh, women receive 5 cents for each $17.99 Disney shirt they sew. Wages like these are not enough to climb the ladder with.

5   There are similar conditions in China. Three million young Chinese women working for wages as low as 12 cents an hour make 80 percent of the sporting goods and toys sold in the United States each year. Companies like Mattel spend 30 times more to advertise a toy than they pay the workers in China to make it.

Each year Americans buy 924 million garments and other textile items made in Bangladesh and $23.5 billion worth of toys and sporting goods from China. Don't we have the consumer and political power to pressure our corporations to end sweatshop wages paid to the people who make these goods? These workers are not demanding stock options and Jazzercise studios. Women in Bangladesh say they could care for their children if their wages rose to 34 cents an hour, two-tenths of 1 percent of the retail price of the Harvard hat.

Some economists argue that even the most exploited and impoverished workers are better off than those who are unemployed or trapped in slave labor. But that argument is not about offering anyone a ladder up, but about which ring of Dante's inferno people in developing nations are consigned to. We don't want Disney, Mattel, Wal-Mart or other major American companies to leave the developing world. We simply want to end the race to the bottom in which companies force countries to compete in offering the lowest wages for their people's labor. There should be a floor beneath which no one has to live.

Our elected officials should end their subservience to corporate donors and begin asking some big questions: Aren't we entitled to know the addresses of corporate sweatshops in developing countries so they can be open to monitoring by local advocates? Why should our tax dollars subsidize government purchases from companies that operate sweatshops?

Under our customs laws, we ban imports made with inmate and indentured labor, so why not extend the ban to include those made with sweatshop and child labor? And if we insist on enforcement of laws against pirate labels and CD's, why not protect 16-year-olds who make CD's for American companies? We should be helping these workers elbow and push their way up from squalor just as American progressives once helped our immigrant forebears.

SUGGESTIONS FOR DISCUSSION

1. With a group of your classmates, make a list of areas where these writers agree. To what extent is it total agreement? Where do their arguments depart?

2. Why do Kristof and WuDunn make it a point to tell their readers that they lived in Asia for fourteen years and began their investigations firmly opposed to sweatshops? How does that information shape the way a reader is likely to receive their argument?

3. Explain why Hayden and Kernaghan compare sweatshop wages and conditions today to the wages and conditions prevalent in the United States at the turn of the twentieth century? What do they hope to accomplish with that comparison?

SUGGESTIONS FOR WRITING

1. Make a survey of the clothes in your closet, the clothes for sale at any local clothing store, or the clothes most popular with your friends. How many of these items are made in countries named in the articles reproduced here and identified with sweatshop labor? How many have union labels? How easy is it to locate union-made clothing? Can you tell if an item that is made in the United States is a sweatshop-free item? After you have completed your investigations, write a brief report in which you indicate your findings and their implications. For example, if you and your friends only want to wear what are called "Sweat Free" clothes, how could you do that, based on what you were able to discover?

2. Reread the two essays, taking care to note where the authors of each article would agree and where they would disagree. Write an essay in which you position yourself within this discussion. What of each or either of these articles is convincing? What is missing in their arguments?

3. United Students Against Sweatshops has organized on campuses across the country such as Yale, Harvard, the University of Michigan, Johns Hopkins, and the University of Pennsylvania to convince their schools not to buy college logo clothes made in sweatshops. Write an editorial for your school paper addressing the issue of sweatshop-made clothing for colleges and universities. Make it clear why you believe your school should stop dealing with or be allowed to deal with companies that rely on sweatshop labor.

CLASSIC READING

I STAND HERE IRONING

— *Tillie Olson*

Tillie Olsen was born in 1912, began writing in the 1930s, and is considered a major voice for women in twentieth-century American literature. Olsen stopped writing for twenty years to raise four children and to work at a series of low-paying jobs to help support the family. She didn't return to writing as a profession until she was in her mid-forties and her last child had started school. The title story in the collection *Tell Me a Riddle* (1961), from which the following selection has been taken, won an O'Henry Prize for short fiction. "I Stand Here Ironing" has become a classic statement of the tensions women face between motherhood and the need to make a living outside the home.

SUGGESTION FOR READING This story has little or no real "action." The woman telling it remains at the ironing board throughout as she recalls the story of her daughter's life. Keep track of that story as you read.

1   I stand here ironing, and what you asked me moves tormented back and forth with the iron.

"I wish you would manage the time to come and talk with me about your daughter. I'm sure you can help me understand her. She's a youngster who needs help and whom I'm deeply interested in helping."

"Who needs help." . . . Even if I came, what good would it do? You think because I am her mother I have a key, or that in some way you could use me as a key? She has lived for nineteen years. There is all that life that has happened outside of me, beyond me.

And when is there time to remember, to sift, to weigh, to estimate, to total? I will start and there will be an interruption and I will have to gather it all together again. Or I will become engulfed with all I did or did not do, with what should have been and what cannot be helped.

5   She was a beautiful baby. The first and only one of our five that was beautiful at birth. You do not guess how new and uneasy her tenancy in her now-loveliness. You did not know her all those years she was thought homely, or see her poring over her baby pictures, making me tell her over and over how beautiful she had been—and would be, I would tell her—and was now, to

the seeing eye. But the seeing eyes were few or nonexistent. Including mine.

I nursed her. They feel that's important nowadays. I nursed all the children, but with her, with all the fierce rigidity of first motherhood, I did like the books then said. Though her cries battered me to trembling and my breasts ached with swollenness, I waited till the clock decreed.

Why do I put that first? I do not even know if it matters, or if it explains anything.

She was a beautiful baby. She blew shining bubbles of sound. She loved motion, loved light, loved color and music and textures. She would lie on the floor in her blue overalls patting the surface so hard in ecstasy her hands and feet would blur. She was a miracle to me, but when she was eight months old I had to leave her daytimes with the woman downstairs to whom she was no miracle at all, for I worked or looked for work and for Emily's father, who "could no longer endure" (he wrote in his good-bye note) "sharing want with us."

I was nineteen. It was the pre-relief, pre-WPA world of the depression. I would start running as soon as I got off the streetcar, running up the stairs, the place smelling sour, and awake or asleep to startle awake, when she saw me she would break into a clogged weeping that could not be comforted, a weeping I can hear yet.

10   After a while I found a job hashing at night so I could be with her days, and it was better. But it came to where I had to bring her to his family and leave her.

It took a long time to raise the money for her fare back. Then she got chicken pox and I had to wait longer. When she finally came, I hardly knew her, walking quick and nervous like her father, looking like her father, thin, and dressed in a shoddy red that yellowed her skin and glared at the pockmarks. All the baby loveliness gone.

She was two. Old enough for nursery school they said, and I did not know then what I know now—the fatigue of the long day, and the lacerations of group life in the kinds of nurseries that are only parking places for children.

Except that it would have made no difference if I had known. It was the only place there was. It was the only way we could be together, the only way I could hold a job.

And even without knowing, I knew. I knew the teacher that was evil because all these years it has curdled into my memory, the little boy hunched in the corner, her rasp, "why aren't you outside, because Alvin hits you? that's no reason, go out, scaredy." I knew Emily hated it even if she did not clutch and implore "don't go Mommy" like the other children, mornings.

15   She always had a reason why we should stay home. Momma, you look sick. Momma, I feel sick. Momma, the teachers aren't there today, they're sick. Momma, we can't go, there was a fire there last night. Momma, it's a holiday today, no school, they told me.

But never a direct protest, never rebellion. I think of our others in their three-, four-year-oldness—the explosions, the tempers, the denunciations, the demands—and I feel suddenly ill. I put the iron down. What in me demanded that goodness in her? And what was the cost, the cost to her of such goodness?

The old man living in the back once said in his gentle way: "You should smile at Emily more when you look at her." What *was* in my face when I looked at her? I loved her. There were all the acts of love.

It was only with the others I remembered what he said, and it was the face of joy, and not of care or tightness or worry I turned to them— too late for Emily. She does not smile easily, let alone almost always as her brothers and sisters do. Her face is closed and sombre, but when she wants, how fluid. You must have seen it in her pantomimes, you spoke of her rare gift for comedy on the stage that rouses laughter out of the audience so dear they applaud and applaud and do not want to let her go.

Where does it come from, that comedy? There was none of it in her when she came back to me that second time, after I had had to send her away again. She had a new daddy now to learn to love, and I think perhaps it was a better time.

20   Except when we left her alone nights, telling ourselves she was old enough.

"Can't you go some other time, Mommy, like tomorrow?" she would ask. "Will it be just a little while you'll be gone? Do you promise?"

The time we came back, the front door open, the clock on the floor in the hall. She rigid awake. "It wasn't just a little while. I didn't cry. Three times I called you, just three times, and then I ran downstairs to open the door so you could come faster. The clock talked loud. I threw it away, it scared me what it talked."

She said the clock talked loud again that night I went to the hospital to have Susan. She was delirious with the fever that comes before red measles, but she was fully conscious all the week I was gone and the week after we were home when she could not come near the new baby or me.

She did not get well. She stayed skeleton thin, not wanting to eat, and night after night she had nightmares. She would call for me, and I would rouse from exhaustion to sleepily call back: "You're all right, darling, go to sleep, it's just a dream," and if she still called, in a sterner voice, "now go to sleep, Emily, there's nothing to hurt you." Twice, only twice, when I had to get up for Susan anyhow, I went in to sit with her.

25   Now when it is too late (as if she would let me hold and comfort her like I do the others) I get up and go to her at once at her moan or restless stirring. "Are you awake, Emily? Can I get you something?" And the answer is always the same: "No, I'm all right, go back to sleep, Mother."

They persuaded me at the clinic to send her away to a convalescent home in the country where "she can have the kind of food and care you can't manage for her, and you'll be free to concentrate on the new baby." They still send children to that place. I see pictures on the society page of sleek young women planning affairs to raise money for it, or dancing at the affairs, or decorating Easter eggs or filling Christmas stockings for the children.

They never have a picture of the children so I do not know if the girls still wear those gigantic red bows and the ravaged looks on the every other Sunday when parents can come to visit "unless otherwise notified"—as we were notified the first six weeks.

Oh it is a handsome place, green lawns and tall trees and fluted flower beds. High up on the balconies of each cottage the children stand, the girls in their red bows and white dresses, the boys in white suits and giant red ties. The parents stand below shrieking up to be heard and the children shriek down to be heard, and between them the invisible wall: "Not to Be Contaminated by Parental Germs or Physical Affection."

There was a tiny girl who always stood hand in hand with Emily. Her parents never came. One visit she was gone. "They moved her to Rose Cottage," Emily shouted in explanation. "They don't like you to love anybody here."

30   She wrote once a week, the labored writing of a seven-year-old. "I am fine. How is the baby. If I write my leter nicly I will have a star. Love." There never was a star. We wrote every other day, letters she could never hold or keep but only hear read—once. "We simply do not have room for children to keep any personal possessions," they patiently explained when we pieced one Sunday's shrieking together to plead how much it would mean to Emily, who loved so to keep things, to be allowed to keep her letters and cards.

Each visit she looked frailer. "She isn't eating," they told us.

(They had runny eggs for breakfast or mush with lumps, Emily said later, I'd hold it in my mouth and not swallow. Nothing ever tasted good, just when they had chicken.)

It took us eight months to get her released home, and only the fact that she gained back so little of her seven lost pounds convinced the social worker.

I used to try to hold and love her after she came back, but her body would stay stiff, and after a while she'd push away. She ate little. Food sickened her, and I think much of life too. Oh she had physical lightness and brightness, twinkling by on skates, bouncing like a ball up and down up and down over the jump rope, skimming over the hill; but these were momentary.

35   She fretted about her appearance, thin and dark and foreign-looking at a time when every little girl was supposed to look or thought she should look a chubby blonde replica of Shirley Temple. The doorbell sometimes rang for her, but no one seemed to come and play in the house or be a best friend. Maybe because we moved so much.

There was a boy she loved painfully through two school semesters. Months later she told me how she had taken pennies from my purse to buy him candy. "Licorice was his favorite and I brought him some every day, but he still liked Jennifer better'n me. Why, Mommy?" The kind of question for which there is no answer.

School was a worry to her. She was not glib or quick in a world where glibness and quickness were easily confused with ability to learn. To her overworked and exasperated teachers she was an overconscientious "slow learner" who kept trying to catch up and was absent entirely too often.

I let her be absent, though sometimes the illness was imaginary. How different from my now-strictness about attendance with the others. I wasn't working. We had a new baby, I was home anyhow. Sometimes, after Susan grew old enough, I would keep her home from school, too, to have them all together.

Mostly Emily had asthma, and her breathing, harsh and labored, would fill the house with a curiously tranquil sound. I would bring the two old dresser mirrors and her boxes of collections to her bed. She would select beads and single earrings, bottle tops and shells, dried flowers and pebbles, old postcards and scraps, all sorts of oddments; then she and Susan would play Kingdom, setting up landscapes and furniture, peopling them with action.

40 Those were the only times of peaceful companionship between her and Susan. I have edged away from it, that poisonous feeling between them, that terrible balancing of hurts and needs I had to do between the two, and did so badly, those earlier years.

Oh there are conflicts between the others too, each one human, needing, demanding, hurting, taking—but only between Emily and Susan, no, Emily toward Susan that corroding resentment. It seems so obvious on the surface, yet it is not obvious. Susan, the second child, Susan, golden- and curly-haired and chubby, quick and articulate and assured, everything in appearance and manner Emily was not; Susan, not able to resist Emily's precious things, losing or sometimes clumsily breaking them; Susan telling jokes and riddles to company for applause while Emily sat silent (to say to me later: that was *my* riddle, Mother, I told it to Susan); Susan, who for all the five years' difference in age was just a year behind Emily in developing physically.

I am glad for that slow physical development that widened the difference between her and her contemporaries, though she suffered over it. She was too vulnerable for that terrible world of youthful competition, of preening and parading, of constant measuring of yourself against every other, of envy, "If I had that copper hair," "If I had that skin . . . " She tormented herself enough about not looking like the others, there was enough of the unsureness, the having to be conscious of words before you speak, the constant caring—what are they thinking of me? without having it all magnified by the merciless physical drives.

Ronnie is calling. He is wet and I change him. It is rare there is such a cry now. That time of motherhood is almost behind me when the ear is not one's own but must always be racked and listening for the child cry, the child call. We sit for a while and I hold him, looking out over the city spread in charcoal with its soft aisles of light. "*Shoogily,*" he breathes and curls closer. I carry him back to bed, asleep. *Shoogily.* A funny word, a family word, inherited from Emily, invented by her to say: *comfort.*

In this and other ways she leaves her seal, I say aloud. And startle at my saying it. What do I mean? What did I start to gather together, to try and make coherent? I was at the terrible, growing years. War years. I do not remember them well. I was working, there were four smaller ones now, there was not time for her. She had to help be a mother, and housekeeper, and shopper. She had to set her seal. Mornings of crisis and near hysteria trying to get lunches packed, hair combed, coats and shoes found, everyone to school or Child Care on time, the baby ready for transportation. And always the paper scribbled on by a smaller one, the book looked at by Susan then mislaid, the homework not done. Running out to that huge school where she was one, she was lost, she was a drop; suffering over the unpreparedness, stammering and unsure in her classes.

45 There was so little time left at night after the kids were bedded down. She would struggle over books, always eating (it was in those years she developed her enormous appetite that is legendary in our family) and I would be ironing, or preparing food for the next day, or writing V-mail to Bill, or tending the baby. Sometimes, to make

me laugh, or out of her despair, she would imitate happenings or types at school.

I think I said once: "Why don't you do something like this in the school amateur show?" One morning she phoned me at work, hardly understandable through the weeping: "Mother, I did it. I won, I won; they gave me first prize; they clapped and clapped and wouldn't let me go."

Now suddenly she was Somebody, and as imprisoned in her difference as she had been in anonymity.

She began to be asked to perform at other high schools, even in colleges, then at city and statewide affairs. The first one we went to, I only recognized her that first moment when thin, shy, she almost drowned herself into the curtains. Then: Was this Emily? The control, the command, the convulsing and deadly clowning, the spell, then the roaring, stamping audience, unwilling to let this rare and precious laughter out of their lives.

Afterwards: You ought to do something about her with a gift like that—but without money or knowing how, what does one do? We have left it all to her, and the gift has as often eddied inside, clogged and clotted, as been used and growing.

50 She is coming. She runs up the stairs two at a time with her light graceful step, and I know she is happy tonight. Whatever it was that occasioned your call did not happen today.

"Aren't you ever going to finish the ironing, Mother? Whistler painted his mother in a rocker. I'd have to paint mine standing over an ironing board." This is one of her communicative nights and she tells me everything and nothing as she fixes herself a plate of food out of the icebox.

She is so lovely. Why did you want me to come in at all? Why were you concerned? She will find her way.

She starts up the stairs to bed. "Don't get me up with the rest in the morning." "But I thought you were having midterms." "Oh, those," she comes back in, kisses me, and says quite lightly, "in a couple of years when we'll all be atom-dead they won't matter a bit."

She has said it before. She *believes* it. But because I have been dredging the past, and all that compounds a human being is so heavy and meaningful in me, I cannot endure it tonight.

55 I will never total it all. I will never come in to say: She was a child seldom smiled at. Her father left me before she was a year old. I had to work her first six years when there was work, or I sent her home and to his relatives. There were years she had care she hated. She was dark and thin and foreign-looking in a world where the prestige went to blondeness and curly hair and dimples, she was slow where glibness was prized. She was a child of anxious, not proud, love. We were poor and could not afford for her the soil of easy growth. I was a young mother, I was a distracted mother. There were other children pushing up, demanding. Her younger sister seemed all that she was not. There were years she did not want me to touch her. She kept too much in herself, her life was such she had to keep too much in herself. My wisdom came too late. She has much to her and probably little will come of it. She is a child of her age, of depression, of war, of fear.

Let her be. So all that is in her will not bloom—but in how many does it? There is still enough left to live by. Only help her to know—help make it so there is cause for her to know—that she is more than this dress on the ironing board, helpless before the iron.

SUGGESTIONS FOR DISCUSSION

1. Sort out the details of the story. What is the setting? Who is the narrator and who is she talking to? What is the situation? What does the narrator mean when she says, "Even if I came, what good would it do? You think because I am her mother I have a key . . . ? There is all that life that has happened outside of me, beyond me."

2. At the end of the story Emily says, "Whistler painted his mother in a rocker. I'd have to paint mine standing over an ironing board." What does Emily mean by that? Is she

joking? Is she criticizing? In terms of how you imagine she spent most of her time, choose a woman in your life and explain how you would "paint" her. What characterizes the way she spends her days?

3. In what ways does the narrator take blame for her daughter's troubles? How much credit does she take for her daughter's successes? What role does Emily's father play in this situation?

SUGGESTIONS FOR WRITING

1. Write a response to this story in which you speculate how Emily might tell the same story. What would she have noticed in her mother's life? What might she miss?

2. Write an analysis of the role that work plays in the narrator's life. How does she use work to explain her daughter? To what extent does she describe herself through work? How does her work or her need to work determine the kind of mother she can be to Emily?

3. This story ends with a plea: "Only help her to know—help make it so there is cause for her to know—that she is more than this dress on the ironing board, helpless before the iron." Write an explanation for that final comment. How does it summarize the dilemma this narrator finds herself in? How might it represent the conflict many mothers have felt over the years as they worked to raise a family and to support that family?

VISUAL CULTURE   Reading Documentary Photography

To learn more about work
photo galleries, visit
www.ablongman.com/george/131

Documentary photography has been at the center of social and political change since the late nineteenth century when reporter Jacob Riis photographed living conditions in the New York City tenement district. His photos of dangerous and horrifying living conditions have long been credited with spurring housing reform at the time. Since then, photographers like Lewis Hine whose photographs documented child labor conditions, Walker Evans who photographed tenant farmers during and after the Great Depression, and Danny Lyon whose photos recorded some of the worst abuses of the civil rights movement have all been credited with opening the public's eyes to events and conditions not available in the mainstream press.

Documentary photography is meant to actually document—to record—events as the photographer sees them. Documentary photography offers evidence of how people are living or that an event occurred in a particular way. The documentarist is a historian, a reporter, and sometimes an artist.

Social historian James Curtis lists the following questions as key to reading documentary photography:

- Who took the photograph? (What do you know about the photographer?)
- Why and for whom was it taken?
- What message is being sent in the photograph?
- How was the photograph taken? (Was it posed? Did the subjects know they were being photographed?)
- What do companion images tell us about the message of the photograph?
- How was the photograph presented? (Is it in a pamphlet advocating change, for example? Is there a caption? How do viewers know what the photograph is about?)

CAMERA OF DIRT: JUÁREZ PHOTOGRAPHER TAKES FORBIDDEN IMAGES IN FOREIGN-OWNED FACTORIES

— *Charles Bowden*

Charles Bowden is a contributing editor for *Esquire* and *Harper's* magazines. He is the author of more than a dozen books, including *Juárez: The Laboratory of Our Future* (1998). He is the recipient of a Lannan Literary Award for Nonfiction and the Sidney Hillman Award. "Camera of Dirt" first appeared in the photography magazine *Aperture* (Spring 2000).

SUGGESTION FOR READING   *Maquiladoras*—the subject of these photos—are foreign-owned and largely untaxed assembly plants located in Mexico along the border between Mexico and the United States. They are not subject to duties or tariffs or to the same labor or environmental regulations that apply in the United States, though most of these plants are U.S. owned. Families might live in cardboard shacks. Young children are allowed to work in these factories. They are typically closed to all outside press.

1   He rises, his lean body unfolds from the chair in the hubbub of the market, and he moves with feline grace, camera in hand. The table hosts short, dark teenagers from Oaxaca, country people who have come up more than a thousand miles to the border because they have heard rumors of work. The boys wear watches, the girls new clothes. He leans into them, his voice soft, face smiling. They have been here six months, they have a shack they share, they have jobs, and today they have Sunday off and can eat in the public market and enjoy the throb of the city. The camera comes up, he slowly bends toward the targets, the film whirls and Julián Cardona feeds. He has been at this for almost twenty years. No one asked him to do this work. That does not matter; he is about his business and his business is this border city of bruises, death, dirt, and love.

Talking about dirt, dust in the air chewing the city, dirt choking the lungs on a windy day, streets of dirt, yards of dirt, a city of dirt and mud and dust, talking about Juárez, two million people huddling in shacks on the flanks of the dunes to the south and west, talking about dirt and dust and mud and Juárez, the city Julián Cardona loves.

"This street," he says, "this street is where I walked with my girl."

The *calle* is dust, rock, and ruts. Here, he wants it known, here when he was a boy, a teenager, he walked with his girl, down this dirt street, and see?—she lived over there, and down there and up the hill, that's where he lived, back then, when he was young and in love in the city of dirt. Smoke from cooking fires floods the air, night is falling, the wind blows, he is in love, he is back there, walking with his girl. The turf is K-13, the most vicious of the hundreds of gangs in the city of dirt. No matter. Love. Here, then, and now.

5   El Paso lights up in the dusk, not even a mile away. He hates it there, it is too cold, he explains. With a ninth-grade education, he managed to learn English. "Do you know this essay," he asks, "by Gore Vidal?" The dust coats the tongue, the smoke sweetens the air, a stench comes off the privies.

He was two, he thinks, when he declared his life for beauty. Ten when he gave up on eternity. About twenty when he was working in a factory here and he stumbled into photography, bought magazines, got a camera, taught himself everything. After that came a time working for

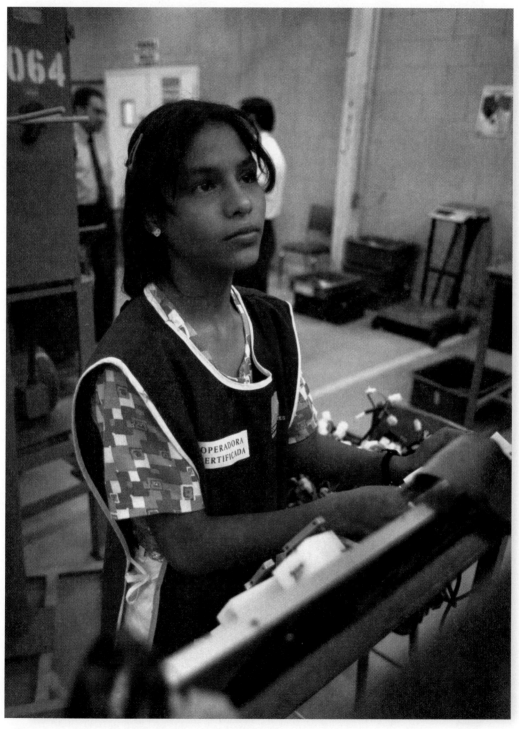

A young girl at work. Electrical Wire (ECM plant.)

A canal of aguas negras (contaminated water) separates one of the ca. 325 maquiladoras in Cd. Juarez from the new home of seven-year-old Guadalupe Valenzuela Rosales, who lives with her parents, two sisters, and brother in a cardboard-and-wood house. (For more about this photo, see page 588.)

Hosiery discarded by El Paso shopkeepers is bought, mended, dyed, and dried in the sun by a Cd. Juarez woman living in Colonia Puerto de Anapra, who then resells the stockings for the equivalent of about $1.

UTA#158 (one of the former Essex plants in Juarez.)
United Technologies Automotive, UTC.

blood-and-guts working-class tabloids, finally the move up to the daily paper, and now, at thirty-nine, the life of beauty. Beauty is everywhere, even in a pebble he spied at age two. Eternity is incomprehensible, there is only now. The photograph, the thing curators call *the image*, is now, this moment of beauty that exists for a second. Until devoured by the camera and made into comprehensible eternity. That's it, it is that simple.

The girl he used to walk with, she married someone else. Julián Cardona lives alone and says with a laugh that the camera is his wife.

And the beauty is here, in this sprawling slum of a city packed with workers in cardboard shacks, racked by drug killings, ruled by endless corruption, ignored by the rest of the planet. Beauty is here in the city of dirt and dust and mud and love and Julián Cardona is here to prove it and taste it and capture it and admire it and love it in turn.

Talking about dirt.

He is a brown man in a brown city. Juárez lacks water and is first and last dust. Grass, trees, flowers, they are for somewhere else. The city is a holding pen for cheap labor sucked north from the hopeless interior of Mexico. Hundreds of factories, mainly owned by Americans, assemble goods for the U.S. market safe within the tariff wall of NAFTA. The wages are 25 to 50 bucks a week. No one can live on them. No one. Turnover runs from 11 percent to 25 percent a week in the plants. And they are plants—General Motors alone has thirty in Juárez. Cheap labor, impossible living conditions, the bottomless U.S. market, violence, and dirt. There is nothing more to say about it, except to tell lies.

10   "I have witnessed a lot of deaths," he offers, "and when you are a photographer you have a chance to die so many times. You see a kid of eleven playing an accordion in the street—what will he become? What if he is you? The woman is dying. What if she is your sister? Photography is a mirror of yourself."

Julián lives in a cement building of two rooms he threw together himself. The patio, a cement slab waiting for some next phase with no due date, looks down on the other little houses and shacks huddling on the bare hillside. Julián Cardona opens a bottle of red wine from Zacatecas. He is a quiet man, a pair of eyes that takes things in and feels no need to speak of what he sees. In his monk's room are a few books of photography with plates he studies, and a simple cot. The other room is a kitchen.

Out here are red wine, night, and talk.

He offers, "I think a photograph uncovers what is hidden and then what is hidden comes before the public eye. You must confront yourself in this mirror of reality. And the photo must seek beauty in even the worst things, it must capture the primitive things that move a human being—loneliness, hope and love. Dreams."

In the *mercado publico*, he eats *menudo* amid the din of Sunday shoppers. A band of old men plays country songs. His eye drifts, the girl two tables away has fine cheekbones and the face of a child. He moves, talks, sits with her.

The camera comes up and feeds. She is a teenager working in an American factory and her face shines with experiments in cosmetics. He never stops. Her name, phone number. He will visit and take yet more images. The photo will nail her in his vision of eternity.

15   He never knew his father, and his mother left Julián to the care of her parents. His grandfather was a farmer who formed an *ejido*, a collective, after the revolution. He tried to teach Julián the earth and its animals. When Julián was in his early twenties, he faltered after working for five years in a *maquiladora* (one eye is permanently damaged from those years of leaning over a lathe), and with two friends he decided to go back to the *ejido* his grandfather had founded. The peasants agreed to let him join and have ground out of respect for his grandfather. It all came to nothing. His friends fell away from the scheme, Julián fell in love with a beautiful and rich woman. So it ends this way: he gives his patch of ground to another peasant and asks that, if possible, someday the *ejido* build a library or clinic and name it after his grandfather because, he says, "He was like millions of farmers and animals. No one will ever know they existed and who they were."

The beautiful rich woman marries someone else. Julián lives on the streets of Juárez for months. He does not explain this period except to make the point that he had it easy since he had money for food. Then he returns to the camera, the beauty. He takes that first shot; two men dressed as clowns standing one atop the other's shoulders in traffic and begging for change. The man on top juggles. The camera clicks. It is twilight, forever.

He spends day after day haunting the central city, the market, the whores, the cathedral, the plaza. He is the thin, silent man, the one almost unnoticed. See him, right over there, in those shadows, that man holding a camera. These spells come and go but now he is in the midst of one. He will capture that eternity, that beauty amid the stench and dust and dirt and broken glass and painted lips on the young girls soliciting in the doorways. And finally, as always, he is broken, worn out, and so he does what he must do. Sometimes he goes to his aunt's house and leaves his camera with her. The house is teeming with cousins and their wives and their children. Everyone sleeps in shifts, everyone works in the *maquiladoras*. This is the safe house for Julián. So he leaves the camera for two weeks.

Then he can rest for a while.

But he can't keep his eyes closed. He retrieves his camera, and creeps into the *maquiladoras*, a zone of work barred to the press except for company-controlled publicity shots. Julián has learned to shoot secretly in low light and so a flow of photographs begins, men and women looking blankly at the camera with eyes chastened by a five-and-a-half-day week. They are a nation of Mexicans from the interior suddenly meeting the culture of the machine and being broken to the habits of presses, drills, and assembly lines. Julián at night leans over the tiny light table in his room and stares at the slides of the place he escaped, the dull grind he fled for the *ejido*, and then the streets and finally the marriage to his camera. No one wants these images. The press of Juárez is in thrall to the economic might of the *maquiladoras*. The press of the United States is oblivious to the carnage just below the surface of the pat phrase "Free Trade." No matter. Julián is on his mission, and he takes his wife, the camera, with him into the mills. And finds the beauty in dead-end lives.

20   For Julián Cardona the entire city of Juárez is the *maquiladora*, a giant factory breathing to the rhythm of the machines. He is the lover of this factory called a city. Forget everything else. Forget the theory, the art of the print, the function of the curator, the various zones. Talking dirt now. Two million people with low wages and constant songs. Young girls everywhere

fresh as flowers and growing out of the din. There will be no folio. There will be no cantos. There will be no show. There will be no audience. The work is instantaneous, a bullet passing through the market and ripping faces off the people. A shot fired in the sterlie void of the factories where brown people meet the machine and wear smocks and sport blank eyes. He is there, everywhere, working with the light or the absence of light.

The photo essay is dead. The video camera is the tool of light now. Julián keeps shooting. He says his camera is his wife. Talking dirt now.

The question is not why he keeps shooting. The question is why not? Like all good questions, it is not asked. Or answered. There is this street where he once walked with his girl. There is this street where he looked down at age two and saw a pebble and it was beautiful. The clock ticks. Do not listen to it. Now, this second, savor eternity, lick it with your tongue.

You gotta wonder. Not why he takes pictures. But why everyone does not walk around with a camera.

Drinking late at night, more of the red wine from Zacatecas, the smoke of the cook-fires drifting up to his tiny house hanging on the dirt of the hillside. He tries to explain why he will not go north, through that nearby fence, into the land of the U.S. and of money. "Mexico is a loose way of living," he says, "a bohemian way of life. We enjoy love. We look at a woman and we say, '*Te adoro,*' I adore you. My pictures are slices of Mexican beauty, but these slices of beauty ask questions. It is a question of love, a love of your country and your people, and by those acts, a love of myself. I know just a little bit of Mexico but it is like knowing just a little bit of a woman you love, still you love her for that little bit. But at the same time, I hate Mexico because I want to change it. But this is impossible because as a lover you must take your love as it is."

SUGGESTIONS FOR DISCUSSION

1. What do you learn about the photographer from Bowden's description? How does knowing that Cordona had to sneak into factories to take the pictures change how you might read them? How does the fact that he lived most of his life in Juárez influence the way you might read the photographs?

2. Compare Julián Cordona's photograph of a young girl at work with Lewis Hine's photograph of a young girl working in a textile mill that appears at the beginning of this chapter. How are the two alike? How do they differ? In what way might color change the way you look at documentary photography? How would this photograph be read differently if it were in black and white?

3. Charles Bowden writes about Cordona not as a documentarist but as an artist—someone pulled to this subject by the beauty he sees in it. He quotes Cordona as saying, "My pictures are slices of Mexican beauty, but these slices of beauty ask questions." What are the questions presented by these photos?

SUGGESTIONS FOR WRITING

1. Look carefully at the images and their captions reprinted with this essay. Then, locate the issue of *Aperture* magazine in which the original essay appeared (*Aperture*, no. 159, Spring 2000, pp. 26–33). Examine all of the photographs together. Using Curtis's questions, listed above, explain the message of these photographs.

2. Curtis asks readers to pay attention to how photographs are presented. Write an essay in which you explain how Charles Bowden's essay printed with these photographs contributes to the way we read them. You might consider, as well, the kind of magazine the photographs appear in. *Aperture* is a magazine about photography. How would these photographs change for a reader if, say, they appeared in a labor rights pamphlet or on a poster opposing NAFTA?

3. Make your own photo documentary of work. You can photograph school work, the workers on campus, a local business, any kind of work that interests you and about which you have something important to say. The kind of work matters much less than what you have to say about it. What is your message? Is it about working conditions? About who does the work? About a lost skill? About uncovering work that must go on daily but that most people don't notice? Present your documentary to the class with a brief explanation of what you were trying to convey with your photo documentary. (In the case of an assignment like this, it is best to get people's permission before you photograph them.)

FILM CLIP   Documentary Film and the Narrator

Like documentary photography, documentary film has been one of the most popular ways to convey labor issues to a large, popular audience. The documentary is meant to tell a factual story about the subject of the film. To do that, a film-

To learn more about famous narrators, visit www.ablongman.com/george/132

maker might follow a story as it happens, in the same way a reporter would for a film news report. The footage would then be edited to tell the story of the event—a strike, changed working conditions, etc.—in the time allotted for the film. Or the filmmaker might take archival footage and work the history of the issue into the actual events to flesh out the story, shape the way the audience understands the story, and give the film historical relevance.

The way the story is narrated might, however, be the element that most influences the way an audience reads a film documentary. Documentary film often uses what is called the *voice-over narrator*—someone who does not appear onscreen but who tells the audience what is happening. A key question for examining the narrator in a documentary, then, is to ask what the narrator's relationship is to the events portrayed in the film.

For this assignment, choose one of the films below. Watch it and then write an essay in which you examine the film's point of view as it is signaled by the narrator.

As you watch the film, pay attention to the following questions concerning the narrator:

- Is the narrator a character in the documentary and thus a part of the story?
- Is the narrator what is called a *noncharacter*, a voice that has sometimes been called "the voice of God" in film circles?
- How does the narrator shape the way you receive the events in the film?
- What position does the narrator take in relation to the events of the film?

The following documentaries all cover labor issues and are widely available for rental:

Roger and Me

Harlan County, USA

American Dream

Wal-Mart: The High Cost of Low Price

FIELDWORK   Reconstructing the Network of a Workplace

In any job you hold, negotiating the workplace involves more than performing the work you were hired to do. You need to understand your coworkers and how they do their jobs, how they relate to each other and to you, how they have established unspoken rules for daily routines and interactions, and where you fit into all of that. As the narrator in Sandra Cisneros's story "The First Job" discovered, the people who have worked at a place for some time seem to know almost automatically how to act, when to speak, when to sit, and when to make sure they are working diligently.

This is what's known as the "social network" established in any job that involves more than two people. Most of these unspoken rules are unique to each workplace and are unknown to those on the outside. If, for example, you entered an office, stood in front of what you thought was the receptionist's desk, and felt frustrated or confused when the person behind the desk pointedly ignored you until you discovered that the receptionist was at the next desk, you probably stumbled onto one of the unspoken rules that has evolved from the social network in that office. Customers often are confused by such networks and, for example, might call the waitress assigned to another area to their table in a restaurant or ask the stocker rather than a sales clerk at a discount store to help them purchase an item. New workers must learn to negotiate these social networks quickly or they are likely to make mistakes in front of the supervisor that veterans in that workplace would never make.

One way that anthropologists have studied the culture of the workplace is to try to understand the social networks established on the job. To do so, they have relied on interviews and on participant-observation studies, such as the one described in the next selection by James Spradley and Brenda Mann.

THE COCKTAIL WAITRESS

— *James P. Spradley and Brenda J. Mann*

James Spradley, a professor of anthropology at MacAlaster College in St. Paul, Minnesota, and Brenda Mann, who has worked as a senior product analyst at Dialog Information Services, spent a year studying the culture of the workplace from the point of view of "cocktail waitresses," as waitresses in bars were still called in 1975 when this study was completed. The selection reprinted below is from *The Cocktail Waitress* and illustrates how workers daily and almost automatically interpret their own workplace so they know whom to go to for information, whom to avoid, or what tasks will hang them up.

SUGGESTION FOR READING Spradley and Mann make a clear distinction between the "social structure" that has been established in Brady's bar and the "social network." Underline/highlight and annotate those places in the selection where Spradley and Mann provide examples or explanations for each. After you complete your reading, review your annotations and use them to write a short explanation of the difference between the two.

1   Denise moves efficiently through her section, stopping at a few of her tables. "Another round here?" she asks at the first table. They nod their assent and she moves on. "Would you like to order now?" "Two more of the usual here?" She takes orders from four of the tables and heads back to the bar to give them to the bartender. The work is not difficult for her now, but when she first started at Brady's, every night on the job was confusing, frustrating, embarrassing, and exhausting. Now it is just exhausting.

Her first night was chaos. When introduced to the bartender, Mark Brady, he responded with: "Haven't I seen you somewhere before?" Flustered, she shook her head. "He's not going to be one of those kind, is he?" she thought. Then later, following previous instruction, she asked two obviously underaged girls for identification, which they didn't have. As she was asking them to leave Mark called Denise over and told her not to card those two particular girls. Embarrassed, Denise returned to their table, explained they could stay, and took their order. A customer at the bar kept grabbing her every time she came to her station, and tried to engage her in conversation. Not knowing what to do, she just smiled and tried to look busy. She asked one customer what he wanted to drink and he said, "the usual" and she had to ask him what that was. An older man seated at the bar smiled and said, "Hello, Denise," as he put a dollar bill on her tray. Again, she didn't know what to say or do so she just smiled and walked away, wondering what she had done or was supposed to do to make her worth the dollar. Another customer at a table grabbed her by the waist each time she walked past his table and persistently questioned her: "Are you new here?" "What nights do you work?" "What are you doing after work?" And so went the rest of the evening. It wasn't until several nights later and following similar encounters that she began to sort out and make sense of all this. She began to learn who these people were, what special identities they had in the bar culture, and where each one was located in the social structure of Brady's Bar.

The bartender's initial question, albeit a rather standard come-on, had been a sincere and friendly inquiry. The two girls she carded were *friends of the Brady family* and often drank there despite their young age. The grabby and talkative customer at the bar was Jerry, a *regular customer* and harmless drinker. The dollar tip came from *Mr. Brady*, the patriarch of the business. The man with the hands and persistent questions was a *regular* from the University who had a reputation with the other waitresses as a *hustler* to be avoided. These people were more than just customers, as Denise had initially categorized them. Nor could she personalize them and treat each one as a unique individual. They were different

kinds of people who came into Brady's, and all required different kinds of services and responses from her.

SOCIAL STRUCTURE

Social structure is a universal feature of culture. It consists of an organized set of social identities and the expected behavior associated with them. Given the infinite possibilities for organizing people, anthropologists have found it crucial to discover the particular social structure in each society they study. It is often necessary to begin by asking informants for the social identity of specific individuals. "He is a *big man*." "That's my *mother*." "She is my *co-wife*." "He is my *uncle*." "She is my *sister*." Then one can go on to examine these categories being used to classify people. A fundamental feature of every social structure is a set of such categories, usually named, for dividing up the social world. In the area of kinship, for example, some societies utilize nearly 100 categories, organizing them in systematic ways for social interaction.

5   When we began our research at Brady's Bar, the various categories of the social structure were not easy to discern. Of course the different activities of waitresses, bartenders, and customers suggested these three groupings, but finer distinctions were often impossible to make without the assistance of informants. At first we thought it would be possible to arrange all the terms for different kinds of people into a single folk taxonomy, much like an anthropologist might do for a set of kinship terms. With this in mind, we began listening, for example, to the way informants talked about customers and asked them specifically, "What are all the different kinds of customers?" This procedure led to a long list of terms, including the following:

girl	regular	cougar
jock	real regular	sweetie
animal	person off street	waitress
bartender	policeman	loner

greaser	party	female
businessman	zoo	drunk
redneck	bore	Johnny
bitch	pig	hands
creep	slob	couple
bastard	hustler	king and his court
obnoxo	Annie	

This list was even more confusing as we checked out the various terms. For example, we asked, "Would a waitress say that a bartender is a kind of customer?" Much to our surprise, the answer was affirmative. Then we discovered that a *regular* could be an *obnoxo* or a *bore*, a *party* could be a *zoo*, a *cougar* was always a *jock*, but a *jock* could also be a *regular* or *person off the street*. Even though it seemed confusing, we knew it was important to the waitresses to make such fine distinctions among types of customers and that they organized all these categories in some way. As our research progressed it became clear that waitresses operated with several different sets of categories. One appeared to be the

basis for the formal social structure of the bar, the others could only be understood in terms of the specific social networks of the waitresses. Let us examine each briefly.

The formal social structure included three major categories of people *customers*, *employees*, and *managers*. When someone first enters the bar and the waitresses look to see who it is, they quickly identify an individual in terms of one or another category in this formal social structure. The terms used form a folk taxonomy shown in Figure 1. Waitresses use these categories to identify who people are, anticipate their behavior, and plan strategies for performing their role.

Although waitresses often learn names and individual identities, it is not necessary. What every girl must know is the category to which people belong. It is essential, for example, to distinguish between a real regular and a person off the street. Both are customers, but both do not receive identical service from her. For example, a waitress should not have to ask a real regular what he's drinking, she should expect some friendly bantering as she waits on him, and she

Kinds of people at Brady's Bar	Managers		
	Employees	Bartenders	Night bartenders
			Day bartenders
		Bouncers	
		Waitresses	Day waitresses
			Night waitresses
	Customers	Regulars	Real regulars
			Regulars
		People off the street	Loners
			Couples
			Businessmen
			People off the street
			Drunks
		Female customers	

FIGURE 1

won't be offended if he puts his arm around her waist. A person off the street, however, receives only minimal attention from the waitress. Denise will have to inquire what he or she wants to drink, she won't be interested in spending her time talking with him, and she will be offended if he makes physical advances. It is important that Denise recognize these differences and not confuse the two kinds of customers. Being a good waitress means she can make such important distinctions. Although a knowledge of this formal social structure is essential to waitresses, it is not sufficient for the complexities of social interaction in Brady's Bar. In order to understand the other categories for identifying people and also to see how waitresses use the social structure, we need to examine the nature of *social networks*.

SOCIAL NETWORK

Social network analysis shifts our attention from the social structure as a formal system to the way it is seen through the eyes of individual members, in this case, the cocktail waitresses. Each waitress is at the center of several social networks. [See Figure 2] Some link her to specific individuals in the bar; other networks have strands that run outside the bar to college professors, roommates, friends, and parents. In addition to the formal social structure, we discovered at least three different sets of identities that make up distinct social networks. Only through an awareness of these networks is it possible to understand the way waitresses view their social world.

10   The first is a social network determined by the behavioral attributes of people. As the girls make their way between the bar and tables each night, identities such as *customer*, *waitress*, and *bartender* become less significant than ones like *bitch* and *obnoxo* based on specific actions of individuals. Sue returns to a table of four men as she balances a tray of drinks. No sooner has she started placing them on the table than she feels a hand on her leg. In the semidarkness no one knows of this encounter but the customer and the waitress. Should she ignore it or call attention to this violation of her personal space? She quietly steps back and the hand disappears, yet every time she serves the table this regular makes a similar advance. By the middle of the evening Sue is

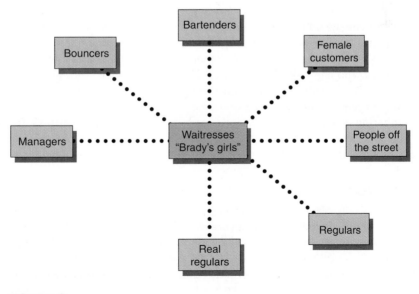

FIGURE 2

saying repeatedly, "Watch the hands." When Sandy takes over for her break, Sue will point out *hands*, a man who has taken on a special social identity in the waitresses' network. The real regular, businessman, loner, person off the street, or almost any kind of male customer can fall into the same network category if his behavior warrants it. A customer who peels paper off the beer bottles and spills wax from the candle becomes a *pig*. The person who slows down the waitress by always engaging her in conversation, perhaps insisting that she sit at his table and talk, becomes a *bore*. As drinking continues during an evening, the behavior of some individuals moves so far outside the bounds of propriety that they become *obnoxos*. *Hustlers* gain their reputation by seeking to engage the waitress in some after-work rendezvous. The bartender who is impatient or rude becomes someone for the waitress to avoid, a real *bastard*. Even another waitress can be a *bitch* by her lack of consideration for the other girls. When a new waitress begins work, she doesn't know what kind of actions to expect nor how to evaluate them. Part of her socialization involves learning the categories and rules for operating within this network.

A second social network is based on social identities from outside the bar itself. Holly's roommate from college often visits the bar and one or another waitress serves her. Although she is a *customer*, they treat her as one of the other girl's *roommates* who has a special place in this social network. Each waitress will reciprocate when the close friends of other waitresses come to the bar, offering special attention to these customers. The colleges attended by customers and employees provide another basis for identifying people. "That's a table of Annie's," Joyce will say about the girls from St. Anne's College. *Cougars* are customers who also play on the university football team. Even *bartenders* and *waitresses* can be terms for kinds of customers when they have these identities from other bars where they work.

Finally, there is a special network of insiders that crosscuts the formal social structure. This is *the Brady family*, made up of managers, employees, and customers—especially real regulars. The new waitress does not know about this select group of people when she first starts work. Sooner or later she will end up hanging around after work to have a drink on the house and talk. In this inner circle she will no longer think of the others as waitresses, bartenders, or customers, but now they are part of the Brady family. This network overarches all the specific categories of people in a dualistic kind of organization, a system not uncommon in non-Western societies. For example, a Nuer tribesman in Africa organizes people primarily on the basis of kinship. He has dozens of kinship terms to sort people into various identities and to anticipate their behavior. But every fellow tribesman, in a general sense, is either *both* or *mar*, distinctions that are important for social interaction. For the waitress, everyone in the bar is either in the Brady family or outside of it.

The social life of Brady's Bar derives its substance and form from the formal social structure as well as the various networks that waitresses and others activate for special purposes. Each waitress finds herself linked in some way to others in the bar with varying degrees of involvement.

SUGGESTIONS FOR DISCUSSION

1. Although this selection opens with a scene of a particular waitress working Brady's Bar, Spradley and Mann are not writing a story of the bar or a description of the shift of one waitress. Why provide this opening scene? How does it help readers to understand the information and analysis provided in the rest of the selection?

2. Recall a place where you have worked or think about the place where you currently work. What are some of the types of people who make up that workplace? Make a "single folk

taxonomy" list the way Spradley and Mann do for Brady's Bar. In what way might your list be divided into a more formal social structure, as the researchers divided their list of types at Brady's?

3. From what you have read here, explain how the social network at Brady's functions to help waitresses do their job and, at the same time, creates what Spradley and Mann call the "social life" of the bar.

Fieldwork Project

For this assignment, reconstruct the social network in a workplace, much like Spradley and Mann did. Do this assignment whether or not you are currently holding a job. If you currently hold a job (even if it is volunteer work, campus work, or work for an organization that is paid or unpaid), spend some time taking field notes (see "Participant Observation Fieldwork" in Chapter 3, Schooling) and keep the questions below in mind. If you currently do not hold a job, write about one you have done before and use the questions below to help you recall details of that workplace. Divide your report into three sections: Background, Analysis, and Conclusion.

Background

Begin your report by giving your audience a general background summary of the workplace. The questions below can help you prepare that summary:

1. What is the nature of this business or organization?
2. When did you begin working there? What was/is your job? What difficulties did you encounter during the initial stages of the job?
3. Who are the people in this workplace, and how many employees typically are on the job at one time?
4. Who supervises the workplace? Is that person always present or only occasionally present?
5. What is the pay, if it is a paying position; if it is not, how many volunteer hours are expected of those who work there?
6. What do people expect from employees in this workplace? (For example, do customers expect to be waited on or are they left to themselves to browse?)
7. What is the workspace like? Describe it. How large is it? Is there enough room here for workers to do a job comfortably? Is there anything in particular that is important to mention about the space? (For example, is it exceptionally dark or open or crowded?)

Analysis: Reconstructing the Social Network of the Workplace

Your aim in this central section of your report is to reconstruct the social network of the workplace. Spradley and Mann use both visual diagrams and descriptive analysis to explain how workers and customers interact in the bar to form the social network at Brady's. You can do the same. Begin by visually mapping out relationships and follow that diagram with a description of the social network you have reconstructed. The following questions can help you with your analysis:

1. Who is in charge (either by actually having a position above others or by virtue of less formal or unstated determinations)? Is the boss or supervisor always in control, or do subordinates have their own ways of doing what they want?

2. How do workers spend their time while on the job?

3. How do workers know what to do and when to do it?

4. What kinds of things happen that help or impede the work done in this place? Are there certain people you would identify as interfering with work and others you would say facilitate the work being done?

5. What seems to be the attitude of those working as they are doing their job?

6. How do workers interact with each other? Do they interact with customers or outside people coming into the workspace? For example, what are the typical informal as well as formal interactions among employees, employees and customers, staff and supervisors, and so on?

7. Is there a person (supervisor or not) who must be pleased or not crossed? How do workers know that?

8. What are some things that go on in the job that you only learned on your own after working there for a time?

9. What are the unspoken rules of this workplace, and how does the social network that has evolved here seem to convey and sustain those rules?

Conclusion

The concluding paragraph of the Spradley and Mann selection offers a quick summary of their descriptive analysis:

> The social life of Brady's Bar derives its form from the formal social structure as well as the various networks that waitresses and others activate for special purposes. Each waitress finds herself linked in some way to others in the bar with varying degrees of involvement.

Your conclusion ought to do the same. Summarize your analysis quickly in this concluding portion of the report.

MINING THE ARCHIVE

Lewis Hine and the Social Uses of Photography

To learn more about sweatshops, visit
www.ablongman.com/george/133

American photographer Lewis Hine believed that photography had an educational and social role to play, and he used his photographs to educate Americans about the conditions of working life in the United States in the first part of the twentieth century. For many years, Hine did work for the National Child Labor Committee. Historian Alan Trachtenberg has written that, for Hine, "social photography means that the photography itself performed a social act,

"Glass Factory Workers."

made a particular communication." Hine believed that pictures could make a difference in the way people thought about issues, such as those surrounding child labor laws. He saw photography as a means of interpreting and revealing the world of work to the public at large.

In 1907, Hine was invited to participate in what came to be called "The Pittsburgh Survey," an investigation of labor conditions in Pittsburgh at the time. Hine's photos from that project were used in six volumes of the magazine the *Survey*, a new publication that had originally been called *Charities and the Commons*. Hine's work was also a familiar feature of the *Survey Graphic*, a monthly magazine begun in 1921.

Both of these publications are still available in many local and college libraries today. Check your library for that publication, and locate Hine's photographs in the early volumes. If you cannot find copies of the *Survey*, enter "Lewis Hine" into the image search engine on your computer and find representative examples of his work in dozens of Internet locations, including sites for the George Eastman House, the Library of Congress, the New York Public Library, the University of Georgia Libraries, and the Chicago Historical Society.

Once you have located photographs by Lewis Hine and information on him and his work, use that material to report on the world of child labor as Hine interpreted it in these photos. In your report, look for what is distinctive about Lewis Hine's vision of child labor in America and speculate about why his photographs remain in the public eye today, even showing up occasionally in labor publicity.

History

> One of the marks of a good professional historian is the consistency with which he reminds his readers of the purely provisional nature of his characterization of events, agents, and agencies found in the always incomplete historical record.
>
> —Hayden White,
> *Tropics of Discourse*

Alfred Stieglitz's "The Steerage," 1907. Library of Congress

When asked what history is, most people say that it is the story of what has happened in the past. They might think of the dates they memorized and the events they learned in school—history as a set of facts about the Louisiana Purchase, the Mexican-American War, or the Homestead Act. Accounts of these events can be verified by records and evidence from the past, and based on these facts, these accounts are taken to be true.

But it is precisely because history claims an authority based on fact that it is important to ask a further question, namely, where do the facts come from? It is true that, in one sense, the facts are simply there—in historical records, newspapers, government documents, archives, and so forth. The facts, however, cannot come forward on their own to speak for themselves. So although it seems incontestable that Columbus did indeed sail from Spain to the West Indies in 1492, the meanings of the event, depending on how people have presented them, can vary considerably.

Students have to learn by heart many things in school. The alphabet. The multiplication tables. The names of the continents and oceans. But students also learn history by heart—and it is worth examining just what "to learn by heart" means. On the one hand, it means memorizing dates, names, and events—and probably getting tested on them. On the other hand, it also suggests an emotional investment. To learn the history of the American Revolution or the Civil War by heart is not just to acquire the facts but to acquire judgments and attitudes and to form social allegiances and loyalties. History, most students understand, despite the ostensibly objective tone of their textbooks, is a moral drama that contains lessons to teach them about which side they belong to in the unfolding story, for example, of the American nation.

The story Americans learn through school and history textbooks is a tale of national destiny—of how hard-working Americans developed a democratic society in the New World and how America prospered and grew bigger and stronger to become an industrial and geopolitical power in the twentieth century. According to this story, the expansion of America's borders and productivity is simply the natural growth and development of the nation, the inevitable unfolding of the country's role in history. This sense of destiny and national purpose is linked closely to Americans' image of themselves and their mission as a people. For many Americans, history is a form of collective memory that joins the country together in a national identity and explains how America became what it is today. American history, in this regard, is not just a matter of the facts. It takes on a mythic dimension by telling of the founding events, heroic acts, and tragic sacrifices that have made this country a powerful nation.

Until fairly recently, there existed a broad consensus about the meaning of American history and its principles of development. Nowadays, however, the version of American history that had prevailed in schools and textbooks has been called into question. Historians have started to reread the historical record to see what voices have been silenced or ignored in the story of America's national development. New perspectives—from women, African Americans, Latinos, Native Americans, Asian Americans, and working-class people—are being added to America's collective history; these alternative accounts complicate the picture of the American past considerably. The westward expansion, for example, from the perspective of Native Americans, looks less like the progressive development of the land and its agricultural and mineral resources and more like the military conquest and occupation of traditional tribal holdings.

The purpose of this chapter is to investigate the writing of history—and why individuals and groups might tell different versions of the past. You will be asked to read, think, and write about the version of American history that you learned in school. You will be asked to recall not only what you learned but also what lessons you were led to draw from the study of the past. You will be asked to think about whose version of the American past you learned, and whose perspectives are included and whose are excluded in the story. You will be asked to consider whether

American history needs to be rewritten to include those perspectives that are absent—the voices from the past that have been silent in the history Americans learn in school.

You will be asked to read for the plot in historians' and other writers' accounts of the past—to describe what their perspectives bring into view about the past and how they have selected and arranged the events to tell a story. By looking at how historians and writers construct versions of the past (always from their particular perspective in the present), you can identify not only the techniques that they use to tell a story but also the different versions of the past that they make available to readers today. In contemporary America, to think about history is to think about competing versions of the past, and you will want to consider how the plots differ—and what is thereby at stake—in the various accounts of the past that you read in the following selections. The chapter's readings have been chosen to include contrasting examples of historical writing—official versions of American history taken from textbooks as well as efforts of revisionist historians and writers to retell the story of the American past. What you will see is that the differences in plots and perspectives raise profound questions about who is entitled to write American history and whose voices are heard.

The answers you get to these and to other questions are concerned finally not just with the study of the past but also with how you as a reader and writer align yourself in the present—how you know what the sides are in American history and where your sympathies reside. The purpose of this chapter, therefore, is to cause you to think about the role that history plays in your own and other people's lives and how it defines (or challenges) Americans' sense of identity as a people and as a nation.

MORE THAN JUST A SHRINE: PAYING HOMAGE TO THE GHOSTS OF ELLIS ISLAND

— Mary Gordon

Mary Gordon is an acclaimed novelist and short-story writer who teaches at Barnard College. Her novels *Final Payments, The Company of Women,* and *The Other Side* explore the history and culture of Irish Catholics in America. In the following selection, an essay originally published in the *New York Times* (1987), Gordon offers her personal reflections on the history of immigration that brought her ancestors—Irish, Italian, and Lithuanian Jews—to the United States by way of Ellis Island, the point of entry in New York Harbor for more than 16 million immigrants between 1892 and 1924. In her essay, Gordon suggests that history is a living relationship to the past, in this case to the "ghosts of Ellis Island" that she wants to honor.

SUGGESTION FOR READING   As you read, notice that Mary Gordon provides a good deal of historical information about Ellis Island, and yet her main point is to establish her own personal connection to this American landmark. Mark passages where Gordon locates herself in relation to what took place in the past.

1 I once sat in a hotel in Bloomsbury trying to have breakfast alone. A Russian with a habit of compulsively licking his lips asked if he could join me. I was afraid to say no; I thought it might be bad for détente. He explained to me that he was a linguist and that he always liked to talk to Americans to see if he could make any connection between their speech and their

ethnic background. When I told him about my mixed ancestry—my mother is Irish and Italian, my father was a Lithuanian Jew—he began jumping up and down in his seat, rubbing his hands together and licking his lips even more frantically.

"Ah," he said, "so you are really somebody who comes from what is called the boiling pot of America." Yes, I told him; yes, I was; but I quickly rose to leave. I thought it would be too hard to explain to him the relation of the boiling potters to the main course, and I wanted to get to the British Museum. I told him that the only thing I could think of that united people whose backgrounds, histories, and points of view were utterly diverse was that their people had landed at a place called Ellis Island.

I didn't tell him that Ellis Island was the only American landmark I'd ever visited. How could I describe to him the estrangement I'd always felt from the kind of traveler who visits shrines to America's past greatness, those rebuilt forts with muskets behind glass and sabers mounted on the walls and gift shops selling maple sugar candy in the shape of Indian headdresses, those reconstructed villages with tables set for fifty and the Paul Revere silver gleaming? All that Americana—Plymouth Rock, Gettysburg, Mount Vernon, Valley Forge—it all inhabits for me a zone of blurred abstraction with far less hold on my imagination than the Bastille or Hampton Court. I suppose I've always known that my uninterest in it contains a large component of the willed: I am American, and those places purport to be my history. But they are not mine.

Ellis Island is, though; it's the one place I can be sure my people are connected to. And so I made a journey there to find my history, like any Rotarian traveling in his Winnebago to Antietam to find his. I had become part of that humbling democracy of people looking in some site for a past that has grown unreal. The monument I traveled to was not, however, a tribute to some old glory. The minute I set foot upon the island I could feel all that it stood for: insecurity, obedience, anxiety, dehumanization, the terrified

and careful deference of the displaced. I hadn't traveled to the Battery and boarded a ferry across from the Statue of Liberty to raise flags or breathe a richer, more triumphant air. I wanted to do homage to the ghosts.

5   I felt them everywhere, from the moment I disembarked and saw the building with its high-minded brick, its hopeful little lawn, its ornamental cornices. The place was derelict when I arrived; it had not functioned for more than thirty years—almost as long as the time it had operated at full capacity as a major immigration center. I was surprised to learn what a small part of history Ellis Island had occupied. The main building was constructed in 1892, then rebuilt between 1898 and 1900 after a fire. Most of the immigrants who arrived during the latter half of the nineteenth century, mainly northern and western Europeans, landed not at Ellis Island but on the western tip of the Battery, at Castle Garden, which had opened as a receiving center for immigrants in 1855.

By the 1880s, the facilities at Castle Garden had grown scandalously inadequate. Officials looked for an island on which to build a new immigration center, because they thought that on an island immigrants could be more easily protected from swindlers and quickly transported to railroad terminals in New Jersey. Bedloe's Island was considered, but New Yorkers were aghast at the idea of a "Babel" ruining their beautiful new treasure, "Liberty Enlightening the World." The statue's sculptor, Frédéric-Auguste Bartholdi, reacted to the prospect of immigrants landing near his masterpiece in horror; he called it a "monstrous plan." So much for Emma Lazarus.

Ellis Island was finally chosen because the citizens of New Jersey petitioned the federal government to remove from the island an old naval powder magazine that they thought dangerously close to the Jersey shore. The explosives were removed; no one wanted the island for anything. It was the perfect place to build an immigration center.

I thought about the island's history as I walked into the building and made my way to the room that was the center in my imagination of the Ellis Island experience: the Great Hall. It had been made real for me in the stark, accusing photographs of Louis Hine and others, who took those pictures to make a point. It was in the Great Hall that everyone had waited—waiting, always, the great vocation of the dispossessed. The room was empty, except for me and a handful of other visitors and the park ranger who showed us around. I felt myself grow insignificant in that room, with its huge semicircular windows, its air, even in dereliction, of solid and official probity.

I walked in the deathlike expansiveness of the room's disuse and tried to think of what it might have been like, filled and swarming. More than sixteen million immigrants came through that room; approximately 250,000 were rejected. Not really a large proportion, but the implications for the rejected were dreadful. For some, there was nothing to go back to, or there was certain death; for others, who left as adventurers, to return would be to adopt in local memory the fool's role, and the failure's. No wonder that the island's history includes reports of three thousand suicides.

10 Sometimes immigrants could pass through Ellis Island in mere hours, though for some the process took days. The particulars of the experience in the Great Hall were often influenced by the political events and attitudes on the mainland. In the 1890s and the first years of the new century, when cheap labor was needed, the newly built receiving center took in its immigrants with comparatively little question. But as the century progressed, the economy worsened, eugenics became both scientifically respectable and popular, and World War I made American xenophobia seem rooted in fact.

Immigration acts were passed; newcomers had to prove, besides moral correctness and financial solvency, their ability to read. Quota laws came into effect, limiting the number of immigrants from southern and eastern Europe to less than 14 percent of the total quota. Intelligence tests were biased against all non-English-speaking persons, and medical examinations

became increasingly strict, until the machinery of immigration nearly collapsed under its own weight. The Second Quota Law of 1924 provided that all immigrants be inspected and issued visas at American consular offices in Europe, rendering the center almost obsolete.

On the day of my visit, my mind fastened upon the medical inspections, which had always seemed to me most emblematic of the ignominy and terror the immigrants ensured. The medical inspectors, sometimes dressed in uniforms like soldiers, were particularly obsessed with a disease of the eyes called trachoma, which they checked for by flipping back the immigrants' top eyelids with a hook used for buttoning gloves— a method that sometimes resulted in the transmission of the disease to healthy people. Mothers feared that if their children cried too much, their red eyes would be mistaken for a symptom of the disease and the whole family would be sent home. Those immigrants suspected of some physical disability had initials chalked on their coats. I remembered the photographs I'd seen of people standing, dumbstruck and innocent as cattle, with their manifest numbers hung around their necks and initials marked in chalk upon their coats: "E" for eye trouble, "K" for hernia, "L" for lameness, "X" for mental defects, "H" for heart disease.

I thought of my grandparents as I stood in the room: my seventeen-year-old grandmother, coming alone from Ireland in 1896, vouched for by a stranger who had found her a place as a domestic servant to some Irish who had done well. I tried to imagine the assault it all must have been for her; I've been to her hometown, a collection of farms with a main street—smaller than the athletic field of my local public school. She must have watched the New York skyline as the first- and second-class passengers were whisked off the gangplank with the most cursory of inspections while she was made to board a ferry to the new immigration center.

What could she have made of it—this buff-painted wooden structure with its towers and its blue slate roof, a place *Harper's Weekly* described as "a latter-day watering place hotel"? It would have been the first time she had heard people speaking something other than English. She would have mingled with people carrying baskets on their heads and eating foods unlike any she had ever seen—dark-eyed people, like the Sicilian she would marry ten years later, who came over with his family at thirteen, the man of the family, responsible even then for his mother and sister. I don't know what they thought, my grandparents, for they were not expansive people, nor romantic; they didn't like to think of what they called "the hard times," and their trip across the ocean was the single adventurous act of lives devoted after landing to security, respectability, and fitting in.

15   What is the potency of Ellis Island for someone like me—an American, obviously, but one who has always felt that the country really belonged to the early settlers, that, as J. F. Powers wrote in *Morte D'Urban*, it had been "handed down to them by the Pilgrims, George Washington and others, and that they were taking a risk in letting you live in it." I have never been the victim of overt discrimination; noth-ing I have wanted has been denied me because of the accidents of blood. But I suppose it is part of being an American to be engaged in a somewhat tiresome but always self-absorbing process of national definition. And in this process, I have found in traveling to Ellis Island an important piece of evidence that could remind me I was right to feel my differentness. Something had happened to my people on that island, a result of the eternal wrongheadedness of American protectionism and the predictabilities of simple greed. I came to the island, too, so I could tell the ghosts that I was one of them, and that I honored them—their stoicism, and their innocence, the fear that turned them inward, and their pride. I wanted to tell them that I liked them better than I did the Americans who made them pass through the Great Hall and stole their names and chalked their weaknesses in public on their clothing. And to tell the ghosts what I have always thought: that American history was a very classy party that was not much fun until they arrived, brought the good food, turned up the music, and taught everyone to dance.

SUGGESTIONS FOR DISCUSSION

1. Mary Gordon describes the "estrangement I'd always felt from the kind of traveler who visits shrines to America's past greatness" and goes on to say that "those places purport to be my history. But they are not mine." Why does Gordon feel this way? What is she suggesting about the way that people experience the history of America? Do some parts belong to you but not others?

2. What historical landmarks have you visited with your family or on class trips in elementary or high school? What were your feelings about those trips? Compare your experience with Gordon's. Did you experience these historical sites as part of your history? Explain.

3. Gordon says that Ellis Island is "the one place I can be sure my people are connected to." Name a place to which your people are connected, where you could, as Gordon puts it, "do homage to the ghosts." To what extent is the place you have named alike or different from the places that your classmates have named?

SUGGESTIONS FOR WRITING

1. Mary Gordon says the one thing that unifies her ancestors—Irish, Italian, and Lithuanian Jews "whose backgrounds, histories, and points of view were utterly diverse"—is that they all landed at Ellis Island. Write an essay that explores the diversity among your ancestors and considers whether there is something—a place such as Ellis Island or a historical event such as immigration—that unites them.

2. Use Gordon's account of her visit to Ellis Island as a model to write an essay that explains your response to visiting a historical site. Explain the historical importance of the place you visited, but also follow Gordon's example to explain your own relation to that history. Did you experience the place as part of a history to which you felt connected, or did you, for some reason, feel estranged?

3. Gordon's essay suggests that history is as much a matter of paying "homage to the ghosts" as it is learning a chronology of events. Pick a historical figure, place, or event in American history with which you feel a strong personal identification. Describe it and then explain the reasons for your identification. Use the essay as an occasion to pay homage—to explain your personal allegiances and why the person, place, or event seems important to you.

OCTOBER 12, 1492

— *Michel-Rolph Trouillot*

Michel-Rolph Trouillot is a professor of anthropology and social sciences at the University of Chicago. He is a leading scholar on Haitian and Caribbean history and culture. This except focuses on the meaning of the familiar date October 12, 1492, when Columbus arrived in the New World. This reading comes from Trouillot's book *Silencing the Past: Power and the Production of History* (1995). Here, Trouillot asks a very fundamental question about the way we understand historical events by calling our attention to the differences between "what happened" and "that which is said to have happened."

SUGGESTION FOR READING Before you start reading, write a short summary of what the date October 12, 1492, calls to mind and the historical significance it has. As you read, consider how the version Michel-Rolph Trouillot offers compares to what you've written.

1 History is messy for the people who must live it. For those within the shaky boundaries of Roman Christendom, the most important event of the year 1492 nearly happened in 1491. Late at night on November 25, 1491, Abu l-Qasim al-Muhli signed the treaties by which the Muslim kingdom of Granada surrendered to the Catholic kingdom of Castile, ending a war the issue of which had become clear a few months earlier. The transfer of power was scheduled for May, but some of the Muslim leaders decided not to wait for the Christian takeover and left town unexpectedly. Granada's Nasrid ruler, Muhammad XII Boabdil, rushed the capitulation. Thus, it was almost by accident that the flag of Castile and the cross of Christendom were raised over the tower of the Alhambra on January 2, 1492, rather than during the previous fall, as first expected, or the following spring, as scheduled.

For actors and witnesses alike, the end of the reconquista was a disorderly series of occurrences, neither a single event, nor a single date. The end of the war and the signing of the treaties—both of which occurred in year 1491 of the Christian calendar—were as significant as the flight of the Muslim leaders, the raising of the Christian flag, or the glorious entry of the Catholic monarchs into the conquered city on January 6, 1492. The capitulation of Granada was, however, as close to a milestone as history in the making can get. Milestones are always set in regard to a past, and the past that Western Christendom had fashioned for itself projected the moving Spanish frontier as the southernmost rampart of the cross.

Since the Council of Clermont (1095), in part as an unexpected effect of three centuries of Islamic influence and control, Christian militants from both sides of the Pyrenees had heralded the reconquest of the Iberian peninsula as a sort of Christian jihad, the via Hispania to the Holy Land, a necessary stage on the road to the Holy Sepulchre. Popes, bishops, and kings had enlisted the limited—but highly symbolic—participation of Catholics from France to Scotland in various campaigns with such incentives as the partial remission of penance.

To be sure, cultural interpenetration between Christians, Moslems, and Jews went on in the peninsula and even north of the Pyrenees long after Alfonso Henriques took Lisbon from the Arabs and placed Portugal under the tutelage of the church early in the twelfth century. But the rhetoric of the popes and the merger of church and state power in the Iberian dominions, which went back to the Visigoths, created an ideological space where religions and cultures that mingled in daily life were seen as officially incompatible. Within that space, the defense of a Christendom, projected as pure and besieged, became a dominant idiom for the military campaigns.

5   Both religious and military ardor declined in the second half of the fourteenth century, yet religion remained by default the closest thing to a "public arena" until the end of the Middle Ages, and religious figures the most able crowd leaders. Thus when religious and military enthusiasm, still intertwined, climbed together once more during Isabella's reign, the ultimate significance of the war for Christendom resurfaced unquestioned. Even then, though, if many of those who lived the fall of Granada saw in it an occurrence of exceptional relevance, it was a milestone only for the peculiar individuals who paid attention to such things in the first place.

It mattered little then, in comparison, that a few months after entering Granada, the Catholic monarchs gave their blessing to a Genoese adventurer eager to reach India via a short-cut through the western seas. It would matter little

that the Genoese was wrong, having grossly underestimated the distance to be traveled. It probably mattered less, at the time, that the Genoese and his Castilian companions reached not the Indies but a tiny islet in the Bahamas on October 12, 1492. The landing in the Bahamas was certainly not the event of the year 1492, if only because the few who cared, on the other side of the Atlantic, did not learn about it until 1493.

How interesting, then, that 1492 has become Columbus's year, and October 12 the day of "The Discovery." Columbus himself has become a quintessential "Spaniard" or a representative of "Italy"—two rather vague entities during his lifetime. The landing has become a clear-cut event much more fixed in time than the prolonged fall of Muslim Granada, the seemingly interminable expulsion of European Jews, or the tortuous consolidation of royal power in the early Renaissance. Whereas these latter issues still appear as convoluted processes—thus the favored turf of academic specialists who break them down into an infinite list of themes for doctoral dissertations—The Discovery has lost its processual character. It has become a single and simple moment.

The creation of that historical moment facilitates the narrativization of history, the transformation of what happened into that which is said to have happened. First, chronology replaces process. All events are placed in a single line leading to the landfall. The years Columbus spent in Portugal, the knowledge he accumulated from Portuguese and North African sailors, his efforts to peddle his project to various monarchs are subsumed among the "antecedents" to The Discovery. Other occurrences, such as the participation of the Pinzon brothers, are included under "the preparations," although in the time lived by the actors, that participation preceded, overlapped, and outlived the landfall. Second, as intermingled processes fade into a linear continuity, context also fades out. For instance, the making of Europe, the rise of the absolutist state, the *reconquista*, and Christian religious intransigence all spread over centuries and paralleled the invention of the Americas. These Old World transformations were not without consequences. Most notably, they created in Castile and elsewhere a number of rejects. Indeed, the first Europeans who made it to the New World were in great majority the rejects of Europe, individuals of modest means who had nothing to lose in a desperate adventure. But in the narrative of The Discovery, Europe becomes a neutral and ageless essence able to function, in turn, as stage for "the preparations," as background for "the voyage," and as supportive cast in a noble epic.

The isolation of a single moment thus creates a historical "fact": on this day, in 1492, Christopher Columbus discovered the Bahamas. As a set event, void of context and marked by a fixed date, this chunk of history becomes much more manageable outside of the academic guild. It returns inevitably: one can await its millenial and prepare its commemoration. It accommodates travel agents, airlines, politicians, the media, or the states who sell it in the prepackaged forms by which the public has come to expect history to present itself for immediate consumption. It is a product of power whose label has been cleansed of traces of power.

10   The naming of the "fact" is itself a narrative of power disguised as innocence. Would anyone care to celebrate the "Castilian invasion of the Bahamas"? Yet this phrasing is somewhat closer to what happened on October 12, 1492, than "the discovery of America." Naming the fact thus already imposes a reading and many historical controversies boil down to who has the power to name what. To call "discovery" the first invasions of inhabited lands by Europeans is an exercise in Eurocentric power that already frames future narratives of the event so described. Contact with the West is seen as the foundation of historicity of different cultures. Once discovered by Europeans, the Other finally enters the human world.

In the 1990s, quite a few observers, historians, and activists worldwide denounced the arrogance implied by this terminology during the quincentennial celebrations of Columbus's Bahamian landing. Some spoke of a Columbian Holocaust. Some proposed "conquest" instead of discovery; others preferred "encounter," which suddenly gained an immense popularity—one more testimony, if needed, of the capacity of liberal discourse to compromise between its premises and its practice. "Encounter" sweetens the horror, polishes the rough edges that do not fit neatly either side of the controversy. Everyone seems to gain.

Not everyone was convinced. Portuguese historian Vitorino Magalhaes Godinho, a former minister of education, reiterated that "discovery" was an appropriate term for the European ventures of the fifteenth and sixteenth centuries, which he compares to Herschel's discovery of Uranus, and Sédillot's discovery of microbes. The problem is, of course, that Uranus did not know that it existed before Herschel, and that Sédillot did not go after the microbes with a sword and a gun.

Yet more than blind arrogance is at issue here. Terminologies demarcate a field, politically and epistemologically. Names set up a field of power. "Discovery" and analogous terms ensure that by just mentioning the event one enters a predetermined lexical field of clichés and predictable categories that foreclose a redefinition of the political and intellectual stakes. Europe becomes the center of "what happened." Whatever else may have happened to other peoples in that process is already reduced to a natural fact: they were discovered. The similarity to planets and microbes precedes their explicit mention by future historians and cabinet ministers.

For this reason, I prefer to say that Columbus "stumbled on the Bahamas," or "discovered the Antilles," and I prefer "conquest" over "discovery" to describe what happened after the landing. Such phrasings are awkward and may raise some eyebrows. They may even annoy some readers. But both the awkwardness and the fact that the entire issue can be dismissed as trivial quibbling suggests that it is not easy to subvert the very language describing the facts of the matter. For the power to decide what is trivial—and annoying—is also part of the power to decide how "what happened" becomes "that which is said to have happened." . . .

15   Commemorations sanitize further the messy history lived by the actors. They contribute to the continuous myth-making process that gives history its more definite shapes: they help to create, modify, or sanction the public meanings attached to historical events deemed worthy of mass celebration. As rituals that package history for public consumption, commemorations play the numbers game to create a past that seems both more real and more elementary.

Numbers matter at the end point, the consumption side of the game: the greater the number of participants in a celebration, the stronger the allusion to the multitude of witnesses for whom the mythicized event is supposed to have meant something from day one. In 1992, when millions of people celebrated a quincentennial staged by states, advertisers, and travel agents, their very mass reinforced the illusion that Columbus's contemporaries must have known— how could they not?—that October 12, 1492, was indeed a momentous event. As we have seen, it was not; and many of our contemporaries, for various reasons, said as much. But few of the 1992 celebrants could accentuate publicly the banality of that date, five hundred years before, without having to admit also that power had intervened between the event and its celebration.

The more varied the participants, the easier also the claim to world historical significance. Numbers matter also as items in the calendar. Years, months, and dates present history as part of the natural cycles of the world. By packaging events within temporal sequences, commemorations adorn the past with certainty: the proof of the happening is in the cyclical inevitability of its celebration.

Cycles may vary, of course, but annual cycles provide a basic element of modern commemorations: an exact date. As a tool of historical production, that date anchors the event in the present. It does so through the simultaneous production of mentions and silences. The recurrence of a predictable date severs Columbus's landfall from the context of emerging Europe on and around 1492. It obliterates the rest of the year now subsumed within a twenty-four hour segment. It imposes a silence upon all events surrounding the one being marked. A potentially endless void now encompasses everything that could be said and is not being said about 1492 and about the years immediately preceding or following.

The void, however, is not left unfilled. The fixed date alone places the event within a new frame with linkages of its own. As a fixed date, October 12 is the fetishized repository for a potentially endless list of disparate events, such as the birth of U.S. activist Dick Gregory or that of Italian tenor Luciano Pavarotti; the independence of Equatorial Guinea; the Broadway opening of the musical *Jesus Christ Superstar*; or the refusal of a Catholic monk, one Martin Luther, to repudiate assertions posted months before on the door of a church in Germany. All these events happened on October 12 of the Christian calendar, in various years from 1518 to 1971. All are likely to be acknowledged publicly by varying numbers of milestone worshippers. Each of them, in turn, can be replaced by another event judged to be equally—or more—noteworthy: Paraguay's break from Argentina in 1811, the 1976 arrest of the Chinese Gang of Four, the beginning of the German occupation of France in 1914, or the approval of the Magna Carta by Edward I of England in 1297.

20   The roster is theoretically expandable in any direction. If the Magna Carta is the most ancient icon mentioned here, that is because these examples have come from the institutionalized memory of what is now the West and were all indexed through Dionysius Exiguus's system. With other modes of counting and another pool of events, October 12 of the Christian calendar could overlap in any given year a number of anniversaries next to which the landing in the Bahamas would look quite recent. As arbitrary

markers of time, dates link a number of dissimilar events, all equally decontextualized and equally susceptible to mythicization. The longer the list of events celebrated on the same date, the more that list looks like an answer in a trivia game. But this is precisely because celebrations trivialize the historical process (historicity 1) at the same time that they mythicize history (historicity 2).

The myth-making process does not operate evenly, however, and the preceding list suggests as much. For if—in theory—all events can be decontextualized to the same point of emptiness, in practice not all are reshaped by the same power plays and not all mean the same to new actors entering the stage and busily reformulating and appropriating the past. In short, celebrations are created, and this creation is part and parcel of the process of historical production. Celebrations straddle the two sides of historicity. They impose a silence upon the events that they ignore, and they fill that silence with narratives of power about the event they celebrate.

The reasons to celebrate Columbus Day and to do so on October 12 are now obvious to most Americans, just as the rationale behind the quincentennial was obvious to many in the West. Most advocates of these celebrations will evoke the obvious significance of "what happened" in 1492 and the no less obvious consequences of that event. But the road between then and now is no more straightforward than the relation between what happened and what is said to have happened. October 12 was certainly not a historical landmark in Columbus's day. It took centuries of battles—both petty and grandiose—and quite a bit of luck to turn it into a significant date. Further, not all those who agree now that the date and the event it indexes are important agree on the significance of its celebration. The images and debates that surround the appropriation of Columbus vary from Spain to the United States and from both Spain and the United States to Latin America, to mention only three areas treated in this chapter. Constructions of Columbus and of Columbus Day vary within these areas according to time and also according to factors such as class and ethnic identification. In short, the road between then and now is itself a history of power.

SUGGESTIONS FOR DISCUSSION

1. Michel-Rolph Trouillot says it is "interesting" that "1492 has become Columbus's year, and October 12 the day of 'The Discovery.' " Why does he think this is so interesting? To answer this question, consider the first six paragraphs of historical background Trouillot gives. How does this provide a context to understand Columbus's voyage to the New World?

2. Work together in a group. Write as many sentences as you can about "what happened" on October 12, 1492. You can begin with the conventional sentence, "Columbus discovered America on October 12, 1492." (Trouillot offers the version "stumbled on the Bahamas" or "discovered the Antilles.") How do these sentences illustrate the distinction Trouillot wants to draw between "what happened" and "that which is said to have happened"? What do you see as the significance of this distinction?

3. Trouillot says it "mattered little" to people in Spain in 1492 that Columbus's ships arrived in the New World. It was "certainly not the event of year," he says. What was the "event of the year" in Spain in 1492? If we now commonly identify the momentous event of 1492 as Columbus's landing in the Bahamas, what has taken place in between? In what sense is this an example of what Trouillot sees as the intervention of power between the "event" and its "celebration"?

SUGGESTIONS FOR WRITING

1. Use the sentences you and your classmates have written about "what happened" on October 12, 1492, to write an essay on what Trouillot means by the difference between "what happened" and "that which is said to have happened."

2. Write a personal essay that explores your own understanding of the date October 12, 1492, and how Trouillot's account relates to the way you understand the significance of the date. You might begin by explaining how you learned the significance of the date. Given this understanding, explain what it was like to read "October 12, 1492." To what extent has your encounter with Trouillot's version caused you to revise your previous perspective on 1492? What do you see as the significance of your response?

3. Write an essay that explains what you see as the significance of Columbus Day as a national holiday in the United States. Consider here Trouillot's comment on how power operates between the "event" and its "celebration."

"INDIANS": TEXTUALISM, MORALITY, AND THE PROBLEM OF HISTORY

— *Jane Tompkins*

Jane Tompkins is a professor of English and education at the University of Illinois, Chicago. She is well known for her literary criticism, including the books *Sensational Designs: The Cultural Work of American Fiction, 1790–1860* (1985) and *West of Everything: The Inner Life of Westerns* (1992). The following essay was written for the journal of literary criticism *Critical Inquiry* and originally appeared in 1986. As you will see, the essay reports on how Tompkins dealt with the conflicting historical interpretations that she encountered in her research on the Puritans' relation with Native Americans.

SUGGESTION FOR READING   Notice that Tompkins's essay can be divided into three parts. The first part raises the problem of conflicting interpretations. The second part—the longest part of the essay—reports on her research and the differing assumptions, perspectives, and interpretations that she has found. In the final part, Tompkins explains how she found a "way out" of the difficulties that these "irreconcilable points of view" posed for her. As you read, annotate the essay to help you keep track of what Tompkins is doing.

1   When I was growing up in New York City, my parents used to take me to an event in Inwood Park at which Indians—real American Indians dressed in feathers and blankets—could be seen and touched by children like me. This event was always a disappointment. It was more fun to imagine that you were an Indian in one of the caves in Inwood Park than to shake the hand of an old man in a headdress who was not overwhelmed at the opportunity of meeting you. After staring at the Indians for a while, we would take a walk in the woods where the caves were, and once I asked my mother if the remains of a fire I had seen in one of them might have been left by the original inhabitants. After that, wandering up some stone steps cut into the side of the hill, I imagined I was a princess in a rude castle. My Indians, like my princesses, were creatures totally of the imagination, and I did not care to have any real exemplars interfering with what I already knew.

I already knew about Indians from having read about them in school. Over and over we were told the story of how Peter Minuit had bought Manhattan Island from the Indians for twenty-four dollars' worth of glass beads. And it was a story we didn't mind hearing because it gave us the rare pleasure of having someone to feel superior to, since the poor Indians had not known (as we eight-year-olds did) how valuable a piece of property Manhattan Island would become. Generally, much was made of the

Indian presence in Manhattan; a poem in one of our readers began: "Where we walk to school today / Indian children used to play," and we were encouraged to write poetry on this topic ourselves. So I had a fairly rich relationship with Indians before I ever met the unprepossessing people in Inwood Park. I felt that I had a lot in common with them. They, too, liked animals (they were often named after animals); they, too, made mistakes—they liked the brightly colored trinkets of little value that the white men were always offering them; they were handsome, war-like, and brave and had led an exciting, roman-tic life in the forest long ago, a life such as I dreamed of leading myself. I felt lucky to be liv-ing in one of the places where they had definitely been. Never mind where they were or what they were doing now.

My story stands for the relationship most non-Indians have to the people who first popu-lated this continent, a relationship characterized by narcissistic fantasies of freedom and adven-ture, of a life lived closer to nature and to spirit than the life we lead now. As Vine Deloria Jr. has pointed out, the American Indian Movement in the early seventies couldn't get people to pay attention to what was happening to Indians who were alive in the present, so powerful was this country's infatuation with people who wore loin-cloths, lived in tepees, and roamed the plains and forests long ago.[1] The present essay, like these fantasies, doesn't have much to do with actual Indians, though its subject matter is the histories of European-Indian relations in seven-teenth-century New England. In a sense, my encounter with Indians as an adult doing "research" replicates the childhood one, for while I started out to learn about Indians, I ended up preoccupied with a problem of my own.

This essay enacts a particular instance of the challenge poststructuralism poses to the study of history. In simpler language, it concerns the dif-ference that point of view makes when people are giving accounts of events, whether at first or second hand. The problem is that if all accounts

of events are determined through and through by the observer's frame of reference, then one will never know, in any given case, what really hap-pened.

5   I encountered this problem in concrete terms while preparing to teach a course in colo-nial American literature. I'd set out to learn what I could about the Puritans' relations with Amer-ican Indians. All I wanted was a general idea of what had happened between the English settlers and the natives in seventeenth-century New Eng-land; poststructuralism and its dilemmas were the furthest thing from my mind. I began, more or less automatically, with Perry Miller, who hardly mentions the Indians at all, then pro-ceeded to the work of historians who had dealt exclusively with the European-Indian encounter. At first, it was a question of deciding which of these authors to believe, for it quickly became apparent that there was no unanimity on the subject. As I read on, however, I discovered that the problem was more complicated than decid-ing whose version of events was correct. Some of the conflicting accounts were not simply con-tradictory, they were completely incommensu-rable, in that their assumptions about what counted as a valid approach to the subject, and what the subject itself was, diverged in funda-mental ways. Faced with an array of mutually irreconcilable points of view, points of view which determined what was being discussed as well as the terms of the discussion, I decided to turn to primary sources for clarification, only to discover that the primary sources reproduced the problem all over again. I found myself, in other words, in an epistemological quandary, not only unable to decide among conflicting versions of events but also unable to believe that any such decision could, in principle, be made. It was a moral quandary as well. Knowledge of what really happened when the Europeans and the Indians first met seemed particularly important, since the result of that encounter was virtual genocide. This was the kind of past "mistake" which, presumably, we studied history in order to avoid repeating. If studying history couldn't

put us in touch with actual events and their causes, then what was to prevent such atrocities from happening again?

For a while, I remained at this impasse. But through analyzing the process by which I had reached it, I eventually arrived at an understanding which seemed to offer a way out. This essay records the concrete experience of meeting and solving the difficulty I have just described (as an abstract problem, I thought I had solved it long ago). My purpose is not to throw new light on antifoundationalist epistemology—the solution I reached is not a new one—but to dramatize and expose the troubles antifoundationalism gets you into when you meet it, so to speak, in the road.

My research began with Perry Miller. Early in the preface to *Errand into the Wilderness*, while explaining how he came to write his history of the New England mind, Miller writes a sentence that stopped me dead. He says that what fascinated him as a young man about his country's history was "the massive narrative of the movement of European culture into the vacant wilderness of America."[2] "Vacant?" Miller, writing in 1956, doesn't pause over the word "vacant," but to people who read his preface thirty years later, the word is shocking. In what circumstances could someone proposing to write a history of colonial New England not take account of the Indian presence there?

The rest of Miller's preface supplies an answer to this question, if one takes the trouble to piece together its details. Miller explains that as a young man, jealous of older compatriots who had had the luck to fight in World War I, he had gone to Africa in search of adventure. "The adventures that Africa afforded," he writes, "were tawdry enough, but it became the setting for a sudden epiphany" (p. vii). "It was given to me," he writes, "disconsolate on the edge of a jungle of central Africa, to have thrust upon me the mission of expounding what I took to be the innermost propulsion of the United States, while supervising, in that barbaric tropic, the unloading

of drums of case oil flowing out of the inexhaustible wilderness of America" (p. viii). Miller's picture of himself on the banks of the Congo furnishes a key to the kind of history he will write and to his mental image of a vacant wilderness; it explains why it was just there, under precisely these conditions, that he should have had his epiphany.

The fuel drums stand, in Miller's mind, for the popular misconception of what this country is about. They are "tangible symbols of [America's] appalling power," a power that everyone but Miller takes for the ultimate reality (p. ix). To Miller, "the mind of man is the basic factor in human history," and he will plead, all unaccommodated as he is among the fuel drums, for the intellect—the intellect for which his fellow historians, with their chapters on "stoves or bathtubs, or tax laws," "the Wilmot Proviso" and "the chain store," "have so little respect" (p. viii, ix). His preface seethes with a hatred of the merely physical and mechanical, and this hatred, which is really a form of moral outrage, explains not only the contempt with which he mentions the stoves and bathtubs but also the nature of his experience in Africa and its relationship to the "massive narrative" he will write.

10   Miller's experiences in Africa are "tawdry," his tropic is barbaric because the jungle he stands on the edge of means nothing to him, no more, indeed something less, than the case oil. It is the nothingness of Africa that precipitates his vision. It is the barbarity of the "dark continent," the obvious (but superficial) parallelism between the jungle at Matadi and America's "vacant wilderness" that releases in Miller the desire to define and vindicate his country's cultural identity. To the young Miller, colonial Africa and colonial America are—but for the history he will bring to light—mirror images of one another. And what he fails to see in the one landscape is the same thing he overlooks in the other: the human beings who people it. As Miller stood with his back to the jungle, thinking about the role of mind in human history, his failure to see that the land into which European culture had

moved was not vacant but already occupied by a varied and numerous population, is of a piece with his failure, in his portrait of himself at Matadi, to notice who was carrying the fuel drums he was supervising the unloading of.

The point is crucial because it suggests that what is invisible to the historian in his own historical moment remains invisible when he turns his gaze to the past. It isn't that Miller didn't "see" the black men, in a literal sense, any more than it's the case that when he looked back he didn't "see" the Indians, in the sense of not realizing they were there. Rather, it's that neither the Indians nor the blacks *counted* for him, in a fundamental way. The way in which Indians can be seen but not counted is illustrated by an entry in Governor John Winthrop's journal, three hundred years before, when he recorded that there had been a great storm with high winds "yet through God's great mercy it did no hurt, but only killed one Indian with the fall of a tree."[3] The juxtaposition suggests that Miller shared with Winthrop a certain colonial point of view, a point of view from which Indians, though present, do not finally matter.

A book entitled *New England Frontier: Puritans and Indians, 1620–1675*, written by Alden Vaughan and published in 1965, promised to rectify Miller's omission. In the outpouring of work on the European-Indian encounter that began in the early sixties, this book is the first major landmark, and to a neophyte it seems definitive. Vaughan acknowledges the absence of Indian sources and emphasizes his use of materials which catch the Puritans "off guard."[4] His announced conclusion that "the New England Puritans followed a remarkably humane, considerate, and just policy in their dealings with the Indians" seems supported by the scope, documentation, and methodicalness of his project (NEF, p. vii). The author's fair-mindedness and equanimity seem everywhere apparent, so that when he asserts "the history of interracial relations from the arrival of the Pilgrims to the outbreak of King Philip's War is a credit to the

integrity of both peoples," one is positively reassured (NEF, p. viii).

But these impressions do not survive an admission that comes late in the book, when, in the course of explaining why works like Helen Hunt Jackson's *Century of Dishonor* had spread misconceptions about Puritan treatment of the Indians, Vaughan finally lays his own cards on the table.

> The root of the misunderstanding [about Puritans and Indians] . . . lie[s] in a failure to recognize the nature of the two societies that met in seventeenth century New England. One was unified, visionary, disciplined, and dynamic. The other was divided, self-satisfied, undisciplined, and static. It would be unreasonable to expect that such societies could live side by side indefinitely with no penetration of the more fragmented and passive by the more consolidated and active. What resulted, then, was not—as many have held—a clash of dissimilar ways of life, but rather the expansion of one into the areas in which the other was lacking. (NEF, p. 323)

From our present vantage point, these remarks seem culturally biased to an incredible degree, not to mention inaccurate: was Puritan society unified? If so, how does one account for its internal dissensions and obsessive need to cast out deviants? Is "unity" necessarily a positive culture trait? From what standpoint can one say that American Indians were neither disciplined nor visionary, when both these characteristics loom so large in the ethnographies? Is it an accident that ways of describing cultural strength and weakness coincide with gender stereotypes—active/passive, and so on? Why is one culture said to "penetrate" the other? Why is the "other" described in terms of "lack"?

Vaughan's fundamental categories of apprehension and judgment will not withstand even the most cursory inspection. For what looked like evenhandedness when he was writing *New England Frontier* does not look that way anymore. In his introduction to *New Directions in American Intellectual History*, John Higham writes that by the end of the sixties the entire conceptual foundation on which [this sort of work] rested [had] crumbled away. . . . Simultaneously, in sociology, anthropology, and history, two working assumptions . . . came under withering attack: first, the assumption that societies tend to be integrated, and second, that a shared culture maintains that integration. . . . By the late 1960s all claims issued in the name of an "American mind" . . . were subject to drastic skepticism.[5]

"Clearly," Higham continues, "the sociocultural upheaval of the sixties created the occasion" for this reaction.[6] Vaughan's book, it seemed, could only have been written before the events of the sixties had sensitized scholars to questions of race and ethnicity. It came as no surprise, therefore, that ten years later there appeared a study of European-Indian relations which reflected the new awareness of social issues the sixties had engendered. And it offered an entirely different picture of the European-Indian encounter.

Francis Jennings's *The Invasion of America* (1975) rips wide open the idea that the Puritans were humane and considerate in their dealings with the Indians. In Jennings's account, even more massively documented than Vaughan's, the early settlers lied to the Indians, stole from them, murdered them, scalped them, captured them, tortured them, raped them, sold them into slavery, confiscated their land, destroyed their crops, burned their homes, scattered their possessions, gave them alcohol, undermined their systems of belief, and infected them with diseases that wiped out ninety percent of their numbers within the first hundred years after contact.[7]

Jennings mounts an all-out attack on the essential decency of the Puritan leadership and their apologists in the twentieth century. The Pequot War, which previous historians had described as an attempt on the part of Massachusetts Bay to protect itself from the fiercest of the New England tribes, becomes, in Jennings's painstakingly researched account, a deliberate war of extermination, waged by whites against Indians. It starts with trumped-up charges, is

carried on through a series of in[...] bloody reprisals, and ends in the ma[...] scores of Indian men, women, and chil[...] so that Massachusetts Bay could gain p[...] and economic control of the southern Con[...] cut Valley. When one reads this and then t[...] over the page and sees a reproduction of the B[...] Colony seal, which depicts an Indian fro[...] whose mouth issue the words "Come over and help us," the effect is shattering.[8]

But even so powerful an argument as Jennings's did not remain unshaken by subsequent work. Reading on, I discovered that if the events of the sixties had revolutionized the study of European-Indian relations, the events of the seventies produced yet another transformation. The American Indian Movement, and in particular the founding of the Native American Rights Fund in 1971 to finance Indian litigation, and a court decision in 1975 which gave the tribes the right to seek redress for past injustices in federal court, created a climate within which historians began to focus on the Indians themselves. "Almost simultaneously," writes James Axtell, "frontier and colonial historians began to discover the necessity of considering the American natives as real determinants of history and the utility of ethnohistory as a way of ensuring parity of focus and impartiality of judgment."[9] In Miller, Indians had been simply beneath notice; in Vaughan, they belonged to an inferior culture; and in Jennings, they were the more or less innocent prey of power-hungry whites. But in the most original and provocative of the ethnohistories, Calvin Martin's *Keepers of the Game*, Indians became complicated, purposeful human beings, whose lives were spiritually motivated to a high degree.[10] Their relationship to the animals they hunted, to the natural environment, and to the whites with whom they traded became intelligible within a system of beliefs that formed the basis for an entirely new perspective on the European-Indian encounter.

20   Within the broader question of why European contact had such a devastating effect on the Indians, Martin's specific aim is to determine

the fur trade which
nk of annihilation.
question had always
ian was introduced to
er kettles, woolen blankets,
erally couldn't keep his hands
ier to acquire these coveted items,
d the animal populations on which
ival depended. In short, the Indian's
vation in participating in the fur trade was
isumed to be the same as the white European's—a desire to accumulate material goods. In direct opposition to this thesis, Martin argues that the reason why Indians ruthlessly exploited their own resources had nothing to do with supply and demand, but stemmed rather from a breakdown of the cosmic worldview that tied them to the game they killed in a spiritual relationship of parity and mutual obligation.

The hunt, according to Martin, was conceived not primarily as a physical activity but as a spiritual quest, in which the spirit of the hunter must overmaster the spirit of the game animal before the kill can take place. The animal, in effect, *allows* itself to be found and killed, once the hunter has mastered its spirit. The hunter prepared himself through rituals of fasting, sweating, or dreaming which revealed the identity of his prey and where he can find it. The physical act of killing is the least important element in the process. Once the animal is killed, eaten, and its parts used for clothing or implements, its remains must be disposed of in ritually prescribed fashion, or the game boss, the "keeper" of that species, will not permit more animals to be killed. The relationship between Indians and animals, then, is contractual; each side must hold up its end of the bargain, or no further transactions can occur.

What happened, according to Martin, was that as a result of diseases introduced into the animal population by Europeans, the game suddenly disappeared, began to act in inexplicable ways, or sickened and died in plain view, and communicated their diseases to the Indians. The Indians, consequently, believed that their

compact with the animals had been broken and that the keepers of the game, the tutelary spirits of each animal species whom they had been so careful to propitiate, had betrayed them. And when missionization, wars with the Europeans, and displacement from their tribal lands had further weakened Indian society and its belief structure, the Indians, no longer restrained by religious sanctions, in effect, turned on the animals in a holy war of revenge.

Whether or not Martin's specific claim about the "holy war" was correct, his analysis made it clear to me that, given the Indians' understanding of economic, religious, and physical processes, an Indian account of what transpired when the European settlers arrived here would look nothing like our own. Their (potential, unwritten) history of the conflict could bear only a marginal resemblance to Eurocentric views. I began to think that the key to understanding European-Indian relations was to see them as an encounter between wholly disparate cultures, and that therefore either defending or attacking the colonists was beside the point since, given the cultural disparity between the two groups, conflict was inevitable and in large part a product of mutual misunderstanding.

But three years after Martin's book appeared, Shepard Krech III edited a collection of seven essays called *Indians, Animals, and the Fur Trade*, attacking Martin's entire project. Here the authors argued that we don't need an ideological or religious explanation for the fur trade. As Charles Hudson writes,

> The Southeastern Indians slaughtered deer (and were prompted to enslave and kill each other) because of their position on the outer fringes of an expanding modern world-system. . . . In the modern world-system there is a core region which establishes *economic* relations with its colonial periphery. . . . If the Indians could not produce commodities, they were on the road to cultural extinction. . . . To maximize his chances for survival, an eighteenth-century Southeastern Indian had to . . . live in the interior, out of range of European cattle, forestry, and agriculture. . . .

He had to produce a commodity which was valuable enough to earn him some protection from English slavers.[11]

25   Though we are talking here about South-eastern Indians, rather than the subarctic and Northeastern tribes Martin studied, what really accounts for these divergent explanations of why Indians slaughtered the game are the assumptions that underlie them. Martin believes that the Indians acted on the basis of perceptions made available to them by their own cosmology; that is, he explains their behavior as the Indians themselves would have explained it (insofar as he can), using a logic and a set of values that are not Eurocentric but derived from within Amerindian culture. Hudson, on the other hand, insists that the Indians' own beliefs are irrelevant to an explanation of how they acted, which can only be understood, as far as he is concerned, in the terms of a Western materialist economic and political analysis. Martin and Hudson, in short, don't agree on what counts as an explanation, and this disagreement sheds light on the pre-ceding accounts as well. From this standpoint, we can see that Vaughan, who thought that the Puritans were superior to the Indians, and Jennings, who thought the reverse, are both, like Hudson, using Eurocentric criteria of description and evaluation. While all three critics (Vaughan, Jennings, and Hudson) acknowledge that Indi-ans and Europeans behave differently from one another, the behavior differs, as it were, within the order of the same: all three assume, though only Hudson makes the assumption explicit, that an understanding of relations between the Euro-peans and the Indians must be elaborated in European terms. In Martin's analysis, however, what we have are not only two different sets of behavior but two incommensurable ways of describing and assigning meaning to events. This difference at the level of explanation calls into question the possibility of obtaining any theory-independent account of interaction between Indians and Europeans.

At this point, dismayed and confused by the wildly divergent views of colonial history the twentieth-century historians had provided, I decided to look at some primary materials. I thought, perhaps, if I looked at some firsthand accounts and at some scholars looking at those accounts, it would be possible to decide which experts were right and which were wrong by com-paring their views with the evidence. Captivity narratives seemed a good place to begin, since it was logical to suppose that the records left by whites who had been captured by Indians would furnish the sort of firsthand information I wanted.

I began with two fascinating essays based on these materials written by the ethnohistorian James Axtell, "The White Indians of Colonial America" and "The Scholastic Philosophy of the Wilderness."[12] These essays suggest that it would have been a privilege to be captured by North American Indians and taken off to Canada to dwell in a wigwam for the rest of one's life. Axtell's reconstruction of the process by which Indians taught European captives to feel com-fortable in the wilderness, first taking their shoes away and giving them moccasins, carrying the children on their backs, sharing the scanty food supply equally, ceremonially cleansing them of their old identities, giving them Indian clothes and jewelry, assiduously teaching them the Indian language, finally adopting them into their families, and even visiting them after many years if, as sometimes happened, they were restored to white society—all of this creates a compelling portrait of Indian culture and helps to explain the extraordinary attraction that Indian culture apparently exercised over Europeans.

But, as I had by now come to expect, this beguiling portrait of the Indians' superior humanity is called into question by other writ-ings on Indian captivity—for example, Norman Heard's *White into Red*, whose summation of the comparative treatment of captive children east and west of the Mississippi seems to contradict some of Axtell's conclusions:

The treatment of captive children seems to have been similar in initial stages. . . . Most children were treated brutally at the time of capture.

Babies and toddlers usually were killed immediately and other small children would be dispatched during the rapid retreat to the Indian villages if they cried, failed to keep the pace, or otherwise indicated a lack of fortitude needed to become a worthy member of the tribe. Upon reaching the village, the child might face such ordeals as running the gauntlet or dancing in the center of a throng of threatening Indians. The prisoner might be so seriously injured at this time that he would no longer be acceptable for adoption.[13]

One account which Heard reprints is particularly arresting. A young girl captured by the Comanches who had not been adopted into a family but used as a slave had been peculiarly mistreated. When they wanted to wake her up the family she belonged to would take a burning brand from the fire and touch it to her nose. When she was returned to her parents, the flesh of her nose was completely burned away, exposing the bone.[14]

30   Since the pictures drawn by Heard and Axtell were in certain respects irreconcilable, it made sense to turn to a firsthand account to see how the Indians treated their captives in a particular instance. Mary Rowlandson's "The Soveraignty and Goodness of God," published in Boston around 1680, suggested itself because it was so widely read and had set the pattern for later narratives. Rowlandson interprets her captivity as God's punishment on her for failing to keep the Sabbath properly on several occasions. She sees everything that happens to her as a sign from God. When the Indians are kind to her, she attributes her good fortune to divine Providence; when they are cruel, she blames her captors. But beyond the question of how Rowlandson interprets events is the question of what she saw in the first place and what she considered worth reporting. The following passage, with its abrupt shifts of focus and peculiar emphases, makes it hard to see her testimony as evidence of anything other than the Puritan point of view:

> Then my heart began to fail: and I fell weeping, which was the first time to my remembrance,

that I wept before them. Although I had met with so much Affliction, and my heart was many times ready to break, yet could I not shed one tear in their sight: but rather had been all this while in a maze, and like one astonished: but not I may say as, Psal. 137.1. *By the Rivers of Babylon, there we sate down; yea, we wept when we remembered Zion.* There one of them asked me, why I wept, I could hardly tell what to say: yet I answered, they would kill me: No, said he, none will hurt you. Then came one of them and gave me two spoon-fulls of Meal to comfort me, and another gave me half a pint of Pease; which was more worth than many Bushels at another time. Then I went to see King Philip, he bade me come in and sit down, and asked me whether I woold smoke it (a usual Complement nowadayes among Saints and Sinners) but this no way suited me. For though I had formerly used Tobacco, yet I had left it ever since I was first taken. It seems to be a Bait, the Devil layes to make men loose their precious time: I remember with shame, how formerly, when I had taken two or three pipes, I was presently ready for another, such a bewitching thing it is: But I thank God, he has now given me power over it; surely there are many who may be better imployed than to ly sucking a stinking Tobacco-pipe.[15]

Anyone who has ever tried to give up smoking has to sympathize with Rowlandson, but it is nonetheless remarkable, first, that a passage which begins with her weeping openly in front of her captors, and comparing herself to Israel in Babylon, should end with her railing against the vice of tobacco; and, second, that it has not a word to say about King Philip, the leader of the Indians who captured her and mastermind of the campaign that devastated the white population of the English colonies. The fact that Rowlandson has just been introduced to the chief of chiefs makes hardly any impression on her at all. What excites her is a moral issue which was being hotly debated in the seventeenth century: to smoke or not to smoke (Puritans frowned on it, apparently, because it wasted time and presented a fire hazard). What seem to us the peculiar emphases in Rowlandson's relation are not the result of her having screened out evidence she couldn't handle, but of her way of constructing the world. She saw what her seventeenth-century English Separatist background made visible. It is when one realizes that the biases of twentieth-century historians like Vaughan or Axtell cannot be corrected for simply by consulting the primary materials, since the primary materials are constructed according to *their* authors' biases, that one begins to envy Miller his vision at Matadi. Not for what he didn't see—the Indian and the black—but for his epistemological confidence.

Since captivity narratives made a poor source of evidence for the nature of European-Indian relations in early New England because they were so relentlessly pietistic, my hope was that a better source of evidence might be writings designed simply to tell Englishmen what the American natives were like. These authors could be presumed to be less severely biased, since they hadn't seen their loved ones killed by Indians or been made to endure the hardships of captivity, and because they weren't writing propaganda calculated to prove that God had delivered his chosen people from the hands of Satan's emissaries.

The problem was that these texts were written with aims no less specific than those of the captivity narratives, though the aims were of a different sort. Here is a passage from William Wood's *New England's Prospect*, published in London in 1634.

To enter into a serious discourse concerning the natural conditions of these Indians might procure admiration from the people of any civilized nations, in regard of their civility and good natures. . . . These Indians are of affable, courteous and well disposed natures, ready to communicate the best of their wealth to the mutual good of one another; . . . so . . . perspicuous is their love . . . that they are as willing to part with a mite in poverty as treasure in plenty. . . . If it were possible to recount the courtesies they have showed the English, since their first arrival in those parts, it would not only

steady belief, that they are a loving people, but also win the love of those that never saw them, and wipe off that needless fear that is too deeply rooted in the conceits of many who think them envious and of such rancorous and inhumane dispositions, that they will one day make an end of their English inmates.[16]

However, in a pamphlet published twenty-one years earlier, Alexander Whitaker of Virginia has this to say of the natives:

These naked slaves . . . serve the divell for feare, after a most base manner, sacrificing sometimes (as I have heere heard) their own Children to him. . . . They live naked in bodie, as if their shame of their sinne deserved no covering: Their names are as naked as their bodie: They esteem it a virtue to lie, deceive and steale as their master the divell teacheth to them.[17]

According to Robert Berkhofer in *The White Man's Indian*, these divergent reports can be explained by looking at the authors' motives. A favorable report like Wood's, intended to encourage new emigrants to America, naturally represented Indians as loving and courteous, civilized and generous, in order to allay the fears of prospective colonists. Whitaker, on the other hand, a minister who wishes to convince his readers that the Indians are in need of conversion, paints them as benighted agents of the devil. Berkhofer's commentary constantly implies that white men were to blame for having represented the Indians in the image of their own desires and needs.[18] But the evidence supplied by Rowlandson's narrative, and by the accounts left by early reporters such as Wood and Whitaker, suggests something rather different. Though it is probably true that in certain cases Europeans did consciously tamper with the evidence, in most cases there is no reason to suppose that they did not record faithfully what they saw. And what they saw was not an illusion, was not determined by selfish motives in any narrow sense, but was there by virtue of a way of seeing which they could no more consciously manipulate than they could choose not to have been born. At this point, it seemed to me, the ethnocentric bias of the firsthand observers invited an investigation of the cultural situation they spoke from. Karen Kupperman's *Settling with the Indians* (1980) supplied just such an analysis.

Kupperman argues that Englishmen inevitably looked at Indians in exactly the same way that they looked at other Englishmen. For instance, if they looked down on Indians and saw them as people to be exploited, it was not because of racial prejudice or antique notions about savagery, it was because they looked down on ordinary English men and women and saw them as subjects for exploitation as well.[19] According to Kupperman, what concerned these writers most when they described the Indians were the insignia of social class, of rank, and of prestige. Indian faces are virtually never described in the earliest accounts, but clothes and hairstyles, tattoos and jewelry, posture and skin color are. "Early modern Englishmen believed that people can create their own identity, and that therefore one communicates to the world through signals such as dress and other forms of decoration who one is, what group or category one belongs to."[20]

Kupperman's book marks a watershed in writings on European-Indian relations, for it reverses the strategy employed by Martin two years before. Whereas Martin had performed an ethnographic analysis of Indian cosmology in order to explain, from within, the Indians' motives for engaging in the fur trade, Kupperman performs an ethnographic study of seventeenth-century England in order to explain, from within, what motivated Englishmen's behavior. The sympathy and understanding that Martin, Axtell, and others extend to the Indians are extended in Kupperman's work to the English themselves. Rather than giving an account of "what happened" between Indians and Europeans, like Martin, she reconstructs the worldview that gave the experience of one group its content. With her study, scholarship on European-Indian relations comes full circle.

It may well seem to you at this point that, given the tremendous variation among the historical accounts, I had no choice but to end in relativism. If the experience of encountering conflicting versions of the "same" events suggests anything certain it is that the attitude a historian takes up in relation to a given event, the way in which he or she judges and even describes "it"— and the "it" has to go in quotation marks because depending on the perspective, that event either did or did not occur—this stance, these judgments and descriptions are a function of the historian's position in relation to the subject. Miller, standing on the banks of the Congo, couldn't see the black men he was supervising because of his background, his assumptions, values, experiences, goals. Jennings, intent on exposing the distortions introduced into the historical record by Vaughan and his predecessors stretching all the way back to Winthrop, couldn't see that Winthrop and his peers were not racists but only Englishmen who looked at other cultures in the way their own culture had taught them to see one another. The historian can never escape the limitations of his or her own position in history and so inevitably gives an account that is an extension of the circumstances from which it springs. But it seems to me that when one is confronted with this particular succession of stories, cultural and historical relativism is not a position that one can comfortably assume. The phenomena to which these histories testify— conquest, massacre, and genocide, on the one hand; torture, slavery, and murder on the other—cry out for judgment. When faced with claims and counterclaims of this magnitude one feels obligated to reach an understanding of what actually did occur. The dilemma posed by the study of European-Indian relations in early America is that the highly charged nature of the materials demands a moral decisiveness which the succession of conflicting accounts effectively precludes. That is the dilemma I found myself in at the end of this course of reading, and which I eventually came to resolve as follows.

After a while it began to seem to me that there was something wrong with the way I had formulated the problem. The statement that the materials on European-Indian relations were so highly charged that they demanded moral judgment, but that the judgment couldn't be made because all possible descriptions of what happened were biased, seemed to contain an internal contradiction. The statement implied that in order to make a moral judgment about something, you have to know something else first—namely, the facts of the case you're being called upon to judge. My complaint was that their perspectival nature would disqualify any facts I might encounter and that therefore I couldn't judge. But to say as I did that the materials I had read were "highly charged" and therefore demanded judgment suggests both that I was reacting to something real—to some facts—*and* that I had judged them. Perhaps I wasn't so much in the lurch morally or epistemologically as I had thought. If you—or I—react with horror to the story of the girl captured and enslaved by Comanches who touched a firebrand to her nose every time they wanted to wake her up, it's because we read this as a story about cruelty and suffering, and not as a story about the conventions of prisoner exchange or the economics of Comanche life. The *seeing* of the story as a cause for alarm rather than as a droll anecdote or a piece of curious information is evidence of values we already hold, of judgments already made, of facts already perceived as facts.

40   My problem presupposed that I couldn't judge because I didn't know what the facts were. All I had, or could have, was a series of different perspectives, and so nothing that would count as an authoritative source on which moral judgments could be based. But, as I have just shown, I did judge, and that is because, as I now think, I did have some facts. I seemed to accept as facts that ninety percent of the native American population of New England died after the first hundred years of contact, that tribes in eastern Canada and the northeastern United States had a compact with the game they killed, that Comanches had subjected a captive girl to casual cruelty, that King Philip smoked a pipe, and so on. It was only where different versions of the same event came into conflict that I doubted the text was a record of something real. And even then, there was no question about certain major catastrophes. I believed that four hundred Pequots were killed near Saybrook, that Winthrop was the Governor of the Massachusetts Bay Colony when it happened, and so on. My sense that certain events, such as the Pequot War, did occur in no way reflected the indecisiveness that overtook me when I tried to choose among the various historical versions. In fact, the need I felt to make up my mind was impelled by the conviction that certain things *had* happened that shouldn't have happened. Hence it was never the case that "what happened" was completely unknowable or unavailable. It's rather that in the process of reading so many different approaches to the same phenomenon I became aware of the difference in the attitudes that informed these approaches. This awareness of the interests motivating each version cast suspicion over everything, in retrospect, and I ended by claiming that there was nothing I could know. This, I now see, was never really the case. But how did it happen?

Someone else, confronted with the same materials, could have decided that one of these historical accounts was correct. Still another person might have decided that more evidence was needed in order to decide among them. Why did I conclude that none of the accounts was accurate because they were all produced from some particular angle of vision? Presumably there was something in my background that enabled me to see the problem in this way. That something, very likely, was poststructuralist theory. I let my discovery that Vaughan was a product of the fifties, Jennings of the sixties, Rowlandson of a Puritan worldview, and so on lead me to the conclusion that all facts are theory dependent because that conclusion was already a thinkable one for me.

My inability to come up with a true account was not the product of being situated nowhere; it was the product of certitude that existed *somewhere else*, namely, in contemporary literary theory. Hence, the level at which my indecision came into play was a function of particular beliefs I held. I was never in a position of epistemological indeterminacy, I was never *en abyme*. The idea that all accounts are perspectival seemed to me a superior standpoint from which to view all the versions of "what happened," and to regard with sympathetic condescension any person so old-fashioned and benighted as to believe that there really was some way of arriving at the truth. But this skeptical standpoint was just as firm as any other. The fact that it was also seriously disabling—it prevented me from coming to any conclusion about what I had read—did not render it any less definite.

At this point something is beginning to show itself that has up to now been hidden. The notion that all facts are only facts within a perspective has the effect of emptying statements of their content. Once I had Miller and Vaughan and Jennings, Martin and Hudson, Axtell and Heard, Rowlandson and Wood and Whitaker, and Kupperman; I had Europeans and Indians, ships and canoes, wigwams and log cabins, bows and arrows and muskets, wigs and tattoos, whiskey and corn, rivers and forts, treaties and battles, fire and blood—and then suddenly all I had was a metastatement about perspectives. The effect of bringing perspectivism to bear on history was to wipe out completely the subject matter of history. And it follows that bringing perspectivism to bear in this way on any subject matter would have a similar effect; everything is wiped out and you are left with nothing but a single idea—perspectivism itself.

But—and it is a crucial but—all this is true only if you believe that there is an alternative. As long as you think that there are or should be facts that exist outside of any perspective, then the notion that facts are perspectival will have this disappearing effect on whatever it touches. But if you are convinced that the alternative does not exist, that there really are no facts except as they are embedded in some particular way of seeing the world, then the argument that a set of facts derives from some particular worldview is no longer an argument against that set of facts. If all facts share this characteristic, to say that any one fact is perspectival doesn't change its factual nature in the slightest. It merely reiterates it.

This doesn't mean that you have to accept just anybody's facts. You can show that what someone else asserts to be a fact is false. But it does mean that you can't argue that someone else's facts are not facts *because they are only the product of a perspective*, since this will be true of the facts that you perceive as well. What this means then is that arguments about "what happened" have to proceed much as they did before poststructuralism broke in with all its talk about language-based reality and culturally produced knowledge. Reasons must be given, evidence adduced, authorities cited, analogies drawn. Being aware that all facts are motivated, believing that people are always operating inside some particular interpretive framework or other is a pertinent argument when what is under discussion is the way beliefs are grounded. But it doesn't give one any leverage on the facts of a particular case.[21]

What this means for the problem I've been addressing is that I must piece together the story of European-Indian relations as best I can, believing this version up to a point, that version not at all, another almost entirely, according to what seems reasonable and plausible, given everything else that I know. And this, as I've shown, is what I was already doing in the back of my mind without realizing it, because there was nothing else I *could* do. If the accounts don't fit together neatly, that is not a reason for rejecting them all in favor of a metadiscourse about epistemology; on the contrary, one encounters contradictory facts and divergent points of view in practically every phase of life, from deciding whom to marry to choosing the right brand of cat food, and one decides as best one can given the evidence available. It is only the nature of the academic situation which makes it appear that one can linger on the threshold of decision in the name of an epistemological principle. What has really happened in such a case is that the subject of debate has changed from the question of what happened in a particular instance to the question of how knowledge is arrived at. The absence of pressure to decide what happened creates the possibility for this change of venue.

The change of venue, however, is itself an action taken. In diverting attention from the original problem and placing it where Miller did, on "the mind of man," it once again ignores what happened and still is happening to American Indians. The moral problem that confronts me now is not that I can never have any facts to go on, but that the work I do is not directed toward solving the kinds of problems that studying the history of European-Indian relations has awakened me to.

NOTES

1. See Vine Deloria Jr., *God Is Red* (New York, 1973), pp. 39–56.
2. Perry Miller, *Errand into the Wilderness* (Cambridge, Mass., 1964), p. vii; all further references will be included in the text.
3. This passage from John Winthrop's *Journal* is excerpted by Perry Miller in his anthology *The American Puritans: Their Prose and Poetry* (Garden City, N.Y., 1956), p. 43. In his headnote to the selections from the *Journal*, Miller speaks of Winthrop's "characteristic objectivity" (p. 37).
4. Alden T. Vaughan, *New England Frontier: Puritans and Indians, 1620–1675* (Boston, 1965), pp. vi–vii; all further references to this work, abbreviated NEF, will be included in the text.
5. John Higham, intro. to *New Directions in American Intellectual History*, ed. Higham and Paul K. Conkin (Baltimore, 1979), p. xii.
6. Ibid.
7. See Francis Jennings, *The Invasion of America: Indians, Colonialism, and the Cant of Conquest* (New York, 1975), pp. 3–31. Jennings writes: "The so-called settlement of America was a resettlement, reoccupation of a land made waste by the diseases and demoralization introduced by the newcomers. Although the source data pertaining to populations have never been compiled, one careful scholar, Henry F. Dobyns, has provided a relatively conservative and meticulously reasoned estimate conforming to the known effects of conquest catastrophe. Dobyns has calculated a total aboriginal population for the western hemisphere within the range of 90 to 112 million, of which 10 to 12 million lived north of the Rio Grande" (p. 30).
8. Jennings, fig. 7, p. 229; and see pp. 186–229.
9. James Axtell, *The European and the Indian: Essays in the Ethnohistory of Colonial North America* (Oxford, 1981), p. viii.
10. See Calvin Martin, *Keepers of the Game: Indian-Animal Relationships and the Fur Trade* (Berkeley and Los Angeles, 1978).
11. See the essay by Charles Hudson in *Indians, Animals, and the Fur Trade: A Critique of "Keepers of the Game,"* ed. Shepard Krech III (Athens, Ga., 1981), pp. 167–69.
12. See Axtell, "The White Indians of Colonial America" and "The Scholastic Philosophy of the Wilderness," *The European and the Indian*, pp. 168–206 and 131–67.
13. J. Norman Heard, *White into Red: A Study of the Assimilation of White Persons Captured by Indians* (Metuchen, N.J., 1973), p. 97.
14. See ibid., p. 98.
15. Mary Rowlandson, "The Sovereignty and Goodness of God, Together with the Faithfulness of His Promises Displayed; Being a Narrative of the Captivity and Restauration of Mrs. Mary Rowlandson (1676)," in *Held Captive by Indians: Selected Narratives, 1642–1836*, ed. Richard VanDerBeets (Knoxville, Tenn., 1973), pp. 57–58.
16. William Wood, *New England's Prospect*, ed. Vaughan (Amherst, Mass., 1977), pp. 88–89.
17. Alexander Whitaker, *Goode Newes from Virginia* (1613), quoted in Robert F. Berkhofer Jr., *The White Man's Indian: Images of the American Indian from Columbus to the Present* (New York, 1978), p. 19.
18. See, for example, Berkhofer's discussion of the passages he quotes from Whitaker (*The White Man's Indian*, pp. 19, 20).
19. See Karen Ordahl Kupperman, *Settling with the Indians: The Meeting of English and Indian Cultures in America, 1580–1640* (Totowa, N.J., 1980), pp. 3, 4.
20. Ibid., p. 35.
21. The position I've been outlining is a version of neopragmatism. For an exposition, see *Against Theory: Literary Studies and the New Pragmatism*, ed. W. J. T. Mitchell (Chicago, 1985).

SUGGESTIONS FOR DISCUSSION

1. What exactly is the problem that Tompkins poses in the opening section of the essay? What does she mean when she says that conflicting historical interpretations posed an "epistemological" and a "moral quandary" for her? According to Tompkins, what is at stake when research turns up "an array of mutually irreconcilable points of view"?

2. Return to Tompkins's essay and notate each of the historians or first-person witnesses discussed in the long middle section. What interpretation of European-Indian relations in colonial New England does each offer? What differing assumptions does each make? It may help to create a chart that notes each historian or eyewitness and the interpretations and assumptions.

3. Think of an occasion or two when you encountered conflicting and irreconcilable interpretations of an event. The event could be one that you studied in a history class or one from personal experience. What differing perspectives and points of view produced the conflicting interpretations? How did you deal with these conflicting interpretations? Explain how Tompkins deals with conflicting interpretations in the final section of the essay. In what sense has she found the "way out" that she describes in the opening section? Compare her resolution of the issue with the way that you handled conflicting interpretations. What do you see as the main similarities and differences? How do you account for them?

SUGGESTIONS FOR WRITING

1. Write an essay that uses Jane Tompkins's account of her research as a model. Choose a research project that you did for a class in school—for example, a term paper, a report, or a history fair exhibit. Following Tompkins's style, explain the connections between the topic that you researched and your personal experience. Then take readers behind the scenes to explain how you did the research and how you dealt with any differing points of view or conflicting interpretations that you encountered. Use your account as a way to pose the problem of historical research and working with other people's accounts of the past.

2. Write a critical review of the historians' points of view and the interpretations that Tompkins presents in her essay. Provide an introduction that generally explains the problems and issues that the historians as a group are addressing. Assess the perspective that each historian brings to his or her research—what it helps you to see and what it obscures—and compare the strengths and weaknesses of the historians' various interpretations. As you review the historians' accounts, explain how you might piece them together and what view of Indian-settler relations in colonial New England ultimately emerges for you.

3. Consult American history textbooks that are used in high school and college and compare their treatment of European-Indian relations in seventeenth-century New England with the perspectives of the various historians in Tompkins's essay. (You can focus on just one textbook or extend your research to several texts.) What point of view and what assumptions seem to determine the treatment of Indians and Europeans in the textbook? How is this treatment similar to or different from the interpretations that you have read in Tompkins's essay? What perspectives seem to dominate? The textbook may well present this material as a factual account. If so, read between the lines to identify the perspective that the textbook author or authors bring to Indian-settler relations in colonial New England.

NECESSARY FICTIONS: WARREN NEIDICH'S EARLY AMERICAN COVER-UPS

Christopher Phillips

> Christopher Phillips is a photography critic who has published in *October, Art in America,* and elsewhere. "Necessary Fictions" introduces the Visual Essay that follows—Warren Neidich's "Contra Curtis: Early American Cover-Ups."

SUGGESTION FOR READING   Edward Sheriff Curtis's images, as Christopher Phillips notes, are "elegiac" depictions of a "vanishing race" of American Indians, seemingly caught in a timeless, aboriginal past. As you read this selection and Neidich's photographic essay, keep in mind Phillips's comments on how images can enable people to forget as well as to remember.

STRATAGEMS FOR FORGETTING

1 "They from the beginning announced that they wanted to maintain their way of life. . . . And we set up these reservations so they could, and have a Bureau of Indian Affairs to help take care of them. . . . Maybe we made a mistake. Maybe we should not have humored them in wanting to stay in that kind of primitive lifestyle. Maybe we should have said, 'No, come join us.' . . . You'd be surprised. Some of them became very wealthy, because some of those reservations were overlaying great pools of oil. And so I don't know what their complaint might be." (Ronald Reagan, in response to a question at Moscow University about the condition of Native Americans, quoted in *Time*, June 13, 1988.)

A CHILDHOOD MEMORY

Only a few days after Reagan provided students in Moscow with this hallucinatory account of the winning of the West, an item in the *New York Times* (June 5, 1988) reported that the designer Oleg Cassini planned a vast "Navajo Nation" complex in Arizona to repackage for the tourist industry the history, art, and culture of that apparently willing tribe. This odd conjunction of events sent me back in thought to the several summers, long ago, when our family paid regular visits to the Appalachian resort town of Cherokee, North Carolina. We were usually accompanied by a friend of my parents . . . a woman whose interest in the trip sprang principally from the fact that one of her own friends, a New York dancer, migrated to Cherokee every summer to earn a few dollars performing in a popular "outdoor historical drama." Minus the feathers and war paint that went with his role as a leaping Cherokee warrior, Louis proved unremarkable, aside from a rasping Brooklyn accent and the purple sports car in which he raced around the mountain roads. I remember, though, being puzzled when I was taken backstage before one evening's performance, and discovered there an assortment of equally improbable characters donning their costumes and makeup. Very interesting, I thought, but where were the real Indians?

The play itself proposed a relatively bland answer to that question. Situated in a past so hazy as to be utterly remote from the concerns of the present day, it unfolded in a series of melodramatic incidents the tale of the Cherokees' encounter with the homespun agents of Manifest Destiny, their expulsion from their mountain homeland, and their arduous trek to a new, ostensibly happier home on the plains of Oklahoma. Nevertheless another, more ominous possibility was planted in my already suspicious ten-year-old mind each time we passed a crowded burger drive-in situated in the heart of Cherokee. It announced its specialty in brazenly flashing red letters that I can still see: Squawburgers.

CONTRA CURTIS

It's from a similar unmarked crossroads of historical representation and popular memory that Warren Neidich's "Contra Curtis" photographs begin. Disinterred from the vast necropolis of American culture comprised of late-night TV's reruns of the pulp entertainment of earlier decades, Neidich's images are at once perfectly innocuous and painfully provoking. All-too-typical examples of the estimated 17,000 acts of mediated mayhem witnessed by all of us who have grown up in the television era, these achingly familiar specimens focus on moments of ritualized violence directed against "Indians." Of course we know that these aren't real Indians being burned, shot, knifed, or burst asunder, but actors, actresses, and stuntmen dressed up for the part. These figures serve as stand-ins or surrogates for a "historical actor" long pushed off the main stage of American life, but preserved in cultural memory in the long line of phantasmic Others against whom any violence is permitted.

5   It's the way that such phantasms weave in and out of our culture's interlocking networks of personal memory, popular memory, and archival memory that furnishes the real subject of much of Neidich's work. But aside from this general predilection, "Contra Curtis" has a more specific target in mind. Neidich seems clearly to wish that these photographs be attached as permanently as a shadow to the famous body of work produced around the turn of the century by the celebrated photographer Edward Sheriff Curtis. Curtis's elegiac images of Native American tribes turned a benign paternal gaze upon the "picturesque" tribespeople whom he singled out, costumed, and directed for his camera. Printed (like Neidich's) on platinum paper, Curtis's photographs were circulated in lavish volumes and portfolios to such discerning patrons as J. P. Morgan and Teddy Roosevelt. Neidich, using images drawn from a later, less discreet cultural sector, suggests the bloody historical preliminaries that were genteelly elided in Curtis's nostalgic account of a "vanishing race." Indeed, like that flashing red sign in Cherokee, his images disclose, behind Curtis's veil of tasteful exoticism, an oblique vision of the return of the historically repressed.

COGITO INTERRUPTUS

Once the very embodiment of the qualities of objectivity, precision, and fidelity, the photographic image occupies an increasingly unstable place in the systems which today generate cultural memory. Certainly the photograph's partaking of the prestige of the indexical sign seemed until very recently to exempt it from the so-called referential illusion that had mired so many other sign-systems in the Slough of Undecidability. Only a decade ago reputable philosophers of history still argued that observing a Brady photograph of the Civil War was, for all practical purposes, equivalent to observing the historical scene itself.

But too often photographs convey a dangerously weak sense of the past . . . substituting a mute and fleeting commemoration for the more active, critical processes of remembering, interrogating, and understanding. Nearly three decades ago Alain Resnais in "Last Year at Marienbad" shared his suspicion that personal memory and photographic images might well lead in different, equally untrustworthy directions. By the 1980s, with the film "Blade Runner" (based on Philip K. Dick's novel) we find android "replicants" conspicuously outfitted with ersatz family snapshots, which provide them with pre-packaged "memories" of a human past that blocks their discovery of their real mechanical origin. This film's implicit allusion to the human condition . . . still camped in Plato's cave . . . is hardly inappropriate as we move into the age of the digitally edited, electronically generated photocomposite: an image indistinguishable from a "real" photograph, an image which renders superfluous the remaining distinctions between photographic fact and fiction.

THE PACIFICATION OF THE PAST

If the camera's images no longer compel unflinching conviction, they nonetheless retain their currency as the standard visual language of the spectacle. Where Warren Neidich's previous work evidenced a fascination with the possibility of fabricating ersatz historical photographs, "Contra Curtis" points not only to the structuring absences of the historical archive but to the historical residue that can be gleaned from spectacle itself. Taking a cue from Duchamp and Breton, these photographs could perhaps be considered "compensation documents," provisional stand-ins for images too often erased from the official picture of the American past.

In regard to the contending claims of the image and the historical sense, Guy Debord's recent "Commentaries on the Society of the Spectacle" affords considerable insight, if small consolation. Writing twenty years after he identified the "spectacle" as the succession of images that provides the contemporary world with its distorting mirror, Debord points out that during the past two decades the discrediting of the historical sense has been increasingly adopted as a tactic of power. He notes that such recently fashionable slogans as "the ruins of post-history" can only bring comfort to those who exercise power now, to all those who can avail themselves of the flagrant historical lie in assurance that no correction will be registered. The self-serving flight of fantasy cited at the head of this essay was dutifully reproduced in Time magazine, after all, without commentary or correction . . . sign of an extraordinary public prudence in regard to power, or confirmation of a jaded reluctance to bother to point to the chasm between fact and phantasmagoria.

CIRCUIT BREAKERS

10 To interrupt the precipitous succession of mutually canceling images that hurdle past us each day, to replace that rhythm, if only for a moment, with another . . . such is the recurrent dream of the art of the 1980s. If they were not disguised as art, Neidich's photographs might be described as attempts at visual sedition, or local campaigns of "critical disinformation." It remains to be determined, of course, whether they (or any other artwork today) can break out of that subcircuit of activity that Debord shrugs off as the "spectacular critique of the spectacle." For the moment, Neidich's photographs modestly propose that the recycled images of popular history available on every channel can be recycled yet again . . . this time to provide an ironic corrective to at least a few of the more transparent idiocies which today parade as public discourse.

VISUAL ESSAY   Contra Curtis: Early American Cover-Ups

To learn more about photography and cover-ups, visit
www.ablongman.com/george/134

Warren Neidich is a photographer living in New York and Los Angeles; his photographs have been exhibited in and collected by museums in Europe and the United States. Neidich is known for his work on the media saturation surrounding the O. J. Simpson murder trial and on Calico, a restored silver mining town in Barstow, California. An ophthalmologist by training, Neidich is interested in cognitive science and sight. Presented here are selections from his photographic essay "Contra Curtis: Early American Cover-Ups," part of his book *American History Reinvented* (1989).

As the title "Contra Curtis" indicates, Warren Neidich locates his work in relation to Edward Sheriff Curtis, the well-known photographer of American Indians in the early twentieth century. Neidich uses platinum prints, just as Curtis did, which give the images an antique glow that seems to assign them to a vanished past. At the same time, Neidich wants to make these images relevant to the present.

Warren Neidich, "Contra Curtis: Early American Cover-Ups," Number 2

"Contra Curtis," Number 5

"Contra Curtis,"
Number 9

"Contra Curtis,"
Number 14

SUGGESTIONS FOR DISCUSSION

1. Warren Neidich joins together two visual codes—the platinum prints Edward Sheriff Curtis used in his photographs and the conventions of the Hollywood western. You can find examples of Curtis's photographs in your library or online at Web sites such as Pastview Gallery (pastview.com/edcuim.html). Find some of Curtis's photographs to consider how Neidach puts the two visual codes together. What viewer response do they provoke?

2. Compare Neidich's photographs with those you have found by Curtis. Do Curtis's photographs prompt historical amnesia, as Christopher Phillips suggests? In what sense are Neidich's photographs a critique of Curtis's work? What is Neidich asking viewers to remember?

3. Compare Neidich's project to "reinvent" American history with Jane Tompkins's struggle to understand the "Indian" in American history.

SUGGESTIONS FOR WRITING

1. What images come to your mind when you hear the term "American Indian"? How have you learned about American Indians? Write an essay that explains your own understanding of American Indians, drawing on Tompkins and Neidich as you see fit.

2. Christopher Phillips says Neidich's photographs "might be described as an act of visual sedition." What does he mean? Write an essay that explains why and how Neidich's photographs are seditious.

3. Write your own introduction to Neidich's photographs. Explain his purposes and the means he has chosen to carry out these purposes.

GOD'S COUNTRY AND AMERICAN KNOW-HOW

— *Loren Baritz*

Loren Baritz taught American Studies for many years at the University of Michigan and is now retired. The following selection, "God's Country and American Know-How," is taken from his book *Backfire: A History of How American Culture Led Us into Vietnam* (1985).

SUGGESTION FOR READING To explain U.S. involvement in Vietnam, Loren Baritz suggests that America's quest for moral leadership, with its deep roots in the past, played an important role. As you read, notice the evidence Baritz offers to support this interpretation. Underline/highlight passages where Baritz provides key examples and reasons.

1 Americans were ignorant about the Vietnamese not because we were stupid, but because we believe certain things about ourselves. Those things necessarily distorted our vision and confused our minds in ways that made learning extraordinarily difficult. To understand our failure we must think about what it means to be an American.

The necessary test for understanding the condition of being an American is a single sentence written by Herman Melville in his novel *White Jacket:* "And we Americans are the peculiar, chosen people—the Israel of our time; we bear the ark of the liberties of the world." This was not the last time this idea was expressed by Americans. It was at the center of thought of the men who brought us the Vietnam War. It was at the center of the most characteristic American myth.

This oldest and most important myth about America has an unusually specific origin. More than 350 years ago, while in mid-passage between England and the American wilderness, John Winthrop told the band of Puritans he was leading to a new and dangerous life that they were engaged in a voyage that God Himself not only approved, but in which He participated. The precise way that Brother Winthrop expressed himself echoes throughout the history of American life. He explained to his fellow travelers, "We shall find that the God of Israel is among us, when ten of us shall be able to resist a thousand of our enemies, when he shall make us a praise and glory, that men shall say of succeeding plantations [settlements]: the Lord make it like that of New England: for we must Consider that we shall be as a City upon a Hill, the eyes of all people are upon us." The myth of America as a city on a hill implies that America is a moral example to the rest of the world, a world that will presumably keep its attention riveted on us. It means that we are a Chosen People, each of whom, because of God's favor and presence, can smite one hundred of our heathen enemies' hip and thigh.

The society Winthrop meant to establish in New England would do God's work, insofar as sinners could. America would become God's country. The Puritans would have understood this to mean that they were creating a nation of, by, and for the Lord. About two centuries later, the pioneers and the farmers who followed the Puritans translated God's country from civilization to the grandeur and nobility of nature, to virgin land, to the purple mountains' majesty. Relocating the country of God from civilization to nature was significant in many ways, but the conclusion that this New World is specially favored by the Lord not only endured but spread.

5   In countless ways Americans know in their gut—the only place myths can live—that we have been Chosen to lead the world in public morality and to instruct it in political virtue. We believe that our own domestic goodness results in strength adequate to destroy our opponents who, by definition, are enemies of virtue, freedom, and God. Over and over, the founding Puritans described their new settlement as a beacon in the darkness, a light whose radiance could keep Christian voyagers from crashing on the rocks, a light that could brighten the world. In his inaugural address John Kennedy said, "The energy, the faith, the devotion which we bring to this endeavor [defending freedom] will light our country and all who serve it—and the glow from that fire can truly light the world." The city on a hill grew from its first tiny society to encompass the entire nation. As we will see, that is one of the reasons why we compelled ourselves to intervene in Vietnam.

An important part of the myth of America as the city on a hill has been lost as American power increased. John Winthrop intended that his tiny settlement should be only an example of rectitude to the cosmos. It could not have occurred to him that his small and weak band of saints should charge about the world to impose the One Right Way on others who were either too wicked, too stupid, or even too oppressed to follow his example. Because they also had domestic distractions, the early American Puritans could not even consider foreign adventures. In almost no time they had their hands full with a variety of local malefactors: Indians, witches, and, worst of all, shrewd Yankees who were more interested in catching fish than in catching the spirit of the Lord. Nathaniel Hawthorne, brooding about these Puritans, wrote that civilization begins by building a jail and a graveyard, but he was only two-thirds right. Within only two generations, the New England saints discovered that there was a brothel in Boston, the hub of the new and correct Christian order.

The New World settlement was puny, but the great ocean was a defensive moat that virtually prohibited an onslaught by foreign predators. The new Americans could therefore go about perfecting their society without distracting anxiety about alien and corrupting intrusions from Europe. This relative powerlessness coupled with defensive security meant that the city on a hill enjoyed a favorable "peculiar situation."

It was peculiarly blessed because the decadent world could not come here, and we did not have to go there. The rest of the world, but especially Europe, with its frippery, pomp, and Catholicism, was thought to be morally leprous. This is what George Washington had in mind when he asked a series of rhetorical questions in his farewell address in 1796:

Why forego the advantages of so peculiar a situation? Why quit our own to stand upon foreign ground? Why, by interweaving our destiny with that of any part of Europe, entangle our peace and prosperity in the toils of European ambition, rivalship, interest, humor, of caprice?

This is also what Thomas Jefferson told his countrymen when he was inaugurated five years later. This enlightened and skeptical philosopher-President announced that this was a "chosen country" which had been "kindly separated by nature and a wide ocean from the exterminating havoc of one quarter of the globe." He said that the young nation could exult in its many blessings if it would only keep clear of foreign evil. His prescription was that America should have "entangling alliances with none."

One final example of the unaggressive, unimperial interpretation of the myth is essential. The entire Adams family had a special affinity for old Winthrop. Perhaps it was that they grew up on the soil in which he was buried. On the Fourth of July, in 1821, John Quincy Adams gave a speech that captured every nuance of the already ancient myth. His speech could have been the text for the Vietnam War critics. He said that America's heart and prayers would always be extended to any free and independent part of the world. "But she goes not abroad in search of monsters to destroy." America, he said, hoped that freedom and independence would spread across the face of the earth. "She will recommend the general cause by the countenance of her voice, and by the benignant sympathy of her example." He said that the new nation understood that it should not actively intervene abroad even if such an adventure would be on the side of freedom because "she would involve herself beyond the power of extrication."

It just might be possible for America to try to impose freedom elsewhere, to assist in the liberation of others. "She might," he said, "become the dictatress of the world. She would no longer be the ruler of her own spirit."

10   In 1966, this speech was quoted by George F. Kennan, the thoughtful analyst of Soviet foreign affairs, to the Senate Foreign Relations Committee which was conducting hearings on the Vietnam War. Perhaps not knowing the myth, Mr. Kennan said that he was not sure what Mr. Adams had in mind when he spoke almost a century and a half earlier. But whatever it was, Mr. Kennan told the senators who were then worrying about Vietnam, "He spoke very directly and very pertinently to us here today."

The myth of the city on a hill became the foundation for the ritualistic thinking of later generations of Americans. This myth helped to establish nationalistic orthodoxy in America. It began to set an American dogma, to fix the limits of thought for Americans about themselves and about the rest of the world, and offered a choice about the appropriate relationship between us and them.

The benevolence of our national motives, the absence of material gain in what we seek, the dedication to principle, and our impenetrable ignorance were all related to the original myth of America. It is temptingly easy to dismiss this as some quaint idea that perhaps once had some significance, but lost it in this more sophisticated, toughminded, modern America. Arthur Schlesinger, Jr., a close aide to President Kennedy, thought otherwise. He was concerned about President Johnson's vastly ambitious plans to create a "Great Society for Asia." Whatever the President meant, according to Professor Schlesinger, such an idea

demands the confrontation of an issue deep in the historical consciousness of the United States: whether this country is a chosen people, uniquely righteous and wise, with a moral mission to all mankind. . . . The ultimate choice is between messianism and maturity.

The city myth should have collapsed during the war. The war should have taught us that we could not continue to play the role of moral adviser and moral enforcer to the world. After the shock of the assassinations, after the shock of Tet, after President Johnson gave up the presidency, after the riots, demonstrations, burned neighborhoods, and the rebellion of the young, it should have been difficult to sustain John Winthrop's optimism. It was not difficult for Robert Kennedy who, after Senator Eugene McCarthy had demonstrated LBJ's vulnerability in New Hampshire, finally announced that he would run for the presidency himself. The language he used in his announcement speech proved that the myth was as alive and as virulent as it had ever been: "At stake," Senator Kennedy said, "is not simply the leadership of our party, and even our own country, it is our right to the moral leadership of this planet." Members of his staff were horrified that he could use such language because they correctly believed that it reflected just the mind-set that had propelled us into Vietnam in the first place. He ignored their protests. This myth could survive in even the toughest of the contemporary, sophisticated, hard-driving politicians. Of course, he may have used this language only to persuade his listeners, to convince the gullible. But, even so, it showed that he believed that the myth was what they wanted to hear. In either case, the city on a hill continued to work its way.

The myth of the city on a hill combined with solipsism in the assumptions about Vietnam made by the American war planners. In other words, we assumed that we had a superior moral claim to be in Vietnam, and because, despite their quite queer ways of doing things, the Vietnamese shared our values, they would applaud our intentions and embrace our physical presence. Thus, Vice President Humphrey later acknowledged that all along we had been ignorant of Vietnam. He said that "to LBJ, the Mekong and the Pedernales were not that far apart." Our claim to virtue was based on the often announced purity of our intentions. It was said, perhaps thousands of times, that all we wanted was freedom for other people, not land, not resources, and not domination.

15   Because we believed that our intentions were virtuous, we could learn nothing from the French experience in Vietnam. After all, they had fought only to maintain their Southeast Asian colonies and as imperialists deserved to lose. We assumed that this was why so mighty a European power lost the important battle of Dien Bien Phu to General Giap's ragged army. America's moral authority was so clear to us that we assumed that it also had to be clear to the Vietnamese. This self-righteousness was the clincher in the debate to intensify the conflict in Vietnam, according to George W. Ball, an undersecretary of state for Presidents Kennedy and Johnson. Washington's war planners, Mr. Ball said in 1973, had been captives of their own myths. Another State Department official also hoped, after the fact, that Americans "will be knocked out of our grandiosity . . . [and] will see the self-righteous, illusory quality of that vision of ourselves offered by the high Washington official who said that while other nations have 'interests' the United States has 'a sense of responsibility.' " Our power, according to this mentality, gives us responsibility, even though we may be reluctant to bear the burden. Other peoples' greed or selfishness gives them interests, even though they may not be strong enough to grab all they want.

Our grandiosity will, however, not be diminished so easily. At least since World War II, America's foreign affairs have been the affairs of Pygmalion. We fall in love with what we create. We create a vision of the world made in what we think is our own image. We are proud of what we create because we are certain that our intentions are pure, our motives good, and our behavior virtuous. We know these things to be true because we believe that we are unique among the nations of the world in our collective idealism. . . .

Implicit in John Winthrop's formulation of the city myth was the idea that the new Americans could, because of their godliness, vanquish their numerically superior enemies. The idea that warriors, because of their virtue, could beat stronger opponents, is very ancient. Pericles spoke of it in his funeral oration to the Athenians. The Christian crusaders counted on it. *Jihad*, Islam's conception of a holy war, is based on it. The Samurai believed it. So did the Nazis.

In time, the history of America proved to Americans that we were militarily invincible. The Vietnam War Presidents naturally cringed at the thought that they could be the first to lose a war. After all, we had already beaten Indians, French, British (twice), Mexicans, Spaniards, Germans (twice), Italians, Japanese, Koreans, and Chinese. Until World War II, the nation necessarily had to rely on the presumed virtue, not the power, of American soldiers to carry the day, and the war. This was also the case in the South during our Civil War.

Starting in the eighteenth century, the nation of farmers began to industrialize. As the outcome of war increasingly came to depend on the ability to inject various forms of flying hardware into the enemy's body, victory increasingly depended on technology. The acceleration of industrialization in the late nineteenth century inevitably quickened the pace of technological evolution. By then no other power could match the Americans' ability to get organized, to commit resources to development, and to invent the gadgets that efficiently produced money in the marketplace, and, when necessary, death on the battlefield. The idea of Yankee ingenuity, American know-how, stretches back beyond the nineteenth century. Our admiration for the tinkerer whose new widget forms the basis of new industry is nowhere better shown than in our national reverence of Thomas Edison.

20   Joining the American sense of its moral superiority with its technological superiority was a marriage made in heaven, at least for American nationalists. We told ourselves that each advantage explained the other, that the success of our standard of living was a result of our virtue, and our virtue was a result of our wealth. Our riches, our technology, provided the strength that had earlier been missing, that once had

forced us to rely only on our virtue. Now, as Hiroshima demonstrated conclusively, we could think of ourselves not only as morally superior, but as the most powerful nation in history. The inevitable offspring of this marriage of an idea with a weapon was the conviction that the United States could not be beaten in war—not by any nation, and not by any combination of nations. For that moment we thought that we could fight where, when, and how we wished, without risking failure. For that moment we thought that we could impose our will on the recalcitrant of the earth.

A great many Americans, in the period just before the war in Vietnam got hot, shared a circular belief that for most was probably not very well formed: America's technological supremacy was a symptom of its uniqueness, and technology made the nation militarily invincible. In 1983, the playwright Arthur Miller said, "I'm an American. I believe in technology. Until the mid-60s I never believed we could lose because we had technology."

The memory of World War II concluding in a mushroom cloud was relatively fresh throughout the 1950s. It was unthinkable that America's military could ever fail to establish its supremacy on the battlefield, that the industrial, scientific, and technological strength of the nation would ever be insufficient for the purposes of war. It was almost as if Americans were technology. The American love affair with the automobile was at its most passionate in the 1950s, our well-equipped armies stopped the Chinese in Korea, for a moment our nuclear supremacy was taken for granted, and affluence for many white Americans seemed to be settling in as a way of life.

It is, of course, unfortunate that the forces of evil may be as strong as the forces of virtue. The Soviet Union exploded its first atomic bomb way ahead of what Americans thought was a likely schedule. This technology is not like others because even a weak bomb is devastating. Even if our bombs are better than theirs, they can still do us in. America's freedom of action after 1949 was not complete. President Eisenhower and

John Foster Dulles, the Secretary of State, threatened "massive retaliation" against the Soviet Union if it stepped over the line. They knew, and we knew, that this threat was not entirely real, and that it freed the Soviets to engage in peripheral adventures because they correctly believed that we would not destroy the world over Korea, Berlin, Hungary, or Czechoslovakia.

Our policy had to become more flexible. We had to invent a theory that would allow us to fight on the edges without nuclear technology. This theory is called "limited war." Its premise is that we and the Soviets can wage little wars, and that each side will refrain from provoking the other to unlock the nuclear armory.

25   Ike threatened the Chinese, who at the time did not have the bomb, with nuclear war in Korea. JFK similarly threatened the Soviets, who had nuclear capability, over Cuba. But, although some military men thought about using nuclear weapons in Vietnam, the fundamental assumption of that war was to keep it limited, not to force either the Soviets or the Chinese, who now had their own sloppy bombs, to enter the war. Thus, we could impose our will on the recalcitrant of the earth if they did not have their own nuclear weapons, and if they could not compel the Soviets or the Chinese to force us to quit.

In Vietnam we had to find a technology to win without broadening the war. The nuclear stalemate reemphasized our need to find a more limited ground, to find, so to speak, a way to fight a domesticated war. We had to find a technology that would prevail locally, but not explode internationally. No assignment is too tough for the technological mentality. In fact, it was made to order for the technicians who were coming into their own throughout all of American life. This war gave them the opportunity to show what they could do. This was to be history's most technologically sophisticated war, most carefully analyzed and managed, using all of the latest wonders of managerial procedures and systems. It was made to order for bureaucracy.

James C. Thomson, who served both JFK and LBJ as an East Asia specialist, understood how the myths converged. He wrote of "*the rise of a new breed of American ideologues who see Vietnam as the ultimate test of their doctrine.*" These new men were the new missionaries and had a trinitarian faith: in military power, technological superiority, and our altruistic idealism. They believed that the reality of American culture "provides us with the opportunity and obligation to ease the nations of the earth toward modernization and stability: toward a full-fledged *Pax Americana Technocratica.*" For these parishioners in the church of the machine, Vietnam was the ideal laboratory.

SUGGESTIONS FOR DISCUSSION

1. Loren Baritz's purpose is to identify reasons the United States got involved in Vietnam. While other historians have examined U.S. foreign policy in the 1950s and 1960s, Baritz suggests that to understand why the United States intervened in Vietnam, we must "think about what it means to be an American." Trace the line of thinking Baritz develops in this selection. How does he connect John Winthrop's "city on the hill" to the politics and policymaking of the Vietnam era? What assumptions enable Baritz to make such a connection?

2. Look closely at the three-paragraph passage (paragraphs 14–16) where Baritz argues that "self-righteousness was the clincher in the debate to intensify the conflict in Vietnam." What does it mean that American policymakers were "captives of their own myths"? What other explanations might historians offer for the escalation of the Vietnam?

3. Baritz describes the "trinitarian faith" of American policymakers in "military power, technological superiority, and altruistic idealism" that he believes led the country into the Vietnam War. Is this "faith" still strongly held today? What, if any, relation do you see between

this faith and the 2003 invasion and ongoing occupation of Iraq? What problems or issues does such "faith" ignore or suppress?

SUGGESTIONS FOR WRITING

1. Read an account of the Vietnam War in an American history textbook. Write an essay that compares the textbook's and Baritz's accounts of the origins of the Vietnam War. Pay attention in particular to how historians identify the causes. End the essay with your own sense of the relative strengths and weaknesses of each way of explaining U.S. involvement in Vietnam.

2. Write an essay on what Baritz calls America's "missionary impulse." What do you see as the problems, if any, with this "altruistic idealism"? Does it invariably lead, as Baritz suggests, to "purity of intention" on the one hand, and "the horror of result" on the other? Look at a particular situation during which the desire to act "in that name of goodness" backfired on the benefactors. Don't limit yourself here to matters of international or military policy. There may be instances closer to home in which some person or some group that seeks to do good actually produces the opposite effect. Your task here is to analyze why and how this is the case.

3. Use Baritz's analysis to write a commentary on President George W. Bush's second inaugural address (for the text of the address, see page 494). Imagine you are writing a column to appear on the op-ed page of a local or campus newspaper.

THE EMPIRE SLINKS BACK

— *Niall Ferguson*

Niall Ferguson is Herzog professor of financial history at the Stern School of Business, New York University, and senior research fellow at Jesus College, Oxford. He has written a number of books, including *Empire: The Rise and Demise of the British World Order and the Lessons for Global Power* (2002) and *Colossus: The Price of America's Empire* (2004). "The Empire Slinks Back" appeared in the *New York Times Magazine* on April 27, 2003, just following the invasion of Iraq.

SUGGESTION FOR READING Niall Ferguson unabashedly says that he is a "fully paid-up member of the neoimperialist gang." As you read this article, notice how Ferguson compares the workings of the British Empire to what he sees as the reluctance of the United States to fully embrace its proper role as an imperialist power.

> Wheresoever the Roman conquers, he inhabits.
>
> —*Seneca*

1 Iraq has fallen. Saddam's statues are face down in the dust. His evil tyranny is at an end.

So—can we, like, go home now?

You didn't have to wait long for a perfect symbol of the fundamental weakness at the heart of the new American imperialism—sorry, humanitarianism. I'm talking about its chronically short time frame. I wasn't counting, but the Stars and Stripes must have been up there on the head of that statue of Saddam for less than a minute. You have to wonder what his commanding officer said to the marine responsible, Cpl. Edward Chin, when he saw Old Glory up there. "Son, get that thing down on the double, or we'll have every TV station from here to Bangladesh denouncing us as Yankee imperialists!"

An echo of Corporal Chin's imperial impulse can be heard in the last letter Cpl. Kemaphoom Chanawongse sent home before he and his Marine unit entered Iraq. Chanawongse joked that his camp in Kuwait was like something out of "M*A*S*H"—except that it would need to be called "M*A*H*T*S*F": "marines are here to stay forever."

5   But the question raised by Corporal Chanawongse's poignant final joke—he was killed a week later, when his amphibious assault vehicle was blown up in Nasiriya—is, Are the marines in Iraq "to stay forever"? No doubt it is true, as President Bush said, that America will "honor forever" Corporal Chanawongse and the more than 120 other service personnel so far killed in the conflict. Honored forever, yes. But *there* forever? In many ways the biggest mystery about the American occupation of Iraq is its probable duration. Recent statements by members of the Bush administration bespeak a time frame a lot closer to ephemeral than eternal. As the president himself told the Iraqi people in a television broadcast shortly after the fall of Baghdad: "The government of Iraq and the future of your country will soon belong to you. . . . We will respect your great religious traditions, whose principles of equality and compassion are essential to Iraq's future. We will help you build a peaceful and representative government that protects the rights of all citizens. *And then our military forces will leave.*"

What the president didn't make entirely clear was whether the departing troops would be accompanied by the retired Lt. Gen. Jay Garner and his "Office of Reconstruction and Humanitarian Assistance," newspeak for what would once have been called Omgus—the Office of Military Government (United States). Nor was he very specific about when exactly he expected to see the handover of power to the "peaceful and representative government" of Iraqis.

But we know the kind of time frame the president has in mind. In a prewar speech to the

American Enterprise Institute, Bush declared, "We will remain in Iraq as long as necessary and not a day more." It is striking that the unit of measure he used was days. Speaking less than a week before the fall of Baghdad, Paul Wolfowitz, the deputy secretary of defense, suggested that Garner would be running Iraq for at least six months. Other administration spokesmen have mentioned two years as the maximum transition period. When Garner himself was asked how long he expected to be in charge, he talked about just three months.

If—as more and more commentators claim—America has embarked on a new age of empire, it may turn out to be the most evanescent empire in all history. Other empire builders have fantasized about ruling subject peoples for a thousand years. This is shaping up to be history's first thousand-day empire. Make that a thousand hours.

Let me come clean. I am a fully paid-up member of the neoimperialist gang. Twelve years ago—when it was not at all fashionable to say so—I was already arguing that it would be "desirable for the United States to depose" tyrants like Saddam Hussein. "Capitalism and democracy," I wrote, "are not naturally occurring, but require strong institutional foundations of law and order. The proper role of an imperial America is to establish these institutions where they are lacking, if necessary . . . by military force." Today this argument is in danger of becoming commonplace, at least among the set who read The National Interest, the latest issue of which is practically an American Empire Special Edition. Elsewhere, writers as diverse as Max Boot, Andrew Bacevich and Thomas Donnelly have drawn explicit (and in Boot's case, approving) comparisons between the pax Britannica of Queen Victoria's reign and the pax Americana they envisage in the reign of George II. Boot has gone so far as to say that the United States should provide places like Afghanistan and other troubled countries with "the sort of enlightened foreign administration once provided by self-confident Englishmen in jodhpurs and pith helmets."

10　I agree. The British Empire has had a pretty lousy press from a generation of "postcolonial" historians anachronistically affronted by its racism. But the reality is that the British were significantly more successful at establishing market economies, the rule of law and the transition to representative government than the majority of postcolonial governments have been. The policy "mix" favored by Victorian imperialists reads like something just published by the International Monetary Fund, if not the World Bank: free trade, balanced budgets, sound money, the common law, incorrupt administration and investment in infrastructure financed by international loans. These are precisely the things Iraq needs right now. If the scary-sounding "American empire" can deliver them, then I am all for it. The catch is whether or not America has the one crucial character trait without which the whole imperial project is doomed: stamina. The more time I spend here in the United States, the more doubtful I become about this.

The United States unquestionably has the raw economic power to build an empire—more, indeed, than the United Kingdom ever had at its disposal. In 1913, for example, Britain's share of total world output was 8 percent, while the equivalent figure for the United States in 1998 was 22 percent. There's "soft" power too—the endlessly innovative consumer culture that Joseph Nye argues is an essential component of American power—but at its core, as we have seen in Afghanistan and now in Iraq, American power is far from soft. It can be very, very hard. The trouble is that it is *ephemeral*. It is not so much Power Lite as Flash Power—here today, with a spectacular bang, but gone tomorrow.

Besides the presidential time frame—which is limited by the four-year election cycle—the most obvious symptom of its short-windedness is the difficulty the American empire finds in recruiting the right sort of people to run it. America's educational institutions excel at producing young men and women who are both academically and professionally very well trained. It's just that the young elites have no desire whatsoever to spend their lives running a screwed-up, sun-scorched sandpit like Iraq. America's brightest and best aspire not to govern Mesopotamia, but to manage MTV; not to rule Hejaz, but to run a hedge fund; not to be a C.B.E., or Commander of the British Empire, but to be a C.E.O. And that, of course, is one reason so many of the Americans currently in Iraq are first-generation immigrants to the United States—men like Cpl. Kemaphoom Chanawongse.

America's British allies have been here before. Having defeated the previous Ottoman rulers in the First World War, Britain ran Iraq as a "mandate" between 1920 and 1932. For the sake of form, the British installed one of their Arab clients, the Hashemite prince Faisal, as king. But there was no doubt who was really running the place. Nor did the British make any bones about why they were there. When two Standard Oil geologists entered Iraq on a prospecting mission, the British civil commissioner handed them over to the chief of police of Baghdad; in 1927 the British takeover paid a handsome dividend when oil was struck at Baba Gurgur, in the northern part of Iraq. Although they formally relinquished power to the ruling dynasty in 1932, the British remained informally in control of Iraq throughout the 1930's. Indeed, they only really lost their grip on Baghdad with the assassination of their clients Faisal II and his prime minister, Nuri es-Said, in the revolution of 1958.

The crucial point is this: when the British went into Iraq, they stuck around. To be precise, there were British government representatives, military and civilian, in Baghdad uninterruptedly for almost exactly 40 years.

15　And that brings up a simple question: Who in today's United States would like to be based in Baghdad as long as the British were—which would be from now until 2043?

"Don't even go there!" is one of those catch phrases you hear every day in New York. Somehow it sums up exactly what is flawed about the whole post-9/11 crypto-imperial project. Despite their vast wealth and devastating weaponry, Americans have no interest in the one crucial activity without which a true empire cannot enduringly be established. They won't actually *go there.*

A British counterexample. Gertrude Bell was the first woman to graduate from Oxford with a First Class degree. She learned to speak Arabic during an archaeological visit to Jerusalem in 1899 and, like T. E. Lawrence, became involved in British military intelligence. In 1920, she was appointed Oriental Secretary to the British High Commission in Baghdad. She died there in 1926, having scarcely visited England in the interim. "I don't care to be in London much," she wrote. "I like Baghdad, and I like Iraq. It's the real East, and it is stirring; things are happening here, and the romance of it all touches me and absorbs me."

Dotted all over the British Empire were thousands of "Orientalists" like Gertrude Bell—simultaneously enamored of the exotic "Other" and yet dominant over it. Her account of Faisal I's coronation in 1921 perfectly illustrates their mode of operation: "Then Saiyid Husain stood up and read Sir Percy's proclamation in which he announced that Faisal had been elected king by 96 percent of the people in Mesopotamia, long live the King! with that we stood up and saluted him, the national flag was broken on the flagstaff by his side and the band played 'God Save the King'—they have no national anthem yet."

The British regarded long-term occupation as an inherent part of their self-appointed "civilizing mission." This did not mean forever. The assumption was that British rule would end once a country had been sufficiently "civilized"—read: anglicized—to ensure the continued rule of law and operation of free markets (not to mention the playing of cricket). But that clearly meant decades, not days; when the British intervened in a country like Iraq, they simply didn't have an exit strategy. The only issue was whether to rule directly—installing a British governor—or indi-rectly, with a British "secretary" offering "advice" to a local puppet like Faisal.

20   In other words, the British did go there. Between 1900 and 1914, 2.6 million Britons left the United Kingdom for imperial destinations (by 1957 the total had reached nearly 6 million). Admittedly, most of them preferred to migrate to the temperate regions of a select few colonies— Canada, Australia, New Zealand and South Africa—that soon became semiautonomous "dominions." Nevertheless, a significant number went to the much less hospitable climes of Asia and Africa. At the end of the 1930's, for example, the official Colonial Service in Africa was staffed by more than 7,500 expat Brits. The sub-stantial expatriate communities they established were crucial to the operation of the British Empire. They provided the indispensable "men on the spot" who learned the local languages, perhaps adopted some local customs—though not usually to the fatal extent of "going native"— and acted as the intermediaries between a remote imperial authority and the indigenous elites upon whose willing collaboration the empire depended.

Expat life was not all tiffin and gin. As Rud-yard Kipling saw it, governing India was a hard slog: "Year by year England sends out fresh drafts for the first fighting-line, which is officially called the Indian Civil Service. These die, or kill themselves by overwork, or are worried to death or broken in health and hope." Yet this was a ser-vice that could confidently expect to attract the very brightest and best products of the elite British universities. Of 927 recruits to the Colo-nial Service between 1927 and 1929, nearly half had been to Oxford or Cambridge. The propor-tion in the Indian Civil Service was even higher.

Why were so many products of Britain's top universities willing to spend their entire work-ing lives so far from the land of their birth, run-ning infernally hot, disease-ridden countries? Why, to pick a typical example, did one Evan Machonochie, an Oxford graduate who passed the grueling Indian Civil Service exam, set off for Bengal in 1887 and spend the next 40 years in India? One clue lies in his Celtic surname. The Scots were heavily overrepresented not just in the colonies of white settlement, but also in the commercial and professional elites of cities like Calcutta and Hong Kong and Cape Town. The Irish too played a disproportionate role in enforcing British rule, supplying a huge proportion of the officers and men of the British army. Not for nothing is Kipling's representative Indian Army N.C.O. named Mulvaney. For young men growing up on the rainy, barren and poorer fringes of the United Kingdom, the empire offered opportunities.

Yet economics alone cannot explain what motivated Machonochie or Bell. The imperial impulse arose from a complex of emotions: racial superiority, yes, but also evangelical zeal; profit, perhaps, but also a sincere belief that spreading "commerce, Christianity and civilization" was not just in Britain's interest but in the interests of her colonial subjects too.

*　*　*

The dilemma is perhaps insoluble. Americans yearn for the quiet life at home. But since 9/11 they have felt impelled to grapple with rogue regimes in the hope that their overthrow will do something to reduce the threat of future terrorist attacks. The trouble is that if they do not undertake these interventions with conviction and commitment, they are unlikely to achieve their stated goals. Anyone who thinks Iraq can become a stable democracy in a matter of months—whether 3, 6 or 24—is simply fantasizing.

25　　Where, then, is the new imperial elite to come from? Not, I hope, exclusively from the reserve army of unemployed generals with good Pentagon connections. The work needs to begin, and swiftly, to encourage American students at the country's leading universities to think more seriously about careers overseas—and by overseas I do not mean in London. Are there, for example, enough good scholarships to attract undergraduates and graduates to study Arabic? How many young men and women currently graduate with a functioning grasp of Chinese?

That, after all, is the language of this country's nearest imperial rival, and the power President Bush urgently needs to woo if he is to deal effectively with North Korea.

After Kipling, John Buchan was perhaps the most readable writer produced by British imperialism. In his 1916 thriller "Greenmantle," he memorably personifies imperial Britain in the person of Sandy Arbuthnot—an Orientalist so talented that he can pass for a Moroccan in Mecca or a Pathan in Peshawar. Arbuthnot's antithesis is the dyspeptic American millionaire John Scantlebury Blenkiron: "a big fellow with a fat, sallow, clean-shaven face" and "a pair of full sleepy eyes, like a ruminating ox." These eyes have seen "nothing gorier than a presidential election," he tells Buchan's hero, Richard Hannay. The symbolism is a little crude, but it has something to it.

Well, now the Blenkirons have seen something gorier than an election. But will it whet their appetites for an empire in the British mode? Only, I think, if Americans radically rethink their attitude to the world beyond their borders. Until there are more Americans not just willing but eager to shoulder the "nation-builder's burden," adventures like the current occupation of Iraq will lack a vital ingredient. For the lesson of Britain's imperial experience is clear: you simply cannot have an empire without imperialists—out there, on the spot—to run it.

Could Blenkiron somehow transform into Arbuthnot? Perhaps. After all, in the years after the Second World War, the generation that had just missed the fighting left Harvard and Yale with something like Buchan's zeal for global rule. Many of them joined the Central Intelligence Agency and devoted their lives to fighting Communism in far-flung lands from Cuba to Cambodia. Yet—as Graham Greene foresaw in "The Quiet American"—their efforts at what the British would have called "indirect rule" were constrained by the need to shore up the local potentates more or less covertly. (The low quality of the locals backed by the United States didn't help, either.) Today, the same fiction that underpinned American strategy in Vietnam—that the United States was not trying to resurrect French colonial rule in Indochina—is peddled in Washington to rationalize what is going on in Iraq. Sure, it may look like the resurrection of British colonial rule in Iraq, but honestly, all we want to do is give the Iraqi people democracy and then go home.

30   So long as the American empire dare not speak its own name—so long as it continues this tradition of organized hypocrisy—today's ambitious young men and women will take one look at the prospects for postwar Iraq and say with one voice, "Don't even go there."

Americans need to go there. If the best and brightest insist on staying home, today's unspoken imperial project may end—unspeakably—tomorrow.

SUGGESTIONS FOR DISCUSSION

1. As noted above, Niall Ferguson considers himself a committed "member of the neoimperialist gang." What exactly does it mean to be a neo-imperialist? What do neo-imperialists see as the role of the United States now that it "has embarked on a new age of empire"? What assumptions is Ferguson making that enable him to argue for the historical necessity of an American empire in the early twenty-first century? What is your evaluation of Ferguson's argument?

2. One of the key moves Ferguson makes in "The Empire Slinks Back" is to compare the British Empire to the current situation in the United States. How does Ferguson represent the British Empire? What function does this comparison perform in Ferguson's overall argument? How might people in Asia and Africa, who lived under British colonialism, respond to Ferguson's representation of the British Empire?

3. Imagine that Loren Baritz, author of "God's Country and American Know-How," and Ferguson were scheduled to appear as guests on *Sixty Minutes* (or some other television news show) to comment on the present state of the American empire. What do you think they would say? How do you think they would respond to each other's analysis?

SUGGESTIONS FOR WRITING

1. Write an analysis of Niall Ferguson's case for the United States as an imperial power. What reasons does he offer, explicitly or implicitly, to justify the United States' embarking "on a new age of empire"? How does he use the history of the British Empire as support for his argument. Use your analysis of Ferguson's argument to clarify your own thinking about the United States as an imperialist power. What is your evaluation of Ferguson's neo-imperialism?

2. Ferguson gives five points to contrast today's "wannabe" imperialists with the genuine article in the British Empire. Write an essay that considers these five points and, more broadly, the relation of most Americans to the rest of the world. Are there alternative ways to interpret the five points Ferguson lists? Are there other models besides the British Empire to assess Americans' interest in the rest of the world?

3. Both Loren Baritz, in "God's Country and American Know-How," and Ferguson think of the "imperial impulse" as motivated in part by the desire to do good for others, though they differ considerably in the conclusions they draw. Write an essay that compares Baritz's and Ferguson's thinking about empire. To what extent do they agree about the nature of empire? What are the main differences? What do you see as the significance of these differences?

WIRED CULTURE   Virtual and Real

To learn more about Iraqi
war images, visit
www.ablongman.com/george/135

Round-the-clock live coverage of the news, pioneered by the Cable News Network (CNN), is made possible by satellite technology and electronic communication networks that promise to link viewers to events as they are happening. In fact, it is now commonplace for viewers to be glued to their televisions at home and in their workplaces to watch history in the making, as such gripping events as the terrorist attacks of 9/11 or the invasion of Iraq in 2003 unfold in real time. Compared to older sources of the news such as the radio and newspaper, CNN's live coverage offers viewers an unprecedented sense of immediacy. The very immediacy of this twenty-four-hour televisual experience, in turn, has raised questions about the nature of the viewing experience and whether it replaces the "real' story with a virtual reality that locates events on the television screen instead of in lived human history. As Marita Sturken notes in the following reading, the Persian Gulf War of 1991 was the "first actual television war," carried live through the new communication technologies instead of being shown after the delay of developing and editing film or video tape. Indeed, the high technology of "night sight," "missile-cams," and "smart" bombs, Sturken further suggests, played a central role in waging the war—and in producing the images that have shaped the public memory.

THE TELEVISION IMAGE: THE IMMEDIATE AND THE VIRTUAL

— Marita Sturken

Marita Sturken teaches in the Annenberg School of Communication at the University of Southern California. This selection is taken from her book *Tangled Memories: The Vietnam War, the AIDS Epidemic, and the Politics of Remembering* (1992), in which she looks at the way watching "national events" such as the Kennedy assassination, the Vietnam War, the first moon walk, and the Persian Gulf War "enables Americans . . . to situate themselves as members of a national culture." In the excerpt that appears here, she is particularly interested in how the technologies of communication and warfare shape our understanding of war.

SUGGESTION FOR READING Notice in the opening three paragraphs how Marita Sturken describes what is new about the television coverage of the Persian Gulf War of 1991. As you read the rest of the selection, consider how she develops the implications of this analysis in her discussion of the "virtual war" and its dominant images.

1 The American public "experienced" the Persian Gulf War through the medium of television, and television's images are central to its history. Yet television images have a slippery relationship to the making of history. The essence of the television image is transmission. It is relentlessly in the present, immediate, simultaneous, and continuous. Hence, television is defined by its capacity to monitor (in the form of surveillance cameras) and to be monitored, transmitting its image regardless of whether we continue to watch it. Raymond Williams wrote

that television is defined by "flow," its capacity to unify fragmentary elements and to incorporate interruption.

Television is coded, like all electronic technology, as immediate and live. It is about the instant present, in which information is more valuable the more quickly we get it, the more immediate it is. Television allows for an immediate participation in the making of history; it produces "instant history." When television images become "historic" images—the lone student halting a tank at Tiananmen Square, the fall of the Berlin Wall, the bombs exploding at night over the city of Baghdad—they retain some of the cultural meaning of electronic technology, connoting the instant and the ephemeral. Their low-resolution, slightly blurred quality allows them to retain a sense of immediacy, as if they were presenting the unfolding of history rather than its image set in the past.

The Persian Gulf War was the first actual television war of the United States. Though the Vietnam War is often termed the first "living room war," its images were shot almost exclusively on film and hence subject to the delays of the developing process. There was always at least a twenty-four-hour delay before images of the Vietnam War reached the United States. The Persian Gulf War, by contrast, took place in the era of satellite technology and highly portable video equipment. It was technologically possible for the world to watch the Persian Gulf War as it happened. This is why military censorship was instituted in such a strict fashion—to make sure that it was *not* seen live. Still, claims of the "immediate" and the "live" reigned. Reporters in the Persian Gulf have noted that many of their stories never aired because they were delayed for a day or two by military censors. Any information that was not "immediate" was considered irrelevant by news producers. The illusion of live coverage given by the twenty-four-hour Cable News Network (CNN) worked in consort with military censorship to mark war news useless unless it was instantaneous.

Thus, one of the ironies of the Persian Gulf War is that although it could have been copiously and immediately documented, it was instead depicted in sterile coverage that yielded very few images. Most of what the American audience saw were maps, still photographs of reporters, and live images of reporters in Israel. CNN's round-the-clock television coverage of the war offered only the illusion that viewers could see everything. The few images that were produced did not accumulate in cultural memory but rushed past in a succession of replays. Ernest Larsen writes: "This was the first war in history that everyone could turn off at night in order to sleep . . . and then switch on again in the morning to know if the world had yet fallen to pieces. The knowledge that such television produces tends not to accumulate, in part because each new moment literally cancels, without a trace, what we have just seen."

5   That the Persian Gulf War was fought in the era of satellite technology affected not only the choice of images that were disseminated in the media but also the surveillance and weapons systems of the war itself. The Gulf War was apparently one of the first in which a computer virus was used as a weapon. Electronic and satellite communications rendered the actual site of the war unclear. As McKenzie Wark writes:

Did the Gulf War take place in Kuwait, Baghdad or Washington? Was the site the Middle East or the whole globe? This is a particularly vexing point. If Iraqi commanders order a SCUD missile launch via radio-telephone from Baghdad, the signal may be intercepted by orbiting US satellites. Another satellite detects the launch using infra-red sensors. Information from both will be relayed to the Pentagon, then again to US command HQ in Saudi Arabia and to Patriot missile bases in Saudi Arabia and Israel.

Wark describes the common notion that the expanded "theater" of the Gulf War included electronic space. This "virtual war" of satellite technology was above all a war of communication vectors. This contributed to the illusion that only those watching CNN, like the TV spectators at a sports event, knew what was "really" happening in the war. As reporter Scott Simon has said:

People around the world often had the sensation of being wired into that war. During the first week, the telephone rang in our workroom in Dhahran. "Get down to the bomb shelter," said an editor on the foreign desk who was watching television. "They've just launched a SCUD at you." And a minute later in eastern Saudi Arabia, the air raid sirens sounded. Weeks later, I stood in line with some soldiers waiting to make phone calls back to the United States. "Calling home before the ground war begins?" I asked. And a paratrooper answered, "Calling to find out what's happening in this war. My folks can really see it." . . . Sometimes I have to remind myself that when I say, "I was there—I saw that," I saw that only on television, just like the people watching the war in Kansas or Kenosha.

Simon evokes the pervasive conflation during the Gulf War of the television experience with the "real" story. Yet it is too simple to allow the Gulf War to be historicized as a virtual high-tech war. Though the image of the war on CNN may have made it appear that the television screen was the war's primary location, this illusion effaced the war that took place among human bodies and communities. The capacity to render the Gulf War in retrospect as a virtual war eclipses the fact that it was still a conventional war, fought with conventional weaponry, in which the body of the other was obliterated. Implicit in many of these statements is the concept that the "real" war is that which is recorded by a camera.

IMAGE ICONS

In this context of censorship and virtual participation, the few images of the war that did filter through took on tremendous significance in defining its narratives. The two images that have emerged as most iconic of the Persian Gulf War—bombs in the night sky over Baghdad and the point-of-view approach of the "smart" bomb to its target—contrast sharply with the iconic images of the Vietnam War.

Baghdad's fiery night sky is an image of both spectacle and the "unseen." Shot by an ABC cameraman with a special "night sight" heat-sensor lens, it is a surreal, otherworldly image that easily evokes the facile appearance of

Night sensor image of Baghdad, Persian Gulf War, 1991

missiles chasing targets in video games. The "beauty" of war is shown here at its most extreme, formally and aesthetically riveting. One pilot said, "I could see the outline of Baghdad lit up like a giant Christmas tree. The entire city was just sparkling." The Vietnam War never produced such images of war as spectacle, the bombs' destructive power sanitized and erased in the darkness. The image of the Baghdad night has commonly been likened to a Fourth of July scene. Indeed, it was reenacted with fireworks at the 1991 Fourth of July celebration in New York, only a month after the huge "welcome home" parade for veterans of the Gulf War, completing the metaphor.

10   The image of the night sky over Baghdad was initially mythologized in the media as depicting Allied Patriot missiles shooting down Iraqi SCUD missiles headed for Israel and Saudi Arabia. However, since the Gulf War, it has been revealed that the video actually depicted the SCUDS coming apart at the end of their flight and falling into pieces onto the Patriots. Yet these qualifying explanations have not changed the meaning of this image as it achieves historic sta-

tus: It signifies the myth of the war as one of clean technology.

The other image icons of the Gulf War—the electronic "missile-cam" footage taken from aircraft and bombs—also emphasize the predominating narrative of the war as a battle of technology. These images portray targeted buildings as seen through the crosshairs (and then exploding) and point-of-view perspectives of a bomb's approach to a site, flashing off the instant before impact. They carry power not only because they are the first popular images of their kind but also because they provide the viewer with a particular experience of military hardware voyeurism. In these images, the technologies of media and war merge to the point of inseparability. It can be said, however, that these technologies have always been inseparable, as television technology has always been derived from technology developed through military research. As Wark notes, "Most of the technologies now accessible to television, including the portable satellite news-gatherers (SNG), are the civilian progeny of equipment developed for military applications."

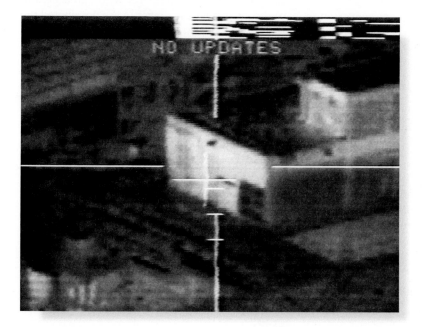

Missile-cam image, Persian Gulf War.

These missile-cam images are "secret" images, shown to audiences in the camaraderie of the military briefing room, usually on a small screen, with a military spokesman using a pointer to brief the "American public" on the interpretive codes needed to understand "our" weaponry. This approach allowed Gen. Norman Schwarzkopf and other military officials to employ sports metaphors, as if they were football coaches narrating their team's plays. Despite the presence of several woman reporters, the military briefing room for the press during the Gulf War was a male domain deliberately constructed as secretive and exclusive. The good-humored inside jokes and comradeship of word jockeying in these press conferences made clear the clubby relationship between the press and the military, masking the fact that many questions went unasked and unanswered. The shared secrecy implied in the presentation of these images is also the result of their visual coding as images of surveillance. In black and white and framed with crosshairs, these images of bombs exploding on their targets thus afforded audiences the feeling of having a special kind of sight, a privileged view.

The camera image has a long history in both the propagation of wars and their documentation and memorialization. Since World War I, camera technology has been integral to the battlefield and image surveillance of the enemy, an essential strategic device. As Paul Virilio has written:

> Thus, alongside the "war machine," there has always existed an ocular (and later optical and electro-optical) "watching machine" capable of providing soldiers, and particularly commanders, with a visual perspective on the military action under way. From the original watch-tower, through the anchored balloon to the reconnaissance aircraft and remote-sensing satellites, one and the same function has been indefinitely repeated, the eye's function being the function of a weapon.

These two roles of the camera—as a device for constructing cultural memory and history and as a device for waging warfare—were inseparable in the production of images of the Gulf War. Yet what distinguishes the Gulf War surveillance images from previous ones is not only their technological proficiency but, more important, their use as the primary *public* images of the war; indeed, they have become the image icons of the war. As part of a well-orchestrated public relations and censorship campaign, these missile-cam images served to screen out images that were never taken or never shown. Hence, American viewers—and, by extension, the rest of the world, watching CNN—not only were given the illusion that they were welcomed into the military briefing room but also were situated as spectators within the frame of reference of the bomb. The camera's point of view was the bomb's point of view and the viewer's point of view. Watching these images, the viewer can imagine being in the bomber, imagine being the bomb itself, blasting forward and exploding in an orgasmic finale, the spectator and the weapon merged. Ironically, the audience did not seem to be implicated. Rather, the bombs took on agency, absolving viewers as distanced spectators.

15   Metaphors of sight were prevalent during the Gulf War; struggles over who had access to and control over the power to see dominated the war. At press briefings, Gen. Norman Schwarzkopf talked initially of blinding Saddam Hussein—"We took out his eyes"—by destroying his air force, and American weaponry was consistently referred to as having vision. For instance, the "thermal night sight" employed by American tanks was described as allowing them to fight at night or in bad weather, when "Iraqi tanks were virtually blind." Thus, "smart weapons" meant weapons that could "see." This emphasis on sight included a concern with concealment through the use of stealth bombers and other stealth technology.

The preoccupation with establishing American technology's ability to see can be directly traced to the representations of American technology in the Vietnam War. The "inpenetrable" jungle foliage of Vietnam has been consistently blamed for the inability of American military technology to win the war (hence the campaign of massive defoliation by Agent Orange perpetrated by the U.S. in Vietnam Not coincidentally, the desert terrain of the Middle East provided the ideal terrain for sight, enabling the American military to see its own technology at work. These "smart" weapons (only 70 percent of which, it was revealed after the war, hit their targets) were awarded intelligence, sight, and even memory— they were said to "hold the characteristics of enemy vehicles in their memory."

SUGGESTIONS FOR DISCUSSION

1. What does it mean for people to see wars televised in live coverage? What does it mean, as reporter Scott Simon says, that people around the world felt "wired into the war"? In what sense was the television screen "the war's primary location"? What does it mean to describe a war as "virtual"?

2. Notice Marita Sturken's remarks on war in an "era of satellite technology." How does high technology enter into the "surveillance and weapon systems of war itself"? How does this change the way we think about war?

3. According to Sturken, the images people remember from the Persian Gulf War of 1991 differ in important ways from the iconic images that have shaped the collective memory of the Vietnam War (and, by extension, of the Iraq invasion and occupation of 2003). Compare the two photos here with photos of war that appear later in the Visual Culture section. Notice the high-tech look of the night sensor and missile-cam images.

SUGGESTIONS FOR WRITING

1. Consider Sturken's discussion of the differences between "real" and virtual war. Write an essay that explains what she sees as the significance of these differences.

2. Sturken says that the iconic images of the Persian Gulf War created a perspective that joined the "smart bombs" and the viewer's point of view. Write an essay that explains the meaning and consequences of such a merger of the spectator and the weapon.

3. Write an essay that compares the iconic images of the night sensor and missile-cam to one or more images of war presented later in this chapter (or other images of war you have found). How are the images alike and different in the way they shape our memory of war?

PERSPECTIVES   George W. Bush's Second Inaugural Address

The 2004 presidential election found Americans deeply divided over George W. Bush's leadership in his first term. The invasion and occupation of Iraq, mounting national debt, growing inequality between rich and poor, and profound differences over such issues as gay marriage and reproductive rights produced widespread uncertainty about the direction of the nation in the first presidential election after 9/11. It was perhaps fitting, then, for President Bush, in his remarkable and, for many, messianic second inaugural address, to articulate a vision of America's historical mission as that of ending tyranny and spreading freedom.

Responses to the inaugural address varied in predictable ways, praising or blaming Bush's policies. But there were also other responses that focused on the president's vision of history. We present the address along with two commentaries written shortly after the inauguration ceremony that raise questions, from the right and the left, about the grandiosity of Bush's address and the role history plays in it. As you read President Bush's address, notice the historical references he makes and the mission he articulates for the future.

SECOND INAUGURAL ADDRESS, JANUARY 17, 2005

— George W. Bush

1 Vice President Cheney, Mr. Chief Justice, President Carter, President Bush, President Clinton, reverend clergy, distinguished guests, fellow citizens:

On this day, prescribed by law and marked by ceremony, we celebrate the durable wisdom of our Constitution, and recall the deep commitments that unite our country. I am grateful for the honor of this hour, mindful of the consequential times in which we live, and determined to fulfill the oath that I have sworn and you have witnessed.

At this second gathering, our duties are defined not by the words I use, but by the history we have seen together. For a half century, America defended our own freedom by standing watch on distant borders. After the shipwreck of communism came years of relative quiet, years of repose, years of sabbatical—and then there came a day of fire.

We have seen our vulnerability—and we have seen its deepest source. For as long as whole regions of the world simmer in resentment and tyranny—prone to ideologies that feed hatred and excuse murder—violence will gather, and multiply in destructive power, and cross the most defended borders, and raise a mortal threat. There is only one force of history that can break the reign of hatred and resentment, and expose the pretensions of tyrants, and reward the hopes of the decent and tolerant, and that is the force of human freedom.

5 We are led, by events and common sense, to one conclusion: The survival of liberty in our land increasingly depends on the success of liberty in other lands. The best hope for peace in our world is the expansion of freedom in all the world.

America's vital interests and our deepest beliefs are now one. From the day of our Founding, we have proclaimed that every man and woman on this earth has rights, and dignity, and matchless value, because they bear the image of the Maker of Heaven and earth. Across the generations we have proclaimed the imperative of self-government, because no one is fit to be a master, and no one deserves to be a slave. Advancing these ideals is the mission that created our Nation. It is the honorable achievement of our fathers. Now it is the urgent requirement of our nation's security, and the calling of our time.

So it is the policy of the United States to seek and support the growth of democratic movements and institutions in every nation and culture, with the ultimate goal of ending tyranny in our world.

This is not primarily the task of arms, though we will defend ourselves and our friends by force of arms when necessary. Freedom, by its nature, must be chosen, and defended by citizens, and sustained by the rule of law and the protection of minorities. And when the soul of a nation finally speaks, the institutions that arise may reflect customs and traditions very different from our own. America will not impose our own style of government on the unwilling. Our goal instead is to help others find their own voice, attain their own freedom, and make their own way.

The great objective of ending tyranny is the concentrated work of generations. The difficulty of the task is no excuse for avoiding it. America's influence is not unlimited, but fortunately for the oppressed, America's influence is considerable, and we will use it confidently in freedom's cause.

10   My most solemn duty is to protect this nation and its people against further attacks and emerging threats. Some have unwisely chosen to test America's resolve, and have found it firm.

We will persistently clarify the choice before every ruler and every nation: the moral choice between oppression, which is always wrong, and freedom, which is eternally right. America will not pretend that jailed dissidents prefer their chains, or that women welcome humiliation and servitude, or that any human being aspires to live at the mercy of bullies.

We will encourage reform in other governments by making clear that success in our relations will require the decent treatment of their own people. America's belief in human dignity will guide our policies, yet rights must be more than the grudging concessions of dictators; they are secured by free dissent and the participation of the governed. In the long run, there is no justice without freedom, and there can be no human rights without human liberty.

Some, I know, have questioned the global appeal of liberty—though this time in history, four decades defined by the swiftest advance of freedom ever seen, is an odd time for doubt. Americans, of all people, should never be surprised by the power of our ideals. Eventually, the call of freedom comes to every mind and every soul. We do not accept the existence of permanent tyranny because we do not accept the possibility of permanent slavery. Liberty will come to those who love it.

Today, America speaks anew to the peoples of the world:

15   All who live in tyranny and hopelessness can know: the United States will not ignore your oppression, or excuse your oppressors. When you stand for your liberty, we will stand with you.

Democratic reformers facing repression, prison, or exile can know: America sees you for who you are: the future leaders of your free country.

The rulers of outlaw regimes can know that we still believe as Abraham Lincoln did: "Those who deny freedom to others deserve it not for themselves; and, under the rule of a just God, cannot long retain it."

The leaders of governments with long habits of control need to know: to serve your people you must learn to trust them. Start on this journey of progress and justice, and America will walk at your side.

And all the allies of the United States can know: we honor your friendship, we rely on your counsel, and we depend on your help. Division among free nations is a primary goal of freedom's enemies. The concerted effort of free nations to promote democracy is a prelude to our enemies' defeat.

20   Today, I also speak anew to my fellow citizens:

From all of you, I have asked patience in the hard task of securing America, which you have granted in good measure. Our country has accepted obligations that are difficult to fulfill, and would be dishonorable to abandon. Yet because we have acted in the great liberating tradition of this nation, tens of millions have achieved their freedom. And as hope kindles hope, millions more will find it. By our efforts, we have lit a fire as well—a fire in the minds of men. It warms those who feel its power, it burns those who fight its progress, and one day this untamed fire of freedom will reach the darkest corners of our world.

A few Americans have accepted the hardest duties in this cause—in the quiet work of intelligence and diplomacy . . . the idealistic work of helping raise up free governments . . . the dangerous and necessary work of fighting our enemies. Some have shown their devotion to our country in deaths that honored their whole lives—and we will always honor their names and their sacrifice.

All Americans have witnessed this idealism, and some for the first time. I ask our youngest citizens to believe the evidence of your eyes. You have seen duty and allegiance in the determined faces of our soldiers. You have seen that life is fragile, and evil is real, and courage triumphs. Make the choice to serve in a cause larger than your wants, larger than yourself—and in your days you will add not just to the wealth of our country, but to its character.

America has need of idealism and courage, because we have essential work at home—the unfinished work of American freedom. In a world moving toward liberty, we are determined to show the meaning and promise of liberty.

25   In America's ideal of freedom, citizens find the dignity and security of economic independence, instead of laboring on the edge of subsistence. This is the broader definition of liberty that motivated the Homestead Act, the Social Security Act, and the G.I. Bill of Rights. And now we will extend this vision by reforming great institutions to serve the needs of our time. To give every American a stake in the promise and future of our country, we will bring the highest standards to our schools, and build an ownership society. We will widen the ownership of homes and businesses, retirement savings and health insurance—preparing our people for the challenges of life in a free society. By making every citizen an agent of his or her own destiny, we will give our fellow Americans greater freedom from want and fear, and make our society more prosperous and just and equal.

In America's ideal of freedom, the public interest depends on private character—on integrity, and tolerance toward others, and the rule of conscience in our own lives. Self-govern-

ment relies, in the end, on the governing of the self. That edifice of character is built in families, supported by communities with standards, and sustained in our national life by the truths of Sinai, the Sermon on the Mount, the words of the Koran, and the varied faiths of our people. Americans move forward in every generation by reaffirming all that is good and true that came before—ideals of justice and conduct that are the same yesterday, today, and forever.

In America's ideal of freedom, the exercise of rights is ennobled by service, and mercy, and a heart for the weak. Liberty for all does not mean independence from one another. Our nation relies on men and women who look after a neighbor and surround the lost with love. Americans, at our best, value the life we see in one another, and must always remember that even the unwanted have worth. And our country must abandon all the habits of racism, because we cannot carry the message of freedom and the baggage of bigotry at the same time.

From the perspective of a single day, including this day of dedication, the issues and questions before our country are many. From the viewpoint of centuries, the questions that come to us are narrowed and few. Did our generation advance the cause of freedom? And did our character bring credit to that cause?

These questions that judge us also unite us, because Americans of every party and background, Americans by choice and by birth, are bound to one another in the cause of freedom. We have known divisions, which must be healed to move forward in great purposes—and I will strive in good faith to heal them. Yet those divisions do not define America. We felt the unity and fellowship of our nation when freedom came under attack, and our response came like a single hand over a single heart. And we can feel that same unity and pride whenever America acts for good, and the victims of disaster are given hope, and the unjust encounter justice, and the captives are set free.

30   We go forward with complete confidence in the eventual triumph of freedom. Not because

history runs on the wheels of inevitability; it is human choices that move events. Not because we consider ourselves a chosen nation; God moves and chooses as He wills. We have confidence because freedom is the permanent hope of mankind, the hunger in dark places, the longing of the soul. When our Founders declared a new order of the ages; when soldiers died in wave upon wave for a union based on liberty; when citizens marched in peaceful outrage under the banner "Freedom Now"—they were acting on an ancient hope that is meant to be fulfilled. History has an ebb and flow of justice, but history also has a visible direction, set by liberty and the Author of Liberty.

When the Declaration of Independence was first read in public and the Liberty Bell was sounded in celebration, a witness said, "It rang as if it meant something." In our time it means something still. America, in this young century, proclaims liberty throughout all the world, and to all the inhabitants thereof. Renewed in our strength—tested, but not weary—we are ready for the greatest achievements in the history of freedom.

May God bless you, and may He watch over the United States of America.

WAY TOO MUCH GOD: WAS THE PRESIDENT'S SPEECH A CASE OF "MISSION INEBRIATION"?

— Peggy Noonan

Peggy Noonan was a speechwriter for President Ronald Reagan and is currently a contributing editor of the *Wall Street Journal*. "Way Too Much God: Was the President's Speech a Case of 'Mission Inebriation'?" appeared just after the inaugural address in her column in the *Wall Street Journal*.

SUGGESTION FOR READING   As you read, notice the distinction Peggy Noonan draws between foreign policy "moralists" and "realists." Consider how she defines the two terms and the assumptions that underlie each approach to history.

1 It was an interesting Inauguration Day. Washington had warmed up, the swift storm of the previous day had passed, the sky was overcast but the air wasn't painful in a wind-chill way, and the capital was full of men in cowboy hats and women in long furs. In fact, the night of the inaugural balls became known this year as The Night of the Long Furs.

Laura Bush's beauty has grown more obvious; she was chic in shades of white, and smiled warmly. The Bush daughters looked exactly as they are, beautiful and young. A well-behaved city was on its best behavior, everyone from cops to doormen to journalists eager to help visitors in any way.

For me there was some unexpected merriness. In my hotel the night before the inauguration, all the guests were evacuated at 1:45 in the morning. There were fire alarms and flashing lights on each floor, and a public address system instructed us to take the stairs, not the elevators. Hundreds of people wound up outside in the slush, eventually gathering inside the lobby, waiting to find out what next.

The staff—kindly, clucking—tried to figure out if the fire existed and, if so, where it was. Hundreds of inaugural revelers wound up observing each other. Over there on the couch was Warren Buffet in bright blue pajamas and a white hotel robe. James Baker was in trench coat and throat scarf. I remembered my keys and eyeglasses but walked out without my shoes. After a while the "all clear" came, and hundreds of us stood in line for elevators to return to our rooms. Later that morning, as I entered an elevator to go to an appointment, I said, "You all look happier than you did last night." A man said, "That was just a dream," and everyone laughed.

5   The inauguration itself was beautiful to see—pomp, panoply, parades, flags and cannonades. America does this well. And the most poignant moment was the manful William Rehnquist, unable to wear a tie and making his way down the long marble steps to swear in the president. The continuation of democracy is made possible by such personal gallantry.

    There were some surprises, one of which was the thrill of a male voice singing "God Bless America," instead of the hyper-coloratura divas who plague our American civic life. But whoever picked the music for the inaugural ceremony itself—modern megachurch hymns, music that sounds like what they'd use for the quiet middle section of a Pixar animated film—was . . . lame. The downbeat orchestral arrangement that followed the president's speech was no doubt an attempt to avoid charges that the ceremony had a triumphalist air. But I wound up thinking: This is America. We have a lot of good songs. And we watch inaugurals in part to hear them.

    Never be defensive in your choice of music.

    The inaugural address itself was startling. It left me with a bad feeling, and reluctant dislike. Rhetorically, it veered from high-class boilerplate to strong and simple sentences, but it was not pedestrian. George W. Bush's second inaugural will no doubt prove historic because it carried a punch, asserting an agenda so sweeping that an observer quipped that by the end he would not have been surprised if the president had announced we were going to colonize Mars.

    A short and self-conscious preamble led quickly to the meat of the speech: the president's evolving thoughts on freedom in the world. Those thoughts seemed marked by deep moral seriousness and no moral modesty.

10   No one will remember what the president said about domestic policy, which was the subject of the last third of the text. This may prove to have been a miscalculation.

    It was a foreign-policy speech. To the extent our foreign policy is marked by a division that

has been (crudely but serviceably) defined as a division between moralists and realists—the moralists taken with a romantic longing to carry democracy and justice to foreign fields, the realists motivated by what might be called cynicism and an acknowledgment of the limits of governmental power—President Bush sided strongly with the moralists, which was not a surprise. But he did it in a way that left this Bush supporter yearning for something she does not normally yearn for, and that is: nuance.

    The administration's approach to history is at odds with what has been described by a communications adviser to the president as the "reality-based community." A dumb phrase, but not a dumb thought: he meant that the administration sees history as dynamic and changeable, not static and impervious to redirection or improvement. That is the Bush administration way, and it happens to be realistic: history is dynamic and changeable. On the other hand, some things are constant, such as human imperfection, injustice, misery and bad government.

    This world is not heaven.

    The president's speech seemed rather heavenish. It was a God-drenched speech. This president, who has been accused of giving too much attention to religious imagery and religious thought, has not let the criticism enter him. God was invoked relentlessly. "The Author of Liberty." "God moves and chooses as He wills. We have confidence because freedom is the permanent hope of mankind . . . the longing of the soul."

15   It seemed a document produced by a White House on a mission. The United States, the speech said, has put the world on notice: good governments that are just to their people are our friends, and those that are not are, essentially, not. We know the way: democracy. The president told every nondemocratic government in the world to shape up. "Success in our relations [with other governments] will require the decent treatment of their own people."

    The speech did not deal with specifics— 9/11, terrorism, particular alliances, Iraq. It was, instead, assertively abstract.

"We are led, by events and common sense, to one conclusion: the survival of liberty in our land increasingly depends on the success of liberty in other lands." "Across the generations we have proclaimed the imperative of self government. . . . Now it is the urgent requirement of our nation's security, and the calling of our time." "It is the policy of the United States to seek and support the growth of democratic movements and institutions in every nation and culture, with the ultimate goal of ending tyranny in the world."

Ending tyranny in the world? Well that's an ambition, and if you're going to have an ambition it might as well be a big one. But this declaration, which is not wrong by any means, seemed to me to land somewhere between dreamy and disturbing. Tyranny is a very bad thing and quite wicked, but one doesn't expect we're going to eradicate it any time soon. Again, this is not heaven, it's earth.

There were moments of eloquence: "America will not pretend that jailed dissidents prefer their chains, or that women welcome humiliation and servitude, or that any human being aspires to live at the mercy of bullies." "We do not accept the existence of permanent tyranny because we do not accept the possibility of permanent slavery." And, to the young people of our country, "You have seen that life is fragile, and evil is real, and courage triumphs." They have, since 9/11, seen exactly that.

20   And yet such promising moments were followed by this, the ending of the speech. "Renewed in our strength—tested, but not weary—we are ready for the greatest achievements in the history of freedom."

This is—how else to put it?—over the top. It is the kind of sentence that makes you wonder if this White House did not, in the preparation period, have a case of what I have called in the past "mission inebriation." A sense that there are few legitimate boundaries to the desires born in the goodness of their good hearts.

One wonders if they shouldn't ease up, calm down, breathe deep, get more securely grounded. The most moving speeches summon us to the cause of what is actually possible. Perfection in the life of man on earth is not.

HISTORIANS IN CAHOOTS

— *Tristram Hunt*

Tristram Hunt is a lecturer in history at Queen Mary, University of London, and the author of *Building Jerusalem: The Rise and Fall of the Victorian City* (2004). "Historians in Cahoots" appeared in the *Guardian* (UK) two weeks after President Bush's inaugural address, when Hunt was a visiting professor at Arizona State University.

SUGGESTION FOR READING   As you read, notice how Tristram Hunt focuses on the role of historians in supporting the Bush administration's vision of history. Consider the distinction he draws between history as "inspiration" and history as "instruction."

1   In his messianic inauguration address, President Bush spoke of America's global duty being defined by "the history we have seen together." Inevitably, this was a reference to the events of 9/11. But given how much a sense of US revolutionary heritage is now informing current policy, the broader history that Americans are experiencing together should be an equal cause for concern.

The latter half of the 20th century saw US scholars lead the way in popular social history. The world of the workplace, family life, native America and civil rights was chronicled with verve and style. The delicate oral histories of social chronicler Studs Terkel opened up the local and working-class past to mass audiences. He showed how the second world war was as much the people's as the statesmen's war. On National Public Radio and the Public Broadcasting Service, history was dissected professionally and polemically.

Today, you would be hard-pressed to find such broad-ranging investigations of the American past. Instead, the bookshelves of Borders and Barnes & Noble are dominated by a very specific reading of the 18th century. This does not, in God-fearing America, represent a new-found interest in the secular ideals of enlightenment and reason. Rather, an obsessive telling and retelling of that great struggle for liberty: the American Revolution.

Heroic biography has become the bestselling history brand of Bush's America. Thomas Jefferson, Alexander Hamilton, George Washington, Benjamin Franklin, John Adams and Abraham Lincoln are all speaking from the grave with new-found loquaciousness. Barely a week passes without another definitive life of a Founding Father, Brother or Sister, each one more adulatory than the last.

5　Not least the vice-president's wife, Dr. Lynne Cheney, whose recent contribution, When Washington Crossed the Delaware: A Wintertime Story for Young Patriots, is the kind of "history" that any ministry of information would have been proud of. Museums and TV schedulers have not been slow to catch the mood. The New York Historical Society currently hosts a vast exhibition celebrating the life of Alexander Hamilton ("The Man who Made Modern America"); the History Channel has even cut into its second world war telethon to offer a series of bio-pics of great American revolutionaries.

Sadly, none of this has resulted in any substantive reinterpretation of the revolution or its principal actors. As Simon Schama rightly puts it, this is history as inspiration, not instruction. Instead of critical analysis, the public is being fed self-serving affirmation: wartime schlock designed to underpin the unique calling, manifest destiny and selfless heroism of the US nation and, above all, its super-human presidents.

Needless to say, this goes down very well at the White House. We are told that the president's current reading matter includes biographies of Washington as well as Alexander Hamilton. For the biographical emphasis on the Great Man who has the character and vision to transcend as well as define his times fits well with a presidency that values personal instinct and prayer above reason and empiricism.

In fact, the historical community seems to be providing the ideal conditions for the Nietzschean approach of the Bush administration. As one senior presidential adviser scarily informed journalist Ron Suskind: "We're an empire now, and when we act, we create our own reality. And while you're studying that reality . . . we'll act again, creating other new realities. . . . We're history's actors . . . and you, all of you, will be left to just study what we do."

Rather than tempering such terrifying ambition, US scholars are happy to play up to it. Historian Eliot Cohen penned an administration-friendly account of how former US presidents have instinctively been right in matters military, compared with their hapless, diffident generals, while prolific biographer Joseph Ellis has sought to offer posthumous suggestions from George Washington to George W.

10　At a time when the US imperium is rampaging across the globe, you might have thought there would be a historical concern to enlighten the domestic citizenry about foreign cultures and peoples. Instead, public scholars are feeding the nation's increasingly insulated mentality with a retreat into the cosy fables of their forebears. Amid the biography and hagiography, stories of Islamic civilisation or Middle East nation-building are among the many histories the American people are not seeing.

SUGGESTIONS FOR DISCUSSION

1. Consider the vision of history in President Bush's second inaugural address. What use does he make of historical references? Note that he does not directly mention the attacks on the World Trade Center and the Pentagon on 9/11. How does he make their presence felt? What role do they play in his articulation of America's mission in the world? Notice too that he makes repeated mention of "freedom." What does he mean by the term? How does he tie it into the vision of history he wants to project? What might other authors in this chapter, such as Loren Baritz and Niall Ferguson, say about Bush's vision of America's mission?

2. Peggy Noonan opens "Too Much God" with a descriptive, chatty account of the inauguration that might seem at first glance to have little relation to the points she makes later about "moralists" and "realists." Why do you think she begins this way? How do these remarks help establish her credentials and credibility? What does she mean by "moralists" and "realists"? What assumptions does each position make about the dynamics of history?

3. Tristram Hunt suggests that the work of historians helps shape the climate of opinion in the United States—and has provided support for the Bush administration's approach to world affairs. What does he mean by "history as inspiration"? How does this differ from history as "instruction"? To what extent could President Bush's second inaugural address be read as an example of "history by inspiration"?

SUGGESTIONS FOR WRITING

1. Write an essay that analyzes the use of the term "freedom" in President Bush's second inaugural address. Explain the role it plays in his vision of America's historical mission. You might consider too how he ties the term to his notion of an "ownership society." What does this mean? Why and how is "ownership" a criteria of freedom?

2. Use President Bush's second inaugural address as the grounds to write an essay that considers the differences between Peggy Noonan's and Tristram Hunt's understandings of the role of history. As you can see, they are both critical of Bush but in very different ways. How can the inaugural address help you bring out and explain these differences?

3. Write an essay that explains what Loren Baritz and Niall Ferguson would say about President Bush's second inaugural address. Both historians are concerned with America's mission in the world, but they differ considerably in their assumptions, analyses, and conclusions. It is likely that both would note the messianic tone of the address. Your task is to explain what they might agree on and what the key differences are that divide them.

THE SIGNIFICANCE OF THE FRONTIER IN AMERICAN HISTORY

Frederick Jackson Turner

Frederick Jackson Turner (1861–1932) taught history at the University of Wisconsin and Harvard. His essay "The Significance of the Frontier in American History," published in 1893, is the classic exposition of what has become known among American historians as the "frontier thesis"—the view that free land and the pioneer experience were formative in shaping the American national character and the country's belief in individualism, democracy, and nationalism.

SUGGESTION FOR READING As you read, notice how Frederick Jackson Turner is offering an overarching interpretation of American development. Underline and annotate those passages where Turner generalizes about the significance of the frontier.

1   In a recent bulletin of the Superintendent of the Census for 1890 appear these significant words: "Up to and including 1880 the country had a frontier of settlement, but at present the unsettled area has been so broken into by isolated bodies of settlement that there can hardly be said to be a frontier line. In the discussion of its extent, its westward movement, etc., it can not, therefore, any longer have a place in the census reports." This brief official statement marks the closing of a great historic movement. Up to our own day American history has been in a large degree the history of the colonization of the Great West. The existence of an area of free land, its continuous recession, and the advance of American settlement westward, explain American development.

Behind institutions, behind constitutional forms and modifications, lie the vital forces that call these organs into life and shape them to meet changing conditions. The peculiarity of American institutions is, the fact that they have been compelled to adapt themselves to the changes of an expanding people—to the changes involved in crossing a continent, in winning a wilderness, and in developing at each area of this progress out of the primitive economic and political conditions of the frontier into the complexity of city life. Said Calhoun in 1817, "We are great, and rapidly—I was about to say fearfully—growing!" So saying, he touched the distinguishing feature of American life. All peoples show development; the germ theory of politics has been sufficiently emphasized. In the case of most nations, however, the development has occurred in a limited area; and if the nation has expanded, it has met other growing peoples whom it has conquered. But in the case of the United States we have a different phenomenon. Limiting our attention to the Atlantic coast, we have the familiar phenomenon of the evolution of institutions in a limited area, such as the rise of representative government; the differentiation of simple colonial governments into complex organs; the progress from primitive industrial society, without division of labor, up to manufacturing civilization. But we have in addition to this a recurrence of the process of evolution in each western area reached in the process of expansion. Thus American development has exhibited not merely advance along a single line, but a return to primitive conditions on a continually advancing frontier line, and a new development for that area. American social development has been continually beginning over again on the frontier. This perennial rebirth, this fluidity of American life, this expansion westward with its new opportunities, its continuous touch with the simplicity of primitive society, furnish the forces dominating American character. The true point of view in the history of this nation is not the Atlantic coast, it is the Great West. Even the slavery struggle, which is made so exclusive an object of attention by writers like Professor von Holst, occupies its important place in American history because of its relation to westward expansion.

In this advance, the frontier is the outer edge of the wave—the meeting point between savagery and civilization. Much has been written about the frontier from the point of view of border warfare and the chase, but as a field for the serious study of the economist and the historian it has been neglected.

The American frontier is sharply distinguished from the European frontier—a fortified boundary line running through dense populations. The most significant thing about the American frontier is, that it lies at the hither edge of free land. In the census reports it is treated as the margin of that settlement which has a density of two or more to the square mile. The term is an elastic one, and for our purposes does not need sharp definition. We shall consider the whole frontier belt, including the Indian country and the outer margin of the "settled area" of the census reports. This paper will make no attempt to treat the subject exhaustively; its aim is simply to call attention to the frontier as a fertile field for investigation, and to suggest some of the problems which arise in connection with it.

5   In the settlement of America we have to observe how European life entered the continent, and how America modified and developed that life and reacted on Europe. Our early history is the study of European germs developing in an American environment. Too exclusive attention has been paid by institutional students to the Germanic origins, too little to the American factors. The frontier is the line of most rapid and effective Americanization. The wilderness masters the colonist. It finds him a European in dress, industries, tools, modes of travel, and thought. It takes him from the railroad car and puts him in the birch canoe. It strips off the garments of civilization and arrays him in the hunting shirt and the

moccasin. It puts him in the log cabin of the Cherokee and Iroquois and runs an Indian palisade around him. Before long he has gone to planting Indian corn and plowing with a sharp stick; he shouts the war cry and takes the scalp in orthodox Indian fashion. In short, at the frontier the environment is at first too strong for the man. He must accept the conditions which it furnishes, or perish, and so he fits himself into the Indian clearings and follows the Indian trails. Little by little he transforms the wilderness, but the outcome is not the old Europe, not simply the development of Germanic germs, any more than the first phenomenon was a case of reversion to the Germanic mark. The fact is, that here is a new product that is American. At first, the frontier was the Atlantic coast. It was the frontier of Europe in a very real sense. Moving westward, the frontier became more and more American. As successive terminal moraines result from successive glaciations, so each frontier leaves its traces behind it, and when it becomes a settled area the region still partakes of the frontier characteristics. Thus the advance of the frontier has meant a steady movement away from the influence of Europe, a steady growth of independence on American lines. And to study this advance, the men who grew up under these conditions, and the political, economic, and social results of it, is to study the really American part of our history. . . .

First, we note that the frontier promoted the formation of a composite nationality for the American people. The coast was preponderantly English, but the later tides of continental immigration flowed across to the free lands. This was the case from the early colonial days. The Scotch-Irish and the Palatine Germans, or "Pennsylvania Dutch," furnished the dominant element in the stock of the colonial frontier. With these peoples were also the freed indented servants, or redemptioners, who at the expiration of their time of service passed to the frontier. Governor Spotswood of Virginia writes in 1717, "The inhabitants of our frontiers are composed generally of such as have been transported hither as servants, and, being out of their time, settle themselves where land is to be taken up and that will produce the necessarys of life with little labour." Very generally these redemptioners were of non-English stock. In the crucible of the frontier the immigrants were Americanized, liberated, and fused into a mixed race, English in neither nationality nor characteristics. The process has gone on from the early days to our own. Burke and other writers in the middle of the eighteenth century believed that Pennsylvania was "threatened with the danger of being wholly foreign in language, manners, and perhaps even inclinations." The German and Scotch-Irish elements in the frontier of the South were only less great. In the middle of the present century the German element in Wisconsin was already so considerable that leading publicists looked to the creation of a German state out of the commonwealth by concentrating their colonization. Such examples teach us to beware of misinterpreting the fact that there is a common English speech in America into a belief that the stock is also English.

In another way the advance of the frontier decreased our dependence on England. The coast, particularly of the South, lacked diversified industries, and was dependent on England for the bulk of its supplies. In the South there was even a dependence on the Northern colonies for articles of food. Governor Glenn, of South Carolina, writes in the middle of the eighteenth century: "Our trade with New York and Philadelphia was of this sort, draining us of all the little money and bills we could gather from other places for their bread, flour, beer, hams, bacon, and other things of their produce, all which, except beer, our new townships begin to supply us with, which are settled with very industrious and thriving Germans. This no doubt diminishes the number of shipping and the appearance of our trade, but it is far from being a detriment to us." Before long the frontier created a demand for merchants. As it retreated from the coast it became less and less possible for England to bring her supplies directly to the consumer's wharfs, and carry away staple crops, and staple crops began to give way to diversified agriculture for a time. The effect of this phase of the frontier action upon the northern section is perceived when we realize how the advance of the frontier

aroused seaboard cities like Boston, New York, and Baltimore, to engage in rivalry for what Washington called "the extensive and valuable trade of a rising empire."

* * *

But the most important effect of the frontier has been in the promotion of democracy here and in Europe. As has been indicated, the frontier is productive of individualism. Complex society is precipitated by the wilderness into a kind of primitive organization based on the family. The tendency is anti-social. It produces antipathy to control, and particularly to any direct control. The tax-gatherer is viewed as a representative of oppression. Prof. Osgood, in an able article, has pointed out that the frontier conditions prevalent in the colonies are important factors in the explanation of the American Revolution, where individual liberty was sometimes confused with absence of all effective government. The same conditions aid in explaining the difficulty of instituting a strong government in the period of the confederacy. The frontier individualism has from the beginning promoted democracy. . . .

From the conditions of frontier life came intellectual traits of profound importance. The works of travelers along each frontier from colonial days onward describe certain common traits, and these traits have, while softening down, still persisted as survivals in the place of their origin, even when a higher social organization succeeded. The result is that to the frontier the American intellect owes its striking characteristics. That coarseness and strength combined with acuteness and inquisitiveness; that practical, inventive turn of mind, quick to find expedients; that masterful grasp of material things, lacking in the artistic but powerful to effect great ends; that restless, nervous energy; that dominant individualism, working for good and for evil, and withal that buoyancy and exuberance which comes with freedom—these are traits of the frontier, or traits called out elsewhere because of the existence of the frontier. Since the days when the fleet of Columbus sailed into the waters of the New World, America has been another name for opportunity, and the people of the United States have taken their tone from the incessant expansion which has not only been open but has even been forced upon them. He would be a rash prophet who should assert that the expansive character of American life has now entirely ceased. Movement has been its dominant fact, and, unless this training has no effect upon a people, the American energy will continually demand a wider field for its exercise. But never again will such gifts of free land offer themselves. For a moment, at the frontier, the bonds of custom are broken and unrestraint is triumphant. There is not *tabula rasa*. The stubborn American environment is there with its imperious summons to accept its conditions; the inherited ways of doing things are also there; and yet, in spite of environment, and in spite of custom, each frontier did indeed furnish a new field of opportunity, a gate of escape from the bondage of the past; and freshness, and confidence, and scorn of older society, impatience of its restraints and its ideas, and indifference to its lessons, have accompanied the frontier. What the Mediterranean Sea was to the Greeks, breaking the bond of custom, offering new experiences, calling out new institutions and activities, that, and more, the ever retreating frontier has been to the United States directly, and to the nations of Europe more remotely. And now, four centuries from the discovery of America, at the end of a hundred years of life under the Constitution, the frontier has gone, and with its going has closed the first period of American history.

SUGGESTIONS FOR DISCUSSION

1. Is this the version of American history you learned in school? To what extent is Turner's "frontier thesis" a familiar one, whether or not you have heard it referred to as such? Can you think of other examples that present the frontier as a shaping influence in the way Americans understand the past?

2. What connections does Turner posit between the frontier, individualism, and democracy? What does he see as the "dangers" and "benefits" of these connections? Do these connections still hold true today?

3. What does Turner mean when he talks about studying the "really American part of our history"? Is there a "really American part"? What is implied by this formulation of the problem? What is left out?

SUGGESTIONS FOR WRITING

1. Write an essay on the "frontier thesis" that explains Turner's ideas and develops your own evaluation of what it brings to light and what it ignores.

2. Write an essay that explains Turner's view that there is a "really American part of our history." Is there something uniquely and characteristically American? If so, what is it? Is it the frontier, as Turner suggests, something else, or something in addition? Or is this the best way to ask questions of American history—to look for the "really American" parts? What might be the benefits of looking at the American past from other perspectives? (You might think here, for example, of how our perspective on Columbus and 1492 changes when we include, as Michel-Rolph Trouillot does, the *reconquista* of Granada by the Catholic monarchs and the expulsion from Spain of Jews and Muslims.)

3. Since Turner published "The Significance of the Frontier" in 1893, the term "frontier" has been applied to any number of political, scientific, and cultural developments. The John F. Kennedy presidency (1961–1963), for example, made the New Frontier a slogan for getting the country moving in new directions—and subsequently, space exploration, computers, neuroscience, and biotechnology have all been called the new frontier. Write an essay that evaluates the metaphor of the frontier. Is the metaphor of the frontier a useful one to describe trends and events? Does it retain symbolic power? Has it been overtaken by other metaphors?

VISUAL CULTURE   Photographing History

To learn more about photographs in history, visit www.ablongman.com/george/136

One of the ways people remember the past is through photographs. Family scrapbooks, photo albums, wedding portraits, high school yearbooks, school pictures exchanged with friends—all record the history of ordinary lives. The same is true of people's collective memory of public history. Single photographic images have taken on the power to contain and represent whole historical events.

From Mathew Brady's photographs of the American Civil War to present-day photojournalism, photographs have created immediately recognizable images of complex historical forces that have been captured in the concrete details of a moment. For example, Alfred Stieglitz's "The Steerage" (1907), which appears at the opening of the chapter, seems to distill the waves of immigration from southern and eastern Europe from 1880 to 1920 in a single frame depicting "huddled masses."

By the same token, the Depression of the 1930s has come to be known and remembered through the photographs of Dorothea Lange, Walker Evans, Arthur Rothstein, and others in the Farm Security Administration. See, for example, Dorothea Lange's famous photograph "Migrant Mother, Florence Thompson and Her Children" in the Guide to Visual Analysis, in the Introduction to this book. People think of these photos as a reliable source, a documentary account of the life experience of workers, sharecroppers, Dust Bowl migrants, and the unemployed. These photos have taken on the authority to bring the past to life and to show how things really were.

Such photographs not only convey images that stand, in immediately recognizable ways, for larger historical events. They also carry attitudes toward these events. Grounded in the relationship that they have with their subjects, photographers' attitudes become visible in the way that they aim the viewfinder and frame the shot. Photographs convey visual images to viewers, not directly but mediated through a lens, from a perspective or way of seeing.

Photographs offer viewers moments of identification as well as information. When people look at a photograph of the flag raising at Iwo Jima, for example, (see page 509) they are likely to recall the story of World War II as one of national unity to fight the "good war." In a sense, the photo seeks to recruit viewers—to have them join the just cause and commemorate American victory. In other instances, such as the picture of John Carlos and Tommy Smith raising their fists on the victory stand at the 1968 Olympics in Mexico City, the insurgent force of a photograph can precipitate a crisis of identification, as viewers respond with fear, anxiety, outrage, pleasure, identification, or some combination of mixed feelings to this powerful image of black power and the freedom struggle of the 1960s. Along similar lines, the two photos of the Vietnam War—the image of Colonel Loan executing a Viet Cong suspect and of children fleeing the bombing of Trang Bang—prompted for many Americans at the time feelings of shock, outrage, and horror and a crisis of confidence in the government's war policies. In turn, these photos have become iconic, summing up in single images the entire history of the war and the way it divided the country.

John Carlos and Tommy Smith at the 1968 Olympics

Colonel Nguyen Ngoc Loan, South Vietnam's police chief, executing a Viet-cong suspect in Saigon

Trang Bang, June 1972

The flag-raising at Iwo Jima, Joe Rosenthal, 1945

READING AMERICAN PHOTOGRAPHS

— *Alan Trachtenberg*

Alan Trachtenberg is a distinguished professor of English and American Studies at Yale and the author of many articles and books, including *The Incorporation of America: Culture and Society in the Gilded Age* (1982). The following selection is an excerpt from the preface to his book *Reading American Photographs: Images as History, Mathew Brady to Walker Evans* (1989). Trachtenberg holds that the historian and photographer share a similar task: "how to make the random, fragmentary, and accidental details of everyday existence meaningful without loss of the details themselves."

SUGGESTION FOR READING As you read, consider what Trachtenberg means when he says that "photographs are not simple depictions but constructions." When you are finished reading, summarize Trachtenberg's argument in three to four sentences.

1 My argument throughout is that American photographs are not simple depictions but constructions, that the history they show is inseparable from the history they enact: a history of photographers employing their medium to make sense of their society. It is also a history of photographers seeking to define themselves, to create a role for photography as an American art. How might the camera be used for social commentary and cultural interpretation? Consisting of images rather than words, photography places its own constraints on interpretation, requiring that pho-

tographers invent new forms of presentation, of collaboration between image and text, between artist and audience.

For the reader of photographs there is always the danger of overreading, of too facile a conversion of images into words. Speaking of "the camera's affinity for the indeterminate," Kracauer remarks that, "however selective," photographs are still "bound to record nature in the raw. Like the natural objects themselves, they will therefore be surrounded by a fringe of indistinct multiple meanings." All photographs have the effect of making their subjects seem at least momentarily strange, capable of meaning several things at once, or nothing at all. Estrangement allows us to see the subject in new and unexpected ways. Photographs entice viewers by their silence, the mysterious beckoning of another world. It is as enigmas, opaque and inexplicable as the living world itself, that they most resemble the data upon which history is based. Just as the meaning of the past is the prerogative of the present to invent and choose, the meaning of an image does not come intact and whole. Indeed, what empowers an image to represent history is not just what it shows but the struggle for meaning we undergo before it, a struggle analogous to the historian's effort to shape an intelligible and usable past. Representing the past, photographs serve the present's need to understand itself and measure its future. Their history lies finally in the political visions they may help us realize.

VISUAL ESSAY The Iraq Invasion and Occupation

To understand the relation of photographs to historical events, it is necessary to begin with the physical presence of the camera at some precisely datable moment in the past. Unlike writing or painting, which necessarily take place over time, shooting a picture occurs in an instant, and the events that the camera records are thereby unrepeatable. This technical ability to capture such unique and distinct moments gives photographs an authority in documenting the past that no other records or accounts can claim.

But the technical character of the photographic image also poses a problem in terms of historical meaning. The photographic image, after all, is visual. It sends a message but, as Roland Barthes says, an "uncoded message," one that cannot immediately and self-evidently be converted into words. The photographic image simultaneously is filled with information and is opaque. The "meaning of the image," as Trachtenberg puts it, "does not come intact and whole." The reason a photograph can stand in for a larger historical event such as the Civil War or the Depression is not just what it shows but how the image has been made memorable—the "struggle for meaning we undergo before it."

The "struggle for meaning" that Trachtenberg refers to is strikingly evident in the photographs assembled here from the U.S.-led invasion of Iraq in 2003 and the ongoing occupation. Alone, each photograph captures a distinct moment that proposes to represent the Iraq war. Taken together, the images stand in an uneasy relationship to each other, bound by common events but divided by what they depict and the meanings that they make available. Just as the meaning of the Iraq war remains volatile and contested in politics, historical interpretation, and popular culture, these images jostle against each other; they call the viewer to different scenes and different ways of seeing the war.

SUGGESTIONS FOR DISCUSSION

1. Look closely at each of the photographs on pages 512 and 513. Read each alone as an icon of the Iraq invasion and occupation. How does each image shape America's understanding and memory of the Iraq war? To what extent do they tell the same version or different versions of the invasion and occupation?

2. The images on pages 512–513 have been arranged in chronological order, but that is not the only way they could be organized. Photographers often create sequences of images so that individual photos interact with each other and enable meanings to emerge that are not available through a single photo. Work together in a group with two or three other students to create your own visual essay about the Iraq invasion and occupation. Use the photos presented here or supplement them with photos from websites or elsewhere. As you assemble your visual essay, take into account what you want your viewers' experience of the photos to be and the story you want the photos to tell. Then compare the visual essay your group composed with those of other groups. Don't argue about whether one set of choices is right or wrong. The issue is how the various visual essays juxtapose photographs and shape the way Americans remember the Iraq war.

3. The written captions that sometimes accompany photographic images can influence the way that viewers understand photos. Depending on the circumstances, captions can be informative by identifying the date, place, and people depicted in the photo. Other times, captions can be interpretive or argumentative by providing not just information but a point of view. Work with a group of classmates and find three photos of historical events (use any of the photos in this chapter if you wish). Write two captions for each photo— one that is informative, the second interpretive or argumentative. Exchange your photos and captions with those from another group. Ask members of the other group how the captions shape or slant their experience of the photo. In turn, respond to the other group's captions in the same way.

SUGGESTED ASSIGNMENT

Select one of the photographs in this chapter or another historical photo of your own choosing. Write a detailed analysis of how the photo brings to life an historical event and how its composition establishes a vantage point for viewers. Look at the photograph closely and carefully and consider these questions:

- *What is depicted in the photo?* How do the details create an impression on viewers? How is the image able to stand in for a larger historical event? What version of the event does it seem to tell?

- *Does the photo have vectors (or eye lines) that establish relationships among the people (and perhaps things) in the photo?* What story do the vectors enable viewers to fill in? (See the discussion of vectors on pages 186–188.)

- *What is the perspective of the camera shot—frontal, oblique, high, low?* How does the use of perspective shape the viewer's attitude toward the event depicted in the photo? (See the discussion of perspective on pages 188–190.)

- *How does the camera space frame the event that it records?* How close does the camera take viewers to its subject? Is the photo a wide shot, full shot, medium shot, or close-up? How does camera space influence the viewer's experience of the photo? (See the discussion of camera space in Chapter 1, "Reading the News.")

FILM CLIP · Film Genres: The Western

To learn more about westerns, visit
www.ablongman.com/george/137

Films can be sorted into genres such as science fiction (the *Star Wars* series or *Space Odyssey 2000*), musicals (*West Side Story* or *Sound of Music*), horror (various Dracula and Frankenstein movies), romantic comedy (*My Best Friend's Wedding* or *Sleepless in Seattle*), and action adventure (*The Terminator* or *Raiders of the Lost Ark*), each of which has a predictable visual look and narrative formula. Of all the genres of Hollywood movies, the western is perhaps the most revered as a central part of American mythology. Although Hollywood is making few westerns today, at one time, from the 1930s into the 1970s, it was a dominant form of filmmaking, with directors such as John Ford and Howard Hawks and stars such as John Wayne, Gary Cooper, Gregory Peck, and James Stewart in leading roles. The western relied on the relatively simple narrative formula that typically located a single heroic figure at the borderland between civilization and savagery, represented variously by Indians, outlaws, or unscrupulous entrepreneurs. The task of the western hero accordingly was to rescue an endangered community from the forces that threatened it. Some of the classic examples of this western formula are *Stagecoach*, *Red River*, *Shane*, and *High Noon*. With the political and moral crisis of the Vietnam War, however, the western was called into question, and a number of "revisionist" westerns, telling a more complex story, arrived in theaters—films such as *McCabe and Mrs. Miller*, *The Wild Bunch*, and *Little Big Man*.

Watch one or more of the classic westerns (there are many in addition to those mentioned here). Consider how they embody the ideas and values in Frederick Jackson Turner's essay "The Significance of the Frontier in American History." What are the qualities that make a western hero? You may then want to watch one or more of the "revisionist" westerns. How do these films retell the story of the "opening of the West"?

FIELDWORK · Oral History

Oral histories offer the personal perspectives of people who are caught up in the history of their time. Oral history is a branch of historical studies that draws on the experience and memories of ordinary people to provide new insight into the meaning and texture of historical events. Sometimes referred to as "history from the bottom up," oral history is an organized effort to record the stories of ordinary people who traditionally have been ignored by historians. In this sense, oral histories are important correctives to older versions of history that focus on "great men," geopolitics, and institutions of power.

This does not mean, however, that oral histories are any more useful or authoritative than traditional historical work that is based on archives, government documents, or the correspondence of national leaders. Their value depends on how the oral historian handles the material once it is collected.

"THE GOOD WAR": AN ORAL HISTORY OF WORLD WAR TWO

▬ Studs Terkel

Studs Terkel has acted in radio soap operas and movies and has been a disk jockey and host of a daily radio show in Chicago, his hometown. He is best known, though, for his oral histories, which include *Division Street: America* (1967), *Hard Times: An Oral History of the Great Depression* (1970), and *Working: People Talk About What They Do All Day and How They Feel About What They Do* (1974). The following excepts, which come from *"The Good War": An Oral History of World War Two* (1984), give a sense of how oral history can provide the perspectives of ordinary people on important historical events.

SUGGESTION FOR READING As you read, notice how each informant remembers the bombing of Pearl Harbor on December 7, 1941, and the beginning of World War II. Consider how their various responses call into question the notion that the United States reacted to the onset of World War II as a unified nation.

YURIKO HOHRI

1   *She lives with her husband in Chicago. He is national chair of the Council for Japanese American Redress. She is active, too.*

The war became real for me when the two FBI agents came to our home in Long Beach. It was a few months after December 7. It was a rainy Saturday morning. My three sisters, my mother, and myself were at home doing the chores. I was twelve.

A black car came right into the driveway. One man went into the kitchen. As I watched, he looked under the sink and he looked into the oven. Then he went into the parlor and opened the glass cases where our most treasured things were. There were several stacks of *shakuhachi* sheet music. It's a bamboo flute. My father played the *shakuhachi* and my mother played the *koto*. At least once a month on a Sunday afternoon, their friends would come over and just enjoy themselves playing music. The man took the music.

I followed the man into my mother and father's bedroom. Strangers do not usually go into our bedrooms when they first come. As I watched, he went into the closet and brought out my father's golf clubs. He turned the bag upside down. I was only concerned about the golf balls, because I played jacks with them. He opened the *tansu*, a chest of drawers. My mother and sisters were weeping.

5   My father was at work. He took care of the vegetable and fruit sections for two grocery stores. He was brought home by the agents. He was taken to a camp in Tujunga Canyon. My grandmother and I went to visit him. It was a different kind of visit. There was a tall barbed-wire fence, so we were unable to touch each other. The only thing we could do was see each other. My father was weeping.

Our family moved to my grandmother's house—my mother's mother. At least six of my uncles were at home, so it was very crowded. My next recollection is that my mother, my three little sisters, and I were on this streetcar. My mother had made a little knapsack for each of us, with our names embroidered. We had a washcloth, a towel, soap, a comb. Just enough for us to carry. It was the first time we took a streetcar. Because we always went by my father's car.

We went to Santa Anita. We lived in a horse stable. We filled a cheesecloth bag with straw—our mattress. The sides of the room did not go up to the ceiling, so there was no privacy at all. They were horse stalls. We'd have fun climbing up. The floors were asphalt. I do remember what we called stinky bugs. They were crunchy, like cockroaches, large, black. Oh, it's really—(Laughs, as she shakes her head.) We had apple butter. To this day, I cannot taste apple butter.

PAUL PISICANO

He is an architect, living in Manhattan. He is fifty-two and "one hundred percent Sicilian."

It was an Italian-speaking neighborhood in New York. We were a whole bunch of people who were just breaking into the system. We all talked Italian at home. We talked a dialect we thought was Italian, but was New York Italian.

10   Mussolini was a hero, a superhero. He made us feel special, especially the southerners, Sicilian, Calabrian. I remember the Abyssinian War, about 1935. I was five. It was talked about as a very positive thing. We had the equivalent of your pep rallies for football teams. To us it was a great victory. We never really got down on Mussolini. He was applauded. Then he went into Greece. He wasn't doing too well (laughs) and had to be bailed out by the Germans, remember? We were awfully disappointed by that.

It was us against the outside. One block against another block. We had less of a sense of nation than, say, the Israelis did. We were never comfortable with the northern Italians. We were Palestinians. (Laughs.)

It was very painful to live in America. You sorta wanted not to talk about it. Prior to Pearl Harbor, you tried not to talk about the Italian thing. We were very disappointed with their performance in the war. They weren't really heroes. They were brought up on this great macho crap. Our heroes were Joe DiMaggio and Phil Rizzuto. When the Yankees won the pennant in '41, they were our biggies. Crosetti was replaced by Rizzuto—I mean, it was an honorary Italian position, shortstop. The Yankee Italians were our heroes. The Cubs ultimately got Cavarretta and Dallessandro, but they didn't count.

You go to movies once a week, right? All you see are Italian guys surrendering to the British. Remember Africa? (Laughs.) That was terrible. You grow up, you're gonna be King Kong. All of a sudden all the guys that look like you are running with their arms in the air. I was ten, eleven, and very impressionable. See, the Italians were chumps.

15   The surrendering happened early. Now the whole neighborhood was not for Mussolini and not really against him. But if he went away, it would be good. We were against Hitler and it was easy to be against the Japanese, but it was still hard to be against Italians.

SUGGESTIONS FOR DISCUSSION

1. Consider each of the reactions to the onset of World War II. How do these accounts compare what you have learned in school about World War II? How do Studs Terkel's informants provide a denser, richer view of the United States at this time?

2. Part of doing oral histories is to ask questions that get people talking. What questions can you imagine Terkel asked to get his informants to talk so eloquently?

3. Consider the point Michel-Rolph Trouillot makes about the difference between "what happened" and "that which is said to have happened." He is commenting on historians, but we can raise the same point about Terkel's informants. How would you apply the distinction to the oral histories presented here?

Fieldwork Project

This fieldwork project asks you to do an oral history. Follow these steps to get started.

1. *Choose a person and an event that will interest readers*—a Vietnam or Gulf War veteran; someone with experience in the antiwar movement or the counterculture of the 1960s; an older person who remembers the Great Depression, the bombing of Pearl Harbor, the end of World War II; a trade unionist involved in an important organizing drive or strike. The events listed here are largely on the national or international scene, but you may also find informants to talk about an important and interesting local event.

2. *Prepare for the interview by familiarizing yourself with the event in question.* Do some background reading. Develop a list of leading questions that will elicit detailed and in-depth responses from your informant (but don't be tied rigidly to them in the interview if it takes another, potentially fruitful, direction). Set a time with your informant, bring a tape recorder, and conduct the interview.

3. *Type up a transcript from the interview that you can edit into an oral history.* For advice on editing your interview, see "Writing the Oral History," below.

Considerations in Doing an Oral History

Selecting a Person to Interview

Not every person will be a good interview subject, even if he or she was intimately involved in an historical event—some people just don't have interesting things to say. Therefore, oral historians usually select an informant who wants to share part of his or her past. Moreover, everyone's memory is selective in some sense. Oral historians expect to get one version of events, though it may be a perspective they didn't foresee.

Interviewing

The interview is not just a matter of turning on the tape recorder and allowing the informant to speak. The oral historian should let the informant know the purpose for the interview and encourage the informant to tell his or her history in detail, but in keeping the informant on track, the historian should be careful not to provide too much direction. The informant may skip over what might be key information or tailor his or her recitation to what the historian seems to want to hear.

Once an interview begins, the historian faces many decisions—about, say, whether a rambling account is going somewhere or if it is time to intervene to redirect the informant, or if stopping an informant to clarify a point will risk interrupting the speaker's train of thought.

Writing the Oral History

The transcript of an interview amounts to a kind of raw data and is likely to be filled with pauses, asides, fragmentary remarks, false starts, and undeveloped trains of thought. The oral historian's task is to fashion an account that is faithful to the informant as well as readable. Oral historians typically face several decisions at this point:

- *How much of the original transcript should be used?* Oral historians rarely use all of the material in the transcript. In the Introduction to *Portraits in Steel* (1993), a collection of photographs and oral histories of Buffalo steel workers, the oral historian Michael Frisch says he used as little as 20 percent of an original transcript and in no case more than 60 percent. When they decide to omit material from the transcript, oral historians are careful to make sure that their editing does not distort the informant's views or suppress important information.

- *How should the material in the transcript be arranged?* Oral historians often decide to rearrange some of the material in the original transcript so that related points appear together and the final version has a coherence that may be missing from the taped interview. The oral historian is by no means obliged to follow the chronological order of the transcript but needs to make sure that any restructuring is faithful to the informant.

- *Should the interviewer's questions appear?* In some cases, oral historians craft the interview into a narrative that is told through the informant's voice. The oral historian stays out of the way, and readers get the sense that the informant is speaking directly to them. In other cases, however, the oral historian may decide to appear in the final text as an interviewer, and the question-and-answer format gives the oral history more of a conversational character, with a greater sense of dialogue and give-and-take.

■ *How much editing should be done at the sentence level?* Oral historians face the task of turning the transcript into readable prose that retains the distinctive qualities of the informant's voice. For example, in *"The Good War,"* Studs Terkel has edited the speech of his informants so that it appears for the most part in complete, grammatically correct sentences. But he does include some exceptions, along with slang and profanity, to suggest the vernacular speech patterns of his informants. Here is an example from Terkel's interview with Roger Tuttrup:

> I wanted to be in it. I was fifteen. I felt I wasn't doing anything constructive. I was spottin' pins in the bowling alley, besides goin' to high school. I figured I should be doin' something else. I guess it was a year later, I went to work in a war plant. Some of my friends started goin' into service. I figured: Why the hell don't I? I'm not dog, right?

MINING THE ARCHIVE   Local Museums and Historical Societies

Telling a story of change

The Mount Zion Albany Civil Rights Movement Museum will tell the story of the impact of the southwest Georgia movement on the rest of the world while focusing on the role of the African American church and the freedom music that emerged during this period.

The stories will be told through oral histories from those who were there—those who lived it, those who breathed it, those who walked it, those who went to jail and those who attended the mass meetings and sang about it.

The museum will restore much of Mount Zion Church as it was in the 1960s. The sanctuary will convey the sense of place as a church where visitors will be treated to stirring renditions of freedom songs and other public performances. Restored pews will seat 100.

A portion of the church will house the museum's artifacts. Educational exhibits will detail the civil rights struggle ranging from voter education and registration to nonviolent protest, song, economic boycott and legal action. The museum will also serve as a center for ongoing academic research and provide school tours and other programs and lectures. Through educational programming, the museum will preserve a part of the history of America and south Georgia and challenge today's and tomorrow's youth to learn more about themselves as citizens.

Promoters of the Mount Zion Albany Civil Rights Movement Museum have a vision beyond restoring the church into a museum. Long-range planning, in coordination with the Albany Dougherty Inner-City Authority and the Albany Convention and Visitors Bureau, includes a historic district and walking tours of restored buildings and residences in the Whitney Avenue neighborhood. These tours will depict life in the African American neighborhood before the end of segregation.

Many towns and cities, as well as colleges and universities, have local museums or historical societies that collect and display historical materials, sponsor research, and put on public programs about local and regional history. There is likely to be one or more in the area near you. Your college library can help you find out where they are and what kind of archival materials they hold.

Visit a local museum or historical society. Sometimes this will require making specific arrangements with its staff. The purpose of your visit should be to acquire an overview of the archival materials and collections. How does the museum or historical society describe its function? What are the nature and scope of the holdings? How were they acquired? What historical

A celebration of courage and freedom

The Mount Zion Albany Civil Rights Movement Museum is a celebration of courage and freedom of ordinary people and their leaders in the Albany and southwest Georgia movements who bore witness to equal rights and helped to spark the national Civil Rights Movement and international struggles for freedom.

The eyes of the nation were on Albany in the early 1960s as thousands of people attended mass meetings and marched in the streets seeking freedom and justice. In December 1961, Dr. Martin Luther King Jr. joined local activists and further inspired overflowing crowds who gathered to hear him at Mount Zion and neighboring Shiloh Baptist Church.

The strength of the Albany Movement gave rise to campaigns in nearby communities:

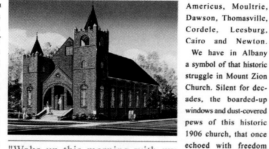

"Woke up this morning with my mind stayed on freedom..."
Freedom Song

Americus, Moultrie, Dawson, Thomasville, Cordele, Leesburg, Cairo and Newton.

We have in Albany a symbol of that historic struggle in Mount Zion Church. Silent for decades, the boarded-up windows and dust-covered pews of this historic 1906 church, that once echoed with freedom songs and the call for nonviolent social change, soon will give voice to a key part of the 1960s history of Albany and southwest Georgia.

The Albany Movement sprang from the community's grass roots. Young and old, rich and poor—citizens of every class, color and occupation were involved in it.

Many of those who participated in the Movement are members of the community today—our neighbors, co-workers and family members. The museum offers us a chance to hear their stories.

periods are represented? What kind of research do they do? Does the archive publish books, pamphlets, or journals? Does it issue an annual report, newsletter, or other informative materials about its holdings and activities? Who uses the collection?

Use your answers to these questions—and other information you picked up during your visit—to prepare a report (either written or oral) on the kinds of historical questions you could answer by drawing on the archive's collection.

WWW

To learn more about museums and historical sites, visit
www.ablongman.com/george/138

Living in a Postcolonial World

Indian taxi driver in New York City, 1977, from *Passport Photos* by Amitava Kumar.

I, too, know something of this immigrant business. I am an emigrant from one country (India) and a newcomer in two (England, where I live, and Pakistan, to which my family moved against my will). And I have a theory that the resentments we mohajirs engender have something to do with our conquest of the force of gravity. We have performed the act of which all men anciently dream, the thing for which they envy the birds; that is to say, we have flown.

—Salman Rushdie

M ost of the readings in this book focus on the United States and what has been called throughout the book "American culture." In the discussion questions and writing assignments, you have examined ways of life, modes of expression, and controversies in the contemporary United States. This makes sense, because the lived experience of many who use this book is firmly rooted in the history and culture of the United States. At the same time, in this closing chapter, it's worth noting that the very idea of American culture can amount to a systematic forgetting that there are many Americas in this hemisphere—Latin America, Central America, Mexico, Canada, and the Caribbean. There is the risk that in focusing on American culture within U.S. borders, it is possible to ignore the fact that since its origins as an English colony, the United States has always been connected in important ways to the rest of the hemisphere and, more broadly, to the rest of the world.

From Columbus's first contact with the Taino tribe in the West Indies, the exploration and settlement of North America has involved a series of encounters with peoples and cultures outside the dominant white, Protestant, middle-class culture in the United States—not only with Native Americans but also with West Africans who were brought forcibly to America through the slave trade; with Mexicans, when the United States appropriated California, Texas, and the Southwest in the Mexican War; with the Irish and Chinese laborers who were recruited to build the transcontinental railroad; and with Italian Catholics and Eastern European Catholics and Jews who immigrated to the United States between 1880 and 1920 to work in mines, steel mills, garment factories, and other industries of an expanding capitalist economy.

To say that the United States has always been a nation of immigrants is true, but the migration of people has never been one way. Though official histories often suggest immigrants came to the United States with the goal of staying and assimilating into an American melting pot, in fact many went back and forth to Italy, Mexico, the West Indies, Central America, the Middle East, and elsewhere. If anything, this movement of people has intensified in recent decades, propelled by the disruptions of the Vietnam War, the effects of the North American Free Trade Agreement (NAFTA), and the impact of an increasingly global economy. The result is that the national borders of the United States are more porous and the national identity less stable than ever, with people from all over the world bringing new languages and ways of life to this country and spreading U.S. culture and language to places they have never been before.

As the events of September 11, 2001, reveal so tellingly, the United States is enmeshed in a world system of economics, politics, and culture. *Globalization* is the term often used to describe the rise of not only multinational corporations but also transnational organizations such as the European Union. Automobiles once built in Detroit now have their parts manufactured in Mexico or Taiwan. The software on your computer may be written in Ireland or India. The clothes and shoes you buy with American brands on them are likely to be made in Indonesia, Vietnam, Malaysia, or elsewhere. Signs of globalization are apparent in the appearance of Coca Cola ads in Saudi Arabia or American sitcoms on French television.

For some, the era of globalization is a brave new world of innovation and opportunity, linked together by the immediacy of communication via the Internet. From another perspective, however, it looks more like a continuation of older relations between the rich American and European countries and their former colonies in the Third World—in Asia, Africa, the Caribbean, and Latin America. This chapter is called "Living in a Postcolonial World" to bring attention to these relationships and help you to think about not just American culture but the world system everyone now lives within.

The term *postcolonial* shows the way the world has changed in the half-century since the end of World War II. In the 1940s, 1950s, and 1960s, former British and French colonies such as Egypt, Kenya, Nigeria, Ghana, Tanzania, Algeria, and Senegal in Africa; India, Pakistan, and Sri Lanka in South Asia; and Vietnam and Laos in

Southeast Asia mounted successful struggles to throw off their colonial status and achieve national independence. In the 1970s, Mozambique, Angola, and Guinea-Bissau became independent of Portugal, and in the 1990s, South Africa threw off the legacy of Dutch and British colonialism and fifty years of apartheid to begin a new era as a democratic nation.

The "post" in "postcolonial" notes these dramatic developments in world history but, at the same time, leaves open the relation of these countries to their colonial past. In a time of globalization, NAFTA, the International Monetary Fund, and the World Bank, the question remains whether the former colonies in Africa and Asia as well as the countries in Central and South America and in the Middle East that gained national liberation have actually secured self-determination and independence from Europe and the United States. Some describe the present situation as "neocolonialism," where formal independence has not necessarily ended economic and political dependence on the West.

In keeping with the main themes discussed throughout the other chapters of *Reading Culture*, this chapter focuses on investigating culture from a postcolonial perspective. This investigation has gone in two main directions. On the one hand, it looks at the way Western powers represented—and continue to represent—former colonial subjects as Others; as people different from "us"; as those in need of Western guidance, expertise, and technology; and as exotic cultures for sophisticated consumption. On the other hand, it looks at the way formerly colonized people view the West and make sense of their relations to it.

Classroom Scenes

One of the best ways to understand the term *postcolonial* is to investigate particular scenes of life, during and after the colonial era. The two readings gathered here are set in classrooms in the former British colonies of Antigua and Sri Lanka. During the heyday of the British Empire, education was a central part of the colonial mission to "civilize" the colonized by promoting loyalty to the empire and identification with British culture and the English language. The classroom in Jamaica Kincaid's "Columbus in Chains" provides a vivid picture of colonial education. As you will see from the second selection, "An English Lesson in Sri Lanka" by A. Suresh Canagarajah, even after political independence, students in postcolonial classrooms continue to encounter the language and culture of the former colonial rulers in complicated ways. Part of the work of coming to grips with life in the postcolonial world is to examine the complex relations of dependence, the ambivalences and ironies, and the moments of resistance and rebellion that can be found in the following classroom scenes.

COLUMBUS IN CHAINS

— Jamaica Kincaid

Jamaica Kincaid is an award-winning novelist, short story writer, and essayist who grew up on the West Indian island of Antigua and now lives in Vermont. Her books include *At the Bottom of the River* (1983), *A Small Place* (1988), and *Autobiography of My Mother* (1996). "Columbus in Chains" was originally published as a short story in the *New Yorker* and then became a chapter in *Annie John* (1985).

SUGGESTION FOR READING "Columbus in Chains" explores the interaction of two cultures in Antigua: the British culture of the schools and the local Antiguan culture. As you read, annotate passages where the narrator Annie John gives us clues about the two cultures and their relationship.

1 Outside, as usual, the sun shone, the trade winds blew; on her way to put some starched clothes on the line, my mother shooed some hens out of her garden; Miss Dewberry baked the buns, some of which my mother would buy for my father and me to eat with our afternoon tea; Miss Henry brought the milk, a glass of which I would drink with my lunch, and another glass of which I would drink with the bun from Miss Dewberry; my mother prepared our lunch; my father noted some perfectly idiotic thing his partner in house-building, Mr. Oatie, had done, so that over lunch he and my mother could have a good laugh.

The Anglican church bell struck eleven o'clock—one hour to go before lunch. I was then sitting at my desk in my classroom. We were having a history lesson—the last lesson of the morning. For taking first place over all the other girls, I had been given a prize, a copy of a book called *Roman Britain*, and I was made prefect of my class. What a mistake the prefect part had been, for I was among the worst-behaved in my class and did not at all believe in setting myself up as a good example, the way a prefect was supposed to do. Now I had to sit in the prefect's seat—the first seat in the front row, the seat from which I could stand up and survey quite easily my classmates. From where I sat I could see out the window. Sometimes when I looked out, I could see the sexton going over to the minister's house. The sexton's daughter, Hilarene, a disgusting model of good behavior and keen attention to scholarship, sat next to me, since she took second place. The minister's daughter, Ruth, sat in the last row, the row reserved for all the dunce girls. Hilarene, of course, I could not stand. A girl that good would never do for me. I would probably not have cared so much for first place if I could be sure it would not go to her. Ruth I liked, because she was such a dunce and came from England and had yellow hair. When I first met her, I used to walk her home and sing bad songs to her just to see her turn pink, as if I had spilled hot water all over her.

Our books, *A History of the West Indies*, were open in front of us. Our day had begun with morning prayers, then a geometry lesson, then it was over to the science building for a lesson in "Introductory Physics" (not a subject we cared much for), taught by the most dingy-toothed Mr. Slacks, a teacher from Canada, then precious recess, and now this, our history lesson. Recess had the usual drama: this time, I coaxed Gwen out of her disappointment at not being allowed to join the junior choir. Her father—how many times had I wished he would become a leper and so be banished to a leper colony for the rest of my long and happy life with Gwen—had forbidden it, giving as his reason that she lived too far away from church, where choir rehearsals were conducted, and that it would be dangerous for her, a young girl, to walk home alone at night in the dark. Of course, all the streets had lamplight, but it was useless to point that out to him. Oh, how it would have pleased us to press and rub our knees together as we sat in our pew while pretending to pay close attention to Mr. Simmons, our choirmaster, as he waved his baton up and down and across, and how it would have pleased us even more to walk home together, alone in the "early dusk" (the way Gwen had phrased it, a ready phrase always on her tongue), stopping, if there was a full moon, to lie down in a pasture and expose our bosoms in the moonlight. We had heard that full moonlight would make our breasts grow to a size we would like. Poor Gwen! When I first heard from her that she was one of ten children, right on the spot I told her that I would love only her, since her mother already had so many other people to love.

Our teacher, Miss Edward, paced up and down in front of the class in her usual way. In front of her desk stood a small table, and on it stood the dunce cap. The dunce cap was in the shape of a coronet, with an adjustable opening in the back, so that it could fit any head. It was made of cardboard with a shiny gold paper covering and the word "DUNCE" in shiny red paper on the front. When the sun shone on it, the dunce cap was all aglitter, almost as if you were being tricked into thinking it a desirable thing to wear. As Miss Edward paced up and down, she would pass between us and the dunce cap like an eclipse. Each Friday morning, we were given a small test to see how well we had learned the things taught to us all week. The girl who scored lowest was made to wear the dunce cap all day the following Monday. On many Mondays, Ruth wore it—only, with her short yellow hair, when the dunce cap was sitting on her head she looked like a girl attending a birthday party in *The Schoolgirl's Own Annual.*

5   It was Miss Edward's way to ask one of us a question the answer to which she was sure the girl would not know and then put the same question to another girl who she was sure would know the answer. The girl who did not answer correctly would then have to repeat the correct answer in the exact words of the other girl. Many times, I had heard my exact words repeated over and over again, and I liked it especially when the girl doing the repeating was one I didn't care about very much. Pointing a finger at Ruth, Miss Edward asked a question the answer to which was "On the third of November 1493, a Sunday morning, Christopher Columbus discovered Dominica." Ruth, of course, did not know the answer, as she did not know the answer to many questions about the West Indies. I could hardly blame her. Ruth had come all the way from England. Perhaps she did not want to be in the West Indies at all. Perhaps she wanted to be in England, where no one would remind her constantly of the terrible things her ancestors had done; perhaps she had felt even worse when her father was a missionary in Africa. I could see how Ruth felt from looking at her face. Her ancestors had been the masters, while ours had been the slaves. She had such a lot to be ashamed of, and

by being with us every day she was always being reminded. We could look everybody in the eye, for our ancestors had done nothing wrong except just sit somewhere, defenseless. Of course, sometimes, what with our teachers and our books, it was hard for us to tell on which side we really now belonged—with the masters or the slaves—for it was all history, it was all in the past, and everybody behaved differently now; all of us celebrated Queen Victoria's birthday, even though she had been dead a long time. But we, the descendants of the slaves, knew quite well what had really happened, and I was sure that if the tables had been turned we would have acted differently; I was sure that if our ancestors had gone from Africa to Europe and come upon the people living there, they would have taken a proper interest in the Europeans on first seeing them, and said, "How nice," and then gone home to tell their friends about it.

I was sitting at my desk, having these thoughts to myself. I don't know how long it had been since I lost track of what was going on around me. I had not noticed that the girl who was asked the question after Ruth failed—a girl named Hyacinth—had only got a part of the answer correct. I had not noticed that after these two attempts Miss Edward had launched into a harangue about what a worthless bunch we were compared to girls of the past. In fact, I was no longer on the same chapter we were studying. I was way ahead, at the end of the chapter about Columbus's third voyage. In this chapter, there was a picture of Columbus that took up a whole page, and it was in color—one of only five color pictures in the book. In this picture, Columbus was seated in the bottom of a ship. He was wearing the usual three-quarter trousers and a shirt with enormous sleeves, both the trousers and shirt made of maroon-colored velvet. His hat, which was cocked up on one side of his head, had a gold feather in it, and his black shoes had huge gold buckles. His hands and feet were bound up in chains, and he was sitting there staring off into space, looking quite dejected and miserable. The picture had as a title

"Columbus in Chains," printed at the bottom of the page. What had happened was that the usually quarrelsome Columbus had got into a disagreement with people who were even more quarrelsome, and a man named Bobadilla, representing King Ferdinand and Queen Isabella, had sent him back to Spain fettered in chains attached to the bottom of a ship. What just deserts, I thought, for I did not like Columbus. How I loved this picture—to see the usually triumphant Columbus, brought so low, seated at the bottom of a boat just watching things go by. Shortly after I first discovered it in my history book, I heard my mother read out loud to my father a letter she had received from her sister, who still lived with her mother and father in the very same Dominica, which is where my mother came from. Ma Chess was fine, wrote my aunt, but Pa Chess was not well. Pa Chess was having a bit of trouble with his limbs; he was not able to go about as he pleased; often he had to depend on someone else to do one thing or another for him. My mother read the letter in quite a state, her voice rising to a higher pitch with each sentence. After she read the part about Pa Chess's stiff limbs, she turned to my father and laughed as she said, "So the great man can no longer just get up and go. How I would love to see his face now!" When I next saw the picture of Columbus sitting there all locked up in his chains, I wrote under it the words "The Great Man Can No Longer Just Get Up and Go." I had written this out with my fountain pen, and in Old English lettering—a script I had recently mastered. As I sat there looking at the picture, I traced the words with my pen over and over, so that the letters grew big and you could read what I had written from not very far away. I don't know how long it was before I heard that my name, Annie John, was being said by this bellowing dragon in the form of Miss Edward bearing down on me.

I had never been a favorite of hers. Her favorite was Hilarene. It must have pained Miss Edward that I so often beat out Hilarene. Not that I liked Miss Edward and wanted her to like

me back, but as the other teachers regarded me with much affection, would always tell my mother that I was the most charming student they had ever had, beamed at me when they saw me coming, and were very sorry when they had to write some version of this on my report card: "Annie is an unusually bright girl. She is well behaved in class, at least in the presence of her masters and mistresses, but behind their backs and outside the classroom quite the opposite is true." When my mother read this or something like it, she would burst into tears. She had hoped to display, with a great flourish, my report card to her friends, along with whatever prize I had won. Instead, the report card would have to take a place at the bottom of the old trunk in which she kept any important thing that had to do with me. I became not a favorite of Miss Edward's in the following way: Each Friday afternoon, the girls in the lower forms were given, instead of a last lesson period, an extra-long recess. We were to use this in ladylike recreation—walks, chats about the novels and poems we were reading, showing each other the new embroidery stitches we had learned to master in home class, or something just as seemly. Instead, some of the girls would play a game of cricket or rounders or stones, but most of us would go to the far end of the school grounds and play band. In this game, of which teachers and parents disapproved and which was sometimes absolutely forbidden, we would place our arms around each other's waist or shoulders, forming lines of ten or so girls, and then we would dance from one end of the school grounds to the other. As we danced, we would sometimes chat these words: "Tee la la la, come go. Tee la la la, come go." At other times we would sing a popular calypso song which usually had lots of unladylike words to it. Up and down the schoolyard, away from our teachers, we would dance and sing. At the end of recess—forty-five minutes—we were missing ribbons and other ornaments from our hair, the pleats of our linen tunics became unset, the collars of our blouses were pulled out, and we were soaking wet all the way down to our bloomers. When the school bell rang, we would make a whooping sound, as if in a great panic, and then we would throw ourselves on top of each other as we laughed and shrieked. We would then run back to our classes, where we prepared to file into the auditorium for evening prayers. After that, it was home for the weekend. But how could we go straight home after all that excitement? No sooner were we on the street than we would form little groups, depending on the direction we were headed in. I was never keen on joining them on the way home, because I was sure I would run into my mother. Instead, my friends and I would go to our usual place near the back of the churchyard and sit on the tombstones of people who had been buried there way before slavery was abolished, in 1833. We would sit and sing bad songs, use forbidden words, and, of course, show each other various parts of our bodies. While some of us watched, the others would walk up and down on the large tombstones showing off their legs. It was immediately a popular idea; everybody soon wanted to do it. It wasn't long before many girls—the ones whose mothers didn't pay strict attention to what they were doing—started to come to school on Fridays wearing not bloomers under their uniforms but underpants trimmed with lace and satin frills. It also wasn't long before an end came to all that. One Friday afternoon, Miss Edward, on her way home from school, took a shortcut through the churchyard. She must have heard the commotion we were making, because there she suddenly was, saying, "What is the meaning of this?"—just the very thing someone like her would say if she came unexpectedly on something like us. It was obvious that I was the ringleader. Oh, how I wished the ground would open up and take her in, but it did not. We all, shamefacedly, slunk home, I with Miss Edward at my side. Tears came to my mother's eyes when she heard what I had done. It was apparently such a bad thing that my mother couldn't bring herself to repeat my misdeed to my father in my presence. I got the usual punishment of dinner alone, outside under the breadfruit tree,

but added on to that, I was not allowed to go to the library on Saturday, and on Sunday, after Sunday school and dinner, I was not allowed to take a stroll in the botanical gardens, where Gwen was waiting for me in the bamboo grove.

That happened when I was in the first form. Now here Miss Edward stood. Her whole face was on fire. Her eyes were bulging out of her head. I was sure that at any minute they would land at my feet and roll away. The small pimples on her face, already looking as if they were constantly irritated, now ballooned into huge, on-the-verge-of-exploding boils. Her head shook from side to side. Her strange bottom, which she carried high in the air, seemed to rise up so high that it almost touched the ceiling. Why did I not pay attention, she said. My impertinence was beyond endurance. She then found a hundred words for the different forms my impertinence took. On she went. I was just getting used to this amazing bellowing when suddenly she was speechless. In fact, everything stopped. Her eyes stopped, her bottom stopped, her pimples stopped. Yes she had got close enough so that her eyes caught a glimpse of what I had done to my textbook. The glimpse soon led to closer inspection. It was bad enough that I had defaced my schoolbook by writing in it. That I should write under the picture of Columbus "The Great Man . . . " etc. was just too much. I had gone too far this time, defaming one of the great men in history, Christopher Columbus, discoverer of the island that was my home. And now look at me. I was not even hanging my head in remorse. Had my peers ever seen anyone so arrogant, so blasphemous?

I was sent to the headmistress, Miss Moore. As punishment, I was removed from my position as prefect, and my place was taken by the odious Hilarene. As an added punishment, I was ordered to copy Books I and II of *Paradise Lost*, by John Milton, and to have it done a week from that day. I then couldn't wait to get home to lunch and the comfort of my mother's kisses and arms. I had nothing to worry about there yet; it would be a while before my mother and father heard of my bad deeds. What a terrible morning! Seeing my mother would be such a tonic—something to pick me up.

10   When I got home, my mother kissed me absentmindedly. My father had got home ahead of me, and they were already deep in conversation, my father regaling her with some unusually outlandish thing the oaf Mr. Oatie had done. I washed my hands and took my place at table. My mother brought me my lunch. I took one smell of it, and I could tell that it was the much hated breadfruit. My mother said not at all, it was a new kind of rice imported from Belgium, and not breadfruit, mashed and forced through a ricer, as I thought. She went back to talking to my father. My father could hardly get a few words out of his mouth before she was a jellyfish of laughter. I sat there, putting my food in my mouth. I could not believe that she couldn't see how miserable I was and so reach

out a hand to comfort me and caress my cheek, the way she usually did when she sensed that something was amiss with me. I could not believe how she laughed at everything he said, and how bitter it made me feel to see how much she liked him. I ate my meal. The more I ate of it, the more I was sure that it was breadfruit. When I finished, my mother got up to remove my plate. As she started out the door, I said, "Tell me, really, the name of the thing I just ate."

My mother said, "You just ate some breadfruit. I made it look like rice so that you would eat it. It's very good for you, filled with lots of vitamins." As she said this, she laughed. She was standing half inside the door, half outside. Her body was in the shade of our house, but her head was in the sun. When she laughed, her mouth opened to show off big, shiny, sharp white teeth. It was as if my mother had suddenly turned into a crocodile.

AN ENGLISH LESSON IN SRI LANKA

— *A. Suresh Canagarajah*

A. Suresh Canagarajah is professor of English at Baruch College of the City University of New York. Previously, he taught English for ten years in the region of Jaffna, Sri Lanka, where the classroom scene that follows takes place in the midst of the civil war between Tamil rebels fighting for self-determination and the central government. This scene appears in *Resisting Linguistic Imperialism in English Teaching* (1999). Canagarajah is also the author of *A Geopolitics of Academic Writing* (2002).

SUGGESTION FOR READING   A. Suresh Canagarajah notes that the following scene "is a reconstruction from the observation notes of a class which took place at the University of Jaffna on December 1st, 1990. The description is slightly dramatized in places to throw certain ironies into relief." As you read, be alert to note these ironies.

ADOPTING A CRITICAL PERSPECTIVE ON PEDAGOGY

1   The students crowded around the thatched classrooms on the university campus, warily eyeing the military helicopter circling overhead. Some suggested it was on the lookout for rebel troops, which could lead to another rocket attack on the nearby town; others said it was just a routine

flight, taking supplies to the army base. As a majority began to favor the first explanation, the students started to look for an excuse to stay away from the English class, which was due to start shortly. Ravi could not make up his mind whether to go home early to join his family, or to stay . . .

As Mrs Kandiah came into view, carrying her teaching material, and walking briskly towards the classroom, the students saw that she was determined to hold the class. Ravi and some of the others quickly made their way into the dilapidated study block, where they could hear the droning sound of the power generator through the classroom wall. This told them that Ravi's friends from secondary school, who had recently joined the resistance movement, were busy making fresh stocks of weapons and ammunition. Ravi always felt guilty when he heard them working, since before the university reopened he had said he wanted to join them. Where should he really be now—in the arms factory, or the classroom?

Mrs Kandiah—known to all as "Mrs K."—marched up to the podium and greeted them in her rather stilted British accent: "Good morning, students." For her students, Mrs K. represented order and discipline in the midst of the chaos and violence outside. She believed that education, and the English language in particular, could provide meaning and hope in an otherwise desperate environment. English could give her students employment, opportunities to get on in life, and access to the cultural and material privileges of more developed countries. Ravi's feelings about the language were more mixed: sometimes English represented a world that was remote and threatening, and far removed from his family and friends; at others, he was tempted by the images of sensual pleasure and material wealth endlessly promoted in foreign movies, magazines, and music.

One of the foreign cultural agencies based in the capital had recently sent the university several sets of ELT textbooks. From one of these books Mrs K. had picked out a particular activity she was sure her students would find interesting. In spite of all the difficulties, she prided herself on being well informed about the latest teaching methods and materials, and was currently championing a combination of process-oriented, collaborative, and task based teaching methods. As usual, having no access to a photocopier or cassette player, she would be reading the text to the class herself. She explained that they should take notes on the short article, which was about a student living in Britain. After the students had heard the passage she would be asking them to practice the simple present, which they had studied in the previous class, as a group activity. Worried that they might be distracted by the noise and confusion outside, and not be able to focus all their attention on the text, she advised them to listen carefully for the main themes, and to look out for the grammatical structures she'd taught them in a recent lesson inductively.

5   Mrs K. began the first passage: "Peter is in his final year at the University of Reading, where he is studying Chemistry. He hopes to obtain first class honors in his final examinations so that he can continue with postgraduate work in photochemistry."

These words set Ravi thinking about his own situation. He had been worried for some time about whether he would ever be able to sit for his own degree. The civil war meant that some graduates had taken up to eight years to complete what was supposed to be a three-year course. Even if he managed to get his degree, he didn't know what he would do after that. The fighting had left more than half the local people without jobs; many had lost their homes as well. Worst of all, Ravi's father and several other local farmers had been arrested earlier in the year, on suspicion of helping the rebel forces, and no one had any idea when they might be freed. If Ravi was to have any hope of finding paid work to support his family, he would almost certainly have to leave his mother with his younger brother and sister, and move to the capital, or even to another country.

"Peter is very well organized, and usually manages a reasonable balance between work and study. Since he has exams this term, he tends to spend about two hours reading in the library after school, and another hour or so at home . . . "

At the sound of a small explosion, Mrs K. paused momentarily in her reading. There was a scream from outside, and several students took cover beside their desks, but the blast had been some distance away. Mrs K. decided that this was hardly sufficient cause for dismissing the class, and carried on with the narration. She didn't consider this distraction to be life threatening—not yet.

"Peter doesn't spend all his time working. He also belongs to the photography club, which he helped to start up last year. He likes sailing, and goes surfing whenever he can in the summer term; in the winter he plays in the university rugby team."

10 In the previous year, when the university was closed, Ravi had tried to keep up with his studies by day while training with the local militia by night, but it hadn't worked out too well. The training exercises and political classes took up too much of his time and energy, and meant he couldn't help his mother with their small-holding.

"At weekends he spends some time relaxing with friends."

Ravi spent much of his time working on the family farm. He watered the plants, manured the soil, and helped his mother take their produce to the Monday market. Seeds and fertilizers were very expensive, but they couldn't afford not to cultivate their small plot of land. Even though the recent harvest had been very poor, the family depended on the rice they grew, and the baskets his mother made.

"On Saturday nights he usually goes to a party or a disco with his girlfriend, Susan, but sometimes they borrow his parents' car and go to a disco or a play in London."

This passage provoked mild excitement in the class. Giggles could be heard coming from the far end of the classroom, where the girls had barricaded themselves behind some empty desks, at a safe distance from the boys. Ravi felt tempted to join his friends, who were teasing the girls. Rajan was calling out to them: "It's party time!", "How about it?", "Who's gonna dance with me?" As an avid watcher of pirated American videos, Rajan's colloquial English was particularly fluent—and as a diligent student, he already felt happier talking about science in English than in his first language.

15 Mrs K. pretended not to hear anything, and divided the class into separate groups of boys and girls. She asked them to draw a chart showing how Peter organized his time. Ravi had been too preoccupied with his own thoughts to remember what Peter did or didn't do, and with the exception of Rajan, the rest of his group hadn't paid much attention to the discussion either. The noise of another helicopter in the distance took their minds away from the work they had been doing in the class, and set them talking in their own language about the latest fighting, and the rumors they'd heard of another military operation. They knew that Mrs K. would go over the passage again at the end, and provide them with the correct answers. After all, that's what she was supposed to do—she was the teacher.

Ravi sat across the aisle from Rajan, who never seemed to have trouble with his English exercises. Apart from that, they had a lot in common; in particular, both detested the poverty, chaos, and corruption that surrounded them, and longed for the sort of full and purposeful life enjoyed by Peter in the story. However, only Rajan believed Mrs K. when she said that English could give him that sort of life—an opportunity to go abroad to study or work. That's why he liked English classes best of all.

SUGGESTIONS FOR DISCUSSION

1. Annie John says, "Of course, sometimes, what with our teachers and our books, it was hard for us to tell on which side we really belonged—with the masters or the slaves—for it was all history, it was all in the past, everybody behaved differently then." Then, however, a line later, Annie says that "we, the descendants of the slaves, knew quite well what had really happened." What is it that Annie knows quite well and why was she hesitant for a moment about "on which side we really belonged"? In what sense is this struggle

over what happened in history and whose side she is on played out in Annie's "defacing" her textbook?

2. A. Suresh Canagarjah says he wanted "to throw certain ironies into relief." What are the ironies in this classroom scene? What larger implications are these ironies meant to illustrate? How are the conflicts Ravi experiences related to these ironies?

3. What does it reveal to think of these two classroom scenes in terms of colonialism and postcolonialism? Consider here, for example, how students in Sri Lanka, which became independent in 1948, continue to encounter English, the language of the British Empire and colonial rule, as well as textbooks from Britain. Compare their experience to the classroom scene in Antigua. Much the same is true of the classroom in Antigua, which, after more than 300 years of colonial rule, achieved limited self-government in 1967 and full independence in 1981. What do the classroom scenes suggest to you about the nature of life in a postcolonial world?

SUGGESTIONS FOR WRITING

1. The key event in "Columbus in Chains" involves an act of writing—when Annie writes "The Great Man Can No Longer Get Up and Go" under the picture of Columbus. Write an essay on the role that reading and writing play in Jamaica Kincaid's short story. Consider, for example, how Annie uses writing to rewrite the textbook history of Columbus. Notice too other passages where reading and writing take place or where Annie mentions written materials of one kind or another. What role, literally and symbolically, do reading and writing play in this story?

2. Write an essay that explains the "ironies" in "An English Lesson in Sri Lanka." Be specific and give examples of ironies A. Suresh Canagarajah wants to highlight. But also make sure you explain what these ironies are meant to reveal about the Sri Lankan classroom and its students.

3. Write an essay that compares the two classroom scenes. Consider how each depicts the language and culture of the British Empire and the relation of students and schooling to the former colonial power. Use the comparison to consider what the term *postcolonial* might mean. Don't feel you have to pin down a definition once and for all. Instead, explore what its possible meanings might reveal.

VISUAL ESSAY Self-Portraits

Samuel Fosso

Samuel Fosso is one of the leading photographers in contemporary Africa. His work has appeared in galleries and museums in Europe and the United States. Fosso was born in Cameroon and grew up in Nigeria until he left during the Biafran war of the 1960s. He eventually set up his own passport, portrait, and wedding photography studio in Bagui, Central African Republic, where he lives and works today. He started taking self-portraits with unused exposures, to send to his grandmother to assure her he was well. From these initial black-and-white self-portraits, Fosso began to experiment with costumes, backdrops, and poses and to photograph himself in color. In many respects, Fosso's self-portraits are an outgrowth of the portraits he has taken of clients in Central African Republic over the past 30 years. "The way I take photographs and the

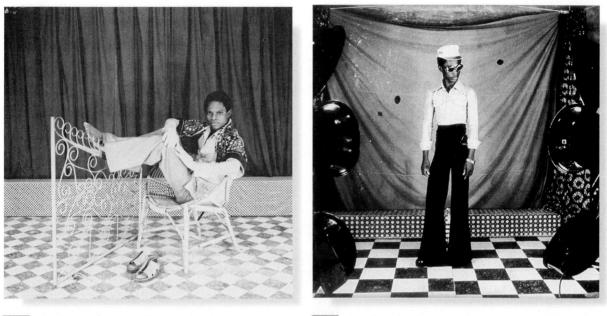

— *Self-Portrait* by Samuel Fosso, 1976.   — *Self-Portrait* by Samuel Fosso, 1977.

way that I use backdrops in order to pose people for their pictures is all about transporting them, taking them to places where they don't go," Fosso says. "It's me who transports them through my photography. It's about taking somebody to a place that they aren't able to get to themselves."

SUGGESTIONS FOR DISCUSSION

1. In the black-and-white self-portrait where Samuel Fosso is standing in front of the camera, viewers also see studio lights along the left and right margins of the photograph. Normally, of course, lights don't appear in photographic portraits. Why do you think Fosso included them? Consider them in relation to what Fosso is wearing and the way he has set up the backdrop. What message is he conveying?

2. The self-portrait of Fosso as a tribal chief is subtitled "Le chef qui a vendu l'Afrique aux colons" ("The chief who sold Africa to the colonizers"). Examine the photograph carefully, noting the backdrop, costume, and pose. What attitude is Fosso conveying? How does he position us as viewers to understand the image he has created?

3. One common assumption about photographic portraits is that they succeed or fail according to how well they reveal the "real" person being photographed. What assumptions does Fosso seem to be making in his self-portraits about the relation between the camera and the person being photographed? Is there even a "real" person involved?

SUGGESTIONS FOR WRITING

1. Imagine that you are an art critic visiting a gallery in which these self-portraits appear. Write a review of the series of four photographs, explaining who Samuel Fosso is and what he is doing. You can find further information about Fosso by doing a Google search.

2. Write an essay that analyzes Fosso's self-portrait as an African chief. Take into account the following remarks by Fosso but do not limit yourself to what he says. Use Fosso's words

— Tati Auto portrait. *Le chef qui a vendu l'Afrique aux colons* by Samuel Fosso, 1997.

to help you shape your own analysis of how the photograph is composed and what it signifies. "With this photo, I wanted to say to westerners, 'Look, we had our own democracy before you came, we had our own rulers, our own presidents, but it was our ruler that you came and got rid of, and in his place, you set up your hierarchies, your systems.' It's about the things they did in the past, and the things that they continue to do. On the surface they cover it up, but beneath the surface it's the same as ever."

3. Write an essay that draws on Fosso self-portraits to consider the issue of identity in a post-colonial world and who has the right to represent self and others.

PASSPORT PHOTOS

▰— *Amitava Kumar*

Amitava Kumar teaches English at the University of Florida. This reading consists of excerpts from the introduction "The Shame of Arrival" and the opening chapter "Language" from Kumar's *Passport Photos* (2000), a multigenre book that combines poetry and photography with literary and cultural analysis. As you can see, Kumar is concerned with the transnational movement of people, encounters at the border, and the condition of immigrants in the Western metropolis.

SUGGESTION
FOR READING
Notice the two photographs that accompany the written text. The photos are not meant, Kumar says, to illustrate an argument. Rather, they "raise the question about how these images are to be seen." As you read, consider how the text and photos offer perspectives to map what Kumar calls "a mixed, postcolonial space."

THE SHAME OF ARRIVAL

> A book is a kind of passport.
>
> —*Salman Rushdie*

1   If it can be allowed that the passport is a kind of book, then the immigration officer, holding a passport in his hand, is also a reader. Like someone in a library or even, in the course of a pleasant afternoon, on a bench beneath a tree. Under the fluorescent lights, he reads the entries made in an unfamiliar hand under categories that are all too familiar. He examines the seals, the stamps, and the signatures on them.

He looks up. He reads the immigrant's responses to his questions, the clothes, the accent. The officer's eyes return to the passport. He appears to be reading it more carefully. He frowns. Suddenly he turns around and tries to catch a colleague's eye. It is nothing, he wants more coffee.

You notice all this if you are an immigrant.

Let us for a moment pretend you are not. Imagine you are drinking your coffee in the café close to your place of work. You notice that the woman who is picking up the cups and then stooping to wipe the floor is someone you have never seen before. She is dark but dressed cleanly in the gray and pink uniform of the employees here. You smile at her and ask if you could please have some more cream. She looks at you but doesn't seem to understand you. You realize she doesn't speak English. Oddly, or perhaps not so oddly, the first thought that crosses your mind is that she is an illegal immigrant in your country. But you don't say anything, you get up and ask someone else for the cream. You smile at her, as if to say, See, nothing to be afraid of here. She probably doesn't smile back. It might or might not occur to you that she doesn't know how to read your smile.

5   Standing in front of the immigration officer, the new arrival from Somalia, El Salvador, or Bangladesh is also a reader. When looking at the American in the café who addresses her—asking her, perhaps, if she wants to have coffee with him—the immigrant reads an unwelcome threat.

If we allow that the passport is a kind of book, we might see the immigrant as a very different kind of reader than the officer seated at his desk with a gleaming badge on his uniform. The immigrant's reading of that book refers to an outside world that is more real. The officer is paid to make a connection only between the book and the person standing in front of him.

The immigrant has a scar on his forehead at the very place his passport says that he does. For the officer this probably means that the man is not a fraud. For the immigrant, that scar is a reminder of his childhood friend in the village, the one whose younger sister he married last May. Or it is likely he doesn't even notice the officer's glance. He is conscious only of a dark weariness behind his eyes because he has not slept for three days.

The officer reads the name of the new arrival's place of birth. He has never heard of it. The immigrant has spent all of the thirty-one years of his life in that village. This difference in itself is quite ordinary. But for some reason that he does not understand, the immigrant is filled with shame.

My attempt, as an immigrant writer, to describe that shame is a part of a historical process.

10 Part of that process is the history of decolonization and the presence, through migration, of formerly colonized populations in the metropolitan centers of the West. What has accompanied this demographic change is the arrival of writers and intellectuals from, say, India or Pakistan, who are giving voice to experiences and identities that Western readers do not encounter in the writings of Saul Bellow or John Updike.

But a crucial part of this narrative and its self-interrogation is the emergence of the discipline that can loosely be called postcolonial studies. Based most prominently in literary and cultural studies, but often engaged in conversations with older projects in the disciplines of history or anthropology, postcolonial scholars have made their task the study of the politics of representing the Other. This has meant, to put it in very reductive terms, not simply that there are more of those people speaking and writing today who are a part of the populations that were formerly solely the object of study by Europeans; it also has meant that a fundamental questioning of the privilege and politics of knowledge has made any representation problematic. There is now no escaping the questions "who is speaking here, and who is being silenced?"

I need to revisit and revise the scene at the customs desk. The new arrival responds to the questions asked by the immigration officer. The postcolonial writer, male, middle-class, skilled in the uses of English, is standing nearby and wants to follow the exchange between the officer and the immigrant. Perhaps he wants to help, perhaps he is interested in this conversation only for professional reasons (or both). But for some reason that he does not understand, that he *cannot* understand, the writer is filled with shame.

The postcolonial writers who are read in the West are mostly migrants. They have traveled to the cities of the West—often for economic reasons, and sometimes for political ones, though it could be argued, of course, that all economic reasons are political too—and in the books they write they undertake more travels.

In Amitav Ghosh's *In An Antique Land*, the writer is a young Indian student in rural Egypt doing research in social anthropology. The book follows Ghosh's archival search for a twelfth-century relationship between a Middle Eastern Jewish trader in India, Abraham Ben Yiju, and his toddy-drinking Indian slave, Bomma. These details are interwoven with the more contemporary relationship that develops between the Indian intellectual and the friends he makes in the Egyptian villages not too far from the Cairo synagogue where for a very long time the papers of Ben Yiju were housed.

15 Ghosh was only twenty-two when he traveled in 1980 to Egypt. One day, while making tea for two young men in his rented room in the village, he is caught short by an observation made by one of his visitors, Nabeel: "It must make you think of all the people you left at home . . . when you put that kettle on the stove with just enough water for yourself."

This comment, Ghosh notes, stayed in his mind. "I was never able to forget it, for it was the first time that anyone in Lataifa or Nashawy had attempted an enterprise similar to mine—to enter my imagination and look at my situation as it might appear to me." Ghosh, the traveler, appreciates the travel undertaken by his friend, Nabeel, in his imagination. That effort brings Nabeel closer to that place where Ghosh himself has traveled—which is not so much Egypt as much as a place away from home, or from that which could be called the familiar. To be where one is not, or where one is not expected to be, and sometimes not even welcome . . . to travel to that place and write about it becomes the credo of the postcolonial writer.

This movement is not always possible. People are held down where they are, or there are intransigent barriers between them. A shared language is an impossibility. In one of the episodes that Ghosh describes with instructive wit, some older Egyptian men at a wedding in the village want to know what is done with the dead in India, whether it is really true that they are cremated, and whether women are "purified" ("you mean you let the clitoris just grow and grow?"), and boys, are they not "purified" either, and you, doctor, are you? Our writer is unable to respond and flees the scene. The trauma of a childhood memory merges with a shared trauma of a public memory and ties his tongue. Ghosh broods over memories of Hindu-Muslim riots in the Indian subcontinent (present in the narrative of his earlier novel *The Shadow Lines*):

The stories of those riots are always the same: tales that grow out of an explosive barrier of symbols—of cities going up in flames because of a cow found dead in a temple or a pig in a mosque; of people killed for wearing a lungi or a dhoti, depending on where they find themselves; of women disembowelled for wearing veils or vermilion, of men dismembered for the state of their foreskins.

But I was never able to explain very much of this to Nabeel or anyone else in Nashawy. The fact was that despite the occasional storms and turbulence their country had seen, despite even the wars that some of them had fought in, theirs was a world that was far gentler, far less violent, very much more humane and innocent than mine.

I could not have expected them to understand an Indian's terror of symbols.

The name that Ghosh gives to the reality—or, at least, the possibility—of travel and historical understanding is "a world of accommodation." When the young writer and a village Imam get into a fight about the West and its advanced status in terms of "guns and tanks and bombs," and then both make claims about India's and Egypt's respective prowess in this regard, Ghosh confesses that he feels crushed because their heated exchange has most indelibly announced an end to that world of accommodation:

[I]t seemed to me that the Imam and I had participated in our own final defeat, in the dissolution of the centuries of dialogue that had linked us: we had demonstrated the irreversible triumph of the language that has usurped all the others in which people once discussed their differences. We had acknowledged that it was no longer possible to speak, as Ben Yiju or his Slave, or any of the thousands of travellers who had crossed the Indian Ocean in the Middle Ages might have done.

But the postcolonial writer need not blame himself here. It is not his debate with the Imam but the might of U.S. armed forces supported by most of the Western nations that rubs out, at the end of Ghosh's narrative, his friend Nabeel—lost among the countless migrant workers in Iraq from countries like Egypt and India, displaced in the desert because of the sudden onset of the Persian Gulf War.

20   In this scenario, the immigrant does not ever appear before the customs officer in the airport of a Western metropolis. As driver, carpenter, servant, or nanny, the immigrant from countries of South and South-East Asia provides service in the Gulf states of the Middle East and Libya. In some of their cases the passport is a missing book.

Lacking proper documents, and much more vulnerable to exploitation and abuse, those immigrants are given the name "contract labor" in the zones of shifting, global capital. In the 1950s and 1960s U.S. capital first attracted foreign labor in the Middle East and today, benefiting from investments of the rentier oil-rich Arab states, still profits from the labor of migrants. And when Western capital's profits were threatened, it was the lives of such migrants, and not only those who were employed in Iraq, that the Gulf War threw into devastating crisis. The postcolonial writer speaking of the migrant worker during the war is doing something rather simple. He is reminding us that the man who said to the foreign visitor in his room one evening, "It must make you think of all the people you left at home . . . when you put that kettle on the stove with just enough water for yourself," is alone now in a distant city threatened with destruction. And that man, when not seen in the footage of the epic exodus shown on television, is then assumed to have "vanished into the anonymity of History."

The migrant laborer might have "vanished into the anonymity of History," but the post-colonial writer clearly has not. By presenting those contrasting conditions, I am making a statement here about class, but besides that fairly obvious fact, what do I say about *writing*?

To ask a question about writing, especially postcolonial writing, perhaps we need to reverse our reading of the passport as a book and, instead, examine the formulation put forward by Rushdie, "A book is a kind of passport." Rushdie's point is on surface a fairly general one. For aspiring writers—"would-be migrants from the World to the Book"—certain books provide permission to travel. Recounting the history of his own formation, Rushdie pays homage, among others, to Günter Grass's *Tin Drum*. Grass's great novel, Rushdie writes, served as a passport to the world of writing. But even when writing of the book as a passport in a *metaphorical* sense, Rushdie is writing about a book—*The Tin Drum*—that is in a *specific* way about migrancy and a migrant's sense of place and language.

That is not a universal trait among writers. The trope of migrancy does not exist as a material fact, in either a metaphorical or literal sense, in the writings of Norman Mailer or John Grisham. But it emerges as an obsession in the pages of a writer like Rushdie. For him, in fact, "the very word *metaphor*, with its roots in the Greek words for *bearing across*, describes a sort of migration, the migration of ideas into images." Rather than oppose the metaphorical to the literal, it is the idea of the metaphorical itself that

Rushdie renders literal and equates with a universal condition: "Migrants—borne-across humans—are metaphorical beings in their very essence; and migration, seen as a metaphor, is everywhere around us. We all cross frontiers; in that sense, we are all migrant peoples."

There is a danger here in migrancy becoming everything and nothing. Aijaz Ahmad points out that exile is a particular fetish of European High Modernism and in Rushdie's case becomes simply ontological rootlessness. And, Ahmad argues, novels like *Shame* display a form of "unbelonging" and an absence of any "existing community of praxis." If we agree with Ahmad and see the obsessive celebration of migrancy in Rushdie as a mere repetition of the desolation experienced by the modernist writer in exile, we might also sense that the inexplicable shame that permeates the postcolonial writer is only that of being taken as a representative by the West but having no one, in any real sense, to represent.

That is a real, hard-to-shake-off, nagging shame. And what complicates it further is that the writer is aware that while the migrant worker has "vanished into the anonymity of History," the writer himself or herself hasn't. But why has the writer escaped that destiny? We can be reductive and attribute the appeal of a writer like Rushdie or Ghosh only to Western tokenism, and indeed much can be said about the subject even without being reductive. But books written by immigrants or writers of immigrant origins are not merely hollow receptacles for the will of the West. This book that you are holding in your hands has been written in the belief that words matter. Words from an alien language. But also words in a familiar language that attest to different realities: words are our defense against invisibility.

I'd like to imagine the immigration officer as a curious reader of my book. But the officer should not assume that this passport doesn't have any missing pages; indeed, he would be wise to be skeptical even of his own interest. I am reminded of the wary response of Mahasweta Devi, an Indian writer who has earned high recognition for her work among the aboriginal or tribal populations in Bihar and Bengal: "Why should American readers want to know from me about Indian tribals, when they have present-day America? How was it built? Only in the names of places the Native American legacy survives." I take Devi's words as a provocation to present in this book, interspersed with my images from India and other places, the photographs that I have also taken in the United States. (The Other shoots back.) In which case, why only quote Devi? In order to go on with this mapping of a mixed, postcolonial space, I would like to frame these images with a line borrowed from the black hip-hop artist Rakim: "It ain't where you're from, it's where you're at."

This is where I'm at: in the spaces claimed or established by these images. These photographs—please see the notes as well as the list of illustrations for more information on them— detail a different kind of immigrant experience. What these images offer cannot be described as "illustrating" any kind of argument; in the image of a woman holding a rubber Miss Liberty, for example, it is for the viewer to construct a story that binds or divides the three female figures in their distinct moments of emergence as objects or subjects. The recording of the difference that I am calling "immigrant experience" also has partly to do with labor and protest. Hence the images of workers and, in some cases, their organized protest, on the streets of New Delhi and New York City. The accompanying narratives, and oftentimes the photographs themselves, raise the question about how these images are to be seen. And from where. As a way of announcing that difference, let me offer at the beginning of this book a photograph that sets itself against the photo of the White House taken by the visiting tourist. This is the photograph of the First House from the viewpoint of the homeless sleeping outside its walls one Christmas Eve.

LANGUAGE

Everytime I think I have forgotten,
I think I have lost the mother tongue,
it blossoms out of my mouth.
Days I try to think in English:
I look up,
paylo kallo kagdo

Homeless outside the White House, 1992

oodto oodto jai, huhvay jzaday pohchay
ainee chanchma kaeek chay
the crow has something in his beak.

               —*Sujata Bhatt*

Name
Place of Birth
Date of Birth
Profession
Nationality
Sex
Identifying Marks

My passport provides no information about my language. It simply presumes I have one.

30   If the immigration officer asks me a question—his voice, if he's speaking English, deliberately slow, and louder than usual—I do not, of course, expect him to be terribly concerned about the nature of language and its entanglement with the very roots of my being. And yet it is in language that all immigrants are defined and in which we all struggle for an identity. That is how I understand the postcolonial writer's declaration about the use of a language like English that came to us from the colonizer:

Those of us who do use English do so in spite of our ambiguity towards it, or perhaps because of that, perhaps because we can find in that linguistic struggle a reflection of other struggles taking place in the real world, struggles between the cultures within ourselves and the influences at work upon our societies. To conquer English may be to complete the process of making ourselves free.

I also do not expect the immigration officer to be very aware of the fact that it is in that country called language that immigrants are reviled. I'd like to know what his thoughts were when he first heard the Guns N' Roses song:

Immigrants
and faggots
They make no sense to me
They come to our country—
And think they'll do as they please
Like start some mini-Iran
Or spread some fuckin' disease.

It is between different words that immigrants must choose to suggest who they are. And if these words, and their meanings, belong to others, then it is in a broken language that we must find refuge. Consider this example.

■■ Shop advertisement,
Brooklyn grocery, 1992

I took this photograph while standing outside an Arab grocery store in Brooklyn. While pressing the shutter I was aware of another grocery store, in the film *Falling Down*, where the following exchange took place between a white American male, played by Michael Douglas, and a Korean grocer:

MR. LEE: Drink eighty-five cent. You pay or go.

FOSTER: This "fie," I don't understand a "fie." There's a "v" in the word. It's "fie-vah." You don't got "v's" in China?

MR. LEE: Not Chinese. I'm Korean.

FOSTER: Whatever. You come to my country, you take my money, you don't even have the grace to learn my language?

What Foster doesn't realize is that not only is it not his country alone, it is also not his language anymore. (That should be obvious to the ordinary American viewer, except that it *wasn't* obvious to every one. And it isn't.) But what I'm interested in asking is this: what is it that Mr. Lee is saying?

35   In saying "Not Chinese. I'm Korean," Mr. Lee is talking about difference. He is trying to tell another story. His story. Except that Foster won't listen. He is more interested in taking apart Mr. Lee's store with a baseball bat—the same way that, as Rita Chaudhry Sethi reminds us, others destroyed Japanese cars before Vincent Chin died. Vincent Chin was a young Chinese American who was murdered, also with a baseball bat, by two white autoworkers in Detroit. Chin was called a "Jap" and told "It's because of you motherfuckers that we're out of work." When I say Mr. Lee is talking about differences, I don't simply mean the difference between someone who is Chinese and someone else who is Korean. Instead, by difference I mean a sense of where it is a person is coming from. Both in terms of a location in place and in history.

Vincent Chin was an American of Chinese origin. The year he was killed marked the hundred-year anniversary of the Chinese Exclusion Act; in the year 1882, lynch mobs had murdered Chinese workers who were working on the West Coast.

Chin's murderers, Ronald Ebens and Michael Nitz, were autoworkers in Detroit, the city that entered the annals of early U.S. industrialism through its success in manufacturing cars. Ebens and Nitz did not know the difference between a worker and a capitalist. They were kept ignorant of the world of transnational capitalism, their very own world in which "General Motors owns 34 percent of Isuzu (which builds the Buick Opel), Ford 25 percent of Mazda (which makes transmissions for the Escort), and Chrysler 15 percent of Mitsubishi (which produces the Colt and the Charger)." Chin's killers did not spend a single night in prison and were fined $3,780 each. A Chinese American protesting the scant sentence is reported to have said, "Three thousand dollars can't even buy a good used car these days."

What does the word "Jap" mean? What is the difference between a Japanese and a Chinese American? What is the difference between a Chinese American and a used car? How does language mean and why does it matter?

As the Swiss linguist Ferdinand de Saussure argued very early in this century, language is a system of signs. And any sign consists of a signifier (the sound or written form) and a signified (the concept). As the two parts of the sign are linked or inseparable (the word "camera," for instance, accompanies the concept "camera" and remains quite distinct in our minds from the concept "car"), what is prompted is the illusion that language is transparent. The relationship between the signifier and the signified, and hence language itself, is assumed to be natural.

40   When we use the word "alien" it seems to stick rather unproblematically and unquestioningly to something or someone, and it is only by a conscious, critical act that we think of something different. Several years ago, in a public speech, Reverend Jesse Jackson seemed to be questioning the fixed and arbitrary assumptions in the dominant ideology when he reminded his audience that undocumented Mexicans were not aliens, they were *migrant workers*.

E.T., Jackson said emphatically, was an *alien*.

California road sign near U.S.-Mexico border, 1994

I took this photograph very close to the U.S.–Mexico border, somewhere between San Diego and Tijuana. There was a tear in the fence; I climbed under it and came up close to the highway to get a better shot. When I went back to the place in the fence, I was startled out of my skin by a Border Patrol van that was very slowly driving past. The officer did not see me, however, and I was soon back in the bar next to my motel.

While sipping my beer, I imagined a conversation with the border patrol officer who had only narrowly missed catching me.

OFFICER: I saw you photographing that sign. That was good, an excellent idea. What do you think about the sign though?

ME: Mmm. I don't know. It's just that—this is the first time I saw that sign. In my country, we have family-planning signs with figures like that. Father, mother, kid. The Health Ministry has a slogan painted beneath it, One or Two Kids. Then Stop.

OFFICER: That's very interesting. This is what I like about multiculturalism. You get to learn about cultural difference.

ME: You really think so? Yes, that's great. What can I learn from *this* sign?

OFFICER: Well, you've gotta get into the semiotics of it, you know what I'm saying?

ME: Uh-huh.

OFFICER: I'll be damned if language is transparent. That's the bottom line here. Just look at that sign—in English it's Caution, but in Spanish, it's *Prohibido*. You don't think those two words mean the same thing, do you?

ME: I don't know. I don't know Spanish.

OFFICER: Okay, well, I'll be patient with you. The sign in English is for folks who drive. They're being cautioned. Now, the sign in Spanish—

ME: Yes, yes, I see what you're driving at! The *Prohibido* sign is for the Spanish speaker—

OFFICER: There you go! Bingo! Bull's eye! They don't have the word *Caución* there. It's plain Prohibited: pure and simple. The picture, the image—it splits, right before your eyes!

ME: The scales have fallen . . .

OFFICER: Well, but you gotta stay alert. 'Cause culture is a moving thing, meanings change. Or sometimes, just get plain run over. All the time.

ME: Yes, yes.

OFFICER: What work do you do?

ME: I teach English.

OFFICER: No kidding! See, this is America! You teaching *English* to our kids, I love it. Say, did you ever watch *Saturday Night Live* when it first came on?

ME: No, I don't think so.

OFFICER: Michael O'Donoghue played a language instructor. He was teaching this confused immigrant played by John Belushi. You know the sentence that O'Donoghue used to introduce the language?

ME: What was it?

OFFICER: I will feed your fingers to the wolverines.

We could have gone on, the officer and I. If we were swapping stories today, I'd have mentioned the news report that the telephone company Sprint, in its billing letter in Spanish, threatens customers with phone cutoff unless their check is received by the end of the month. According to the news report, the Anti-Defamation League and the National Council of La Raza have filed complaints. Why? Because the billing letter in English is somewhat differently worded: "As a customer you are Sprint's number one priority. We . . . look forward to serving your communication needs for many years to come."

45   And, if the officer had had more time, we might have arrived at an understanding that language, especially English, has been used as a racial weapon in immigration.

To cite a historical example: in 1896 a colonial official argued against the restrictions imposed on the entry of Indians in South Africa, adding that this would be "most painful" for Queen Victoria to approve. At the same time, he sanctioned a European literacy test that would automatically exclude Indians while preserving the facade of racial equality.

Almost a hundred years later a Texas judge ordered the mother of a five-year-old to stop speaking in Spanish to her child. Judge Samuel Kiser reminded the mother that her daughter was a "full-blooded American." "Now, get this straight. You start speaking English to this child because if she doesn't do good in school, then I can remove her because it's not in her best interest to be ignorant. The child will only hear English."

Who is permitted to proceed beyond the gates into the mansion of full citizenship? And on what terms? These are the questions that the episode in the Texas courthouse raises. Apart from the issue of gross paternalism and an entirely injudicious jingoism, what comes into play here is the class bias in North American society that promotes bilingualism in the upper class but frowns on it when it becomes an aspect of lower-class life.

More revealing of the ties between language and U.S. Immigration is the following newspaper report: "School and city officials expressed outrage this week over the Border Patrol's arrest of three Hispanic students outside an English as Second Language class."

50   For the Chicano poet Alfred Arteaga, the above story about arrest and deportation has a double irony: "irony, not only that 'officials expressed outrage' at so typical an INS action, but irony also, that the story made it into print in the first place." Arteaga knows too well that what Chicanos say and do in their own language is rarely found worthy of printing.

I think it is equally significant to remark on the fact that the officers who conducted the arrest were patrolling the borders of the dominant language to pick up the illegals. They are ably assisted by the likes of the California state assemblyman William J. Knight, who distributed among his fellow legislators a poem, "I Love America." That poem begins with the words "I come for visit, get treated regal, / So I stay, who care illegal." This little ditty makes its way through the slime of a racist fantasy. Its landscape is filled with greedy swindlers and dishonest migrant workers. The breeding subhumans speak in a broken syntax and mispronounce the name Chevy, the heartbeat of America, as (call the National Guard, please!) Chebby. The poem ends with a call that emanates like a howl from the guts of the Ku Klux Klan:

We think America damn good place,
Too damn good for white man's race.
If they no like us, they can go,
Got lots of room in Mexico.

If the immigration officer were to ask me about my language, what would I say? That any precious life-giving sense of language loses all form in this arid landscape of Buchanan-speak? Perhaps. That any answer I could possibly give is nothing more defined than a blur moving on the infrared scopes of those guarding the borders of fixed identity.

Homi Bhabha writes: "The enchantment of art lies in looking in a glass darkly—a wall, stone, a screen, paper, canvas, steel—that turns suddenly into the almost unbearable lightness of being." But where is this buoyancy, the refulgence, the mix of new life and new art? As the case of Fauziya Kasinga reminds us—the young woman who fled Togo to avoid genital mutilation and was held for long in detention by the U.S. Immigration authorities—grim reality so often persists in its unenchanting rudeness.

In such conditions to speak is only to declare any speech a station of loss.

I brought two bags from home, but there was a
   third that I left behind. In this new country,
   apart from the struggles that made me a
   stranger, were your needs, of the ones who
   bid me goodbye, those I left behind. Among
   the papers I collected, you had put a small
   bag of sweets, I left behind.
There were divisions at home, there were other
   possibilities;
there were communities in my town, there were
   communities where I came;
I found a job, called it a struggle for survival,
   everything else I left behind. I didn't want to

forget my traditions, the tradition of forgetting
   I left behind.
Bags, passport, my shoes crossed the yellow
   lines, something was left behind.
Here I am, a sum of different parts; travel agents
   everywhere are selling ads for the parts that
   were left behind.

And yet, while speaking of the patrolling of the borders of dominant identity, I must note the presence of one who is still eluding arrest: a border-artist/poet-performer/hoarder-of-hypehs/warrior-for-Gringostroika. Officer, meet Guillermo Gómez-Peña. You have been looking for him not only because Gómez-Peña declares "I speak in English therefore you listen/I speak in English therefore I hate you." But also because, like a "Pablo Neruda gone punk," this "border brujo" threatens mainstream America with the swaggering banditry of language, demanding as ransom a pure reality-reversal:

What if the U.S. was Mexico?
What if 200,000 Anglo-Saxicans
Were to cross the border each month
to work as gardeners, waiters
3rd chair musicians, movie extras
bouncers, babysitters, chauffeurs
syndicated cartoons, feather-weight boxers,
   fruit-pickers
and anonymous poets?
What if they were called Waspanos
Waspitos, Wasperos or Waspbacks?
What if literature was life, eh?

SUGGESTIONS FOR DISCUSSION

1. One of the threads running through Amitava Kumar's writing is the idea that a passport is a book that enables different and complex readings. He also uses a line from Salman Rushdie, "A book is a kind of passport," as an epigram to the introduction. What is the relationship between these two ideas? What comes to light if you put the emphasis on the passport (as a kind of book) or on the book (as a kind of passport)?

2. In the excerpt from the introduction, Kumar defines the "task" of postcolonial scholars as "the study of the politics of representing the Other." Later in the same paragraph, he says a "fundamental questioning of the privilege and politics of knowledge have made any representation problematic. There is now no escaping the questions 'who is speaking here, and who is being silenced?' " What does Kumar mean here? Put in your own words what you think he is saying about the purposes of a postcolonial perspective and the kinds of questions raised by such a perspective. Draw on the rest of the reading selection to give examples of what a postcolonial perspective looks like as Kumar presents it.

3. In these excerpts and throughout *Passport Photos*, Kumar uses a mixed and episodic style that combines, among other things, photos, poetry, song lyrics, movie dialogue, imagined conversations, reporting, and analysis instead of straightforward exposition. Why do you think Kumar has chosen this writing strategy? In what sense is the writing strategy linked to Kumar's themes of migration, borders, postcolonialism, and globalization? Consider, for example, the imagined conversation with the border patrol officer. To hear how this passage fits into the mosaic of styles Kumar uses, have two people in class take the two parts and read them aloud.

SUGGESTIONS FOR WRITING

1. Write a letter to a friend at another college that explains what the term *postcolonial* means in these excerpts from *Passport Photos*. Assume your friend is curious about the term but hasn't read this selection. Explain how Kumar defines and illustrates the term, but it may help your friend, who hasn't read these excerpts, to use other examples from your shared knowledge and experience as well. Because this is a letter to a friend, describe your own experience working through Kumar's writing and explain what you see as the value and significance of the term *postcolonial*.

2. Many of these excerpts from *Passport Photos* are devoted to the idea of international borders or actually take place at the U.S. border. Here is a passage from an essay by Richard Rodriquez, "Illegal Immigrants: Prophets of a Borderless World."

> Before professors in business schools were talking about global economics, illegals knew all about it. Before fax machines punctured the Iron Curtin, coyotes knew the most efficient ways to infiltrate southern California. Before businessmen flew into Mexico City to sign big deals, illegals were picking peaches in the fields of California or flipping pancakes at the roadside diner.
>
> We live in a world in which economies overlap, in which we no longer know where our automobiles are assembled. We are headed for a century in which the great question will be exactly this: What is a border?
>
> The illegal immigrant is the bravest among us. The most modern among us. The prophet. "The border, señor?" the illegal immigrant sighs. The border is an inconvenience surely. A danger in the dark. But the border does not hold. The peasant knows the reality of our world decades before the California suburbanites will ever get the point.

    Write an essay that takes seriously Rodriquez's claim that the "great question" of the twenty-first century will be "What is a border?" Explain Rodriquez's and Kumar's perspectives on the question, noting similarities and differences. Use this discussion to set up your own commentary on what you see as the implications of the question "What is a border?"

3. Write an essay that imitates Kumar's mixed, episodic style. Draw upon any or all of the genres Kumar does to create your own reflections on life in a postcolonial world.

HOW TO TAME A WILD TONGUE

— *Gloria Anzaldúa*

Gloria Anzaldúa writes in a language that grows out of the multiple cultures in the American Southwest—a mosaic of English (both standard and slang), Spanish (both Castilian and Mexican), northern Mexican and Chicano Spanish dialects, Tex-Mex, *Pachuco* (the vernacular of urban zoot suiters), and the Aztec language Nahuatl. The following selection is a chapter from her book *Borderlands/La Frontera* (1987). As the title of her book indicates, Anzaldúa sees herself as a "border woman." "I grew up between two cultures," she says, "the Mexican (with a heavy Indian influence) and the Anglo (as a member of a colonized people in our own territory). I have been straddling that *tejas*-Mexican border, and others, all my life." Anzaldúa's "borderland" refers to those places "where two or more cultures edge each other, where people of different races occupy the same territory, where under, lower, middle, and upper classes touch, where the space between two individuals shrinks with intimacy."

SUGGESTION FOR READING As you read, you will notice how Gloria Anzaldúa combines English and Spanish in a sentence or a paragraph. Consider the effects of Anzaldúa's prose and how it locates you as a reader on the border where two cultures and languages touch.

1 "We're going to have to control your tongue," the dentist says, pulling out all the metal from my mouth. Silver bits plop and tinkle into the basin. My mouth is a motherlode. The dentist is cleaning out my roots. I get a whiff of the stench when I gasp. "I can't cap that tooth yet, you're still draining," he says.

"We're going to have to do something about your tongue," I hear the anger rising in his voice. My tongue keeps pushing out the wads of cotton, pushing back the drills, the long thin needles. "I've never seen anything as strong or as stubborn," he says. And I think, how do you tame a wild tongue, train it to be quiet, how do you bridle and saddle it? How do you make it lie down?

Who is to say that robbing a people of its
language is less violent than war?
—*Ray Gwyn Smith*[1]

I remember being caught speaking Spanish at recess—that was good for three licks on the knuckles with a sharp ruler. I remember being sent to the corner of the classroom for "talking back" to the Anglo teacher when all I was trying to do was tell her how to pronounce my name. "If you want to be American, speak 'American.' If you don't like it, go back to Mexico where you belong."

"I want you to speak English. *Pa' hallar buen trabajo tienes que saber hablar el inglés bien. Qué vale toda tu educatión si todavía hablas inglés con un* 'accent,' " my mother would say, mortified that I spoke English like a Mexican. At Pan American University, I and all Chicano students were required to take two speech classes. Their purpose: to get rid of our accents.

5 Attacks on one's form of expression with the intent to censor are a violation of the First Amendment. *El Anglo con care de inocente nos arrancó la lengua.* Wild tongues can't be tamed, they can only be cut out.

OVERCOMING THE TRADITION OF SILENCE

Ahogadas, escupimos el oscuro. Peleando con nuestra propia sombra el silencio nos sepulta.

En boca cerrada no entran moscas. "Flies don't enter a closed mouth" is a saying I kept hearing when I was a child. *Ser habladora* was to be a gossip and a liar, to talk too much. *Muchachitas bien criadas*, well-bred girls don't answer back. *Es una falta de respeto* to talk back to one's mother or father. I remember one of the sins I'd recite to the priest in the confession box the few times I went to confession: talking back to my mother, *hablar pa' 'tras, repelar. Hocicona, repelona, chismosa*, having a big mouth, questioning, carrying tales are all signs of being *mal criada*. In my culture they are all words that are derogatory if applied to women—I've never heard them applied to men.

The first time I heard two women, a Puerto Rican and a Cuban, say the word "*nosotras*," I was shocked. I had not known the word existed. Chicanas use *nosotros* whether we're male or female. We are robbed of our female being by the masculine plural. Language is a male discourse.

And our tongues have become dry the
wilderness has dried out our tongues and we
have forgotten speech.
—*Irena Klepfisz*[2]

Even our own people, other Spanish speakers *nos quieren poner candados en la boca.* They would hold us back with their bag of *reglas de academia.*

OYÉ COMO LADRA: EL LENGUAJE DE LA FRONTERA

Quien tiene boca se equivoca.

—*Mexican saying*

"*Pocho*, cultural traitor, you're speaking the oppressor's language by speaking English, you're ruining the Spanish language," I have been accused by various Latinos and Latinas. Chicano Spanish is considered by the purist and by most Latinos deficient, a mutilation of Spanish.

10   But Chicano Spanish is a border tongue which developed naturally. Change, *evolución, enriquecimiento de palabras nuevas por invención o adopción* have created variants of Chicano Spanish, *un nuevo lenguaje. Un lenguaje que corresponde a un modo de vivir.* Chicano Spanish is not incorrect, it is a living language.

For a people who are neither Spanish nor live in a country in which Spanish is the first language; for a people who live in a country in which English is the reigning tongue but who are not Anglo; for a people who cannot entirely identify with either standard (formal, Castilian) Spanish nor standard English, what recourse is left to them but to create their own language? A language which they can connect their identity to, one capable of communicating the realities and values true to themselves—a language with terms that are neither *español ni inglés*, but both. We speak a patois, a forked tongue, a variation of two languages.

Chicano Spanish sprang out of the Chicanos' need to identify ourselves as a distinct people. We need a language with which we could communicate with ourselves, a secret language. For some of us, language is a homeland closer than the Southwest—for many Chicanos today live in the Midwest and the East. And because we are a complex, heterogeneous people, we speak many languages. Some of the languages we speak are

1. Standard English
2. Working-class and slang English
3. Standard Spanish
4. Standard Mexican Spanish
5. North Mexican Spanish dialect
6. Chicano Spanish (Texas, New Mexico, Arizona, and California have regional variations)
7. Tex-Mex
8. *Pachuco* (called *caló*)

My "home" tongues are the languages I speak with my sister and brothers, with my friends. They are the last five listed, with 6 and 7 being closest to my heart. From school, the media, and job situations, I've picked up standard and working class English. From Mamagrande Locha and from reading Spanish and Mexican literature, I've picked up Standard Spanish and Standard Mexican Spanish. From *los recién llegados*, Mexican immigrants, and *braceros*, I learned the North Mexican dialect. With Mexicans I'll try to speak either Standard Mexican Spanish or the North Mexican dialect. From my parents and Chicanos living in the Valley, I picked up Chicano Texas Spanish, and I speak it with my mom, younger brother (who married a Mexican and who rarely mixes Spanish with English), aunts, and older relatives.

With Chicanas from *Nuevo México* or *Arizona* I will speak Chicano Spanish a little, but often they don't understand what I'm saying. With most California Chicanas I speak entirely in English (unless I forget). When I first moved to San Francisco, I'd rattle off something in Spanish, unintentionally embarrassing them. Often it is only with another Chicana *tejano* that I can talk freely.

15   Words distorted by English are known as anglicisms or *pochismos.* The *pocho* is an anglicized Mexican or American of Mexican origin who speaks Spanish with an accent characteristic of North Americans and who distorts and reconstructs the language according to the influence of English.[3] Tex-Mex, or Spanglish, comes most naturally to me. I may switch back and forth from English to Spanish in the same sentence or in the same word. With my sister and my brother Nune and with Chicano *tejano* contemporaries I speak in Tex-Mex.

From kids and people my own age I picked up *Pachuco*. *Pachuco* (the language of the zoot suiters) is a language of rebellion, both against Standard Spanish and Standard English. It is a secret language. Adults of the culture and outsiders cannot understand it. It is made up of slang words from both English and Spanish. *Ruca* means girl or woman, *vato* means guy or dude, *chale* means no, *simón* means yes, *churro* is sure, talk is *periquiar*, *pigionear* means petting, *que gacho* means how nerdy, *ponte águila* means watch out, death is called *la pelona*. Through lack of practice and not having others who can speak it, I've lost most of the *Pachuco* tongue.

CHICANO SPANISH

Chicanos, after 250 years of Spanish/Anglo colonization, have developed significant differences in the Spanish we speak. We collapse two adjacent vowels into a single syllable and sometimes shift the stress in certain words such as *maíz/maiz, cohete/cuete*. We leave out certain consonants when they appear between vowels: *lado/lao, mojado/mojao*. Chicanos from South Texas pronounce *f* as *j* as in *jue* (*fue*). Chicanos use "archaisms," words that are no longer in the Spanish language, words that have been evolved out. We say *semos, truje, haiga, ansina*, and *naiden*. We retain the "archaic" *j*, as in *jalar*, that derives from an earlier *h* (the French *halar* or the Germanic *halon* which was lost to standard Spanish in the sixteenth century), but which is still found in several regional dialects such as the one spoken in South Texas. (Due to geography, Chicanos from the Valley of South Texas were cut off linguistically from other Spanish speakers. We tend to use words that the Spaniards brought over from Medieval Spain. The majority of the Spanish colonizers in Mexico and the Southwest came from Extremadura—Hernán Cortés was one of them—and Andalucía. Andalucians pronounce *ll* like a *y*, and their *d*'s tend to be absorbed by adjacent vowels: *tirado* becomes *tirao*. They brought *el lenguaje popular, dialectos y regionalismos*.)[4]

Chicanos and other Spanish speakers also shift *ll* to *y* and *z* to *s*.[5] We leave out initial syllables, saying *tar* for *estar*, *toy* for *estoy*, *hora* for *ahora* (*cubanos* and *puertorriqueños* also leave out initial letters of some words). We also leave out the final syllable such as *pa* for *para*. The intervocalic *y*, the *ll* as in *tortilla, ella, botella*, gets replaced by *tortia* or *tortiya, ea, botea*. We add an additional syllable at the beginning of certain words: *atocar* for *tocar*, *agastar* for *gastar*. Sometimes we'll say *lavaste las vacijas*, other times *lavates* (substituting the *ates* verb endings for the *aste*).

We used anglicisms, words borrowed from English: *bola* from ball, *carpeta* from carpet, *máchina de lavar* (instead of *lavadora*) from washing machine. Tex-Mex argot, created by adding a Spanish sound at the beginning or end of an English word such as *cookiar* for cook, *watchar* for watch, *parkiar* for park, and *rapiar* for rape, is the result of the pressures on Spanish speakers to adapt to English.

20   We don't use the word *vosotros/as* or its accompanying verb form. We don't say *claro* (to mean yes), *imagínate*, or *me emociona*, unless we picked up Spanish from Latinas, out of a book, or in a classroom. Other Spanish-speaking groups are going through the same, or similar, development in their Spanish.

LINGUISTIC TERRORISM

Deslenguadas. Somos los del español deficiente.
We are your linguistic nightmare, your linguistic aberration, your linguistic *mestisaje*, the subject of your *burla*. Because we speak with tongues of fire we are culturally crucified. Racially, culturally, and linguistically *somos huérfanos*—we speak an orphan tongue.

Chicanas who grew up speaking Chicano Spanish have internalized the belief that we speak poor Spanish. It is illegitimate, a bastard language. And because we internalize how our language has been used against us by the dominant culture, we use our language differences against each other.

Chicana feminists often skirt around each other with suspicion and hesitation. For the longest time I couldn't figure it out. Then it dawned on me. To be close to another Chicana is like looking into the mirror. We are afraid of what we'll see there. *Pena.* Shame. Low estimation of self. In childhood we are told that our language is wrong. Repeated attacks on our native tongue diminish our sense of self. The attacks continue throughout our lives.

Chicanas feel uncomfortable talking in Spanish to Latinas, afraid of their censure. Their language was not outlawed in their countries. They had a whole lifetime of being immersed in their native tongue; generations, centuries in which Spanish was a first language, taught in school, heard on radio and TV, and read in the newspaper.

If a person, Chicana or Latina, has a low estimation of my native tongue, she also has a low estimation of me. Often with *mexicanas y latinas* we'll speak English as a neutral language. Even among Chicanas we tend to speak English at parties or conferences. Yet, at the same time, we're afraid the other will think we're *agringadas* because we don't speak Chicano Spanish. We oppress each other trying to out-Chicano each other, vying to be the "real" Chicanas, to speak like Chicanos. There is no one Chicano language just as there is no one Chicano experience. A monolingual Chicana whose first language is English or Spanish is just as much a Chicana as one who speaks several variants of Spanish. A Chicana from Michigan or Chicago or Detroit is just as much a Chicana as one from the Southwest. Chicano Spanish is as diverse linguistically as it is regionally.

25   By the end of this century, Spanish speakers will comprise the biggest minority group in the United States, a country where students in high schools and colleges are encouraged to take French classes because French is considered more "cultured." But for a language to remain alive it must be used.[6] By the end of this century English, and not Spanish, will be the mother tongue of most Chicanos and Latinos.

So, if you want to really hurt me, talk badly about my language. Ethnic identity is twin skin to linguistic identity—I am my language. Until I can take pride in my language, I cannot take pride in myself. Until I can accept as legitimate Chicano Texas Spanish, Tex-Mex, and all the other languages I speak, I cannot accept the legitimacy of myself. Until I am free to write bilingually and to switch codes without having always to translate, while I still have to speak English or Spanish when I would rather speak Spanglish, and as long as I have to accommodate the English speakers rather than having them accommodate me, my tongue will be illegitimate.

I will no longer be made to feel ashamed of existing. I will have my voice: Indian, Spanish, white. I will have my serpent's tongue—my woman's voice, my sexual voice, my poet's voice. I will overcome the tradition of silence.

My fingers
move sly against your palm
Like women everywhere, we speak in code
—*Melanie Kaye/Kantrowitz[7]*

"VISTAS," CORRIDOS, Y COMIDA: MY NATIVE TONGUE

In the 1960s, I read my first Chicano novel. It was *City of Night* by John Rechy, a gay Texan, son of a Scottish father and a Mexican mother. For days I walked around in stunned amazement that a Chicano could write and could get published. When I read *I Am Joaquín*[8] I was surprised to see a bilingual book by a Chicano in print. When I saw poetry written in Tex-Mex for the first time, a feeling of pure joy flashed through me. I felt like we really existed as a people. In 1971, when I started teaching High School English to Chicano students, I tried to supplement the required texts with works by Chicanos, only to be reprimanded and forbidden to do so by the principal. He claimed that I was supposed to teach "American" and English literature. At the risk of being fired, I swore my students to secrecy and slipped in Chicano short stories, poems, a play. In graduate school, while working toward a Ph.D., I had to "argue" with one adviser after the other, semester after semester, before I was allowed to make Chicano literature an area of focus.

Even before I read books by Chicanos or Mexicans, it was the Mexican movies I saw at the drive-in—the Thursday night special of $1.00 a carload—that gave me a sense of belonging. "*Vámonos a las vistas*," my mother would call out and we'd all—grandmother, brothers, sister, and cousins—squeeze into the car. We'd wolf down cheese and bologna white bread sandwiches while watching Pedro Infante in melodramatic tearjerkers like *Nosotros los pobres*, the first "real" Mexican movie (that was not an imitation of European movies). I remember seeing *Cuando los hijos se van* and surmising that all Mexican movies played up the love a mother has for her children and what ungrateful sons and daughters suffer when they are not devoted to their mothers. I remember the singing-type "westerns" of Jorge Negrete and Miquel Aceves Mejía. When watching Mexican movies, I felt a sense of homecoming as well as alienation. People who were to amount to something didn't go to Mexican movies, or bailes, or tune their radios to *bolero, rancherita*, and *corrido* music.

30   The whole time I was growing up, there was *norteño* music sometimes called North Mexican border music, or Tex-Mex music, or Chicano music, or *cantina* (bar) music. I grew up listening to *conjuntos*, three- or four-piece bands made up of folk musicians playing guitar, *bajo sexto*, drums, and button accordion, which Chicanos had borrowed from the German immigrants who had come to Central Texas and Mexico to farm and build breweries. In the Rio Grande Valley, Steve Jordan and Little Joe Hernández were popular, and Flaco Jiménez was the accordion king. The rhythms of Tex-Mex music are those of the polka, also adapted from the Germans, who in turn had borrowed the polka from the Czechs and Bohemians.

I remember the hot, sultry evenings when *corridos*—songs of love and death on the Texas-Mexican borderlands—reverberated out of cheap amplifiers from the local *cantinas* and wafted in through my bedroom window.

Corridos first became widely used along the South Texas/Mexican border during the early conflict between Chicanos and Anglos. The *corridos* are usually about Mexican heroes who do valiant deeds against the Anglo oppressors. Pancho Villa's song, "*La cucaracha*," is the most famous one. *Corridos* of John F. Kennedy and his death are still very popular in the Valley. Older Chicanos remember Lydia Mendoza, one of the great border *corrido* singers who was called *la Gloria de Tejas*. Her "*El tango negro*," sung during the Great Depression, made her a singer of the people. The ever-present *corridos* narrated one hundred years of border history, bringing news of events as well as entertaining. These folk musicians and folk songs are our chief cultural mythmakers, and they made our hard lives seem bearable.

I grew up feeling ambivalent about our music. Country-western and rock-and-roll had more status. In the fifties and sixties, for the slightly educated and *agringado* Chicanos, there existed a sense of shame at being caught listening to our music. Yet I couldn't stop my feet from thumping to the music, could not stop humming the words, nor hide from myself the exhilaration I felt when I heard it.

There are more subtle ways that we internalize identification, especially in the forms of images and emotions. For me food and certain smells are tied to my identity, to my homeland. Woodsmoke curling up to an immense blue sky; woodsmoke perfuming my grandmother's clothes, her skin. The stench of cow manure and the yellow patches on the ground; the crack of a .22 rifle and the reek of cordite. Homemade white cheese sizzling in a pan, melting inside a folded *tortilla*. My sister Hilda's hot, spicy *menudo, chile colorado* making it deep red, pieces of *panza* and hominy floating on top. My brother Carito barbequing *fajitas* in the backyard. Even now and 3,000 miles away, I can see my mother spicing the ground beef, pork, and venison with chile. My mouth salivates at the thought of the hot steaming *tamales* I would be eating if I were home.

SÍ LE PREGUNTAS A MI MAMÁ, "¿QUÉ ERES?"

> Identity is the essential core of who we are as individuals, the conscious experience of the self inside.
>
> —*Gershen Kaufman*[9]

35   *Nosotros los* Chicanos straddle the borderlands. On one side of us, we are constantly exposed to the Spanish of the Mexicans, on the other side we hear the Anglos' incessant clamoring so that we forget our language. Among ourselves we don't say *nosotros los americanos, o nosotros los españoles, o nosotros los hispanos.* We say *nosotros los mexicanos* (by *mexicanos* we do not mean citizens of Mexico; we do not mean a national identity, but a racial one). We distinguish between *mexicanos del otro lado* and *mexicanos de este lado.* Deep in our hearts we believe that being Mexican has nothing to do with which country one lives in. Being Mexican is a state of soul—not one of mind, not one of citizenship. Neither eagle nor serpent, but both. And like the ocean, neither animal respects borders.

> *Dime con quien andas y te diré quien eres.*
> (Tell me who your friends are and I'll tell you who you are.)
>
> —*Mexican saying*

Si le preguntas a mi mamá, "¿Qué eres?" te dirá, "Soy mexicana." My brothers and sister say the same. I sometimes will answer *"soy mexicana"* and at others will say *"soy Chicana" o "soy tejana."* But I identified as *"Raza"* before I ever identified as *"mexicana"* or *"Chicana."*

As a culture, we call ourselves Spanish when referring to ourselves as a linguistic group and when copping out. It is then that we forget our predominant Indian genes. We are 70–80 percent Indian.[10] We call ourselves Hispanic[11] or Spanish American or Latin American or Latin when linking ourselves to other Spanish-speaking peoples of the Western hemisphere and when copping out. We call ourselves Mexican American[12] to signify we are neither Mexican nor American, but more the noun "American" than the adjective "Mexican" (and when copping out).

Chicanos and other people of color suffer economically for not acculturating. This voluntary (yet forced) alienation makes for psychological conflict, a kind of dual identity—we don't identify with the Anglo-American cultural values and we don't totally identify with the Mexican cultural values. We are a synergy of two cultures with various degrees of Mexicanness or Angloness. I have so internalized the borderland conflict that sometimes I feel like one cancels out the other and we are zero, nothing, no one. *A veces no soy nada ni nadie. Pero hasta cuando no lo soy, lo soy.*

When not copping out, when we know we are more than nothing, we call ourselves Mexican, referring to race and ancestry; *mestizo* when affirming both our Indian and Spanish (but we hardly ever own our Black) ancestry; Chicano when referring to a politically aware people born and/or raised in the United States; *Raza* when referring to Chicanos; *tejanos* when we are Chicanos from Texas.

40   Chicanos did not know we were a people until 1965 when Cesar Chavez and the farmworkers united and *I Am Joaquin* was published and *la Raza Unida* party was formed in Texas. With that recognition, we became a distinct people. Something momentous happened to the Chicano soul—we became aware of our reality and acquired a name and a language (Chicano Spanish) that reflected that reality. Now that we had a name, some of the fragmented pieces began to fall together—who we were, what we were, how we had evolved. We began to get glimpses of what we might eventually become.

Yet the struggle of identities continues, the struggle of borders is our reality still. One day the inner struggle will cease and a true integration take place. In the meantime, *tenémos que hacer la lucha. ¿Quién está protegiendo los ranchos de mi gente? ¿Quién está tratando de cerrar la fisura entre la india y el blanco en nuestra sangre? El Chicano, si, el Chicano que anda como un ladrón en su propia casa.*

Los Chicanos, how patient we seem, how very patient. There is the quiet of the Indian about us.[13] We know how to survive. When other races have given up their tongue we've kept ours. We know what it is to live under the hammer blow of the dominant *norteamericano* culture. But more than we count the blows, we count the days the weeks the years the centuries the aeons until the white laws and commerce and customs will rot in the deserts they've created, lie bleached. *Humildes* yet proud, *quietos* yet wild, *nosotros los mexicanos-Chicanos* will walk by the crumbling ashes as we go about our business. Stubborn, persevering, impenetrable as stone, yet possessing a malleability that renders us unbreakable, we, the *mestizas* and *mestizos*, will remain.

NOTES

1. Ray Gwyn Smith, *Moorland Is Cold Country*, unpublished book.
2. Irena Klepfisz, *"Di rayze aheym*/The Journey Home," in *The Tribe of Dina: A Jewish Women's Anthology*, Melanie Kaye/Kantrowitz and Irena Klepfisz, eds. (Montpelier, VT: Sinister Wisdom Books, 1986), 49.
3. R. C. Ortega, *Dialectologia Del Barrio*, trans. Hortencia S. Alwan (Los Angeles, CA: R. C. Ortega Publisher & Bookseller, 1977), 132.
4. Eduardo Hernandéz-Chávez, Andrew D. Cohen, and Anthony F. Beltramo, *El Lenguaje de los Chicanos: Regional and Social Characteristics of Language Used by Mexican Americans* (Arlington, VA: Center for Applied Linguistics, 1975), 39.
5. Hernandéz-Chávez, xvii.
6. Irena Klepfisz, "Secular Jewish Identity: Yidishkayt in America," in *The Tribe of Dina*, Kaye/Kantrowitz and Klepfisz, eds., 43.
7. Melanie Kaye/Kantrowitz, "Sign," in *We Speak in Code: Poems and Other Writings* (Pittsburgh, PA: Motheroot Publications, Inc., 1980), 85.
8. Rodolfo Gonzales, *I Am Joaquín/Yo Soy Joaquín* (New York, NY: Bantam Books, 1972). It was first published in 1967.
9. Gershen Kaufman, *Shame: The Power of Caring* (Cambridge, MA: Schenkman Books, Inc., 1980), 68.
10. John R. Chávez, *The Lost Land: The Chicano Images of the Southwest* (Albuquerque, NM: University of New Mexico Press, 1984), 88–90.
11. "Hispanic" is derived from *Hispanis* (*España*, a name given to the Iberian Peninsula in ancient times when it was a part of the Roman Empire) and is a term designated by the U.S. government to make it easier to handle us on paper.
12. The Treaty of Guadalupe Hidalgo created the Mexican American in 1848.
13. Anglos, in order to alleviate their guilt for dispossessing the Chicano, stressed the Spanish part of us and perpetrated the myth of the Spanish Southwest. We have accepted the fiction that we are Hispanic, that is Spanish, in order to accommodate ourselves to the dominant culture and its abhorrence of Indians. Chávez, 88–91.

SUGGESTIONS FOR DISCUSSION

1. Compare your experience of reading Gloria Anzaldúa's polyglot prose with the experiences of others in your class. As we have suggested, the purpose of Anzaldúa's mix of language is to recreate the conditions of the borderland, where the use of one language leaves out or excludes those who know only the other language. But what are readers to do with such prose? If you don't know Spanish, how did you try to make sense of the Spanish words and phrases Anzaldúa uses? Even if you do know Spanish, are you familiar with the terms that she draws from regional dialects? What does your experience reading "How to Tame a Wild Tongue" reveal to you about the nature of cultural encounters at the borderlands?

2. Anzaldúa has composed the chapter "How to Tame a Wild Tongue" like a mosaic, in which she juxtaposes seven separate sections without offering an overarching statement of purpose or meaning to unify the sections. At the same time, the sections do seem to go together in an associative, nonlinear way. Look back over the sections of the chapter to identify how (or whether) the separate parts work together to form a whole. What in your view is the principle of combination that links them together?

3. How is Anzaldúa's representation of the border similar to and different from the one you find in Amitava Kumar's "Passport Photos"?

SUGGESTIONS FOR WRITING

1. Write an essay describing and analyzing your experience reading "How to Tame a Wild Tongue." How do the mix of languages and the fragmentary character of the text put special demands on you as a reader? How and in what sense is this reading experience equivalent to what Anzaldúa calls the "borderland"? What does your position as a reader on the border reveal to you about the nature of encounters across cultures in multicultural America?

2. Write an essay that compares the representations of the border found in "How to Tame a Wild Tongue" and in "Passport Photos." How does Anzaldúa's representation of herself as a *mestiza* of the borderlands compare to Kumar's picture of himself as a passport holder crossing the border? What does each reveal about the movement of people in a postcolonial world? What does each reveal about the position of the United States in a globalized world?

3. Use Anzaldúa's chapter as a model to write your own essay about the contradictory and conflicting meanings of language use and cultural expression in your life. This assignment is meant to be an experiment in writing that asks you to emulate Anzaldúa in incorporating multiple voices, dialects, slangs, and languages and in composing by way of a collage that juxtaposes fragments of thought and experience instead of developing a linear piece of writing with a main point and supporting evidence. To develop ideas for this essay, you might begin by thinking of the different voices, musics, foods, and other cultural forms that are part of your experience, the conflicting ways of life that you have lived, and the multiple identities that you inhabit.

WORKS IN TRANSLATION: GHADA AMER'S HYBRID PLEASURES

— Laura Auricchio

Laura Auricchio teaches in the Critical Studies program at Parsons School of Design. "Works in Translation: Ghada Amer's Hybrid Pleasures" appeared in *Art Journal* in 2001. Auricchio offers an introduction to the installations and embroidery of the Egyptian feminist artist Ghada Amer.

SUGGESTION FOR READING   Laura Auricchio is introducing the artist Ghada Amer to an American audience. Notice how Auricchio opens by describing Ghada Amer's artwork as "uneasy alliances among feminist, Islamic, and postcolonial ideologies." As you read, consider what makes these "alliances" so "uneasy."

1 Ghada Amer's elaborately embroidered paintings, sculptures, and installations add discomfiting overtones to the needlework that has played an important role in feminist art for the past thirty years. Her works forge uneasy alliances among feminist, Islamic, and postcolonial ideologies, yielding hybrids that settle in no one place, culture, or political position. For example, viewers of Amer's *Private Room* (1999) encounter hanging garment bags made of richly colored satin and embroidered with extensive texts culled from the Qur'an. By presenting the

holy Arabic words in French translation, Amer creates a double obstacle that blocks English-speakers' access to the original meanings.

The unsatisfied desire to understand is transformed into material pleasure in Amer's more recent stitched canvases. In *Gray Lisa* (2000) pornographic images of women traced or copied from sex-industry magazines challenge us to rethink female sexuality, while unmotivated drips and tangles of brightly colored thread revel in their own excess, and in an embrace of bodily enjoyment. Amer is one in an emerging generation of artists working to reclaim female pleasure as a subject for feminist art.

A BRIEF HISTORY OF FEMINIST EMBROIDERY ART

Since the 1970s, feminist artists have been challenging the boundaries that divide art from craft, public from domestic, and masculine from feminine by incorporating embroidery into their work. By appropriating this traditionally feminine and domestic form of creativity, artists ranging from Kate Walker to Judy Chicago to Elaine Reichek have called attention to the complicated history of women's needlework. Their sewn

— *Private Rooms* by Ghada Amer, 1999. Embroidery on satin garment bags, variable dimensions (fifteen elements).

objects, canvases, and samplers critique the tradition that has classified sewing as hobby, craft, or ornament, in opposition to the rarefied professional arts of painting and sculpture.

In *The Subversive Stitch: Embroidery and the Making of the Feminine*, Rozsika Parker locates these artists in the context of English sewing practices from the Middle Ages through the twentieth century. "Embroidery," she points out, "has provided a source of pleasure and power for women, while being indissolubly linked to their powerlessness. . . . Paradoxically, while embroidery was employed to inculcate femininity in women, it also enabled them to negotiate the constraints of femininity."[1] Feminist artists who have incorporated embroidery into their work are operating within this paradox, using a traditionally feminine endeavor to forge new models of womanhood and claiming high-art identity for an activity usually relegated to the status of craft.

In the 1970s Kate Walker and Judy Chicago called on the domestic and communal connotations of women's needlework to foster a new model of collaborative art practice. At the Women's Art Alliance in London, Walker took part in a postal art project known as *Feministo* that questioned whether the categories of public and private, home and work, were separate, gendered, and incompatible spheres.[2] The artist members of *Feministo* were women dispersed throughout England who created works of art in their homes and sent them to one another by mail. Walker contributed a sewn work entitled *Sampler* (1978) that featured the embroidered text, "Wife is a four-letter word." One year later, Chicago first displayed her *Dinner Party*, for which more than four hundred men and women had created a table with thirty-nine place settings, each devoted to a woman from the past or to a mythological female figure.[3] Embroidery, used to decorate the place mats, was combined with other traditional crafts, including pottery and china painting.

Elaine Reichek's embroidered works from the 1990s follow in this vein. *When This You See . . .* , Reichek's 1999 installation in the Museum

Manjun by Ghada Amer, 1997. Embroidery on plastic storage closets, 64 x 69¾ in. (163 x 176.9 cm).

of Modern Art, New York, consisted of twenty-five samplers that encourage viewers to consider embroidery in relation to both the history of women and the history of modernism. Speaking of her choice of materials, Reichek explained, "It is deliberate that for tools historically associated with 'male' art—paint, brush, canvas—I substitute media usually seen as related to 'female' activities."[4] In *Sampler (Andy Warhol)* (1997) she performs a double substitution: with its horizontal format, all-over composition, and intertwined "drips" of red, black, and yellow thread, the work appears to be a reduced and sewn version of a Jackson Pollock drip painting. Yet the title does not reference Pollock. Instead, Reichek directs our attention to Andy Warhol's 1983 *Yarn Painting*, which was itself a comment on Pollock's enormous, hyper-masculine paintings of the late 1940s.[5]

PROBLEMS OF HYBRIDITY

Although Amer shares some of her feminist predecessors' sensibilities, her works complicate both their Western focus and their gender ideologies. *Private Room* (2000) introduces the main themes

that course through her oeuvre. In addition to challenging received wisdom regarding both femininity and embroidery, this piece addresses problems of sensual pleasure and cultural hybridity. Installed at the Greater New York Exhibition at P.S. 1, the visually enticing *Private Room* presented fifteen satin garment bags suspended from a rod stretched between two walls. Dyed in rich saturated colors, set off against white walls, and shimmering with reflected light, these otherwise prosaic sacks became a field of visual pleasure. Their sheer beauty beckoned visitors closer; the curious were rewarded with embroidered texts stitched across the surface of each suspended object.

The physical presence of heavy, life-size garment bags evokes the figures of women concealed in chadors increasingly seen in Amer's native Egypt. Amer has expressed dismay at the religious conservatism that often circumscribes the sartorial, personal, and professional choices of Egyptian women. Recalling the less constrained lives of Egyptian women in the 1970s, when her family moved to France, she laments the impact of conservative Islamic law on women's attitudes toward their own bodies. In a recent interview, she described her own experience of this effect: "When I go home, I feel so conscious of my body, every time, conscious of the relationship to the body of everything I wear. Everything is so hidden that if you have a finger out, it becomes the focus of sexuality."[6] Amer has identified her work as "a vengeance against this."

The texts embroidered on the garment bags of *Private Room* present the multiplicity of Islamic attitudes toward women, countering the sometimes monolithic gender politics of religious conservatism. As Amer explains, she "took all the sentences that speak about women from the Qur'an and embroidered them in French." The words of the Qur'an are sacred when written in Arabic. Not wanting to give offense, Amer offers the text in the secular French. Although religious concerns may have loomed large for Amer, the translation nonetheless has a significant impact on viewers' experiences of the work.[7] The scale of the piece was partly determined by the Qur'an itself, as the number of embroidered bags was set by her wish to include every text in which women are mentioned. Setting all of the statements side by side, she highlights the diversity of viewpoints expressed in the holy book and takes issue with the narrow perspective on women promulgated by some Egyptian authorities today.

10   Turning our attention from content to form, we find that Amer's text functions like the Egyptian woman's exposed finger: it is the unattainable focus of the viewer's desire.[8] Written out in near rows of clear capital letters in a Western European language familiar to Amer's fellow residents of France, the words of the Qur'an promise to yield their meanings to the attentive reader. Even so, *Private Room* requires us to grapple with the problem of reading across languages and among cultures. First exhibited at ARCO in Madrid, and later in New York, the work addressed local audiences in a language native neither to them nor to the Qur'an's original readers. Spanish- or English-speaking audiences who encountered the Qur'an as mediated by Amer's French translation struggled, to a greater or lesser degree, to understand the foreign words. Amer insists that the linguistic and cultural distances between viewer and work cannot be fully bridged. Try as we may to capture the original meaning, satisfaction will always be denied us.

For instance, English-speaking readers may wrestle with the meaning of one passage that offers guidance in selecting a bride. Amer's translation reads: "Une esclave qui croit, a plus de valeur qu'une femme libre et polythéiste." (A slave who believes is more valuable than a free and polytheistic woman.) The original text is from the Qur'anic book Sura al-Baqarah 2:221 (The Cow). English translations struggle with the terms that Amer has rendered in French as *polythéiste* and *libre*. Three translations available on the Internet provide a sampling: "Wed not idolatresses till they believe; for lo! A believing bondwoman is better than an idolatress though she please you; and give not your daughters in marriage to idolaters till they believe, for lo! A believing slave is better than an idolater though he please you." Or, "Do not marry unbelieving women, until they believe: A slave woman who believes is better than an unbelieving woman, even though she allures you. Nor marry [your girls] to unbelievers until they believe: A man slave who believes is better than an unbeliever, even though he allures you." One also finds this rendering: "And do not marry the idolatresses until they believe, and certainly a believing maid is better than an idolatrous woman, even though she should please you; and do not give [believing women] in marriage to idolaters until they believe, and certainly a believing servant is better than an idolater, even though he should please you."[9] These fine distinctions will always escape us, confounding our attempts to pin down a meaning.

Just as the Qur'an, already uprooted from its native tongue in her art, will never fully settle into one language, Amer herself is almost always identified as a figure in exile. In the exhibition reviews that have introduced her to an international public her name, like Homer's "rosy-fingered" Dawn, is rarely seen without an epithet. Barry Schwabsky tells of "the Egyptian-born, French-educated" artist.[10] Writing for the French magazine *L'Oeil*, Eric de Chassey discusses Amer, "born in Cairo . . . lives in New York, following a lengthy stay in Paris."[11] Amer's exhibiting venues have also highlighted her condition of exile. At the 1999 Venice Biennale, her works were in the large *Aperto* section, devoted to an international mixture of artists rather than those selected to represent their homelands, housed in pavilions sponsored by their countries. Amer is always out of place. Her international past defies attempts to pin her to any one nation or culture. Whether in Paris or New York, Venice or Madrid, she appears in translation. Wherever she may be, her identity is inflected with the traces of other cultures, and she continually spills across local boundaries.

In interviews Amer both calls attention to and voices concerns about her identity as a "postcolonial subject," with claims to several cultures but fully embraced by none.[12] Recently, she described herself as feeling "a little French," having lived in Paris for twenty-one years.[13] Her feeling, though, was not sufficient for the French government, which has three times rejected her applications for citizenship. Speaking with Nigel Ryan in 1998, she granted that seeing her work as the product of "a woman from a Muslim society" can be "liberating" and can help to "command an audience."[14] Yet, acknowledging the potential pitfalls of that tag, she warned that such an exclusive focus could also serve "simply to stereotype, to restrict." "I cannot resent people's interest on this level," she said, "but I cannot embrace it fully."

Amer's concerns about the stultifying effect of a "postcolonial" label echo anxieties voiced by several contemporary theorists about the resurrection of the postcolonial "hybrid" as a figure of fascination. In a historical analysis of hybridity, now an important term in cultural criticism, Robert J. C. Young offers a deceptively simple definition of the term: "Hybridity implies a disruption and forcing together of any unlike living things."[15] Young reminds us that hybridity emerged from nineteenth-century investigations of botanical or biological cross-breeding. Indeed, apprehensions about hybridity gained currency within an anxious discourse on racial identity, as the fear of miscegenation found expression in debates over whether Africans belonged to the same human species as Europeans. Young suggests that a similar presupposition of clear and separate races, if not breeds, remains latent in the writings of some postcolonial thinkers who see and use cultural hybridity as a liberating strategy. The very concept of hybridity, he warns, runs the risk of reifying difference by positing a prior state of unadulterated purity, when cultural identities were both distinct and intact.

15   A more optimistic perspective, however, might see the hybridity of Amer's *Private Room*—and, more generally, the hybridity of postcolonial societies—as revealing the essentially mixed and always unstable nature of language and social relations. Rather than presuming preexisting differences among cultures, the artist who makes hybridity visible highlights a constant state of interaction among all cultures and shatters illusions of cultural purity. The critic Yuri Lotman's notion of the "semiosphere" offers one such optimistic model. His semiosphere encompasses "the semiotic space necessary for the existence and functioning of languages," which are marked by asymmetry, heterogeneity, and interaction.[16] Not a simple "sum total of different languages," the semiosphere is intricately "transected by boundaries of different levels, boundaries of different languages and even of texts."[17]

Perhaps we can recast Amer's series of literal and implied translations as an ever-changing system. Rather than understanding the process of translation as an inevitably failed attempt at replication, Lotman sees translation as a crucial and on-going process that creates meaning. He calls translation "a primary mechanism of consciousness. To express something in another language is a way of understanding it."[18] Since two languages often do not possess exactly equivalent words, every translation generates information by introducing or uncovering additional meanings.

Problems of dialogue and translation take center stage once again in Amer's *Majnun* (1997). Similar in structure to *Private Room*, *Majnun* features a row of life-size storage closets formed from orange plastic stretched over internal rectangular frames. A French text translated from an older Arabic text is embroidered in red thread across the surface. The embroidered fragment is from a tragic Persian love story in which a young suitor named Majnun writes letter after letter to his beloved Leila, but receives no response. Devastated by the apparent rejection, Majnun dies of a broken heart, and the silent but desiring Leila follows him to the grave. Amer gives form to Leila's voicelessness by imagining her as an Arabian Echo, who can form no words of her own but only reproduce the words of Majnun, her Narcissus. It is these words that Amer embroiders. When written by Majnun, the text conveys desire and longing. Yet when mimicked by the powerless Leila, the words become travesties that block fulfillment. The impossibility of dialogue sounds the lovers' death knell.

By giving voice to Leila's silence, *Majnun* offers an equivocal answer to the questions posed by Gayatri Spivak in her seminal essay, "Can the Subaltern Speak?"[19] Spivak maintains that the logic of colonialism permits the colonized to attain representation only through the language and voice of the colonizer. Focusing on the conditions that relegate women from former European colonies to political and social silence, Spivak encourages these women to create their own voices by interrupting the colonist's monologue. Although Amer's Leila can speak only in the colonizer's language (French, in this case), and can voice only the words of the man who desires her, Amer herself performs the kind of intervention that Spivak advocates. Like generations of women before her, Amer uses the medium of embroidery for her text, employing a traditional realm of women's subordination to speak about and against that oppression.

NOTES

1. Rozsika Parker, *The Subversive Stitch: Embroidery and the Making of the Feminine* (London: The Women's Press, 1994), 11.
2. Ibid., 207–9.
3. Ibid., 209–10. On Chicago's more recent collaborative embroidery projects see Paula Harper, "The Chicago Resolutions," *Art in America* 88, no. 6 (June 2000): 112–5, 137–8.
4. Elaine Reichek and Laura Engel, "Commentary: Mother/Daughter Dresses," *Fiberarts* 20, no. 3 (November–December 1993): 9, and cited in Beth Handler, "Projects 67: Elaine Reichek," exhibition brochure (New York: Museum of Modern Art, 1999).
5. Handler, "Reichek."
6. Sarah Robbins, "Love in Threads," *Australian Style* 49 (March 2001): 66–70, esp. 69.
7. Marilu Knode, "Interview with Ghada Amer," *New Art Examiner* 27, no. 4 (December 1999–January 2000): 38–39, esp. 38.
8. On desire in Amer, see Candice Breitz, "Ghada Amer/The Modeling of Desire," *NKA Journal of Contemporary African Art*, no. 5 (Fall–Winter, 1996): 14–16.
9. M. M. Pickthall, *Meaning of the Glorious Quran* (London: Islamic Computing Centre); M. H. Shakir, *The Holy Qur'an* (Elmhurst, New York: Tahrike Tarsile Qur'an, Inc.); and A. Yusufali, *Meanings of the Glorious Quran* (London: Islamic Computing Centre).
10. Barry Schwabsky, "Ghada Amer: Deitch Projects, New York," *Artext*, no. 70 (August–October 2000): 84.
11. Eric de Chassey, "La peinture est vivante: Dix artistes de moins de 40 ans," *L'Oeil*, no. 489 (October 1997): 52–61, esp. 56.
12. Homi Bhabha, arguably one of the most influential figures in postcolonial criticism, has described "postcolonial perspectives" as emerging "from the colonial testimony of Third World countries. They formulate their critical revisions around issues of cultural difference, social authority, and political discrimination in order to reveal the antagonistic and ambivalent moments within the 'rationalizations' of modernity." Homi K. Bhabha, *The Location of Culture* (London: Routledge, 1994), 171.
13. Sarah Robbins, "Love in Threads," *Australian Style* 49 (March 2001): 66–70, esp. 66.
14. Nigel Ryan, "A Stitch in Time," *Medina* (April 1998): 80.
15. Robert J. C. Young, *Colonial Desire: Hybridity in Theory, Culture, and Race* (London: Routledge, 1995), 26.
16. Yuri Lotman, *Universe of the Mind: A Semiotic Theory of Culture* (Bloomington: Indiana University Press, 2000), 123. For a summary of approaches to this hybridity, see Nikos Papastergiadis, "Restless Hybrids," *Third Text*, no. 32 (Autumn 1995): 9–18.
17. Lotman, 138.
18. Ibid., 127.
19. Gayatri Spivak, "Can the Subaltern Speak?" in Patrick Williams and Laura Chrisman, eds., *Colonial Discourse and Post-Colonial Theory: A Reader* (London: Harvester Whatsheaf, 1993), 66–111.

SUGGESTIONS FOR DISCUSSION

1. Laura Auricchio locates Ghada Amer's artwork in a tradition of feminist embroidery but then says Amer complicates "both their Western focus and their gender ideologies." What is Auricchio getting at here? What is the nature of this complication?

2. As you can see from the title of this reading, translation is one of its main themes. What does Auricchio see at stake in the fact that Amer has translated the Arabic text of the Qur'an into French? Notice Auricchio offers a number of translations of the passage from the Qur'anic book Sura al-Baqarah (The Cow). What is the point of these multiple translations?

3. Auricchio titles one of the sections of this reading "The Problems of Hybridity." What exactly does the term *hybridity* mean in this context? What is the "problem" Auricchio refers to? Consider here the two different perspectives on hybridity offered by Robert J. C. Young and Yuri Lotman. How is the term *hybridity* linked to the notion of the postcolonial?

SUGGESTIONS FOR WRITING

1. Use the information and analysis in this reading to write your own explanation of Ghada Amer's installation *Private Room*. Consider what the title *Private Room* signifies about the design and meaning of this installation.

2. Auricchio says that Ghada Amer is "almost always identified as a figure in exile." Write an essay that explains why this is so.

3. As Auricchio notes, *hybridity* is "an important term in cultural criticism." What makes this term so important? What does it reveal? Write an essay that offers your own definition of hybridity and that explains what the "problem" of hybridity is, as Auricchio describes it. Use this discussion to analyze an example of hybridity you have chosen to illustrate the concept.

WIRED CULTURE   Transnational Networks

To learn more about political organizations, visit www.ablongman.com/george/139

The Internet has provided a new platform for political organizing that groups around the world now use routinely to publicize their causes. It has also enabled the formation of transnational networks of activists to organize campaigns and demonstrations, to work out shared political positions, and to keep their ideas before the public eye. The Zapatista National Liberation Army (EZLN) in Mexico pioneered the political use of the Internet in the 1980s to overcome their geographical and media isolation in the Mexican state of Chiapas, to communicate their uprising for social justice, to establish support networks internationally, and to link their struggle to an emerging worldwide antiglobalization movement. Since the demonstrations against the World Trade Organization (WTO) in Seattle in 1999, antiglobalization activists have formed transnational networks such as the World Social Forum (WSF) to organize an international opposition to the neoliberal policies of the transnational corporations and the WTO, the International Monetary Fund (IMF), and the World Bank. The Call from Social Movements below will give you an idea of how the WSF seeks to build globalization-from-below on an international scale.

WORLD SOCIAL FORUM: CALL FROM SOCIAL MOVEMENTS

The first World Social Forum (WSF) was held in Porto Allegre, Brazil, in January 2001, when 10,000 gathered for a week of workshops, speeches, and concerts. The following year, 70,000 attended the second WSF in Porto Allegre. The WSF is not a political party. Instead it is a loose network of social movements linked to one another much as their Web sites are linked on the Internet in nonhierarchical and intensely interactive ways. The following "Call from Social Movements" comes from the Fifth World Social Forum that took place in India in 2005.

SUGGESTION FOR READING Notice that the "Call from Social Movements" is written in the genre and classic style of a political manifesto. The opening paragraphs form a preamble that marks the occasion and presents general principles. As you read the "Agenda of Struggles" that follows, consider what the WSF supports, what it demands, and what are its calls for action.

Call From Social Movements For Mobilizations Against The War, Neoliberalism, Exploitation And Exclusion

Another World Is Possible

1   We are social movements gathered in the 5th World Social Forum. The great success of the plural and massive participation in the Forum gives us the possibility and the responsibility to organize more and better our campaigns and mobilizations, to expand and strengthen our struggles.

Four years ago the collective and global call for ANOTHER WORLD IS POSSIBLE broke the lie that neoliberal domination is unavoidable as well as the acceptance of the "normality" of war, of social inequalities, racism, casts, patriarchy, imperialism and the destruction of the environment. As people take this truth as their own their strength becomes unstoppable and it starts materialising in concrete actions of resistance, for demands and proposals.

Therefore what is new about our proposal is the outbreak and the scale of the social movements in all continents and their ability to build within diversity new convergences and common actions at global level.

In that frame, tens of millions of men and women were mobilized in all corners of the world for peace, against the war and the invasion led by Bush against Iraq. Summits like the G8 and the WTO, the IMF and the World Bank, where few intend to decide for everybody, were questioned and de-legitimized by the action of social movements. Popular struggles in defence of nature, the rights of people and the common good, against their privatization, such as in Bolivia, Uruguay and other peoples, demonstrated the possibility of creating a crisis for neoliberal domination. New spaces for political and social struggle were opened to us.

5   Neoliberalism is incapable of offering a dignified and democratic future to humanity. Nevertheless, nowadays it again takes the initiative responding to its crisis of legitimacy with force, militarization, repression, criminalization of social struggles, political authoritarianism and ideological reaction. Millions of men and women suffer every day. We want here to remember the war in Congo that has already caused four million victims. For all that, another world is not only possible, but necessary and urgent.

Conscious that we still have a long way ahead of us, we call all movements of the world to fight for peace, human, social and democratic rights, for the right of people to decide their destiny and for the immediate cancellation of foreign debt from the countries of the South, from the AGENDA that we share in the 5th World Social Forum:

AGENDA OF STRUGGLES

- We call all organizations and social movements which have participated in the World Social Forum and those who could not be in Porto Alegre, to work together in the campaign for the IMMEDIATE and UNCONDITIONAL CANCELLATION OF THE FOREIGN and illegitimate DEBT of the countries of the South, beginning with the countries victims of tsunami and other that have undergone terrible disasters and crisis in the recent months.

- We support Social Movements from the South that declare themselves CREDITORS of historical, social and ecological debts. We demand the end of the implementation of projects and "integration agreements" which facilitate the looting of natural resources form the countries of the South.

- We support demands from peasant and fisherfolk Social Movements in areas affected by the Tsunami, in order to have the resources for emergency aid and reconstruction managed directly by local communities in order to avoid new debts, colonization and militarization.

10
- After two years of the Iraq invasion, global opposition to the war is constantly increasing. It is time for the anti-war movement to increase actions and do not retreat.

- We demand the end of the Iraq occupation. We demand the US to stop threatening Iran, Venezuela and other countries. We commit to establish more contacts with the occupation forces in Iraq and the Middle East. We will strengthen our campaigns against transnationals committed with the invasion, we support soldiers who oppose to participate in the war and we defend activists that have been persecuted for being against the war. We call all movements to organize on March 19th a global day of actions to demand the retreat of US troops from Iraq. No more war!

- We support all campaigns for disarmament and demilitarization, including the campaign against US military bases in the world, the campaigns for nuclear disarmament, for the control of arms trade and the cut on military spending.

- Under the pretext of "Free Trade" neoliberal capitalism advances under the weakness of the US, in the de-regulation of economies and the "legalization" of privileges for transnational corporations through free trade Agreements (FTAs). After the failure of FTAA due to popular pressure, now Central America and other countries have been obliged to subscribe to Bilateral Free Trade Agreements that we the people reject. In Europe the European Union Bolkenstein directive wants to impose the complete privatization of public services. We call everyone to mobilize during the Global Action Rally, from April 10th to 17th, in the Summit of the People of the Americas, in Mar del Plata, Argentina, in November 2005; and during the 6th WTO meeting in Hong Kong, in December 2005.

- We support the Women's World March which is organizing a campaign of global feminist actions throughout the world starting from São Paulo on March 8th and ending on October 17th in Burkina Faso, to restate their commitment with in the struggle against neoliberalism, patriarchy, exclusion and domination. We call all movements to organize feminist actions during this period against free trade, sex trade, militarization and food sovereignty.

15
- We support the efforts of social movements and organizations that promote the struggle for dignity, justice, equality and human rights specially the dalit movement; afro-descendents, indigenous people, romas, burakumins and the most oppressed and repressed sectors of society.

- We call for mass mobilization against the G8 meeting in Scotland on July 2nd to 8th. We will take to the streets and will participate in the counter-meeting in Edinburgh and Gleneagles. We demand: poverty to go to history, to stop the war, to cancel debt and impose a global tax on financial transactions to finance development.

- We protest against neoliberal policies and the EU military support in Latin America. We call for a solidarity mobilization among the peoples during the Meeting from Latin American and European Union Presidents in May 2006, in Vienna, Austria.

■ We struggle for the universal right to healthy and sufficient food. We struggle for the right of the peoples, nations and peasants to produce their own food. We manifest against subsidies to exports which destroy the economies of rural communities. Let's avoid food dumping.

■ We reject GMO foods because besides threatening our health and the environment, they are an instrument for five transnationals to have control of all markets. We reject patents on any form of life and in special on seeds, since the intention is the appropriation of our resources and the knowledge associated to them. We demand the Agrarian Reform as a strategy to allow the access of peasants to land, and healthy and sufficient food, and not to be concentrated in the hands of transnationals and latifundiários.

20 ■ We demand for actions against peasants around the world to be called off, for the immediate liberation of peasants and political prisoners in the world, and the end of militarization of rural areas.

■ We support sustainable production based in the preservation of natural resources: soil, water, forest, air, biodiversity, water resources etc. We support the development of organic and agro-ecological production.

■ We call for mobilizations during the national peasant day on April 17th; and on the anniversary of the death of Mr. Lee on September 10th against the WTO.

■ We support campaigns and struggles in defence of water as a common good, against its privatization and for the recognition of the right to access to water as a human right, such as the campaign "No to Suez in Latin America". We invite all to participate in International Forum from March 18th to 20th in Geneva.

■ We share the demands to build an alliance between social movements and networks for a "World contract on climate: a solar world is possible". Energy is the right to life and it is a common good. The struggle against poverty and climate change demands sustainable energy to be among the priorities of initiatives

and campaigns from social movements. We support the international march on climate in November.

25 ■ The "Social Responsibility of Transnationals" did not manage to eliminate abuses and crimes committed by transnationals. It must be seriously challenged. Movements will work together to take power away from transnationals and stop their abuses and crimes. Communities must have the freedom to protect themselves, their environment and society against the power of transnationals.

■ We support campaigns against transnationals that violate human, social and trade union's rights, such as those against Nestlé and Coca-Cola in Colombia; and Pepsi and Coca-Cola in India.

■ We support the struggle of the Palestinian people for their fundamental and national rights, including the right to return, based on the international law and in the UN resolutions.

■ We ask the international community and governments to impose political and economic sanctions to Israel, including an embargo on Arms. We call social movements to also mobilize for de-investments and boycotts. These efforts aim at pressuring Israel to implement international resolutions and to respect the decision of the International Court of Justice for the immediate stop and destruction of the illegal apartheid wall and the end of occupation.

■ We support Israeli activists for peace and the refusnik for their struggle against the occupation.

30 ■ We condemn the unfair embargo of Cuba and demand a fair trial to the five Cubans who have been arrested in the US. We also demand the withdrawal of military foreign troops in Haiti.

■ We recognize diversity in sexual orientation as an expression of an alternative world and we condemn mercantilization. Movements commit to participate in the struggle against exclusion based on identity, gender and homophobia. We will unite our voices against all forms of mercantilization of the body of women and GLBT.

■ We support the process of building a global network of social movements committed to defend migrants, refugees and displaced peoples. Neoliberalism and the policies of "the war against terror" have increased the criminalization of migrants, the militarization of borders, clandestine operations and the access to cheap labour. We support the campaign to ratify the United Nations Convention for the rights of migrants, which no government from the North wants to accept. We support the campaign to establish an independent organism to sanction governments that do not respect the Geneva Convention for refugees and the rights of migrants.

■ We support campaigns and struggles for children's rights, against labour and sexual exploitation, against the trade of children and sexual tourism.

■ We support the call of the excluded, of those with no voice, to develop an active solidarity campaign to propel a world march in which the oppressed and excluded of the planet will raise their voice to conquer the right to a dignified life.

35   ■ From September 14th to 16th, in the general Assembly of the UN, government heads of the whole world will make decisions about the agrarian reform in the United Nations and will revise their commitments to eradicate poverty. They are mainly responsible for the critical situation of humanity now. We support the call for international networks which invite to mobilize globally on September 10th for a new world democratic order and against poverty and the war.

■ We support the call for a mobilization on November 17th, international student day, in defence of public education, against privatization and the trans-nationalization of education.

■ In solidarity with Venezuela , the youth of the world is calling to participate in the 16th World Youth Festival and of the Students from Venezuela between August 7th and 15th.

■ Communication is a fundamental human right. We support the call for mobilizations during the World Conference of the Communication Society, in Tunis from November 16th to 18th. We support the call for a strong international convention about Cultural Diversity and we oppose the mercantilization of information and communication from the WTO.

■ We support social economy as a concrete expression of an alternative for a fair, mutual, democratic and equitable development.

40   ■ In defence of public health and against its privatization, we call all peoples of the world for a permanent struggle. We call for mobilizations during the General Assembly in Defence of the Health of the People, in Cuenca, Ecuador, in 2005 and in the World Health Forum during the World Social Forum in Africa in 2007.

This is a small demonstration of the struggles of social movements

GLOBALISE STRUGGLE, GLOBALISE HOPE!

SUGGESTIONS FOR DISCUSSION

1. The slogan of the World Social Forum is "Another World Is Possible." What does this mean? What are the political principles that form the basis of the WSF? What is the WSF's criticism of "neoliberal capitalism"? You may need to share information or do a bit of research to understand the term *neoliberalism* because it is central to the WSF's analysis of contemporary politics.

2. Visit the WSF Web site, browse through it, and follow some of the links. What do you learn about the nature and purpose of the WSF and its allied social movements?

3. Consider the Internet as a tool of political organizing and networking. What does it make possible that activists and organizations could not do before? In what sense is the Internet changing the nature of political life, in the United States and worldwide? What examples besides the WSF can you cite as evidence of these changes?

SUGGESTIONS FOR WRITING

1. Imagine you are writing to a friend to explain what the World Social Forum is and what it stands for. You may or may not be sympathetic with its goals and you can certainly indicate your own views of the WSF. Make sure, however, that you accurately describe the WSF and explain what it is seeking to accomplish.

2. As noted above, the Zapatistas in Chiapas, Mexico, were one of the first political movements to make extensive use of the Web. Do some research on the Zapatistas to write a report on their struggles and how they have used the Internet. (A good place to start is the Web site "Zapatistas in Cyberspace: A Guide to Analysis and Resources" at http://www.eco.utexas.edu/Homepages/Faculty/Cleaver/zapsincyber.html.)

3. Write an essay on the political uses of the Internet that focuses on a particular group, cause, or organization. Use the essay to do a case study of how the Web can be used to form political networks. Pay particular attention to the design of the group's Web site. How is it set up? What information does it contain? What links does it have? What does it ask visitors to do?

PERSPECTIVES — Bob Marley, Reggae, and Rastas

To learn more about world music, visit
www.ablongman.com/george/140

Lee "Scratch" Perry, an early producer of reggae and one of its "conceptular" innovators in Jamaica, explains the beginning of the sound in the late 1960s:

> See, at them time, me used to go out town and stay late, drink some beer, thing like that. And one night me walking past a Pocomania church and hear the people inside a wail. And me catch the vibration and say, "Boy! Let's make a sound fe catch the vibration of the people!" Them was in the spirit and them tune me spiritually. That's where the thing come from, 'cos them Poco people getting sweet!"

Perry goes on to describe the reggae beat he helped to pioneer: "And when the people hear what I man do them hear a different beat, a waxy beat—like you stepping in glue. Them hear a different bass, a rebel bass, coming at you like sticking a gun." With its roots in Afro-Jamaican religious traditions and the secular sounds of the Caribbean islands and American R&B, the "waxy beat" and "rebel bass" of reggae became the music of the oppressed, a revolutionary chant against neocolonialism that arose from the ghettoes and shantytowns of Jamaica and quickly spread the message of the Rastafari movement and Third World liberation to Europe, North America, and Africa. There are many influential and important reggae musicians—Jimmy Cliff, Toots and the Maytals, Burning Spear, Peter Tosh, and Steel Pulse, to name just a few. None, however, has so captured the popular imagination as Bob Marley and the Wailers. If anything, Marley's life and music have, since his death in 1981, taken on the stature of a prophetic performance to "chant down Babylon." The two readings in this section offer perspectives on the meaning of Marley's life and music and the complex intertwining of reggae, rastas, and revolution.

GET UP, STAND UP: THE REDEMPTIVE POETICS OF BOB MARLEY

— Anthony Bogues

Anthony Bogues is currently chair of Africana Studies at Brown University and was formerly a journalist, labor organizer, and political activist in Jamaica. "Get Up, Stand Up" appears in his book *Black Heretics, Black Prophets: Radical Political Intellectuals* (2003).

SUGGESTION FOR READING   Anthony Bogues opens by noting "two competing contemporary representations of Marley." By the time he reaches the final paragraph, however, Bogues says, "In the end, there is no mystery about Marley's international appeal." As you read, consider how Bogues moves from the competing representations in the beginning to his unequivocal judgment at the end.

> Mi see myself as a revolutionary . . . who nah tek no bribe. Fight it single-handed with Music.
>
> —*Bob Marley*, Catch a Fire *(video)*

> I man know sey is my work to go out in a Babylon to do the work I do.
>
> —*Bob Marley*

> Revelation reveals the truth . . .
>
> —*Bob Marley* (Revolution, 1974)

INTRODUCTION

1 The figure of Robert Nesta Marley is iconic. T-shirts, videos, the entire paraphernalia of international commodification and communication, including the Walt Disney theme park of freedom, seem to work overtime to make the Rastaman who "chanted down Babylon" into a fangless musician, a symbol of exotic difference, trapped and captured in an illusionary rainbow world of dreamers. Whenever I listen to, think of, or teach about Marley, two impulses take hold of me. The first is that of Caribbean pride, that a figure from "region" could have such a high international profile. The second is recognition of the ways in which hegemonic ideology operates, how it is able to rework the most radical ideas and practices of individuals into a mélange of difference, and then claim ownership. This process, which Joy James has called "depoliticizing representations," can also be seen in the dominant representation of Martin Luther King, Jr. King's life, thought, and praxis fold into the "I have a dream" speech, and he becomes the dreamer who adorns a U.S. postage stamp. In the case of Bob Marley's "One Love," a Rastafarian phrase meaning unity and respect becomes the theme song of the former British empire to greet the new millennium.

In both these processes radicalism is expunged. Erased is the radical King who is his last years attempted to put together a coalition of labor, the poor, and African-Americans in an effort to fight against what he called the triple evils: "the problem of racism, the problem of economic exploitation and the problem of war." Marley is no longer the defiant Rasta rebel from the Jamaican ghetto of Trench Town, railing against the "Babylon system . . . as vampire, sucking the blood of the sufferer," but the light-skinned Jamaican Rastafarian who in transcending racial boundaries and countries also moves beyond race, and therefore belongs no longer to the black radical tradition out of which he sprang. Common to both King and Marley was a universalism, a commitment to social change, and the fact that both were prophetic voices whose visions of a new world were rooted in struggles against racial domination and oppression. It is the irony of ironies that in death the "Buffalo soldier" has been co-opted by the ideological processes of capitalism, and that the man who, the night before he was murdered, saw the coming of the Lord in the masses of the people of the world rising up for freedom, has a public holiday declared for him while thousands of young black men continue to live in America's prisons.

In this essay I want to resituate Marley, to suggest that he, like King, belonged to a prophetic black radical tradition. Furthermore, I hope to demonstrate that Marley *saw* himself as part of this tradition. Marley represented one segment of the voice of Rastafari. His lyrical and musical weapons were used in an effort to describe events while signaling hope for the oppressed. The revolution he sang and spoke about was a form of *symbolic insurgency*, a way to replace the old ideas about racial oppression and exploitation in general and to promote a radical desire for a new life. Such an analysis of Marley does not ignore the way in which black popular culture is commodified, becomes deformed and incorporated. Rather, it agrees with Stuart Hall that while commodification occurs, we should

see in the figures and the repertoires on which popular culture draws . . . [that] black popular culture has enabled the surfacing, inside the mixed and contradictory modes even of some mainstream popular culture, of elements of a discourse that is different—other forms of life, other traditions of representation.

Marley understood this process of commodification in the ways he referred to the producer Chris Blackwell as his "translator." He consistently navigated the music business, trying not to get trapped in its glitz and glamour, since for him the justification for the entire enterprise was the use of his artistic gifts as a medium of prophetic social criticism. Thus we get two competing contemporary representations of Marley. The first is his incorporation into hegemonic modes of representation symbolized by the prominent billboard with his picture in Times Square in New York City, and the second is the way he is appropriated by people who are marginalized by their own societies. This latter mode of representation is demonstrated by the many instances of his music being played and sung with hope in the *musseques*, *favelas*, *bidonvilles*, and inner cities of the world.

5   Adebayo Ojo writes about this kind of representation and appropriation in Nigeria: "It is fascinating to see so many ardent militant fans prance away to Marley's tunes, mumbling substitute phrases for his lyrics . . . many fans are only sustained by [a] knowledge of Bob Marley's . . . uncompromising stand for equal rights and justice." It is Marley's prophetic call for the oppressed to "Get Up, Stand Up" that has made him such a popular radical icon for many today. If, as Raymond Williams argues, hegemony is not static but constantly shifts its internal arguments and symbols while renewing and re-creating itself, then inside the contestation within the domain of the popular, the successful integration of Marley was crucial. The "depoliticized representation" of Marley, then, is of a successful singer and cultural icon, not a prophetic social critic, since hegemony selects, bends, and reshapes figures who contest it. Thus one secondary purpose of this chapter is to attempt to untangle some of those bends done on Marley. . . .

SYMBOLIC INSURGENCY AND PROPHECY

Sylvia Wynter argues that within the framework of the symbolic, the central "strategy of the politics of black culture is the counter invention of the self." Attached to this counterinvention, Wynter tells us, is an ultimate "revolutionary demand, the demand for happiness now." However, this demand for immediate happiness can be fulfilled only in the symbolic counterworld. Wynter tells us:

. . . the power of the black counter culture lies in its symbolic negativity, thus its politics is a politics that can never be realized except in that symbolic world—Zion—in which all structures of power having been overturned, the autonomous, separate concept of politics—will have been made obsolescent and meaningless.

I want to suggest that to achieve this "symbolic negativity," Marley engages in practices of *symbolic insurgency*. The nature of this insurgency resides in two things. First are the ways in which Marley uses words in his texts, and second is the reordering of questions of history of the black diaspora and the emphasis he places upon mental slavery. We know that a central aspect of domination is what Pierre Bourdieu calls the "formation and reformation of mental structures." The crucial orders for this process are of course knowledge production and the creation of a symbolic universe. Symbolic power, Bourdieu suggests, is "a power of constructing reality." To practice *symbolic insurgency* means that an individual is engaged in consistent efforts to rearrange the ways in which mainstream reality is both constructed and explained. This of course breaks the pattern of social integration and shatters the legitimacy of the dominant order. *Symbolic insurgency* does not have to lead to the overthrow of an oppressive system, but it creates everyday spaces of hope. Its primary preoccupation is with creating and contesting the old order at the level of ideas and the self. It punctures the self-image of the old order, critiquing its moral bankruptcy while seeking to profoundly influence people. In Marley's case it is a call for people to sing "redemption songs," to emancipate oneself from mental slavery.

Second, we should note that in the Jewish tradition, Michael Walzer has pointed out, prophecy, because of its rootedness in local particularism, is not utopian. In the black tradition this is not so. What makes Marley an outstanding prophetic critic is that he was able to weave together some of the doctrinal tenets of Rastafari, join them to the local knowledge embodied in proverbs, and then present them in a powerful critique of the system, producing a Zion train that would leave Babylon oppression behind. Within the Africana tradition of prophecy we can distinguish the feature of *mantic* (a possession and declaration of knowledge) and concern for the wider "moral community at a social and political level." On all these accounts Marley qualifies as prophet. What was distinctive about his practice is what

is distinctive about Rastafari, its capacity to overturn core elements of the dominant symbolic order. Of course Marley took the teachings of Rastafari to the world and was centrally responsible for making reggae an international phenomenon. But the overarching motivation for his work was, as he said, doing the business of "my fathers work." In Marley's practice, popular culture became a site for ideological struggle. Marley as prophet practiced *symbolic insurgency* in a struggle for the minds of the oppressed, rallying them to Zion in the chants against Babylon. His last three albums are ample evidence of this.

From all reports it seems that sometime in 1978, Marley decided that he needed to do a trilogy. The names of the albums were chosen: *Black Survival*, *Uprising*, and *Confrontation*. Given Rastafari attention to the meaning of words, we can be assured that the names of the albums had profound significance. One possible meaning is that at this moment of history, black people had been able to survive, but that continued black survival meant first an uprising and then confrontation. These three titles are also moments of struggle for the dethroning of the hegemonic symbolic order of Babylon. The *Confrontation* album cover is interesting in this regard, since it has Marley on a white horse, dressed in white tunic and gold shirt with a green breastplate, barefooted, his riding blanket red and gold with a faint touch of green on the inside, dreadlocks flying while he is about to slay a dragon. He is dressed in the manner of an Ethiopian, but he is about to slay a dragon. So a cover that at first blush would make the Western mind, and those of us trained in its tradition, think about English mythology and St. George is not quite accurate. On the other side of the album cover is an Ethiopian illustration featuring the famous nineteenth century battle of Adowa. Taken together, this album jacket indicates a line of continuity between Marley's work and that of defeating the colonial attempt to conquer Ethiopia. What is happening here in this strange symbolic portrait is what has been called "symbolic inversion."

At another level, when we think about these album covers and their possible meanings, we should also see that they resemble historic moments in concrete revolutionary praxis. The oppressed survive, and then rise up to confront their oppressors. In Marley's case the first moment, survival, depends upon the last moment in a historical cycle. Given all of this, I therefore suggest that these three concept albums are a piece of *one* musical movement, both symbolically and as musical verbal text. However, I will limit my present analysis to some of the songs on one of the albums—*Survival.*

IN THE BEGINNING—BLACK SURVIVAL

10 Against the backdrop of the flags of independent African nations and blazoned in white, the word *survival* is written inside the plan of a slave ship that wraps around the album cover. The liner notes tell us about the slave ship: "This plan of a slave ship shows the stowage for the dreaded crossing of the Atlantic. The bounded slaves were packed like so many non-human commodities." The center spread of the album jacket has a wide photograph of members of the Wailers cooking outside in a tenement yard with an epigraph from Marcus Garvey: "A people without the knowledge of their past history, origin and culture is like a tree without roots." What is interesting about this photograph is that the fire for the cooking is being stoked by a long stick taken from a tree and that two men are sitting around the fire with small sticks or branches in their hands. The message from this visual production is clear: fire, roots, and branches—all central images in the Rastafari symbolic order— are critical to various ways in which black people have survived. There is also another possible reading of this album cover: that it is a realist depiction of the many "boats" in Jamaica, where men cook once a day, so that different people in the tenement yard are able to eat. Whatever interpretation one puts on this photograph, it is clear that Marley and Neville Garrick, the talented visual artist, were putting together an unusual album.

The album opens with the recording mike catching Marley instructing, "A little more drums"; then there is a drum roll lick accompanied with a high-pitched guitar that draws our attention to the opening announcement of the album—that there is "so much trouble in the world." The ability to see that there is "so much trouble in the world" is possible because this is Jah's world and there is a prophet who has knowledge of the trouble. What is the nature of this trouble? For Marley it has the following dimensions: the fact that men are sailing on ego trips, using spaceships that take them away from the realities of the earth. And as they do this, they have no care for the ordinary person—"No care for you. No care for me." And who are these persons who do not care? They are the current rulers of the world with their plans for conquering space while humans on earth suffer. In the opening lines of this song Marley is drawing the stark contrast between the use of wealth and the condition of many people on earth.

From these opening lines Marley engages in something that is common in all his verbal texts: he weaves a story that moves from point to counterpoint, at each stage speaking to different actors in the drama of the song. At one moment he is addressing the powerful, and the next he is speaking in the personage of the oppressed. So the verbal text says, "You think you have found the solution, but it is just another illusion"; this is followed by a warning to the world's rulers: "Do not leave the cornerstone standing there behind." Why? Because "We the street people talking, we the people struggling." Because of this struggle of the street people, the rulers and the powerful are sitting on a "time bomb" that will soon explode, since in Jamaican folk wisdom and the law of gravity, "What goes up is coming down." This song, which opens the album, calls our attention to trouble in the world and is a warning to the rulers and powerful that their time is up and redemptive judgment is nigh. Then, with an offbeat organ chord accompanied by a militant stand-up bass, Marley changes from his warning mood to one of rebellious defiance, and to the militant verbal text "Zimbabwe."

This song, written in Ethiopia, became one of the anthems of the national liberation guerrillas in Zimbabwe. Horace Campbell gives us a flavor of the night that Marley played in Zimbabwe in 1980:

> After 15 minutes of the supposed two minutes, the Wailers sang "Africans a liberate Zimbabwe." In one section of the stadium the whole gathering stood and joined in chanting this song of freedom, saying that they did not want to be fooled by mercenaries. It was an experience filled with emotion, and Bob Marley responded with the slogans of Pan-African Unity which were an essential . . . part of his outlook as Rastafari.

In listening to a recording of the entire concert, what emerges is a Bob Marley whose stage presence seems to be organically linked with the audience's responses to him. Therefore, both in performance and in recording, "Zimbabwe" leaves the realm of symbolic African struggles and becomes an integral part of revolutionary struggles all over the world. In other words, the national liberation struggle in Zimbabwe of that period becomes the canvas on which all struggles to free colonial Africa, as well as other oppressed people, are played out. The verbal text begins with the statement "Every Man gotta right to decide his own destiny." This statement of self-determination can be read at two levels. The first is the level of the fight against colonialism—political freedom and decolonization. But at the second level the statement is about the nature of human existence and the nature of autonomy. This autonomy is a complex one, because it can be achieved only "arms in arms with arms." This is one of Marley's most complex lines in the song, and shows his ability to weave stories with the use of words that, when shifted in position, invoke different meanings— so arms become arms of human collectivity as well as weaponry. It is a brilliant play on words.

Marley then turns his attention to the concrete struggle of Zimbabwe and Africa. He announces, "We will fight this little struggle 'cause that the only way we can overcome our little trouble." Here Marley's Jamaican roots are clear. In Jamaican "nation-language" the word "little," pronounced "likl," is used in different ways. It can be used in front of the words "more" or "most" to mean two different things. "Likl more" means "in a little while." On the other hand, "likl most" means "almost." However, a "likl" trouble can be a major problem, but by describing it as small, the Jamaican nation-language reorders the significance of the difficulty. So for Marley the overcoming of the colonial relationship and the fight for self-determination was a small but important matter that was secondary to the real issue: "To overcome the little trouble soon we will find out who is the real revolutionary."

15   It seems that this "little trouble" has two dimensions. In the first there is the general colonial problem, and in the second there is the internal conflict between the colonized peoples. Coming from Jamaica, where he had seen the devastating effects of manufactured intraclass violence, Marley was alert to its consequences in Zimbabwe. He also was aware of the history of the colonial practice, which would rule by creating a native elite or transforming the new political elite into its ally. With this in mind, Marley appeals in the song for the revolutionaries not to allow themselves to be divided. This is then followed by the proclamation, "And I don't want my people to be tricked by mercenaries." The song then moves to merge Africans and "natty dread," indicating that Marley thought blacks in the Caribbean were exiled Africans and, since Rastafari recognized this fact, then they, too, had claims to being called Africans. The three lines of the final verse indicate this: "Natty trash it up in Zimbabwe Africans a liberate Zimbabwe I and I a liberate Zimbabwe." The song ends the way it began, with the explicit political statement "Every Man gotta right to decide his own destiny." It was a clarion call for African liberation, but it was also a call for that revolution to be pure. There is, in addition, a certain universal-

ism as the song speaks to the deepest emotional structures of all those who are oppressed. The song is rooted in the Jamaican and Zimbabwean experiences, but it resonated with people engaged in political and social struggles where questions about social division, revolutionaries who have other political agendas, and the nature of community that explodes in moments of revolution are posed.

The final song I wish to pay some attention to on the *Survival* album is "Babylon System." Slowing down the music, this track is the only one on the album that is musically constructed in a Rastafari Nyabingi format. All the instruments surround the bass drum, and the repeater drum fills the spaces between lyrics as the organ and I-Threes chorus carry us along in this prophetic meditation. In a cool but militant voice, Marley begins by announcing, "We refuse to be what you wanted us to be, we are what we are that's the way its going to be." Several things are remarkable about these lines. Not only are they an eloquent testimony of resistance, but they begin a song whose lyrical construction continuously shifts. The next lines, which continue to speak to the oppressor group, make one of the most profound points in radical politics. Marley asserts that the typical solution of education as a means of social mobility and equal opportunity is a false one, since "you can't educate for no equal opportunity, talking about my freedom people, freedom and liberty." By juxtaposing education to freedom, Marley is intimating that freedom is a higher value. Why should this be so? We find the answer in the third verse, where Marley sings to the oppressed people, claiming knowledge about the system:

Babylon System is the vampire
Sucking the children Day by Day
Babylon System is the vampire
Sucking the Blood of the Sufferers
Building Church and University
Deceiving the People Continually
Me say Them Graduating Thieves
And Murderers look out now
Sucking the Blood of the Sufferers.

It is clear from the above that the problem is that education as presently constructed, along the with the teachings of mainstream Christianity, produces individuals who are morally unfit. Therefore both churches and universities are involved in a massive deception. As a consequence, education cannot be a substitute for freedom. The system of oppression is metaphorically described as a vampire that sucks blood. It is therefore evil, with no redeeming features.

In the fourth verse Marley enunciates his prophetic calling by chanting, "tell the children the truth." This truth is that the oppressed " . . . 've been trodding on the winepress much too long," and therefore should now "Rebel." This call for rebellion continues to the last verse, in which Marley paints a historical picture of the nature of black oppression:

From the very day we left the shores
Of our Father's land
We've been trampled on.
Oh Now, Now we know everything we got
    to rebel.

For Marley the time has come when full knowledge is revealed about the history and present condition of people of African descent. Thus there are no more reasons for remaining quiescent. Marley's call for rebellion is a general one. He does not state the nature of the rebellion. What he is clear on is that resistance must now turn to rebellion and freedom. It is not in the nature of prophetic criticism to always be specific or have a defined political program of change. Therefore one should not expect this from Marley. What Marley does is to call the system to order, to create an alternative mental universe, and to rally people toward this new possibility.

SOME CONCLUSIONS

In the end there is no mystery about Marley's international appeal. In a time of pessimism, when radical thought seems to be on the retreat and skepticism abounds, finding, in one element of the popular, defiance and hope that can also give joy is rare. Mario Vargas Llosa, in a commentary on Marley and Rastafari, notes their "bid against moral disintegration and human injustice." In a world where both these things are the order of the day, it should be no surprise that Marley's appeal a decade after his death still resonates. In the end, whenever I think of Marley, I cannot help recalling my arrival in Mexico City in the mid-1980s, seating myself in cab with a driver who spoke only Spanish and who, after I finally communicated my destination, wondered if I was a Jamaican. Receiving an affirmative answer, he stopped the car, searched under the seat for a set of tapes, placed one in the cassette player of the car, and proclaimed with joy on his face, "Jah! Jah lives!" He was not a Rastafarian, and did not seem to have profound understanding of the doctrine, but somehow he had heard the voice of prophetic criticism, and it was that which he was celebrating. Surely the time has come for us to chant down Babylon one more time.

ONE LOVE

— *Robert Palmer*

Robert Palmer was a renowned music critic, record producer, and documentary filmmaker. He was the first full-time rock critic at the *New York Times*, where he worked for over a decade in the 1970s and 1980s, and the author of *Deep Blues* (1981) and *Rock and Roll: An Unruly History* (1995). Palmer's tribute to Bob Marley, written on the occasion of Marley's election to the Rock and Roll Hall of Fame, appeared in the February 24, 1994, issue of *Rolling Stone*.

SUGGESTION FOR READING Robert Palmer says in the early part of his essay that the election of Bob Marley to the Rock and Roll Hall of Fame "provides the opportunity for a reassessment" of the relation between reggae and rock and roll. As you read, consider to what extent Palmer's essay offers such a "reassessment."

1 Memory pictures coming in: two snapshots of Bob Marley. In the first, the Wailers are playing one of their mid-'70s New York City concerts to a theater thick with ganja and dreads. The music unwinds from the first note like an impossibly sinuous Slinky, the groove steady, one song shading into the next without pause or change of key. Marley is a blur of motion, bobbing, weaving, dreadlocks flying, never seeming to quite touch the stage. It's as if the thick clouds of smoke and the rapt concentration of the mostly Jamaican audience are somehow buoying him up; he's hovering. No matter how much I squint and stare, his feet seem to be floating a few inches above the boards. Maybe it's the ganja. Maybe not.

In the second picture, Marley is sitting on the couch in a posh midtown hotel suite, surrounded by protectively huddling brethren and sistren, looking pale, drawn, severe. It's 1980, and the Wailers—now playing Madison Square Garden—have taken over an entire floor of the hotel, muting the lights in the hall to perpetual twilight, filling their stuffy, carpeted precinct with the unaccustomed smells of ital cooking and, of course, ganja.

There's been a disquieting change in Marley's demeanor. In the past, he would deliver even his most biting critiques of Babylon with an unmistakable generosity of spirit, his face friendly and open, his body language expansive. Each toss of his head set his mane of dreadlocks flying.

"It take many a year, mon, and maybe some bloodshed must be, but righteousness someday prevail," Marley would say. And it would come across more like a prayer than a warning.

5   This time, Marley sits very still, his head almost swallowed by the knitted cap he's wearing. His critique of the "politricks" of exploitation is as trenchant as ever, but now it's straight on, lacking the warmth and humor that were once such outstanding signifiers of his Rasta state of grace. Warmth? Humor? In less than a year, Marley will succumb to the cancer that only his inner circle knows is eating him alive.

The world Bob Marley came from, the Third World of the political philosophers, is a dog-eat-dog world: Trenchtown, a chaotic maze of shacks and dirt and footpaths and concrete jungle slung precariously along the edge of the 20th-century abyss. His life story has many of this century's most characteristic and horrific leitmotifs—the New World Order's rape of the planet's organic and spiritual resources; the obscenity of plenty and poverty living cheek to jowl under the gun; naked force opposed by visionary religion and deep cultural magic.

There really is only one way out, as Marley sang in "Trenchtown Rock": "One good thing about music / When it hits, you feel no pain." With his induction this year into the Rock & Roll Hall of Fame, he is being honored for his music, which celebrates life even as it embodies struggle. But the music will not let us forget that this is a dog-eat-dog story and that even the big dog gets eaten in the end.

Marley's extraordinary body of work spans the entire history of modern Jamaican music, from ska to rock steady to reggae. But he never lost sight of the emotional center of his art—his people, the sufferers of Trenchtown, of greater Kingston, of all the world's ghettos. They placed their faith and hope in him, and he did not let them down. Later works such as "Survival," "Zimbabwe" and "Coming in from the Cold" are as passionately committed as anything from earlier years.

"It something really serious, is not entertainment," Marley once said of his music. "You entertain people who are satisfied. Hungry people can't be entertained—or people who are afraid. You can't entertain a man who has no food."

10   No one in rock & roll has left a musical legacy that matters more or one that matters in such fundamental ways. Yet there has been a reluctance in some quarters to accept Marley's music and reggae in general as a part of rock & roll. For their part, reggae musicians have been understandably reluctant to identify themselves with rock & roll's passing parade.

"Me have to laugh sometimes when dem scribes seh me like Mick Jagger or some superstar thing like that," Marley told *Rolling Stone* in 1976. "Dem have to listen close to the music, 'cause the message not the same. Nooo, mon, the reggae not the twist, mon!"

That was Marley's sense of humor at work. He clarified his position in an interview with author Stephen Davis: "Reggae music, soul music, rock music—every song is a sign. But ya have te be careful of this type of song and vibration that ya give te the people, for 'Woe be unto them they who lead my people astray.' "

Marley's election to the Hall of Fame provides the opportunity for a reassessment of this issue—or perhaps a reintegration. He was right to make a distinction between his music's singleness of purpose and various pop ephemeras; that doesn't mean one should separate it from the rest of music in its own proud but insulated ghetto. Because it isn't enough to identify the man as the crown prince of reggae or the Third World's first pop-music superstar. As an artist, he was always playing in the big leagues. No matter what category you put him in, his stature stands undiminished.

For that matter, it's probably high time we stopped looking at Jamaican music as a reflection or derivation of developments on the American mainland. The realities are more complex than that. Memphis, Tenn., and New Orleans created and sustained their own distinctive rock & roll traditions, and so did Jamaica. The processes that shaped all these musics are, in fact, very nearly identical. Arguably, the way these processes work defines rock & roll itself.

15   It works something like this. Ships come in bringing slaves from Africa, bringing music. In

a climate of brutal oppression, the music toughs it out, assuming the importance it had in Africa as the culture's psychic and social foundation. As in Africa, there is an emphasis on rhythms, and the rhythms have a story to tell—often literally as speech-inflected patterns—and work to do. They bring people together, draw them into participation and serve as mediators between the individual, the community and the world beyond the world, the world of the spirits.

As the culture evolves and slavery's death grip at last begins to falter, rhythmic fundamentals begin to spread beyond the ritual setting. As populations leave the countryside for the cities looking for opportunity, dance music built on sacred rhythms spreads into urban dance halls, bars and theaters. There the music encounters the mediums of radio and recording: flashpoint. Suddenly, the venerable rhythms are the latest thing, a pop sensation. From plantation drumming and voodoo ceremonies to country-church "shouts" to Bo Diddley to James Brown: That's the North American version of the tale. The Jamaican version runs from the drumming of the Maroons (runaway-slave societies) to the pocomania and Revival Zion churches to the Rastafarians to mento, ska, rock steady, reggae and Bob Marley.

Robert Nesta Marley was born Feb. 6, 1945, in the heavily forested country of St. Ann's Parish, the child of 19-year-old country girl Cedella Booker and a white colonial then working in the area, Captain Norval Sinclair Marley. The captain did marry Cedella, then abandoned her. Bob grew up in a back-country world whose values and beliefs were still profoundly African, a world more permeable to superhuman forces both natural and supernatural than any city child could know. His grandfather Omeriah Malcolm was a respected man in the parish, a myalman adept in the ways of sorcery and spirit propitiation. Long before he embraced Rastafarianism as a spiritual philosophy and a way of life, Bob Marley was on intimate terms with his culture's deepest mysteries.

When the teen-age Marley arrived in Kingston, Jamaican music was entering a period of unprecedented expansion and growth. Mento, an acoustic popular music comparable to the calypso of Trinidad and Tobago, was being displaced from the forefront by an increasingly Jamaicanized take on Southern R&B and soul music. As the new ska sound developed, it began to exert a subtle but increasingly significant influence on North American soul.

Island rhythms had been an important ingredient in New Orleans' musical gumbo since the early days of jazz. Professor Longhair, the founding father of New Orleans' piano-based R&B, specifically mentioned his wartime experience playing with "West Indian boys" as a factor shaping his influential polyrhythms of the 1940s and '50s. By the mid-'60s—when Jamaican tempos slowed, its grooves deepened, and its bass moved out front in the mix, creating the style dubbed rock steady—Jamaican rhythmic ideas were beginning to surface in Memphis soul music as well.

20   Al Jackson Jr., the seminal Booker T. and the MG's-Stax Records session drummer, began vacationing in Jamaica, buying records, visiting sessions. Listen to Jackson's rhythm arrangement on Wilson Pickett's "In the Midnight Hour" back to back with the Silvertones' rock-steady cover of the tune, and you will readily hear the connections. All rock & roll styles are derivative of earlier musics in the beginning. Jamaican music quickly grew out of this phase, becoming part of a two-way rhythmic dialogue, transcending geographical and national boundaries.

Marley did not spend much time watching these events from the sidelines. A precocious musician with an already distinctive vocal style, he began making records in 1962. He sounded nervous, high-pitched, painfully adolescent on his debut ska recording, "Judge Not." But already he was drawing on Biblical imagery and themes in original lyrics that had an important social dimension as well as a spiritual and moral imperative: "While you talk about me / Someone else is judging you."

Marley's earliest ska recordings were solo efforts, but the '60s were the heyday of Jamaican vocal groups, and Marley had been wood-shedding with a loose group of friends from Trenchtown. When he became dissatisfied with his original recording situation, he auditioned with the group for No. 1 sound-system man Clement "Sir Coxsone" Dodd.

Of the original group members, Junior Braithwaite and Beverly Kelso soon dropped out, leaving a tighter-than-tight trio of running partners to carry on. Neville "Bunny" Livingston, later Bunny Wailer, was one of Bob's earliest and closest childhood friends from St. Ann's Parish. Marley's mother and Wailer's father were living together in Trenchtown when Bob and Bunny met Peter McIntosh, later Peter Tosh, who completed the triumvirate.

This trio's mesh of voices was never conventionally pretty. The three voices didn't so much blend as create a constantly shifting ensemble texture, tightly interwoven but with each singer's timbre remaining distinct. Unlike most singers on the way up, Marley, Tosh and Livingston refused to cosmeticize their back-of-town rawness, realizing from the first that their origins were one of their greatest strengths. They had in fact chosen a group name that called attention to these origins; they were Wailers, they said, because they were ghetto sufferers, born wailing. Dog eat dog; that was the reality of life in the ghetto and in Kingston's music and recording scene. Producers ruled the roost, paying musicians and singers a nominal one-time fee for recording and reaping the subsequent profits. Nevertheless, in 1966, the Wailers took on the system, leaving Sir Coxsone's stable (a move tantamount to professional suicide) to start their own record label, Wail 'M' Soul 'M', and produce the sessions themselves.

25   "Yes, people rob me and try te trick me, but now I have experience," Marley said, adding later, "I know, and I see, and I don't get tricked. Everybody that deals with West Indian music . . . thieves!"

If you're listening chronologically to Island's exemplary four-CD set *Bob Marley: Songs of Freedom*, the move into self-production comes as a dramatic departure. For the first time, the singers and musicians seem to be breathing the same air, producing a superbly organic group sound. The Wailers' 1967–68 rock-steady sides for Wail 'M' Soul 'M' are the trio's first unalloyed masterpieces: "Mellow Mood," "Bend Down Low," "Thank You Lord" and the rest still move, instruct and delight.

After Marley took time off to write songs for the American pop-soul singer Johnny Nash (who recorded "Stir It Up" and "Guava Jelly"), the Wailers met Lee Perry, a former sound-system DJ for Sir Coxsone who was beginning to bring a new sense of space and mystery to Jamaican music. Among the session players who worked for Perry were the two Barrett brothers, drummer Carlton ("Carly") and bassist Aston ("Family Man"). As rock steady mutated into the even trickier, more fluid grooves of reggae, the Barrett brothers staked their claim as the music's definitive rhythm section. With the hyper-creative Perry, aka Dread at the Control, behind the mixing desk, the wailing Wailers and the Barrett brothers made an imaginative leap into a new and entirely unanticipated sonic landscape. Marley was now a songwriter in a class by himself, and the Wailers-Barretts-Perry team was able to create and sustain a powerfully specific mood and presence for each of his gems. Many hardcore reggae fans consider these recordings, collected on such albums as *Soul Rebels* and *African Herbsman*, the high point of Marley's entire career. That's debatable; the music's blinding brilliance is not.

DOG EAT DOG

Almost 10 years in the forefront of one of the most hectic, intensely creative music scenes on the planet, and what did the Wailers have to show for it? They were still living in Trenchtown, below the poverty line. They never heard their records played on Jamaican radio. "It's because the music shows the real situation in Jamaica,"

Marley said. "Some people don't like to hear the real truth." And outside Jamaica and the West Indian communities in the U.K., they were utterly unknown, as was reggae itself.

Through Marley's Johnny Nash connection, the Wailers, Barretts in tow, went to England, hoping to tour and stir up some interest on the part of a major record label. They managed to secure a bit of session work, record some demos and play a handful of dates in clubs and schools. They awoke one morning—cold and hungry—to find that their erstwhile management had left the country, stranding them cold and penniless.

30   Enter Chris Blackwell, a white Jamaican who had done well leasing hits from Kingston for the U.K. on his Island Records label and who was currently scoring major pop successes with the likes of Traffic and Cat Stevens. He still thought reggae could win an audience in the wider world, and to that end he gave the Wailers the budget to record an album. This in itself was an innovative move. Any other label honcho would surely have seen the group's outspoken stand against oppression and exploitation and its embrace of a Rastafarian belief system as potential impediments to commercial success at best. Blackwell encouraged the Wailers to be themselves.

The Wailers' first two Island albums, *Catch a Fire* and *Burnin'* (both from 1973), represent another new beginning for Marley. Both albums freely raided his enormous back catalog of songs, and while some of the versions issued earlier may be the definitive ones, as albums, *Catch a Fire* and *Burnin'* are themselves definitive Marley records. They are the powerful, unified masterworks of an artist at the height of his powers.

With the release of *Catch a Fire*, the pressure was on. After a U.S. tour that found the Wailers driving thousands of miles to play for audiences that were frequently small and uncomprehending, Wailer and Tosh elected to drop out of the rat race and go solo. This development broke up one of the era's greatest vocal groups, but Marley assembled the I-Threes (Rita Marley, Marcia Griffiths, Judy Mowatt) to fill out the band's vocal sound and kept touring. He was a man with a mission.

"God sent me on earth," Marley once said. "He send me to do something, and nobody can stop me. If God want to stop me, then I stop. Man never can." Marley's next three studio albums—*Natty Dread* (1974), *Rastaman Vibration* (1976) and *Exodus* (1977)—made him an international star. The Wailers were now officially Bob Marley's band, still piloted through the rhythmic rapids by the incomparable Barrett brothers but now expanded to include a clutch of superb musical individualists who were fundamentally team players, including guitarists Al Anderson and Junior Marvin and keyboard men Earl "Wia" Lindo and Bernard "Touter" Harvey.

Brutal as the Wailers' nonstop touring schedule was, the real brutality was waiting for Marley back home. Jamaica in the middle and late '70s seemed to be a society coming apart at the seams. The country's two rival political parties both employed gangs of ghetto gunmen to settle their differences. They also leaned hard on Marley for public support. At the same time, there was a great deal of resentment in the air. Jamaica's ruling class traditionally despised the Rastafarians for offering scathing critiques of the "shitstem" while refusing to take part in it. The emergence of a dreadlocked Rasta as Jamaica's No. 1 citizen to the world was seen as a public-relations disaster and, for many, a personal affront.

35   No rock & roller has ever had so many formidable and sinister forces arrayed against him. Marley found it expedient to maintain social relationships with gunmen and politicians from both political parties. "The devil ain't got no power over me," he asserted. "The devil come, and me shake hands with the devil. Devil have his part to play. Devil's a good friend, too . . . because when you don't know him, that's the time he can mosh you down."

Marley proved miraculously adept at advocating justice and an end to neocolonial exploitation of the increasingly beleaguered island while maintaining a sovereign's indifference to the machinations of partisan politics. But attempts to manipulate him for political gain continued unabated, and Marley well knew that the slightest miscalculation could have fatal consequences.

In 1976, representatives of the country's ruling, nominally socialist government persuaded Marley to headline a free outdoor concert in Kingston that would be strictly apolitical, a plea for peace among the ghetto's warring factions and a celebration of "one love, one heart." Two nights before the concert, two carloads of gunmen broke into Marley's house with barrels blazing. Astonishingly, no one was killed, though Marley and several associates were wounded. Showing remarkable courage, Marley honored his promise to sing at the concert. Showing good sense, he left the island the next day and didn't return for more than a year.

"They claim that I was supporting a political party, which is not true," Marley insisted afterward. "If it was really true that I was defending politics, then I would have died that night, because me know that the politician is the devil. . . . My job is to come between these politicians and become something else for the people."

Throughout these difficult years, Marley remained committed to his Rastafarian ideals and to self-determination for his people. In the Third World, especially where liberation struggles were in progress, he was seen as both a popular musician and a revolutionary ally. When Zimbabwe won its freedom from the white Rhodesian regime in 1980, the Wailers played at the independence celebration. Through it all, Marley continued to forge a visionary music that opposed the tide of violence and celebrated the rhythms of life.

40 His diligence never faltered; finally, it was his own rebellious cells that brought him down. The cancer that finally killed him on May 11, 1981, had apparently developed from an untreated soccer injury—although in circumstances such as these, one can never be entirely certain what happened or why. One can only be certain of Marley's enduring musical legacy.

The beauty of Marley's music is that while it holds a special significance for the sufferers of this world, it speaks to any listener with an open heart. You don't have to understand the sociopolitical background or the Rasta subculture—or even Marley's Trenchtown patois—to get it. The rhythms are as close as your heartbeat, the voice speaks a language the spirit understands. And, yes, when it hits, you feel no pain.

SUGGESTIONS FOR DISCUSSION

1. Consider what Anthony Bogues means by the "two competing contemporary representations" of Bob Marley. What is Bogues bringing to light by comparing the "depoliticization" of Marley and Martin Luther King? How does Bogues go about developing his analysis of Marley as a prophetic social critic rather than simply a cultural icon and successful entertainer?

2. Consider the issue that Robert Palmer raises about the reluctance, on one hand, of some to accept reggae as a part of rock and roll and the reluctance, on the other, of reggae musicians to identify themselves with rock and roll. What is at stake in this mutual reluctance? What do Palmer's views seem to be?

3. In the closing paragraph of "One Love," Palmer says you "don't have to understand the sociopolitical background or the Rasta subculture" to "get" Bob Marley's music. How do you think Bogues would respond to this statement? Consider here, for example, how Bogues accounts in the final paragraph of "Get Up, Stand Up" for Marley's international appeal. What assumptions does each writer seem to be making that lead them to their final words about Marley's music?

SUGGESTIONS FOR WRITING

1. Write an essay that examines Anthony Bogues's claim that Bob Marley and Martin Luther King have been "depoliticized" and turned into "feel good" cultural icons. Summarize Bogues's analysis and provide your own evaluation of its usefulness in understanding how public figures such as Marley and King are incorporated into historical memory. You may want to continue by extending Bogues's line of analysis in order to account for other public figures, whether musicians or social activists.

2. Write an essay that compares and critically evaluates Bogues's and Palmer's perspectives on Marley's life and music. Identify views they hold in common, but pay particular attention to their differences. What is the significance of these differences and their underlying assumptions?

3. Choose a song by Bob Marley (or another reggae musician) to analyze. Use the writings by Bogues and Palmer to examine the meaning and significance of the song. Consider the message in the lyrics but also analyze the sound of the song and how the beat and music convey the message.

CLASSIC READING

THE SOULS OF OUR STRIVING

— *W. E. B. Du Bois*

W. E. B. Du Bois (1868–1963) was the cofounder of the National Association for the Advancement of Colored People in 1909, a prolific author on issues of race, and a political and intellectual leader of the African American struggle for equal rights. Toward the end of his life, Du Bois grew increasingly disillusioned with the United States. At the age of ninety-one, he renounced his American citizenship and lived in exile in Ghana until his death in 1963. The following selection comes from a time much earlier in Du Bois's life. "The Souls of Our Striving" is the opening chapter of his classic work *The Souls of Black Folk*, published in 1903.

SUGGESTION FOR READING   In this opening chapter, Du Bois presents the idea of "double consciousness"—a concept that has become widely influential in explaining the relations between whites and African Americans in the United States and colonizers and the colonized throughout the world. He sets the context from the beginning sentence by dividing "me and the other world." Notice how this lays the groundwork for the third paragraph, in which Du Bois first mentions "double consciousness."

O water, voice of my heart, crying in the sand,
  All night long crying with a mournful cry,
As I lie and listen, and cannot understand
    The voice of my heart in my side or the
      voice of the sea,
  O water, crying for rest, is it I, is it I?
  All night long the water is crying to me.

Unresting water, there shall never be rest
  Till the last moon droop and the last tide fail,
And the fire of the end begin to burn in the west;
    And the heart shall be weary and wonder
      and cry like the sea,
  All life long crying without avail,
    As the water all night long is crying to me.
                —*Arthur Symons*

1 Between me and the other world there is ever an unasked question: unasked by some through feelings of delicacy; by others through the difficulty of rightly framing it. All, nevertheless, flutter round it. They approach me in a half-hesitant sort of way, eye me curiously or compassionately, and then, instead of saying directly, How does it feel to be a Problem? they say, I know an excellent colored man in my town; or, I fought at Mechanicsville; or, Do not these Southern outrages make your blood boil? At these I smile, or am interested, or reduce the boiling to a simmer, as the occasion may require. To the real question, How does it feel to be a problem? I answer seldom a word.

And yet, being a problem is a strange experience,—peculiar even for one who has never been anything else, save perhaps in babyhood and in Europe. It is in the early days of rollicking boyhood that the revelation first bursts upon one, all in a day, as it were. I remember well when the shadow swept across me. I was a little thing, away up in the hills of New England, where the dark Housatonic winds between Hoosac and Taghkanic to the sea. In a wee wooden schoolhouse, something put it into the boys' and girls' heads to buy gorgeous visiting-cards—ten cents a package—and exchange. The exchange was merry, till one girl, a tall newcomer, refused my card,—refused it peremptorily, with a glance. Then it dawned upon me with a certain suddenness that I was different from the others; or like, mayhap, in heart and life and longing, but shut out from their world by a vast veil. I had thereafter no desire to tear down that veil, to creep through; I held all beyond it in common contempt, and lived above it in a region of blue sky and great wandering shadows. That sky was bluest when I could beat my mates at examination-time, or beat them at a foot-race, or even beat their stringy heads. Alas, with the years all this fine contempt began to fade; for the words I longed for, and all their dazzling opportunities, were theirs, not mine. But they should not keep these prizes, I said; some, all, I would wrest from them. Just how I would do it I could never decide: by reading law, by healing the sick, by telling the wonderful tales that swam in my head,—some way. With other black boys the strife was not so fiercely sunny: their youth shrunk into tasteless sycophancy, or into silent hatred of the pale world about them and mocking distrust of everything white; or wasted itself in a bitter cry, Why did God make me an outcast and a stranger in mine own house? The shades of the prison-house closed round about us all: walls strait and stubborn to the whitest, but relentlessly narrow, tall, and unscalable to sons of night who must plod darkly on in resignation, or beat unavailing palms against the stone, or steadily, half hopelessly, watch the streak of blue above.

After the Egyptian and Indian, the Greek and Roman, the Teuton and Mongolian, the Negro is a sort of seventh son, born with a veil, and gifted with second-sight in this American world,—a world which yields him no true self-consciousness, but only lets him see himself through the revelation of the other world. It is a peculiar sensation, this double-consciousness, this sense of always looking at one's self through the eyes of others, of measuring one's soul by the tape of a world that looks on in amused contempt and pity. One ever feels his twoness,—an American, a Negro; two souls, two thoughts, two unreconciled strivings; two warring ideals in one dark body, whose dogged strength alone keeps it from being torn asunder.

The history of the American Negro is the history of this strife,—this longing to attain self-conscious manhood, to merge his double self into a better and truer self. In this merging he wishes neither of the older selves to be lost. He would not Africanize America, for America has too much to teach the world and Africa. He would not bleach his Negro soul in a flood of white Americanism, for he knows that Negro blood has a message for the world. He simply wishes to make it possible for a man to be both a Negro and an American, without being cursed and spit upon by his fellows, without having the doors of Opportunity closed roughly in his face.

5   This, then, is the end of his striving: to be a co-worker in the kingdom of culture, to escape both death and isolation, to husband and use his best powers and his latent genius. These powers of body and mind have in the past been strangely wasted, dispersed, or forgotten. The shadow of a mighty Negro past flits through the tale of Ethiopia the Shadowy and of Egypt the Sphinx. Through history, the powers of single black men flash here and there like falling stars, and die sometimes before the world has rightly gauged their brightness. Here in America, in the few days since Emancipation, the black man's turning hither and thither in hesitant and doubtful striving has often made his very strength to lose effectiveness, to seem like absence of power, like weakness. And yet it is not weakness,—it is the contradiction of double aims. The double-aimed struggle of the black artisan—on the one hand to escape white contempt for a nation of mere hewers of wood and drawers of water, and on the other hand to plough and nail and dig for a poverty-stricken horde—could only result in making him a poor craftsman, for he had but half a heart in either cause. By the poverty and ignorance of his people, the Negro minister or doctor was tempted toward quackery and demagogy; and by the criticism of the other world, toward ideals that made him ashamed of his lowly tasks. The would-be black *savant* was confronted by the paradox that the knowledge his people needed was a twice-told tale to his white neighbors, while the knowledge which would teach the white world was Greek to his own flesh and blood. The innate love of harmony and beauty that set the ruder souls of his people a-dancing and a-singing raised but confusion and doubt in the soul of the black artist; for the beauty revealed to him was the soul-beauty of a race which his larger audience despised, and he could not articulate the message of another people. This waste of double aims, this seeking to satisfy two unreconciled ideals, has wrought sad havoc with the courage and faith and deeds of ten thousand thousand people,—has sent them often wooing false gods and invoking false means of salvation, and at times has even seemed about to make them ashamed of themselves.

Away back in the days of bondage they thought to see in one divine event the end of all doubt and disappointment; few men ever worshipped Freedom with half such unquestioning faith as did the American Negro for two centuries. To him, so far as he thought and dreamed, slavery was indeed the sum of all villainies, the cause of all sorrow, the root of all prejudice; Emancipation was the key to a promised land of sweeter beauty than ever stretched before the eyes of wearied Israelites. In song and exhortation swelled one refrain—Liberty; in his tears and curses the God he implored had Freedom in his right hand. At last it came,—suddenly, fearfully, like a dream. With one wild carnival of blood and passion came the message in his own plaintive cadences:—

> "Shout, O children!
> Shout, you're free!
> For God has bought your liberty!"

Years have passed away since then,—ten, twenty, forty; forty years of national life, forty years of renewal and development, and yet the swarthy spectre sits in its accustomed seat at the Nation's feast. In vain do we cry to this our vastest social problem:—

> "Take any shape but that, and my firm nerves
> Shall never tremble!"

The Nation has not yet found peace from its sins; the freedman has not yet found in freedom his promised land. Whatever of good may have come in these years of change, the shadow of a deep disappointment rests upon the Negro people,—a disappointment all the more bitter because the unattained ideal was unbounded save by the simple ignorance of a lowly people.

The first decade was merely a prolongation of the vain search for freedom, the boon that seemed ever barely to elude their grasp,—like a tantalizing will-o'-the-wisp, maddening and misleading the headless host. The holocaust of war, the terrors of the Ku-Klux Klan, the lies of carpet-baggers, the disorganization of industry, and the contradictory advice of friends and foes, left the bewildered serf with no new watchword beyond the old cry for freedom. As the time flew, however, he began to grasp a new idea. The ideal of liberty demanded for its attainment powerful means, and these the Fifteenth Amendment gave him. The ballot, which before he had looked upon as a visible sign of freedom, he now regarded as the chief means of gaining and perfecting the liberty with which war had partially endowed him. And why not? Had not votes made war and emancipated millions? Had not votes enfranchised the freedmen? Was anything impossible to a power that had done all this? A million black men started with renewed zeal to vote themselves into the kingdom. So the decade flew away, the revolution of 1876 came, and left the half-free serf weary, wondering, but still inspired. Slowly but steadily, in the following years, a new vision began gradually to replace the dream of political power,—a powerful movement, the rise of another ideal to guide the unguided, another pillar of fire by night after a clouded day. It was the ideal of "book-learning"; the curiosity, born of compulsory ignorance, to know and test the power of the cabalistic letters of the white man, the longing to know. Here at last seemed to have been discovered the mountain path to Canaan; longer than the highway of Emancipation and law, steep and rugged, but straight, leading to heights high enough to overlook life.

10   Up the new path the advance guard toiled, slowly, heavily, doggedly; only those who have watched and guided the faltering feet, the misty minds, the dull understandings, of the dark pupils of these schools know how faithfully, how piteously, this people strove to learn. It was weary work. The cold statistician wrote down the inches of progress here and there, noted also where here and there a foot had slipped or some one had fallen. To the tired climbers, the horizon was ever dark, the mists were often cold, the Canaan was always dim and far away. If,

however, the vistas disclosed as yet no goal, no resting-place, little but flattery and criticism, the journey at least gave leisure for reflection and self-examination; it changed the child of Emancipation to the youth with dawning self-consciousness, self-realization, self-respect. In those sombre forests of his striving his own soul rose before him, and he saw himself,—darkly as through a veil; and yet he saw in himself some faint revelation of his power, of his mission. He began to have a dim feeling that, to attain his place in the world, he must be himself, and not another. For the first time he sought to analyze the burden he bore upon his back, that dead-weight of social degradation partially masked behind a half-named Negro problem. He felt his poverty; without a cent, without a home, without land, tools, or savings, he had entered into competition with rich, landed, skilled neighbors. To be a poor man is hard, but to be a poor race in a land of dollars is the very bottom of hardships. He felt the weight of his ignorance,—not simply of letters, but of life, of business, of the humanities; the accumulated sloth and shirking and awkwardness of decades and centuries shackled his hands and feet. Nor was his burden all poverty and ignorance. The red stain of bastardy, which two centuries of systematic legal defilement of Negro women had stamped upon his race, meant not only the loss of ancient African chastity, but also the hereditary weight of a mass of corruption from white adulterers, threatening almost the obliteration of the Negro home.

A people thus handicapped ought not to be asked to race with the world, but rather allowed to give all its time and thought to its own social problems. But alas! while sociologists gleefully count his bastards and his prostitutes, the very soul of the toiling, sweating black man is darkened by the shadow of a vast despair. Men call the shadow prejudice, and learnedly explain it as the natural defence of culture against barbarism, learning against ignorance, purity against crime, the "higher" against the "lower" races. To which the Negro cries Amen! and swears that to so much of this strange prejudice as is founded on just homage to civilization, culture, righteousness, and progress, he humbly bows and meekly does obeisance. But before that nameless prejudice that leaps beyond all this he stands helpless, dismayed, and well-nigh speechless; before that personal disrespect and mockery, the ridicule and systematic humiliation, the distortion of fact and wanton license of fancy, the cynical ignoring of the better and the boisterous welcoming of the worse, the all-pervading desire to inculcate disdain for everything black, from Toussaint to the devil,—before this there rises a sickening despair that would disarm and discourage any nation save that black host to whom "discouragement" is an unwritten word.

But the facing of so vast a prejudice could not but bring the inevitable self-questioning, self-disparagement, and lowering of ideals which ever accompany repression and breed in an atmosphere of contempt and hate. Whisperings and portents came borne upon the four winds: Lo! we are diseased and dying, cried the dark hosts; we cannot write, our voting is vain; what need of education, since we must always cook and serve? And the Nation echoed and enforced this self-criticism, saying: Be content to be servants, and nothing more; what need of higher culture for half-men? Away with the black man's ballot, by force or fraud,—and behold the suicide of a race! Nevertheless, out of the evil came something of good,—the more careful adjustment of education to real life, the clearer perception of the Negroes' social responsibilities, and the sobering realization of the meaning of progress.

So dawned the time of *Sturm und Drang*: storm and stress to-day rocks our little boat on the mad waters of the world-sea; there is within and without the sound of conflict, the burning of body and rending of soul; inspiration strives with doubt, and faith with vain questionings. The bright ideals of the past,—physical freedom, political power, the training of brains and the training of hands,—all these in turn have waxed and waned, until even the last grows dim and overcast. Are they all wrong,—all false? No, not that, but each alone was over-simple and incomplete,—the dreams of a credulous race-childhood, or the fond imaginings of the other world which does not know and does not want to know our power. To be really true, all these ideals must be melted and welded into one. The training of the schools we need to-day more than ever,—the training of deft hands, quick eyes and ears, and above all the broader, deeper, higher culture of gifted minds and pure hearts. The power of the ballot we need in sheer self-defence,—else what shall save us from a second slavery? Freedom, too, the long-sought, we still seek,—the freedom of life and limb, the freedom to work and think, the freedom to love and aspire. Work, culture, liberty,—all these we need, not singly but together, not successively but together, each growing and aiding each, and all striving toward that vaster ideal that swims before the Negro people, the ideal of human brotherhood, gained through the unifying ideal of Race; the ideal of fostering and developing the traits and talents of the Negro, not in opposition to or contempt for other races, but rather in large conformity to the greater ideals of the American Republic, in order that some day on American soil two world-races may give each to each those characteristics both so sadly lack. We the darker ones come even now not altogether empty-handed: there are to-day no truer exponents of the pure human spirit of the Declaration of Independence than the American Negroes; there is no true American music but the wild sweet melodies of the Negro slave; the American fairy tales and folk-lore are Indian and African; and, all in all, we black men seem the sole oasis of simple faith and reverence in a dusty desert of dollars and smartness. Will America be poorer if she replace her brutal dyspeptic blundering with light-hearted but determined Negro humility? or her coarse and cruel wit with loving jovial good-humor? or her vulgar music with the soul of the Sorrow Songs?

Merely a concrete test of the underlying principles of the great republic is the Negro Problem, and the spiritual striving of the freedmen's sons is the travail of souls whose burden is almost beyond the measure of their strength, but who bear it in the name of an historic race, in the name of this the land of their fathers' fathers, and in the name of human opportunity.

15   And now what I have briefly sketched in large outline let me on coming pages tell again in many ways, with loving emphasis and deeper detail, that men may listen to the striving in the souls of black folk.

SUGGESTIONS FOR DISCUSSION

1. What does Du Bois mean by "double consciousness"? What is he trying to explain? How does he define the term? What examples does he offer? Does the term have relevance for social life in the United States today? Where would you look for evidence of "always looking at one's self through the eyes of others?" What are the effects?

2. At the end of this chapter, Du Bois says that the "Negro Problem" is a "concrete test of the underlying principles of the great republic." What does he mean here? Exactly how does the question of race in the United States "test" the nation's principles? In another part of *The Souls of Black Folks*, Du Bois claims more widely that the "problem of the Twentieth Century is the problem of the color line." Now that you are living in a postcolonial world in the twenty-first century, what is the current status of the "problem of the color line"—in the United States and internationally?

3. Compare Du Bois's notion of "double consciousness" with the notion of hybridity in "Works in Translation: Ghada Amer's Hybrid Pleasures." To what extent are the ideas getting at the same thing? To what extent do they differ? What do you see as the significance of their differences and similarities?

SUGGESTIONS FOR WRITING

1. In the contemporary world of visual images and the mass media, viewers are constantly encountering representations of nonwhites, whether American racial minorities or people of color from around the world. Pick an example from an ad, a film, a television show, or elsewhere. Write an essay that uses Du Bois's concept of "double consciousness" to analyze the representation as a "revelation of the other world," where the dominant white culture presents nonwhites with images of themselves. Take into account here how the dominant culture defines others and what the effects might be.

2. Many of the other readings in this chapter, in one way or another, take up notions similar to Du Bois's concept of "double consciousness" such as in the image of the border that turns up in Amitava Kumar's and Gloria Anzaldúa's essays and in the idea of hybridity in "Works in Translation: Ghada Amer's Hybrid Pleasures." Pick one or more of the other readings in this chapter and write an essay that compares the sense, in Edward Said's words, of not being "purely *one* thing" with Du Bois' notion of "double consciousness."

3. Write an essay in which you locate yourself in a postcolonial world. Draw on your ancestry and family history, but do not simply report on the paths of migration and patterns of settlement that brought you to where you are today. Answer this question: in an era of globalization and the movements of people, where and how do you fit in? Think in terms of how culture is changing in the United States and the world—in part becoming more standardized and more Americanized, in part more diverse and polycultural. Think in terms of your identity and the identity of those around you. Can you say you have a single identity, or is the identity of you and others more complicated and perhaps more contradictory?

VISUAL CULTURE

Coco Fusco and Guillermo Gómez-Peña: Postcolonial Representation

To learn more about postcolonial representation, visit
www.ablongman.com/george/141

Coco Fusco and Guillermo Gómez-Peña are writers, critics, and performance artists who call into question representations in popular culture and the media of Latino cultures, the U.S.-Mexican border, globalization, and national identity. Their techniques, which resemble those of "rewriting the image" in Chapter 4, involve exaggerating common images to expose the ethnocentric stereotyping and scapegoating that create the "we" and "they" of mainstream America and its cultural Others. Here are three examples of their work.

"Two Undiscovered Amerindians Visit the West." The cage performance pictured here, in which Fusco and Gómez-Peña are "undiscovered Amerindians" from an island in the Gulf of Mexico, is part of a larger interdisciplinary arts project including multimedia, installation, and experimental radio soundtrack that premiered at the Walker Art Center in Minneapolis in 1992 and subsequently appeared in Madrid, London, and Washington, D.C.

"Better Yet When Dead." Coco Fusco's performance installation raises questions about why Latina artists such as Selena, Ar Mendieta, Sara Gomez, Frida Kahlo, and Sor Juana become celebrated figures once they are dead. The installation, which premiered in 1997, resembles a funeral parlor in which the spectators become guests at a wake.

SUGGESTIONS FOR DISCUSSION

1. Coco Fusco and Guillermo Gómez-Peña's cage performance in "Two Undiscovered Amerindians Visit the West" puts spectators in the uncomfortable position of viewing the "undiscovered Amerindians" as exotic curiosities. Notice particularly the image of a family posing in front of the cage while someone takes its picture. What commentary does the cage performance make about American history? What does it tell about representations of American Indians?

2. Visit Coco Fusco's Virtual Laboratory at http://www.thing.net/~cocofusco, and on the home page, click on "Performances" for descriptions of performance art projects Fusco has created. Check out "Better Yet When Dead" and the other performances. How would you describe Fusco's method as an artist? What do you see her trying to do? In what ways do her performances involve the audience?

3. Visit "The Shame Man and El Mexican't Meet the CyberVato" Web site at http://www.rice.edu/projects/CyberVato. Click on "Techno-Ethno-Graphic Profile" and check out the various questionnaires it leads to. What kind of position do the questions

put you in? Do you think this is really a survey? Are you supposed to answer or think about the logic of the questions? What is the relationship between the questionnaires and the larger themes of this arts project?

SUGGESTED ASSIGNMENT

Design your own instance of performance art. Follow Coco Fusco and Guillermo Gómez-Peña's example by involving the audience directly in issues such as cultural representation, stereotyping, and scapegoating.

FILM CLIP   Film Genres: Bollywood

To learn more about Bollywood, visit www.ablongman.com/george/142

The Indian film industry is the largest in the world, producing over 800 films a year (or more than two per day) for movie-goers in India, Pakistan, and South Asian communities in Europe, Africa, and North America. Bollywood, the name often given to the Indian film industry, combines "Hollywood" and "Bombay." As is true of the movie industry in Hollywood, Bollywood has a long history of filmmaking that dates back to the silent film era of the early twentieth century and includes its own classics. And like Hollywood, Bollywood has a number of large studios and popular stars who are featured in extravagantly made commercial films, as well as independent filmmakers who make smaller art films. Although Bollywood productions can be wide-ranging in subject matter and style, several central characteristics have come to define Bollywood. Bollywood films are typically longer than Hollywood films, running up to three hours, and often combine in a single film elements of romance, melodrama, and action adventure with lavish musical productions featuring singers and dancers in brightly colored costumes performing on elaborate studio sets.

To get a sense of what is unique about Bollywood, you will need, of course, to watch some Bollywood films. A few representative examples are listed here, but there are many others.

Kuch Kuch Hota Hai (1998)	*Dil Chahta Hai* (2001)
Dil Se (1998)	*Zakhm* (1998)
Satya (1998)	*Lagaan* (2001)
Dilwale Dulhaniya Le Jayenge (1995)	*Satta* (2003)
1942: A Love Story (1994)	*Qayamat Se Qayamat Tak* (1988)

As you watch one or more Bollywood films, notice the role of the stars and their romantic relationships. Does the film combine romance with action or melodrama? Consider how the musical scenes are integrated. You may want to compare Bollywood films to classic Hollywood musicals such as *Singing in the Rain* or *My Fair Lady*).

MINING THE ARCHIVE   Nineteenth-Century Orientalist Painting

The Snake Charmer by Jean-Leon Gérôme, c. 1880. Oil on canvas. Acc: 1955.51. Sterling and Francine Clark Art Institute, Williamstown, Massachusetts, USA.

Representations of the Arab world in North Africa and the Middle East were favorite subjects in nineteenth-century European art. Often called Orientalist painting, with its scenes of Turkish baths, snake charmers, slave markets, and harems, this style represented Arab culture as exotic and alien. As you can see from the two paintings reproduced here— "The Slave Market" and "The Snake Charmer" by Jean-Leon Gérôme, perhaps the most important nineteenth-century French painter of Orientalist subjects—Orientalist art offered European viewers the titillation of sexual power and forbidden pleasures while assuring them such unthinkable desires and practices belonged to an Oriental Other, not to "us."

To learn more about representations of Orientalist painting, visit www.ablongman.com/george/143

Nineteenth-century Orientalist painting forms an important archive for understanding how representations of Arab culture were quite literally fantastic figments of the European imagination. An art museum near you may have Orientalist paintings in its collection. There are also several excellent books that have plenty of examples of paintings, such as the exhibition catalogue *The Orientalists: Delacroix to Matisse: The Allure of North Africa and the Near East*, edited by MaryAnne Stevens (London: Thames and Hudson, 1984). And you can find Web sites by entering "orientalism" and "art" in your search engine. Look for definitions of the term *Orientalism* so that you understand how art historians and cultural critics use it. As you look at the paintings, consider what they reveal about Western representations of the Arab world and how these representations continue to shape perceptions today. For example, compare images of the Arab world that appear in nineteenth-century paintings and in *National Geographic*. Linda Street's book *Veils and Daggers: A Century of National Geographic's Representation of the Arab World* (Philadelphia: Temple University Press, 2000) is a good source for this project.

The Slave Market by Jean-Leon Gérôme, 1866. Oil on canvas. 1955.53. Sterling and Francine Clark Art Institute, Williamstown, Massachusetts, USA.

Credits

Text Credits

Chabon, Michael. From *The Amazing Adventures of Kavalier & Clay* by Michael Chabon, copyright © 2000 by Michael Chabon. Used by permission of Random House, Inc.

"Bringing Emotions to Video Games" reprinted by permission of MSNBC.com

Gilchrist, Todd. Review of *Spider-Man 2*. Copyright © Todd Gilchrist and FilmStew.com. Reprinted by permission.

Ebert, Roger. "Review of Spiderman 2." *Chicago Sun Times,* June 30, 2004. Reprinted by permission of Roger Ebert.

Warshow, Robert. "The Gangster as Tragic Hero" from *The Immediate Experience* by Robert Warshow.

Satrapi, Marjane. "Introduction" from *Persepolis: The Story of a Childhood* by Marjane Satrapi, translated by Mattias Ripa and Blake Ferris, copyright © 2003 by L'Asociation, Paris, France. Used by permission of Pantheon Books, a division of Random House, Inc.

Chapter 8

Cisneros, Sandra. From *The House on Mango Street.* Copyright © 1984 by Sandra Cisneros. Published by Vintage Books, a division of Random House, Inc. and in hardcover by Alfred A. Knopf in 1994. Reprinted by permission of Susan Bergholz Literary Services, New York. All rights reserved.

Espada, Martin. "Alabanza: In Praise of Local 100," from *Alabanza* by Martin Espada. Copyright © 2003 by Martin Espada. Used by permission of W. W. Norton & Company, Inc.

Adams, Scott. Pages 11–15 from *The Dilbert Principle* by Scott Adams. Copyright © 1996 by United Features Syndicate, Inc. Reprinted by permission of HarperCollins Publishers, Inc.

Ehrenreich, Barbara. "Nickel-and-Dimed" by Barbara Ehrenreich. Copyright © 1999 by Barbara Ehrenreich. Reprinted by permission of International Creative Management.

Friedman, Thomas L. "The Great Indian Dream," *The New York Times,* 3/11/04. Copyright © 2004 The New York Times Company. Reprinted with permission.

Moberg, David. "High-Tech Hijack," *In These Times,* January 2005. Reprinted by permission of *In These Times.*

Kristof, Nicholas D. and Sheryl WuDunn. "Two Cheers for Sweatshops" from *Thunder from the East* by Nicholas D. Kristof and Sheryl WuDunn, copyright © 2000 by Nicholas D. Kristof and Sheryl WuDunn. Used by permission of Alfred A. Knopf, a division of Random House, Inc.

"Pennies an Hour and No Way Up," *The New York Times,* 7/6/02. Copyright © 2002 The New York Times Company. Reprinted by permission.

Olson, Tillie. "I Stand Here Ironing," copyright © 1956, 1957, 1960, 1961 by Tillie Olsen, from *Tell Me a Riddle* by Tillie Olsen, Introduction by John Leonard. Used by permission of Dell Publishing, a division of Random House, Inc.

Spradley, J. From *The Cocktail Waitress: Women's Work in a Man's World* by J. Spradley. Copyright © 1975. Reprinted by permission of the McGraw-Hill Companies.

Chapter 9

Gordon, Mary. "More Than Just a Shrine." Copyright © 1985 by the New York Times Co. Reprinted by permission.

Trouillot, Michel-Rolph. "October 12, 1492" from *Silencing the Past* by Michel-Rolph Trouillot. Copyright © 1995 by Michel-Rolph Trouillot. Reprinted by permission of Beacon Press, Boston.

Tomkins, J. "'Indians,' Textualism, Morality and the Problem of History." *Critical Inquiry* 13:1 (1986) pp. 101–119. Reprinted by permission of The University of Chicago Press.

Phillips, Christopher. "Necessary Fictions: Warren Neidich's Early American Cover-ups" from *American History Reinvented: Photographs of Warren Neidich.* Essay copyright © 1989 by Christopher Phillips. Reprinted by permission of the author.

Baritz, Loren. "God's Country and American Know-How" from *Backfire* by Loren Baritz. Copyright © 1985 by Loren Baritz. Reprinted by permission of Gerard McCauley Literary Agency.

Ferguson, Niall. "The Empire Slinks Back." Copyright © 2003 by Niall Ferguson, reprinted with the permission of The Wylie Agency.

Noonan, Peggy. "Too Much God: Was the President's Speech a Case of "Mission Inebriation?" *The Wall Street Journal,* 1/21/05. Reprinted by permission of Dow Jones & Co. via Copyright Clearance Center.

Hunt, Tristram. "Historians in Cahoots." Copyright Guardian Newspapers Limited 2005.

Trachtenberg, Alan. Excerpt from *Preface* from *Reading American Photographs: Images as History From Matthew Brady to Walker Evans* by Alan Trachtenberg. Copyright © 1989 by Allen Trachtenberg. Reprinted by permission of Hill & Wang, a division of Farrar, Straus and Giroux, LLC.

From *The Good War* by Studs Terkel. Reprinted by permission of Donadio & Olson, Inc. Copyright © 1984 by Studs Terkel.

Chapter 10

Canagarajah, A. Suresh. "An English Lesson in Sri Lanka" from *Adopting a Critical Perspective of Pedagogy* by A. S. Canagarajah. Copyright © 1999. Reprinted by permission of Oxford University Press.

Kumar, Amitava. "The Shame of Arrival" from *Passport Photos*, copyright © 2000. Reprinted by permission of the University of California Press.

Anzaldúa, Gloria. "How to Tame a Wild Tongue" from *Borderlands/La Frontera: The New Mestiza*. Copyright © 1987, 1999 by Gloria Anzaldúa. Reprinted by permission of Aunt Lute Books.

Auricchio, Laura. "Works in Translation: Ghada Amer's Hybrid Pleasures." *Art Journal,* Winter, 2001, pp. 27–34. Reprinted by permission of the author, Laura Auricchio, full-time faculty member, Department of Art & Design Studies, Parsons The New School for Design.

Bogues, B. Anthony. "Get Up, Stand Up: The Redemptive Poetics of Bob Marley" Copyright © 2003 from *Black Heretics, Black Prophets* by B. Anthony Bogues. Reproduced by permission of Routledge/Taylor & Francis Group, LLC.

Photo Credits

Introduction   Page 2: ©The Absolut Company. **Page 7:** Library of Congress. **Page 10:** Courtesy Everett Collection.

Chapter 1   Page 14: Paul Hawthorne/Getty Images. **Page 35 (Right):** *The Wall Street Journal* front page: Top: AP/Wide World Photos; Bottom Left: Rohan/Getty Images; Bottom Center: Stephanie Wunderlich/Three In A Box; Bottom Right: Kenneth Chen.

Chapter 2   Page 83: Big Cheese Photo/Index Stock Imagery, Inc. **Page 113:** Courtesy of U.S. English. **Page 120 (Left):** COLUMBIA/THE KOBAL COLLECTION. **Page 120 (Right):** Courtesy Everett Collection. **Page 121:** WARNER BROS/THE KOBAL COLLECTION. **Page 128:** Nina Leen/Life Magazine, Copyright Time Inc./Time Life Pictures/Getty Images.

Chapter 3   Page 171 (Top): AP/Wide World Photos. **Page 187:** Courtesy of Hampton University Archives. **Page 188:** Jane Addams Memorial Collection (JAMC neg. 613), Special Collections, The University Library, The University of Illinois at Chicago. **Page 197:** Text and illustrations pp. 18-19 from THE NEW FUN WITH DICK AND JANE by Williams S. Gray, et al., illustrated by Keith Ward and Eleanor Campbell. Copyright 1951 by Scott, Foresman and Company. Reprinted by permission of Pearson Education, Inc.

Chapter 4   Page 200: Courtesy of Craig Frazier, Designer. **Page 201:** Courtesy of Coach. **Page 203:** The JEEP® is a registered trademark of DaimlerChrysler Corporation and the JEEP® advertisement is used with permission. **Page 204:** "Down & Out in Discount America Cover" by Nation Magazine. Reprinted with permission from the January 3, 2005, issue of *The Nation*. For subscription information, call 1-800-333-8536. Portions of each week's Nation magazine can be accessed at http://www.thenation.com. **Page 220:** Courtesy of Diamond Trading Company. **Page 221 (Top Left):** Courtesy of National Fluid Milk Processor Promotion Board. **Page 221 (Top Right):** Courtesy of Mandalay Bay. **Page 221 (Bottom):** Courtesy of Diesel. **Page 224 (Left):** Erich Lessing/Art Resource, NY. **Page 224 (Right):** Cameraphoto Arte, Venice/Art Resource, NY. **Page 225 (Top):** Photograph by Hervé Lewandoswki. Réunion des Musées Nationaux/Art Resource, NY. **Page 225 (Bottom):** Courtesy of Guerrilla Girls. **Page 226:** Image courtesy of www.adbusters.org. **Page 228:** The Candie's Foundation. **Page 229 (Top Left, Right):** Courtesy of National Archives. **Page 229 (Bottom Left):** RAJ Publications, Lakewood, CO. **Page 232:** Courtesy of Vertamae Grosvenor. **Page 249:** Private Collection.

Chapter 5   Page 258: Courtesy of Mike Szabo and N.A.S.A. **Page 260:** Courtesy of Alison Jackson, photographer. **Page 267 (Top, Center):** AP/Wide World Photos. **Page 267 (Bottom):** Steve McCurry/Magnum Photos, Inc. **Pages 290–291:** General Research Division, The New York Public Library, Astor, Lenox and Tilden Foundations. **Page 293:** Hulton Archive/Getty Images. **Page 295:** AP/Wide World Photos.

Chapter 6   Page 296: The Metropolitan Museum of Art, Walker Evans Archive, 1994 (1994.251.283) © The Walker Evans Achive, The Metropolitan Museum of Art. All rights reserved, The Metropolitan Museum of Art. **Pages 336–337:** Courtesy of the artist.

Chapter 8   Pages 431–433: Courtesy of Julián Cardona. **Page 432 (Top):** A canal of aguas negras (contaminated water, such as untreated sewage, or waste water from the maquiladoras) separates one of the ca. 325 maquiladoras in Cd. Juarez-this one in the Rio Bravo industrial park (in the background)-from the new home of seven-year-old Guadalupe Valenzuela Rosales, who live with her parents, two sisters, and brother in a cardboard-and-wood house. Her family and many of their neighbors came to Cd. Juarez from the southern states of Coahuila and Durango in search of employment and better living conditions. In 1997, a fire razed ten of these houses and also the wooden bridges that cross the canal to the Rio Bravo industrial park, where Guadalupe's family and their neighbors work. **Page 445:** Bettmann/CORBIS.

Chapter 9   Pages 474–475: Courtesy of Warren Neidich. **Page 491:** CNN/Getty Images. **Pages 507–509:** AP/Wide World Photos. **Page 512 (Top):** Goran Tomasevic/Reuters/CORBIS. **Page 513 (Bottom):** Larry Downing/Reuters/CORBIS. **Page 513 (Top):** AP/Wide World Photos. **Page 513 (Bottom Left):** AFP/Getty Images. **Page 513 (Bottom Right):** AP/Wide World Photos.

Chapter 10   Page 520: Photography by Amitava Kumar. **Pages 531–532:** Courtesy of Jack Shainman Gallery, New York. **Pages 537–538:** Photography by Amitava Kumar. **Page 540:** Photography by Amitava Kumar. **Pages 552–553:** Courtesy of the artist and of Deitch Projects, NY. **Page 581 (Top):** Courtesy of Coco Fusco, Unknown photographer. **Page 581 (Bottom):** Courtesy of Coco Fusco, Photography by Peter Barker. **Page 582:** Courtesy of Coco Fusco, *Better Yet When Dead*, performance, 1996–97.

Index

Note to reader: All titles (of text selections, books, magazines, newspapers, television shows, movies, and songs) are printed in italic type. Names of authors of text selections are printed in bold type. Names of images are printed in regular type.